Osmanlı History and Institutions

# Osmanlı History and Institutions

Prof. Dr. Mehmet Maksudoğlu

*Classical and Contemporary Books on Islam and Sufism*

Copyright © Prof. Dr. Mehmet Maksudoğlu., 2023 C.E./1445 AH

Osmanlı History and Institutions

| | |
|---|---|
| Published by: | Diwan Press Ltd. |
| | 311 Allerton Road |
| | Bradford |
| | BD15 7HA |
| | UK |
| Website: | www.diwanpress.com |
| E-mail: | info@diwanpress.com |

All rights reserved. No part of this publication may be reproduced, stored in any retrieval system or transmitted in any form or by any means, electronic, mechanical, photocopying, recording or otherwise without the prior permission of the publishers.

Author:                    Prof. Dr. Mehmet Maksudoğlu

A catalogue record of this book is available from the British Library.

ISBN-13:            978-1-914397-03-5  (paperback)

                    978-1-914397-04-2  (casebound)

                    978-1-914397-05-9  (ePub and Kindle)

The cover image is in the public domain courtesy of Wikimedia (https://commons.wikimedia.org/wiki/File:Abdulhamid_II_at_Selânik.jpg) and is from The Awakening of Turkey, by Edward Frederick Knight. J. B. Lippincott Company, Philadelphia 1909.

# Contents

| | |
|---|---|
| Terms and Names | ix |
| Pronunciation of Turkish Sounds | ix |
| Abbreviations | ix |
| Footnotes and Endnotes | x |
| Introduction | 1 |

**Part One:**
**The Foundation of the Osmanlı Devlet 1288-1453**    25

    Chapter One: Islam in Anatolia    27

    Chapter Two: The Foundation of the Osmanlı Devlet    41

    Chapter Three: Restoration    115

**Part Two:**
**Expansion 1453-1699**    147

    Chapter Four: Expansion    149

    Chapter Five: Sultân Bâyezîd Velî (1481-1512)    195

    Chapter Six: The Struggle For Islamic Unity    209

    Chapter Seven: The Superpower of the World    237

    Chapter Eight: The Beginning of Decline    268

Chapter Nine: The Osmanlı Sultan's Descent to Equality With Emperors  285

Chapter Ten: Rejuvenation  290

Chapter Eleven: Decline and Restoration  293

Part Three:
Decline 1699-1922  311

Chapter Twelve: The Resumption of Decline  312

Chapter Thirteen: The Attempt at Restoration  319

Chapter Fourteen: Crisis and Struggle  324

Chapter Fifteen: Another Attempt at Restoration  328

Chapter Sixteen: Preservation and Rejuvenation  385

Chapter Seventeen: The İttihâd ve Teraqqî Society – The Committee of Union and Progress  404

Conclusion  421

Osmanlı Sovereigns  430

Addendum:
The Osmanlı Socio-Political Entity: Empire or Devlet?  433

# Osmanlı Institutions  451

Introduction  453

I. Administrative Organisation  456

II – Economic Institutions  473

| | |
|---|---|
| III – The Legal System | 482 |
| IV – Military Organisation | 493 |
| V – Social Institutions | 508 |
| Conclusion | 529 |
| Bibliography | 531 |
| Endnotes | 541 |
| Glossary | 577 |
| Places Mentioned in the Text | 584 |
| Full Table of Contents | 608 |

# Terms and Names

Note that since the Osmanlı khalifate was the final fully functioning one, the author has preferred Osmanlı spellings to words. Because of the global character of this work, it necessarily has terms from several different languages, most importantly Turkish, Arabic and Farsi all of them in their English transliterations and translations. It has not proved possible to reduce these to a single convention, so we beg the reader's patience while navigating this terrain.

## Pronunciation of Turkish Sounds

| | |
|---|---|
| *a* | short, like u in sun; long, like a in father. |
| *ch* | like ch in child. |
| *e* | like e in get. |
| *ğ* | not pronounced but lengthens the preceding letter, like the gh in night. |
| *ı* | like i in cousin or i in cushion. |
| *i* | like i in hit. |
| *ö* | like i in girl (actually, like French eu or German ö). |
| *u* | like u in June. |
| *ü* | like u in French "tu". |
| ^ | lengthens the sound and makes it thinner. |

## Abbreviations

| | |
|---|---|
| ﷺ | *sall-Allahu 'alayhi wa sallam* (May Allah bless him and give him peace) |
| ﷻ | *subhânahu wa ta'âlâ* (glorious is He and exalted) |

    ☪    *'alayhi-s-salâm* (peace be with him)
    ☪    *radyAllahu 'anhu* (may Allah be pleased with him)
BOA   Başbakanlık Osmanlı Arşivi (Prime Minister's Osmanlı Archive – Now, President's Osmanlı Archive)
TSMK  Topkapı Sarayı Müzesi Kitaplığı (Library of the Topkapı Sarayı Museum)

## Footnotes and Endnotes

Footnotes numbered i, ii, iii etc. contain explanatory material and are placed at the bottom of the page for easy reference. The numbering starts afresh on each page.

Endnotes numbered 1, 2, 3 etc. are placed at the end of the book and contain references to books and articles consulted and cited.

# Introduction

Many books have been written in Western literature on Osmanlı[i] history, but the overwhelming majority of them are based on secondary sources alone. In this book, however, which is based on Osmanlı sources first and foremost, but also takes into account the work of academics, I do not intend to give a critique of existing literature on Osmanlı history, but it may be appropriate in this introduction to discuss its methodological and conceptual problems and to explain my own methodology as well as my objectives and conclusions.

An abstract of this book will also be given here. All historians of Osmanlı history should be expected to depend primarily on Osmanlı sources. But this has been totally ignored and neglected for a long time, as Stanford Shaw explicitly mentions in his *History of the Ottoman Empire and Modern Turkey:* "Of course Ottoman history has been discussed many times before, and in considerable detail, but always from the European perspective, through the light of European prejudice, and largely on the basis of European sources."[1] He and his wife Ezel Kural Shaw attempted, courageously, to use

---

i   Proper names and nomenclatures should not be changed; for every change involves distortion. Therefore there is no reason whatsoever to change "Osmanlı" into "Ottoman." Nevertheless, even in the West, the correct term, "Osmanlı," has occasionally been used. See for example: Z. Duckett Ferriman, *Turkey and the Turks* (London: Mills and Boon Limited; 1911) pp. 50-51; H.A. Gibbons, *The Foundation of the Ottoman Empire: A History of the Osmanlis up to the Death of Bâyezîd I, 1300- 1403,* (Frank Cass & Co. 1968) pp. 158-159, 163, 173-179, 183 and 184.

Osmanlı sources in their *History of the Ottoman Empire and Modern Turkey* expressing it thus:

> "We make no apology for using Ottoman sources for a history of the Ottoman Empire. For too long the Ottomans have been studied without the use of *any* of their sources, resulting in serious distortion and error. No history of France would be considered methodologically sound and balanced if it were written on the basis of English and Italian observations. At the same time, however, we have made use of a mass of relevant non-Ottoman materials, as is evident in the Bibliography."[2]

Coming from an entirely different background, Western writers have certain "mindsets". They underestimate and even ignore the fact that "countries and peoples are unique and are not so easily lured into identity with each other save on limited, and specific points."[3]

Thus, it is necessary to understand and define many terms related to the Osmanlıs and their history. To begin with, the very name of this socio-political structure should be clarified. Nearly all scholarly works in English use the term "Ottoman Empire." But when looking at Osmanlı documents, official correspondence, treaties, and books written during their era and by *their* official historians, we notice that the title "*Imparatoriyye-i Osmaniyye*" is never used. They called their socio-political entity دولت علیه عثمانیه (*Devlet-i 'Alîyye-i Osmâniyye* – The Sublime Osmanlı Devlet) and sometimes called it سلطنة سنیة (*Saltanat-ı Senîyye* – The Splendid Sultanate). This term *devlet* was in fact used by the Osmanlıs themselves throughout the centuries.

It is a general and universal rule that proper names should be kept as they are and never translated. The term empire, in particular, does not suit the Osmanlı socio-political structure at all. It is sufficient to remember that a great majority of the Osmanlı *sadrazams* and *vazîrs* were generally of non-Turkish descent, while the janissaries continued to be so up until the end of the sixteenth century. Thus both racism and nationalism were alien to the Osmanlı structure. They never imposed their language on other communities but, on the contrary, used Arabic largely in their educational institutions. Moreover, they used the Arabic Qur'ânic script for their own language, Osmanlı Turkish.

From an economic perspective, it is wrong and misleading to claim that the Osmanlıs expanded into other territories for the sake of raw materials for their industry. When they went to Yemen for example, it was not for the sake of oil but to prevent European powers from gaining access to the Red Sea and the two most sacred cities of Islam, Makkah and Medîna. In short, the Osmanlı Devlet did not intend to exploit people in the annexed territories. Trade and industry were, in fact, in the hands of non-Muslim people, as Bernard Lewis himself admitted: "Industry and trade were left to non-Muslim conquered subjects, who continued to practise their inherited crafts."[4]

It seems that the late Professor Kemâl Karpat was aware of this wrong usage and preferred "state" in *The Ottoman State and its Place in World History* (Leiden, Brill, 1974) to avoid this misnomer:

But, even the word "state" does not correspond to "*Devlet*." Since the Treaty of Westphalia of 1648, the concept of state has acquired additional dimensions and an expanded jurisdiction; in the West parliament replaced Church. The authorities of the state can legislate almost absolutely, but *devlet* in the Islamic understanding and practice is only a tool to implement the *Sharî'at*, which has already been ordained by the Creator. The structure of *devlet* is completely different from that of the state.

A state has 3 powers:
Legislative (Parliament), Executive, Judiciary.

> A *devlet* has 2 powers only:
> Executive, Judiciary (*Dîvân-ı Hümâyûn* and *Qudât* – judges)

A *devlet* does not legislate. There is already legislation: *Sharî'at*, which has been ordained by Allah, the Creator, and the Devlet is a tool to implement these orders on the earth.

The *Qânûnnâmes* are only administrative regulations about how *Sharî'at* (the Heavenly Orders of the Creator) should be carried out according to circumstances; and NOT "secular" orders, as some orientalists claim. They are not aware that in the Muslim socio-political entity called *Devlet* secular regulations are not used.

1648 (The Treaty of Westphalia) is a very important date in secularism. However, according to those learned orientalists Qânûnî Sultân Süleymân (r.1520-1566), for example, issues "secular" *Qânûnnâme* before the beginnings of secularism!

Another mistaken nomenclature for the Osmanlı Devlet is calling it the Ottoman Empire. Almost all the orientalists who have written about the Osmanlı Devlet stubbornly insist on using the term empire[5] for the Osmanlıs. This word "empire" certainly applies to *their* socio-political entities, but it has no relation at all to the Osmanlı Devlet.

First of all, the structure is completely different. In the Osmanlı Devlet, the governed people, *ra'iyyet* (plural: *ra'âyâ*) are considered *emânet-i ilâhî* (the security and well-being of those under the administration are entrusted by Allah to the Devlet) while in Europe the governed people were *serfs* (those who served), later called *subjects* (those who have been subjected).

In Arabic the verb رَعَى *ra'â* has two infinitives: رَعْيٌ *ra'yun* – putting cattle in fields to graze, and رِعَايَةٌ *ri'âyatun* – taking care of, consideration, observance, regard. And *ra'iyyet* means: those who are taken care of, treated well.

In Europe when a piece of land was sold to another feudal lord, the ownership of the people living on it was also changed, as if they were farm animals. And a marrying girl spent her first night with the feudal lord, not with her husband. This practice was called: *jus primae noctis*! In Osmanlı administration, the *tımarlı sipâhî* was responsible for the people's security of life, property and honour. He collected *kharâj* or *'ushr* on behalf of the Devlet and prepared a certain number of well trained *mujâhid*s for *jihâd*.

Almost all of the "supposed" specialists in Osmanlı History, call the *tımarlı sipâhî* "feudal cavalry"! What relation does that have to the real meaning?

Differences of structure are very important: the raw material of diamond and coal is the same, carbon, but the structure, the arrangement of the atoms makes the difference.

When speaking or writing about empires generally, the Osmanlı socio-political entity comes to no one's mind:

> "From the fifteenth century onwards, Spain, Portugal, Holland, France and Britain began building overseas empires.[6]

> "some of the old imperial powers continued to enlarge their empires impressively, such were Russia, France and Great Britain. Others stood still and found theirs reduced; this group included the Dutch, Spanish and Portuguese."[7]

Secondly : What is the reason to change a proper name? It is a universal rule that proper names are not changed, but they stubbornly insist distorting almost everything about the Osmanlı Devlet although they claim to be objective scholars!

There was a learned gathering about the Gulf of Basra in Boğaziçi University, Istanbul where I met a British professor who came from Cambridge. I told him that I was also at the University of Cambridge, in the Faculty of Oriental Studies, and that this term of empire for the Osmanlı Devlet should be changed.

He replied: "You will never be able to change it!"

In my view, this explains everything. There is an international consensus about presenting the Osmanlıs as imperial bandits like their own socio-political bodies of whom they are so proud, which they maintain stubbornly. I wrote about the incident in an article, advising the Turkish academics responsible not to allow *any* foreign researcher who uses the term "empire" about the Osmanlı Devlet into the Osmanlı Archives (after cleansing *our* textbooks of this word.) There I mentioned a sentence of Yûnus Emre:

*Dağ nice yüce olsa, Yol onun üstünden aşar.*
  However high the mountain, the Way (Method) passes over it.

Apparently that person relied upon libraries full of books containing this false label. But there are and will be honest researchers who will correct many distorted points about Osmanlı history.

Imâm A'zam Nu'mân bin Sâbit says :

I have persuaded forty scholars using one proof only
  But I could not persuade one ignoramus using forty proofs.

Having established the reason for using the name "Osmanlı Devlet", we should now explain the meaning and implication of the *dîvân*, the Osmanlı government. *Dîvân* originally meant registers concerning administrative, military, and fiscal affairs, and the place that was used to keep these registers and account books was called, by extension, *Dîvân*. In a *hadîth sharîf* (saying of the Prophet ﷺ) that came down from Ummul Mu'minîn 'Aishah ؓ he said: "There are three *dîvâns* in the presence of Allah."[8] The Prophet ﷺ employed

*Introduction*

scribes for writing the *wahy*, and it may be argued that these scribes comprised the first *dîvân* in Islam.⁹

The list of the companions of the Final Messenger ﷺ in Medîna, about 1500,¹⁰ may also be seen as a kind of *dîvân*. For the Final Messenger ﷺ used to give them *'atâ* (*ma'âsh* – stipend) on the same day he received the *fay'* (amount obtained from unbelievers as a tribute, without involving war) in accordance to that *dîvân* (register): two shares for the married and one share to the bachelor.¹¹ When distributing *'atiyyah* (*ma'âsh*) to the Muslims, the first *khalîfah* Abû Bakr ؓ used to ask the person: "Do you have property to pay *zakât* on?" If he replied "yes," the *khalîfah* would then take the *zakât* from his *'ata (ma'âsh)*.¹²

But the second *khalîfah*, Umar b. al-Khattâb ؓ, was the first in the history of Islam to form a *dîvân* in an administrative sense.¹³ This institution continued to exist throughout the Muslim administration of the Umawîs (Umayyids – 661-750), the Abbâsîs (Abbasids – 750-1258), the Great Selçuklus (Seljuks – 1075-1157), and Anatolian Selçuklus (1079-1308). When the Osmanlı dynasty replaced the Anatolian Selçuklu dynasty, it continued to have the same Islamic administrative structure and institutions, including the *dîvân*.

Since they perceived themselves as those who bore the responsibility of representing and implementing the heavenly message of Islam, the Osmanlıs called their *dîvân*, *Dîvân-ı Hümâyûn*. *Hümâyûn* (همايون) pertains to *Hümâ* (هما), a mythical bird whose egg is believed to hatch in the sky and which always lives in the sky without touching Earth. Since it always lives in the sky, *Hümâyûn* means "heavenly" or "belonging to the sky". The Osmanlıs perceived themselves to be bearers of the Final Heavenly Message, Islam, and they therefore related every important item to this word *Hümâyûn*¹⁴ – hence, the *Ordu-yu Hümâyûn* or the Heavenly Army, and *Khatt-ı Hümâyûn* or the Heavenly Decree of the *khalîfah*-sultân. The first gate of the *khalîfah*'s residence, Topkapı Palace, was called *Bâb-ı Hümâyûn*: The

Heavenly Gate. Therefore, *Dîvân-ı Hümâyûn* is the Heavenly *Dîvân*. To translate it as "Imperial Council," as Stanford Shaw does,[15] is a mistake. It does not reflect the meaning; moreover, nomenclatures should not in any case be translated.

There are *vazîrs* (*wazīrs*) in the *Dîvân*. The word *vazîr* occurs in the Qur'ân in the sense of "helper," "assistant," and "supporter," when the Messenger Moses ﷺ asks Allah the Almighty: *"And appoint a vazîr for me from my family, Aaron, my brother."*[16] The word *vazîr* is also mentioned in the sayings of the Final Messenger Muhammad ﷺ: "If Allah wants an *amîr* (administrator) to be successful, He gives him a straight, trustworthy *vazîr*. When he forgets, he reminds him, when he remembers, he helps him"[17]; "If anyone of you undertakes a task and if Allah wants it to succeed, He gives him a good *vazîr*. If he forgets, the *vazîr* reminds him, when he remembers, he helps him."[18] The word *vazîr* is derived from وزر – *w z r*, which signifies responsibility. *Vazîr* (وزير) means a man who assumes responsibility and undertakes the *burden* of the people. The Qur'ân states: لَا تَزِرُ وَازِرَةٌ وِزْرَ أُخْرَىٰ ("*Lâ taziru wâziratun wizra ukhra*[19] – *No soul bears the burden of another*").

The *Dîvân* in the Osmanlı administration was first set up by Orhan Gâzi (1324-1362), following the practice of the Anatolian Selçuklus, and the number of its *vazîrs* increased in due course. During the rule of Chelebi Mehemmed (1413-1421) and his son Murâd II (1421-1451), one of the *vazîrs* was called "*ulu vazîr*" (Grand Vazîr), and subsequently *vazîr-i a'zam*. The latter continued until the time of Süleymân the Magnificent (1520-1566) who changed it to *sadr-ı a'zam* (*sadrâzam*). The Osmanlı *sadrâzam* was a *vazîr* of *tafwîz* – تفويض – an authorised *vazîr*, who was given full authority and acted on behalf of the Sultân, having his *mühr-i hümâyûn* – the seal of the Sultân. Nevertheless, he would be held accountable if he committed a major sin and could lose his life altogether. But it is incorrect to refer to the *sadrâzam*, as Shaw did, as "the chief executive officer of state beginning about 1360."²⁰ For the *vazîr* had an executive capacity (*tanfîdh* – تنفيذ) only at the beginning. But when the number of the *vazîrs* increased in due course, one of them was selected to be *sadrâzam*, and was known as the *vazîr* of *tafwîz* (the authorised *vazîr* – وزيــر مفــوض – *vezîr mufawwaz*). In addition, with respect to the Osmanlı administration the *vazîr* should not be translated as minister.

Another concept that needs clarification is *fath*. Many writers translate it as conquest, hence *al-Fâtih* becomes the *Conqueror*. But "conquest" is not the same as *fath*. While conquest implies subduing by force, the *fath* of a country literally means opening it, its jurisprudence (*Sharî'at*) and values, to Islam but without compelling people in any way to embrace Islam. Islam advocates religious tolerance and all non-Muslims are entitled to complete freedom of belief. Only male adults from among them are asked to pay *jizyah* in return for protection of their lives and property, and *kharâj* on their land possession. In this and other respects they are treated on a similar basis with the Muslims who are asked to pay *zakât* on their property, and *'ushr* on their crops.

*Zakât* is instituted in the *Noble Qur'ân* and is frequently mentioned in it together with *salât* (prayer).ⁱ *Zakât* in Arabic implies purity, and Muslims are therefore obliged to pay it on their property and belongings in order to "cleanse" themselves from the rights of Allah/ rights of His slaves.

When a Muslim pays *zakât* his wealth will also increase, just like a tree that grows bigger when its branches are pruned. The Creator ordained this duty, and the Qur'ân explicitly specified the areas for

---

i   *al-Qur'ân al-Karîm, al-Baqarah (2) 43, 110, 177; an Nisa (4) 162; al-Mâidah (5) 55, 'Ushr* means one-tenth. Farmers could, however, pay one-twentieth if they spent time and effort and incurred expenditure on their fields.

its expenditure.²¹ The motivation of the *zakât* should therefore be an important feature of the fiscal system for any Muslim Devlet. The Osmanlıs, who were keen to implement Islam in all aspects of life, maintained this institution in their *devlet* throughout the centuries.ⁱ We should remember that many well-versed scholars in Islamic jurisprudence (*fiqh*) continuously flowed into Osmanlı domains while others graduated from its *madrasahs*. The important reference work *ash-Shaqâ'iqu'n-Nu'mâniyyah fî 'Ulamâ'i-d-Dawlati'l 'Othmâniyyah* by Tashköprüzâde²² gives us a long list of those who lived as early as the time of Osman Gâzi. The Osmanlı Devlet observed the Islamic principles of justice to such an extent that there were usually no destitute Muslims who needed the *zakât* during the time of Orhan Gâzi (1324 -1362).²³

Indeed it was much more advanced than the Roman Empire in terms of social and charitable organisation. The assertion of Shaw that the Osmanlıs maintained, with little change, "the tax structure" and the "feudal practices" of the Byzantine Empireⁱⁱ is therefore incorrect. We also object to the term "feudal practice" because the Osmanlı *tımar*ⁱⁱⁱ system was nothing like feudalism.ⁱᵛ It was, in fact, a continuation of the concept of *iqtâ'* initiated by the Final Messenger ﷺ and adopted

---

i  They also maintained the *jizyah*, which is mentioned in the Qur'ân (*at Tawbah* (9), *âyat*: 29). It was taken by the Prophet ﷺ from the people of 'Aqabah (Eyle) during his expedition to Tabûk in 9/630.

ii  *op. cit.*, I, p. 26. On the other hand it is a very common mistake among Western writers to call the "Roman Empire" the "Byzantine Empire".

iii *Tımar* means looking after, caring for the horse in Turkish

iv Western writers usually equate the *tımar* system with feudalism, and *tımarlı sipâhî* (provincial cavalry) thus automatically becomes "the feudal army" in their writings. See for example: Walter Livingstone Wright, *Sarı Mehmed Pasha, the Defterdar, Ottoman Statecraft, Turkish Text with Introduction, Translation, and Notes* (Princeton University Press: 1935) p. 43.

*Introduction*

by *al-Khulafâ ar-Râshidûn* in the first Muslim Devlet in history. Under the *tımar* system, the *sipâhîs* were given administrative rights (not ownership) and the right to collect revenues from certain pieces of land in recognition of their bravery, and on condition that they provide the *devlet* with a specified number of well-trained and fully equipped soldiers. People who lived in these lands were known as *ra'iyyet* (those cared for), but they were not in any way considered slaves, as was the case in feudalism. While they could be sold together with the farm and animals in feudalism and their newly-married brides be asked to comply with the wish of the feudal landlords to spend their first night with him, there was no room for such inhuman practices in the *tımar* system. On the contrary, the *sipâhî* was responsible for protecting the *ra'iyyet*'s honour, life, and property.

The literature used in this book is derived mainly from Osmanlı sources contemporaneous with events, although Western academic authors are also cited. When relating events, I judge them against their own background and occasionally compare them with the situation in other countries at that time. Such comparison is probably the best way to understand and evaluate facts and events. I also try to look at the Osmanlı socio-political entity as it was perceived by its own citizens, giving the facts in their own circumstances.

This is probably a completely different approach from that in existing Osmanlı historiography whose oversights and mistakes are occasionally referred to in this work.

**Sources**

The sources that I have used are as follows. For Osmanlı genealogy, my main source is the manuscript written by Yazıjızâde, *Selchûqnâme*, which is deposited in the Topkapı Sarayı Museum, İstanbul (TSMK, Revân 1391). As for the foundation of the Osmanlı Devlet, the well-known book by Ferîdûn Beğ, *Munsheât-i Selâtîn*, has been used to a large extent. Ferîdûn Beğ was the scribe of the famous Osmanlı *sadrâzam* Sokollu Mehmed Pasha (1505-1579), who served Süleymân the Magnificent (1520-1566), his son, Selîm II (1566-1574), and Murâd III (1574-1595). In his two-volume work Ferîdûn Bey collected and compiled the correspondence of the Osmanlı rulers. Though open to some criticism concerning the correspondences of Osman Gâzi and Orhan Gâzi, this work is an important source that gives abundant information. At least it reflects the Osmanlı concept about and attitude of mind toward events. It shows in particular that the Osmanlı Devlet – unlike many other emirates – did not emerge upon the collapse of the Selçuklu Devlet in Anatolia. On the contrary, the Selçuklu sultân appointed Osman Gâzi ruler of Söğüt and saw his prospective successor in him, as is explicitly stated in Neshrî's book *Cihân-nümâ* also.

For this period I also made use of Neshrî's two-volume work, *Cihân-nümâ*, which was published by the Turkish Historical Society in Ankara in 1949. Neshrî lived during the time of Fâtih (1451-1481) and his son Bâyezîd II (1481-1512). His book is one of the earliest sources for Osmanlı history, which was – directly and indirectly – used by later Osmanlı historians like Sa'deddîn, Ali, Solaqzâde, and Münejjimbashı. Reference is also made to the work of İbn Battûta (703-770/1307-1369), who visited Anatolia during the time of Orhan Gâzi (1326-1362). Though not a historian as such, İbn Battûta's book, *Tuhfatu'n Nuzzâr,* is important because it gives "an admirable and unbiased account of Asia Minor"[24] at that time.

For early Osmanlı history I have used the book by Âshıqpashazâde (803/1400-), *Tevârîh-i Âl-i Osmân* (Histories of the House of Osman), published as *Aşıkpashaoğlu Tarihi*, and edited by Atsız. Âshıqpashazâde obtained his information from Yahshı Faqîh, imâm of the Orhan mosque in Bursa. Oruc Beğ's work and Enverî's *Düstûrnâme* on the period were also consulted.

For al-Fâtih's period (1451-1481), my main sources are Tursun Beğ's *Târîh-i Ebu'l Feth* and Neshrî's *Cihân-nümâ*. Tursun Beğ lived in the fifteenth century C.E., and wrote his book between 903-905/1497-1500. It covers the events of the period 848-893/1444-1488.

For Bâyezîd II (1481-1512) I relied mainly on Neshrî's *Cihânnümâ*.

For the period of Selîm I (1512-1520) my main references are Jelâlzâde Koja Nishânjı Mustafa (d. 975/1567), *Kitâb-ı Meâsir-i Selîm Khânî*, which is in TSMK, H 1415, and İbn Iyâs' book (b.852/1448), *Badâi'uz Zuhûr*, which covers the period 928/1521. The works of Kemâl Pasha-zâde (İbn Kemâl) were also consulted, particularly his seventh *defter* (volume). This reference work was published in ten *defters* that cover Osmanlı history from the beginning up to 1527. İbn Kemâl Shamsu'd Dîn Ahmed was born in 873/1468-69 in Edirne and belonged to a distinguished family. His grandfather Kemâl Pasha, after whom he was named, was a commander during the era of Fâtih Mehemmed (r.1451-1481), while his father Süleymân Pasha was a commander during the reign of Bâyezîd II (1481-1512). İbn Kemâl became Qâdıasker of Anatolia in 922/1516, participated in the campaign against the Mamlûks, and was appointed *sheyhülislâm* in 932/1526. He died in 940/1534.[25]

Hoja Sa'deddîn (1536-1599), son of Hasan Jân, a *nedîm* of Selîm I (1512-1520), was a *müderris* (professor) during Süleymân the Magnificent's reign (1520-1566). His work *Tâju't-Tevârîh* (The Crown of Histories) provides valuable information about Osmanlı history up to the death of Selîm I. Hoja Sa'deddîn himself was instrumental in changing the defeat of the Osmanlı army to victory at the Battle of Hachova in 1596.

For the period of Süleymân the Magnificent (1520-1566) my sources are the works of Selânikî (d.1600), Solaqzâde (d.1657), Na'îmâ (1665-1716), the first Osmanlı court chronicler, Pîrî Reîs (d.1553), and the one-time *sadrâzam* Lütfî Pasha (1539-1541). I also consulted the works of Kâtip Chelebi (1609-1657), Pechûyî Ibrâhîm

(1574-1649), and Silahdâr Fındıqlılı Mehmed Ağa. The works of the Osmanlı chroniclers like those of Naʿîmâ (1665-1716), his successors Mehmed Râshid (d.1735), Ahmed Vâsıf (1739-1807), Ahmed ʿÂsim (1755-1819), and Shânizâde Mehmed Atâullâh (d.1827) were also used.

The work of Mustafa Nûrî Pasha (d.1307/1889), *Netâyijul Vuqûʿât* (4 volumes in one; İstanbul 1327), and İ.H. Uzunçarşılı, *Osmanlı Tarihi* (I-IV) are also reference works for this book. The former was *Defter-i Hâqânî Nâzırı* for five years (1293-1298/1876-1881) and, as such, his work is very valuable in giving detailed information and the personal experience of an insider. The latter is indeed a prolific historian, who lived during the last decades of the Osmanlı Devlet, and over half a century in republican Turkey. His *Osmanlı Tarihi* I-IV, which is based on Osmanlı sources and archival data, is a standard work on the Osmanlı polity. The work of İ. Hakkı Uzunçarşılı was continued by Enver Ziyâ Karal who wrote another four standard volumes in Turkish (V-VIII) that dealt mainly with the nineteenth century. Besides the above-mentioned sources, I consulted other material related to the topic, including archival data.

**Important Observations**

While studying Osmanlı sources one comes across interesting and perhaps new information. They show, for example, that the Osmanlı Devlet was founded in 1288 and not in 1299 as is generally assumed. Having no sons himself, in 688/1288 the Selçuklu sovereign sent a big drum and a white flag to Osman Gâzi whom he saw as his son.[i]

---

i Neşrî, *Kitâb-ı Cihân-Nümâ* (Ankara: Türk Tarih Kurumu, 1949) I, 109; Ferîdûn Beğ, *Munsheât-i Selâtîn* (İstanbul: 1274) I, p. 56. In both works the Selçuklu sultân who sent the flag and drum to Osman Gâzi is Alâeddîn b. Ferâmurz. The Selçuklu sultân's view of Osman Gâzi as his son is mentioned in *Cihânnümâ* (I,109), while the flag (Aq Sancaq) is

The latter had, in fact, planned to go to Qonya, the Selçuklu capital, with precious gifts in the hope that he would become the *wely'ahd* to the Selçuklu sultân, but he could not because of the Sultân's death. Though continuing to observe the Friday *khutbah* and *sikkah* (coinage) in the name of the Sultân out of respect for him, Osman Gâzi had attained a large measure of independence by that time.[26] The *khutbah* on Friday is a token of sovereignty and independence: it is delivered in the name of the ruler of the country. The Osmanlı Devlet was founded at the moment the *khutbah* of *Jum'ah* (Friday) was delivered in the name of Osman Gazi by Tursun Faqîh, at Qaraja Hisâr in 687/1288.[27] (The first *Jum'ah* Prayer was performed by Muhammad ﷺ during the Hijrah (emigration), at Rânûnâ valley, when he was completely free.[28] The second token of sovereignty is the *sikkah* (coinage), but it is not as important: Muslims used Roman and Sassanid (Persian) coins until the Umawî *Khalîfah* 'Abdulmalik bin Marwân (65-86/685-705) who minted coins in 696.

Osman Gâzi received the *menshûr*, drum, sword, and flag from the Selçuklu sovereign in 687/1288. Nevertheless, Osmân Gâzi and his successors continued the practice of listening while standing to the *mehter*, the Osmanlı military band, in the mid-afternoon out of sheer respect for the Selçuklus. This practice was, however, discontinued in the time of Mehemmed Fâtih (855-886/1451-1481) who, after opening Constantinople to Islam in 857/1453, listened to the *mehter* while seated.

It is generally claimed that the Khalifate ended after the fall of the Abbâsîs in 656/1258. But Osmanlı sources show that this is not true since the 'Abbâsî Khalifate in Baghdad was transferred to and continued with the Anatolian Selçuklus (1075-1308). On giving

---

mentioned in the *Munsheât* (I,56). But there may be a mistake concerning the name of the Selçuklu sultân. What is certain is that the Selçuklu sultân of the time did send a big drum and a white flag to Osman Gâzi in 1288.

Osman Gâzi Söğüt a small town in north-western Anatolia on the border of the Roman Empire, the Anatolian Selçuklu sultân referred to himself in the *menshûr* dated Ramadân 683/November 1284 as "*ve mansıb-i mâ be-dereje-i nisbet-i zillullâh fi'l Arz* – Our standing is that of the rank of shadow of Allah in the world."[29] Since *zillullâh* (Shadow of Allah) is known to be the title of the *khalîfah*, this means that the Selçuklu sultân saw himself as the *khalîfah*. Subsequently, on the Mongol invasion of the Abbâsî domains (1258), this central institution survived in the Anatolian Selçuklus (1075-1308).

We should keep in mind that it is impossible for Muslims not to have a *khalîfah*: a Hadith Sharif states that "any Muslim who spends a single night without a *bay'at* on his neck, spends that night as a person living in Jahiliyyah circumstances."[30] To swear allegiance (*bay'at*) to a Muslim leader who undertakes to govern Muslims implementing *Sharî'at* means gathering people into a political Islamic body. So, Muslims did have *khalîfah*s in their socio-political entities because any Muslim Devlet that calls itself thus has to implement the *Sharî'at*, Islamic law, and the head of that structure is the *Khalîfah*. According to this saying of the Final Messenger 🌿, every Muslim has to obey the leader who implements the *Sharî'at*. Thus, the leader certainly has to possess military and consequently political power, and becomes head of the *devlet* (state, état, staat etc. are not the same as a *devlet*; because the former legislate, whereas the *devlet* is only a tool for implementing the law already Divinely legislated called *Sharî'at*).

The attainment of the *khalîfah* seems to have become the goal of the Osmanlıs as early as 1332, when Orhan Gâzi had then explicitly written in his *berât* to his elder son, Süleymân Pasha, in which he appointed him member of the *dîvân*: "because it is incumbent upon us to revive functions of the religion and the *devlet* modelled on the practice of the great sultâns who functioned as *khalîfah*s."[31] His son,

*Introduction*

Murâd I (1362-1389), perceived himself as *khalîfah*.[i] Murâd's son Bâyezîd (1389-1402) was also addressed by the sovereign of Egypt, Hajj b. Shaʻbân, in 1391 as *"Zillullâh fil Khâfiqayn"* and "Sultân of the Muslims."[32] Bâyezîd's son, Chelebi Mehammed (1412-1421) sent *surre* (gifts) to Kaʻba and money to the people of Makkah and Medîna, while the title of Fâtih Mehammed (1451-1481) was "Sultân of the two continents, Khâqân of the two seas (the Mediterranean and the Black Sea), Amîrul Mu'minîn (Prince of Believers)."[33] Amîrul Mu'minîn, first used by ʻUmar b. Al Khattâb ﷺ, as is well known, is the title of the *khalîfah*. Fâtih's son Bâyezîd II (1481-1512) was addressed by Hüseyin Bayqara (795-819 AH/1392-1416 C.E.), Pâdishâh of Horasan, as "Khalîfetullâh fil anâm – The *Khalîfah* (vicegerent) of Allah among His creatures."[ii] The sovereign of India, Yaʻqûb Shâh, and his son Baysungur Mirza addressed Bâyezîd II as *khalîfah*,[34] while his son Sultân Selîm (1512-1520) was aware of his position as *khalîfah*. ʻUbeyd Khân of Samarqand recognised him as the *khalîfah* in 920/1514 well before he took over Egypt in 923/1517.[35] Thus, the Osmanlı sultâns continued to have the title as well as the practical power of the *khalîfah* until the end of their *devlet*. What Abdülhamîd II (1876-1909) added was simply the emphasis he put on the necessity of Islamic unity, but he did not "invent" the notion of the *khalîfah* as some Western writers claim.

Osmanlı sources also reveal that Sultân Selîm was determined to eradicate Shiʻism from Iran, and had actually planned to march

---

i *Ibid.*, I, 87. In his *berât* to Evrenos Beğ. Murâd I mentions that the lands in Rumeli (the European part of the Osmanlı Devlet) annexed by Evrenos Beğ belonged to "Allah, then to His Messenger ﷺ and then to the *Khalîfah* of His Messenger (i.e. Murâd I himself)." line 9.

ii *Munsheat*, I, p. 306; Hüseyin Bayqara continues: "appointed for the Sultanate and the Khalifate… Master of the *jihâd* (Ebu'l Magâzi) Sultân Bâyezîd."

against İsmâil Safavî in 1516. But the advance of the Mamlûk sultân Qansu Gavri (1440-1516) towards Anatolia in that year forced him to stop this venture. Had it not been for this, Sultân Selîm would probably have eradicated Shi'ism in Iran, and united the western Sunnî Muslim domain with Turkestan.

The social history of Anatolia in the last decades of the thirteenth and the first decades of the fourteenth century can be adequately found in İbn Battûta's famous book. Anatolia suffered a great deal, no doubt, after the Mongol invasion, but the picture was not so gloomy as generally assumed. Society was well organised and the *akhîs* acted as voluntary security forces that maintained – following *sûfî* spiritual training – a very high professional and moral standard such as we do not find among the police in many so-called developed countries today. Thus, it is reasonable to assume that the people of Anatolia – regardless of their race and religion – enjoyed better security during the Osmanlı era than many peoples living today in some cities of Germany, Russia, and the USA, not to mention Europeans in the fourteenth century.

The Osmanlı sources demonstrate that the Osmanlı Devlet was in fact a continuation of the Muslim Devlet of the four rightly-guided *khalîfah*s, the dynasties of the Umawîs (661-750), the Abbâsîs (750-1258), the Selçuklus (1038-1157), and the Anatolian Selçuklus (1075-1308). Many of the Osmanlı documents emphasise this fact, and I will quote only a few examples here. Sultân Murâd I (1362-1389) addressed Evrenos Beğ as "Amîrul Mu'minîn" when appointing him supreme commander over *gâzis* in Osmanlı Europe.[36] He probably did this in a parallel with the Final Messenger Muhammad ﷺ who used this title for the first time in connection with 'Abdullâh b. Jahsh, who led a small group of *muhâjirîn* to monitor the activities of Quraish in 2/624. Moreover, the Osmanlı archers at the first Battle of Kosova (791/1389) were compared to Sa'd b. Abî Waqqâs, the famous Muslim archer, who shot one thousand arrows during the battle of Uhud (3/625).[37]

*Introduction*

Kâtib Chelebi, the great Osmanlı writer and historian, says, "the Venetian Doce (Duke) is equivalent in rank to Beğlerbeği in a Muslim administration."³⁸ By using the Turkish word *beğlerbeği* in this Muslim context, this writer demonstrates that the Osmanlı Turks had fully submerged their identity in Islam. Another indication of this fact can be seen from the information given by Neshrî in his two-volume book on the formation of the famous *yenicheri* (janissary) corps. The Osmanlıs abided strictly by the laws of the Creator in the Qur'ân by taking one-fifth of the *ganîmet*³⁹ for the *devlet*.⁴⁰ Moreover, the ex-Christian children, who were taken as part of the *ganîmet*, were well treated. Once they accepted Islam, they were not discriminated against in public posts, and many of them became *pashas*, *vazîrs* and grand *vazîrs*.

Perhaps the most significant aspect of this continuity appears in the Osmanlı attitude towards the great *sahâbî* (companion of the Final Messenger ﷺ) Abû Ayyûb Khâlid b. Zayd al-Ansârî. The Turks called him Eyüb Sultân. Even now, almost a century after the destruction of the Osmanlı Devlet, the tomb of Eyüb Sultân is visited by newly-weds and circumcised children. In Turkish, this circumcision ceremony is significantly called *sünnet düğünü* (feast of the Sunnat), after the tradition of Muhammad ﷺ. The fact that this *sahâbî* has been given the title of "sultân" signifies the utmost respect given to him by the Osmanlı Muslims.⁴¹

Osmanlı aid to the Andalusian Muslims is also very clear in Osmanlı sources: Hızır Hayreddîn Reîs (afterwards Pasha: 1466-1546) rescued 70,000 Muslims from the Inquisition in Spain, and took them to Muslim North Africa.⁴² Kemâl Reîs (?-1511), who was appointed by Bâyezîd II as *qaptân-ı deryâ* (commander-in-chief of the Osmanlı navy), succeeded in helping the Muslims of Andalusia in 829/1487.⁴³ The Osmanlı presence in North Africa furthermore saved those countries from becoming a second Andalusia or "Latin Africa." Had the Osmanlıs not gone there, the people of Libya,

Tunisia, and Algeria would have probably become "Spanish-speaking Catholics" and those in Morocco "Portuguese-speaking Catholics." It is worth mentioning here that Oruch Reîs (d. 1518), elder brother of Hayreddîn Pasha, went from Tunis to Algeria[48] at the request of the notables of Algeria[44] to protect their city and country from the invasion of the Spaniards.

An entirely new dimension concerning the motives of the Osmanlı drive into Europe emerges when we read the account of the Osmanlı Sultân Süleymân the Magnificent (1520-1566) and a poem by an *aqınjı* commander.[i] After the victory of Mohac (932/1526), Süleymân the Magnificent said to the Hungarian ambassador who visited him in İstanbul: "Christendom used to accumulate threatening clouds over my ancestors, but those clouds did not result in rain. If they (the Europeans) had not caused these battles, that bloodshed would not have been necessary."[45]

In his poem *aqınjı* commander Mihaloğlu Ali Beğ, says:

*Eğer def olmaz ise bu beliyye*
   *Ne İznik kala ne Konstantiniyye*[46]
If this challenge is not repulsed.
   Neither Nicaea nor İstanbul will remain in our possession.

This shows that Europeans were determined to drive the Muslims out of Europe from the moment the Osmanlıs crossed the Marmara Sea. So the Osmanlıs had to fight their way to establish and consolidate their authority on that continent.

*Târîh* by Solaqzâde (ca.1000-1068/ca.1590-1657) gives detailed information about the Osmanlı annexation of Crimea. As mentioned elsewhere in this book, Fâtih took the shores and Azak (Azov)

---

i  The Aqınjıs were an Osmanlı voluntary force that fought beside the central and provincial armies. They were usually employed to make advance raids against the enemy.

*Introduction*

from the Genoese, while the rest of Crimea was annexed through diplomacy by his grandson Sultân Selîm (1512-1520).[i]

Osmanlı sources also reveal the main motive for the Osmanlı presence in Yemen, namely the protection of the two sacred cities of Islam from Portuguese aggression in the sixteenth century, and the subsequent hostility of other European powers. Being the protectors of the Holy Cities, the Osmanlıs were obliged to secure the *hajj* (pilgrimage) route from the Indian subcontinent and Jawa (Java) against Portuguese naval supremacy in the Indian Ocean. If the Osmanlı Devlet had not protected Yemen, the Portuguese would have occupied Makkah al-Mukarramah and Medîna al-Munawwarah! The calamity was carried out by Britain in the 20th Century during the destruction of Osmanlı Devlet (First World War).

It should be said here that the study of those Osmanlı sources requires a good knowledge of the Osmanlı language as well as a working knowledge of both Arabic and Persian. In addition, one should be very well versed in Islam, its culture, and history to understand and evaluate Osmanlı history. Psychological common ground is also a great help in this respect – so much so that even a non-practising Muslim Turk is bound to have some deficits and shortcomings in understanding Osmanlı history.

**Outline of the Book**

Unlike other works in the field, this book divides Osmanlı history into three main parts.

---

i   In the books written in European languages, the annexation of Crimea is generally accepted as actualised by Fâtih: see, for example, the map showing "The Rise of the Ottoman Empire: 1280-1683" in Shaw, *The History of Ottoman Empire and Modern Turkey* (Cambridge: C.U.P.), 1976) I, XIV-XV. Some – because they do not use Osmanlı sources – state that it is not certain if Fâtih acquired the whole of Crimea or only the shores. But there is no mention of Sultân Selîm, who accomplished this important task in a very diplomatic way.

Part One (1288-1453) deals with the foundation of the Osmanlı Devlet which began in 1288 (and not the oft-repeated date of 1299) and continued up to the opening of Constantinople (İstanbul) to Islam (857/1453). Indeed the Osmanlı Devlet became an important *beğlik* (emirate) during the reign of Orhan Gâzi, and a major power during the period of Sultân Murâd I, who defeated the combined European armies and reduced the (Eastern) Roman Empire to a tribute-paying vassal of the Osmanlıs. Nevertheless, the Osmanlı Devlet remained insecure until they put an end to the (Eastern) Roman Empire in 1453.

Part Two (1453-1699) deals with the expansion of the Osmanlı Devlet. The expansion of this *devlet* is generally assumed to have lasted until 1579, the year the famous *vazîr* Sokollu Mehmed Pasha died. But we now know that this expansion continued afterwards. Eğri was opened to Islam in 1596, Kanije in 1600, and Estergon in 1605. Until 1606, the year in which the famous Treaty of Zitvatorok was concluded, the status of all the kings of Europe was equal to that of the Osmanlı *sadrâzam*, while the Osmanlı Sultân remained superior to them all. With this treaty, the Osmanlıs had, however, recognised the Austrian king as a *caesar*, and henceforth an equal to their sultân. Thus this treaty marks a turning point in Osmanlı history.

Though it annexed Crete and besieged Vienna, the capital of Austria (1683), towards the last decades of the seventeenth century the Osmanlı Devlet seemed to have lost its vigour, dynamics, and zeal, and the Treaty of Karlofcha/Karlowitz (1699) stipulated its first loss of territory.

Part Three (1699-1922) studies the gradual decline of the Osmanlı Devlet. It is true that the Osmanlıs defeated the Russian czar, Peter, at Prut in 1711 and there were attempts at modernisation and rejuvenation, but the general feature of the *devlet* at the time was decay and deterioration.

*Introduction*

The capable Sultân Abdülhamîd II (1876-1909) did his best to revive the Osmanlı Devlet. In spite of the intrigues of the superpowers at the time, this political genius succeeded in maintaining the unity of peoples of different races and cultures in a single socio-political body that continued for 33 years. This credible achievement was realised without any undue economic burden on the people. In addition, Abdülhamîd set up scores of learning institutions that many great intellectuals graduated from. He was also a major champion of Islamic unity, which was in line with tradition and the basic principles of the Osmanlı Devlet.

But with his deposition in 1909 the Osmanlı Devlet steadily disintegrated at the hands of the leaders of the Ittihâd and Teraqqî Party until it was finally destroyed during the First World War (1914-1918) and officially ceased to exist on November 4, 1922.

# Part One

# The Foundation of the Osmanlı Devlet 1288-1453

# Chapter One

# Islam in Anatolia

The Seal of the Prophets, Muhammad 🌿, received the first revelation in the year 610 C.E. Immediately after his historic Hijrah (emigration) to Medîna he founded in 622 the first Muslim Devlet in history. This young and dynamic *devlet* rapidly expanded in all directions and addressed the glorious and revolutionary message of Islam to all humanity. It soon challenged the authority and the very existence of the two then decaying superpowers in the world: the Roman Empire and Sassanid Persia.

The Muslims, however, made their first incursion into Anatolia during the Umawî Khalifate (41-132 A.H./661-750 C.E.), when its army marched through that country until it reached Scutari, opposite the capital Constantinople on the European side of the Bosphorus. Subsequently another force commanded by Sufyân b. 'Awf made an assault on Constantinople itself. Meanwhile, the Muslim navy sailed into the Mediterranean and the Aegean Sea until it firmly established itself in the Qapıdağı Isthmus on the southern shore of the Marmara Sea. From this strategic naval base it proceeded to defeat the Eastern Roman navy and subsequently supported the Muslim army in its siege of Constantinople.

It is worth mentioning here that amongst the warriors of this Muslim army was Abû Ayyûb Khâlid b. Zayd al-Ansârî, the famous *sahâbî* (companion of the Prophet) who was the Prophet's 🌿 host on his migration to Medîna. Abû Ayyûb died there in 49/669 and was buried outside the city walls of Constantinople in a place that remained unidentified for the next eight centuries. When opening[i] Constantinople to Islam in 857/1453 the Osmanlı Sultân Mehemmed II (al-Fâtih) is reported to have appealed to *Shaykh* (*sûfî* leader) Akshemseddîn to locate this place, which he did. A tomb was then constructed on Abû Ayyûb's grave, and a mosque was built nearby in honour of his memory. The Turks give this great *sahâbî* the sovereign title of sultân, and he is consequently known among them as "Eyüb Sultân." The Osmanlı sultâns were inaugurated in that spot in a ceremony called *Qılıch Alayı* (The Sword Pageant), and they used to visit Ansârî's tomb with their army commanders for a blessing just before proceeding on *jihâd* against the infidel Europeans.

Another Muslim army besieged Constantinople in 99/717-718 but was unable to open it to Islam. The famous commander Maslamah b. 'Abd il-Malik (d. 120/738) had, however, managed to enter Anatolia and captured the city of Qayseri in 108/726. His famous and brave friend Sayyid Battâl Gâzi died a martyr of Islam in western Anatolia in 122/740. When this area was subsequently annexed by the Selçuklu Turks, a tomb and mosque were built on his grave. In due course this area became very famous, and the town nearby is now named after him: Seyitgâzi.

The Abbâsîs made fresh assaults on Anatolia. *Khalîfah* Hârûn ar-Rashîd (170-193/786-809) defeated the Roman Emperor Nikephoros at a battle near Ereğli, Qonya, in 190/806 and forced him to pay the *jizyah*.[ii] Another 'Abbâsî *khalîfah*, al-Ma'mûn (198-218/813-833),

---

i   The term "opening" is used in this book with some discretion to avoid the unsatisfactory usage of "invasion" and "conquest".

ii  The word *jizyah* derived from Arabic root *jazâ,* which means to compensate. *Jizyah* was thus a tax levied on able, male non-Muslims who lived under the protection of a Muslim Devlet because they were not entitled to serve in the Muslim army. It varied in amount, and there were exemptions for the poor, women, children, slaves, monks, and hermits. It was ordained by

## Chapter One – Islam in Anatolia

defeated the Eastern Romans after a fierce war of three years (215-218/ 830-833). But he died in 218/833 and was buried in a small but historic town, Tarsus. His grave is now in the great mosque of this town.

*Great Mosque, Tarsus*

*Al Ma'mûn's sarcophagus*

In 222/837 his successor, al-Mu'tasim (218-227/833-842), inflicted another humiliating defeat on the Roman Emperor Theophilos, destroying Amorium, an important centre and the Emperor's hometown. Al-Mu'tasim also dominated the "'Awâsim" area that extended from Malatya to Tarsus. But all these victories were temporary in nature, and Islam only won a stronghold in Anatolia during the time of the Selçuklu Turks who dominated most of this land, and firmly established their rule there.

### 1.1 Islam and the Turks

The ancient Turks lived in the Altay mountain area south of the Yenisey River. They claimed descent from Yâfeth, son of the Prophet Nûh 🌸. Their most outstanding character is Oğuz Khân,

---

the Creator in the Qur'ân Karîm (Sûrat al-Tawbah [9] *âyat*: 29), and was first adopted by the Final Messenger 🌸 when he went on a *jihâd* to Tabûk in 9/630: Yuhanna the Bishop of 'Aqabah (Aylah) came to him with a golden cross on his chest and paid *jizyah*, thus obtaining the protection of the Muslim Devlet.

a contemporary of the Prophet İbrâhîm ﷺ, who willingly accepted Islam. The Turks see him as Zulqarnayn. Oğuz Khân had six sons: Gün, Ay, Yıldız, Gök, Dağ, and Deniz. Four tribes descended from each of these sons:

| | |
|---|---|
| Gün Khân | – Qayı, Bayat, Alqaevli, Qaraevli |
| Ay Khân | – Yazır, Döğer, Dodurga, Yabırlı |
| Yıldız Khân | – Avshar, Qarıq, Beg-dili, Qarqın |

These tribes lived in the right-hand side of the domain and were consequently known as the right-hand Oğuz tribes.

| | |
|---|---|
| Gök Khân | – Bayındır, Pechenek, Chavundur, Chebni |
| Dağ Khân | – Salur, Eymür, Alayundlu, Üreğir |
| Deniz Khân | – Igdır, Büküdüz, Yıva, Qınıq |

These tribes were known as the left-hand tribes.[47]

Salur, the founding-forefather of the Salur tribe, lived during the time of the Prophet Muhammad ﷺ, and his successor Chanaq Khân accepted Islam. Other Turkish tribes and families converted to Islam and were thus called Türk-i İmân (Türks of Belief, i.e. Muslim Türks). In due course this word was read as Türkimân (Türcoman) and is pronounced today as Türkmen.

Islam spread in Turkestan via merchants. Although Qutaybah b. Muslim opened Bukhârâ to Islam and built the first mosque there in 94/713, this act did not cause the Turks to embrace Islam. But as they became familiar with Islam through Muslim merchants and understood that Islam was in harmony with their worldview and way of life, Turks embraced Islam willingly and voluntarily. It should be mentioned that Turks' becoming Muslim is regarded as one of the most important events in world history.

On the other hand, it seems that Islam spread quite early among the northern Turks. We see the Bulgars (in Arabic sources: Saqâlibah) emerging as the first Muslim Turkish *devlet* in history. "The name of 'Bulgar' seems to occur the first time in 482 C.E. After Atillâ's death in 453 C.E., the Hun unity disintegrated and the

## Chapter One – Islam in Anatolia

Bulgar Turks established their sovereignty from the Caucasus to the Danube."⁴⁸ Some of the Bulgar Turks moved to the Dobruja region under Esperih, son of Quvrat Khân, due to pressure by the Khazars. This branch of the Bulgars, i.e. the Danube Bulgars, enjoyed their most splendid period under Qurum Khân (803-814) and Omurtag Khân (814-831). Pars Khân (859-890) converted to Christianity in 864 and became Boris Khân, and consequently the Danube Bulgars became Christian and in due course mixed with Slavs to become a Slavonic people. Some Turkish words that remained in the Bulgarian language from pre-Islamic era indicate this fact.

*İdil Mosque*
*Picture designed to commemorate the Bulgar Turks*
*converting to Islam in 310/922*

The other branch of the Bulgars settled near the middle of the İdil (Volga) river in the second half of the seventh century. Their important cities were Bulgar, Biler, Suvar, Oshal, and Tetish. Islam spread quickly among them by means of merchants coming from Muslim countries. The Bulgarian Khân Almısh, son of Yaltavar,ⁱ embraced Islam and in 920 sent an envoy to the 'Abbâsî *Khalîfah* in Baghdad, asking him to send *'ulamâ* to teach Islam to the Bulgar people, as well as architects to build mosques and castles. *Khalîfah*

---

i His Muslim name is Ja'far b. 'Abdullah: Akdes Nimet Kurat, "Bulgar" M.E.B. *İslâm Ansiklopedisi*, İstanbul 1979, v.II, p.791.

## Osmanli History and Institutions

al-Muqtedir Billâh Ja'far sent an ambassadorial committee in 310/922.[49] The Bulgars of the İdil (Volga) embraced Islam in 922, thus becoming the first Turkish Muslim Devlet. Bulgars of the İdil lived happily until the second half of the thirteenth century. But their assault on and defeat of the Mongols who returned to the Aral area after a battle against Qumans in the Don region in 1223 prepared the way for their own disaster. So, on the orders of Batu Khân, after a lengthy preparation the Mongols attacked the Bulgars in 1236 and destroyed all their cities, putting the people to the sword.

The Bulgars recovered to some extent during the Golden Horde epoch (1282-1452) and survived. But they were attacked by Pulat Timur, the Khân of the Golden Horde, in 1361 and their main cities were destroyed. When later Emîr Timur carried out a campaign against Toktamısh, the Khân of the Golden Horde, in 1391, the Bulgars' cities were also destroyed. After that, the Bulgars lived on in the Khanate of Qazan.[50]

Another Muslim Turkish political entity was the Qarakhânlı (İligkhânlı) or Kara-Khanid *Devlet* (840-1212 C.E.), which was established in Afghanistan and parts of Turkestan, and whose most famous sovereign was Satuq Buğra Khân whose Arabic name was 'Abd ul-Karîm, who died in 344/959. The Turks, whose identity was by now immersed in Islam, fought their previous brothers the Shamanists and Buddhists. They also played an active role in spreading Islam in India to which they sent many *ghazwas* (*jihâd* expeditions) during the period 351-582/963-1186. Mahmûd of Ghazni (388-421/998-1186) and his successors led seventeen such expeditions. The Turkish Muslim army that fought these battles contained Arab, Persian, and other local soldiers. They spoke a pidgin language called Ordu, which in Turkish means "army." The present day word Urdu seems to have its origin in this Turkish word *ordu*.

The founder of the great Selçuklu Devlet (429-552/1038-1157) was a son of Duqaq of the Qınıq Clan of Oğuz. Its sultân, Tuğrul Beğ, son of Mîkâîl, son of Selçuk, marched to Baghdad at the head of his army in 447/1055 to rescue the 'Abbâsî *Khalîfah* from a Shî'î-Bûyî (Buyid) conspiracy. In honour of and respect for this *khalîfah*, Tuğrul himself led the *khalîfah*'s horse. He married his daughter afterwards, and it is related that, during the wedding festivities, the Turks of the *Harmandallı* clan performed their dance which is known today as *harmandalı* and which is still performed in western Anatolia. The *khalîfah* turned over his mundane authority to Tuğrul Beğ and invested him with the title of sultân.[51]

## 1.2 THE OPENING OF ANATOLIA TO ISLAM

*Fath* is an Arabic word, meaning "to open." In Islamic practice and terminology, it means "to open a country to Islam," i.e. "to enable inhabitants of that country to become familiar with Islam and its values" and "to remove artificial barriers between the created and the commands of the Creator."

As the religion of *fitrah* (natural disposition), Islam is presented to the inhabitants of that country to enable them to recognise and perceive that these commands are in conformity with their inner instincts and natural structures. The people in the country opened to Islam are not compelled to convert to Islam, which would only result in many hypocrites. Muslims pay *'ushr*, one-tenth of the crops, and the non-Muslims pay *kharâj* on their produce. The best way to evaluate the historical facts is to make a comparison; it should be remembered that at that time and afterwards the non-Christians in Europe were greatly oppressed.

Muslims came to Anatolia for the first time in a *jihâd* expedition at the time of the second *khalîfah* Umar b. al-Khattâb (13-23/634-644) under the *sahâbî* 'İyâz b. Ghanm in 18/639. Having arrived at Harrân, 'İyâz proceeded to Diyârbakır. Afterwards, the Muslims carried out another *jihâd* expedition to Anatolia at the time of the third *khalîfah* Uthmân b. 'Affân 23-35/644-656). They arrived in

Anatolia under the Umayyads; Sufyan b. ʿAwf arrived at Scutari at the head of the Muslim army and the navy came to the Qapıdağı peninsula on the southern shore of the Marmara Sea, helping the besieging army. The Muslims' siege of Constantinople continued until 60/679, and they concluded a peace treaty of thirty years with the Roman Empire.[52]

The ʿAbbâsî *Khalîfah* Harûn ar-Rashîd defeated Nikephoros, the Roman Emperor near Ereğli, Qonya in 192/807 and imposed the *jizyah*[i] on him and his family to humiliate him. Another ʿAbbâsî *Khalîfah*, al-Maʾmûn, also defeated an Eastern Roman army at Ereğli in 215/830. The *khalîfah* Muʿtasim defeated the Roman Emperor Theophilos in 222/837 and destroyed Amorium,[ii] the main Eastern Roman centre in Anatolia. But all these victories were of a temporary nature; the Muslims did not establish themselves in Anatolia firmly until the Selçuklu Turks opened it to Islam.

The Selçuklu Turks who had dominated Persia, Syria, and the Caucasus resumed the *jihâd* in Anatolia.[iii] Çağrı Beğ, son of Mîkâîl

---

i   *Jizyah* is an Islamic tax levied on non-Muslims by the Muslim ruler; the Muslim Devlet undertakes the protection of the *dhimmî* (non-Muslim living under Islamic rule) with regard to his life, dignity, and property.

ii  Amorium is mentioned in Arabic sources as Amûriyyah; it lies between Ankara and Emirdağ. When young Salmân al-Fârisî was in search of the true religion, he visited Mosul, Nusaybin, and Amûriyyah, residing in these centres together with the priests, the representatives of the religion taught by the Muslim Prophet Îsâ b. Maryam ﷺ – all Prophets are Muslims submitted to the commands and will of Allah; Islam means submission to the will of the Creator – just before the emergence of the Final Messenger, and then set out to the Arabian Peninsula where he met the Prophet Muhammad ﷺ and embraced the Final Message.

iii They called Anatolia Bilâd-ı Rûm or Rûm because of the fact that it was under Eastern Roman (Rûm) rule at that time. In fact, that empire was of

*Chapter One – Islam in Anatolia*

*Amorium in Western Anatolia, near Emirdağı under the village of Hisârköy. Westerners excavated their historic sites – after twelve centuries – to undermine the Islamic presence and, in the long run, to claim that those areas belonged to them.*

*The Westerners excavated their cultural past, undermining the Muslim presence in Anatolia, having lulled the educated elite and the administrators of the country to sleep with the concept of "human heritage." (On the other hand, and at the very same time, the destruction of Osmanlı mosques, buildings in Bosnia and Kosova (not to speak of other previously Osmanlı countries), has not been given any importance: they must be annihilated – those buildings are not part of the "human heritage"; they are to be expunged from the record!)*

Beğ, son of Selchuq Beğ, came to the Caucasus in 1015 C.E. and engaged in *jihâd* activities against Eastern Anatolia. Tuğrul Beğ, the other son of Mîkâîl Beğ, entered Anatolia in 1054 C.E. and arrived at Erzurum. All these achievements were reconnaissance activities. The war that decided the future of Anatolia took place at Manzikert on 26 August 1071 C.E. Selçuklu Sultân Muhammad Alp Arslan ibn Dâvûd (r. 455-465/1063-1072) commanded a Muslim army that marched through Persia to Anatolia. In a gesture of support and sympathy for this Muslim army, the 'Abbâsî *khalîfah* ordered that a prayer be said during *jum'ah* prayer in all the mosques of his khalifate. An attempt was made, however, to reach a peaceful settlement. In

---

Latin (Roman) origin, but it had been Hellenized culturally.

a heated dialogue between the arrogant Roman Emperor, Romanus Diogenus (r.1068-1071), and the Muslims' chief negotiator, Sav Tigin, the former sarcastically asserted that his horses would soon be watered at Hemedân, the capital of the Selçuklus. But the latter defiantly replied that the horses would indeed be in Hemedân, but he was not sure where the emperor would spend the next winter, i.e. the horses would be taken as booty and the emperor's future would be at stake. When diplomacy failed to achieve peace, the two armies fought a fierce battle at Malazgirt (Manzikert) in Eastern Anatolia on Friday afternoon, 26 August 1071. Though the Muslim army of only 54,000 men met a huge Christian army of 200,000 warriors, the forces of Islam were victorious in this memorable battle which determined the future of Anatolia. The infidels were dispersed and their emperor was captured.[i] Though released by the Selçuklus, Emperor Romanus was killed by his own people.

On the capture of Anatolia by the Selçuklu Devlet, the commander Süleymân, son of Kutalmish,[ii] was appointed ruler over the central part of Anatolia. He established his capital at Qonya and treated his people in a decent and courteous manner. He asked them to pay reasonable taxes and never interfered with their religious beliefs. At the same time, he intelligently exploited the inner feuds and conflicts within the Eastern Roman ruling family to acquire more territories.

i   This was the first time a Roman emperor was captured by a Muslim army. Claude Cahen: *La Turquie Pre-Ottomane* (İstanbul-Paris, 1988), p. 8.

ii   Neşrî, *op. cit.*, I, p. 26. *Kut almısh* means one who has aquired *kut* (holiness), i.e. is blessed. But Western writers read this name as Kutlumush, which does not make sense. (See for example: S. Shaw, *op. cit.*, I, 7; C. Cahen, *La Turquie pre-Ottomane,* (İstanbul-Paris: 1988), p. 1, and Bertold Spuler, *The Muslim World, Part I The Age of the Caliphs* (Leiden: 1960), p. 118.) Being alien to the Muslim world, they lack the necessary background and insight and often blindly repeat each others' mistakes and erroneous views.

*Chapter One – Islam in Anatolia*

He was, in fact, able to annex many parts of the Roman Empire, including İznik (Nicea) which he made his capital.[53] By 473/1080 he had extended his holdings as far as the Marmara and Aegean Seas, and the Roman Emperor, Aleksi Komnen, was compelled to pay him an annual tax. The territories that were under this branch of the Selçuklu dynasty became known as the "Sultanate of Rûm," and the Sultâns were called "Caesars of Rome" in Arabic to indicate their rule over the eastern part of the "Roman" Empire. By the end of the eleventh century, the Anatolian Selçuklus had fought the first wave of Crusaders. A monk called Pierre l'Hermit, travelling from one village to another on a donkey, had incited the Christians of Europe to take Jerusalem and other places venerated by Christians from the Muslims; thus, he was instrumental in the looting wars that started in 1097 C.E. called the "Crusades."

For example, during the Fourth Crusade, the European Christians occupied Constantinople in 1204 C.E. and looted it. The Eastern Roman dynasty had to flee the city; one branch continued at Trebizond as the Pontus Empire, the other branch continued at Nicea in Anatolia and was able to return to Constantinople in 1261.

Immediately after the death of Süleymân Shâh, his commanders were engaged in a bitter struggle for power that led to the disintegration of Anatolia into petty provinces, each under an autonomous governor. The most famous of those governors was Emîr Chaka, who opened many parts of western Anatolia to Islam in 488/1095: Focha, Urla, and the islands of Sockia and Sisam (Samos) in the Aegean Sea. Meanwhile, the Selçuklu sultân Börküyaruk in 487/1094 appointed Süleymân's son, Qılıch Arslan, governor of Anatolia. In 603/1206 the Selçuklu Turks terminated Christian rule over Antalya on the Mediterranean coast and opened this important city to Islam. During the time of the Selçuklu sultân Giyâseddîn Keyhusrev, the Selçuklu Turks fought their last battle with the Eastern Romans over Anatolia in Antaqiyya (Antioch) in 607/1210.

## OSMANLI HISTORY AND INSTITUTIONS

The greatest sultân of the Anatolian Selçuklus was Alâeddîn Keyqubâd. Coming to power in 616/1219, he set up an arsenal for the Selçuklu navy at Alâiyye on the Mediterranean coast. On the other hand, the people of Sudaq in Crimea mistreated the merchants engaged in trade with Anatolia, and Alâeddîn Keyqubâd sent Husâmeddîn Chobân there. Sailing from Sinop, Husâmeddîn Chobân went to Sudaq in 625/1228 and, after establishing sovereignty, imposed taxes on them.

*Chifte Minâreli Madrasah, Erzurum (from the Selçuklu period)*

On the approach of the Mongol threat, the 'Abbâsî *khalîfah* al-Mustansir Billâh reconciled the Anatolian Selçuklus with the Ayyûbîs in 633/1236. 'Alâeddîn Keyqubâd died in 634/1237 from eating wild fowl at a banquet.

### 1.3 THE MONGOLIAN OCCUPATION OF ANATOLIA

The Mongols, who were called "Tatars"[i] at that time, occupied the

---

i Contemporary sources always refer to the Mongols as Tatars. Barthold says that after Genghis Khân the name "Mongol'" replaced "Tatar": "Tatar,"

## Chapter One – Islam in Anatolia

area north of the Caspian and the Black Seas, Persia, Iraq, and Syria in the 13th century. The Mongol commander Bayju Noyin occupied Erzurum in Anatolia in 640/1242 and destroyed the city. The Selçuklu Sultân Giyâsuddîn Keyhusrev II came to Sivas at the head of 50,000 cavalry. The experienced commanders advised him to wait for reinforcements, but the commanders under him thought that the Mongols had only 40,000 horsemen and that there was no need for reinforcements. The Mongols, in fact, had 60,000 and the Selçuklu army was defeated at the Battle of Kösedağı in 641/1243. And the Selçuklus were obliged to pay the Tatars a certain amount of taxes and animals every year.

Some of the Tatars settled in Anatolia after the Battle of Kösedağı, and the Selçuklu sultâns became figureheads and puppets in the hands of the occupying Tatars. The Turkish tribes who had been settled by the Selçuklus in the area bordering on the Roman Empire found themselves in a position trying to survive on their own. The last Selçuklu sultân, Giyâsuddîn Mes'ûd, passed away in 1308. The administration of Anatolia was subsequently left to a Tatar governor-general.

The Tatar population was not enough to dominate all of Anatolia, so many Turkish *beğliks* (emirates) emerged in the debris of the Selçuklus. The largest ones were Qaramân, which included the capital Qonya, and the Germiyân Beğliks, and the smallest one was the Osmanlı *Beğlik*. Lands of the Osmanlı *Beğlik* were on the Silk Road. The Osmanlı winter seat of Söğüt was close to this

---

*Encyclopedia of Islam* (Leiden: 1934) IV, p. 701. But the term "Mongol" was used in the eastern part, and "Tatar" continued in the Western part. So, the Pechenek, Kipchak, and other Turkish peoples living under the Tatar administration were also called "Tatars" after their administrators. This fact explains why the Turks living north of the Caspian Sea and the Black Sea are called "Tatars" even today.

historical road. Nicea had become the capital of the Roman Empire in 1204 during the Fourth Crusade when the Crusaders invaded Constantinople. When the Roman Empire restored Constantinople in 1261, it became its capital again. This weakened the hold of the empire on the local governors, *tekfûrs* in Anatolia. Every *tekfûr* behaved as if he were an independent ruler. This event made the region vulnerable, but the most important factor was the "human" element. The first rulers and administrators of the Osmanlı *Beğlik* were the most committed to Islam, the prescription of salvation and happiness of all humankind. Thus they were appointed to realise the unity of Muslim Anatolia.

# Chapter Two

# The Foundation of the Osmanlı Devleti

*Ertuğrul Gâzi's sarcophagus, Söğüt*

i  The official name is: *Devlet-i 'Aliyye-*i Osmâniyye (The Sublime Osmanlı Devlet) and afterwards: Saltanat-ı Saniyya (The Brilliant Sultanate). The Osmanlı sociopolitical entity ***never*** called itself an empire (*imparatoriyye*). Even state is not relevant for the Osmanlıs; because the *devlet* is only a "tool" to implement the

## 2.1 ERTUĞRUL GÂZI

The founders of the Osmanlı Devlet came from the Qayı tribe of Oğuz. Ertuğrul Beğ entered the service of the Selçuklu Sultân Giyâsuddîn Keyhusrev III (1264-1283) in 1279.[54] He served as the *uch beği* of the Selçuklus and was given the small town of Söğüt by the Selçuklu sultân as a winter residence and Domanich as a summer one. Ertuğrul Beğ died and was buried in Söğüt. The year of his death is given as 1281. The Qayı tribe selected his son Osmân as the leader.[55]

*The infant Osmân was swung on a swing made of this pine (cham) tree by his grandmother. The tree is in the Domur village of Domanich, Kütahya*

---

already ordered rules (the revealed heavenly commands by the Creator); on the other hand, the socio-political entities called *state*, *état*, *reich*, and *staat* in Western languages are legislative as well as executive bodies; they assumed power "to legislate" after the Treaty of Westphalia (1648).

Moreover, it is impossible for Muslims not to have a *Khalîfah*: a *hadith sharif* states that "any Muslim who spends a single night without a *bay'at* on his neck, spends that night as a person living in Jahiliyyah circumstances." Abû Ya'lâ al-Farrâ Muhammad, *al-Ahkâmus Sultâniyyah* (Surabaya: 1394 /1974 ) p. 20.

## 2.2 OSMÂN GÂZI (1288-1324)

Osmân Gâzi was born in Söğüt in 652/1255.[56] He was appointed *beğ* (bey) of Söğüt by the Selçuklu Sultân in 683/1284. The *menshûr* (appointment decree) began with the Qur'ânic *âyat*: *"(O Muhammad) say: O Lord God, Owner of sovereignty! You bestow sovereignty on whom you will ...."*[57] The Selçuklu Sultân expressed his position as ظـل اللــه في الأرض *zillullâhi fil Arz* – Shadow of Allah on Earth.[i] As is well known, this was the title of the *khalîfah*.

The Selçuklu Khalîfah-Sultân asked the newly appointed *beğ* to be thankful to the Creator and to be affectionate towards the people, the created ones for whom he was about to assume the throne. In contrast, at that time, around 1284, the population of Europe consisted mainly of peasants, called serfs. No serf was allowed to leave the land on which he worked; he was a slave together with all his family. When the land was sold, they were also sold along with it as if they were farm animals; when a girl was married, she was obliged to spend her first night with the feudal lord. It is interesting to note that, while people in Europe were treated as if they were not full human beings, people in Anatolia were regarded as "those whose well-being was entrusted by the Creator to the rulers" (*emânet-i ilâhî*). In fact, the naming of the ruled ones in Muslim and non-Muslim countries does reveal those two very different approaches and treatment of them by rulers. In Islam, the ruled one is called

---

i  Feridûn Bey, *Mejmûa-i Münsheât-i Selâtîn*, İstanbul 1274, vol. I, pp. 48-49. It is interesting to note that almost none of the orientalists mentions the fact that the Anatolian Selçuklu sultân was the *khalîfah*. After the destruction of the 'Abbâsî khalifate in Baghdad in 656/1258, the Anatolian Selçuklus (446-718/1074-1308) became the major Muslim power that represented the *de facto* khalifate. The 'Abbâsî *khalîfah*s, then under the tutelage of the Mamlûks, were mere figureheads.

*ra'iyyat* (plural: *ra'âyâ*) meaning "one who is looked after, taken care of." In Europe these people were called *subjects*, in English, meaning "those who were brought under control."

*Anatolia under Ilhanlı (Mongol) sovereignty*

The Selçuklu Khalîfah-Sultân had no son. It seems that he saw great ability and a potential successor in Osman Gâzi. He pointed out his hopes for the future of this newly appointed *beğ* and his *beğlik* (emirate) stating:

*wa awwalul gaythi rashshun thumma yansakib*

وأول الغيث رش ثم ينسكب

"The beginning of bountiful rain is a tiny drop, then it pours."

He thus implied that the small Osmanlı *beğlik* (emirate) would evolve in the future to a huge ocean.

The *Khalîfah* goes on, urging Osmân Bey to be straightforward and to act in accordance with Islamic values: "*Fa man khâfa Allaha khawwafa 'anhu kulla shay' wa man lam yakhafillâha khawwafahu kullu shay'* – Whoever fears Allah, Allah causes everything to fear him, and whoever does not fear Allah, Allah causes him to fear

## Chapter Two – The Foundation of the Osmanlı Devlet

everything." The Sultân advised the *beğ* about fiscal affairs as well, quoting from the Qur'an: وَلَا تَجْعَلْ يَدَكَ مَغْلُولَةً إِلَىٰ عُنُقِكَ وَلَا تَبْسُطْهَا كُلَّ الْبَسْطِ – *Do not make your hand (as if it was) tied to your neck (being miserly) and do not stretch it (in giving) entirely* (17: 29).[i]

The Osmanlı Devlet in fact observed those guidelines and was known in particular for its piety and sympathy for the people. Osmân Gâzi used to invite the poor and the pious to dinner once every three days as well as clothing the needy and aiding widows.[ii]

Among the people of Osmân was a certain Shaykh Edebalı, who was a pious, educated, knowledgeable, and rich *sûfî*, though he lived a modest and ascetic life. Osmân Gâzi was reported to have had a

---

i  *Munsheât*, vol. I, pp. 48-55. We do know that the Selçuklu sultân sent a drum and a standard, tokens of inauguration to Osmân Gâzi (Neşrî, I, 110), and it is only very natural that a *menshûr* was sent with them. Even if the one quoted in the *Munsheât* is not the original, it reflects at least the essence and concept of what it should have been.

ii  Neşrî, *Kitâb-ı Cihân-Nümâ* (Ankara: Türk Tarih Kurumu, 1949), vol. I, p. 72. Not only Osmanlı history, but the history of Islam as a whole has been subject to non-Muslim Western cultural invasion and distortion; (the whole history of Islam) has been "made", "constructed" as they (orientalists) like and many Muslim scholars repeat their writings blindly, without being aware of the fact that the Muslim world has been living under cultural invasion for the last two centuries. The Muslim historians are in a position to rewrite their history on the basis of original (Arabic, Turkish, Persian) sources, using analytical methodology. One of the points that Westerners infused even into Muslims' minds is the fallacy that the Khalifate came to an end when the Mongols (called Tatars at that time) invaded Baghdad in 1258 and killed the *khalîfah*. It is true that the 'Abbâsî *khalîfah* who was installed in Egypt in 1260 was merely a figurehead and a symbolic one; but the *de facto* khalifate did continue with the Great Selçuklus who represented the military and political power of Islam, and, after them, with their successors, the Anatolian Selçuklus.

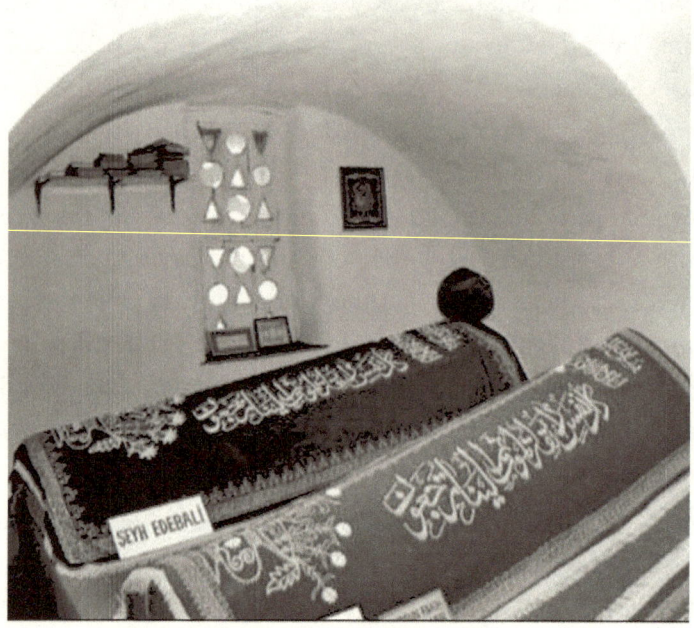

*Shaykh Edebalı's sarcophagus at Bilejik*

dream in which he saw a moon coming out of this *shaykh*'s chest and entering his own and a tree coming out of Osmân Gâzi's navel and spreading over a vast area, under whose shadow were mountains and rivers. When Osmân related this dream to the shaykh, Edebalı joyfully told him that Allah the Almighty had vested sovereignty over the whole world in him and his descendants. Shaykh Edebalı gave his daughter Malhun Hâtûn to Osmân in marriage.[58]

At that time there was an Islamic youth organisation in Anatolia called *Akhiyyah*, which represented a continuation of the *Futuwwah* organisation. İbn Battûtah, who visited Anatolia in 736/1336, gives a fairly detailed account of it:

> "We stayed here at the college mosque of the town, the principal of which was Shaykh Shihâbu'd Dîn al-Hamawî. Now in all the lands inhabited by the Turkmens in Anatolia, in every district, town and village, members of the

## Chapter Two – The Foundation of the Osmanlı Devlet

organisation known as the Akhiyya or Young Brotherhood can be found. Nowhere in the world will you find men so eager to welcome strangers, so prompt to serve food and to satisfy the wants of others, and so ready to suppress the cruel and kill their helpers[i] who join them."[59]

Edebalı was a *shaykh* in this organisation, which gave Osmân Gâzi considerable support, and its leaders Akhî Shemseddîn, his son Akhî Hasan, and Jendereli[ii] Kara Halîl were of particular importance in establishing the Osmanlı *Beğlik* (Principality) and in its development.[60] The important *futuwwah* groups, which represented a kind of Islamic chivalry, generally became the fashion throughout the central Muslim world at the beginning of the thirteenth century. Reorganised under the leadership of the last powerful 'Abbâsî *Khalîfah* an-Nâsir li Dînillâh (575-622/1180-1225), *futuwwah* had a very strong following in Anatolia at that time. Its members were given the title of *akhî*, *kardesh* (brother), or *javânmard* (brave, manly).

The *futuwwah* organisation existed not only in cities but also in rural areas. It had meeting places and lodges that were built in imitation of those of the *sûfî* brotherhoods, which had spread throughout the entire Islamic world in the thirteenth century. It also instituted rules and rituals that were similar to these brotherhoods' rites. People from everywhere in society, from leading political figures to rich merchants, *shaykhs*, scholars, master craftsmen, even unemployed vagabonds, were included in this organisation. All the artisans in the cities eventually joined it. In the largest cities in particular, young apprentices constituted the most numerous element in this organisation. In the

---

i    The word used in the text is the Arabic word *shurat* and it is not related to *shurta* (police force) as Gibb claims. It may be "injurers".

ii   This title was derived from Jendere, a village belonging to the municipality of Sivrihisar between Ankara and Eskişehir.

second half of the thirteenth century, when the authority of the central administration was especially shaken, this powerful organisation constantly made its presence felt. It played an active role in city life and was always taken into account as a political factor.⁶¹

From this account it is fairly clear that the Muslim inhabitants of Anatolia were very well organised. Among them were, in fact, four major such organisations in the fourteenth century:

1. *Akhiyân-ı Rûm*: the youth organisation of Anatolia
2. *Bâjiyân-ı Rûm*: the ladies' organisation of Anatolia
3. *Abdâlân-ı Rûm*: the *sûfî* organisation of Anatolia
4. *Gâziyân-ı Rûm*: the Holy War fighters' organisation of Anatolia.⁶²

These organisations indicate a very high standard of discipline in the Selçuklu Muslim Devlet even after its military defeat by the Mongols. The *akhiyya* (*futuwwah*) organisation seems to have its roots in a remark of the Final Messenger Muhammad ﷺ during one of his battles in which he called a warrior, Safwân, a *fatâ* (gallant, brave young man). Hence his *futuwwah* (*sûfî* youth) organisation was institutionalised and continued throughout the centuries.

> "[It] was an exemplary expression of the qualities of nobility, honesty, loyalty, and courage. The brothers of the *fityân* were expected to lead lives approaching these ideal qualities, which included demonstrations of generous hospitality to visiting strangers."ⁱ

---

i   In his book *The Adventures of İbn Battuta: A Muslim Traveler of the Fourteenth Century* (London: 1986), Ross E. Dunn claims that *futuwwah* "appears to have entered Asia Minor from Iran …" (p. 146). In fact, the Selçuklu Turks captured Iran while they were advancing from Turkestan, and the Anatolian (Rûm) Selçuklu rulers were their descendants. We have now sufficient evidence to assume that they brought the *futuwwah*

## Chapter Two – The Foundation of the Osmanlı Devlet

"With regard to its economic development and social division of labour, Turkish society in Anatolia in the thirteenth century was one of the most advanced of the late Middle Ages. The Selçuklu Devlet of the thirteenth century Anatolia that was the political expression of that society, was a centralised *devlet* having well-organised and sound institutions. It maintained the political and administrative traditions of the Great Selchûq *Devlet* which, in the eleventh century, ruled the area from Eastern Turkestan to the shores of the Sea of Marmara, and from the Caucasus to the Persian Gulf. With respect to the culture of mind, Selchûq Anatolia also reached a rather high level. In addition to the primary schools that were established next to every mosque to teach children reading and writing, *madrasah*s were built everywhere. Furthermore, because of the Mongol invasion, a great many scholars, poets, and mystics went to Anatolia from the eastern regions [of the Muslim World] and settled there. They increased the intellectual activity in Anatolia and won well-deserved fame for Selçuklu *madrasah*s."[63]

This provided a solid background for the Osmanlı Devlet.

The *akhîs* were bachelors; they worked during the day and came to their *tekke* in mid-afternoon. They ate together and welcomed anyone, regardless of race, religion, etc., who was visiting the town. Moreover, they acted as a volunteer police force. The *akhiyya* was an ideal non-governmental organisation. It is by no means an exaggeration to say that people in Anatolia in the thirteenth century, despite living under Mongol occupation, lived in better conditions than the citizens of

---

institution from Turkestan, which they ruled according to Islamic principles. So it is by no means an exaggeration to suggest that the Muslim society in Anatolia at that time was highly cultured and well organised.

49

New York, Chicago, Moscow, or St. Petersburg, and non-Germans in Germany in the 20th century, in terms of safety.

According to one report, Osmân Gâzi was the guest of an imam in a village one night. In those days homes had thick walls and wide windows that allowed putting some objects on them. The host said to Osmân Gâzi: "Would you mind bowing a little, there is something behind you in the window, let me have it." Osmân Gâzi asked what it was, and the host replied that it was the Word of Allah that had been revealed to the Final Messenger. Osmân Gâzi remained silent and steady. But when the host left him at bedtime he stood up, made *ghusl* (great ablution), and spent the whole night in a respectful posture towards the Qur'ân.[64]

According to an anecdote about Mawlânâ Jalâluddîn Rûmî, Ertuğrul Beğ used to visit him whenever he went to Qonya. On one of his visits to the great Shaykh, he was accompanied by his little son Osmân. Mawlânâ had heard that the Selçuklu sultân of the time had been connected to a *qalandarî shaykh* and said: "If the Sultân has found a father for himself, we, in our turn, we have found a son," and prayed for little Osmân.[65]

*Mehter (Osmanlı Military Band)*

## Chapter Two – The Foundation of the Osmanlı Devlet

Osmân Beğ opened Karajahisar to Islam in 687/1288[i] and captured its *tekfur* (governor). He sent his nephew Aq Temür with *khumsul ghanâim*[ii] to the Selçuklu sultân Giyâseddîn Mes'ûd II, who was very pleased with this victory against the Romans. In appreciation of this, he sent Osmân Beğ a flag, a *tuğ*, a drum, and trumpet, and a robe of honour together with a precious horse. These gifts arrived at mid-afternoon when Osmân Beğ ordered the drum and trumpet to be played at his door, where he stood and listened. The Sultân also gave him the town of Eskişehir.[66] Since the Selçuklu Sultân had no son,[67] he seemed to have seriously seen Osmân Beğ as his heir. Drums and trumpets increased in number and shape and in due course formed the *mehter*, the Osmanlı military band that subsequently became a model for European bands.

*Tablkhâne (Mehter)* was sent to Osmân Beğ in 1288. The Osmanlı Sultâns and the military and administrative people listened to the *mehter* while standing during their *jihâd* campaigns until Sultân Mehemmed II (Fâtih) listened to it while seated.[68] He did so because the Selçuklu Devlet had come to an end a long time previously and the Osmanlı Devlet was at that time a major power.

The monuments of the Anatolian Selçuklus bear the symbol of a two-headed falcon. We may conclude that the two-headed falcon was on the Selçuklu flags. We do not know if the two-headed falcon

---

i   Neşrî I, 86; İbn Kemâl, *Tevârîh-i Al–i Osmân*. ed. by Şerafettin Turan (Ankara: 1991), vol. I, pp. 105-106. According to Neşrî, the Sultân was Alâeddîn II, and according to İbn Kemâl Giyâseddîn, at that time the Sultân must have been Giyâseddîn. It should be noted that Eskişehir was given as a gift by the Selçuklu sultân to Osmân Beğ and that there is a mosque called Alâeddîn Jâmii (Alaeddîn Mosque) in the old part of Eskişehir, in the park in front of Atatürk Lisesi.

ii  It is an Islamic practice that *khums* (one-fifth) of the *ghanîmet* (spoils of the war) is sent to the *Baytul Mâl* (central treasury of the *devlet*).

was on the flag sent to Osmân Gâzi by the Anatolian Selçuklu sultân.

On the other hand, we know that the first *khutbah* in the name of Osmân Gâzi was recited during *jum'ah* (Friday) *prayer* in 688/1288 in Karajahisâr.[69] Since mentioning someone's name during *jum'ah khutba* is a sign of his being the ruler, it should be accepted that the *foundation* of the Osmanlı Devlet was proclaimed in 1288, not the often cited 1299.[i] It should be remembered that the first *jum'ah prayer* was performed by the Final Messenger Muhammad ﷺ at Rânûnâ valley during the *hijrah* from Makkah to Medîna;[70] when he was completely free, and there was no other authority; he was independent. As is well known, the *jum'ah prayer* is a strict obligation (*farz 'ayn mu'akkad*) for every free, independent Muslim; but a slave is not expected to perform it. According to Islamic jurisprudence (*fiqh*) there must be a certain amount of believers to perform the *jum'ah prayer*, and in the Hanafi school it must be performed with the permission of the authority. When Tursun Faqiyh and Edebalı were debating in Karajahisâr, since it was populated and the people were in need of *jum'ah prayer*, Osmân Beğ asked what the matter was. On learning that the permission of the Sultân of the time was needed for performing the *jum'ah prayer* in congregation, he responded sharply: "I am not under anyone's sovereignty (*taht-ı hukûmet*); I am a sultân myself, I have opened this country to Islam with my sword. I have not been a subordinate to anyone. I have neither master nor sultân. Is my permission not enough, is my authorisation not sufficient? If you mean by 'Sultân of the Age' the sovereign of Anatolia, what authority can he hold in my domain? Who is he? Neither are the people of my

---

i Neşrî states (*op. cit.*, I, 110) that the Selçuklu sultân Alâeddîn, sent the drum and flag to Osmân Beğ with Aq Temür many years before the opening of Bilejik (which occurred in 698/1299) to Islam (as tokens of sovereignty).

*Chapter Two – The Foundation of the Osmanlı Devlet*

country in need of him, nor does my sovereignty depend on him, and my lineage is not inferior to his."[71] Hence Osmân Beğ appointed Tursun Faqîh as the *Khatîb* who delivered the *khutbah* on Fridays and gave *ijâzet* (permission, authority) to perform the *jum'ah Prayer* in congregation in 688/1288. The first *jum'ah Prayer* was performed at Karajahisâr and the first *bayram* (*'Iyd*) *prayer* was performed at Eskişehir in the name of Osmân Beğ.[72] On the other hand, one of the earliest Osmanlı sources points out that "Osmân Gâzi had already acquired independence to some extent but had kept *khutbah* in the name of the Selçuklu Sultân out of sheer respect for him."[73]

The socio-political entity established by Osmân Beğ was later called by them *Devlet-i Aliyye-i Osmâniyyeh* – دولت علیه عثمانیه – The Sublime Osmanlı Devlet. In Islamic understanding and practice a *devlet* is only a tool for implementing already existing rules called *sharî'at* that *all* Muslims believe to have been revealed by Allah, the Creator. The *devlet* does not legislate; it only implements. The state, état, staat etc. in European countries are completely *different* socio-political entities from *legal, structural,* and *functional* points of view. In other words, to translate *devlet* as *state*, *état* or *staat*, let alone *empire*, is incorrect and unacceptable. Those socio-political entities called state, état or staat in European countries assumed legislative power after the Westphalia Treaty (1648). They *legislate*; the *qânûns* issued by the Osmanlı administration are not legislation; they depended in essence on Islam and on local tradition as long as it was not essentially incongruous with Islam. In other words, a *qânûn* is equivalent to a list of instructions. It must not be ignored that "Countries and peoples are unique and are not so easily lured into identity with each other save on limited, and specific points."[74] It is a basic rule that proper names, nomenclature are not translated; so, translating *devlet* into *state* or *état*, let alone *empire* is unacceptable.[i]

---

i   Chris Cook, *Dictionary of Historical Terms* (London: Macmillan, 1983),

The Islamic leaven put by Shaykh Edebalı into the Osmanlı dough during the process of its making is essential and very important. If the continuous, overwhelming effect of this very well-educated, knowledgeable shaykh on the founder of the Osmanlı Devlet and his son Orhân Beğ is ignored, any writing of its history is bound to follow a wrong path. Osman Beğ was a very brave and able ruler, but a founder needs other qualifications as well. Shaykh Edebalı guided him and he was effective in founding the *devlet* on solid Islamic foundations. Enver Pasha, who played a destructive role in the collapse of the Osmanlı Devlet, was also a determined, able,

*Osmanlı Beğlik (Hüseyin Dağtekin)*

---

p. 152: "From the fifteenth century onwards, Spain, Portugal, Holland, France and Britain began building overseas empires."

J.M. Roberts, *The Hutchinson History of the World* (London: Hutchinson, 1987), p. 835 (emphasis added). "... some of the old imperial powers continued to enlarge their empires impressively, such were Russia, France and Great Britain. Others stood still and found theirs reduced; this group included the Dutch, Spanish and Portuguese."

## Chapter Two – The Foundation of the Osmanlı Devlet

and extremely brave man, but his qualifications did not lead him to success.

During a skirmish, Osmân Beğ arrested Köse Mihâl, *tekfur* of Harmankaya, but soon released him in appreciation of his bravery. Köse Mihâl subsequently declared loyalty to Osmân Gâzi, and disclosed to him a plot organised by the neighbouring *tekfurs* to assassinate him during a wedding to which he had been invited. But Osmân Beğ managed to out-manoeuvre them, and succeeded in annexing both Bilejik and Yarhisâr to Islam. He married the daughter of the *tekfur* of Yarhisâr to his own son Orhan in 698/1299.[75] This woman, Nilufer Khâtûn, was the mother of Süleymân Pasha and Murâd Gâzi. Subsequently, Osmân Beğ sent one of his commanders, Turgut Alp, to besiege the castle of İnegöl and later joined him to open İnegöl to Islam in the same year. Then Yenişehir was opened to Islam to become the new capital for the *beğlik*. The Turkmens (Turkomans) adopted the urban way of life at this new town.

When the European armies who set out on the Fourth Crusade occupied Constantinople and plundered it in 1204, the Roman Empire shifted her capital to İznik (Nicea). When Constantinople was restored in 1261, the capital was shifted there from İznik, so its grip on the *tekfurs* in Anatolia eased. On the other hand, many Turks of Oğuz descent, who came to Anatolia while fleeing from the Mongols, joined the Osmanlı forces that were in the process of opening town after town to Islam at the expense of the Roman Empire.

However, the *tekfurs* resumed their anti-Osmanlı activities with the support of Constantinople, which sent them a force of 2,000 soldiers for this purpose. Osmân Beğ defeated this combined force at Qoyunhisâr in 701/1302, and annexed most of the land surrounding Bursa for the Osmanlıs. The way was now open to İzmit. When the region of Ulubâd was opened to Islam, the *tekfur* of Ulubâd handed over to him the *tekfur* of Kite (Kütahya), who had fled from

Osmân Beğ, after Osmân Beğ promised that neither he nor any of his descendants would cross the bridge over the Ulubâd River. This promise was honoured throughout the centuries: Osmanlı Sultâns opened large areas not only in Anatolia, but also in the heart of Europe, but none of the Osmanlı Sultâns crossed the bridge over the Ulubâd river in their Anatolian campaigns. They did, however, cross the river by boat![76]

Faced with this serious challenge and in an attempt to solicit the support of the Mongols against the Osmanlıs, in 708/1308 the Roman Emperor, Andronikos II, offered to marry his sister Maria Despina to the Mongol ruler (who made her a concubine) in Persia. But the latter was too engaged in internal troubles and in war with the Sultân of the Mamlûks, who ruled Egypt, the Hejâz, and Syria, to give active support to the Emperor. Nevertheless, Osmân Beğ prepared himself for a confrontation, particularly when he was informed that the Ilkhanlı (Mongol) Sultân (680-716/1281-1316) ordered a Mongol army of 30,000 men to be formed against the Osmanlıs.[77]

Meanwhile, after getting to know the early Osmanlıs, who lived according to their beliefs, Köse Mihâl embraced Islam voluntarily in 713/1313; he was called Abdullah Mihâl and fought numerous battles alongside Osmân Beğ, which resulted in the opening of Mekeje, Akhisâr, and Geyve to Islam.[78] Mihâl Gâzi's descendants commanded *aqınjı* (raiding forces) in Europe until the mid-sixteenth century C.E., and some of them were very famous commanders.[i]

---

i   Yılmaz Öztuna includes Taraklı among those towns and gives 1308 as the year of its being opened to Islam (*Başlangıcından Zamanımıza Kadar Türkiye Tarihi* (Hayat Kitapları, İstanbul: 1964), v. III, p. 25). There is a very old buttonwood tree assumed by the local people to have been planted at the opening of Taraklı to Islam, which they hold is 1293-94.

   *Aqınjı* forces were light cavalry; they were extremely brave and fit, very

## Chapter Two – The Foundation of the Osmanlı Devlet

Osmân Beğ was not, however, personally engaged in any battle after 720/1320 because of a serious disease that made him unable to ride. His son, Orhan Beğ assumed the *devlet*'s affairs and Osmân Beğ died in 726/1326 during the opening of Bursa to Islam and was buried there in Gümüşlü Kümbet.[79]

In his will to his son Orhan Gâzi, Osmân Gâzi advised him, "If anyone advises you to do something that the Sublime Truth (Haqq Te'âla, i.e. Allah subhânahu wa ta'âla) has not ordered, do not accept it. Do not carry out anything which Allah ﷻ has not ordered. Consult the *'ulamâ* of *sharî'at* about matters you do not know."[80]

Osmân Gâzi set the regulations for his *devlet*, which was founded on a *jihâd* principle:

> "Whoever I give a *tımar* it must not be taken back without reason; when he dies, the *tımar* will be given to his son. If the son is too young to participate in a *jihâd* campaign, his servants will represent him until he is able to fight. May Allah be pleased with whoever complies with this regulation. May Allah not be pleased with anyone who misleads my descendants concerning this rule."[81]

As is well known, the *iqtâ'* system was practised in early Islam by

---

well-trained *mujâhids*. An *aqınjı beği* (aqınjı commander) knew more than half a dozen local languages; he personally selected his soldiers, trained them well, commanded thousands of *aqınjıs*, and was directly answerable to the *Dîvân-ı Hümâyûn* (central Osmanlı Government) in İstanbul; no local administrator, *sanjak beği* or even *beğlerbeği* was entitled to interfere with his administrative or organisational affairs. *Aqınjı* forces entered enemy lands in advance of the main army and, scattered around in the form of tree branches, raided towns and villages. No village or town in central Europe in the sixteenth century could be certain that there would not be any *aqınjı* cavalry in its streets in the morning.

## Osmanlı History and Institutions

*Osmân Gâzi's sarcophagus Bursa*

the Final Messenger Muhammad ﷺ; this practice continued with the Osmanlıs under the name of *tımar*: a piece of land was given to the administration of a soldier or commander for his bravery in *jihâd* and, in return, he would train a certain number of soldiers for *jihâd*.

Thus Osmân Gâzi laid the foundation of an Islamic *devlet* and carried out *jihâd* to "open new lands to Islam" in compliance with "the Heavenly commands."

### 2.3 ORHAN BEĞ (1324-1362)

Orhan Beğ, or "İkhtiyârud Dîn Orhan Beğ" as he was called by İbn Battûta,[i] took charge of the army while his father was still alive.

---

i  *Rihlatubni Battûta* (Beirut, 1384/1964), p. 308. He referred to himself, however, as "Shujâuddîn Orhan bin Fakhruddîn Osmân." See: İ.H. Uzunçarşılı, "Gazi Orhan Beğ Vakfiyesi," in *Belleten* (Ankara: Türk Tarih Kurumu, 1941), vol. 19, pp. 280-283. Pitcher wrote on İbn Battûta's work: "An admirable and unbiased account of Asia Minor is given by the famous traveller who went right through the Peninsula in 1333." D.E. Pitcher, *An*

## Chapter Two – The Foundation of the Osmanlı Devlet

He opened Mudanya to Islam in 721/1321 and during the siege of Bursa, Qonur Alp opened the area between the Osmanlı borders and the Black Sea, while Aqchaqoja annexed the lands around İzmit. Subsequently, Gâzi Orhan Beğ controlled Atranos (Orhaneli), a key position for Bursa, and continued to besiege Bursa itself until it surrendered in 726/1326.[82]

When Orhan Beğ became ruler, his brother Alâeddîn Beğ took command of the army and became *beğlerbeği*. However, he retired afterwards to his farm on the plain of Kütahya. While he was *beğlerbeği*, he changed the colour of the Osmanlı soldiers' *börk*[i] from red to white. Alâeddîn Beğ helped Chandarlı (Jendereli) Kara Halîl set up infantry units.[83]

Orhan Beğ made Bursa his capital. In the meantime, Aqchaqoja opened Qandıra to Islam, and Qaramürsel Gâzi annexed the southern shores of İzmit Bay. Aqchakoja and his lieutenant Abdurrahman Gâzi opened Aydos and Samandıra to Islam, thus pushing the Osmanlı border to the Bosphorus and the shores of the Black Sea. This frightened the Roman Emperor Andronikos III (r.1328-1341), who crossed the Bosphorus and met Orhan Gâzi at Pelecanon between Darıja and Eskihisâr. But he was defeated and fled to save his life in 728/1328. İznik (Nicea), which had been besieged by Osmanlıs for some time, surrendered in 731/1331.[84] Women in the city who had lost their husbands because of starvation or in battle, were married to the Osmanlı *gâzis* who stayed in İznik to protect the town.[ii] Because

---

*Historical Geography of the Ottoman Empire*, (Leiden: E.J. Brill, 1972), p. 5.

i This headgear, called *börk*, was made of tailored felt during the Osmanlı era. The *börk* of the Göktürks in Turkestan was made of lamb skin, with the wool still on it.

ii Neşrî, I, 158. In İznik, at the Council of Nicea in 325 C.E., the number of gospels accepted as canonical by Christians was reduced from 72 to 4.

*The Buttonwood Tree at Taraklı*

the Osmanlıs treated the people of the lands that were opened to Islam fairly, many Christian people from those areas came to İznik while it was under siege, and advised those being besieged to surrender and live in comfort.[85] This attitude explains the comparative ease with which the Osmanlıs opened large areas to Islam in a very short time. For example, when Orhan Gâzi's elder son, Süleymân Pasha, approached Taraklı, the Christian inhabitants gave up the castle without any fight and were happy to live under Muslim rule. Many peasants from neighbouring villages willingly accepted Islam.[86]

## Chapter Two – The Foundation of the Osmanlı Devlet

It was the Osmanlı Devlet's custom to plant a buttonwood (plane tree) as a symbol for its length of life in a town newly opened to Islam. There is still a buttonwood tree that is assumed by the local people to have been planted in 1293-94 at the opening of Taraklı to Islam. It is very old, and eleven people are needed to circle it holding hands. It is clear that the Osmanlıs did not open that town in the name of the Selçuklu Sultân.

İznik temporarily succeeded Bursa as the Osmanlı capital, and Orhan Gâzi transformed İznik's Ayasofya (Hagia Sophia), the cathedral church, into a mosque. He also converted a monastery into a *madrasah* and built an *imâret*, an institution for the elderly and the poor. He appointed al-Hâj Hasan, a *murîd* of the famous Shaykh Edebalı, the head of the *imâret*.[87]

It is significant to note that the Muslims had such charitable and philanthropic institutions as early as the fourteenth century while Europe still practised slavery and despotism. Indeed, the Mediaeval Ages (395-1453) are Dark Ages for Europeans, but they should logically be considered "Brilliant Ages" for Muslims. Orhan Gâzi appointed Mevlânâ Dâvûd Qayserî as *müderris* (professor) of the *madrasah*.[88] Another *imâret* was built in İznik in the name of Nilüfer Khâtûn, Orhan Gâzi's wife, while his son Süleymân Pasha (1316-1358) built a *madrasah*.

Thus, by the first half of the fourteenth century, the Osmanlıs were superior to the Eastern Romans in terms of social and educational activities. At that time, there was in fact a clash between Islamic and Christian civilisations. Those who lived under the administration of the Muslim Devlet were far better off than their Christian counterparts in the Roman Empire, not to speak of Europe which experienced all kinds of exploitation then and had no time for or interest in such philanthropic institutions. Muslims had public and private baths at that time, but Christians used to destroy them. While the concept of cleanliness is of utmost importance in Islam, it

*The madrasah of Süleymân Pasha, İznik*

was despised among the Christians of that time. Robert J. Scrutton elaborates on this in the following quotation:[89]

> "Self-torturing monks gloried in their own filth. In his *History of the Inquisition,* Llorente mentions many instances of converts from mohammedanism being scourged almost to death, then thrown into filthy prisons because they continued the daily ablutions of their former faith. The Inquisition abolished public and personal cleansing of the body. As bathing was a heathenish custom, all public baths were to be destroyed and even all large baths in private homes."[90]

Indeed public and private baths were well known in the Muslim countries at that time, while Christians were accustomed to destroying them. When the Muslims opened İznik to Islam, they built public baths there; at that time the situation in Europe is described by a Westerner in the following passage:

> "The streets and dwellings were foul with human and animal excretions. Filthy, louse-ridden Christians, from kings to commoners, were infested with sores and riddled

*Chapter Two – The Foundation of the Osmanlı Devlet*

with disease. The madness brought its own punishment, the terrible plagues. The people believed God was punishing them for their sins, and failed to realise they had brought the punishment upon themselves. The cosmos pattern of health taught by prophets of God cannot be ignored with impunity."[91]

The spiritual and moral atmosphere that emanated from Shaykh Edebalı and his followers prevailed in Osmanlı social life. Society was well organised, justice was well established. There were scarcely any poor people, so much so that, "it was very difficult, even impossible, to find any poor person to pay *zakât* to."[92]

## 2.4 THE KHALIFATE: THE OSMANLI GOAL AND IDEAL

Being the most devout Muslims among the other *beğliks*, the Osmanlıs were aware of their responsibility towards Islam. They strove in particular to revive the Khalifate through the *jihâd* they carried out against the then superior but internally decayed Roman Empire. This is clear from a *berât* Orhan Gâzi sent to his elder son, Süleymân Pasha, in 734/1332, appointing him a member of the *Dîvân* (the Osmanlı government) and *Mîrimîrân* (supreme commander) of the Osmanlı forces. After reminding him of his duties to defend the borders of Islam, to look after the people's wellbeing, and to maintain justice, he explicitly told his son that "all the people in our domain" should be represented in "our Dîvân … because it is incumbent upon us to revive functions of the religion and the *devlet* after the practice of the great sultâns who functioned as Khalîfahs."[93]

While the people in Europe had few rights, lived in serfdom, and were sold together with animals when the piece of land on which they lived was sold, people of all faiths in the Osmanlı Devlet lived under the most humane conditions: their lives, honour, beliefs, property were protected by the *devlet*, this practice being accepted *as a heavenly duty*. As is well known, people in Europe were bound to the land they cultivated by the decree of Constantine, the Roman Emperor,[94] and they became slaves who were not able to leave the place.

The Osmanlıs opened Gemlik to Islam in 734/1334, then Armutlu on the southern shore of the Marmara Sea, and the city of İzmit in 737/1337, whose administration was entrusted to Süleymân Pasha, the elder son of Orhan Gâzi. The next year Üsküdar (Scutari) was annexed.[95] Eventually, when the famous and important city of İznik became the capital of the Osmanlıs, the previous capital Bursa was placed under the administration of Murâd Beğ, the second son of Orhan Gâzi, who had the name of *Beğ Sanjağı*.[96]

The Osmanlı Devlet had so far refrained from fighting any Muslim country, but they were engaged in *jihâd* activities against the (Eastern) Roman Empire. Like many other governors, Ajlân Beğ remained sovereign over Qaresi *Beğlik* after the collapse of the Selçuklu Devlet. He died in 1335, leaving two sons: Tursun Beğ, who joined Orhan Gâzi, and Demirhan Beğ, who assumed the administration of the *beğlik*. But the people of Qaresi did not accept Demirhan and sent for Tursun Beğ. The latter, however, told Orhan Gâzi that he would be satisfied with Qızılja Tuzla and Mahrama, and that he was therefore free to dispense with Balıkesri, Bergama, and Edremit as he wished.[97] To encourage the opening of new areas to Islam, Osmanlı rulers used to allocate the administration of the newly annexed territories to the relevant commanders of the troops. Some of these areas still bear the names of those commanders: Qojaeli (Qoja's country), the *vilâyat* whose administrative centre is İzmit, was named after Aqchaqoja, and Qaramürsel, on the south shore of the Marmara Sea, named after Qaramürsel Gâzi. Thus, Orhan Gâzi accepted Tursun Beğ's offer, and they marched together to Balıkesri while Demirhan Beğ fled to Bergama. When

## Chapter Two – The Foundation of the Osmanlı Devlet

he approached the castle to speak to his brother, however, Tursun Beğ was killed by an arrow. Nevertheless, Orhan Gâzi proclaimed a general amnesty and consequently many people offered obedience to him in 735/1334-1335. The life of Demirhan Beğ was spared; he was sent to Bursa to die there of a plague two years later. Orhan Beğ left the administration of the Qaresi country to his elder son Süleymân Pasha and returned to Bursa.[98]

The Osmanlı annexation of the Qaresi *Beğlik* with its lands up to Chanaqqale in 735/1334-1335, facilitated their advance into Europe. The able and famous commanders of Qaresi *Beğlik* such as Hâjı İlbeği, Eje Halîl, and Gâzi Fâzıl joined the Osmanlı Army and did it great service.[99] As far as they were concerned, this was the continuation of the same *jihâd* activity against the same infidel in collaboration with the neighbouring Muslim force of the same race, the same faith, the same language, the same tradition, and the same worldview. With his ultimate aim *"kefereyi qam' ve Müslimîni jem* – to subdue the infidels and to unite the Muslims", Orhan Gâzi seriously contemplated the idea of crossing the Marmara Sea and spreading Islam on its other side.[100] But it is important to note that he did not think of expanding his territory at the expense of other Muslim *beğliks* in Anatolia, while most of the other *beğliks* were engaged in that futile activity. When he disclosed his wish to his son Süleymân Pasha, the latter gallantly responded: "If you order me, your humble servant, I will cross the sea by the grace of Allah, and the miraculous help of the Final Messenger. I will remove the darkness of disbelief in those areas and enlighten them by the light of Islam."[i]

---

i Neşrî, I, 172. The writer of *Münsheât* was criticised for the documents related to the beginnings of the Osmanlı Devlet. But Neşrî, who is one of the writers of the earliest sources for Osmanlı History, mentions here this "attitude of mind, worldview, and ready-to-act spirit." I am of the opinion

*The Balkans in the mid-fourteenth century*

Süleymân Pasha, after obtaining permission from his father, consulted two ex-Qaresi commanders, Eje Beğ and Gâzi Fâzıl, who advised crossing the sea at its narrowest spot. They then crossed it on a raft, captured a peasant, and took him back with them. Süleymân Pasha gave this man a number of presents to secure his help in attacking Chimbeni castle. With a selected group of 80 brave soldiers, Süleymân Pasha crossed the Dardanelles and entered Chimbeni castle by night. The next day he captured some ships to convey more than 200 *mujâhids* from Anatolia to Chimbeni. Eje Beğ went to Aqcha Liman, where he burnt the moored Roman ships, and the Muslims opened another castle called Ayashilunye. Many people came from Edinjik, south of the Marmara Sea, to the Muslim liberated areas in Europe, while the Christian soldiers of those two castles were conveyed to Qaresi in Anatolia. Volunteer *gâzis* continued to flow to the newly-acquired Muslim territories. Subsequently, a united Christian force entered into a fierce battle with the Muslim army, in which they were defeated and dispersed

---

that this line of conduct on the part of the Osmanlıs, as mentioned by Neşrî, is to be taken into consideration.

## Chapter Two – The Foundation of the Osmanlı Devlet

in 758/1357.[i] Yaqûb Eje opened the area called today Ejeâbâd in Gelibolu (Gallipoli) Peninsula to Islam, and Gâzi Fâzıl accompanied him. The two heroes' tombs are there now.[101]

European Christian countries noted the Osmanlı activity in Gelibolu, but they could not find time to struggle with those newcomers because of conflicts among themselves. The Osmanlıs, nevertheless, provided against the possibility of a Serbian, Bulgarian, and Hungarian attack or a Rome-Venetian alliance; they captured the whole Marmara coast up to Tekirdağ and settled Muslims there, bringing them from Anatolia, and they sent some of the Christians who were potential soldiers to Qaresi in Anatolia, and settled them there.[102]

Gâzi Süleymân Pasha opened Malkara and Keşan to Islam, thus blocking the Constantinople-Edirne road. He died in an accident while hunting in Bolayır in 760/1359. His father, Orhan Gâzi kept on sending Turkmens to European Muslim lands to settle there, but he died two months after his son[103] and was buried at Bursa.

When he appointed his elder son Süleymân commander-in-chief of the areas newly-opened to Islam in 733/1332, Orhan Gâzi specified his responsibilities as follows: "to defend the boundaries of Islam, to look after the people and care about their well being. If we do not, the Creator will not be happy with us and hence our *Devlet* will not continue to survive." Orhan Gâzi goes on to say that "The great Khalîfahs behaved in accordance with the

---

i *Oruç Beğ Tarihi*, ed. by Atsız, Tercüman 1001 Temel Eser, İstanbul 1972, p. 36; *Aşıkpaşaoğlu Tarihi*, ed. by A. Nihal Atsız, Kültür ve Turizm Bakanlığı, Ankara 1985, pp. 52-53; Neşrî, I, 176. Westerners generally depend on what Cantacuzen wrote on this topic. But he lost the struggle for power and retired in 1355 to a monastery; and many points in his work were criticised and refuted by his contemporary writer Grigoras: İ.H. Uzunçarşılı, *Osmanlı Tarihi*, vol. I, p. 138, footnote 3.

directive of the Qur'ân: '*Stand out firmly for Allah, as a witness to fair dealing, and let not the hatred of others make you swerve to do wrong and depart from justice. Be just: that is next to piety*' (*al-Mâidah* [5]: 8)." He went on to remind his son of the need to protect Muslim territories and to open new lands to Islam. In this respect, he quoted a number of *âyât* from the Qur'ân: "*They rejoice in the bounty provided by Allah*" (*Âlu Îmrân* [3]: 170). "*If any do transgress the limits ordained by Allah such persons wrong (themselves as well as others)*" (*al-Baqarah* [2]: 229).

He also quoted from the Final Messenger's sayings: "To carry out justice for one hour is better than worshipping for seventy years" (i.e. in addition to the five prayers). Finally, Orhan Gâzi urged his son to be generous and to reward people for their services.[104] When informing his father of the acquisition of new areas to Islam in Rumelia, Süleymân Pasha mentioned that he gave the *dizdâr* (the commander of a castle) and the *erenler* (*sûfî gâzis*) their *ulûfe* (salary) and *tımar* (*iqtâ'*).[105] His use of the word *eren* is very interesting as it implies that most, if not all, of the volunteer soldiers in the newly-acquired castles were *sûfî gâzis* who acted in accordance with the *ribât* tradition of early Islam. This indicates that the Osmanlı Devlet had based itself right from the beginning on high Islamic values and principles that secured happiness in this world as well as in the hereafter for humanity. Those *sûfî gâzis* were morally and spiritually very well educated under a *shaykh* (a spiritual master), who had acquired a high spiritual level; they were dedicated to *jihâd* activity after winning victory over their inner selves, egos, having attained a high moral standard. They were stationed on the borders in continuation of the *ribât* tradition. Their aim and ideal was "to please the Creator," which is the utmost goal for every conscientious Muslim.

The Osmanlı Devlet was in fact a means to implement the Creator's commands on this earth. On the other hand, Western historians,

*Chapter Two – The Foundation of the Osmanlı Devlet*

who were "taught" that Islam is in itself most dangerous for Europe and the West, and this prejudice was imprinted on their mind and conscience, can hardly understand and evaluate the victories won by Muslims; they view and interpret Muslims' victories within the framework of their own armies' imperialistic victories. They are bound to fail to see that "the motive and the point of departure" is completely different.

Not only Western historians and writers, who come from an entirely different cultural background, but some so-called Muslim-born Turkish historians, who find themselves "alien" and "cool" toward Islam, cannot understand "this Osmanlı fact" either, because they lack the "psychological participation" that is essential to be able to understand the Osmanlı reality. While Orhan Gâzi was actually engaged in securing the "rights of the people", Europeans were virtually living in bondage. The Osmanlı expansion in Europe had thus brought two different visions and civilisations (Islam and Christendom) into direct confrontation with each other.

Under Osmân Gâzi every able-bodied man had to enlist in the army, particularly in the cavalry, whose swift movement was necessary to protect the frontier areas. The soldiers were summoned during the *ghazawât* (holy wars), and were allowed to return to cultivate their lands when hostilities ceased. During the siege of Bursa, however, Orhan Gâzi realised that the cavalry was excellent during skirmishes but not during long-term struggles, where infantry were essential. Hence, he formed the force called *yaya* (foot soldiers), and set up regular units of horsemen called *müsellem*,[i] which means "exempt from taxes."

---

i  İ.H.Uzunçarşılı, *Osmanlı Devleti Teşkilâtından Kapukulu Ocakları* (Ankara, 1984) vol. I, pp. 1-3.
   S. Shaw says that "The new army included both Christians and Muslim Turks, but as the Ottomans moved into the Balkans under Murâd, the former largely prevailed," cited in *History of the Ottoman Empire*

## Osmanli History and Institutions

Thus those soldiers were given this privilege in return for their military service. Both units, the *yaya* and *müsellem*, composed the Osmanlı regular army. Orhan Gâzi assigned allowances for the *huffâz* (memorisers of the Glorious Qur'ân by heart) and for scholars. The people in general enjoyed a high standard of living, and very few deserved or needed the *zakât*.[106] İkhtiyâruddîn Orhan Beğ was perhaps the greatest, strongest, and richest of all the Turkmen Beğs.

*Orhan Gâzi's sarcophagus, Bursa*

## 2.5 GÂZI SULTÂN MURÂD (1362-1389)

Murâd Beğ came to Bursa after the death of his father and assumed

---

*and Modern Turkey* (Cambridge, 1976) vol. I, p. 25. But this assertion is incorrect. It is true that the Osmanlıs employed a certain number of Christian soldiers in their army whom the Christian rulers were obliged to give as a tribute, but these were only a minority. It is indeed illogical and ridiculous for a Muslim army to be manned mainly by Christians, as its main function is to open new lands to Islam and to implement the *Sharî'at*.

## Chapter Two – The Foundation of the Osmanlı Devlet

the leadership of the Osmanlı Devlet on the decision of the *akhîs* (*fityân*).[107] In fact, Murâd Gâzi was head of the *akhîs*,[108] and they were instrumental in his becoming ruler. But the Roman Empire took advantage of the death of Orhan Beğ to seize some newly acquired Muslim territories in Europe. Lala Shâhin Pasha, Hâjı İlbeği, and Evrenos Beğ established themselves on the coast of the Marmara Sea and waited for the new Khân to come after settling the affairs of the *devlet* in Anatolia. They were keen to protect the tomb of Süleymân Pasha at Bolayır.[109] Murâd Khân's brother Süleymân Pasha had acquired Ankara in 755/1354, but the *beğ* of Qaramân had incited the *akhîs* to assume power there upon the death of Orhan Gâzi.

The famous traveller İbn Battûtah gives us extensive information about the *akhîs:* "A young brother, or *akhî* in their language, is one who is chosen by all members of his trade (guild), or by other young unmarried men, or those who live in ascetic retreat, to be their leader. This organisation is known also as the Futuwwa, or Order of Youth. The leader builds a hospice and furnishes it with rugs, lamps, and other necessary appliances. The members of his community work during the day for their livelihood, and bring him what they have earned in the late afternoon. With this they buy fruit, food, and other things which the hospice requires for their use. If a traveller comes to the town that day they lodge him in their hospice; these provisions serve as his entertainment as their guest, and he stays with them until he goes away. If there are no travellers they themselves assemble to partake of the food, and having eaten it they sing and dance. On the morrow they return to their occupations and bring their earnings to their leader in the late afternoon. The members are called *fityân* (youths) and their leader, as we have said, is the *akhî*."[110]

The *akhîs* apparently felt that the Osmanlı Devlet was in the process of uniting the Muslims in Anatolia. Hence, when Murâd Khân marched upon Ankara in 763/1362 they willingly handed the city to him.¹¹¹ Furthermore, Murâd Khân was himself an *akhî shaykh*¹¹² (head of *akhîs*); this factor also may have played an important role in that decision.

Taking over Ankara resulted in the expansion of Osmanlı territory to the east and enabled them to collect warriors to be sent to open new lands to Islam on European soil.

Murâd Khân returned to Bursa where Lala Shâhîn Pasha had also arrived. The Sultân appointed him the first *beğlerbeği* and they crossed the Sea of Marmara together to the European side.

### The Situation in the Balkans

When the Osmanlıs were engaged in *jihâd* activities in the Balkans, the political situation there was as follows:

Eastern Thrace, Salonica, and its environs, some of the coast of Peloponnesus, and southern Epir were dependent on the Roman Empire. The north-eastern region of the Balkans was under Bulgarian administration. High Serbia and Serez were under Serbian hegemony in bits and pieces. There were Serbian, Albanian, and Latin Albanian princedoms of various sizes in the north of Epir; those princedoms were under the influence of the Republic of Venice and the Kingdom of Naples.¹¹³

Murâd Khân opened Chorlu and Lüleburgaz to Islam in 763/1361-62,¹¹⁴ demolished their walls, and ordered the Turkmens of Anatolia to settle there. The Osmanlıs continued their advance in that region to prevent any reinforcements and help from Constantinople, the capital, to Edirne (Adrianapolis). Evrenos Beğ annexed Malkara and İpsala while Hâji İlbeği took Alexandroupolis (Dedeağaç) and its harbour in 761/1360. Subsequently, Dimetoka (Dydimothikhon) was opened to Islam. The Osmanlıs defeated the Roman forces who were keen to retrieve those areas. By 762/1361 Sultân Murâd opened Edirne to Islam and made it his capital in 770/1368. Edirne was the centre of Thrace, and the second most important city after

*Chapter Two – The Foundation of the Osmanlı Devlet*

Constantinople in the Roman Empire. It stood at the junction of the rivers Meriç (Maritsa) and Tunja, at the junction of the roads of the Balkans, and on the Constantinople-Vienna route. So, opening Edirne to Islam was a very important military acquisition on the part of the Osmanlıs. The Osmanlıs firmly established themselves on the European continent in this way.[115]

The Osmanlı Turks were actively engaged in conveying Muslims from Anatolia to settle in these newly acquired territories. They treated the people very well, giving them complete religious freedom and reasonable living conditions. According to regulations set by Stefan Dushan, the Serbian king, the villagers had, for example, to work two days a week for their lord, while the Osmanlıs asked them to work only three days per year for their *sipâhî*, their Osmanlı administrator. The Osmanlıs had also prohibited usurpation of the villagers by their local chieftains. This humane treatment persuaded the villagers to keep quiet and willingly accept Osmanlı rule. The summons of the lords or rulers to resist the rule of the Osmanlıs had, for example, been negatively received by the Christian population of the Balkans.[116]

The ideal of *ghazwâh*, Holy War, was not only an essential factor in the foundation and development of the Osmanlı Devlet, but was its very *raison d'être*. But *jihâd* does not necessarily mean destroying the infidel world, *dârulharb*, but essentially subduing it and making it *dârulislâm* (the realm of Islamic values). Thus, the first Osmanlı sultâns were primarily concerned with the spread of Islam and not with the spoils of war as such. They therefore never hesitated in giving large tracts of lands to their commanders who opened new areas to Islam.[117] When Sultân Murâd sent a *Nâme-i Hümâyûn* (letter) to the sovereign of the Qaramân Emirate on 1 Rabî' Thâni 767/16 December 1365, he referred to his capital Bursa as *Dârulkhilâfet* (Seat of the Khalifate).[118] When the commander Evrenos Beğ opened the cities of Gümüljine, Serez (Siroz), and

Bitola (Monastir) to Islam, the Osmanlı sultân Murâd gave him all those areas as a *sanjaq*, appointing him Emîrul Mu'minîn[i] over all *gâzis* (*mujâhids*) in those *vilâyats*. He added: "But do not be deceived into thinking that 'I have opened *vilâyats* of Rumeli with my sword.' On the contrary, do know for certain that those *vilâyats* belong to Allah ﷻ, then to His Messenger, then, by order of Allah, after His Messenger they belong to his *khalîfah*. It is true that you rendered us truthfulness and favour. And we in response to your truthfulness and service, have favoured you; we have enhanced you through three ways. First, we addressed you as Emîrul Mu'minîn, second, we gave you a cloak of honour (*khil'at-i fâkhirah*), third, we sent you a drum and the Standard[ii] of the Honourable Respected Prophet and a *tuğ* ...."[119] It is clear from his *berât* that the third Osmanlı sultân Murâd saw himself as the *Khalîfah*. As early as 1332 his father had particularly expressed the Osmanlı zeal to revive the khalifate and to give it its due, and Sultân Murâd was addressed as such by the then largest emirate in Anatolia, the *beğlik* of Qaramân, as well as by Janıbek Khân of the Golden Horde.[iii] Indeed, the Osmanlı Devlet had by that time become *the* Muslim fighting force that was actively engaged in a continuous *jihâd* against the infidels.

---

i   The title was first given by Muhammad ﷺ to 'Abdullâh b. Jahsh when the latter was sent at the head of a group of *muhâjirîn* to monitor the activities of Quraysh. The usage of the same title by the Osmanlıs many centuries later reveals the continuity of Islamic culture and values.

ii   We may assume that *kalimat ush-shahâdah* was inscribed on this standard.

iii   *Münsheât*, I, 95; Qaramân Oğlu congratulates Sultân Murâd, mentioning the latter's title as *zillullâh* on the occasion of opening of Edirne, Filibe, Zağra, and Gümüljine to Islam. Janıbek Khân congratulated him on the latter's making Edirne his capital, referring to this new capital as *dârulkhalifate*: I, 97 (Seat of the Khalifate).

*Chapter Two – The Foundation of the Osmanlı Devlet*

In fact, as Abû Ya'lâ al-Farrâ' states, "When a Muslim rules Muslims and becomes a *khalîfah* it is not legitimate for anyone who believes in Allah and the Last Day to spend the night without accepting him as his leader (*Imâman 'aleyhi*). Be he a pious man or a sinner, he is the leader of the Muslims."[120] But Sultân Murâd was a very pious man.

### The Roman Empire Becomes Subordinate to the Osmanlı Devlet

Sultân Murâd continued his *fath* (opening new lands to Islam) activities; using the strategical position of Edirne, he sent Lala Shâhîn Pasha northward to Filibe and Zağra (Zagora), Evrenos Beğ to western Thrace, to open Gümüljine to Islam. Lala Shâhîn Pasha opened Filibe to Islam, thus depriving the Roman Empire of rice and the taxes it used to collect that arose from the Meriç (Maritsa) valley. The opening of Filibe to Islam resulted in the expansion of Osmanlı territory as a barrier between the Bulgarians and the Greeks, who had been trying to resist on the shores of the Aegean, hindering contact between them.[121]

The Roman Emperor John (1341-1391) concluded a treaty with the Venetian Doge in July 1361, but he soon realised that this treaty would not enable him to drive the Osmanlı forces out of Thrace because the Osmanlıs had settled Turks from Anatolia there and protected the shores very efficiently. And the Roman Empire was in the process of collapse, having become very weak; its total income consisted of the taxes obtained from the customs of Selânik (Thessaloniki) and Constantinople, and the municipal taxes of Constantinople. So, he concluded a pact with the Osmanlı Devlet in 1364, according to which he recognised that the lands opened to Islam by Osmanlıs belonged to them. By this treaty the Emperor agreed that he would not try to retrieve those areas directly or indirectly, would not collaborate with enemies of the Osmanlıs, and would send forces to

Sultân Murâd whenever he wanted against the possible assault of the emirates in Anatolia. He thus became subordinate to the Osmanlı sultân. This treaty meant that Sultân Murâd became the ruler of the Roman Empire in an official and legal sense.[122]

### The Battle of Sırpsındığı (Rout of the Serbs) 1364

The commander of the (Eastern) Roman Empire forces, who surrendered Filibe to the Osmanlıs and went with his family to Serbia, told Pope Urban V that the Turkish soldiers were few in number and encouraged him to attack the Osmanlı forces, warning him that otherwise the present situation would become worse. Urban V incited the Christians to form a united front against the Osmanlı Muslims. So, the kings of Hungary, Serbia, and Bulgaria, and the Prince of Wallachia formed a Crusader army of 50-60,000 headed by the Hungarian king, Louis. At that time, Murâd Khân was engaged in Anatolia, besieging Biga, and the Crusaders were determined to drive the Osmanlıs from Europe. If King Louis had been successful in this campaign, this would presumably have given him control over the Bulgarians and enabled him to spread Catholicism in eastern Europe.[123] The united Christian armies marched on Edirne. Beğlerbeği Lala Shâhîn informed Sultân Murâd of this dangerous situation and sent a reconnoitring force under Hâjı İlbeği, who was able to arrive at the scene only after the united Christian armies had crossed the Meriç (Maritsa) river. The Crusaders were apparently confident of victory because they did not face any tangible resistance until their arrival at Edirne. Though his soldiers were far fewer in number than the Europeans, Hâjı İlbeği attacked the enemy at night from three different directions. The reportedly drunken Christians were confused and defeated, and some of them even drowned in the river Meriç, while King Louis barely escaped death.

This battle took place in 765/1364 and is called *Sırpsındığı* (Rout of the Serbs).[124] It was the first of many Christian attempts at united

*Chapter Two – The Foundation of the Osmanlı Devlet*

action against the Osmanlıs.[125] Louis built Maria Zell Church in Istirya as a token of gratitude to Mary.[126] Murâd Hüdâvendigâr built a mosque in Bilejik, an *imâret* in Yenişehir, a *tekke* for Pustin Push Baba, a mosque in Bursa, a castle, an *imâret*, a *madrasah*, a *hammâm* (public bath) a *khân* (hostel for travellers) at Chekirge, Bursa as tokens of gratitude to Allah for this victory over Christian armies.[127]

Due to the vast expansion of their territory and army, the Osmanlıs instituted the post of Qâdıasker to administer the *shar'î* (religio-judicial) affairs of the soldiers, and the first to fill it was the *qadi* of Bursa, Jendereli Kara Halîl (d. 789/1387).[128] The Osmanlıs tried to recruit captives into their army, but this did not work out well, as some of them deserted. Hence, they developed a new method of raising Muslim soldiers among the conquered peoples of the Balkans. A scholar, Mevlâna Qara Rüstem, argued that, since *Sharî'at* gives the *devlet* one-fifth of the spoils of war, one of every five captives should go to the *Beytü'l mâl*, the treasury of the Islamic *devlet*.[129] Hence, Qâdıasker Qara Halîl adopted this method to recruit soldiers for the Osmanlı Devlet.[130] Consequently, those captives were sent to the countryside to learn the Turkish language and to be brought up in an Islamic environment. It was through this practice, which is called *Türke vermek* ("giving to Turks") that the Osmanlı *yenicheri* force (janissaries) was formed.[131] The word *yenicheri* means "new soldier." It is worth noting that the headgear worn by the *yenicheris* was called *börük* or *börk*; the very same name used by Göktürks in Turkestan even before the advent of Islam, though its form had changed.

It is extremely significant to note that the Islamic orientation of these young people in the fourteenth and fifteenth centuries was not achieved in formal educational institutions with a developed curriculum and specialised teachers. On the contrary, it was realised informally through contact with the people, which indicated that Islam had by then become a way of life and a code of morality that could easily be adopted. In other words, the Osmanlı Turkish population of Anatolia had, in sociological terms, their own distinctive Islamic culture that excelled that of the Christianised Europeans of the fourteenth and fifteenth centuries. Indeed, history tells us that when two cultures compete with each other, the stronger one supersedes the other altogether. This was the case of the ancient Greek culture versus the Roman, and that of the Mongols versus the culture of Islam, though both the Romans and the Mongols achieved military victory on the battlefields. Had the Islamic culture of the Osmanlıs not been strong enough to inspire those young people to accept Islam and its code of ethics, it would probably been impossible for the Osmanlı Devlet to survive and expand.

Under Osmân Gâzi every able Muslim was a *mujâhid*. Nevertheless, the vast expansion of the Osmanlı Devlet made it essential for the *devlet* to have a regular army. Orhan Gâzi (1324-1362) founded the regular Osmanlı army for the first time, with infantry troops called *yaya* and cavalry called *müsellem*. Since newly annexed areas were predominantly inhabited by Christians, the Osmanlıs adopted a new method during the rule of Sultân Murâd (1362-1389) to recruit them into their army, namely *devshirme*. Christian children in those areas were taken and brought up in an Islamic environment. Hence, they accepted Islam and were eventually recruited for a new Osmanlı force called *yenicheri* (new soldiers).

### The Opening of Biga to Islam

Biga, on Anatolian soil, was under the control of Catalonia. Sultân Murâd Hüdâvendigâr wanted to open that town to Islam, so that no enemy force would be left behind when he went to Europe to confront the Christian forces. This *fath* (opening to Islam) took place in 1363 or 1364.

The Catalan company consisted of European mercenaries. They were taken into service by the Roman Emperor Andronikos II Palaiologos in 1303, and this force included vagabonds from Sicily,

## Chapter Two – The Foundation of the Osmanlı Devlet

Aragon, Navarre, France, Italy, Germany, and other areas of Europe. Whoever paid them was entitled to use them against whomever they wanted. They were commanded by a German, Roger de Flor. His surname was Blum in German, which means flower; when he became head of these troops, his surname was translated into Spanish and became "Flor." Recruiting about 10,000 vagabonds, Roger entered the service of the King of Sicily and fought against Naples. Finding himself jobless when a peace treaty was concluded, he offered his services to the Roman Emperor, who accepted his offer, wearied by the Turkish advances in Anatolia. Roger de Flor and his vagabonds left Sicily in 26 ships and arrived in Constantinople; he received the title "Megadukas" (Grand Duke) from the Emperor in accordance with the agreement, and was given a princess, the Emperor's niece, as a bride.

The mercenaries were deployed in 1304 at Erdek on Anatolian soil and began attacking. But the Christian population also suffered along with the Muslims in Anatolia. So they were transferred to the European part of the Roman Empire in 1306 on the pretext of fighting the Bulgarians. The Catalan Company left some forces in Biga and Erdek in Anatolia. Catalans continued to increase in number with new recruits from France, Italy, and Spain, and they were a disaster for the Christian population of that part of the empire. The Emperor decided to use them against the Osmanlıs in Anatolia again and concluded a new agreement with Roger, bestowing on him the title of Caesar, which was below Emperor in rank in Eastern Roman usage. Roger is regarded as the first foreigner to obtain this title in the history of the Roman Empire. But the Emperor's son and co-regent Michael was in Edirne (Adrianapolis) at that time. When Caesar Roger de Flor came to Edirne in 1307 before departing for Anatolia to greet Michael, he and some of his comrades were killed during the feast. The Catalan Companies in Anatolia were defeated by Sultân Murâd Hüdâvendigâr.[132]

### Dubrovnik Enters Osmanlı Protection (1365)

The Republic of Dubrovnik (Raguza), was in the south-western part of Bosnia and on the shores of Adriatic Sea. Being a small country with little arable land, it engaged in commercial activities. This republic made an agreement with the Osmanlı Devlet in 1365, according to which it agreed to pay the Osmanlıs 500 gold pieces per year in return for Osmanlı protection and freedom of commerce in the eastern Mediterranean. The *tuğra* (the Sultân's signature) was put on agreements during the administration of the Selçuklus and other Turkmen *beğliks* in Anatolia; so the *tuğra* of Sultân Murâd was put on the agreement. The official who put the *tuğra* on the document was called *tuğra-kesh* and this art was an important one. The claim that Sultân Murâd plunged his hand into ink and put it on the agreement for signature is incorrect. It is known for certain that his father, Orhan Gâzi, had his *tuğra* even prior to this; this sort of statement only reflects bias and prejudice on some writers' part. This agreement is regarded as the first continuous peace treaty with a European socio-political entity on the Osmanlıs' part and the first document for the Osmanlı Devlet's becoming the heir of the (Eastern) Roman Empire.[133]

### The Loss of Gallipoli (Gelibolu)

The Roman Emperor John V Palaiologos, who had accepted Murâd Hüdâvendigâr as his suzerain, could not get over this situation and went secretly to Hungary, met with King Louis, and incited him against the Osmanlıs. While returning through Bulgaria, John was arrested and imprisoned in the castle of Nicopolis by the order of the Bulgarian King, Shisman, who wanted to please the Osmanlı Sultân.[134] Meanwhile, the Pope proclaimed a new Crusade against Osmanlıs on Christmas 1366. The Roman Emperor, the King of Hungary, and the city-rulers of Italy were all invited to participate

## Chapter Two – The Foundation of the Osmanlı Devlet

in that Crusade. The sole serious response came from the Duke of Savoy Amadeus II, whose fleet took over Gallipoli and handed it over to the Roman Empire.[135] But the Osmanlı Devlet was not affected by the loss of Gallipoli very much, since they had firmly established themselves at Thrace. Murâd Hüdâvendigâr conveyed Turkmens from Anatolia to Thrace in response and transferred part of the Christian population from Thrace to Anatolia.

The Osmanlıs continued to tolerate Jews and Christians, who were called *Ehl-i Kitâb* (People of the Book) in Islamic terminology, protected them, their souls, property, and honour, requiring only *jizyah* from them.[i] Due to good treatment by the Osmanlı Devlet, some Christians in the Balkans voluntarily accepted Islam. And some groups such as Bogomils preferred Islam to escape Christian oppression.[136] The claim by some Westerners that people entered

---

i  Almost all Western writers erroneously claim that the Osmanlı Devlet inherited all its institutions from Constantinople. S. Shaw is no exception when he claims: "The existing tax structure as well as feudal practices developed under Byzantine rule were retained with little change" (*op. cit.*, I, p. 26). But it is well known that the Osmanlıs in fact made Islam the *raison d'être* of their *devlet*. Consequently, they implemented *Sharî'at* and its institutions as clearly spelled out in the Qur'ân and Sunna in every aspect of life, e.g., the *jizyah* institution by which Muslims were authorised to collect money from unbelievers in return for the security that the Muslim Devlet gives them. *"Fight those who do not believe in Allah, nor in the Last Day, nor hold forbidden which has been forbidden by Allah and His Messenger, nor acknowledge the Religion of Truth, from among the People of the Book, until they pay jizyah with willing submission and feel themselves subdued"* (*Tawbah* [9], *âyat*: 29). And the Final Messenger Muhammad ﷺ received *jizyah* from the bishop of Aylah in 9/630, and the people of Jarbâ' and Azruh also paid *jizyah* to the Muslims then: İbn Hishâm, *as-Siyrat un-Nabawiyyah*, Cairo, 1375/1955, v. II, p. 525.

Islam to escape *jizyah* is wrong and unacceptable because those who entered Islam, were to pay *zakât*, the tax paid by Muslims.

## The Return to Opening New Lands in Europe

The Osmanlıs continued their drive to open fresh areas in Europe to Islam. Timurtash Pasha (d. 1404) took Qızılağach and Yanbolu from the Bulgarians, and Lala Shâhin Pasha annexed İhtiman and Samokov in 768/1367. In the next year Sultân Murâd took Bulgars Aydos (Aytes), Qarinabad, and Sozopol from the Bulgarians, and Hayrabolu from the Roman Empire in 769/1368. He also reopened Qırqlareli to Islam.[137] Lala Shâhin Pasha defeated the Bulgarian Tsar Ivan Shishman, and the Serbian King at Samokov in 774/1371. The Osmanlıs fought the Serbs again in 774/1372 at Chirmen and scattered their army. This success gave them access to the trade routes to Macedonia while Gâzi Evrenos Beğ opened Gümüljine to Islam after this battle. Qara Halîl, who had been promoted to the rank of *vazîr* and was called Hayreddîn Pasha, opened Qavala, Drama, Zihne (Alistati), Serez, and Veroia (Qaraferye) to Islam. Evrenos Beğ established himself at Serez and made it his base. Köstendil was opened to Islam in 774/1372 while Sultân Murâd subdued the castles of İnjegiz and Chatalburgaz in 775/1373. Following their success at the Battle of Sırpsındığı, the Osmanlıs held Rumeli and established themselves firmly at Macedonia after their second victory at Chirmen in 1372. It was assumed at first that the Osmanlıs came to Rumeli for the spoils of war, as was the case with the emirates of Aydın, Saruhan, and Qaresi. But when they annexed Macedonia after the second Battle of Chirmen, it was realised that they were there to stay. Sultân Murâd had, however, stopped military operations in Rumeli after 1373 and directed his attention to Anatolia.[138]

On the other hand, the Roman Emperor went to Rome to secure the support of Pope Urban V in 771/1369, asked God's pardon for having been Orthodox, repented, and became a Catholic. But the

## Chapter Two – The Foundation of the Osmanlı Devlet

people of the empire did not agree to become Catholic with him. When Chatalja and İnjeğiz were opened to Islam, John V Palaiologos, being unable to leave even İstanbul, sent envoys to Sultân Murâd Hüdâvendigâr and asked for his protection. On this occasion the pact of suzerainty, which had been concluded and infringed by John, was renewed with John's assurance: according to this treaty, John sent his son Theodoros as a hostage to the Osmanlı court and accepted the obligation of fighting with his soldiers under Sultân Murâd whenever the latter ordered.[139]

On the recommendation of Timurtash Pasha, the Osmanlıs formed regular and salaried cavalry units called *sipâhî* who were the sons of *devshirme*. They also improved the *tımar* organisation that was based on the practice of the Final Messenger Muhammad ﷺ, who gave lands in areas newly opened to Islam to certain individuals in return for specific services to his *devlet*. Since Muslims are asked in the Qur'ân to follow the Sunnat (practice of the Prophet ﷺ), "*Certainly there is a very good example for you in the Messenger of Allah*" (*al-Ahzâb* [33] *âyat* 21), they did so. This system was called *iqtâ'* and had been practised and developed by various Islamic *devlets*. While inheriting this system from their predecessors, the Selçuklus, the Osmanlıs called it *tımar*. The *sipâhîs* would, according to this system, make use of the lands given to them in return for their formation of a certain number of fully equipped cavalry, and active participation in the *jihâd* whenever called. But this system of *tımar* was not like the feudalism of Europe where the landlord possessed the land as well as the people who lived on it. In the Osmanlı *tımar* system, the *sipâhî*[i] was responsible for the lives, honour, and property of the people who

---

i This is not to be confused with the central cavalry, who were also called *sipâhîs*; the *tımarlı sipâhî* was a soldier who was brave in *jihâd* activity and was given a certain piece of land with villages on it, with authority to collect taxes in the name of the *devlet*; he did not possess the land or the villages.

lived on his *tımar*. The people were known as *ra'iyyet* (those looked after and cared for)[i] and enjoyed complete freedom of religion. The Muslim *ra'iyyet* paid *zakât* and *'ushr*, and non-Muslims paid *jizyah*.[ii]

A peaceful period followed the cessation of hostilities in 1373 during which Sultân Murâd married his elder son Yıldırım Bâyezîd to Devlet Hâtûn, daughter of Süleymân Shâh, the ruler of the Germiyân Emirate in 780/1378. As dowry, the latter offered the Osmanlıs the towns of Kütahya, Tavşanlı, Emet, and Simav and

---

i  Some uninformed writers translate *tımar* or *iqtâ'* as "feudalism." One should keep in mind that such terms should be kept as they are because they entail specific meanings that are peculiar to Muslim societies. Their translation into other languages would therefore distort their meaning.

ii *Jizyah* is translated as "poll tax," but it should be remembered that *jizyah* means "a kind of compensation", derived from the root *jezê* (to recompense). Since the non-Muslim was not obligated to participate in *jihâd* activity, instead of military service he paid, "as compensation", a certain amount of money, according to his financial means. Women, aged, children, and religious officials did not pay it.

*Timurtash Pasha Mosque, Bursa*

## Chapter Two – The Foundation of the Osmanlı Devlet

retired to the small town of Qula.[140] This is significant because the Germiyân Emirate, one of the largest *beğliks* that inherited the Anatolian Selçuklu Devlet, had by then become part of the Osmanlı Devlet without any bloodshed. By then the Osmanlı Devlet, which incorporated part of Europe, had certainly become the most powerful of the *beğliks*, and the Turkmens of Anatolia were prone to unite under its leadership.

Sultân Murâd bought the towns of Aqshehir from Hüseyin Beğ of Hamîdeli, Yalvach, Beğshehri, Seydishehri, Qaraağach, and Isparta, which were assumed to be his private property, for 80,000 gold pieces.[141] This is another significant event indicating the supremacy of the Osmanlıs in the area. Rather than wait for their inevitable incorporation into the Osmanlı Devlet by force if necessary, neighbouring *beğliks* in Anatolia preferred to do this voluntarily. Being of the same religious, cultural, and ethnic background as the Osmanlıs, the populations of those areas welcomed their unification with this large and supreme political entity.

The Osmanlıs could have, however, annexed these as well as other neighbouring territories by force and without paying such a large sum of money. But being the bearers of the banner of Islam, they felt it their responsibility to do their best to unite all the believers in one *devlet* without unnecessarily shedding the blood of their Muslim brothers, no matter how much money they paid for this religious duty and noble cause. This attitude, which can be traced throughout Osmanlı history, did not prevail at that time in Europe.

Resuming their drive in Europe, the Osmanlıs took Ishtip on the left bank of the Vardar river in 782/1380, and Sofia in 787/1385, while Yahshi Beğ, son of Timurtash Pasha, annexed Nish in 788/1386. Christians in general were now apprehensive of Osmanlı military might. To play it safe, Lazar, the despot of Serbia, voluntarily offered to increase the levy and soldiers that he had to give by a previous treaty to Osmanlıs.[142]

85

"The treaty concluded between the Byzantines and Genoese in 1386 affords a striking illustration of Murâd's power after the Nish campaign. This treaty, whose text has been preserved, was signed by John Andronikos Palaiologos, the *podesta* of Pera, and the Genoese ambassador. John Palaiologos bound himself to live in peace with his son Andronikus and to mobilise his army against all enemies of Genoa 'except Morat Bey and his Turks.' The Genoese in turn promised to defend Constantinople 'against all enemies of whatever nationality except the said Morat Bey and his Turks who acted according to the will of the said Morat Bey.'" [143] Throughout the treaty Murâd is carefully accepted on both sides to avoid his retaliation. It should be remembered that Genoa was at that time an important power in Europe, had a very powerful naval force, possessed colonies on many shores as far as the Crimea.

Edirne was on the route from Constantinople to the Balkan mountains and was the second most important city of the empire. With the opening of Filibe to Islam, the Osmanlıs entered between the Bulgarians and the Greeks. Nish was also located at an important strategic point. All these acquisitions necessitated a considerable knowledge of Europe's strategic geography.[144]

Assisted by Evrenos Beğ of the *aqınjıs*, Jendereli Halîl Hayreddîn Pasha opened Bitola (Monastir) and Ohrid to Islam in 787/1385. It is perhaps appropriate to mention here that Islam protects the rights of the *dhimmîs* under Muslim administration. The following *âyât* demonstrate this:

> *Allah commands you when you judge between people (not only Muslims) that you judge with justice. (an-Nisâ [4]: 58).*
>
> *We have sent down to you the Book (the Qur'ân) in truth, that you may judge between people by that which Allah has shown you ... (an-Nisâ [4]: 105.).*

## Chapter Two – The Foundation of the Osmanlı Devlet

*O you who believe! Stand out firmly for justice, as witnesses to Allah even against yourselves, or your parents, or your kin, and whether it be (against) rich or poor. For Allah can best protect both. Do not follow the lusts (of your hearts), lest you swerve, and if you distort (justice) or decline to do justice, verily Allah is well acquainted with all that you do. (an-Nisâ [4]: 135.).*

There are also many *hadîths* that make it mandatory for Muslims to safeguard the rights of the *dhimmîs* under their protection. The Osmanlıs were very keen to implement this directive. The conquered peoples in the Balkans were so happy under Osmanlı rule that they kept quiet during the Osmanlı wars against the united European Christian armies.[145]

There was an effort in Europe to form a Balkan alliance including Serbs, Bulgarians, and Vlachs (Romanians). To prevent this alliance, Ali Pasha, who was installed as *vazîr-i a'zam* on the death of his father Halîl Hayreddîn Pasha in 789/1387, quickly crossed the Balkan mountains, opened Pravadi, Shumnu, and Tırnova, the capital of the Bulgarian kingdom at that time, to Islam. The Bulgarian king, Shishman, took shelter in the castle of Niğbolu (Nicopolis). Sultân Murâd came with another army and opened Niğbolu to Islam in 790/1388. Central Bulgaria was thus opened to Islam, Shishman was forgiven and remained as an Osmanlı governor.[146]

Before 772/1370, Alâeddîn Beğ of Qaramân had married Melek Hâtûn, daughter of Sultân Murâd.[147] Qaramân Beğlik was the largest among the *beğliks* of Anatolia that emerged after the Selçuklu Devlet. Furthermore, the rulers of Qaramân Beğlik had become related to those of the Selçuklus and this *beğlik* had inherited the capital, Qonya. Therefore, they saw themselves, not incorrectly, as the heirs of the Selçuklus.

However, the Osmanlıs were the *beğs* most committed to Islam, engaged in *jihâd* activities, opened large areas in Europe to Islam, and became rulers over the Roman Empire. Being apprehensive of the Osmanlı expansion in Anatolia as well, Alâeddîn Beğ, however, planned to capture the towns the Osmanlıs bought from the Hamîdoğlu Beğlik. While the Osmanlıs were busy in Rumelia, he incited the king of Bosnia against them and captured Beğshehri in 788/1386 himself. Upon this act of enmity on the part of this Muslim leader, Murâd summoned the notables and addressed them emotionally: "I have been doing my best for the cause of Islam, leaving my home, leaving every comfort, proceeding one month's distance into the *kâfirs'* territory, and this stupid man has attacked the Muslims and caused them harm. O *mujâhids!* What should I do with that cruel host? They distract me from *jihâd* and cause me to fight Muslims! If I leave them alone and pursue *jihâd*, the Muslims would suffer from their actions. If I attack him, it would entail the shifting of the swords of *mujâhids* onto them."

Murâd, however, overcame this dilemma by a bold decision to fight the Qaramân army on the grounds that its *beğ* prevented him every year from waging *jihâd* against unbelievers. And to engage in war against those who prevented Muslims from *jihâd* is the greatest *jihâd*.[148] Therefore, he marched upon the *beğ* of Qaramân and defeated him in 789/1387, and retook Beğshehri. At his daughter's request, however, he pardoned his son-in-law who totally and unconditionally submitted to him.

The Osmanlıs' victory over the largest and at one time the strongest of the *beğliks* of Anatolia, the Qaramân Beğlik, enhanced their reputation immensely. Consequently, the other *beğliks* sent units of their soldiers to fight against the Christian enemies at the Battle of Kosova.[149] It is said that the Osmanlıs experimented with artillery against Qaramân for the first time, and that their success there encouraged Murâd to employ it to considerable effect in his wars against Lazar's Christian armies.[150] With this success against the once greatest *beğlik* (emirate) of Anatolia, the Osmanlı

*Chapter Two – The Foundation of the Osmanlı Devlet*

Devlet emerged as the major Muslim power. Nevertheless, the *de facto Khalîfah* felt it desirable to secure the official recognition of the nominal 'Abbâsî *Khalîfah*, then staying in Cairo. He therefore sent an envoy with gifts to Egypt, who came back with an *ijâzet* (authorisation) for a *Sharî'at* government to implement *Sharî'at* (in Osmanlı Turkish: *tenfîz-i hükûmet-i sher'îyye*) in every walk of life, and the title of Sultân of Rûm (Sultân of Anatolia) to Murâd Khân. He thus became officially Sultân Murâd, and his *devlet* Devlet-i 'Aliyye-i Osmâniyye (Sublime Osmanlı Devlet), his followers and people Osmanlı (pertaining to Osmân).[151] This title of Sultân consolidated and made his position official, and, consequently, minor Anatolian emirates felt obliged to send military units to participate in the Osmanlı *jihâd* against the infidels.

### The First Battle of Kosova (791/1389)

After thus consolidating Osmanlı sovereignty in Anatolia, Sultân Murâd went to Europe to confront the united Christian army formed by the Serbian despot Lazar (r. 1371-1389). By that time Evrenos Beğ had returned from the Hejâz after performing the *hajj*, and his presence was decisive in boosting the morale of the Osmanlı army, which was reinforced by units from the *beğliks* of Qastamonu, Germiyân, Hamîd, Teke, Menteshe, and Aydın.[152] The *yenicheris* were placed in the front and the centre, while the artillery was stationed in front of them. Upon Evrenos Beğ's suggestion, 1,000 archers were placed at the front of each flank of the Osmanlı Muslim army and each of these archers was as skilful and strong as Sa'd b. Abî Waqqâs.[i]

---

i Neşrî, I, 294. It is interesting to note that the Osmanlı Muslim archers at Kosova in 791/1389 were equated to the famous archer of the Prophet ﷺ Sa'd b. Abî Waqqâs, who shot 1,000 arrows at the Battle of Uhud in 3/625, a fact that indicates that Sa'd b. Abî Waqqâs is the example for the

"The sources differ widely on the number of soldiers involved, but apparently the Balkan Union managed to gather about 100,000 men, while Murat had no more than 60,000 at best."[153] The Osmanlıs entertained the idea of putting camels in front of their army for protection, but this was eventually dropped. The allied European army was composed of Serbian, Hungarian, Vlach (Romanian), Polish, and Czech units.

While these preparations were in progress, 'Ali Pasha quoted the *âyat "How often has a small force vanquished a big one, with Allah's permission! Allah is with those who steadfastly persevere"* (al-Qur'ân, al-Baqarah [2]: 249) and the *hadîth* "whoever breathes the dust of *jihâd* will not smell the smoke of Hell" (al-Bukhârî, *al-Jâmi'us Sahîh, Kitâbul Jihâd*: 17).[154] While everybody was sleeping on that dark night "in which it was impossible to discern human being from horse," Sultân Murâd stood up, made his ablutions, prayed two cycles of *salât al-hâjah*, put his face on the ground in prostration (*sujûd*), and prayed till dawn in this position. He addressed Allah: "Lord! sovereignty, property, and human beings belong to You. You give the sovereignty to whom You like.[155] As for me, I am a humble servant of Yours. You know what I have on my mind, and You know my innermost intentions.[i] Sovereignty, reign, and wealth are not my aim at all. I have not come here for the sake of attaining male and female slaves. I do implore most sincerely Your pleasure (*ridâ*)[ii].

---

Muslim archer, and the Osmanlıs' motive in their advance into Europe was Islam. Again, this demonstrates the continuation of the same values in the Osmanlı Devlet as well as its Islamic nature.

i  A Muslim believes that *"Allah does know what is secret and what is yet more hidden"* (al-Qur'ân, Tâ Hâ [20]: 7).

ii *Jihâd* (Holy War) is incumbent on Muslims: *"Fighting is prescribed upon you, and you dislike it. But it is possible that you dislike something which is good for you, and that you love something which is bad for you. Allah knows*

*Chapter Two – The Foundation of the Osmanlı Devlet*

O Lord! I sacrifice myself earnestly to these Muslims over here. Please do not allow those *kâfirs* (unbelievers in the Final Message) to defeat and annihilate these believers at the battle. O my Lord! do not make me the cause of death of so many Muslim souls.[i] Make these Muslims *mansûr* and *muzaffar* (i.e. victorious).[ii] I consent and I am prepared to sacrifice myself for the sake of the soldiers of Islam. Please do not show me the death of these believers. O my God! make me host in Your neighbourhood (*jiwâr*), ransom the souls of the believers with my soul. You have made me a *gâzi* (warrior in a holy war) beforehand, make me achieve the rank of *shahîd* (martyr) at the end."[156] This quotation and others reveal the fatherly, loving, and caring attitude of Osmanlı sultâns towards their people and their earnest desire not to shed their blood unnecessarily.

Finally, the fierce first Battle of Kosova took place in 791/1389 in which the Osmanlıs used artillery with great success. In the beginning, the left flank of the Muslim army was driven back under heavy attack, but its right flank soon counter-attacked and scattered the enemy. The battle continued till noon, and Murâd Gâzi was stabbed towards its end by a Serbian noble, Milosh

---

*and you do not* (al-Baqarah [2]: 216.). So, Sultân Murâd was carrying out a duty to please his Creator.

i  Sultân Murâd, who was known for his piety, seems to have been thinking of a *hadith sharîf* of the Final Messenger that asks rulers to attend to their personal conduct (Muslim, *Kitâbul Îmârah:* 21). Murâd, however, is generally considered a *waly* (singular of *Awliyâ*) as Neşrî puts it: "Everyone was sure of his *Welâyat*" (Neşrî, *op. cit.*, I, p. 306).

ii  It is significant to note that Sultân Murâd used the Arabic words *mansûr* and *muzaffar* to emphasize his commitment to the Islamic concept that victory always comes from Allah alone. Both words mean "victorious," and they are passive participles (*ism mafʿûl*) in Arabic; the implication is that one is made victorious.

Obilic, who pretended to want to kiss his stirrups but struck him deceitfully with a dagger hidden in his sleeve.[157] Nevertheless, Murâd Gâzi continued to lead his forces but soon realised that his wound was fatal. Therefore, he called his elder son Bâyezîd and appointed him Khân with the consent of the dignitaries of the Osmanlı Devlet. While Murâd died as a courageous martyr, Lazar, who had already been captured, was executed.[158] Sultân Murâd's internal organs were buried where he was martyred,[i] and his body was taken to and buried in Bursa. The Battle of Kosova was the first Osmanlı success against a major allied European military force. It destroyed the last organised resistance in the Balkans south of the Danube, opened northern Serbia to the Osmanlı *fath*, and left Hungary as the only important opponent in south-eastern Europe. It meant that Serbia, like Bulgaria, was now firmly under Osmanlı control, although as before the Osmanlı continued to establish their rule through vassal princes.[159]

## The Osmanlı Administrative Structure

It is customary for Turks to give the eldest son the title *pasha*. Thus, Süleymân, the eldest son of Orhan Gâzi, was called Süleymân Pasha. Sultân Murâd appointed Jendereli Qara Halîl *vazîr* with the title "Hayreddîn Pasha" who was replaced at his death in 787/1385 by his son 'Ali Pasha (d. 809/1407). Senior officials were considered elder sons of the Sultân, and consequently given the title of pasha. After opening lands in Europe, Lala Shâhin Pasha was appointed *beğlerbeği* (*emîrul umerâ*) of Rumelia, and was succeeded in this post by Timurtash Pasha. When the latter and some other *beğs* were promoted to the rank of *vazîr*, Ali Pasha was distinguished from them

---

i   A tomb was erected there, and the place was called Meshhed-i Hüdâvendigâr (Place of the Martyrdom of Hüdâvendigâr). Muslims in the area visit it. The Serbs erected a huge statue of Milosh Obilic in the twentieth century.

*Chapter Two – The Foundation of the Osmanlı Devlet*

by the title *vazîr-i a'zam*. As for Anatolia, they appointed another *beğlerbeği* with his seat at Ankara. The Osmanlıs appointed a *sanjaqbeği* for each *sanjaq* (region), and a *qâdi (qâzi – Sharî'at* judge) who had both judiciary and executive powers in each *qazâ* (town). During *jihâd*, the *qâdi* of the Osmanlı capital would accompany the army. Jendereli Qara Halîl was appointed during the first years of Sultân Murâd's rule to the newly founded post of *qâdıasker (qâziasker* military judge), while the *Shâhzâdas* (sons of the Sultân) were appointed *sanjaqbeğis* in Anatolia to be trained in administration. Another post was the *defterdâr*, responsible for the fiscal affairs of the *devlet*.[160] *Qazâ* means a "district for which a *qâdi* is responsible." In other words, an Osmanlı *qâdi* carried out the duties of a mayor and governor of a town, public prosecutor, judge, director of education, and director of *awqâf* (pious foundations).

*Tomb of Devlet Hâtûn, Bursa*

## 2.6 SULTÂN YILDIRIM BÂYEZÎD KHÂN (1389-1402)

After the victory at the Battle of Kosova[i] the Osmanlıs annexed a sizable part of Serbia. Meanwhile, the body of Sultân Murâd was sent to Bursa to be buried there. A tomb and a mosque were erected there in his memory. Yıldırım Bâyezîd married Olivera Despina, daughter of Lazar, thus gaining the friendship and loyalty of the Serbs. They agreed to supply soldiers to the army of Yıldırım Bâyezîd, but at the same time drink and amusement entered the Osmanlı

---

i  The standard (*sanjaq*) hoisted at Kosova is on display at the Military Museum, Harbiye, İstanbul; *kalimah shâhâdah* is inscribed on it.

*Osmanlı boundaries at the time of the death of Sultân Murâd Hüdâvendigâr*

court through this woman.¹⁶¹

Hoja Fîrûz Beğ entered northern Bulgaria, opened Vidin to Islam, crossed the Danube, and raided some districts in Wallachia.¹⁶² Yıldırım Bâyezîd received representatives from Venice and Genoa who came to Edirne to congratulate him. He renewed commercial agreements with them but did not neglect to mention his intention of advancing even to Rome. Thus Yıldırım Bâyezîd declared his position regarding Christendom and tried to conclude a pact with Mamlûks against the Crusader spirit in Europe.¹⁶³

On the other hand, the *beğliks* of Aydın, Saruhan, Menteshe, Germiyân, Hamîd, Teke, and Qâdi Burhâneddîn formed an alliance under the leadership of Qaramân Beğlik. They entered Osmanlı territory while Yıldırım Bâyezîd was busy in Rumelia. In response, Yıldırım went to Anatolia with a strong army. Bâyezîd Khân directed his attention to Aydınoğlu *Beğlik*.¹⁶⁴ The *beğ* of Aydın declared homage to the Osmanlı Devlet. He instructed the recitation of the *khutbah* of the *jum'ah* prayer in the name of the Osmanlı ruler, and the usage of the Osmanlı *sikkah* (coinage), both of which are symbols of sovereignty. The Osmanlıs, however, left the administration of the *waqfs* to the ex-rulers, the sons of the *beğ* of Aydın,¹⁶⁵ who remained prosperous and respected under Osmanlı rule. The administration of a *waqf* meant the guarantee of a fairly well-off life; the *mutawally* (administrator) of the *waqf* collected all revenue, spent the necessary amount on prescribed places and lived on the salary paid out of the revenue of the *waqf*. In other words, the post of *mutawally* secured a

*Chapter Two – The Foundation of the Osmanlı Devlet*

*Meşhed-i Hüdâvendigâr*

good living for oneself as well as for one's descendants.

In 792/1390 Bâyezîd Khân took the *beğlik* (emirate) of Saruhan, and the province of Menteshe without any serious fighting.¹⁶⁶ Other Anatolian *beğliks* soon realised that the Osmanlıs were serious about the unity of all Muslim forces in Anatolia; hence, they gradually joined the Osmanlı Devlet in one form or another.

Bâyezîd Khân opened Alaşehir (Philadelphia) to Islam, taking it from the Roman Empire. It had been like an island among Muslim *beğliks*. It is interesting that Bâyezîd Khân used John V, who had attained the throne of the Roman Empire through the help of Bâyezîd, together with John's son Manuel II and the Roman Empire forces to take the Alaşehir castle.¹⁶⁷

Meanwhile, as the head of the socio-political body whose *raison d'être* was to carry out the duty of *jihâd*, Bâyezîd Khân marched to Europe through Gelibolu to spread Islam and to annex Hungary. A spy was caught *en route*, presumably sent by the Roman Empire to tip off Hungary about an expected Osmanlı drive. Upon the suggestion of Beğlerbeği Qara Timurtash Pasha, Bâyezîd Khân decided at first to take Constantinople itself, the capital of the Roman Empire, and actually besieged it. Yıldırım Bâyezîd Khân asked John V Palaiologos to remove the repairers of the walls of İstanbul, and the emperor complied with this wish. When this emperor died, Yıldırım Bâyezîd wanted his son Manuel II Palaiologos, the new emperor to allow a Turkish quarter to be set up in İstanbul, to build a mosque,

*Shehâdet Mosque (in commemoration of the martyrdom of Sultân Murâd) in Bursa*

establish a court of justice with an Osmanlı *qâdi*, and to increase the tribute paid to the Osmanlı Treasury. Trusting in the walls of the city and help from Europe, the emperor refused to accept these wishes. So, Yıldırım Bâyezîd besieged the city, taking over all the surrounding land up to the walls.

This siege lasted seven months, during which the city began to suffer from hunger. Emperor Manuel wanted help from Europe. When he learned that the Hungarian king Sigismund was preparing to march on Bulgaria, Yıldırım Bâyezîd consented to raise the siege on the condition that:

1 – The Roman Empire would give 700 houses to Muslims who would set up a Turkish quarter in Constantinople;

2 – A Muslim court of justice would be set up at Sirkeji in İstanbul;

3 – The Osmanlı Devlet would appoint a *qâdi* to that court;

*Chapter Two – The Foundation of the Osmanlı Devlet*

4 – A mosque would be built in Constantinople;

5 – The land between Galata and Kâğıthâne (outside the city walls); would be given to Osmanlıs and they would station a garrison there;

6 – The amount paid by the Roman Empire to the Osmanlı Treasury as tribute would be increased;

7 – One-tenth of the tax collected on the orchards and vegetable gardens outside the city walls would be paid to the Osmanlı Treasury.

Emperor Manuel II accepted these conditions and an Osmanlı garrison of 6,000 was placed in the area between Galata, which was under Genoese rule, and Kâğıthâne.[i]

Having rendered the Roman Empire ineffective with this treaty, Yıldırım Bâyezîd directed his attention to the Rumelia front, met a huge Hungarian army at Nagy-Olosz, and defeated it in 793/1391.[168]

The Mamlûk sultân of Egypt, who was the host of the exiled 'Abbâsî *Khalîfah*, addressed Yıldırım Bâyezîd as "The Shadow of Allah in the World" and "The Sultân of the Muslims" in 793/1391,[ii] a fact that shows the political and military power that the Osmanlı Devlet had attained.

Bâyezîd Khân built Güzelje Hisâr castle on the Anatolian shore of the Bosphorus.[iii] Following sieges at intervals, the Roman Empire agreed to pay 10,000 gold pieces annually as tribute.[169]

---

i   Dânişmend, I, 94-95. It is understood that a Turkish quarter and a court of justice was set up in Constantinople in 1400; *op. cit.*, I, 123.

ii  Ferîdûn Beğ, *Mejmû'a-i Münsheât-i Selâtîn*, I, 116. Zillullâh signifies that the *khalîfah*, unlike the Pope, has both spiritual and temporal powers in his community.

iii The date of building Güzelje Hisâr differs from 1391 to 1397, depending on the sources. *OT*, I, 291, footnote 2.

With the Roman Empire, Bulgarians, and Serbians under Osmanlı rule, the only power left in Europe to resist the Osmanlı advance was Hungary. Its direct sovereignty extended to Dalmatia and Belgrade in the south and it was recognised by the princes of the Vlachs and Moldavians as their suzerain. The Hungarian king, Sigismund (1387-1437), tried to incite Christendom against the Turks, but the Western European rulers were preoccupied with their own problems. Moreover, the situation in Hungary was not in a good state because of internal troubles between the local barons and the central administration, and between the Orthodox peasants and the Catholic nobles.[170]

Sigismund was descended from the Luxembourg dynasty. When the last Hungarian King, Louis, died without an heir, he was elected to the throne of Hungary on the grounds that he was his son-in-law. Receiving tribute from the Republic of Venice, Sigismund's first aim was to become emperor of the Holy Roman Empire, Poland and Bohemia. Nevertheless, he was not completely indifferent toward the Osmanlı drive into Europe and the spread of Islam there. Sigismund attacked Niğbolu, which the Osmanlıs had taken from the Bulgarian king Shishman, capturing it in 794/1392, but Yıldırım (Thunderbolt) Bâyezîd immediately arrived from Anatolia. Sigismund left Niğbolu and fled, narrowly escaping capture.[171] Yıldırım Bâyezîd abolished the vassal Bulgarian kingdom, capturing its capital of Tırnova in 795/1393 and most of the rest of the country, except for Dobruja and Vidin, which remained under the rule of minor Bulgarian princes.[172]

Continuing to carry out the duty of *jihâd*, Yıldırım Bâyezîd opened Salonica and Yenişehir (Larissa) to Islam in Jumâdal Akhira 796/April 1394. The Osmanlıs advanced in northern Albania along the rivers Boyana and Drina and took areas south and southwest of Lake Ishqodra (Shkodër). At that time, there were feudal lords among the local and other races in Albania. These feudal lords were in a position to rely either on the Venetians from the west, or on

*Chapter Two – The Foundation of the Osmanlı Devlet*

the Osmanlıs who came from the east and were in the process of spreading Islam in the region.[173]

Meanwhile, the *beğ* of Qaramân, once the most powerful of the *beğliks* in Anatolia, harboured plans to enlarge his territories in Anatolia at the expense of the Osmanlıs who were busy with their *jihâd* in Europe. When he attacked Osmanlı territories, Bâyezîd Khân proceeded to Anatolia until he reached Qonya, the capital of the Qaramân Beğlik. But the *beğ* fled, and the people of Qonya voluntarily placed their city under Osmanlı rule and sovereignty. Aqsaray, Niğde, and Qayseri followed suit, which demonstrated the benevolence and justice of the Osmanlı administration. Bâyezîd Khân marched to take Qastamonu from Jandaroğlu *Beğlik* in 794/1392.[174]

He took Samsun from the Janik *Beğlik* in 800/1398, and Sivas, Toqat, and Qayseri from Qâdi Burhâneddîn *Devlet* in 801/1399,[175] while the city of Sivas voluntarily joined the Osmanlı Devlet, and the *beğ* of Erzinjan declared his allegiance, thereupon to be appointed its governor under the suzerainty of the Osmanlıs. Yıldırım Bâyezîd Khân proceeded to take the city of Malatya and the towns of Dârende and Divriği in 798/1396.[176] The city of Amasya also voluntarily joined the Osmanlı Devlet. By that time the Osmanlı Devlet became well known for its commitment to the cause of Islam and its earnest desire to unite the Muslims of Anatolia under its rule. Hence, they flocked to join it.

At the suggestion of Jendereli Halîl Pasha's son, Ali Pasha, the incomes of the *qâdis* were increased. It was decided that a *qâdi* would receive 20 *aqchas* for every 1,000 *aqchas* in deciding distribution of the amount of the heritage and 2 *aqchas* for drafting a legal document.[177]

## The Battle of Niğbolu (Nicopolis) (798/1396)

Sigismund, the king of Catholic Hungary (r. 1386-1437), became apprehensive of the Osmanlı presence near his kingdom. Being unwilling to negotiate or compromise with the Muslim Devlet, he approached European countries to form a united Christian front against it. At the same time, the Roman Empire had continued to exist like a small island in the surrounding Osmanlı lands; a situation that embarrassed Christian Europe very much. Under these circumstances, the Roman Emperor Manuel's having recourse to the European socio-political entities and the call by Pope Boniface IX for a Crusade against the Osmanlı Devlet proved effective. Hence in 1394 the Pope proclaimed another Crusade against the Muslims and another formidable army of 200,000 was formed under the leadership of the Hungarian king. Hungarians, famous French knights, three cousins of the French king, the Bavarian Knights of Germany, Belgians, Dutch, Venetians, the knights of Switzerland, Crusaders from Britain, the knights of Scotland, Savoy, and Rhodes, Vlachs (Romanians), and Bulgarians all participated in this force. This huge Crusader army was assisted by the Christian naval forces as well: the Venetian navy, which was one of the strongest naval forces of the time, together with the important naval power of the Knights of Rhodes (Saint John), and the Eastern Roman navy undertook to control the Dardanelles and the Bosphorus. They advanced in 798/1396 to rescue the city of Constantinople, which had been besieged for five years, and the Holy Land from Muslim domination. They seem to have been confident of victory and boasted, "Were the sky to fall we would hold it up with our spears." The allied Christian army plundered Serbia, but the Orthodox king remained true to his treaty, presumably out of fear of retaliation by Bâyezîd.

Due to this massive European advance, Sultân Bâyezîd partially lifted the siege of Constantinople and advanced to Edirne until he quickly reached Nicopolis (Niğbolu), which had been taken by Sultân Murâd from the Bulgarian king Shisman, whose castle was surrounded by the Christian forces. The Crusaders did not

## Chapter Two – The Foundation of the Osmanlı Devlet

think that Bâyezîd would reach the scene quickly and were taken by surprise. Yıldırım Bâyezîd, an extremely brave soldier, passed through the surrounding lines of the Crusaders at night by himself, approached the castle, and addressed the commander of the castle "Bre Doğan! (O Doğan!)." "Order me, my Sultân!" the commander replied, knowing that no one, except Yıldırım Bâyezîd, would call him by name. After a short conversation about the situation, thus enhancing the morale of the besieged *mujâhids*, Yıldırım Bâyezîd returned to his army.

The Osmanlı army, arrayed in the form of a crescent, was first attacked by the French cavalry who did not want to lose the honour of the victory to the Hungarians despite Sigismund's advice of caution. Its centre retreated a bit, and the French cavalry continued its onslaught. Sigismund tried in vain to rescue them, but his own life was threatened, and he finally fled by boat to the Christian fleet that was stationed on the Danube to support the Crusader army. Sigismund sailed to Constantinople via the Black Sea, and on through the Dardanelles to Dalmatia until he reached his own country Hungary by land.[178] A certain Schiltberger of Bavaria, who was captured in this battle by the Osmanlıs and spent some time in Gelibolu, states that the Osmanlıs lined up the captives of Niğbolu on the shores of Gelibolu while the ship on which Sigismund was passing and shouted to him to take these captives with him.

"Bayezit brought together contingents from Anatolia and routed the attackers (September 25, 1396), with thousands of knights and their leaders being either killed on the battlefield or drowned as they attempted to cross the Danube. Thousands more were taken prisoner, including nobles from all over Europe, who were freed only after the payment of heavy ransom."[179] Among them were Jean sans Peur, the arrogant grandchild of the French king and more than twenty French nobles who were sent to Bursa and Mihalıç.

They remained in captivity for more than a year and were released in exchange for a ransom of 200,000 gold pieces. Heavy taxes were imposed on people in the whole of France, and, in addition, money was collected from the Republic of Venice, Hungary, and Cyprus to ransom them. This battle consolidated Osmanlı rule in the Balkans, making it beyond dispute.[180] Sultân Bâyezîd used the spoils of this victory to build Ulujâmi (the Grand Mosque)[i] in Bursa. This fact underlines the difference between the two sides: in the West they erected statues or arches of triumph to commemorate victories. Osmanlıs built mosques, hospices, etc. for public use, because Islam prohibits useless expenditure (*isrâf*).

Yıldırım's horse was shot dead and he himself was wounded during the battle, but he switched to another horse and fought on, not caring about his wound.

Following this great victory against the allied Christian forces of Europe at the Battle of Nicopolis on 21 Zilhijjah 798/25 September 1396, the Osmanlıs annexed the remaining parts of the Bulgarian kingdom, and the Muslim *gâzis* known as *aqınjı* (raiders) attacked Wallachia and Hungary.

Meanwhile Sultân Bâyezîd resumed the siege of Constantinople. The Osmanlı Devlet was, however, careful to maintain peaceful relations at that time with the Genoese and the Venetians. Being supreme on the high seas, these powers could, if they wanted,

---

i   Süleymân Chelebi was *imâm* at Ulujâmi, Bursa. When he heard that a *wâiz* (speaker) understood and interpreted the *âyat* "*we make no distinction between any of His messengers*" (*al-Baqarah* [2]: 285) as "all the messengers are equal in degree," he wrote *wasîlatun najât* in Osmanlı Turkish, generally known as *mavlid* and recited on many occasions such as circumcisions, weddings, funerals, etc. to emphasise the superiority of the Final Messenger Muhammad ﷺ recounting his life. The theme is that there is no distinction among the prophets in terms of being Messengers.

*Chapter Two – The Foundation of the Osmanlı Devlet*

prevent the Osmanlı army from crossing the Bosphorus or the Dardanelles.[181] Having no guns big enough to destroy the strong walls of Constantinople, Yıldırım Bâyezîd's strategy was to besiege the city until it ran out of food and consequently surrendered to the Osmanlıs. In fact, there were incidents of people climbing down the walls of the city to safety. Had not Emîr Timur come with a huge army, Yıldırım Bâyezîd could most probably have opened Constantinople to Islam at that time.[i]

Sultân Bâyezîd sent *aqınjı* forces to Morea. Meanwhile, the *beğ* of Qaramân, 'Alâeddîn 'Ali, took advantage of the Osmanlı preoccupation in Europe to attack the city of Ankara, and took Sarı Timurtash Pasha prisoner. Learning that Yıldırım Bâyezîd defeated the Crusaders at Niğbolu, he released Timurtash Pasha and wanted

*Ulujâmi, Bursa*

i    *OT*, I, 291. In his book *History of the Ottoman Empire and Modern Turkey* (Cambridge, 1988), p. 34, S. Shaw claims that Bâyezîd abandoned the siege because "his Christian advisors pleaded with him to do so." But he does not give any of their names, and Bâyezîd was, moreover, not the type of man to be guided by others. Rather, this tactical withdrawal was dictated by the rising threat posed by Emîr Timur.

to be on good terms with the Osmanlı sultân. But Yıldırım Bâyezîd, after putting the situation in order in Rumelia and leaving *aqınjı* forces in Morea, went to Anatolia in 799/1397 and advanced to the city of Qonya, the capital of the Qaramân Beğlik. The Osmanlı army defeated the *beğ* of Qaramân at the battle that took place at Aqchây. When the Osmanlı army came to Qonya, it was harvest time; when the people of Qonya saw that Osmanlı soldiers did not plunder their grain, which was spread on the ground outside the city, but purchased it, they decided to hand over the city,[182] and they did so on condition that their lives and property would be spared.[183] The cities of Aqsaray, Niğde, and Lârende also were annexed in 800/1398; some parts of Qaramân land south of the Taurus mountains remained beyond Osmanlı reach at that time, but the Qaramân *beğlik*, which was the largest one, came to an actual end and this situation increased the prestige of the Osmanlı Devlet. And Ahmed Beğ, Emîr of Amasya, who was tired of the pressure by Qâdi Burhâneddîn, applied in 795/1393 to Yıldırım Bâyezîd, informing him that he wanted to hand over the city of Amasya in return for an appointment as a *sanjaqbeği*, which was granted.[184] Yıldırım Bâyezîd annexed the cities of Sivas, Toqat, and Qayseri from the Qâdi Burhâneddîn *beğlik* in 801/1399 and returned to Bursa. Qâdi Burhâneddîn had accepted the suzerainty of the Mamlûks of Egypt and ash-Shâm when he saw that the Osmanlı Devlet had become very strong and prestigious after the battle of Niğbolu and its victory over the Qaramân Beğlik. The city of Malatya belonged to the Qâdi Burhâneddîn *Beğlik*. Yıldırım Bâyezîd wanted the Mamlûk sultân Nâsirud Dîn Farac to hand the city of Malatya to him on the grounds that it had put an end to the *beğlik* of Qâdi Burhâneddîn and, consequently, Malatya should also be within Osmanlı borders. When his wish was not fulfilled, Yıldırım Bâyezîd marched to the city of Malatya and the people handed over the city. Yıldırım annexed the towns of Divriği and Dârende, which belonged to the

*Chapter Two – The Foundation of the Osmanlı Devlet*

*Tomb of Süleymân Chelebi, Bursa*

Mamlûks. Mutahharten the Beğ of Erzinjan, who had accepted the suzerainty of Emîr Timur, declared allegiance to Yıldırım Bâyezîd, and was left as *beğ* of the city under Osmanlı rule. It was generally accepted at that time that the Osmanlı Devlet was going to unite all the Muslims of Anatolia under its standard.

Before the Battle of Ankara in 804/1402, the Osmanlı Devlet had taken over almost all of the Muslim territories under the Selçuklu Devlet and opened vast areas in Europe to Islam as far as the Danube. This magnificent achievement was miraculously accomplished in just over one century. Mustapha Nûrî Pasha, a famous statesman, summarises the causes of this unique success as follows.

1. The early Osmanlı sultâns obeyed *Sharî'at* law unquestioningly.[i]

---

[i] Sultân Yıldırım Bâyezîd was supposed to testify, but the *qâdi* of Bursa Shamsaddîn Fanârî hesitated to accept him as a witness on the grounds that he neglected to attend the worship services (*salâtu Jamâ'ah*) even though this was because of his preoccupation with official affairs; upon this, Yıldırım Bâyezîd built a mosque in front of his palace to be able to attend services: Osmân-zâde Tâib, *Hadîqatus Selâtîn*, cited in Dânişmend, I, 141.

105

They put the administration of law exclusively in the hands of the *qâdis* whom they appointed to every city and town in the *devlet*.
2. The Osmanlıs remained consistently loyal to the Selçuklu Muslim Devlet and never revolted against it. The Creator rewarded them for this, as it is mandatory for the Muslims to obey the ruler who implements Islam, as revealed in the Qur'ân, *"Obey Allah and the Messenger and the Ulu'l Amr (those charged with authority) among you"* (*an-Nisâ* 4: 59).
3. The collapse of the Selçuklu Devlet and the weakness of the Roman Empire prepared the grounds for expansion of the Osmanlı Devlet.
4. The Osmanlıs' strategic location enabled them to wage *jihâd* against the *kâfirs* (infidels) and to acquire much booty which encouraged more *gâzis* (*mujâhids*) to participate in their *jihâd*.
5. The Osmanlıs respected the *'ulamâ* (scholars) and invested their commanders with authority over and administration of the areas, thus encouraging them to be loyal to the new Muslim Devlet. They were also very keen to spread Islam and implement the *Sharî'at* in those areas where they built public and charitable institutions, such as baths, *madrasahs*, mosques, and so on.[185]

### Emîr Timur and Yıldırım Bâyezîd

While Bâyezîd was engaged in *jihâd* activities in Europe, another strong Turkish ruler emerged in Turkestan. This was Emîr Timur or Tamerlane as he is popularly known in the West. His capital was Samarqand in today's Özbekistan,[i] but he kept moving,[ii] acquiring

---

i  Uzbek is a distortion of Özbek, and Uzbekistan a distortion of Özbekistan.
ii Emîr Timur ordered his cooks to prepare a meal that his army would be able to eat on horseback, without wasting time to stop to eat. So they prepared a meal of rice, some vegetables and onions, which is still consumed in Özbekistan even today, thus complying with his order.

## Chapter Two – The Foundation of the Osmanlı Devlet

new territories in Asia. His expansionist campaign frightened both the ruler of Baghdad, Ahmed of Jelâyir (784-813/1382-1410), and his vassal Qara Yusuf, ruler of Tabrîz.[186] Emîr Timur (736-807/1336-1405) approached Yıldırım Bâyezîd to extradite these two rulers, but the latter angrily refused on the grounds that this was unethical. Further diplomatic efforts (envoys and correspondence) failed to settle the dispute between the two, and Emîr Timur finally advanced and stormed the Osmanlı garrison at Sivas. Many were executed in 802/1400.

The Sultân learned of the fall of Sivas during the siege of Constantinople. He hurriedly left for Anatolia but missed Timur, who had marched south against the Mamlûks of Egypt[187] and occupied Bilâdush Shâm (Syria) in 803/1401. The Sultân of the Mamlûks had died by that time and had been succeeded by a child. This led to quarrels and feuds among the ruling Mamlûks and consequently paved the way for Timur's advance.

> "Timur, who hesitated for a while to march against Yıldırım who had acquired a great fame through the Niğbolu victory, saw himself the heir of İlhanlıs and the Anatolian Selçuklus and was keen to keep the *status quo* in Anatolia and made it his aim to remove any entity who opposed him. In fact, he saw the Osmanlıs as one of the *beğliks* in western Anatolia that should obey him. Yıldırım's efforts to disturb the balance in Anatolia and to unite it meant a blow to his capacity of patronageandguardianship."[188]

---

Hitler also wanted his armies not to waste time eating and ordered them to have their ration in the form of pills that contained enough protein, starch, vitamins, etc. to meet one's daily needs. But it proved futile because they became constipated due to a lack of cellulose.

Emîr Timur appreciated the situation and knew that he could not achieve anything against Bâyezîd with the forces with him; so he brought select units from Turkestan and spent the winter at Qarabağ, Azerbayjân. He could have then captured China, which was passing through a state of chaos and confusion after the death of its Emperor, but he felt it essential to deal first with Sultân Bâyezîd who threatened Iraq, al-Jazîrah, and Azerbayjân.[189] The real reason for the Timur-Bâyezîd conflict was Timur's desire for world hegemony and Bâyezîd's sense of personal supremacy, having gone from one victory to another until that point.

The Osmanlı administrators, who appreciated the situation and valued Timur's power, got Yıldırım to agree to peace and to send an envoy to Timur. Bâyezîd stated in his letter that there was no reason for mutual aversion and that he had been engaged in *jihâd* like all his forefathers.

Emîr Timur, however, wanted Bâyezîd to immediately accept a number of humiliating conditions: he was to accept the supremacy of Timur unconditionally, send him one of his sons as a hostage, and hand Qara Yusuf over to him. Furthermore, he had to return the town of Kemah to its previous rulers and to surrender all the territories that the Osmanlıs took in Anatolia to their previous rulers.

Bâyezîd, who had not experienced defeat so far, refused these conditions contemptuously, and the two armies met on the plain of Chubuq near Ankara in 804/1402.[190] While Timur had elephants in his army, the Osmanlıs employed artillery and Serbian soldiers who had been given to the Osmanlıs as a tribute. During the battle that followed, some cavalrymen from Anatolia went over to Timur's army when they saw their former *beğs*' flags on the other side.[191] The Mongols, who were called Tatars when they occupied Anatolia and defeated the Selçuklus at Kösedağı in 1243, had left some of their units in Anatolia to prevent the Selçuklus' return. Yıldırım Bâyezîd, who annexed the areas where those Tatars had settled, did not

## Chapter Two – The Foundation of the Osmanlı Devlet

impose any taxes on them but used them during war. Emîr Timur contacted those Mongols (who are referred to as "Qara Tatar" in Osmanlı sources) in secrecy, promised them Anatolia as theirs to rule. So, those Qara Tatars also went over to Timur's army.[192] The Osmanlı army retreated, and the Grand Vazîr Ali Pasha fled with Shâhzâda (Prince) Süleymân Chelebi, while the other *shâhzâda*, Mehemmed Chelebi, who was in the rear guard, made his way to Amasya. Yıldırım Bâyezîd fought courageously but was surrounded by Timur's soldiers, and eventually captured.[193] He died in grief in Aqshehir[194] and was buried in Bursa. He was carried in a barred litter, which popularised a legend that he had been kept in an iron cage.

Emîr Timur achieved more victories by occupying İznik (Nicea), Bursa, and the cities on the coast. He took İzmir (Smyrna) from the valiant Knights of St. John, and restored the various petty *beğliks* that the Osmanlıs had taken in Anatolia to their former rulers.[195] The Knights of St. John had taken the harbour of İzmir from the Aydınoğlu *beğlik* in 745/1344. Emîr Timur's taking the castle of İzmir in 805/1402 was a great success. He gave İzmir to Aydınoğlu *beğlik* which was among the *beğliks* of Anatolia that he had revived.[i] Timur did not cross the Marmara Sea to Europe, thus the European part of the Osmanlı Devlet remained untouched. Yıldırım Bâyezîd's elder son, Süleymân Chelebi, ruled the European part of the Osmanlı domain.

Emîr Timur sent letters to the French king Charles VI and the king of England Henry IV informing them about his success and that he had defeated the person they could not at Niğbolu.[196]

---

i Dânişmend, *op. cit.*, I, pp. 138-139. The "Knights of St. John" was a religious-military order. Youth from all over Europe came and entered this order, they were militarily very well trained to fight Muslims, especially the "infidel Turk" (because they did not accept Jesus ﷺ as God).

Mustafa Nûrî Pasha[i] criticised Bâyezîd for being "short tempered and proud" and went on to say: "He should have taken his time before annexing all the *beğliks* of Aydın, Menteshe, Hamîd, Germiyân, and İsfendiyâr."[197] Stanley Lane-Poole had this to say about the Osmanlı defeat: "The Osmanlı power seemed gone forever. At one blow Timur, the 'Noble Tartarian,'[ii] had apparently swept away its sovereignty in

---

i   He was 'Defter-i Hâqânî Nâzırı' under Sultân Abdülhamîd II, and his book is invaluable.

ii  Timur was not exclusively a Tatar. The name itself indicates his Turkish origin. It is pronounced in Eastern (Chagatay) Turkish as "Timur," and in Western (Osmanlı) Turkish "Demîr," which means "iron." "Tatar" or "Tartar" indicates the Mongols who invaded most of the known world at that time, including vast Turkish areas that stretched east of the Caspian Sea to China, and north of the Caspian and Black Seas. For example, İbn al-Athîr writes in his *al-Kâmil fit Târîkh* (Beirut, 1398/1978), when relating the events of the year 617/1220, "of the coming of Tatars to Turkestan" (p. 329); "Their sovereign Jinghis Khân" (p. 329); "Tatars' entrance to Diyâr Bakr and al-Jazîrah, 628/1231" (p. 384). Therefore, it is obvious that the Mongols were called "Tatars" at that time. The Turks in Turkestan and north of the Caspian and Black Seas were invaded by the Mongols and lived under their rule, and they were called "Tatar" after their rulers. In due course, the term "Mongol" prevailed in the eastern region of the Mongol domain, while "Tatar" continued to be used in the remaining part: Barthold, "Tatar," *Encyclopaedia of Islam* (Leiden: 1934), vol. iv, p. 701. The real Tatars in those areas merged over time with the much more numerous Turkish people. A good example of this is Tataristan in today's Russian Federation. The Muslim people of Tataristan speak the Kipchaq dialect of the Turkish language and are descendants of the Bolgar (Kipchaq) Turks. As for Timur, he spoke the eastern (Chagatay) dialect of the Turkish language. His great-great grandfather might have been in the entourage of Chagatay Khân, grandson of Jinghis Khân, but

## Chapter Two – The Foundation of the Osmanlı Devlet

Anatolia, and there were too many foes awaiting their opportunity in Europe for the hold of the Turks on their European provinces to be anything but precarious. Hungarians, Poles, Bulgarians, Albanians, Vlachs, and many more hovered on the brink of the Turkish provinces or were ready to rise in revolt within their borders. Their enemy was fallen, they thought, for ever."[198]

### Evaluation

The defeat of the Osmanlıs at the hands of Timur may be attributed to many reasons.

Timur's army was very disciplined and it substantially outnumbered the Osmanlı army. The Osmanlı army contained about 8,000 non-Muslim Serbian soldiers, whose participation in a battle against Muslims was presumably considered a bad omen for the Osmanlıs. Incidentally, it is rightly or wrongly asserted that Sultân Murâd was penalised for his fight with the Muslim *beğ* of Qaramân by the subsequent Battle of Kosova in which he was killed. Moreover, the newly annexed territories had not experienced Osmanlı rule long enough to accept it, and they switched to Timur's side once they saw their former *beğs* on his side. Besides all this, it was reported that high-ranking officials and officers were not enthusiastic about this battle with Muslims and had therefore not fought valiantly against Timur. Nevertheless, being well aware that all the responsibility of this battle rested on his shoulders, the Sultân continued the fight with only a few hundred soldiers to the bitter end, though he could have fled to safety if he had chosen to.[199]

---

the ruling Mongols (Tatars) had become Turkified after four generations, as the name Timur indicates. It is certain that Emîr Timur did not speak Mongolian but eastern Turkish, like the people in Özbekistan. Shaw also thinks that Timur was a Tatar, for he writes "the powerful Tartar invader of Iran, Tamerlane" (Shaw, *op. cit.*, I, p. 32).

The Battle of Ankara was an immense cause of joy for the Roman Empire. The Emperor John VII immediately sent envoys to Emîr Timur, presenting his homage, and paying tribute to him instead of the Osmanlıs. Timur thus wanted him to prepare a navy for him to convey his troops to Europe. Now, fearing that they were falling into Timur's hands, the Roman Emperor sent envoys to the Pope and the Senate of Venice asking for help. But Timur did not want to sever his ties to Anatolia by crossing the Marmara Sea and gave up the idea. He preferred to march on China instead. Meanwhile, he accepted the suzerainty of Faraj, the Mamlûk sultân.

The Osmanlı *shâhzâdas* also paid homage to Timur: Süleymân Chelebi, who proclaimed his rule at Edirne, sent Shaykh Ramadân to Timur. İsâ Chelebi, who controlled Bursa and Balıkesir, sent Shaykh Qutbeddîn, and Mehemmed Chelebi,[i] who was at Amasya, sent Sofu Bâyezîd to Timur. Emîr Timur, on the other hand, sent Shâhzâda Mustafa together with his father's corpse. Timur's name is seen on Mehemmed Chelebi's coins, dated 806/1403-4 as a token of homage.[200]

### The Period of Tumult (1402-1413)

After Yıldırım's capture, his sons tried to take over the *devlet*. Emîr

---

i  The correct pronunciation of this name at that time should be "Mehemmed" and not "Mehmed" as generally used. See, for example: H.A.R. Gibb, *A History of Ottoman Poetry* (London: 1900, reprint 1958), pp. 392-393. The name of the poet occurs there as "Mehemmed" which many would read as "Mehmed" today. It shows that this name was pronounced "Mehemmed" in the fifteenth century. Another example is *Gazavât-ı Sultân Murâd b. Mehemmed Hân,* ed. by Halîl İnalcık and Mevlüt Oğuz (Ankara: 1978), which relates Sultân Murâd II's (Chelebi Mehemmed's son) battles at İzladi and Varna (1443-1444). The title of the book refers to this Osmanlı ruler, Mehemmed I.

## Chapter Two – The Foundation of the Osmanlı Devlet

Süleymân and Mûsâ Chelebi consecutively ruled the Osmanlı territories of Europe while Mehemmed Chelebi ruled the Anatolian part of the Osmanlı Devlet, after having overthrown his brother İsâ Chelebi.

Subsequently Mehemmed Chelebi went to Europe, where he defeated his brother Mûsâ and became the sole sultân in 815/1412.[201] The Period of Tumult, however, continued for eleven years. It is interesting to note that while the Osmanlıs were engaged in civil war, no serious revolt took place in the newly annexed European territories. The Christians in those areas, for example, remained peaceful during the successful campaigns of Mûsâ Chelebi against the Serbians. Had they been unhappy under Osmanlı rule, they would have revolted against it and diverted its attention from the *jihâd* against other Christians. This indicates that the Osmanlı administration was just and tolerant towards its *dhimmîs*, and we now have sufficient evidence to assume that they preferred the Osmanlıs to Christian rule. The Orthodox Christians of the Balkan Peninsula had, for example, preferred the Muslim administration to the Catholic one,[202] as Donald Edgar Pitcher emphasised by writing: "The most striking feature of the ten-year struggle for the Empire between the four sons of Bayazid is that within the boundaries of the Sultanate as established by Murâd I there was astonishing fidelity to the house of Osman. Support might be transferred from one brother to another according to character and circumstance, but there was little or no inclination to break away from Ottoman rule. Participation in the war naturally employed the main energies of the troops, but that the *gazi* impulse was still strong is shown by the continuation of raids into Christian territory even as far afield as Motting (1408) in the extreme northwest."[203] In this respect, the Osmanlıs were much more tolerant towards the Christian people under their rule than most of the Christian countries in the present day so-called developed world towards the Muslims living in their

*Tomb of Shaykh Qutbuddin, İznik*

domains. In other words, what the Muslims achieved in this respect five centuries ago has not yet been attained by the Christian West. This is a unique credit to Islam for which the Muslims should all and always be proud and honoured.

# Chapter Three

# Restoration

## 3.1 MEHEMMED CHELEBI (1413-1421)

Mehemmed Chelebi[i] came to Bursa when Timur left Anatolia, but İsâ Chelebi, the other *shâhzâda*, was there. They fought, and İsâ Chelebi was defeated and retreated, and Mehemmed Chelebi entered Bursa. He wanted Germiyanoğlu Yaqûb Beğ to send him Yıldırım Bâyezîd's corpse, which Yaqûb had. He sent it with Mûsâ Chelebi, and the funeral was held in 806/1403-04.

Süleymân Chelebi, who governed the European part, intended to annex the Anatolian part since he was Bâyezîd's elder son. But Ali Pasha, the *vazîr-i a'zam*, thought that sending the other *shâhzâda* İsâ Chelebi was more convenient. Accordingly, İsâ Chelebi was sent with troops. But he was defeated by Mehemmed Chelebi and fled to İsfendiyâr Beğ of Qastamonu. Then İsâ Chelebi attempted once more, with the help of some Anatolian *beğliks* to defeat Mehemmed Chelebi but was himself defeated and killed. Chelebi Mehemmed marched against the *beğs* of İzmir, Saruhan, and Menteshe, who had supported İsâ Chelebi. After defeating them, Mehemmed Chelebi

---

i *Chelebi* is a Turkish word that means *prince* or *noble* and occasionally "brother-in-law" of the bride. But in this context it is indication of the fact that all of the sons of Sultân Bâyezîd were descendants of Mewlânâ; because "their mother *Devlet* Hâtûn was daughter of Mutahhara Hâtûn, granddaughter of Mewlânâ Jelâleddîn Rûmî." Ahmet Şimşirgil, *KAYI – I Osmanlı Tarihi*, İstanbul, 2014 (15. printing) p. 95.

annexed Saruhan *Beğlik*, and Jüneyd, the *beğ* of İzmir, accepted Chelebi Mehemmed as ruler.

Thus, Mehemmed Chelebi first had to deal with the rebellious *beğliks* (emirates, principalities) of Anatolia that had been reestablished by Emîr Timur. While he was busy in Rumelia, fighting Mûsâ Chelebi (d.1413), who had defeated Süleymân Chelebi and had ruled the European part of the Osmanlı Devlet, Mehmed, the *beğ* of Qaramân, besieged Bursa. But the Osmanlı troops forced him to flee. Chelebi Mehemmed now appointed his son Murâd as *sanjaqbeği*[i] of Amasya and entrusted Hamza Beğ to be his *lala*.[ii] He also acquired İzmir from Juneyd Beğ, appointed Juneyd Beğ *sanjaqbeği* of Niğbolu (Nicopolis), and Alexander, a convert to Islam and son of the Bulgarian King, to be the *beğ* of İzmir and the surrounding area in 817/1414.[204] Those who called themselves "Knights of St. John," with their headquarters on the island of Rhodes, had been building a castle on the shore of İzmir. Chelebi Mehemmed demolished that incomplete castle in one night. The head of the Knights was furious and said that if the Osmanlıs did not permit the castle to be built, a violent struggle would ensue between the Osmanlı Devlet and the papal powers that would entail the destruction of many parts of the Osmanlı country. Mehemmed Chelebi listened to this threat quietly. He replied that he was just to everyone but that the castle had been a pirate den and the Muslims of the environment had suffered very much because of it, and that the people in that area insisted that it

---

i   In the Osmanlı administration a *sanjaq* was part of a province. The *sanjaqbeği* was head of a military and administrative structure. Originally, however, *sanjaq* means a flag or standard flown during a battle.

ii  *Lala* (consonant *l* has a deep voice in this word) for the Osmanlıs was similar in meaning to *Atabeğ* for the Selçuklus; an experienced and well-educated man trusted with the upbringing and education of the *Shâhzâda* (son of the Sultân).

be destroyed. He added that he would not permit the castle to be built there but assigned another place in the south. So, the European pirates built Petroniyon castle at Bodrum (Halicarnassos). Once the Osmanlıs established themselves on the shores of the Aegean sea, the Genoese administrators of Focha, Midilli, and Sakız accepted Osmanlı suzerainty and paid taxes to them.[205]

Qaramânoğlu Beğlik was not satisfied with being re-established by Emîr Timur and given some other cities in addition to previous lands that belonged to it. It also occupied the *beğlik* of Germiyân.[206] Having inherited Qonya, the capital of the Selçuklus, this large *beğlik* saw itself as uniting Anatolia under its standard instead of the Osmanlı Devlet, which at that time appeared to be in decline.

The Osmanlı army marched against Qaramânoğlu, with the support of Yaqûb Beğ of Germiyân and İsfendiyâr Beğ of Jandar, who sent his son Qâsim Beğ at the head of his forces.

The Osmanlı army retook, without resistance, Aqshehir, Saideli, Beğshehri, Otlukhisarı that had previously belonged to the Osmanlı Devlet, and some other places. They besieged Qonya but could not take it because of heavy rains. Peace was concluded with Mehmed Beğ of Qaramân. Then, seeing that the Osmanlı army was tired and Chelebi Mehemmed was busy at Janik, Mehmed Beğ of Qaramân attacked again. The battle took place in the plain of Qonya, and Mehmed Beğ was defeated and fled to Tasheli. His son Mustafa Beğ remained at Qonya. Bâyezîd Pasha, the Grand Vazîr, was instrumental in the pardon that Mehmed Beğ received from the Osmanlıs, and a treaty was concluded in 818/1415, according to which the Osmanlıs regained Beğpazarı, Sivrihisâr, Aqshehir, Yalvach, Beğshehri, and Seydishehri, which had belonged to them and had been given to Qaramânoğlu by Emîr Timur. With this treaty Qaramânoğlu accepted the obligation to support the Osmanlıs by providing soldiers whenever they wanted.[207] Thus it became evident that the Osmanlı Devlet had become the one to unite the Anatolian

Muslims by subduing the Germiyân *beğlik* to being its vassal and placing the Qaramân *beğlik* in a position to pay tribute, putting some of its soldiers under Osmanlı command.

### The First Osmanlı-Venetian Naval Conflict

The Osmanlı navy began developing towards the end of the fourteenth century with their annexation of the *beğliks* of Saruhan, Menteshe, and Aydın, thus giving them direct access to the Aegean Sea. Yıldırım Bâyezîd set up a dockyard at Gelibolu and began naval activities with the help of volunteer seamen. The Republic of Venice, with its large navy, was the dominant force in the Mediterranean at that time. Having colonies in Albania, Greece, and on the shores of Morea, it wanted to dominate the eastern Mediterranean; even Cyprus was under Venetian rule.

The Kiklad islands were on this sea-route and were rocky places. The Republic sold these islands to Pietro Zeno, stipulating that the dukedom that would be founded would be dependent on Venice. Because of Pietro Zeno's bad treatment of Muslim sailors, the Osmanlıs prepared a fleet at Gelibolu and raided the Kiklad islands and then Eğriboz Island, in 818/1415, taking captives and booty. Admiral Pietro Lorendano came to Gelibolu and defeated the Osmanlı fleet the next year.[208] While the Osmanlı Devlet prepared to make up for this defeat, the uprising of Shaykh Bedreddîn at that time became a threat; so the preparations remained incomplete.[209]

### Tribute of Mircea, the Voyvoda of Wallachia

Mûsâ Chelebi had married the daughter of Mircea, the *voyvoda* of Wallachia. One of his relatives, Dan, contested Mircea on the position. Mehemmed Chelebi supported Dan, and Mircea turned to King Sigismund of Hungary for help. Mehemmed Chelebi marched against Mircea and defeated him, levied tribute on him, took his son as hostage, and Mircea accepted the obligation of sending soldiers to

Mehemmed Chelebi on his campaigns. The Osmanlı Devlet built the castle of Yergöğü (Giurgu) on the other side of the Danube in 819/1416 to guarantee Mircea's obedience. Mehemmed Chelebi marched against the Hungarians because of Sigismund's support for Mircea, took the castle of Saint Severin and besieged the city of Radkersburg. The Osmanlı forces could not open that city to Islam because of the troops coming from Austria.[210]

## Jandaroğlu Beğlik

Qâsim Beğ, of the Jandaroğlu *Beğlik*, requested the help of the Osmanlıs against his own father, İsfendiyâr Beğ. They responded favourably and besieged the town of Sinop in Jandaroğlu *Beğlik*. But the latter accepted Osmanlı rule and, as a token of this, had the *khutbah* delivered in the name of the Osmanlı Sultân during *jum'ah* prayer and accepted the *sikkah* (coinage) of the Osmanlı Sultân to be used as currency in his country. İsfendiyâr Beğ surrendered all his *beğlik* (with the exception of the towns of Qastamonu and Baqır küresi) to the Osmanlıs, and not to his son Qâsim Beğ.[211] The Osmanlı towns of Tosya, Çankırı, and Qalecik, which had been previously taken by Timur and given to this *beğlik* of Jandâr, were now claimed back by Mehemmed Chelebi. He acquired them without any resistance.[212]

## Mustafa Chelebi as a Hostage

Meanwhile, Mustafa Chelebi (d.1422), who had been taken captive along with his father Yıldırım Bâyezîd, was released and stayed for a while in the town of Niğde, in the Qaramân Beğlik. Subsequently, the Roman Emperor Manuel (r. 1391-1425) transported him to Europe as part of his campaign to foment trouble in the Osmanlı Devlet by playing one *shâhzâda* against the other. Mehemmed Chelebi therefore marched against Mustafa, who took refuge in the castle of Selânik (Thessaloniki), which was under the control of the Roman

Empire. When Mehemmed asked the Roman Emperor to hand him over, the latter refused, saying: "Mustafa will be imprisoned as long as you live." Mehemmed Chelebi then lifted the siege of the Selânik castle and agreed to pay Manuel an annual amount of 300,000 *aqchas* to cover the expenses of Mustafa Chelebi and his men while indetention.[213]

### The End of the Interregnum

During the tumult and after the capture of Yıldırım Bâyezîd, the Osmanlı territory in Anatolia was reduced to a few *sanjaqs*: Bursa, İzmit, Ankara, and Amasya. The Osmanlıs lost Selânik in Greece and some areas in Serbia. In this situation, the tax-paying Christian countries stopped payment to the Osmanlıs, but they could not find the courage and power to form a united front against the Osmanlıs. In spite of this trouble in the Osmanlı Devlet, no new political identities emerged, and strong and famous military leaders, such as the sons of Mihal and Evrenos, remained loyal to the Osmanlıs and their *devlet*.[214]

If Yıldırım Bâyezîd had not been defeated, his eldest son Emîr Süleymân would have been likely to succeed him, and hence continue living the luxurious and pompous life that was routine during his father's time. But Mehemmed Chelebi, who had already gone through considerable hardship and difficulties, was able to take over. He was a resolute and mature man, and hence succeeded in uniting the *devlet* and maintaining its stability.[215]

Emîr Süleymân began building a mosque in Edirne, the capital, and Mûsâ Chelebi continued with its construction. It was finally finished by Mehemmed Chelebi in 816/January 1414. This became known as Eski Jâmi (the old mosque). Mehemmed Chelebi built the Green Mosque, a *madrasah*, an *imâret*, and the Green Tomb in Bursa. He captured Hereke, Darıja, Gebze, Kartal, and Pendik on the Sea of Marmara in 823/1420, and allocated their revenue as a *waqf* for

*Chapter Three – Restoration*

*Eski Jâmi, Edirne*

these institutions. Taking over these towns from the Roman Empire was his response to their support of Mustafa Chelebi. Emperor Manuel's fear was so great he sent an envoy to Edirne to propose friendship and, in fact, to find out if Mehemmed Chelebi intended to march against Constantinople, since there were rumours that he was going to do so.[216]

Mehemmed Chelebi fell ill in Edirne. Knowing that he would not recover, he invited his *vazîrs* Bâyezîd, Chandarlı-zâde İbrâhîm and Hâjı İvaz Pashas, and willed that his death be kept a secret until his son Murâd, the *sanjaqbeği* of Amasya arrived and took over as ruler, because Mustafa Chelebi's detention by the Roman Emperor on Limni Island was limited to his lifetime. It was obvious that the Roman Emperor would release Mustafa Chelebi upon his death in order to provoke civil war in the Osmanlı domains. Shâhzâda Murâd was invited, but before he arrived his father Mehemmed Chelebi passed away. The death of the Sultân was kept secret until the new sultân arrived.[217] Mehemmed Chelebi is known as the Renewer (*Mujaddid*) of the Ninth Century (of the Hegira).

## 3.2 Sultân Murâd II (1421-1451)

During the change in power between Mehemmed Chelebi's death and his son Murâd's taking over, some *beğs* who wanted to become independent of the Osmanlıs, began to move: the *beğs* of Aydın, Menteshe, Saruhan and Hamîd rebelled.[218] The power was passed down from father to son in almost every country at that time. And the Osmanlı Devlet had just come out of an interregnum of eleven years. The death of Mehemmed Chelebi thus encouraged some *beğs* to attempt to become independent. Therefore, it was not an easy task at all to re-establish the *devlet* uniting all *beğliks*.

On the other hand, the Roman Empire discussed the situation and evaluated it from its viewpoint. The group headed by John, son of the emperor, and his co-regent held that they should support Mustafa Chelebi and make him the Sultân in Rumelia. The old Emperor Manuel and his group preferred Murâd. John and his group insisted they support Mustafa Chelebi, who promised to give Gelibolu to them, and this view was accepted. General Dimitriyos Lascarius was sent to Mustafa Chelebi on Limni Island. An agreement was concluded according to which Mustafa Chelebi would obey the emperor, would send his son to him as a hostage, would relinquish Tesalya (Thessaly), Gelibolu, and the western shores of the Black Sea up to Wallachia to the Roman Empire. After signing the agreement, Mustafa Chelebi went with Jüneyd Beğ and some Roman units to Gelibolu, then to Edirne and proclaimed his sultanate there in Zilka'de 824/ October 1421.[219] Jüneyd Beğ of İzmir (Aydınoğlu beğlik) became the *vazîr* of this new sultân. Thus, the European part came under his rule, while the Anatolian part of the Osmanlı Devlet remained under Murâd's rule.[220] The Roman Empire thus succeeded in its plot to split the Osmanlı Devlet in two.

Though called "Düzme (False) Mustafa" by the Osmanlı administration, this *shâhzâda* was joined by the famous *aqınjı*

*Chapter Three – Restoration*

*Yeshil Türbe of Chelebi Mehemmed, Bursa*

*beğs*, the sons of Evrenos, and others. Mustafa Chelebi moved to Anatolia, and the two Osmanlı armies thus met near Ulubad where a catastrophe was about to take place. It was at this critical juncture that an *aqınjı* (raider) *beğ*, Mihaloğlu Mehmed (d.1423), came by night to the river of Ulubad and secured the support of certain *aqınjı beğs* for Sultân Murâd. In addition, Hajı İvaz Pasha, Sultân Murâd's *vazîr*, sent a letter to Mustafa Chelebi in which he claimed that the *beğs* and other influential personalities in Osmanlı Europe had decided to desert him and cooperate with the Sultân. In another letter to Jüneyd Beğ, Mustafa Chelebi's *vazîr*, İvaz Pasha, wrote "You are a noble man, a *beğ*, and it is not certain that this man whose *vazîr* you agreed to be is the real Mustafa Chelebi. Sultân Murâd promises you a good position in the Osmanlı administration." That night, Hâjı İvaz Pasha himself took some soldiers to the spot he specified in his letter and shouted: "Sultân Murâd mükâfâtına selâm! (Greetings to the reward from Sultân Murâd)." Mustafa Chelebi suspected that he was about to be arrested and therefore fled. Jüneyd Beğ also fled. Consequently, in 825/1422 Mustafa's troops joined the Sultân, who pursued Mustafa Chelebi.[221] The latter was caught and executed in Edirne.[222] Had it not been for Hâjı İvaz Pasha's shrewdness, thousands of warriors might have been killed in this civil war. The Osmanlıs, in fact, usually opted to sacrifice the lives of the *Shâhzâdas* to avoid any civil war that might endanger the unity of the *devlet*, however remote it was. To them, "everything was dedicated to the *devlet* and the *devlet* was dedicated to the well-being of the people."

Sultân Murâd was determined to punish the Roman Empire for this terrible plot. On the other hand, Emperor Manuel and his co-regent John became anxious. They sent Lakanas and Marco Ganis to Sultân Murâd with gifts on the pretext of congratulating him but actually to find out the Sultân's intention. But Sultân Murâd refused to receive them and rejected their gifts.[223]

Sultân Murâd besieged Constantinople in retaliation for the activities of the Roman Empire which brought the Osmanlı Devlet to the brink of catastrophe in 1422. But during that siege, Manuel incited İlyâs, the *lala* of Mustafa, Murâd's younger brother and the *sanjaqbeği* of Hamîdeli, to revolt and proclaim independence. The *beğs* of Qaramân and Germiyân were also involved in this act. This army arrived at Bursa, which avoided invasion by giving gifts to the *lala*. They went to İznik and formed a government there. Faced with this serious threat, Murâd withdrew from Constantinople to attack İznik and execute Mustafa.[224] It is perhaps reasonable to believe that the Osmanlıs learned and adopted this practice of fratricide from the administrators of the Roman Empire who did this quite regularly.[i] On the other hand, "It appears to be a rule that a Turkish prince (was) never satisfied with anything short of the Sultanate; and it becomes a matter of sheer necessity, not a question of jealous suspicion, to make it impossible for him to attain his ambition."[225]

The Roman Empire was saved from the siege through using and victimising the young Mustafa. Western writers mention fratricide in the Osmanlı Devlet, but they do not mention that the Turks learned and adopted this practice from Romans. It is certain that

---

[i] Anthony Bryer, *Peoples and Settlement in Anatolia and Caucasus, 800-1900* (London, 1988, Variorum reprints), IV, p. 485, note 3. This information was previously published in an article entitled "Greek Historians on the Turks: The Case of the First Byzantine-Ottoman Marriage," in *The Writing of History in the Middle Ages* (Oxford: Clarendon Press, 1981) in which the following is mentioned: "As for fratricide, it is true that Andronikos III Grand Komnenos executed his brothers Michael and George on his accession to the throne of Trebizond in 1332, *before any known cases of Ottoman fratricide*" (emphasis added).

Moreover, it is well known that Irene blinded her six-year-old son, Constantine VI, and ruled the Roman Empire under the name of Augusta for five years: "She (Irene) transformed her regency for her son Constantine VI into a co-rule, and after his deposition and blinding (797) governed the Empire as sole ruler" (*The Cambridge Medieval History*, ed. by J.M. Hussey, Cambridge: 1967) IV, part II, p. 5.

"... the Empress Irene, the imperious beauty, who as regent brought up her son in utter dissipation in order to unfit him for the exercise of his royal prerogatives, and, when he nevertheless asserted himself, had him dethroned and blinded. She later became St. Irene, because the Church remembered only her devotion to images..." Herbert J. Muller, *The Uses of the Past: Profiles of Former Societies* (New York: New American Library, 1954), p. 16. And, needless to say, we do not know of any fratricide or similar practice among the Turks before the Osmanlıs.

Michael and George were the victims of fratricide in 1332 and that the first fratricide in the Osmanlı practice took place in 1389!

### The Situation in Rumelia

While Sultân Murâd was preoccupied with these problems in Anatolia, Prince Vlad Drakul of Wallachia (at present southern Romania) crossed the Danube and plundered Osmanlı territories. Vlad had overthrown Dan and replaced him. His title *drakul* means Satan. Fîrûz Beğ was sent against this Satan and defeated him. Taxes were levied on Vlad, and he sent his two sons to the Osmanlıs as hostages.[226] It was necessary for the Osmanlı Devlet to retrieve the lands it lost in Albania during the Interregnum to assert and establish its dominance in the Balkans. İsa Beğ, son of Evrenos Beğ, was sent with a large army to Albania, and he went as far as the Adriatic Sea. Ghion Kastriot was defeated during this campaign and his son Yorgi was brought to Edirne as a hostage. He converted to Islam there, and was called İskender Beğ. He later abandoned Islam and caused trouble for the Osmanlı Devlet. İsa Beğ, son of Evrenos Beğ, demolished the walls of Corinth and entered Morea in 826/1423.[227]

### The Situation in Anatolia

While Sultân Murâd was busy with his brother Mustafa, İsfendiyâr Beğ of Jandaroğlu *Beğlik* invaded Chanqırı, Tosya, and Qalecik, which had been annexed by the Osmanlıs in Mehemmed Chelebi's time. The Osmanlı army met İsfendiyâr Beğ's army near Bolu. The latter was defeated and fled to Sinop. He was, however, pardoned in 827/1423 after pledging loyalty and support to the Osmanlıs.[228]

### The Annexation of the Menteshe Beğlik 829/1425

Mehmed Beğ of Menteshe was among the *beğs* whose *beğliks* were revived by Emîr Timur after the Battle of Ankara. After his death, his son İlyâs became the beğ of Menteshe. İlyâs Beğ supported İsa

Chelebi during the struggle for power among the Osmanlı shâhzâdas but finally recognised the suzerainty of Mehemmed Chelebi in 817/1414 and minted coins in his name as a token of his rule. Upon the death of İlyâs Beğ in 824/1421, his two sons, who were hostages at the Osmanlı palace, fled and went to Menteshe and became rulers there. But Sultân Murâd was determined to establish the unity of Anatolia under the Osmanlı banner and went to Menteshe, captured them, and sent them to Tokat castle to be kept there. He thus annexed the Menteshe Beğlik in 829/1425.[229]

### The Annexation of Aydınoğlu Beğlik 829/1426

Jüneyd Beğ had been given his previous Aydınoğlu (İzmir) Beğlik, and he used every opportunity to enlarge his *beğlik* at Osmanlı expense. He retreated whenever Osmanlı forces were sent against him, but when they went back, he was again busy enlarging his *beğlik*. Upon this, the *beğlerbeği* of Anatolia Hamza Beğ and Yahshi Beğ were sent against Jüneyd Beğ and defeated him. Aydınoğlu *Beğlik* was also annexed in 829/1426.[230]

### Qaramânoğlu Beğlik

While Sultân Murâd was in the European part of his *devlet*, Mehemmed Beğ of Qaramân tried to capture the castle of Antalya in 830/1426 but died during the siege.[i] His son İbrâhîm Beğ went to Qonya, but his uncle Ali Beğ had already captured Qaramân. İbrâhîm thus fled with his brother İsa and took refuge

---

i When the *beğ* of Qaramân attacked the Osmanlı territory during the absence of the Sultân in Europe, one of his courtiers sarcastically said, "Our sultân from this side and your brother Yanko from the other side are trying to destroy the Osmanlıs; it is hoped that in a short time Muslims will be trampled under the infidels' feet." Cited in Osman Turan, *Türk Cihan Hakimiyeti Mefküresi Tarihi* (İstanbul: Nakışlar Yayınevi, 1979), II, p. 341.

with Sultân Murâd. The latter gave them protection and married them to two of his sisters.²³¹

### The Annexation of Germiyân Beğlik 832/1429

Yâqûb Beğ II of Germiyân (r.1387-1390, 1402-1429) had no son to succeed him in his *beğlik*. He liked his sister's (the wife of Yıldırım Bâyezîd, Devlet Hâtûn) grandson, Sultân Murâd, very much. More than 80 years old, Yâqûb Beğ II set out in 831/1428 to visit Sultân Murâd II. He was met with utmost respect in all Osmanlı cities on his journey, and in Bursa he was met by all the people, visited the tombs of Osmanlı sultâns there, and distributed money to people. He also visited Shaykh Emîr Sultân, the great *sûfî*, and kissed his hand in respect. When he arrived at Edirne he was shown great respect, and Sultân Murâd gave him a large amount of money as gift. A very generous man, Yâqûb Beğ gave away all his wealth on his journey."²³²

Yâqûb Beğ made Sultân Murâd his heir and successor in his will, was seen off, and he returned to Kütahya. Despite the fact that Yâqûb Beğ II had two brothers, İlyâs and Hızır, and nephews, he preferred Murâd II as his heir. "It is certain that the impossibility of resisting the Osmanlı Devlet had its effect in this preference, but in any case, this action of this old man deserves appreciation."²³³ When he died the next year, Kütahya was also annexed by the Osmanlı Devlet in 832/1429. Thus, with the exception of Qaramân and Jandaroğlu *beğliks*, all Anatolia was united under Osmanlı rule. The rulers of these two *beğliks* were in power with Osmanlı support, however, and were therefore also under Osmanlı influence.²³⁴

### The Opening of Selânik and Yanya to Islam

The castle of Selânik that was taken by Yıldırım Bâyezîd was recaptured by the Roman Empire after the Battle of Ankara. Sultân Murâd sent Evrenos Beğ's sons and Turahan Beğ to besiege Selânik.

*Chapter Three – Restoration*

*Emîr Sultân Mosque*

Manuel's son Andronikos was the despot of Selânik. The people, suffering from hunger, decided to sell the city to the Republic of Venice on the condition that the Venetians give them food and treat them well regardless of Andronikos' views. The Venetians agreed to the offer on the condition that the people would be loyal to them and bought Selânik for 50,000 pieces of gold. Andronikos, who had fallen ill, was sent to Morea in 826/1423.

Sultân Murâd did not agree to the Venetians' purchase of Selânik, but he had more important problems to deal with at that time. Therefore, Sultân Murâd did not renew the peace treaty with the Republic of Venice as he did with the rulers of Midilli, Sakız, and Rhodes. The Republic sent envoys to Edirne to renew the treaty, but Sultân Murâd told them: "Selânik is my city, which I inherited from my father; my grandfather Bâyezîd captured it by force from the Roman Empire; if its administration were in the hands of the

Romans, it would have been reasonable for them to complain if they had incurred any injustice; on the other hand, you are the Latins, people of Italy, what is the reason for your intrusion in this region? Leave it and depart of your own accord, or I will come."

Sultân Murâd besieged Selânik in 833/1430 and opened it to Islam. This event caused great grief in Venice and western Europe. Sultân Murâd settled Muslim families in Selânik, bringing them from Vardar Yenijesi and other cities, assigned the Ayadimitri (St. Demetrius) Church to the Christians, and converted other churches into mosques.

The despot of Epir Qarlotoji, who had recognised Osmanlı suzerainty, died, and his sons started a struggle for power. One of them, Menon, requested the support of the Osmanlıs. Qaraja Pasha was sent and helped Menon to succeed. But the people, who were tired of this struggle and preferred the direct rule of the Osmanlıs, applied to the Sultân. Having accepted their wish, the Sultân sent Qaraja Pasha, to whom the people surrendered Yanya. Muslims were sent there to settle in 835/1431.[235]

### The Serbian-Hungarian and Qaramân Alliance

The Serbian despot Vulakoğlu was instrumental in concluding an alliance between the Hungarian king, Sigismund, and İbrâhîm Beğ of Qaramân Beğlik (r. 1426-1464). The Hungarians besieged Güverjinlik (Kolomboc) on the banks of the Danube, and İbrâhîm Beğ attacked at Beğshehri, which had been bought by the Osmanlıs from the Hamîdoğlu Beğlik, and invaded it. Murâd did not fight against either of the attackers from two different sides but remained at Edirne, waiting. He sent Sinân Pasha, Beğlerbeği of Rumelia, to the aid of Güverjinlik. While Sinân Pasha was waiting for captives from the enemy to get information about the besiegers, Akınjı Sinân, *sanjaqbeği* of Vidin, attacked the Hungarians, saying that "our horses will demolish their stables because of panic resulting from

*Chapter Three – Restoration*

the uproar of the artillery," and Sinân Pasha also attacked, playing drums and shouting *takbîrs*. The besiegers were defeated and fled, trampling each other. Sigismund (King of Hungary 1388-1437 and Emperor of Germany 1411-1437) barely escaped death. Many of his soldiers were drowned in the Danube. The castle of Güverjinlik was thus saved in 837/1434.[236]

Sultân Murâd went on to Anatolia next year and marched against İbrâhîm Beğ of Qaramân, who fled to Tasheli. He wrote a letter of apology to the Sultân, who forgave him at the request of his sister who was İbrâhîm Beğ's wife.[237]

## Campaign in Rumelia

When Sultân Murâd returned from his campaign against Qaramân, it was the Serbian despot's turn to be punished. İshâq Beğ, the *sanjaqbeği* of Üsküp, had informed the Sultân that the Serbian despot had been instrumental in the alliance of Qaramânoğlu with the Hungarian King.

While Sultân Murâd was preparing to march against the Serbian despot, the latter informed him that his daughter, who was to be given in marriage to the Sultân, was ready to be sent. The Sultân received the bride[238] but did not arrange a wedding ceremony, saying "There is no need for festivities for this *kâfir's* daughter," and did not keep her at Edirne, the capital, because he was still angry with her father, and sent her to Bursa. He brought his other wife, Hatîje Hâtûn, the granddaughter of İsfendiyâr Beğ of Jandar, to Edirne. This woman was the mother of the future *Fâtih* (opener) of İstanbul (to Islam).[239]

Beğlerbeği Sinân Pasha, İshâq Beğ, and Turahan Beğ raided Albania.[240] While Sultân Murâd was busy with Qaramânoğlu in Anatolia, the Hungarian king, Sigismund, had sent units to plunder the environs of Alajahisâr.[241] Sultân Murâd, having punished and intimidated the allies of this king, thus isolating him, now decided to march against him. After returning from the Qaramân campaign, the Sultân ordered Ali Beğ, son of Evrenos Beğ in 840/1437 to carry out raids to open up access to Hungary. Ali Beğ raided Hungarian lands for a month. Upon his return, he said: "O my Sultân! is it not a pity that such a nice country should remain in the *kâfir's* hands!"[242] This expression manifests the *raison d'être* of the Osmanlı Devlet: they saw themselves as the representatives and disseminators of the Final Message, Islam, and the tool of implementing the Sacred Order of the Creator all over the world. And the Qur'ân states: *"My righteous slaves shall inherit the earth"* (al-Anbiyâ [21]: 105). Therefore, it was only very natural that, in every place, especially in the best parts of the world, those who submitted themselves to the commands of the Creator (i.e. Muslims), and tried to disseminate those orders and make them supreme, should rule.

This point is extremely important: the Osmanlı expansion followed necessarily from the belief that it was "a socio-political entity (*devlet*) to implement the Sacred Order on the Earth." Western imperialist expansion was nothing more than the understanding and practice that "those who possess the power can do whatever they want, and they may use this power for their profit"[i] as a primitive person would do because their stance is not dependent on *haqq*.[ii] In Islamic terminology, *haqq* is one of the attributes of Allah. Muslims call him *Haqq Te'âlâ* (The Sublime Haqq). (It seems that there is no concept in the western mind for '*haqq*'; you cannot translate '*haqq*' to a western language!).

---

i   It seems that the Western mentality has not changed very much, as can be seen nowadays all over the world: hunger, deprivation are everywhere in their sphere of influence.

ii  The word *haqq* has many meanings, some of which are truth, reality, justice, right, due. No single word in Western languages can give the same concept.

*Chapter Three – Restoration*

In this great raid, the previous allies of Hungary, Branković, the despot of Serbia, and the *voyvoda* of Wallachia, Vlad Drakul, had received orders from the Sultân and served with their soldiers under the command of Ali Beğ.[243]

In 841/1437 Sultân Murâd crossed the Danube and entered Transylvania. Branković, the Serbian despot (r. 1427-1450), and Vlad Drakul, prince of Wallachia (r. 1432-1446), joined the Osmanlı army in taking six castles, while the king of Hungary was nowhere present.[244] At that time Sigismund, the Holy Roman Emperor and king of Hungary, had died and his son-in-law Albert had become king of Hungary, and a year later he was elected the Holy Roman Emperor.[245]

*Murâdiye Madrasah, Bursa*

After this campaign to Hungary, Jorj Branković, whose loyalty to the Osmanlıs had been fading, was invited to come to Edirne with the keys of Semendire. But he fled to Albert, Holy Roman Emperor and king of Hungary. The Osmanlı forces besieged Semendire, and İshâq Bey, who had returned to the area – which he knew very well – after performing his *hajj* duty, took command of the Muslim forces and opened the castle to Islam. A huge Hungarian army arrived at the scene, but Gâzi İshâq Bey and Osmân Bey, the grandson of Timurtash Pasha, confronted that army and defeated it. They took many captives and a great amount of *ghanîmet*. The famous historian Aşık Paşazâde participated in that battle.[246] Shaw explained the reasons for these overwhelming victories admirably in the following words: "In all these advances into Europe Murat took advantage of the social, religious, and economic stresses that were rending society within the lands of his enemies. He was able to offer the downtrodden Balkan peasants what amounted to a social revolution, freedom from the tyranny of their feudal masters. Within the Balkan countries struggles for power at the center had ended real central authority, allowing the feudal magnates to increase their power and subject the cultivators to increasingly tyrannical conditions of tax payments and forced labor. In contrast, whenever the Ottomans established direct administration, all the land became the property of the Sultân, the state established close control and supervision over the fief holders, and manorial dues and forced labor were abolished, the latter being replaced by an easily payable tax known as the plough tax *(çift resmi)*. The Balkan masses, therefore, were at best lukewarm in support of the armies of their rulers, as well as those of the Crusaders, against the Muslims."[247]

There was a power struggle in Bohemia, and conflicts that started with the death of Albert; a situation that prepared favourable conditions for the Osmanlı Devlet. Therefore, Sultân Murâd left it to Ali Beğ, son of Evrenos Beğ, to take Belgrade, which was on the south bank of the Danube and of great strategical importance. They besieged Belgrade in 843/1439 and were able to enter the city, but the *fath* was not accomplished.[248]

The conflict with the Hungarians continued. Mezîd Beğ entered Transylvania with an *aqınjı* force in 845/1442, defeated a Hungarian force and besieged Hermanstad. At that time, Jan Hunyad arrived at the scene, and Mezîd Beğ, who remained between the two forces, was martyred and the Osmanlı forces were defeated. This battle secured great fame for Jan Hunyad throughout Europe. To make up for this defeat, Qula Shâhin Pasha, the *beğlerbeği* of Rumelia was sent against the Hungarians, but, because of his pride in his army and neglect in taking precautions, he was also defeated at Vazağ by Jan Hunyad. Upon these consecutive victories against the Osmanlıs a Crusader army was formed, and Ladislas, the king of Hungary and Poland, was put in command of this army, Jan Hunyad being commander-in-chief. This huge army defeated the Osmanlıs at Morava and İzladi. Then a ten-year peace treaty of Edirne-Segedin between the Osmanlı Devlet and Ladislas was concluded on Rabî'ul Awwal 25, 848/ July 12, 1444.[249]

Thus, secure on the European border, Sultân Murâd marched against İbrâhîm Bey of Qaramân, who had attacked Osmanlı territories in Anatolia. Murâd needed a *fetvâ* (*fatwâ* – legal opinion and permission) to fight a Muslim Devlet, and he obtained a *fatwâ* to fight the *beğ* of Qaramân from jurists of the four *madhhabs*: ash-Shâfi'î jurist İbn Hajar al-Asqalânî (d. 852/1448), al-Hanefî Qâdilqudât and Sheyhulislâm Sa'deddîn ad-Deyrî (d. 868/1462), al-Mâlikî Qâdilqudât Shaykhuyislâm Bedreddîn at-Tûnisî (d. 853/1449), al-Hanbalî Qâdilqudât and Shaykhulislâm Bedreddîn Bagdâdî (d.857/1453).[250] İbrâhîm Bey could not defeat Sultân Murâd and fled to Tasheli. He was married to Murâd's sister and, sending his wife to apologise, sued for peace. Sultân Murâd pardoned him, and a peace treaty was concluded with the Qaramân Beğlik.

## 3.3 THE ABDICATION OF SULTÂN MURÂD

Unlike his contemporaries in Europe and elsewhere, Sultân Murâd was not an absolute sovereign who would cling to power right up until he died. Instead, he was a *gâzi* (warrior in the holy war against unbelievers), a rational ruler, and a devout *sûfî* and *wely*. According to

*The three marble pillars in the courtyard of Üch Sherefeli Jâmi*

one story, he dreamed about three angels alighting in three different spots of the courtyard of the mosque that he built in Edirne.[i] He erected a green marble pillar at each of these spots to protect them from being trodden on by human feet, and these three pillars are still there to this day.

Like the great *sûfî* İbrâhîm ibn Adham *(quddise sirruhu)*[ii] (d.166/783), Murâd voluntarily abdicated the throne. Before doing so, however, he consulted Vazîr Halîl Pasha on the issue and made

i  Though famous as *üch sherefeli* (possessor of three *sherefes* or *ezân* reciting places of minarets), this mosque actually has four minarets.

ii İbrâhîm ibn Adham ibn Mansûr was a prince in Balkh who became a great *sûfî* (*wely*) and relinquished his throne. He was martyred during a *jihâd* against the Roman Empire (IA, v. V, p. 886.).

*Chapter Three – Restoration*

the necessary arrangements for the peaceful transfer of power to his son Mehemmed, the *sanjaqbeği* of Manisa. Murâd retired in 1444 to Manisa in the hope of spending the rest of his life in peaceful and calm prayer.[i]

He had done his best to protect the unity of the *devlet*, to secure the unity of the Muslims in his country, but he was able to show great unselfishness and courage by relinquishing power when he saw that it was time to do so. We should keep in mind that he could not have done so beforehand. He could have left power to his uncle Mustafa Chelebi and retired to a farm. But before long some people would have gathered around him, urging him to retake power, and hoping thereby to obtain some positions in the new administration, as some party supporters do in our time. On the other hand, some of the officials might have aroused Mustafa's suspicion about Murâd's intentions. So, Murâd could not have led a calm and quiet life at all; at that time there was no democracy allowing former rulers to retire to their calm residences in a peaceful environment.[ii]

The enemies of the Osmanlı Devlet perceived this transfer of power from the veteran Murâd to the inexperienced son as a great advantage. Cardinal Caesarini, the representative of the Pope turned immediately to King Ladislas, stating that this was a unique opportunity to drive the Turks out of Europe. Cardinal Condolmieri, who was in charge of the papal fleet of 65-70 vessels in the Aegean

---

i   Neşrî, *op. cit.*, II, 647; Oruç Bey, *op. cit.*, p. 92; Solakzâde Mehmed Hemdemî, *Solakzâde Tarihi* (İstanbul, 1298), p. 173. Osmanlı sources inform that he retired to Manisa.

ii  Yavuz Bahadıroğlu's opinion concerning the abdication of Sultân Murâd is that Sultân Murâd left the power to his son because he strictly believed that Constantinople would be opened to Islam (There is a *hadith sherîf* [saying of the Final Messenger] about it), he did not succeed in that task; so his son would realise it.

at that time, wrote a letter to the Hungarian king urging him to take advantage of the opportunity, adding that he was going to Gallipoli to prevent the Turks from crossing the Dardanelles Strait into Europe. The Roman Emperor John Palaiologos also wrote a letter to the Hungarian king on the same topic.[251]

On the other hand, İbrâhîm Beğ of Qaramân also wanted to take advantage of the situation and informed the European enemies of the Osmanlı Devlet that he was prepared to attack from the Anatolian side if the Europeans attacked from the other. He claimed that Sultân Murâd was compelled to abdicate the caliphate (leadership) to his twelve-year-old son[252] because of his insanity. Hence, on the initiative of the famous Hungarian commander John Hunyadi, the rulers of Hungary, Germany, Hercegovina, Wallachia, Bogdan, and Venice formed a united army against the Osmanlıs. The Pope absolved them from their previous commitment to observe a truce for ten years on the grounds that oaths taken with "infidels" were not binding.[253]

The combined Christian army crossed the Osmanlı border, and the Venetian fleet blockaded the Dardanelles Strait to prevent any Osmanlı advance from Anatolia to Europe. Faced with this critical situation and urged by his *vazîrs*, Sultân Mehemmed II called his father, Murâd, who crossed the Bosphorus to Europe because the Dardanelles Strait was blockaded by the Christian vessels. This crossing was carried out by paying the Genoese one gold piece for each Osmanlı soldier.[254] The Osmanlı army, although much inferior in numbers, fought the Christian army near Varna on 28 Rajab 848/10 November 1444. Sultân Murâd hoisted the Treaty of Szegedin on a lance and erected it in front of the Muslim Army, reminding the Christians of their violation of their oath. John Hunyadi attacked and dispersed the left wing of the Osmanlı army. But the attacking Vlachs on the right wing were repulsed. The main part of the Osmanlı army was forced to disperse, though Sultân Murâd remained in the battlefield with a small number of janissaries. When pressed hard, he entertained the idea of retreating. But his commander Qaraja Beğ was aware of the devastating impact such a move would have on the morale of the army, and therefore prevented him from doing so by seizing the reins of his horse. Being anxious to capture the throne of Hungary, John Hunyadi would provoke the Hungarian nobles against the Turks but always deserted them in the battlefield at the last moment, leaving them to be defeated by the Turks. Thus, he urged the king of Hungary to attack by claiming "The Turkish army has been routed; you had better attack the Sultân." Incited by John Hunyadi, King Ladislas advanced up to the standards of the Sultân, where Timurtash, a janissary, hit the leg of the king's horse with an axe and dropped the horse and the king. A janissary officer, Hızır, cut off Ladislas' head, which was immediately impaled on a spear, and the Muslim soldiers shouted *takbîr* in unison. This frightened the Christian soldiers who took to their heels, but many of them were killed in the battlefield and en route.[i] "Hunyadi was able to escape only with great difficulty, while thousands of knights were killed. European hopes for a Crusade victory were shattered. The fate of Byzantium was sealed. Ottoman prestige throughout the Muslim world was immensely enhanced, and once again Ottoman rule of Southeastern Europe was assured."[255]

Infuriated by the treachery of İbrâhîm Beğ, Mehemmed, son of Sultân Murâd II, sent him an angry letter, which began by quoting from the Qur'ân: *"those who have disease in their hearts"* (al-Baqarah

---

i   Neşrî, II, p. 653; *Âşıkpaşaoğlu Tarihi*, p. 128. Lord Kinross, *The Ottoman Centuries, the Rise and Fall of the Turkish Empire* (New York, 1977), p. 91: The Hungarian king "was unhorsed and put to death on the field, his head in its helmet raised upon a lance, while another lance beside it transfixed a copy of the broken treaty to serve as a lesson in Christian perfidy for the Ottoman troops."

[2]: 10), and went on to say, "on the incitement and seduction of the unbelievers of this area (Anatolia), the hordes of unbelievers broke the agreement and transgressed ... but with the help of Allah the Muslims defeated them at Varna." He concluded his message with the famous remark the Prophet ﷺ made after opening Makkah to Islam in 8/630, "Praise be to Allah who helped His slave and supported his army."[256]

After the Battle of Varna in 1444 and at the request of his son Mehemmed, Sultân Murâd assumed power once again, and the son went back to his *sanjaq* of Manisa. While going to Varna, Sultân Murâd tried to cross the Dardanelles Strait, but this was blocked by the Venetian fleet, the strongest naval force of the fifteenth century. The Osmanlıs retaliated against this aggression by proceeding to annex the Morea (Peloponnesus) peninsula, then under Venetian rule. Sultân Murâd managed to destroy the fortifications and gained control of the peninsula in 850/1446, and its despot begged for pardon.[257]

### The Second Battle of Kosova (852/1448)

John Hunyadi was instrumental in the conclusion of yet another treaty between the rulers of the Poles, Czechs, Wallachia, and Bogdan against the Osmanlıs. They mustered a huge Christian army that crossed the Danube and arrived at Kosova. Sultân Murâd, for his part, assembled a large army that confronted the enemy at the second Battle of Kosova in 852/1448. Before the actual engagement, Sultân Murâd prayed two cycles of the *hâjet* prayer and implored the Creator for victory over the unbelievers.[258] Sultân Murâd sent an envoy to Hunyadi to discuss peace but was not accepted.[259] The two armies waited one day and one night, then exchanged artillery, rifle, and arrow shots.[260] The battle continued for two days and two nights, and the Christian army was defeated; John Hunyadi fled at night, two *bans* (notables)[261] were killed and the *bans* of the Czechs and Poles were captured. The Polish *ban* succeeded in disguising himself, was sold as an ordinary captive, then several times to different individuals, and finally gained his freedom.[262] Sultân Murâd asked the Czech *ban*: "Although we did not show enmity towards you, why did you come against us?" He replied that it was predetermined that he would be a captive in that position, and then he offered Sultân Murâd ten castles together with their lands, to allow the representative of the Sultân to collect taxes in every place of his country and to provide 5,000 soldiers to the Sultân every year. But the Sultân said: "I do not need those things you offer." Then that *kâfir* said: "Whoever marches against you, a powerful and rich sultân, deserves judgement." And then the Sultân ordered him to be executed.[263] This attitude of Sultân Murâd is in conformity with the *âyat* that was revealed about the captives of the battle of Badr (2/624).[i] This attitude shows that Islamic values continued on

---

i *Âyats* 67 and 68 of *al-Anfâl* (8) were revealed about the captives of Badr. Sultân Murâd's attitude is in conformity with those *âyats*. An ordinary war may be for territory or trade, revenge, or military glory – all "temporal goods of this world." Such a war is condemned. But a *jihâd* is fought under strict conditions laid down by Islam, and solely for the cause of Allah. All baser motives, therefore, are strictly excluded. Even Jesus, whose mission was more limited, said: "Think not that I am come to send peace on earth: I came not to send peace but a sword" (Matthew 10:34), cited in 'Abdullah Yûsuf 'Ali, *The Holy Qur'ân*, p. 431, footnote 1234.

Verses 67-69 of *al-Anfâl* (8) were revealed when the Prophet ﷺ had decided to spare the lives of the prisoners taken at Badr, and hold them for ransom, against the wishes of 'Umar who wished them to be executed for their past crimes. The Prophet ﷺ took the verses as a reproof, and they are generally understood to mean that no quarter ought to have been given in that first battle.

another continent after centuries and that the Osmanlıs had been acting in conformity with those principles. Indeed, it would had been more convenient and much easier for Sultân Murâd to collect taxes every year and gain worldly riches instead of threatening and intimidating potential enemies.

It is worth mentioning here that the Osmanlı army was extremely careful not to cause unnecessary damage to the people and their property. "Any of its soldiers," Neshrî wrote, "who caused harm even to a piece of straw, would be beaten (in punishment). So, it was the custom of the cavalry to raise their horses' heads while passing by crops and not to allow their horses to eat from the crops."[264] This civilised and human conduct is indeed governed and required by the principles of Islam and was in fact followed by the Muslims. Abû Bakr ؓ (r.11-13/632-634) had, for example, issued strict orders to the Muslim army to abide by this disciplined conduct that was unthinkable to Westerners in the dark Middle Ages, and perhaps even today.

After the Battle of Kosova, Sultân Murâd married his son Mehemmed to Sitti Mükrime Hâtûn, daughter of Süleymân Beğ of Dulqadir.[265]

Security and welfare during the time of Sultân Murâd prevailed so widely and was so firmly established that many people from different religious and racial backgrounds came to Anatolia and lived there in comfort.[266] Sultân Murâd Khân Gâzi treated his soldiers and *ra'iyyet*[i] very well. The *'ulamâ*, *sulahâ*, and *ahlut tasawwuf* in general

---

While prisoners of war are to be treated honourably (*al-İnsân* [76] 8), one should not be afraid to kill the enemy in battle.

i   A governed people is called *ra'iyyet* (plural: *ra'âyâ*) in the Osmanlı Devlet. *Ra'iyyet* means "taken care of," "cared for," "looked after." It is an Islamic concept and extremely different from the "subject" of European rulers of the Middle Ages.

*Chapter Three – Restoration*

*Murâdiye, Bursa*

lived in very good conditions. In 829/1426 he built an *imâret*[i] and a mosque in Bursa. "He appointed thirty *hâfiz*[ii] and fourteen *muhallil*[iii] to recite seventy thousand *tahlîl* every day and to present the *sevâb*[iv] to the soul of "Master of the Two Universes" *(Sayyidul Kawnayn)*, Muhammad Mustafa, to the souls of all the Prophets, to the souls of his forefathers, and to the souls of all the male and female believers. He built a *madrasah* beside his mosque and a tomb for himself between the mosque and the *madrasah*. He arranged in his will that the Qur'ân would be recited round the clock at his tomb after his death. Apart from that, he built a mosque, a *madrasah*, a *dârul*

---

i   An institution to feed people twice daily.
ii  A *hâfiz* is one who memorises the whole Qur'ân, quite a common practice among the imams in Turkey, even today.
iii *Muhallil*: the one who recites *tahlîl* (*Lâ ilâha illAllah* – There is no god but Allah).
iv  Allah's reward for a pious act.

*hadîth*,[i] and a *mevlevîhâne*[ii] at Edirne that took ten years (1437-1447) to build. He appointed another forty men to recite the *surah of An'âm* and present the *sevâb* to the soul of his father Mehemmed Khân. He appointed another five men to recite *salawât to the soul of the Final Messenger Muhammad* ﷺ. He appointed many people to recite *Lâ ilâha illAllah* every day and to present the *sevâb* to the souls of the believers. He built another *imâret* at Ergene (Uzunköprü). He sent 3,500 pieces of gold to Khalîlur Rahmân (the resting place of the Prophet İbrâhîm ﷺ in Hebron), Makkah, and Medîna every year. He turned the villages of Balıq Hisâr near Ankara into a *waqf* whose revenue was to be sent to Makkah. He used to distribute 1,000 gold pieces to the *sayyids* in whatever city he happened to be in with them. Al-Hâjj İsâ Dede, one of the followers *(murîds)* of Emîr Sultân, told Sultân Murâd that he should prepare because his death was near. He took his advice seriously, invited his son Mehemmed from Manisa, then fell ill in Edirne and passed away in 855/1451.[iii] His death was not announced however, until his son arrived from Manisa, and his body was subsequently conveyed to Bursa for burial.[267]

The best way to understand and evaluate historical events and the situation of societies in history is comparison. During the first half of the fifteenth century, Muslim society was in very good condition materially and morally. European society was indeed still in the "dark" Middle Ages. The people in Osmanlı society were fed at

i *Dârul hadîth*: an institution dedicated to the teaching traditions of the Final Messenger Muhammad ﷺ.

ii *Mevlevîhâne*: a building with all the requirements for the followers of the *Jalâleddîn Rûmî* (the whirling derwishes) to perform their rituals and live in; a *tekye* of the Mevlevî Order.

iii Neşrî, II, p. 680. It is noteworthy that his tomb has not been covered by a roof, presumably to allow rain to drop on his grave, for rain is a sign of mercy from Allah and in Turkish is called *rahmet* (mercy).

## Chapter Three – Restoration

*imârets* if they were poor, and their social welfare was guaranteed through the Islamic institution of *zakât*. On the moral side, leaders and followers of religious orders, *ahlut tasawwuf*, secured and established a good position in society. Individuals were not isolated or lost in society; on the contrary, people met at mosques, *tekyes*, and those who were in need were supported by others. Many *waqfs* were utilised since the time of Orhân Gâzi. People recited the poem *Wasîlatun Nejât*, which was popularly known as *mawlid* and related the life of the Final Messenger. It was composed by Süleymân Chelebi, who was the imam of Ulu Jâmi at Bursa during the time of Yıldırım Bâyezîd, and was read at births, marriages, and deaths. The Muhammadiyya, written by Shaykh Yazıjıoğlu Mehemmed, was also read widely by the public. Thus, Osmanlı society was, in the fifteenth century, an elevated one. The people in Europe lived in dirt, struggled with preventable illnesses, and most were serfs.

This solid foundation prepared by Sultân Murâd paved the way for Mehemmed to emerge in convenient circumstances and to achieve great success.

*Tomb of Sultân Murâd, Bursa*

# Part Two

# Expansion
# 1453-1699

# Chapter Four

# Expansion

## 4.1 FÂTIH SULTÂN MEHEMMED KHÂN (1451-1481)

Mehemmed II came to the throne in 855/1451.[268] He was very well educated, had learned half a dozen languages, and was a fairly good poet, like many Osmanlı rulers. His *makhlas* (pen name) in poetry is *'awnî*. Moreover, he had a distinguished political and military career, and right up to the present is particularly reputed for his unique success in putting an end to the Roman Empire.

As is well known, there are three elements that compose the cultural background of the West: Ancient Greece, Roman order, and Christianity. Therefore, Westerners cannot forget that Fâtih put an end to the Roman Empire; they criticise him unjustly on one hand and admire him on the other. They try to turn him into a non-Turk on his mother's side, distorting historical facts. As part of their persistent campaign to distort Osmanlı history, Western writers tried to undermine his Turkish origins by claiming that his mother was Maria, Stella, or a French princess. Indeed this is another gross mistake since she was a Turkish woman by the name of Hümâ Hâtûn.[i] The *hammâm* (bath) that she was bathed in while

---

i Bursa Court Registers, No. 31 (p. 35), 201 (p. 64), and 375 (p. 40), cited in Günvar Otmanbölük, "Fâtih'in Annesi Özbeöz Türktür" (Fâtih's mother is of pure Turkish stock), *Türkiye* (newspaper) January 13, 1992, p. 8. To reiterate her being of Turkish descent, it is also mentioned that she was a daughter of the *beğ* of İsfendiyâr: Mehmed Süreyyâ, *Sijill-i*

going to marry Fâtih's father, Murâd II, in 827/1424, still exists in the Chayırjıq village of Qastamonu city. The ruins of that *hammâm* are still called *gelin hamamı* (bath of the bride) and people carry out festivities nearby every year called *fetih shenlikleri*. Khatîje Hümâ is the daughter of İbrâhîm Beğ, son of İsfendiyâr Beğ of Qastamonu. And it is interesting to note that the revenues from this bath were allotted to the people of Makkah and Medîna; it was a *waqf* for al-Haramayn ash-Sharîfayn![269]

Sultân Murâd's other wife, Despina Maria, daughter of the Serbian despot, was sent to her father upon Sultân Murâd's death; if she had been the mother of Fâtih, she certainly would have stayed on as *vâlide sultân* (the mother sultân of the ruler). But the last Roman Emperor, Constantine, asked the Serbian despot for her hand, and they agreed. Despina Maria asserted, however, that she had vowed

*Hâtûniye Künbedi (Sarcophagus of Fâtih's mother), Murâdiye, Bursa*

---

*Osmânî* (İstanbul, 1308), p. 121; Neşrî, II, p. 682; Dânişmend, I, p. 190. Some Europeans claim that Fâtih's mother was a Christian, and her tomb is at Galata, İstanbul. But this claim is baseless: his mother was a Turkish Muslim and her tomb is at Bursa: Dânişmend, *op. cit.*, I, p. 202.

that if God saved her from unbelievers[i] she would not get married again, and so she refused the Emperor's proposal.[270]

A second claim that was forged to blur Fâtih's origins was advanced by Henry Mathieu, in his *La Turque et ses differents peuples*. Without presenting *any* documentary evidence, he claims that Fâtih's mother was not a Serbian but an Italian called Stella; she was captured by the Turkish pirates when she was seven years old. Changing masters, she was married to Sultân Murâd at last. In fact, it is necessary to wait at least eighty years, up to 1510 and even years after that date to see the Turkish volunteer *mujâhids*, called pirates by the Europeans, emerge in the Mediterranean as a sizable power. This ridiculous claim has no base at all. This claim shows how some Europeans handle Osmanlı history.

*Gelin hamamı, Chayırcıq, Devrekâni, Qastamonu*

i  As far as those who called themselves "Christians," Turks were "unbelievers" because of the fact that they did not accept Jesus Christ ﷺ as God, son of God, etc. As far as Muslims are concerned, those who called themselves "Christians" were followers of an abrogated Book, but they were called *Ahlul Kitâb* (People of the Book), and a Muslim man is allowed to marry a woman of the People of the Book.

Another similar claim arising from the imagination of a French ambassador also has been refuted by Osmanlı historians such as Pechûyi and Javrî. In fact, Fâtih's mother was a Muslim, and her tomb is at Murâdiye, Bursa, and it is called *Hâtûniye* Künbedi.[271]

İbrâhîm Beğ of Qaramân tried once more to utilise this delicate situation against the Osmanlı Devlet. He concluded a treaty with the Republic of Venice, invaded Alâiye, and urged some notables of the Germiyân, Menteshe, Saruhan, and Aydın emirates to retrieve their lands from the Osmanlı Devlet, and sent reinforcements to them when they attacked Osmanlı territory.[272]

To guard against any probable assault by John Hunyadi, the young Sultân left Dayı Qaraja Pasha, the *beğlerbeği* of Rumeli, behind in his European territories[273] and hurriedly advanced to Aqshehir and Beğshehri. İbrâhîm Beğ of Qaramân fled to Tasheli; where he asked for peace. İbrâhîm Beğ gave the cities of Aqshehir, Beğshehri, and Seydishehri back to the Osmanlı Devlet, cities that Sultân Murâd had been obliged to give to him during the critical situation just before the Battle of Varna. The border between the two *devlets* was the town of Ilgın. İbrâhîm Beğ agreed to provide soldiers to the Osmanlı Devlet during *jihâd* campaigns.[274]

The Osmanlıs had to pay the Genoese 40,000 gold pieces to cross the Bosphorus while going to meet the Christian armies at Varna in 848/1444. And as long as Constantinople, an enemy entity, existed in the middle of the Osmanlı territories, the unity of the Osmanlı Devlet on two continents was not secure. On top of that, while Mehemmed II was preoccupied with the Qaramân Beğlik, the Roman Emperor Constantine and the Senate asked the Osmanlı Devlet to double the amount the latter had been paying to them for the "expenses" of Shâhzâda Orhan who had been kept in Constantinople as a hostage; they added that they would otherwise send Shâhzâda Orhan to Osmanlı territory in Rumeli, an act that was sure to incite a civil war in the Osmanlı domain. Therefore,

## Chapter Four – Expansion

it became a dire necessity for the Osmanlı Devlet to remove that source of mischief from its territories.

While returning to his capital Edirne, Sultân Mehemmed II was also unable to go through Gelibolu to the European part of his *Devlet* because of the blockade of the Dardanelles Strait by Christian ships. Thus, he crossed the Bosphorus from Güzelje Hisâr, the castle built by Bâyezîd on the Anatolian shore of the Bosphorus, and ordered the construction of another on its European shore.[275] He appointed Fîrûz Ağa *dizdâr* (commander) of this new castle, which was also known as Rumeli Hisârı and Boğazkesen (that which cuts off the Bosphorus).

*Rumeli Hisarı, İstanbul*

### The Opening of Constantinople to Islam (857/29 May 1453)

According to a *hadîth sharîf* reported by Ahmad b. Hanbal[276] the Final Messenger Muhammad ﷺ said: "The city of Constantine will certainly be opened to Islam; what a fine commander he who opens it is and what a fine army under his command."

Though the city of Constantinople had stubbornly resisted many previous Muslim assaults, Sultân Mehemmed was determined to open it to Islam. There was no one of calibre in Europe able to

*The walls of Constantinople*

organise yet another Crusade, or to direct and carry out such a campaign. The Christian forces had been exhausted in the previous four years, suffering heavy losses at the battles of Varna and Kosova. Faced with this imminent danger, the Roman Emperor approached European powers for help.[277] Pope Nicholas V was willing to cooperate, provided the emperor would agree to implement the decision taken in Florence to unify the Catholic and Orthodox Churches, to mention his name during the holy communion in the Hagia Sophia Cathedral in Constantinople, and to reinstate Cardinal Gregorius who had been dismissed in 1450. But some of the notables in Constantinople were not in favour of this unity between the two churches, including Grand Duke Notaras and Gennadios. The former was reported to have said: "I would prefer seeing the Turkish turban in Constantinople than the Cardinal's hat." Gennadios, whom Fâtih was to appoint Patriarch after the *fath*, was also opposed to the unification of the Orthodox and Catholic Churches. Because

*Chapter Four – Expansion*

the tolerance practised by the Osmanlıs towards non-Muslims under their sovereignty was largely known, their administration was preferred to others.[278] As is well known, tolerance and modesty are peculiar only to those who are powerful and self-reliant. The weak person is far from tolerant and tries to conceal his weakness by an imposing appearance.

It is only natural for any society to be at the same level in every respect: socially, culturally, economically, technologically, in literature and the arts. In fact, the social and cultural levels are bound to be strictly interconnected just as the law of the equilibrium of liquids in physics is. A society cannot be at a high level in moral values and at a low level in material affairs. If it is at a low level materially, it is very difficult for it to attain a high level in moral matters. The Osmanlıs at that time were at a very high level morally as well as materially; it is no wonder that they had outstripped Europe technologically as well.

The *shâhî* (royal) cannon, which was produced in Edirne over a period of three months, was very large; it was pulled by 50 teams of oxen, 200 men were needed to secure its balance while proceeding toward Constantinople. The road between Edirne and Constantinople was levelled beforehand by 200 workers and 50 carriage drivers. It took two months to transport the cannon to the scene. The fact that Urban produced that cannon has been greatly over-emphasised by some writers. First of all, Urban was only one of the craftsmen employed by the Sultân; he applied to Fâtih while the *fath* was being prepared and the castle of Boğazkesen was being constructed. There were many able craftsmen in arms, such as Saruja Pasha and Mi'mâr Muslihuddîn, who had produced many cannons before and contributed to designing and carrying out the project. Hoja Sa'duddîn states that "the cannon that Saruja Pasha produced was made of 300 *qantâr* of copper." The historian Alî also indicates that fact in his book *Künhül Akhbâr*.[279]

Urban's talent had to do with casting, but the important aspect was found in its ballistic calculations, which were carried out by the Sultân himself.[i]

In addition, the huge gun that Urban manufactured cracked after the first firing, and the cannons cast by Muslim craftsmen were used during the siege. Constantinople had been successful in defending itself against many previous Muslim attacks. Therefore Sultân Mehemmed was very careful and painstaking in making his preparations for opening the city to Islam.

*The chain*

The siege of Constantinople began on Friday, 6 April 1453. Its walls were strong, high, and double lined, and there was a seven-metre wide moat outside that the Osmanlı army had to cross to capture this strongly fortified city. The walls along the Golden Horn (*Khalîj*: gulf) were relatively weak, but the Romans made it very difficult for the Osmanlı fleet to enter because they stretched a strong chain across the mouth of the gulf.[ii]

The Osmanlı army made its first attack during the night of 18th April when it tried to penetrate through some holes that it made in

---

i   Schlumberger, *Le Siege et la prise de Constantinople par les Turcs*, Paris: 1915, p. 57: "Il (Orban) avouait cependant ne pas connaitres les question de jet et de protee des projectiles, on dirait aujourd'hui les questions de balistique. Mais Mahomet se fit fort de regler par luimeme ces details, pourvu qu'Orban lui fournit l'instrument tant desire," cited in Dânişmend, *Loc. cit.*

ii  *OT,* I, p. 470. This chain is now on display in the Military Museum, Harbiye, İstanbul.

the walls of the city, but it was repulsed. Meanwhile the Pope sent three Genoese ships that arrived at Constantinople on 20th April. In spite of his gallant resistance and the loss of an eye during the naval battle, the Osmanlı Kapudân-ı Deryâ (commander of the navy), Baltaoğlu Süleymân Beğ, was unable to stop them[280] because of the inferiority of his ships. Nevertheless, he was dismissed, and Hamza Beğ was appointed Kapudân-ı Deryâ.[281] The Osmanlıs made another attempt on the night of 21-22 April: they slid seventy ships from Tophâne to Qasim Pasha on the wooden slipway and into the Khalîj[i] to attack the relatively weaker single walls. This achievement greatly demoralised the Romans. Fâtih Sultân Mehemmed invented mortars, making all the necessary ballistic calculations, and used this new weapon to pound the Roman and Latin ships in the gulf.

The demoralised Romans asked for a peace treaty, offering all the lands up to the walls of Constantinople to the Osmanlıs, appointment of the officials responsible for security in the city by the Osmanlı Devlet, and a tribute whose amount was to be decided by the Osmanlıs. But the young Osmanlı Sultân said that "either I take Constantinople or it takes me" and asked for the surrender of the city.[282]

The Muslim army engaged in another attack on 6th May, after sunset, four hours later, but they could not enter the city.[283] Some Osmanlı soldiers succeeded in entering through the holes on 12th May but were repulsed by the Romans who were very

---

i   İbn-i Kemâl, *Tevârîh-i Âl–i Osmân, VII. Defter*, p. 52; *OT,* I, p. 481. Lord Kinross imagined, in an example of wishful thinking, that Fatih's ingenious idea of transporting his ships overland was "probably put into his head by an Italian in his service" (*The Ottoman Centuries; the Rise and Fall of the Turkish Empire,* New York 1977, p. 103). There was no one in his service known to be Italian at that time.

swift in getting reinforcements to the vulnerable spots.[284] Sultân Mehemmed II constructed mobile war towers. The first was constructed by engineers and workers in four hours beside the ditch in front of the Topkapı walls. It stood on wheels and could be moved; it was higher than the city walls. The Romans burnt that huge tower down, but the Osmanlıs constructed others. This event shows that the Osmanlıs were superior to the Romans technologically as well. The battle continued with the exchange of volleys of arrows and gunfire.

Towards the end of the siege, some Hungarian ambassadors arrived to warn that John Hunyadi was no longer in charge of the government in Hungary, and the young king, Ladislas, was determined to march upon Osmanlı territory at the head of a huge army if the Osmanlıs did not lift the siege immediately. They informed him that the Hungarians had annulled the three-year peace treaty. This threat and the announcement that the Venetian navy was on the move to help the Roman Empire put the young Sultân in an awkward position. He met with his advisors, and they discussed the situation. Vazîr-i A'zam Khalîl Pasha, who knew the scope and volume of the Crusader armies by experience, was of the opinion that the Osmanlıs should lift the siege, imposing a heavy tribute on the Roman Empire. On the other hand, Zağanos Pasha asserted that the Romans could not get help, and even if they did get any, such help would not be sufficient to affect the situation. Shaykh Aqshemseddîn and other notables supported this view and the decision was made to carry on the siege.

It was learned that a sizable Christian navy from Venice or the Pope had arrived at Sakız Island in the Aegean Sea. So the Osmanlıs detained the Hungarian ambassadors to see the result of the last attack. There were whispers and unhappy talk among the soldiers because of the long siege, and the Sultân was concerned.

*Chapter Four – Expansion*

*One of the sanjaks (standards) that was actually used during the fath of Constantinople to Islam*

But the encouraging letter from Shaykh Aqshemseddîn, the Sultân's spiritual master, to the Sultân raised his morale.[285] On Shaykh Akshemseddîn's advice, the *mujâhids* attacked just after the *subh* (dawn) prayer[286] on Tuesday, May 29th, and the Muslim army victoriously entered the city through Topkapusu Gate. The Roman Emperor was reported to have been killed during the tumult, though he was actually trying to escape, running towards Pemton Gate.[287] Because İstanbul (Constantinople) changed hands on Tuesday, the Roman Greeks regarded that day as bringing bad luck.

The siege of Constantinople lasted 53 days. The honour of opening it to Islam was given to the young Osmanlı sultân, Mehemmed II, who was only twenty-one at the time, and he has been called Fâtih (opener of an important place to Islam) since then. Thus, the Osmanlı Devlet was given a strong foundation. Now the way was open for the Osmanlıs to expand and spread Islam, their main mission and their *raison d'etre*. Fâtih converted the Hagia Sophia Cathedral, where the Roman emperors were crowned, into the *Masjid Jâmi'* and performed the first *jum'ah*

## Osmanli History and Institutions

prayer there; the *khutbah* was recited by Shaykh Akshemseddîn[i] in the name of the Sultân.[288]

The Sultân's title was Sultânul Berreyn, Khâqânul Bahreyn, Amîrul Mu'minîn[ii] Qâmi'ul Fejereti wel Mushrikîn, es Sultân ibnus Sultân

i Shams ad-Dîn ibn Muhammad ibn Hamzah, born in Damascus in 792/1390, and a descendant of Shihâbud'd Dîn 'Umar Suhrawardî (d. 632/1234), author of *'Awârif ul Ma'ârif*, whose lineage reaches to Abû Bakr Siddîq ⚜. Akshemseddîn became a *murîd* of the famous *wely* Hajı Bayram, who lived during the time of Sultân Murâd II. When his *shaykh*, Haji Bayram, passed away in 833/1429-30, he succeeded him as spiritual master. Fâtih Mehemmed wanted to be his full and devoted *murîd* but the *shaykh* did not agree to that, because he wanted him to allocate all his time to the administration of the *devlet*. The *shaykh* went to Göynük where he lived the rest of his life (Orhan F. Köprülü-Mustafa Uzun, "Akşemseddin" *Türkiye Diyanet Vakfı İslam Ansiklopedisi*, vol. II, pp. 299-301).

ii *Amîrul Mu'minîn* is the title of the *Khalîfah*. The majority of Western historians and writers assert that when Sultân Selîm annexed Egypt in 1517 the Osmanlıs did not gain the *khalifate* (Caliphate). In support of this view they assert that there was no mention of any ceremony related to this transmission in the contemporary Osmanlı sources. This is true; there was no need for that kind of ceremony. But the Osmanlı ideal, beginning with the second ruler Orhan Gâzi, had been to become sultâns who represented the khalifate at the same time (Feridun Beğ, *Münsheât*, I, p. 69; Sultân Murâd perceived himself as *Khalîfah*: *Münsheât*, I, p. 87); His son Yıldırım Bâyezîd was addressed in 1391 as *Zillullah* (The Shadow of Allah), which is the title of the *khalîfah* of the Sultân of Egypt, who hosted the symbolic 'Abbâsî *Khalîfah* in his realm. The Sultân of Khorasân, Huseyn Bayqara, addressed Yıldırım Bâyezîd by the same title (*Münsheât*, I, p. 306). (On this topic see: *Münsheât*, I, pp. 307, 326, 327, 330, 345, 346, 365, 375-377, 379, 500, 515.) *Amîrul Mu'minîn* is another title for the *khalîfah*. It was first used by the second *khalîfah*, Umar b. al-Khattâb.

Mehemmed bin Murâd Khân (The Sultân of the Two Continents, the Khâqân of the Two Seas, Prince of the Believers, Subduer of the Swervers from the Truth and the Polytheists, Sultân, Son of the Sultân, Mehemmed Khân, Son of Murâd Khân).[289]

The Osmanlı Devlet was the sole Islamic power to confront the unbelievers. By opening Constantinople, Fâtih achieved a very high position in the Islamic world. The role of Shaykh Edebalı in the founding of the *devlet* is very important; and Shaykh Aqshemseddîn's role in promoting the Osmanlı Devlet to a superpower by directing his disciple Fâtih is equally important. In fact, it is very difficult,

*Ayasofya in İstanbul*

if not impossible to evaluate the Osmanlı reality and mission, the social structure, or anything related to the Osmanlı Devlet without understanding the scope of the effect of *Tasawwuf* on that entity. Foreigners aside, even Turkish historians who are not deeply aware of and do not appreciate the role of Tasawwuf in forming and developing Osmanlı society are very similar to the hotel receptionist who asks the writer his profession and, hearing that the author makes his living by his pen, concludes that he "sells pens".

This honour of opening İstanbul to Islam that Mehemmed deservedly had, could have been bestowed 50 years earlier on Yıldırım Bâyezîd, had Timur not come to Anatolia[290] and consequently delayed the drive of the Osmanlı Devlet in becoming a major power.

Fâtih Sultân Mehemmed offered a general amnesty and brought a large number of Muslim people from Anatolia to İstanbul (Constantinople). He named Gennadios Patriarch of the Orthodox Church and generously offered full religious freedom to all non-Muslims. Such religious tolerance was then unthinkable in Europe, and Muslims are generally not tolerated by Western politicians even today.

Sharing the same culture, the Osmanlıs were aware that the great Sahâbî Abû Ayyûb al-Ansârî was buried outside the city walls when he came with the Muslim army in 49/669 to Constantinople and died there; but they did not know the exact spot. Sultân Fâtih Mehemmed requested his spiritual master Shaykh Aqshemseddîn

*Eyüb Sultân Mosque, İstanbul*

to identify this spot, which he did by way of *mukâshefe*.ⁱ Then, Fâtih erected a beautiful tomb and a mosque in memory of this great *sahâbî*. Successive *Khalîfahs* visited his tomb for *barakah* (blessing) and started their *jihâd* into Europe from that spot. It is also popular among the Muslim population of İstanbul to visit his tomb before marriage and circumcision ceremonies. The whole district is called Eyüb (the Turkish version of Ayyûb), and the great *sahâbî* is known as Eyüb Sultân. Indeed, the reputation and profound respect that this *sahâbî* has demonstrates the continuity throughout the centuries of the Islamic culture and heritage among the Muslim peoples in different and distant areas.

According to the Western division of history, the opening of İstanbul to Islam is one of the turning points that marks the end of the Middle Ages and the beginning of the modern era. The Osmanlıs made İstanbul an Islamic metropolis, but its Christian inhabitants were not oppressed in any way. On the contrary they were allowed to stay, were treated mercifully and courteously, and continued to enjoy full religious freedom until the present. İstanbul is still the seat of the Greek Orthodox Patriarchate. Had Christendom managed to achieve such a victory over a major Muslim city at that time, it is perhaps not difficult to envisage the devastating repercussions since "most of the peoples of Europe have, at one time or another, been exterminators. The French exterminated the Albigensians in the thirteenth century and the Huguenots in the seventeenth; the Spaniards exterminated the Moors; the English exterminated the North American Indians and attempted in the seventeenth century to exterminate the Irish."[291]

---

i *Mukâshefe*: A *wely*'s (beloved believer) heart, purified from stains of worldly and transitory concerns, is ready to receive and to reflect, like a bright mirror, knowledge from the unseen.

Shortly after the annexation of İstanbul, which became an important Islamic metropolis, Sultân Fâtih communicated a *fathnâma* (letter of victory) to İnal Shâh, sovereign of Egypt (r. 857-865/1453-1460). After the *besmeleh*, the letter quoted two *âyats* from the Qur'ân: *"O Allah! Lord of Sovereignty! You bestow sovereignty on whom You will, and take it from whom You will; You exalt whom You will and abase whom You will, in Your hand lies all that is good; You have power over all things"* (Alu İmrân [3] :26). *"Fight those who do not believe in Allah nor in the Last Day"* (at Tawbah [9]: 29). Then it quoted a saying by the Final Messenger ﷺ: "Whoever's feet get dusty in the cause of Allah, the Creator forbids him from entering Hell." The letter concluded by saying that the Prophet ﷺ had assured the Muslims that they would open this famous city to Islam and that the Osmanlıs had undertaken this *jihâd* in compliance with the heavenly order as mentioned in the Qur'ân: *"Fight the unbelievers who are near you"* (at Tawbah [9]: 23). With this *fathnâma* the Osmanlı sultân sent precious gifts to the sovereign of Egypt.[292]

Another *fathnâma* was sent to the *sharîf* of Makkah al-Mukarramah, in which Sultân Fâtih said, "We send this letter heralding what Allah granted us this year, a victory that no eye has ever seen and no ear has ever heard: the opening of Constantinople to Islam." The letter then quoted *âyat* 20 from *Sûrat al-Fath:* "*Allah has promised you many gains that you will acquire and He has given you these beforehand,*" and a saying of the Prophet ﷺ: "Paradise has a hundred grades, Allah has prepared them for those who fight in His Cause (for Islam), and the distance between two grades is like the distance between the Heavens and the Earth."[293]

A third *fathnâma* was dispatched to the sovereign of Iran, Jahân Shâh (1405?-1467) in which Sultân Fâtih said that the Muslim *mujâhids* were able to open this city to Islam through the spiritual help of the Creator and in compliance with the *âyah* that was revealed at the opening of Makkah to Islam: "*We have given you (O Muhammad) a great victory*" *(al-Fath* [48]: 1*)*. He goes on to assure the sovereign that the *mujâhids* had the same zeal as their co-religionists who opened Makkah to Islam, and quotes in this respect the *âyat*: "*It is He Who sent tranquillity into the hearts of the believers ...*" *(al-Fath* [48]: 4*)*.[294]

It is significant to note that, in his reply, Jahân Shâh quoted some *âyât* from the Qur'ân: "*We did indeed make you khalîfah on earth*" *(*Sâd [38]: 26*)*. By this he presumably admitted that, after opening Constantinople to Islam, which put an end to the Roman Empire, the Osmanlı sultân became the *de facto* spokesman and leader of the Muslims. In fact, all other Muslim powers were then more or less engaged in conflicts and feuds with one another, and the Osmanlıs were thus the only Muslims fighting for the cause of Islam deep in the heart of Christian Europe. The opening of Constantinople to Islam had far-reaching repercussions for Christian Europe, as Abbâs Hamdani puts it: "The fall of Constantinople in 1453 revived crusading activities in Europe. Prince Henry (of Portugal) saw this in terms of circumnavigating Africa and reaching the elusive Christian rulers of the East. He saw this also in terms of trade monopoly and exemption from payment of the customary tithe to the Pope. All this was confirmed by a papal bull on 8 January 1455. The next Portuguese ruler, Dom Joao II, sent a reconnaissance mission overland through the Mamlûk Middle East, charged with contacting the Emperor of Ethiopia as well as with discovering the sources of the spice trade in the East. This was led by two Arabic-speaking men, Pero de Covilha and Alfonso de Pavia. At the same time Bartholomew Diaz reached the Cape of Good Hope."[295]

Europeans saw the date of opening Constantinople to Islam, which, from the Europeans' point of view, is the "fall" of Constantinople to "Turkish unbelievers,"[i] as a turning point in world history, wanting to guarantee that 1453 not be forgotten. They claim that the dark medieval age (as far as Europe is concerned) ended on that date thanks to the scholars fleeing from Constantinople; they were instrumental in starting the Renaissance. In fact, the social and cultural levels are bound to be strictly interconnected just as the law of the equilibrium of liquids in physics is. The Roman scholars had been discussing the sex of angels and the number of their wings, how a rich person has as little chance of entering Paradise as a camel has of passing through the eye of a needle. Constantinople was corrupt in every respect in 1453, and it is absolutely illogical to hope that *any* good, any seed of contribution to civilisation, came from it. When the Osmanlı army besieged the city, the people did not care very much and flocked to the Hippodrome to watch the Greens and the Blues. As is well known, the scholars who were effective in starting the Renaissance went from Morea (Peloponnesus) to Central and Western Europe.

In fact, instead of Eurocentric division of world history, the most important turning points could be viewed as follows:

The Flood of Noah happened about 4000 B.C. (Werner Keller, *The Bible as History* (trans. by William Neil) Great Britain: 1967, p. 51.)

| YEAR | EVENT |
|---|---|
| 1 | 1. Flood of Noah |
| 4000 | 2. Birth of Jesus Christ |
| 4622 | 3. *Hegira* of Muhammad |
| 5260 | 4. Battle of Ayn Jâlût: The first and major defeat of Mongols |

---

[i] Christians believe that Jesus Christ is the son of God, while Muslims believe that he is a prophet, and a Muslim believes in all prophets. Hence, Christians regard Muslims as "unbelievers" because they do not believe the prophet Jesus Christ is God, the Creator, the Sustainer, etc.

who were previously deemed "invincible" (1260 C.E. plus 4000).
5517   5. Martin Luther starts Protestantism (1517 C.E. plus 4000)
5789   6. The French Revolution (1789 C.E.)
5991   7. Disintegration of the Soviet Union (1991 C.E.)

Thus 2020 C.E. corresponds to 6020 which should be acceptable to most of the world population.

The Roman Emperor had concluded a treaty with the Pope to get help from Christian Europe, and, accordingly, Cardinal Isidore, sent by the Pope, led a religious ceremony on 12 December 1452 at the Hagia Sophia Cathedral, thus proclaiming that the Catholic and the Orthodox Religions were united. It meant that when İstanbul (Constantinople) was opened to Islam by Fâtih Mehemmed in 1453, there was no controversy between Catholicism and Orthodoxy, and Eastern Christianity was under the hegemony of the Western church. This was completely against the wishes, trends, and traditions of the Greeks of İstanbul. On the other hand, the Osmanlı Devlet was not in favour of a united Christendom. Therefore, Sultân Fâtih appointed Gennadios Skholarios, who was against the unification of the two churches, patriarch in a fabulous ceremony. Thus, the Orthodox Church became independent of the Catholic Church.

The first *qâdi* of İstanbul was Hızır Beğ, of the family of the famous Nasreddîn Khoja (Juha). The district where he settled at that time was called Qadıköyü (the village of the *qâdi*), and it is called Qadıköy today. Many Turkish families were brought from Anatolia to İstanbul, and the districts where they settled are still called after the towns from which they came – for example, Qaramân, Aqsaray,[296] Charshamba.

Congratulations came from Islamic countries upon the opening of İstanbul to Islam, and many committees from Christian administrations came to İstanbul for the same reason, such as the

Pontus Empire of Trebizond, the Kingdom of Serbia, the Republic of Dubrovnik (Raguza), Despotic Morea which was governed by Dimitrios and Thomas, brothers of the last Roman Emperor Constantine Palaiologos, the Genoese administration of the Sakız Island colony, the Genoese Dukedom of the Island of Midilli. Some were pledged to pay tribute to the Osmanlı Devlet.

The opening of İstanbul to Islam by Mehemmed II was so important that, rightly aware of it, he assumed leadership of the Muslim world: "With the conquest of Constantinople the Muslim world acknowledged Mehmet as leader of the Holy War against Christianity. He now claimed superiority over all other Muslim rulers, including the neighbouring Mamlûk sultâns, and demanded the right to replace the latter as leaders of the pilgrimage to the Holy Cities."[297]

### The Jihâd against Serbia

The Serbian king, George Branković, invaded Osmanlı territory in 858/1454 with the help of the Hungarians. Fâtih marched on Serbia and took over Ostrovicha castle, one of the two most important castles of Serbia, and returned to Edirne, leaving Mehemmed[i] Beğ, son of Fîrûz Beğ, with 30,000 men to protect the area. John Hunyadi, the Hungarian commander-in-chief, utilised this opportunity and, together with Branković, leading a huge army attacked suddenly, and captured Mehemmed Beğ at Kreshevach. Upon this, Fâtih Mehemmed directed his army to Serbia, but Hunyadi fled to Hungary. The Serbian king submitted and promised to pay a tribute of 30,000 gold pieces every year.

Fâtih Mehemmed continued to open new areas in Serbia to Islam in the following year and took over the town of Novobërda.

---

i  The correct pronunciation of this name was "Mehemmed" at that time, not "Mehmed" as it afterwards became.

Meanwhile, Hunyadi encouraged Branković to resist the Osmanlı drive, but relations between them had cooled because of sectarian differences. In contrast, Fâtih was very tolerant of other beliefs. Branković asked Hunyadi: "If we defeat the Turks, what will be your attitude towards Serbian Orthodoxy?" Hunyadi replied, "I will construct Catholic churches all over Serbia." On the other hand, when asked the same question, Fâtih Mehemmed replied, "Construction of an orthodox church beside every mosque is permitted." This tolerance of the Osmanlıs had an important influence on their expansion in the Balkans.

### Victory at Berat in Albania

While Mehemmed II was busily engaged in the siege of Constantinople, the Albanians made use of this situation and attacked the Osmanlı forces in the area, defeating them on 12 Rabî'ulâhir 846/22 April 1453. Fâtih Mehemmed sent İsâ Beğ, the son of Evrenos Beğ, at the head of 40,000 cavalry to avenge this defeat as well as to continue the vocation of spreading Islam in the region. İsâ Beğ defeated the Albanian leader Alexander on the 10 Sha'bân 857/26 July 1453 at Berat, a town in Albania, despite the fact that the latter had received reinforcements from the King of Naples. More than half of the united Albanian-Italian army was annihilated at the battle, and many of the survivors were captured.[298]

### The Siege of Belgrade

The Danube River was the boundary between the Islamic realm in Europe and Christendom; the south belonged to Muslims and the north to Christians. Belgrade is on the south bank of the Danube River and was then under Hungarian rule. The Osmanlıs felt it necessary to gain control of it so they could maintain a Muslim presence in Serbia to confront the attacking waves of the combined Christian armies from the north and to be able to continue the *jihâd* against Hungary. Thus, Sultân Fâtih Mehemmed marched on Belgrade in 860/1456, and a group of Muslim ships arrived at the Danube. But he faced formidable difficulties in his efforts to subdue this city because of its strategic situation at the confluence of the Danube and Sava rivers, which allowed reinforcements to get to it quickly and safely. The city itself was, moreover, very well fortified with a full moat surrounding it, and the siege was not yet complete. Qaraja Beğ had, in fact, asked for permission to cross the Danube, but this suggestion was not accepted by the *beğs* operating in Rumeli on the grounds that it would endanger all the Muslim troops at the other end. Belgrade also received reinforcements from the Hungarian king via the Danube. Due to all these factors, the Muslims could not capture the city, and, in fact, left after fierce battles with the enemy.[299]

The Christian powers had formed a Crusader alliance against the Osmanlıs during the siege of Belgrade. At the incitement of Pope Callixtus III the Borgia, and the efforts of the Italian priest Giovanni di Capistrano, a 60,000 strong army was formed, recruiting soldiers from Italy, Germany, and Bohemia to defend Belgrade against the Osmanlıs. Hunyadi came with a sizable force to help and brought 200 vessels via the Danube as well. The Osmanlı fleet had to retreat and the Christian fleet dominated the Danube. On one occasion, the Osmanlı army was able to enter the city, but Capistrano, with the help of reinforcements, was able to drive these forces back. Fâtih Mehemmed led his army in person and tried to enter the city, but he was wounded by a lance and the attack had to stop. During these fights, the *beğlerbeği* of Rumeli, Qaraja Pasha, and Hasan Ağa of the janissaries were martyred. On the other side, Hunyadi and Capistrano were wounded and later succumbed to their wounds.

### The Opening of Serbia to Islam (863/1459)

The Serbian king, George Branković, died in 860/1456, and was replaced by his son Lazar, but the latter also died shortly afterwards, and the problem of a successor arose with regard to rule and administration. Branković's daughter Maria had been married to the Osmanlı Sultân Murâd II, and was Fâtih Mehemmed's stepmother. The Serbs called her Czaritche. Thus, Fâtih was also among those who claimed the right to rule Serbia. The other claimants were Maria's two brothers, Lazar's widow, Eleni, and Lazar's son-in-law the Bosnian King. Queen Eleni, knowing that she was unable to defend Serbia against Turks by herself, transferred her right to the Pope, who sent a cardinal there and agreed to take over the rule of Serbia.[300]

The Osmanlı army marched upon the Morea (Peloponnesus) Peninsula and opened part of it to Islam in 861/1457, and Fâtih himself spent the winter in Üsküp (Skopje). He also sent Vazîr-i A'zam Mahmûd Pasha to some parts of Serbia to open those areas to Islam while he marched in the meantime on Semendire, the capital of Serbia at that time. The castle of Semendire finally surrendered to Fâtih, and thus the annexation of Serbia was completed by 863/1459.[301] This act was justified in accordance with the understanding of the time that Fâtih had a say as one of the heirs.[302] As a result, Serbia was saved from the struggles that were sure to occur among the various claimants. And throughout the centuries the Serbs lived absolutely free in terms of Greek Orthodox religious beliefs and practice under Osmanlı rule; on the other hand, if the supporters of the Pope, who acted in the name of Eleni, had been successful, it was certain that the Serbs would have been forced to change their religion from Orthodoxy to Catholicism; they would not have been allowed to remain Orthodox.

### The Opening of Pontus to Islam (865/1461)

The fact that İstanbul was now in Osmanlı control frightened the European powers, confusing and alarming them. And the Venetians and the Genoese, who were the great naval powers of that time and used to make a very good living through colonialism and trade, found themselves in an awkward position. It was concluded that an alliance with the other countries on the eastern boundaries of the Osmanlıs, which saw the expansion of the latter against their interests, was necessary to surround their common adversary.

Pope Pius II initiated the campaign by sending Lodovico to Georgia in 862/1458. He was successful in carrying out an alliance between the Pontus Empire of Trebizond, Georgia, and the Turkoman Aq Qoyunlu Devlet.[303] The Emperor of Pontus had married his daughter Catherine (Despina) to Uzun Hasan, Pâdishâh of Aq Qoyunlu Devlet, in the hope that the latter would help him when necessary against the Osmanlıs. Uzun Hasan (r.1453-1478), sovereign of Western Persia and Eastern Anatolia, attacked the Osmanlı town of Amasya. Hence, after due preparations Sultân Fâtih directed his army towards the East; the Osmanlı Fleet sailed in the Black Sea as well. Fâtih never told anyone of where he was headed during his *jihâd* campaigns; his saying "If a single strand of my beard had known where I am going, I would have cut it off immediately" is famous. He first, marched on Amasra, on the shore of the Black Sea and under Genoese rule. The Genoese paid tribute to the Osmanlıs but inflicted harm on their Muslim neighbours. The Osmanlı fleet also arrived at the scene. The Genoese ruler, knowing that resistance was useless, surrendered, and Amasra was annexed by the Osmanlıs without fighting in 864/1460.[304]

Then the Osmanlı army came to Sinop, which was in the Jandaroğlu Turkoman Beğlik. Its ruler, İsmâil Beğ, was very well educated and knowledgeable. The Osmanlıs asked him to join in compliance with *ad-Dînu an-Nasîha* ("religion is good counsel"), so that there would be no fighting. Being a very well-educated and conscientious man, İsmâil Beğ surrendered his *beğlik* and joined the Osmanlı Devlet, even though Sinop had a very well fortified castle, 400 guns with 2,000 artillerymen, and some ships in the harbour; but he avoided bloodshed. He was very well treated, highly honoured, and the revenues of Yenişehir, İnegöl, and Yarhisâr were assigned as *dirlik* to him. He was then appointed *sanjaqbeği* of Filibe in Europe and lived an honourable life.[305] This act gained him a reputable position in society, while the Osmanlıs achieved a further success in the unification of Anatolia. By then, the Qaramân Beğlik was the only outpost of Anatolia that remained outside Osmanlı control.

This act of İsmâil Beğ is indeed an important and significant one; he relinquished his authority as an independent ruler but became an important person in the Osmanlı administration, the *devlet* that united the Muslims in Anatolia and in Europe.

Uzun Hasan, the *pâdishâh*, sent his mother Sâre Khâtûn to Sultân Mehemmed to apologise and to dissuade him from taking over Trebizond, which he guessed was Fâtih's intention. Indeed, Sultân Fâtih was a strict adherent to the morality of Islam and had great respect for the woman, but he felt religiously committed to put an end to the Pontus Empire.[306] He sent Mahmûd Pasha at the head of the main army to prevent the emperor from fleeing anywhere else. Accompanied by Sâre Khâtûn herself, Sultân Fâtih gallantly proceeded on his expedition, although the road was sometimes impassable on horseback. Sâre Khâtûn expressed her concern by saying to Fâtih, "O son, what a great toil you have been undertaking for this city of Trebizond." But he quickly responded: "Mother, this toil is not for the sake of Trebizond, but for Allah's. We carry the sword of Islam. If we do not undertake this toil, we do not deserve to be called *gâzi* [a warrior in a holy war], and we would be in a position of shame in the Hereafter before the Sublime Haqq (Allah)."[307] In these few sharp and expressive words, the Sultân accurately summarised the objectives and mission of the Osmanlı Devlet.

Sultân Fâtih finally arrived at Trebizond, which was already besieged by the Osmanlı ships that he had sent there. The emperor,

*Hammâm of Ismâil Beğ, Devrekâni, Kastamonu*

David Comnenos, was obliged to surrender, and consequently the Pontus Empire, founded by members of the Roman Empire dynasty in 1204 C.E. when the Europeans of the Fourth Crusade occupied Constantinople, came to an end in 865/1461.[i] The last emperor, David Comnenos and his family, were sent to İstanbul, and then to Edirne where the Osmanlıs generously granted him a *khâs* (a large piece of land to live on) near Ustruma Qarasu, and an annual subsidy of 300,000 *akcha* (Osmanlı currency). The ex-emperor corresponded with Uzun Hasan's wife about family affairs, but it was a connection any way. This could have been dangerous for the Osmanlıs because Uzun Hasan was the head of the powerful Aq Qoyunlu Devlet and rival of the Osmanlıs. Determined to maintain the unity and solidarity

---

i   Tursun Beğ, *op. cit.*, p. 110; *OT,* II, p. 55. While relating the opening of Pontus to Islam, İbn Kemâl tells us that Sultân Fâtih was the *khalîfah*: ... *ol vilâyat havza-i himâyat-i Pâdishâh-ı Khilâfet-penâhda dâhil olduğunu beyân eyler,*" *op. cit.*, VII, p. 194. He gave him the same title when he related the ceremony of the circumcision of Fâtih's son Jem: "*Hazret-i Pâdishâh-ı Khilâfet-penâh...,*" *op. cit.*, VII, p. 296.

of their *devlet* at any expense, the Osmanlıs dealt swiftly and firmly with this potential danger. The emperor and his son were imprisoned in Edirne, and were subsequently executed in İstanbul in 867/1463.[308]

## The Opening of New Lands to Islam in Albania

Some places in Albania had been opened to Islam during the time of Sultân Murâd II. It was difficult to proceed in that steep and inaccessible land. Alphonso V, the king of Naples and Aragon, wanted to build an empire in the Balkans and the Mediterranean. Therefore, he encouraged and incited İskender Beğ (Yorgi Kastriyota or George Kastriota), who, after having been brought up in the Osmanlı palace, fled and was engaged in hostile activities in Albania against the Osmanlı Devlet.

On the Pope's urging, a treaty was concluded between İskender Beğ and the king of Naples in 855/1451. According to that treaty, the king of Naples was to support and help İskender Beğ who was afraid of the Osmanlı Devlet, and, in return, he would recognise the king as his sovereign. Thus, trying to avoid Osmanlı sovereignty, İskender Beğ was in the process of accepting the king of Naples' supremacy. Three years after that treaty, money was coined in the name of the king of Naples in Albania. There was a representative of the king in the town of Kroya. The Republic of Venice also had interests in the region and actually had some lands, but when the Osmanlı Devlet took over İstanbul in 857/1453, Venice suffered a heavy loss in the East and thought it more important to direct its energy there, and thus gave up its conflict with İskender Beğ.

In 859/1455 İskender Beğ besieged the town of Berat that was in the Osmanlı Devlet but could not achieve anything. Moreover, the Albanian army, which was supported by a large number of Neapolitan soldiers, was put to rout by an *akınjı beğ*, a son of Evrenos Beğ. This delivered a major blow to the reputation of İskender Beğ. The king of Naples, who did not want to lose his hegemony in Albania, rushed to support İskender Beğ and persuaded the Pope to do the same. Thus, a large number of soldiers from France, Germany, and Serbia gathered in 860/1456 to save Albania.

With the death of Alphonso V, the king of Naples and Aragon, in 862/1458 İskender Beğ lost a good protector. He was therefore obliged to recognise Osmanlı suzerainty and to pay tribute to the Osmanlı Devlet in 864/1460. But he violated the treaty at the incitement of the Pope and the Venetian ambassador in 866/1462, and returned to a stance of hostility. The Turkish *aqınjıs* attacked; there was no clear-cut result, but the position of İskender Beğ continued to deteriorate.

Pope Pius II was in the process of preparing a new Crusade against the Osmanlı Devlet. Therefore, the Osmanlı Devlet, leaving the problem of İskender Beğ, who used to take refuge in the steep mountains whenever he found himself in a difficult situation, for a more convenient time, concluded a peace treaty with him in 867/1463.[309]

İskender Beğ, who became a tool and puppet in the hands of the Venetians and the Hungarians, violated the peace treaty once more at the incitement of those Christian powers in 868/1464 and attacked Osmanlı soldiers. There were various skirmishes, and Balaban Beğ defeated the Albanians. Upon the martyrdom of Yaqûb Beğ during the final skirmishes, Sultân Fâtih decided to march against Albania in person.

Sultân Fâtih captured some important castles during his campaign in 870/1466 and besieged Kroya, the capital of George Kastriota/İskender Beğ. It was very difficult, if not nearly impossible, to subdue the castle, which was built on a very steep point. Therefore, Sultân Fâtih constructed the castle of Elbasan near it to control the town and peopled the region, thus securing continuous control of the region. Balaban Beğ was assigned to maintain the siege of Kroya castle.

George Kastriota/İskender Beğ died of malaria in 872/1468 at Lesh Alessio, and Kroya was taken over by the Venetians. Kastriota had lived as a hostage in the Osmanlı court in İstanbul, became a Muslim, and was named İskender Beğ. But he fled and abandoned Islam, so he was buried at Saint Nicholas Church in Lesh Alessio. Kroya had been taken over by the Osmanlıs, but when Kastriota fled and went there, he gained control of it through deception. But the Osmanlı Devlet finally opened it to Islam in 883/1478. As a result, the struggle for Albania between the then powerful Republic of Venice and the Osmanlı Devlet ended with the victory of the latter.[310]

### Prince Vlad of Wallachia, the Impaler

With the help of the Osmanlıs, Vlad Jepesh (r. 1446-1462), son of Drakul (r. 1432-1446), who grew in the Osmanlı palace, became Voyvoda (Prince) of Wallachia in 1456. Initially, he demonstrated his loyalty to the Osmanlı Devlet and paid his tribute regularly.[311] But he became antagonistic to the Osmanlıs after their annexation of Trebizond and conspired with the Hungarians against them. He even killed Hamza Beğ of Nish and became notorious for impaling his victims. Infuriated by his deception, in 866/1462 Sultân Fâtih marched on Vlad until he arrived at Vidin. An Osmanlı fleet arrived via the Danube, but the Osmanlıs could not find Vlad. Vlad then plotted to kill Fâtih in a night raid but failed and consequently fled to Hungary. Hence, Fâtih appointed his brother Radul (r.1462-1479) in his place as Voyvoda of Wallachia.[312] The Hungarian King, Matyas Korven (r. 1458-1490), turned down Vlad's request for help and imprisoned him. He died there[313] in disgrace.

In the meantime, the Osmanlı fleet blockaded the island of Midilli, which is very close to the Anatolian coast and was under Genoese dominion and had become a source of annoyance for the Muslims until it surrendered in 866/1462.[i]

---

i  Enverî, *Düstürnâme,* edited by M. Halîl Yinanç (İstanbul, 1928), p. 100; Dânişmend, I, p. 298. Enverî, who wrote his book in 869/1464-5 for

## The Opening of Bosnia to Islam

The opening of İstanbul to Islam, the coming of the commercial route between the Black Sea and the Mediterranean under Osmanlı rule, and the opening of Serbia to Islam – in short, the expansion of the Osmanlıs towards the west – very quickly caused great concern and alarm in the Christian West. The Pope started organising a new Crusade, and Christians of Europe initiated the establishment of secret relations between Uzun Hasan, the eastern rival of the Osmanlıs, and the great naval power of the time, the Republic of Venice. One of the most enthusiastic answers to the call of Pope Pius II for a Crusade came from the king of Bosnia, Stephan Tomashevich. Sultân Fâtih, having a very effective spy organisation, learned all about these events in time and considered what should be done.

Sadrâzam Mahmûd Pasha proceeded at the head of the vanguard, and Sultân Fâtih succeeded in annexing Bosnia to the Osmanlı Devlet in 867/1463.[314] The Bogomil Christians in Bosnia were very similar to the Muslims in terms of belief: they recognised and accepted Jesus Christ as a prophet and a servant of God but not as the son of God. The Bogomils had another name: Pataren. Therefore, Osmanlıs called them *Potur oğulları* (sons of Potur). This large group entered Islam in a short time. Fâtih, being very pleased because of this mass conversion to Islam, wanted to do something for them; and they were taken into service in the army and in the palace as they wished, and served faithfully.[315]

---

Mahmûd Pasha, Sadrâzam of Fâtih, states that the *ezân* was recited by himself after the opening of the island to Islam / p. 101. It is the Osmanlı practice to recite *ezân* as soon as a place is opened to Islam, proclaiming that it is no more in unbelievers' hands and has become *Dârulislâm*.

*Chapter Four – Expansion*

The next target of the Osmanlıs was Hercegovina, whose king surrendered half of his country to the Osmanlı Devlet, and as a gesture of loyalty and good will offered his son for the service of the Osmanlı Sultân. The king died shortly after these events, and the remaining part of Hercegovina was annexed by the Osmanlıs. His son, the famous Hersekzâde Ahmed Pasha, converted to Islam and was subsequently appointed *vazîr* and then *sadrâzam*.[i] Fâtih's and his successors' humane treatment of the inhabitants of the region inspired them to join Islam *en masse*.

## The Republic of Raguza

Venetian strength was always a reason for concern to the Republic of Dubrovnik (Raguza). It therefore voluntarily recognised the Osmanlı presence in Bosnia, offered its loyalty to the *devlet*, and promised to pay it 75,000 *qurush* every three years. As a further gesture and to guard against any future Venetian aggression, they also offered the Osmanlıs part of their territory bordering Venice. The width of the territory they left to the Osmanlı Devlet was one hour and a half's walking distance. Hence the inhabitants of Dubrovnik lived safely and happily under Osmanlı protection for more than 400 years until

---

i   A convert becomes *the* first man after the Sultân. This proves that the Osmanlı Sublime Devlet acted according to Islamic principles: whoever deserved a post attained it, regardless of his racial background. There was no such national socio-political entity at that time. But Westerners insist on painting the Islamic Osmanlı Devlet as "Turkish," stripping it of its Islamic identity, and they thus present it to other Muslim peoples as an "alien," "imperial" power. It is rare even today for a Western country to have a president or prime minister of a different race who has "recently" become a citizen. Which one is "humane," "acting according to humane principles," "modern" – the Osmanlı Sublime Devlet or *any* contemporary Western society/state?

Napoleon Bonaparte invaded their republic in 1215/1800, which was later incorporated into Austria.[316]

## The Opening of Morea to Islam

A slave of the Osmanlıs stole a great amount of money from the Athens treasury and fled to Koron, in southern Morea (Peloponnesus) which was under Venetian rule. İsâ Beğ, son of Evrenos Beğ, asked for the return of the slave together with the money he stole. But the Venetians refused to give the slave back on the grounds that he was a Christian and denied the theft had taken place. Upon this, the Osmanlıs opened Argos, a town under Venetian rule, to Islam and annexed the neighbouring lands of İnebahtı (Lepanto). Thus the sixteen years Osmanlı-Venice war (1463-1479) began. In fact, this event was only the pretext for the war; the real reason lay in the fact that the Pope had been busily engaged in concluding a new alliance of the Christian powers against the Osmanlıs, the contacts between the Christian Europeans and Qaramânoğlu Beğlik as well as Uzun Hasan Padishâh of Aq Qoyunlu against the Osmanlıs. Within this framework, a treaty was signed by the Kingdom of Hungary and the Republic of Venice on 12 September 1463 at Petervaradin, according to which the Venetians would attack Morea and Albania by sea and the Hungarians would attack Bosnia. In that context, the Republic of Venice took İskender Beğ into its service, helped him by sending soldiers, money, and ammunition to him. The king of Hungary, Matyas Corven, entered Bosnia but was swift in leaving the country when Mahmûd Pasha approached the region the next year. After that, the Osmanlı army left Bosnia, marched on Morea and opened all the towns in that peninsula to Islam again. The Republic of Venice preserved only a few castles in the region that they had before the war in 870/1466.

*Chapter Four – Expansion*

## The Annexation of the Beğlik of Qaramân

İbrâhîm Beğ of Qaramân died in 868/1464 and was succeeded in the *beğlik* by İshâq, his elder son from a concubine. But his younger brother, a son of a daughter of the Osmanlı Sultân Chelebi Mehemmed, Pîr Ahmed Beğ, appealed to Sultân Fâtih against him. Fâtih appointed Pîr Ahmed Beğ ruler of the Qaramân Beğlik in 868/1464.³¹⁷

Initially, Pîr Ahmed Beğ gave the towns of Aqshehir, Beğshehri, Ilgın, and Saqlanhisâr to the Osmanlı Devlet as a token of gratitude. But later on he concluded a treaty with the Republic of Venice against the Osmanlıs, and, although he had promised unconditional loyalty and obedience to the Osmanlıs, he failed to honour his word to support the military operations of Sultân Fâtih against Uzun Hasan, Pâdishâh of the Aq Qoyunlu Devlet in Iran. Hence, Sultân Fâtih postponed these operations and marched on Qaramân Beğlik, captured its capital Qonya, and sent Mahmûd Pasha to Lârende (Qaramân) who was captured. He thus annexed this last *beğlik*, last with the exception of Tasheli, to his *devlet* in 871/1466.³¹⁸ He appointed his son, Shâhzâda Mustafa, to lead the administration in this new province. It should be pointed out that Qaramân Beğlik thus lost all its territory except Tasheli, but they were in a close relationship with the Republic of Venice and Uzun Hasan. This family left the stage of history when their last post, Silifke, was taken over by the Osmanlıs in 879/1474.

Meanwhile Mahmûd Pasha commanded the Osmanlı fleet from Gelibolu and in 873/1469 annexed the island of Eğriboz, the largest island in the Aegean, from the Venetians with whom they were at war.³¹⁹ Thus the 260 years of hegemony that the Republic of Venice exercised, the strongest naval power of that time, came to an end on this island.

### The Battle of Otluqbeli (878/1473)

After his escape from Qonya, Pîr Ahmed Beğ tried to rally the support of Uzun Hasan, an Aq Qoyunlu Turk who established his *devlet* in İrân, captured Iraq and Azerbayjân, and defeated Abû Sa'îd, khân of Turkestân (830-873/1427-1469) at the battle of Aras in 1469. He now rightly saw himself as the legitimate heir to the İl-Khânlıs and Timurîs. He sent Yûsuf Mirzâ, son of his paternal uncle to Osmanlı territory and destroyed the town of Toqat.[320] He allied himself with the Republic of Venice against the Osmanlı Devlet and sent envoys to Rhodes, trying to make an alliance with those who called themselves the "Knights of St. John."[i] He kept in touch with the Pope, the Kings of Hungary, Poland, Naples, the *voyvoda* of Bogdan (Moldova) against the Osmanlıs. Meanwhile the Christian naval forces came and destroyed the coast of Muğla and the town of Antalya, contacted Uzun Hasan Beğ's envoys and returned to Rhodes. Uzun Hasan asked his allies for guns, and artillerymen, etc. They actually sent what he wanted, but they did not arrive in time. To justify his fight with the Osmanlıs, Uzun Hasan asked them to give him Trebizond on the grounds that he was related to its last emperor.[321] And when the Aq Qoyunlu forces entered Osmanlı territory, the battle became imminent. Sultân Fâtih wanted to secure

---

i  The soldiers on the island of Rhodes called themselves the "Knights of St. John." They were from different races and backgrounds and came from various countries of Europe "to fight the "Turkish unbelievers", as they described the Osmanlıs, and went through a very intense military training. At that time "Turk" meant not only Osmanlıs but was also a synonym for "Muslim" because Islam was represented by the Osmanlı Turks, so much so that "a Western convert to Islam was said to have turned 'Turk', even when the conversion took place in Fez or Isfahan." Bernard Lewis, *The Emergence of Modern Turkey* (Oxford University Press, 1968), p. 13.

## Chapter Four – Expansion

the western boundaries of the Osmanlı Devlet before marching against Uzun Hasan. Therefore, he sought a peace treaty with the Republic of Venice, but they wanted Eğriboz which had recently been opened to Islam by the Osmanlıs, and the negotiations therefore proved futile.[322]

Sultân Fâtih marched upon Uzun Hasan, and they met at Otluqbeli, near Erzurum in eastern Anatolia. Initially, the Osmanlıs suffered heavy casualties, but they soon made a successful fresh attack with artillery and rifles against the centre of the Aq Qoyunlu army. Uzun Hasan narrowly escaped death at the Battle of Otluqbeli in 878/1473. The victorious Osmanlı army did not pursue the fleeing Aq Qoyunlu soldiers and did not go further; they did not want to destroy a Muslim country. The purpose of that campaign was to teach Uzun Hasan a lesson, and this had been achieved.[323] Sultân Fâtih released 4,000 slaves and concubines as a token of gratitude for this victory.

Sultân Fâtih Mehemmed, regretted the fact that Uzun Hasan, a Turk and a Muslim, was allied with Christians against him; he referred to this unbecoming act of Uzun Hasan in the *fathnâma* that he sent to Huseyin Bayqara, the ruler of Khorasân.[324]

The custodian of Shabinqarahisâr in Anatolia, Dârâb Beğ, surrendered the city without a fight, and the Osmanlıs rewarded him by appointing him *sanjaqbeği* of Chirmen in Osmanlı Europe.[325] This was a customary way that the Osmanlıs rewarded other Muslims who did not actually oppose them. Indeed, this was dictated by their keen desire to unite all Muslims and to avoid any shedding of their blood as much as possible. İsmâil Beğ of İsfendiyâr and Dârâb Beğ of Shabinqarahisâr were treated in this manner, and they became *beğs* of the Osmanlı Devlet.

### The Opening of Kefe and Azak (Azov) to Islam (880/1475)

Genoa was a great naval power in the fifteenth century, with colonies at Kefe, Azak (Azov), and Manqup on the northern shores of the Black Sea, and on the Sea of Azak. Merchandise coming from Kabul through Astrakhan and two roads in Persia was conveyed to Europe from those ports on the Black Sea.

Fâtih Sultân Mehemmed directed his attention towards Crimea to press the *voyvoda* of Bogdan (Moldova) on two fronts, and to prevent the further expansion of the holdings of the *Knez* of Moscow further – at that time Ivan III Vasilyevich. He had been trying to get rid of the hegemony of the Qıpchaq *devlets* that emerged after the disintegration of the *Kok Orda* (Golden Horde) when it was defeated by Emîr Timur in 1396. The Knez of Moscow had been trying to expand his lands to the north and west. His wife Zoe (Sophia) had been very influential with Ivan III. She was the daughter of Thomas, brother of the last Roman Emperor Constantine Palaiologos.

Meanwhile, in 1460 when Fâtih annexed the southern part of Morea, its despot Thomas Palaiologos fled to Italy on a Venetian ship and took refuge with the Pope. He died in Rome, and his daughter Sophia remained in the Pope's protection. Pope Paul II planned to marry this girl to someone who could be of use against the Osmanlı Devlet. Cardinal Bessarion, of Greek descent, recommended that he marry her to the Prince of Moscow, Ivan III. Envoys were sent to him, and he accepted the proposal with gratitude. Princess Sophia was sent by the Pope to Moscow in 877/1472. Many Greek scholars and men of art from Greece, Rome, and other places went to Moscow on this occasion and settled there, starting a new Greek-Italian cultural centre. Thus, this wedding, which occurred in 1472, was very important in forming Russia.

The Prince of Moscow had been trying to become entirely independent of the Qıpchaq *devlets*; on the other hand, he had established political links with the European kingdoms and had contacted Uzun Hasan, the most powerful rival of the Osmanlıs in the East. Now when he married a Roman princess, he began to claim that he was the heir of the Roman Empire, and adopted the Roman coat of arms in the form of double-headed eagle. He did his best to make Moscow the centre of Orthodoxy; this claim became a strong current in the politics of the Czars afterwards.

Fâtih Sultân Mehemmed was very careful in following what was happening worldwide, especially in matters concerning the Osmanlı Devlet. Therefore, he could not neglect such important and dangerous events. He sent Gedik Ahmed Pasha at the head of an Osmanlı fleet of 300 vessels to Crimea. The Osmanlı soldiers landed at Kefe, the most important Genoese colony on the Black Sea and besieged the castle with Crimean soldiers. Through the actions of Squerciafico, a Genoese who had been previously captured by Fâtih, and the Crimeans and Armenians in the city, Kefe surrendered. Azak (Azov) and other Genoese colonies followed suit. Manqup was opened to Islam in 880/1475.[326] At the request of *ulemâ* and notables of Crimea (Qırım), the Osmanlıs invested Mengli Gırây (d.1515) as Khân of Qırım in 880/1475.[i] Thus, Fâtih acted against a probable Russian expansion towards the south, putting a Qıpchaq barrier between the Osmanlı territories and Russia. Those openings to Islam in the north expanded as far as Circassia.[327] The Black Sea was in the process of becoming a Muslim lake; only the Caucasian shores in the East and the shores of Bogdan (Moldova) in the West remained outside the Osmanlı borders.

### The Opening of New Regions in Europe to Islam

The *voyvoda* of Bogdan, Petru Aaron, submitted to Osmanlı domination in 859/1455, paying 2,000 pieces of gold yearly when he saw that it was impossible for him to resist this powerful *devlet*. At Rakovitza, his successor, Ştefan cel Mare, with the help of the

---

i  *Netâyij*, I, p.46. The other parts of Crimea were annexed afterwards through peaceful means by Sultân Selîm, Fâtih's grandson.

Hungarians and Poles, led an army of 50,000 men and defeated the tired Osmanlı units who were on their way back after the siege of Ishkodra in 879/1475. The Pope endowed him with the title of Athleta Christi (The Champion of Christ). It was impossible for the Osmanlıs to understand this act. Therefore, Fâtih marched against Ștefan cel Mare. While he himself entered Bogdan at the head of the *Ordu-yu Hümâyûn*, as the Osmanlıs called their army,[i] the Osmanlı *inje donanma* (light vessels) proceeded via the Danube and captured the shores of Basarabia, dominated the river-mouth of the Danube, and opened Aqkerman (Bilhorod-Dnistrovskyi) to Islam. Fâtih defeated the Bogdan army at Aqdere (Valea Alba) in 881/1476. The Osmanlıs could have taken all of Bogdan after this victory if a plague had not broken out in the army. It was for that reason that the Osmanlıs returned and not because of the resistance of the Bogdan army.

The Osmanlıs continued to open new lands to Islam in Europe: Ömer Beğ, son of Turhan Beğ even raided places very close to Venice itself, among them Kroya (Akçahisâr) castle was taken over for good in 883/1478. İshkodra was besieged but could not be opened to Islam; Fâtih could not bring guns there because of the steep terrain, but he made some very large guns while besieging the castle. The defending commander was the Venetian Antonio de Lezze. During this siege the Osmanlı army used fire bombs made of olive oil, wax,

---

i  Seeing themselves as "the representatives of Islam," "the Final Heavenly Message," the Osmanlıs named some important objects *hümâyûn*, referring to the *hümâ*, a very high flying bird, or the legendary phoenix. Therefore, *hümâyûn* means "pertaining to the sky, heavenly." Thus, the *Ordu-yu Hümâyûn* means "heavenly army"; *Dîvân-ı Hümâyûn*, "Heavenly Dîvân"; *Mühr-i Hümâyûn*, "Heavenly Seal" (Seal of the Sultân); *Donanma-yı Hümâyûn* "Heavenly Navy"; *Khatt-ı Hümâyûn*, "Heavenly writing" (handwriting of the Sultân); etc.

sulphur, and some other substances. It seems that the Osmanlıs were superior in technology at that time. Ahmed Beğ, son of Evrenos Beğ, continued to besiege the Ishkodra castle with 40,000 men.

The Republic of Venice was obliged to conclude a peace treaty with the Osmanlı Devlet which brought the fifteen years of war to an end; because it saw that the Osmanlıs continued to expand in Europe despite the alliance between the Pope, Venice, Naples, Hungary, Aq Qoyunlu, and Qaramân against them. On the other hand, the king of Naples, Ferdinand, his son-in-law, Mathias Corven, and the king of Hungary were also in the process of concluding a peace treaty with the Osmanlıs; they had also reached the conclusion that they were not able to contend against the Osmanlıs. The Republic of Venice saw that Ishkodra castle could not resist any more, and the Republic suffered heavy commercial losses because of the ongoing war. A peace treaty was concluded on 3 Zilqaʿda 883/26 January 1479 in İstanbul, according to which the Republic of Venice left Ishkodra and some places in Albania to the Osmanlı Devlet and the Republic would pay the Osmanlı Devlet 200,000 pieces of gold as a war indemnity. In addition, it would pay 12,000 pieces of gold every year for permission to use Osmanlı harbours. This treaty was a political success for the Osmanlı *sadrâzam* Pîrî Mehemmed Pasha; it secured a permanent Osmanlı presence in Albania.

Now the next step was towards Italy. Rome also was about to come to an end at the hands of Fâtih Sultân Mehemmed following the end of the Roman Empire.[328] Fâtih sent Gedik Ahmed Pasha to open Otranto in Italy to Islam, capturing it and some castles in the environs from the Kingdom of Naples in 884/1479. The presence of the Osmanlıs in Italian territory frightened Christians very much: "Rome panicked, and the Pope planned to flee northward along with most of the population of the city."[329] But two years later, when Sultân Bâyezîd II was busy dealing with his brother Jem, the Osmanlı Devlet lost its Italian territory to the Christians.[330]

## The Death of Sultân Fâtih

These overwhelming victories were not enough to satisfy the religious zeal of Sultân Fâtih. He therefore led another army that marched towards Anatolia but without specifying his exact destination. He was perhaps planning to take the enemy by surprise in compliance with the famous wisdom: "Get help in your affairs by concealment." But Sultân Fâtih died prematurely in 886/1481 at the age of 51 while he was at Gebze.[331] Stanley Lane-Poole wrote in this respect:

> "Muhammad was preparing an immense expedition, whither destined no man knew but he, when he suddenly died. It is hard to say what might have been followed by the sack of Rome. *Sed Dis aliter visium.* The death of the conqueror saved Europe."[i]

During Sultân Fâtih's *Khalifate*, the Osmanlı Devlet was technologically superior to Europe, and the two guns it manufactured for the siege of Constantinople were a novelty at that time. The castle built by Gedik Ahmed Pasha at Otranto in Italy proved so strong that it took the Christians quite some time to conquer. The Osmanlıs attained a high level of industrial expertise, producing goods such as porcelain and carpets. Moreover, they were, even at that early time in the fifteenth century, so conscious of environmental hazards that they prohibited agriculture on the hills near the Golden Horn to prevent erosion and sowed plants on the slopes to hold its soil firmly.[332] Safranbolu, near Qastamonu in Anatolia, is a typical Osmanlı town that has luckily kept its original form until today: it is a good example of a Muslim city, reminding us how people could live as "human beings", constructing houses in such a way

---

i  Stanley Lane-Poole, *Turkey* (London, 1986), p. 139. Though generally considered outdated, this book gives reliable information on and evaluation of some issues.

that no one could hinder the sun or air from any other, each home independent and having been designed according to Islamic daily life.ⁱ High buildings in Japan pay an indemnity to other buildings if they prevent the sun from reaching these other buildings. This is a very civilised notion. A similar attitude prevailed in Osmanlı society centuries ago.

During Sultân Fâtih's *khalifate*, the Osmanlı Devlet shared a border with Iran (Persia), one with the Mamlûks in Asia, and one with Venice, Hungary, and Poland in Europe. In many cases, these countries were so incapable of inflicting a defeat on Sultân Fâtih that they sent envoys to the Osmanlıs requesting peace and pardon. When, if ever, the Sultân decided to respond favourably, he would hand them a *fermân-ı âli* (sublime decree) that warned them they would be safe as long as they remained friendly to the other side, and the Osmanlıs did not deign to accept any document from them.³³³

Sultân Fâtih's worldview he himself expressed in his famous poem:

*İmtisâl-i "Jâhidû fillâh" olubdur niyyetüm*

امتثال (جاهدوا في الله) اولوبدر نيتم

*Dîn-i İslâmun mujerred gayretüdür gayretüm*

دين اسلامك مجرد غيرتيدر غيرتم

*Fazl-ı Haqq u himmet-i Jünd-i Rijâlullâh ile*

فضل حق و همت جند رجال الله ايله

*Ehl-i Küfrü ser te ser qahr eylemekdür niyyetüm.*

أهل كفرى س ته سر قهر أيلمكدر نيتم

---

i There is an original part like Safranbolu in Qastamonu also. The house of a certain lieutenant-colonel from the Osmanlı Era in Safranbolu has been converted into a museum, called *Qaymakam Qonağı* (Mansion of the Lieutenant-Colonel), it is worth visiting: the interior has been designed to make the Islamic way of life very easy.

"My intention and determination are to comply with Allah's commands: strive and fight in the way of Allah ﷻ.

All my efforts are only for the sake of the Islamic religion. I try my best to encourage Muslims.

By the grace of Allah and by the spiritual help of an army of the great Muslims (many *shaykhs* of *sûfî* orders)

I am resolved to destroy the unbelievers before and after."

Sultân Fâtih Mehemmed converted the Hagia Sophia (Aya Sofya) Cathedral, where the Roman emperors were crowned, into a mosque for which he made many *waqfs*, as Lord Kinross explains in the following passage: "As part of the endowment of Aya Sofya, the first great mosque of İstanbul, Mehmed the Conqueror ordered the building of a *bedesten,* a large bazaar or covered market, with some hundred shops and storerooms, together with another thousand shops in the streets and markets around it. It was, in effect, a business and trade center, where merchants could securely store their goods and congregate to do business. When Mehmed built his own great mosque, there were eight *madrasahs* around it, where six hundred students studied each day, a children's school, a library, two hostels for travellers, a refectory, kitchens where the poor were given food, and a hospital, which employed for their free treatment an eye specialist, a surgeon, a pharmacist, and cooks to prepare food under the doctors' orders. Here was the free education and health service of a medieval Islamic welfare state."[334] This *madrasah* was thus at university level. Indeed, Sultân Fâtih showed a profound respect for scholars, men of letters, and artists whom he attracted to İstanbul. For example, he invited Ali Qushchu from Samarkand with his family and gave him an immeasurable amount of money. During Sultân Fâtih's *Khalifate*, highway robbery and prostitution were almost forgotten; if a woman set out by herself with a great amount of gold for a two-day trip, everybody was certain she would return safely. And he inflicted severe punishment on the few transgressors.³³⁵

In short, Osmanlı society during the middle of the fifteenth century was a very fine and decent one: everybody, regardless of race, religion, etc. lived in peace and security, without fear. It represented civil society at the highest level. On the other hand, social vices were prevalent in the society of the Roman Empire. Jenkins has this to say about that deplorable situation: "In all ranks of society harlotry was rife, and was certainly encouraged by the rigorous seclusion of women in polite society …. This seclusion tended as usual, to promote associations of a criminal character between the sexes. Though the slender license granted to prostitution by Constantine the Great was reportedly revoked, and though severe penalties were pronounced against keepers of disorderly houses, the evil was never checked. Inn-keepers, tavern-keepers and bath-keepers regularly augmented their gains by maintaining whores, of whom penury and the deceitful promises of itinerant pimps procured an inexhaustible supply. The large majority of these wretched creatures lived in the most abject squalor, providing their services for a few half-pence and widely disseminating the filth and diseases incident to their profession. They were commonly at the centre of drunkenness, riot and disorder. Their number cannot be computed with any accuracy; but we shall not err in putting it at many thousands."³³⁶

Equally, when compared to their position in the society of the Roman Empire, slaves enjoyed a prestigious status in the Osmanlı Devlet. They could, and in fact did, become *vazîrs*, statesmen and other high ranking officials. Jenkins gives this gloomy picture about the position of slaves in the Roman Empire: "… The conditions of the slaves themselves varied very greatly according to the circumstances and temper of their masters. The darling of a wealthy citizen might be in a better plight, and entrusted with greater authority, than many free men; he might be bosom friend of the children of aristocrats. He might be perfumed and in silk. But he had few or no rights at law. And the servile labourer on an estate, or the wretched chattel of some inhumane and immoral tyrant, might live a life so deeply prostituted and degraded that death, even when it came, as it often did, in cruel torments, could not be regarded as anything but a merciful release. The frequency and vigour with which churches at all times inveighed against the ill-treatment of slaves makes it only too certain that such ill-treatment was common enough."[337]

From the above evidence, it is reasonable to believe that Muslim society of the fifteenth century was far better than any of the so-called civilised societies of the twenty-first century, not to speak of Western society in general at that time. In other words, the present technologically advanced but spiritually and morally bankrupt Western civilisation has not yet reached the standard that the Muslims attained five centuries ago. Moreover, in contrast to the barbaric treatment given by the Christians to the defeated Muslims in Spain and Portugal, Sultân Fâtih gave the defeated non-Muslims complete freedom of religion and appointed Gennadios the Greek Orthodox Patriarch.

Civilisation is for the "human being", living in comfort and without fear. The fact that Western civilisation cannot grant this, gives cause to scrutinise its defects, and Islam will automatically come up. Thinkers, scholars, and writers should think about it without prejudice. If the maintainers of Western civilisation were brave enough to face this fact and to evaluate it, they would come to terms with Islam and adopt its main values. It is the dominant civilisation that has the chance of survival; otherwise, one can see that there is no future for it, since it includes and supports everything except the "human being". Undoubtedly, scientific and technological development in the hands of those who have no moral considerations can only serve destruction. And the dominant religion in the Western world, which is called "Christianity", including all its sects, denominations and church organisations, is far from being the religion that Jesus Christ preached,[i] and is not sufficient to satisfy humanity's moral needs. There is no need to be a soothsayer to see this fact; it is enough to get rid of prejudice about Islam and to stop being brainwashed against it.

Muslim superiority was so overwhelming that Christians resorted in desperation to magic and superstition to find consolation for themselves. Thus, it was rumoured that a deliverer would appear to save them from Muslim domination. As Arthur Goldschmidt said "Indeed, Europeans believed that somewhere beyond the lands of Islam they might find a mighty Christian ruler, whom they called Prester John. They hoped that this mythical potentate, of course, would attack the Muslim menace from the rear and save Western Christendom. In the late thirteenth century Prester John was thought to be a Mongol; two centuries later Europeans would seek him in Ethiopia. Driven by this strange combination of hope and fear, the Popes sent missions to make contact with the Mongol empire and, if possible, convert them to Christianity. Catholicism had little in those days to offer the Mongols, but some did adopt a form of Christianity already common in Iraq, Iran, and Central Asia, namely Nestorianism."[338]

Abbâs Hamdani wrote the following on the same theme: "The Portuguese and the Spanish carried over the medieval spirit of the *Reconquista* in their discoveries of the new route to India and the

---

i   To see this fact, it is enough to remember that Jesus Christ ﷺ spoke Aramaic, was a Prophet, but had been made into a member of the divine Trinity; the actual time of his birth differs up to eight years from the accepted date of his official birth, the beginning of the C.E. era; he must have been born in spring (Luke 2:8), and not in December, none of the Gospels was written during his lifetime, the earliest ones were written decades after him in Latin, Hebrew and ancient Greek.

New World respectively. The Portuguese aimed at taking Makkah with the hope of exchanging it for Jerusalem. They also established links with the king of Ethiopia, identifying him as Prester John. ... Columbus' *Journals* reveal that his *empresa de las Indias* involved a master-plan for contacting the Mongols and pro-Christian Grand Khân in the East, circumventing and encircling the Islamic lands of the Middle East, opening a new trade-route to the East to bypass Mamlûk territories, and combining the forces of western and eastern Christendom in an enveloping movement for the recovery of Jerusalem and its *casa santa*. Columbus' plan was a later example in a long tradition already developed by Marco Polo (1295), Marino Sanudo's *Liber secretorum* (1321), the life-work of Pope Pius II (1458-65), and such writings as Campanus' *Oratio* (1471)."[339]

The Osmanlı Devlet, in my opinion, was not established firmly and for good until it annexed İstanbul; it is true that it had become a powerful socio-political entity, but it was vulnerable from its very centre through the intrigues designed by the Roman Empire inciting the European powers as well as Anatolian *beğliks* against it. It was not safe; it was in constant danger from within, at the heart of its domain. It became possible for the Osmanlı Devlet to become *the* superpower only after it opened Constantinople to Islam. Therefore, the period until the opening of İstanbul to Islam may be regarded as the foundation of the Osmanlı Sublime Devlet.

# Chapter Five

# Sultân Bâyezîd Velî (1481-1512)

Bâyezîd, Fâtih's elder son and *sanjaqbeği* of Amasya, succeeded his father as sultân. But his younger brother Jem (1459-1495), the *sanjaqbeği* of Qaramân (Qonya), challenged his authority, controlled the city of Bursa, and in the *khutbah* of the *jum'ah* prayer asserted his claim to the throne. The two brothers fought a fierce battle on the plain of Yenişehir in which Jem was defeated and compelled to retreat to Qonya.[340] He subsequently went to the Mamlûk sultân, Qayıtbây, in Egypt and from there he performed the *hajj* with his family in 1481.[i]

---

i   Westerners try to undermine the Osmanlı Devlet's Islamic profile by stating that Osmanlı sultâns did not perform *hajj*. It is very simple trick: reading history backwards, anachronistically, looking at conditions from the fourteenth to the nineteenth centuries from the perspective of the twentieth. Until 1517 Hejâz, where the Ka'bah is situated, was not in the Osmanlı domain but in Mamlûk territory, a rival *devlet*. To perform the *hajj*, the Osmanlı sultân would have to cross through Mamlûk territory with his entourage and army. This would entail a "security problem" for both *devlets*. When Shâhzâda Jem performed *hajj*, he was completely free; he did not have any responsibility in the Osmanlı *devlet*. It would take about 8-9 months for an Osmanlı sultân to leave İstanbul for Hejâz and come back. It should be remembered that even in the twentieth century, with telecommunication facilities, Gaddafi usurped power in 1969 while the king of Libya was out of his country. It was impossible for an Osmanlı sultân to spend such a long time away from his country.

When Jem returned to Cairo³⁴¹ Sultân Bâyezîd sent him envoys with letters offering him asylum in the holy city of Jerusalem, and the whole revenue of Qonya (Qaramân) province. But the latter insisted on having the whole of the Anatolian part of the Osmanlı territories, which entailed the partition of the *devlet,* and the Sultân therefore had no option but to send Gedik Ahmed Pasha

> Another important reason is that, in the sixteenth century, when Hejâz had voluntarily joined the Osmanlı Devlet, Portugal and Spain were very strong Christian powers; so much so that the Pope divided power over the world between them. The two colonised Central and South America; even today that part of the world is called "Latin" (i.e. Catholic) America, speaking Spanish and Portuguese. The Indian Ocean had become a "Portuguese Ocean." They actually entered the Red Sea but were driven back. The Portuguese wanted to capture Makkah and to exchange it for Jerusalem. Therefore, a sultân's journey there would necessitate being accompanied by thousands of soldiers for security and their accommodation, etc. on one hand, and would expose the borders with the infidel world, on the other, since his absence from İstanbul would certainly be known to them. After the Portuguese, other Christian powers replaced them in those waters. The *Ordu-yu Hümâyûn* did not leave İstanbul for *jihâd* in Europe *en masse;* the central part remained in İstanbul, and the huge body joined it on the way, just like streams joining a river.
>
> Another point is this: the Osmanlı sultâns sent *surreh* to Hejâz every year, beginning with Mehemmed Çhelebi and well into the First World War. *Surreh* was a commission carrying gifts, money, and goods to the People of al-Haramayn ash-Sharîfayn (Makkah and Medîna). The chief of this commission was the *surreh emîni* who represented the Sultân. He certainly performed *hajj,* and, as *wakîl* of the Sultân, performed for him as well. Sending *wakîl* (*bedel*) is acceptable even today and is practised by many Muslims; the *bedel/wakîl* performs *hajj* for himself and for the one who sends him, who pays his expenses.

to crush this mutiny. Jem, however, planned to go to Osmanlı Europe to renew his opposition to his brother's authority[342] with the help of the Knights of St. John on the island of Rhodes who promised to receive him hospitably and to find him a way to Europe. These developments were described by Lane-Poole as follows: "D'Abusson, the Grand Master of Rhodes, however, was too astute a diplomatist to sacrifice the solid gains that he perceived would accrue to his Order for the sake of a few paltry twinges of conscience; and he no sooner made sure of Prince Jem's person, and induced him to sign a treaty, by which, in the event of his coming to the throne, the Order was to reap many sterling advantages, then he ingeniously opened negotiations with Sultân Bâyezîd, with a view to ascertain how much gold that sovereign was willing to pay for the safe custody of his refractory brother. It is only fair to say that Bâyezîd, who had no particle of cruelty in his nature, did all he could to come to terms with Jem. He had indeed been stern and uncompromising while his brother was in open hostility, and to the entreaty of their grand-aunt that he would be gentle and accommodating to his own flesh and blood, he had replied that 'there is no kinship among princes'; yet had he offered to restore to his brother the profits, though not the power, of the province of Qaramân, which Jem had formerly governed, on condition that he should retire and live peaceable at Jerusalem. Jem, however, would have nothing less than independent authority, and this the Sultân could not be expected to allow. 'An empire,'[i] said he, 'is a bride whose favours cannot be shared.' All negotiations and compromise having proved ineffectual, he listened to the proposals of the crafty Grand Master, and finally agreed to pay him 45,000 ducats a year, so long as he kept Jem under his surveillance."[343] The

---

i  The word used by Sultân Bâyezîd is *saltanat* (sultanate) and *not İmparatoriyye* (Empire), as S. Lane-Poole distortingly claims, *op. cit.*, p. 142.

same Christian writer has these revealing remarks to say about the deception of the Knights of St. John:

> "The Knights of St. John possessed many commanderies, and the one they now selected for Jem's entertainment was at Nice, in the south of France. In 1482 he arrived there, wholly unconscious of the plots that were being woven about him.
>
> "He desired to start at once for Hungary, whence he proposed to raise his adherents in Turkey. But he was gently restrained from his purpose. On one pretext or another the knights contrived to keep their prisoner at Nice for several months …. Meanwhile, Grand Master D'Aubusson was driving a handsome trade in his capacity of jailer. All the potentates of Europe were anxious to obtain possession of the claimant to the Ottoman throne, and were ready to pay large sums in hard cash to enjoy the privileges of using this specially dangerous instrument against the Sultân's peace. D'Aubusson was not averse to taking the money, but he did not wish to give up his captive; and his knightly honour felt no smirch in taking 20,000 ducats from Jem's desolate wife as the price of her husband's release, while he held him all the tighter. Of such chivalrous stuff were made the famous knights of Rhodes: and of such men as D'Aubusson the Church made cardinals!"[344]

The king of France intended to use Jem against the Osmanlı Devlet. But he took him from the Knights and put him in the custody of the Pope. The same Western writer explicitly explains the morality of Europe at that time: "The curious conclusion one draws from the whole melancholy tale is that there was not apparently a single honest man in Christendom to take compassion upon the captive; nor one to reprobate the ungenerous and venal intrigues of the Grand Master, the Pope, and Charles VIII. Each contended with the other for the prize of perfidy and shame. Bâyezîd may be excused for his desire to see his brother in safe keeping; but what can be said for the head of the Christian Church, and the leader of an Order of religious knights, who eagerly betrayed a helpless refugee for the sake of the infidel's gold? When we come to read of the heroism of the Knights of Rhodes and Malta, it may be well to recall the history of Prince Jem, and to weigh well the chivalry that could fatten upon such treason."[345]

Another European writer emphasises this point by stating: "Needless to say a most able Ottoman sultân could have not attempted a grand-scale campaign against European powers while his own brother and claimant to the Ottoman throne had been kept by them. In the event of Jem's being free, the whole Ottoman domain would have been split automatically into two, and tens of thousands of Muslim warriors have been killed in the civil wars.... The possession of an important hostage was used on many occasions as a threat to Bayezid's security, and undoubtedly acted as a brake on his activities ...."[346]

This incident clearly explains the determination of the Osmanlı sultâns to maintain the unity of the Devlet at any expense. They never hesitated to dispense with men of their own flesh and blood if and when they dared to rebel. The constitutional framework of the Sultanate had exclusively invested power and restricted it to the House of Osman. But the Turks did not initiate the hereditary system in Islam; it had actually been pioneered by the Umawîs. The Turks who entered Islam voluntarily had, however, found this system compatible and in line with their pre-Islamic practice. Moreover, we should remember that the monarchical system was prevalent in all of Europe at that time. When dealing with the Osmanlı practice of fratricide, we should always recall the fact that "this was a Roman practice which was in fact followed by the Osmanlıs."[i]

---

i  Anthony Bryer, *Peoples and Settlement in Anatolia and Caucasus 800-1900* (Variorum reprints, London: 1988), IV, p. 485, footnote 3, previously

Until that time European sovereigns had not shown any opposition to the authority of the Pope. But the French King, Charles VIII, who was then anxious to have Jem away from the Pope, entered Rome and challenged the Pope's authority. Jem went to Naples together with the French King, whose plan was to go to Drech and Avlonya and march on İstanbul, using Jem to challenge the authority of the Sultân Bâyezîd.[347] But, out of annoyance and frustration, the Pope had given Jem a poison that took effect slowly, and Jem died in 900/1495 in despair. In his will Jem asked to be buried in Dârul Islâm so that no European would assume his identity in the future in order to attain territory and cause bloodshed among the Muslims. His body was taken to Bursa and buried there.[i]

---

published in an article entitled "Greek Historians on the Turks: The Case of the First Byzantine-Ottoman Marriage," in *The Writing of History in the Middle Ages, Essays Presented to Richard William Southern* (ed. by R.M.C. Davis and J.M. Wallace-Hadrill) Oxford:Clarendon Press, 1981. Needless to say: NOT "Byzantine" but: ROMAN.

It is interesting to note that Bryer tries to play down the impact of the Roman practice of fratricide on the Osmanlıs by asserting that the Romans were a small entity while the Osmanlıs were a great power. But the crucial point is not whether they were large or small but that this was originally a Roman practice.

i  Solaqzâde, *Târîh* (İstanbul: 1297AH), pp. 290-291. The Osmanlıs could not find a solution to the problem of the Sultanate practice they had inherited from the Umawîs through the Abbâsîs and Selçuklus. They victimised their own brothers to avoid civil war; trying to solve the problem in the family circle. It should be remembered that the Osmanlıs learned and adapted fratricide from the Roman Empire: Anthony Bryer, *Peoples and Settlement in Anatolia and the Caucasus, 800-1900* (London: Variorum reprints, 1988), IV, p. 485, footnote 3, published previously as: *The Writing of History in the Middle Ages: Essays presented to Richard*

Even Jem's body was reduced to a matter of money for the Europeans: Sultân Bâyezîd II sent an envoy to Naples in Sha'bân 900/May 1495 to ask the French who were in power there at that time for the body of his brother, but they refused. The Sultân sent another envoy in February 1496, and the French stated that they would sell the body for 50,000 pieces of gold. When the king of Naples, Frederic, saved Italy from the French, the Sultân asked him for Jem's body, but Frederic asked 5,000 pieces of gold for it. Meanwhile, the Pope also asked the king of Naples for the body so he could sell it to the Osmanlıs. Then Sultân Bâyezîd II sent an envoy on board a warship in 904/1498 to the king of Naples, and asked him to deliver the body within eight days, stating that the Osmanlı forces would otherwise attack Italy's coast. The king had to surrender the body.[348]

## The Expedition to Bogdan

While Bâyezîd was preoccupied with Jem, the king of Bogdan attacked the Osmanlı territory of Wallachia.[349] Hence, Bâyezîd II set out at the head of the *Ordu-yu Hümâyûn* in 889/1484. The Osmanlı Devlet had concluded peace treaties with the Republic of Venice and Hungary; therefore, the Balkan borders were secure. The situation was convenient for the Osmanlı Devlet, which dominated three-quarters of the western shores of the Black Sea, to annex the remaining quarter. Sultân Bâyezîd

---

*William Southern*, ed. by R.M.C. Davis and J.M. Wallace-Hadrill (Oxford: Clarendon Press, 1981). "Greek Historians on the Turks: The Case of the First Byzantine-Ottoman Marriage." In his contribution Bryer states that Andronikos Grand Comnenos III executed his brothers Michael (Mihail) and George on the day he became emperor at Trebizond in 1332, and the Osmanlıs did not practise fratricide before that date. Therefore, there is no doubt that fratricide in the Osmanlıs has its origin in the Romans.

started building his *imâret, madrasah,* and *bîmârhâne*[350] on the banks of the Tunja River at Edirne.[351]

*The Bîmârhâne, at Edirne*

The *voyvoda* of Wallachia and the Khân of Crimea, Mengli Gıray, were invited to participate in that campaign. First, Kili castle, which stood on the left bank of the Danube and was Bogdan's access to the Black Sea, was captured. Then, the Osmanlı army besieged the castle of Aqkerman at the mouth of Dinyester (Dniester) River in the north. Mengli Gıray led 50,000 cavalry. The castle was very well fortified and there was a ditch on the land side, but it surrendered after twelve days. Thus, the Osmanlı border stretched to the north and reached to and joined with the northern Turks, the people of Crimea. Kili and Aqkerman on the Black Sea shore were the vital spots for Bogdan since they were its commercial ports. Thus, it became easier for the Osmanlıs to dominate Bogdan afterwards. The *voyvoda* of Bogdan, Ştefan cel Mare, tried to capture these ports but failed. He finally understood that it was impossible to struggle with the Osmanlı Devlet and accepted Osmanlı sovereignty; he paid 4,000 pieces of gold to the treasury of the Osmanlı Devlet. As part of this campaign, Mengli Gıray opened all the north-western shores of the Black Sea to Islam, which became an important entity in the region. A great amount of the *ganîmet* (spoils of war) was given by the Osmanlı Devlet to the Khân and the *voyvoda* of Wallachia. Sultân Bâyezîd II allocated the share of the Osmanlı Devlet in the *ganîmet* to public and educational institutions such as a mosque, *madrasah*, *imâret*, and *bîmârhâne*, which were built at Edirne.³⁵²

### Aid for the Muslims of Andalusia

By that time, the Muslims of Andalusia had been defeated by the Christians. Andalusia was in the process of being lost to Christianity. The Osmanlı navy was not strong enough to dominate the Mediterranean, and had to wait another half-century to do so.[i] Nevertheless Bâyezîd II sent Kemâl Reîs to help his co-religionists in Andalusia. This venture was described in the following words: "Mention must be made of one striking employment of the Turkish navy when, in response to an appeal for help from Granada engaged in the final struggle with Castille, Bâyezîd dispatched Kemâl Reis to harry the Spanish coast. The fleet was also employed in 1487 and after the fall of Granada in 1492 to rescue numbers of refugees and to ferry them across to North Africa. This was the first Osmanlı venture into the western Mediterranean, but it foreshadowed the great achievements of Turkish sailors in the next century, of which only the first falls within this period, the raid of Kemâl Reis to the Balearic Isles, Sardinia, and Pianosa (near Elba) in 1501."[ii]

---

i   Western writers and historians engage in anachronism when they say that the Osmanlı Devlet, which claimed to be the champion of Islam, did not save Andalusia. In fact they did their best. They could not have reached Spain through land – that would have required eliminating all Christendom. At sea, they became superior only after the sea battle of Preveza on 28 September 1538 when they defeated the Christian navy. The last Muslim city Gırnata (Granada) in Andalusia (Spain) fell in 1492.

ii  D.E. Pitcher, *op. cit.*, p. 99. The Osmanlı Sultân Bâyezîd II appointed

The Muslims of Andalusia asked Hızır Hayreddîn Beğ (afterwards Pasha) for help, and he sent 36 ships from Algeria for this purpose. The Osmanlı volunteer *gâzis* were able to convey 70,000 Muslims from Andalusia to Algeria.[353] After Jem's death, the Osmanlıs were free to attack European territories and managed to annex İnebahtı (Lepanto) from the Venetians in 904/1499, and the Moton and Koron castles in Morea in 905/1500.[354]

**The Jihâd in Lehistân (Poland)**

A peace treaty of three years between Bâyezîd II and the King of Lehistân (Poland), Casimir Jagellon IV, was concluded in 895/1484. The Osmanlı Devlet had some interests in Bogdan. On the other hand, Hungary in the west and Poland to the north-west of Bogdan were also interested in Bogdan. The *voyvodas* of Bogdan used to pay tribute to the Kings of Hungary. Thus, there were three rivals for Bogdan. The Osmanlı Sultân Bâyezîd II, preoccupied with other affairs elsewhere, concluded a treaty with the king of Poland for three years, which was renewed for successive periods of three years.[355]

Casimir's son, Jan Albert, who became the king of Poland in 897/1492, marched against Bogdan in 902/1497, which was under Osmanlı protection, and the *voyvoda* of Bogdan, Stephan, applied to the Osmanlı Devlet, complaining about the assault. The king of Hungary, Vladislas, tried to include Poland in the treaty between Hungary and the Osmanlı Devlet in an effort to prevent an Osmanlı march against Poland, but the Osmanlı Devlet did not accept it. The *sanjaqbeği* of Silistre and a commander of *aqınjıs*, Malqochoğlu Bâli Beğ was dispatched to lead 40,000 men to Lehistân (Poland) in the spring of 903/1498. The *voyvoda* of Bogdan guided those *aqınjıs* in

---

Kemâl Reîs as "Kaptan Pasha" in 1495. He was engaged in a number of successful naval battles against European powers. See Pîrî Reîs, *Kitâb-ı Bahriye* (İstanbul: 1935), p. 11.

this campaign. They crossed the Turla (Dniester) River on the bridge constructed on the river-ships, and entered Lehistân. They took over Qarqova castle on the banks of the Turla, and the castles of Dreczny, Glagori, Qanczuga, Gelenbanya in the interior, even the castle at Braqlav, which was the royal summer residence, and destroyed all of them. The *aqınjıs* then returned and entered Osmanlı territory at Aqkerman.[356]

### Osmanlı-Mamlûk Relations

The political relations between the Osmanlıs and the Mamlûks began during the time of Sultân Murâd I and deepened, beginning with Yıldırım Bâyezîd especially, when the Osmanlıs annexed Qaramân Beğlik and other *beğliks* in Anatolia. The two major powers became neighbours. At that time, the Mamlûks dominated Egypt, Hejâz, Syria, Yemen, and some regions in Anatolia. The Osmanlıs did not approve of the attitude of the Mamlûks towards the Ramazanoğlu and Dulqadiroğlu *beğliks* in Anatolia. On the other hand, the Mamlûks did not like the Osmanlıs annexing Qaramân Beğlik in Anatolia. The Mamlûks received Jem in Cairo as if he were a sultân. This fact also added to the tension, and some skirmishes actually took place between the two sides in Chuqurova beginning in 890/1485. But Abû Zekeriyya Yahyâ, the Hafsî sultân of Tunisia, contained the crisis and was instrumental in attaining peace between the two Muslim powers in 896/1491.[357]

### The Completion of the Opening of Morea to Islam

After the death of Shâhzâda Jem, the Osmanlıs felt much more comfortable about activities in Europe; the Christians had no other *shâhzâda* able to incite a civil war in the Osmanlı domain. The Venetians who dominated the western part of Morea, sought to organise a Crusade against the Osmanlıs. They applied to the Holy Roman Emperor, the Pope, the Kings of England,

France, Spain, Naples, Poland, and Hungary for help against the Osmanlıs.

The Pope tried to incite a new Crusade against the Osmanlıs. A treaty was concluded between Venice, the Pope, and Hungary in the spring of 1500 and was proclaimed on a Sunday during a Christian feast in 1501. They planned to attack by land and sea at the same time. The Venetian admiral Pisaro occupied the Osmanlı island of Egine (Aegina). The navies of Spain and Venice occupied the island of Kefalonya. Another fleet carrying 15,000 French soldiers came and moored at the island of Zanta. The fleet of the king of Aragon and Sicily came to the island of Corfu. More important than all of these, a French fleet of 200 vessels under Admiral Ravensteyn came and blockaded the island of Midilli (Mitylene) which is very close to the Anatolian shore of the Aegean. The nephew of the French king was with them. The *sanjaqbeği* of Manisa, Shâhzâda Qorqut, dispatched soldiers to help the Osmanlı garrison on the island. When the Osmanlı navy arrived, the French fleet fled. The nephew of the French King was killed and his head displayed in public.

On the other hand, the Osmanlı *gâzis* completed the opening of Morea to Islam in 907/1502, taking it from the Venetians. A treaty was concluded between the Osmanlı Devlet and the Republic of Venice in Rajab 908/December 1502, according to which İnebahtı (Lepanto), Moton, Qoron and other small castles remained in Osmanlı hands, Kefalonya was taken possession of by Venice, and the island of Santamavra was retrieved by the Osmanlıs.[358]

### The Spread of Shî'ism in Anatolia

Though his predecessors were Sunnî sûfîs, Shâh İsmâîl Safawî (r.1502-1524) deliberately and for political reasons changed Iran from a Sunnî to a Shî'î realm and mercilessly executed religious leaders who opposed this change.[359] After the establishment of their Safavî realm, they "deliberately falsified the evidence of their own origins. Their fundamental object in claiming a Shî'î origin was to differentiate themselves from the Ottomans and to enable them to enlist the sympathies of all heterodox elements. To this end they systematically destroyed any evidence that Shaykh Safi al-Dîn Ishâq, the founder of the Safavid *tarîqa*, was not a Shî'î (he was probably a Sunnî of the Shâfi'î *madhhab*), and they fabricated evidence to prove that the Safavids were *sayyids,* that is, direct descendants of the Prophet ﷺ. They constructed a dubious genealogy tracing the descent of the Safavid family from the seventh of the Twelver Imams, Mûsâ al-Kâzim, a genealogy which is sedulously followed by later Safavid sources and introduced into the text of a hagiological work on the life of Shaykh Safi al-Dîn, a number of anecdotes designed to validate the Safavid claim to be *sayyids*. Viewed dispassionately, the majority of these anecdotes appear ingenuous, not to say naive."[360]

All these acts were committed because of the fact that Shâh İsmâîl had two options: either defeat the Mamlûks and the Osmanlıs, who were the "representatives" of Islam, or obey one of them, since there could only be one head of Islam. He did not want to obey either of these powers, but it was very difficult, if not impossible, to defeat them.

Therefore, the switch to Shî'ism seemed the only way. In fact, there was no reason whatsoever for Iran, which was dominated by Turks, to switch to Shî'ism. The disagreement between Hz Ali and Mu'âwiya was a thing of the distant past. When Mu'âwiya b. Abî Sufyân came to power in 40/661 the supporters (Shî'a) of Hz. Ali continued their struggle, and the Umawî house that Mu'âwiya initiated was overthrown in 132/750 and replaced by the House of Abbâs, the uncle of the Prophet ﷺ. The Umavîs dominated the Muslim world for 90 years (661-750), and the Muslims lived under 'Abbâsî rule (751-1258) after them. The Turks lived in Turkestân in 40/661 and had not become Muslims. When the Tragedy of Kerbelâ took place on the 10 Muharram 61/10 October 680 the Turks were still in Turkestân; they had nothing to do with it. If it is a question of honouring the Ahlul Bayt (Hz. Muhammad's ﷺ family) and love for them, it is impossible to find a Sunnî (Follower of the *Sunnat* {tradition} of the Messenger ﷺ) who does not love and honour the Ahlul Bayt; there is no one among the Sunnîs bearing Yazîd's name. Therefore, it was only for secular, mundane motives, through oppression, that Iran was converted to Shî'ism.

Shâh İsmâîl conducted an active campaign to spread Shî'ism in Anatolia, and sent many agents for this purpose. Meanwhile the aging Bâyezîd II seriously thought of abdication in favour of his elder son Shâhzâda Ahmed, *sanjaqbeği* of Amasya, who was reputed to be benign, generous, and popular among the *vazîrs*. But Qorqut, the second *shâhzâda* (1470-1513), who was a patron of scholars and sailors, conspired against him and tried to gain the support of the military. He failed, however, and was taken from Manisa to Antalya. Ahmed was appointed to Manisa, and was sent in 1511 to suppress, unsuccessfully, an uprising organised by one of Shâh İsmâîl's agents called Shâhqulu in western Anatolia. In fact, Shâhqulu was killed in the battle, but Ali Pasha, who was instrumental in the success, advanced unnecessarily and was martyred. The Osmanlı forces did not pursue the rioters. This uncertain situation in Anatolia encouraged many members of the army and the government to call upon Selîm, the third and very able *shâhzâda*, for help against this rising danger.[361]

# Chapter Six

# The Struggle For Islamic Unity

## 6.1 SULTÂN SELÎM KHÂN (1512-1520)

The third *shâhzâda*, Selîm, the *sanjaqbeği* of Trabzon, was well aware of Shâh İsmâîl's activities in Anatolia. Upon learning of the planned accession to the throne of his brother Ahmed, Selîm asked to be appointed *sanjaqbeği* in Rumeli (Osmanlı Europe). But this was refused on the grounds that the Osmanlı traditional practice did not allow the appointment of any *shâhzâda* as *sanjaqbeği* in Rumeli. Hence, Selîm went to Kefe in the Crimean peninsula and then to Rumeli with a force of 10,000 men. On his arrival at Silistre, he asked to talk to his father in person. After some deliberations it was, however, decided that he would be appointed *sanjaqbeği* of Semendire in Rumeli and that none of the *Shâhzâdas* would be nominated *welyahd* (crown prince). Knowing that Sultân Bâyezîd was still very anxious to secure the Sultanate for Ahmed, his eldest son, and that he was actually about to call him to İstanbul, Selîm reached Chorlu, and the *vazîrs* raised the curtains of Bâyezîd's carriage to tell him: "Behold, the army of your son who claims that he came only with the intention of kissing your hand." They simultaneously fired their guns at Selîm who was obliged, though reluctantly, to fight. After a while, however, Selîm retreated and Sultân Bâyezîd returned to İstanbul.

Meanwhile, Shâhzâda Ahmed was anxiously waiting in Maltepe for an invitation to go to İstanbul. But the *yenicheris* (janissaries) admired Selîm's courage and heroism during the fighting; they were not in favour of Ahmed who had not solved the Shî'î problem.

The other *shâhzâda*, Qorqut, was a learned and refined man, had an artist's spirit, but he was not a good warrior; besides, he had no son to keep up the Osmanlı line. Therefore the *yenicheris* (core of the Osmanlı army) defiantly insisted, "We do not accept anyone as sultân except Selîm." Shâhzâda Ahmed was thus sent back to his *sanjaq*, and Selîm received letters from the notables inviting him to İstanbul. He crossed the frozen Danube and arrived in İstanbul in 918/1512 to meet his father, both of them on horseback. Sultân Bâyezîd offered him the post of commander-in-chief of the army on the condition that he march immediately against Shâh İsmâîl. But Selîm insisted that it was essential for him to assume the Sultanate if this task was to be achieved successfully. Sultân Bâyezîd, thus, abdicated[362] at the age of 65. He set out for Malkara and died on the way there at Söğütlüdere.[363]

Meanwhile, important imperialistic and adventurous activities were taking place in Europe. Abbâs Hamdani summarises them as follows: "In Europe, Portugal and Spain began their naval expansion after the discovery of America and the Cape of Good Hope. Diaz' report in 1488 and that of Covilha in 1492 convinced Dom Joao of the feasibility of reaching India and the Orient by a sea-route via the Cape of Good Hope. News of Columbus' discovery of the Indies may have delayed Joao's plans, but later realisation that Columbus had discovered a new continent which was not India revived the Portuguese ruler's determination to equip a new expedition to the south. Rounding the Cape in 1479, Vasco da Gama followed the African coast northward to Malindi (now Zanzibar). There he contacted a renowned Arab navigator who was the author of books on navigation, Ahmed ibn Majîd. The latter helped the Portuguese to cross the Indian Ocean to reach Calicut on the west coast of southern India, a major emporium of the Eastern spice-trade. Indian spice was thus added to West African gold, ivory, and slaves. The Portuguese established colonies along the new route to India ...."[364]

The Portuguese actively pursued their ambitions and occupied new ports in the Indian Ocean. In effect, they turned it into a "Portuguese Ocean" and prevented Muslim navigation there. It was an open secret that the Christians wanted to occupy the holy city of Makkah and exchange it for Jerusalem. They even thought of starving Egypt by diverting the Nile through Ethiopia to the Red Sea.³⁶⁵ Sultân Selîm was still suspicious of the intentions of his brothers Ahmed and Qorqut, even though he gave the latter Midilli in addition to his *sanjaq* of Saruhan (Manisa). Ahmed besieged Qonya but was driven back and forced to flee to Malatya. To discover his brothers' intentions, Selîm sent them forged letters in the names of Osmanlı notables in which they were "invited" to assume the Sultanate in İstanbul. Both came to the capital and were executed. Later Osmanlı history has been dominated by such troubles between members of the ruling house that had cost the Devlet a great deal. To avoid further chaos and instability, Sultân Selîm had therefore no option but to deal with his brothers in this harsh manner. The majority of Osmanlı historians declare that if one of the two *shâhzâdas* had escaped to Iran or Egypt, the Osmanlı sultân would have been unable to take any action. The Sultân was full of sorrow, and he even wept.³⁶⁶ But this regrettably violent course was presumably unavoidable for the Sultân to assume power, maintain the unity and stability of the Devlet, and carry out its historical responsibilities.

## The Struggle Between Selîm and İsmâîl

Sultân Selîm was a devoted Sunnî and, as such, committed to the ideal of Islamic unity. He expressed his intentions and worldview in his famous poem:

*Milletümde ikhtilâf u tefrika endîshesi*
ملتمده اختلاف و تفرقه أنديشه سى
*Kûshe-yi qabrimde hattâ bî-qarâr eyler beni*
كوشه قبرمده حتى بي قرار أيلر بني

*İttihâd oldu hüjûm-ı hasmı def'a châremüz*
اتحاد اولدی هجوم خصمی دفعه چاره مز
*İttihâd etmezse millet dağidâr eyler beni*³⁶⁷.
اتحاد ایتمز سه ملت داغدار ایلر بنی

*Apprehension of discord among Muslims*
 *Disturbs me even when I am in my grave.*
*Unity is our means to repulse the enemy's attack.*
*If the Muslims do not unite, this hurts me greatly.*

Once he was in full control of the Osmanlı Devlet, Sultân Selîm ordered his administration to probe into the question of Shî'ism in Anatolia. This study claimed that Shî'î propaganda had succeeded in enlisting the support of some 40,000 people in Anatolia on the side of Shâh İsmâîl who assertively executed 60,000 Sunnîs in Âzerbeyjân. In retaliation for this crime, Sultân Selîm executed many of the Shî'î leaders in Anatolia and imprisoned others. After inflicting this heavy blow on Shî'ism in Anatolia, Sultân Selîm set out in 1514 for Iran to deal with the Shî'î threat by the Safavîs there. Shâh İsmâîl then also threatened the Mamlûks' rule and had, in fact, offered to attack Syria from the north if the Christians in Europe would attack simultaneously from the Mediterranean.³⁶⁸ The Osmanlıs tried to conclude a deal with the Mamlûks against the Safavîs of Iran, but nothing concrete came out of this attempt. The Mamlûks had previously preferred neutrality in this conflict, and all they did was to dispatch some troops to Aleppo to protect their borders there against both of the two northern powers.³⁶⁹

Sultân Selîm sent a letter to Shâh İsmâîl, urging him to repent and refrain from hostility and aggression, quoting the Noble Qur'ân: *"Those who have committed wrongdoing or done injustice to themselves should call on Allah and ask for forgiveness, they will find Allah Forgiving and Merciful"*³⁷⁰ (*an-Nisâ'* 4: 110). But the Shâh remained stubborn and uncompromising. Then Sultân Selîm sent

## Chapter Six – The Struggle for Islamic Unity

a letter to Shâh İsmâil stating: "I am coming against you, let it be what Haqq Te'âlâ decreed; do not say that you have been taken by surprise, you could not find time to gather soldiers!"[371] Sultân Selîm advanced against him with an army of 100,000 men and sent him a strongly-worded message in which he challenged him to battle. But Shâh İsmâil did not have the ability or courage at that time for such a confrontation and consequently retreated to Iran in disgrace. The Osmanlı army searched for his army in western Iran for two months[372] but to no avail. Ustajlu Mehmed Khân was Shâh İsmâîl's commander on the western front. Knowing that he was not able to confront the Osmanlı army, he left the province after destroying cities, towns, villages, everything there, and joined the Shâh in the interior. The Osmanlı army was tired, and the enemy was not in sight. So, the janissaries revolted, firing at the tent of Sultân Selîm on the plain of Eleshgird: they wanted to go back! And there the steel will of Sultân Selîm emerged: without the slightest sign of fear, he rode his horse and addressed the janissaries: "We have not arrived yet where we want, and we have not met the enemy; there is no probability of going back without confrontation; so much so that, even thinking about it is a mischievous illusion. It is very regrettable that the followers of the Shâh are prepared to sacrifice themselves for his sake, and we, while we came to the border to put those who behave contrary to the *Sharî'at* on the Right Path, some slackers are trying to abort this *jihâd* campaign. I most certainly will not swerve and go back; I will go together with those who obey *Ulul Emr* (those in command) until we arrive where we are going. Those whose hearts are weak, those who think about their families and want to go back on the pretext of the difficulties of advancing, it is up to them: if they return, it means they go back, leave the campaign, for the sake of *Dîn-i Mübîn*. If the excuse is the absence of the enemy – they are in front. If you are men, then come with me, otherwise I am going alone!" With that, he drove his horse forward; the janissaries, feeling ashamed, followed him.[373] His speech summarises the *raison d'être* of the Osmanlı Devlet: the Osmanlı presence and life is dedicated to Islam, the Osmanlıs were about to fight their kin, Turks, for the sake of Islam because the Osmanlı Devlet represented Sunnî Islam and held that their adversary was no longer part of Islam. The Osmanlı believed that whosoever abandoned a *jihâd* campaign, such as this one, was an apostate. The important point here is that there was no hesitation whatsoever on the part of anyone in the Osmanlı army. Western writers who try to show the Osmanlı Devlet to be an imperialist Turkish power cannot explain the Battle of Chaldıran between two Turkish armies. This fearless behaviour of Sultân Selîm changed the course of history: if he had relented and obeyed the wishes of the janissaries there, Shâh İsmâîl, whose domain stretched to India, would have expanded his authority to Anatolia. His secret propaganda had even gained supporters in Rumeli; therefore, it would have been very difficult for the Osmanlı Devlet to maintain itself in Europe, and it would have been annihilated before Christian Europe.

Shâh İsmâîl finally confronted the Osmanlı army in 920/August 1514 at Chaldıran; the Osmanlı cavalry was tired, and the Safavî cavalry was vigorous, but that situation was counterbalanced by Osmanlı artillery. The Osmanlı army arrived there after travelling a distance of 2,500 kilometres. As a matter of fact, the Shâh planned to tire the Osmanlı army out that way and then annihilate the tired and weary Osmanlı army.

Upon his arrival at Chaldıran, Sultân Selîm convened a council of war to decide either to let the army rest or to engage the enemy. The *vazîrs* held that the army should rest; only *bashdefterdâr* Pîrî Mehmed Chelebi argued that there could be secret Shîʿîs in the Osmanlı army, and they could be propagandising against fighting the Shâh. Therefore, he felt that the engagement should take place immediately. Sultân Selîm, admiring this opinion, said: "This is the

## Chapter Six – The Struggle for Islamic Unity

only man of opinion, it is regrettable that he is not a *vazîr* yet!" and it was decided that they engage the enemy at dawn the next morning.[374] This Pîrî Mehemmed Chelebi (afterwards Pasha) became a *vazîr* later on, and then *sadrâzam* in 1518. He did not have enough seniority at that time (1514) to be appointed *vazîr*. The important point is that one be able to judge the abilities and values of people; Sultân Selîm was good at this as well. "Pîrî Mehemmed Pasha, who became *vazîr-i a'zam* (Grand Vazîr) towards the end of Sultân Selîm's rule and continued his work during the early period of Sultân Süleymân (the Magnificent) was of Turkish descent, which is a rare occurrence in the Osmanlı administration, and a great administrator."[375]

The battle began at dawn on 2 Rajab 920/23 August 1514; the Safavî cavalry attacked the left flank of the Osmanlı army, and the *a'zeb* (light infantry) could not be drawn from in front of the guns in time, so the left flank of the Osmanlı army suffered heavy casualties. The *beğlerbeği* of Rumeli and some other *beğs* were martyred.[376] But the *beğlerbeği* of Anatolia, Sinân Pasha, fired heavy artillery that confused the enemy and forced its cavalry to disperse and flee. Shâh İsmâîl himself was almost killed[377] and finally took to his heels with some injuries. The Osmanlı army thus inflicted a heavy defeat on the Safavî army,[i] and Selîm entered Tabrîz, the

---

i  R.M. Savory is unable to conceal his sorrow and regret at the Osmanlı victory over the Shî'î Safavîs: "[A]nd there is no doubt at all that the Safavids could have developed the use of artillery and hand-guns had they chosen to do so. It has been suggested that the Safavids, like their contemporaries the Mamlûks of Egypt and Syria, considered the use of firearms to be unchivalrous and unmanly. Whatever the reasons for Safavid neglect in this regard, it is clear that it was primarily Ottoman superiority in firearms which enabled them to inflict a signal defeat on the Safavids at Chaldiran." "Safavid Persia" in *The Cambridge History of Islam* (Cambridge: C.U.P., 1980), 1 A, p. 400.

capital of the Safavîs. The *khutbah* was recited there in his name on 18 Rajab 920/8 September 1514. He brought about 1,000 scholars and artists from Tabrîz to İstanbul, many of whom Shâh İsmâîl had brought from Khorasân, and they were of Turkish descent. It was a tradition that began with Fâtih: to bring scholars and artists

---

By contrast, the same author is quite happy with Iran's becoming a source of annoyance in the midst of Sunnî Muslim world: "Ismâîl's first action on his accession, the proclamation of the Shî'î form of Islam as the religion of the new state, was unquestionably the most significant act of his whole reign. By taking this step, he not only clearly differentiated the new state from the Ottoman empire, the major power in the Islamic world at the time, which otherwise might well have incorporated Persia in its dominions, but imparted to his subjects a sense of unity which permitted the rise of a state in the modern sense of the term. Ever since the Arab conquest in the first/seventh century, Persia had been a geographical rather then a political entity." *op. cit.*, p. 398.

According to Savory, this switch from Sunnism to Shî'ism "permitted the rise of a state in the modern sense of the term." But, in fact, the most significant aspect of the "modern" state is secularism, while the movement was in fact based entirely on a religious view. On the other hand, to use the phrase "Arab conquest" for the opening of Persia to Islam is absolutely irrelevant; for Persia was conquered in the name of and for Islam.

For the disastrous results on the Islamic world of Iran's becoming a Shî'î power see: M.A. Hraydi, *al-Hurûb'l Uthmâniyya-al-Fârisiyyah wa âthâruhâ fî inhisâri'l maddi'l Islamî 'an Urubbâ* (The Osmanlı-Persian Wars and Their Effect in Restricting the Islamic Tide from Europe), Cairo: 1408/1987.

Savory's other two mistakes are calling the Osmanlı political entity an "empire" and claiming that Osmanlı territories were "dominions."

## Chapter Six – The Struggle for Islamic Unity

to İstanbul. Among them were *muezzin*[i] Hâfiz[ii] Mehmed of Isfahân and his son Hasan Jân.[iii]

Sultân Selîm stayed in Tabrîz for some time. His intention was to spend the winter at Qarabağ[iv] and to march against Shâh İsmâîl the next year.[378] But the Osmanlı army was tired and homesick, and the Sultân therefore returned. "[N]ever again was there to be such an opportunity for pan-Turanism as when Selîm I, victorious at the battle of Chaldıran in 1514, might have marched through Iran to join hands with Özbek Turkmens against this Shi'a heresy to bolster the nomadic front against the threat from Muscovy. But the janissaries refused to follow, so Selîm turned against the Mamlûks. Babur adventured into India, and the Islamic steppe-country began its long and losing battle against Russia."[379] Sultân Selîm spent the winter at Amasya and captured Kemah and Diyarbakır from Safavî commandants in the spring of 1515. In the meantime, Mawsil, Urfa, some parts of eastern Anatolia, and Iraq were all annexed by the Osmanlıs.

The two armies at the battle of Chaldıran were mainly Turkish, but the struggle was not racial or national since neither of these considerations counted at all in the sixteenth century. On the

---

i   *Muezzin* is an *ezân* reciter and assistant to the imam in other religious duties.
ii  A *hâfiz* is one who memorises the Noble Qur'ân, a practice that still takes place in Turkey. The majority of the imams in mosques, and some *müezzins* memorise the whole Noble Qur'ân.
iii Dânişmend, *op. cit.*, vol. II, p. 15. Hasan Jân is the father of Khoja Sa'deddîn Efendi, the famous *shaykhulislâm*, historian, and writer of *Tâju't Tevârîh*.
iv  The Armenians were settled in Qarabağ by the British in the twentieth century, and the Russians sent some more of them there. To obscure the Turkish name Qarabağ (dark orchard), Russians added another word, Nagorno, so it became Nagorno-Karabagh.

*Sultân Selîm Mosque*

contrary, it was basically a doctrinal one in which the Osmanlı Turks fought for the sake of *sunnah* while the Turks under the Safavî administration struggled for the dominance of Shî'ism.

### The Campaign against the Mamlûks

Alâüddevle, the *beğ* of Dulqadir Beğlik (r. 1479-1515), favoured the Mamlûks, and attacked some Osmanlı units. So Sinân Pasha, the *vazîr-i a'zam*, was sent against him with Alâüddevle's nephew, Ali Beğ, the son of Shehsuvar Beğ (1515-1522). Alâüddevle and his officers were killed in battle, the *beğlik* of Dulqadir was annexed to the Osmanlı domain, and Ali Beğ was appointed governor of this newprovince.[380]

Qansu Ghawri, the Mamlûk sultân, was disturbed by the Osmanlı expansion in this direction, and therefore demanded that the *khutbah* of the *jum'ah* prayer in the province of Dulqadir be in his name. Since this is an important symbol of sovereignty in Islamic practice, the Osmanlı Sultân adamantly refused. Being a committed Sunnî, Sultân Selîm planned to annex Iran to his *Devlet*, and to implement Sunnî Islam there. He gave his instructions to *Dîvân-ı Hümâyûn* to

## Chapter Six – The Struggle for Islamic Unity

prepare an army for this task and to provide it with enough food and ammunition for a *sefer*[i] of three years.

In 922/1516 the Sultân sent an advance force of 40,000 men commanded by Vazîr Sinân Pasha. But when he arrived at Malatya the provincial emîrs did not allow him to proceed. After his defeat at Chaldıran, Shâh İsmâîl had approached the Mamlûks of Egypt to enlist their support against the Osmanlı Sultân by claiming that his ulterior motive, after taking over Iran, would be the capture of Egypt itself. The Mamlûks of Egypt, then a major power in the area, were receptive to this propaganda and had furthermore used their strength and diplomacy to convince the small emirates along the Osmanlı-Mamlûk border that it was in their interest to prevent an Osmanlı advance into Iran. The Mamlûk sultân Qansu Ghawri himself thus led a force of 50,000 men to Syria, which was then under Mamlûk rule. This move was perhaps feasible from a worldly perspective, but, on the other hand, it undermined the Mamlûks' own legitimacy as protectors of Sunnî Islam who gave asylum in Cairo to the Sunnî 'Abbâsî *Khalîfah*, and were officially the protectors of the holy places of Makkah, Medîna, and Jerusalem. They were now actually supporting the Shî'î forces of Iran against Sunnî champions of the faith, the Osmanlıs. When the Osmanlı sultân learned from Sinân Pasha of the arrival of the Mamlûk Sultân in Syria, he discussed the situation thoroughly with his *dîvân*. He also sent envoys to the Mamlûk Sultân in Aleppo (Halab) to explain to

---

i The Osmanlıs called a *jihâd* campaign *sefer* (Arabic: *safar*). Their meals were *sofra* (*ta'âmul musâfir*). It is interesting to note that the name of the fifth *sûrah* in the Noble Qur'ân is *al-Mâidah* ("the Table Spread"). The Osmanlı Turks called their eating utensil *sofra* because of the fact that most of their time was spent at *sefer*. Only 28 years (1740-1768) in all Osmanlı history was without a *sefer* (*jihâd* campaign). The word *sofra*, which is still used in Turkish, is, therefore a reminder of *jihâd*.

him the Osmanlı intention to purify Iran of Shî'ism before it became rooted there. But the Mamlûks imprisoned the Osmanlı envoys, and they were only released under pressure from the advancing *Ordu-yu Hümâyûn*. Though Qansu Ghawri apologised and sent envoys to Sultân Selîm, the latter was convinced that the Mamlûks were not sincere and were perhaps conspiring secretly with Iran. It might have been dangerous if the *Ordu-yu Hümâyûn* had gone to Iran, for the rear of the army would have been vulnerable and the country would have been exposed to an invasion by the Mamlûk forces, or the *Ordu-yu Hümâyûn* could have been trapped between the two rival armies. Since Shâh İsmâîl was not in sight, there was no imminent danger from the east; he therefore directed his army to the south, and fought a battle with Qansu Ghawri at Marj Dâbiq near Aleppo in 922/1516.[381] The Mamlûk army was defeated, Qansu Ghawri was killed, and Bilâdu's Shâm (Syria and Palestine) was annexed by the Osmanlıs.

> "The Turks entered the Arab lands at a time when a great economic change was taking place throughout the Middle East, a change that was rapidly rendering those lands economically insignificant and, in fact, threatening them with complete ruin. In the first years of the sixteenth century the mainstay of the Arabs' economic structure had been shattered, and the consequences of that disaster had become evident long before the advent of the Turks upon the scene. Until the early sixteenth century the foundation of Arab prosperity was the trade from India to Europe which passed mostly through their hands and yielded to the Mameluke Empire, including Syria, and the Hejaz, much revenue from customs duties alone. But by the early years of the sixteenth century the trade route to India had shifted away from Arab lands to Portugal, via the Cape of

## Chapter Six – The Struggle for Islamic Unity

Good Hope, and the resulting decrease in revenue took its toll in more ways than in the lessening receipts from direct taxes on the Indian and European wares."[382]

By that time the Mamlûk Devlet was weak and unable to confront the new Europe of the fifteenth and sixteenth centuries. Its trade and economy dwindled, particularly after the discovery of the new route around the Cape of Good Hope. The Christian powers were now in the Indian Ocean, the Red Sea, and Jeddah, and the Portuguese had completely annihilated the navy of the Mamlûks at the battle of Diu near the Indian coast. Being anxious to protect *al-Haramayn ash-Sharîfayn* against the Portuguese threat, the Osmanlı Devlet sent 30 warships and 300 guns to Egypt as a gesture of Islamic support. But the pirates who called themselves the Knights of St. John captured them. The Osmanlı sultân, Selîm, sent another 400 guns and two tons of gunpowder to Egypt with materials, Osmanlı officers, and military technicians to build warships for the Egyptian arsenal. After his defeat of Qansu Ghawri at Marj Dâbiq, Sultân Selîm also offered Tomânbây, the new Mamlûk sultân, the undisputed rule of Egypt and the complete cessation of hostilities in Zilkade 922/ December 1516 on condition that the Mamlûks recognise Osmanlı sovereignty by performing the *khutbah* in the name of the Sultân and by using Osmanlı coinage. In his letter to Tomânbây, Sultân Selîm wrote that the latter was "a slave changing masters, he himself was the son of rulers going back twenty generations, if Tomânbây would send the *kharâj* of Egypt every year and obey him, he would be *vâli* of Egypt and the land stretching until Gazze (Gaza); otherwise, Sultân Selîm would treat him very harshly. When he read that letter, Tomânbây feared and wept."[383] Incited by some narrow-minded Mamlûks he refused this offer.[384]

The new sultân of the Mamlûks and the notables of Egypt thought that annexation of Kilikya and Syria by the Osmanlıs would be temporary and Sultân Selîm would not be able to get to Egypt and would retreat from Palestine as had the forces of Genghis Khân and Tamerlane. They hoped to retrieve those lands when the Osmanlı sultân returned to Anatolia. In fact, when the Osmanlı Sultân asked his *vazîr* Yunus Pasha about marching against Egypt, the latter replied that it was dangerous; but Sultân Selîm thought that the victory would be temporary if he did not take over Egypt, and thus he decided to annex it.[385]

Historian Ali Efendi, writer of *Künhü'l Akhbâr*, stated that when Sultân Selîm annexed Damascus, there was a learned, knowledgeable man living in *i'tikâf* at the tomb of ash-Shaykh al-Akbar (Muhyiddîn İbn 'Arabî) who was good at *'ilmi'l Jefr*. It was Sultân Selîm's custom, whenever he went to visit the tomb of Muhyiddîn İbn 'Arabî, to converse with that *mu'takif*. One day Sultân Selîm asked that knowledgeable man about his attempt to cross the waterless land to Egypt. The latter replied that "Your taking over Egypt is mentioned in the Great Qur'ân; direct yourself there without wasting time." When Selîm asked, "How and where is that explained?" the man replied:

$$\text{وَلَقَدْ كَتَبْنَا فِى ٱلزَّبُورِ مِن بَعْدِ ٱلذِّكْرِ}$$
$$\text{أَنَّ ٱلْأَرْضَ يَرِثُهَا عِبَادِىَ ٱلصَّٰلِحُونَ}$$

*Wa laqad katabnâ fiz Zabûri min ba'didh Dhikri annal Arda yarithuhâ 'Ibâdiyas Sâlihûn (al-Anbiyâ 21:105)*

*We wrote down in the Zabūr, after the Reminder came: 'It is My slaves who are righteous who will inherit the earth.'*

and he added: "When the word *arz* is mentioned with *al-(mu'arraf bil lâm – the definite article:* الأرض), it means Egypt, and when the same word is mentioned without *alif lâm*, the land of the Romans

## Chapter Six – The Struggle for Islamic Unity

is meant." And the numerical value of *wa laqad* that occurs in the *âyah* is 140; the numerical value of your name (Selîm) is also 140. The numerical value of the word *Dhikr* is 920 which indicates the date of this act, especially '*Our good slaves will inherit*' indicates you as 'a good slave of Allah.'[i] It might be supposed that this herald also affected Sultân Selîm's decision, since this kind of knowledge was regarded as acceptable at the time. The people and the events should be evaluated in connection with the circumstances in which they lived and took place, against their backgrounds.

Hence, Sultân Selîm spent the winter in Damascus and set out towards Egypt. But it was not an easy task at all to reach Egypt: before the Osmanlı army lay the Sinai desert that neither Alexander of Macedonia nor the Mongols were brave enough to cross. He entered the desert, crossed it, and reached Egypt. The Mamlûks were waiting for the Osmanlı army at Raydâniyyah. Tomânbây had 20,000 soldiers and employed artillery and riflemen whom he had brought from Frangistân (Europe), and his soldiers were armoured.[386] Their cannons were fixed in the expected direction of the Osmanlı approach. But Sultân Selîm went round the Muqattam mountain with his army and caught the Mamlûk army by complete surprise whereby the Mamlûk artillery became useless.[387] Tomânbây, a very brave soldier, was obliged to flee. Some of his soldiers, however, had attacked Sultân Selîm's quarters directly, although he was not hurt since at that time he was at the head of the units going round the Muqattam mountain.

The Battle of Raydâniyyah took place on 28 Zilhijjah (Dhil Hijja) 922/22 January 1517 and a unit of the Osmanlı army was stationed

---

i Solaqzâde, *op. cit.*, pp. 427-428. The *Abjad* (*jefr*) values of the letters mentioned are as follow: *waw* 6, *lâm* 30, *qaf* 100, *dâl* 4, *wa laqad* 140, *sîn* 60, *lâm* 30, *yâ* 10, *mîm* 40, *selîm* 140, *dhâl* 700, *kâf* 20, *râ* 200, *dhikr* 920. But it should be noted that Selîm entered Egypt in Zilhicca 922/ January 1517 (after 920).

at Cairo to protect the city. Sultân Selîm was somehow fond of Tomânbây's bravery, and in fact entertained the idea of appointing him *vâli* of this new *eyâlet*[i] (province). He made his offer through an envoy, but Tomânbây refused it and killed the envoy.[388] A few days later Tomânbây attacked suddenly, and street battles went on for three days in Cairo. Tomânbây fled but was eventually arrested. Finally, Sultân Selîm entered Cairo in victory on 23 Muharram 923/15 February 1517.[389] Sultân Selîm performed the *jum'ah* prayer at the Melik Muayyad Mosque, and when the *khatîb* mentioned his name during the *khutbah* as *Khâdimu'l-Haramayn ash-Sharîfayn*, he turned his *sajjâdah* (prayer rug) over and put his face on the ground and wept out of enthusiasm.[390]

Sultân Selîm wanted to appoint Tomânbây *vâli* of this new Osmanlı province, but the latter did not accept it; he was stubborn and difficult to please. So, in due course, he was surrendered to Ali Beğ, son of Shehsuvâr Beğ. Tomânbây was finally hanged at Bâbuz Zuwaylah where Shehsuvâr Beğ (1467-1473) had been previously executed by the Mamlûks.[391] His body was left hanging from the rope for three days to convince the people of his death, and his funeral was a ruler's one; Sultân Selîm participated in his *salâtul Janâzah* and distributed money as alms for the benefit of Tomânbây's soul.[392]

Ruling over a devout and zealous Muslim Devlet that had implemented Islamic law (*Sharî'at*) in every aspect of life, the Osmanlıs needed a *fetvâ* to engage in this war against the Mamlûks. Two *fetvâs* were at issue here, one of which was based on the well-known Muslim principle, *"Man a'âna mulhidan fa-huwa mulhid* – Whoever assists an unbeliever is an unbeliever," indicating the Mamlûks' indirect support for Shâh Ismâîl. The

---

i  An *eyâlet* was a large region in the Osmanlı administration. The number of *eyâlets* fluctuated over time, between 32 to 36. Egypt was an *eyâlet*, as were Libya and Budin (the Osmanlı part of Hungary).

## Chapter Six – The Struggle for Islamic Unity

second was based on the view that "Muslims should see to it that their coins on which the *kalimatu'sh shâhâdah* is printed should not be used by unbelievers since they could touch this sacred *kalimah* with their dirty hands after coming out of the privy. But if these Muslims do not strictly observe and implement this directive, then it becomes necessary to kill them."[393]

Sultân Selîm organised the administration in Egypt. Abû'l Barakât ibn Muhammad al-Hasanî, the *sharîf* of Makkah and Medîna, sent his son with the keys of the holy places to Sultân Selîm to assure his loyalty and obedience to the Sultân. For his part, Sultân Selîm, confirmed the *sharîf* in his position and sent him *sürre* (money and presents) for the people of Makkah and Medîna. He also appointed two famous *kadıs* to al-Haramayn ash-Sharîfayn, and sent 200,000 ducats (golden coins) with them to be distributed to the poor there.[394]

Thus the Hejâz joined voluntarily, without *any* dispute about the question of who was the Muslim superpower, and the Mamlûk commanders who ruled some parts of Yemen at that time followed suit. By that time, the Red Sea almost became an Osmanlı Sea that was employed by the Osmanlı Devlet to check the activities of the Portuguese and to obstruct their attempts to form, with the Abyssinians, a Christian front against neighbouring Muslim Arab powers.[395]

Sharîf Abû Numay, son of Sharîf Abû'l-Barakât, stayed one month in Cairo and returned with the *berât* confirming the latter at his post. Every year the Osmanlı Devlet sent units in rotation from seven *ojaks* that were stationed in Egypt to protect Makkah and Medîna. And when, needed, some units were sent from Syria as well. The *sharîf* of Makkah had an allowance from the treasury of Egypt and revenue from the customs of Jeddah. The money sent from Egypt was called *'atiyye-i hümâyûn*; in addition, the *sharîf* received gold pieces through *sürre-i hümâyûn*. When his father died in 941/1525, the 25-year-old Sharîf Abû Numay was appointed Emîr of Makkah.

The Portuguese suddenly entered the Red Sea in 948/1542, deployed soldiers at Jeddah, and tried to occupy the castle. The *sanjaqbeği* of Jeddah gallantly resisted and Sharîf Abû Numay reached the scene with the nomads that he collected, and the Portuguese were repulsed. Sharîf Abû Numay was rewarded with the allocation of half the revenue from the Jeddah customs, and this practice was continued with his successors.[396]

The Republic of Venice, which owned Cyprus at the time and used to pay *kharâj* for it to the Mamlûks, began to pay it to the Osmanlı Devlet after the latter annexed Egypt.[i]

### The Osmanlı Khalifate

According to a *hadîth sharîf*, the Muslim *ummat* must have a *khalîfah*.[397] Therefore, it is only very natural for *any strong* Muslim Devlet to have the *khalifate*, and to represent Islam. And the Osmanlıs also seem to have thought that – given that they were *the* Muslim force in Europe, the heart of Christendom, and the *only* power carrying out *jihâd* – they were *the* representative of Islam, and the head of their *devlet* was the *Khalîfah*. This fact is shown explicitly in Murâd Hüdâvendigâr's (1362-1389) letter to the *beğ* of Qaramân dated 1 Rabî' Thâni 767/16 December 1365, referring to his capital as *Dârul Khilâfah* (Seat of the Khalifate).[398] As a matter of fact, the Osmanlı Devlet had represented the Khalifate since the time of Murâd Hüdâvendigâr. For example, on the occasion of the Osmanlı Devlet opening Edirne to Islam, Janıbek Khân of Kök Orda (the Golden Horde) addressed Murâd Hüdâvendigâr as "Sultânul Guzât wel Mujâhidîn, *Zillullâh* – The Sultân of the

---

i   Dânişmend, *op. cit.*, II, p. 45. The Venetians sent Kontarini and Mochenigo to Cairo stating that they would pay 8,000 ducats yearly, which they used to pay to the Mamlûks who ruled Egypt and Syria, to the Osmanlı Devlet: *OT*, II, pp. 292-293.

## Chapter Six – The Struggle for Islamic Unity

Gâzis and Mujâhidîn, the Shadow of Allah," referred to Edirne as "Edirne *maqarr-ı Khilâfet* (the seat of Khilâfet)."³⁹⁹ İsfendiyâr Beğ of Qastamonu also addressed Murâd Hüdâvendigâr as "Hazret-i Khilâfetmenqabet."⁴⁰⁰ His son, Yıldırım Bâyezîd, was addressed in 793/1391 by the Sultân of Egypt who sheltered the "shadow" 'Abbâsî *Khalîfah* in his country, as "Zillullâh – Shadow of Allah" (a title for the *khalîfah*).⁴⁰¹ In fact, when the Osmanlı Devlet defeated the united European Christian armies in 798/1396 at the battle of Niğbolu (Nicopolis), the head of the *devlet*, Yıldırım Bâyezîd became the *de facto* supreme head of the Muslims, the *khalîfah*. It is interesting to note that he built Ulu Jâmi<sup>i</sup> at Bursa with the *ghanîmet* (booty) obtained from the Crusader army at Niğbolu. With the opening in 1453 of Constantinople to Islam,

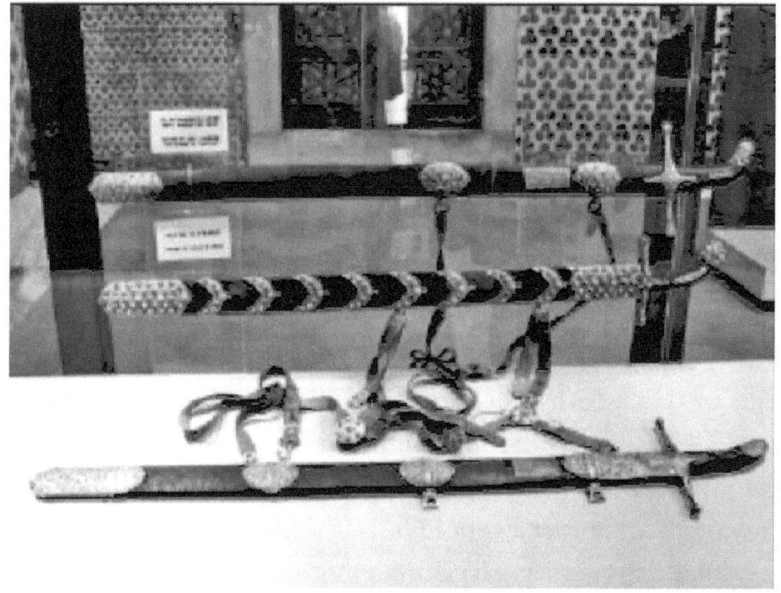

*Al-Amânât al-Mukaddasah in Topkapı Palace: The Swords of Rasûlullâh*

---

i   Ulu Jâmi is the Great Mosque where the *Jum'ah* prayer takes place, the *khutbah* in which the sovereign's name is mentioned.

which virtually ended the Roman Empire, the Osmanlı Devlet became the superpower of its age, and its sultân was the actual *Khalîfah* of the Muslims. The nominal 'Abbâsî *Khalîfah* in Cairo was nothing more than a figurehead and a puppet in the hands of the Circassian Mamlûk rulers. The Osmanlı historian İbn Kemâl calls Fâtih Sultân Mehemmed *Khalîfah*.[402] Fâtih's son, Bâyezîd II, was addressed by Hüseyn Bayqara, Pâdishâh of Khorasân, as "Khalîfat Allah fi'l anâm, Hâfizu thugûri'l Islam – The *Khalîfah* of Allah among His Creatures, the Defender of the boundaries of Islam", and "al-Mu'ayyad bi ta'yîdi'llâh, al-Maliku'l Majîd, mu'ayyanan li's Saltanati wa'l Khilâfati – supported by Allah the Glorious Sovereign, assigned to the Sultanate and Khalîfate by Allah".[403] Similarly, Yâqûb Shâh referred in official correspondence to Bâyezîd II as the *Khalîfah*.[404] Upon his death, Bâyezîd II sent his condolences to his son, Baysungur Mirza, who addressed Bâyezîd II in his reply as sultân and *khalîfah*.[405] On other occasions the Sunnî Muslim Devlet in Iran[406] and the notables of the Aq Qoyunlu Devlet also addressed him in the same way.[407] Even Shâh İsmâîl, who replaced the Sunnî Aq Qoyunlu Devlet in Iran with a Shî'î one[408] and the Shaykhu'l Islam of Herât, Ahmad Taftazânî,[409] addressed Bâyezîd II in the same manner. His successor, Sultân Selîm, was well aware of his position as *khalîfah* and was addressed thus by 'Ubayd Khân of Samarkand in 929/1514[410] before taking over Egypt. Sultân Selîm continued to use this title in his correspondence with Shâh İsmâîl before the battle of Chaldıran[411] and after taking over Egypt in 923/1517. Actually, the *khutbah* of the khalifate was recited in Cairo in his name.[412] On the voluntary incorporation of the Hejâz into the Osmanlı Devlet, Islamic unity in the central Muslim lands was achieved, combining all the spiritual, temporal, historical, traditional, and functional aspects of the *ummat*. Selîm's son, Süleymân the Magnificent, was addressed by the same title.[413] In fact, the khalifate continued to be

## Chapter Six – The Struggle for Islamic Unity

represented by Sultâns[i] up to the end of the Osmanlı Devlet, and even for a period during the Republic of Turkey, until it was finally abolished by the Grand National Assembly of Turkey on 3 March 1924. Khayri Beğ, the governor of Aleppo under the Mamlûks and who did not resist the Osmanlıs, was therefore rewarded by being appointed the *vâli* of Osmanlı Egypt. Sultân Selîm returned to Damascus where he built a tomb over the burial place of the great Sûfî Muhyiddîn İbn al-'Arabî, with an adjacent mosque and an *imâret*. He took part in the first *Jum'ah* prayer in this mosque, and allocated a *wâqf* for those charitable institutions.[414]

Palestine remained an Osmanlı country up to the First World War. During these long centuries, there was no trouble among the people there, because of the justice the Osmanlı Devlet practised. It is interesting to note that Ehud Barak, the former prime minister of Israel, said to Süleymân Demirel, the former president of Turkey, "An Osmanlı Corporal quietly governed this place with his twenty men; we have difficulty governing it now with an army!"[415] It explains the Osmanlı attitude toward the governed, the *ra'iyyet*, the Osmanlı worldview and practice.

The governing class in the domains of the Mamlûks was of Turkish (Qıpchaq) and Circassian stock, and not Arab. Qıpchaq

---

i  For example, when the Osmanlı sultân Genç Osmân (1618-1622) was deposed and took refuge with the janissaries in 1622, they shouted in unison: "We do not accept you as *khalîfah*, but we do not agree to your being executed either" (Na'îmâ, *Târîh*, II, p. 227); the Osmanlı Sultân Mehemmed IV was addressed on his accession in 1648 by the ruler of Morocco as the "Shadow of Allah over His Creatures," which is the title of the *khalîfah*, and "flyer of the flags of the *Sharî'at* in the fields of justice" (BOA, NMD 7, pp. 246-247). And Sultân 'Abdulmajîd (1839-1861) was addressed in 1263/1846-47 by the Ruler of Khokand as *khalîfah* (Zillu's-Subhân) (BOA, NMD, 12, p. 56).

Turks governed first, then Circassians took over. But sovereignty in Egypt and Bilâdu's Shâm had only shifted from one Muslim governing body to another stronger Muslim Devlet. By then the Osmanlı Devlet included Nubia as well, and its boundary reached to Sawâkin. Having taken over the khalifate from the nominal 'Abbâsî *khalîfah*[i] in Egypt, Sultân Selîm gave himself the title of *Khâdimu'l-Haramayn ash-Sharîfayn* – The Servant of the Two Holy Honourable Places.

On his way back from Egypt at the head of the *Ordu-yu Hümâyûn*, Sultân Selîm called on the *qâdıasker* of Anatolia, Shamsuddîn Ahmed ibn Kemâl, to talk to him; they were conversing on horseback when İbn Kemâl's horse trod in a puddle and covered Sultân Selîm's *qaftân* (outer garment) with mud. Naturally, the *qâdıasker* was very sorry, but Sultân Selîm, taking off his *qaftân*, said: "the mud splashed on me from the foot of the horse of an *'âlim* (Muslim scholar) is an honour for me; let them spread this *qaftân* on my *sanduqa* (sarcophagus) when I die." And, that *qaftân* was actually put on his *sanduqa*.[416]

This annexation of the Mamlûk lands was a great success for the Osmanlıs. The people in İstanbul were anxiously waiting to meet the Sultân in great festive mood. But, because he was a committed Sunnî who adhered to the ethics of Islam, Sultân Selîm entered the city quietly, at night by sea, and the people learned of his arrival the

---

i  The nominal *Khalîfah* Mutawakkil 'Alallâh took refuge with Sultân Selîm after the Battle of Marj Dâbiq. So, his father, the previous *Khalîfah* Mustamsik Billâh was appointed *khalîfah* as representative of his son in Egypt. When Sultân Selîm took over Cairo, he seated Mutawakkil whom he brought with him at his 'nominal' post. After his removal to İstanbul, Mutawakkil fell from favour because of his ethical conduct on the complaint of his cousins and was imprisoned in 925/1520. After Sultân Selîm's death, Süleymân the Magnificent allowed him and some others to return to Cairo. He died there afterwards: *OT*, II, pp. 293-294.

## Chapter Six – The Struggle for Islamic Unity

next morning. His action reminds us of that of the Holy Prophet ﷺ when Makkah was opened to Islam, when he leaned forward so much so that his beard almost touched the saddle of his mount. To be modest and not arrogant and rude at the time of success and victory is indeed a basic Islamic value.

Sultân Selîm initiated the practice of reciting the Noble Qur'ân around the clock at the quarters of *Emânât-ı Muqaddese* (the Holy Relics), which he built in the Topqapı Palace in İstanbul. He appointed forty *huffâz* (memorisers of the Noble Qur'ân) for this duty, and participated in person in reading the Qur'ân. This practice continued until the end of the Osmanlı Devlet.

### Naval Affairs

Sultân Selîm did not ignore the importance of navigation. While in Egypt, he received Selmân Reîs, the commander of the navy on the Red Sea during the Mamlûk Devlet. Then he was ordered to go to İstanbul. After returning from Egypt, Sultân Selîm constructed a dockyard at Khalich (the Golden Horn) and ordered 150 ships to be built in addition to the existing 150 ships. The Republic of Venice panicked and continued to pay the *kharâj* for Cyprus, fortified the island as a precaution and looked for allies in Europe also. On the other hand, Pope Leon X was preparing a new Crusade against the Osmanlı Devlet; he sent cardinals to Austria, France, England, and Spain to conclude an alliance against the Osmanlıs. Sultân Selîm paved the way for Spain to divert it from that attempted alliance, speaking to its ambassador who came to İstanbul in 1519 regarding the conditions for Christian visitors' to the Qamâme Church in Jerusalem. If the King of Spain wanted to conclude a peace treaty with him, he should send his delegate.[417]

### The Annexation of Crimea

In 880/1475 the Osmanlı Devlet took over some coastal areas and the city of Kefe from the Genoese who had established colonies there. Mengli Gıray was appointed Khân by Fâtih Sultân Mehemmed (1451-1481) at the request of the notables and *ulemâ* of Crimea. Sultân Selîm saw a strong rival in this northern Turkish khânate, for "it took their horsemen one day to cover a distance that would take the Osmanlı cavalry five or six days, while their horses did not need horseshoes, and their soldiers crossed dangerous rivers swimming with horses, whereas the Osmanlı soldiers would wait for a bridge or boats to do so, the Crimean soldiers lived on a very limited food, etc. ...."[418] Being a good diplomat as well, Sultân Selîm sent 20,000 *aqchas* to the Khân of Crimea Mengli Gıray, and 300 *aqchas* as salary to each of the notables, asking the Osmanlı standard to be flown and Mengli Gıray's son Sa'âdet Gıray to be sent to the Osmanlı palace to be educated (in fact as hostage). The notables opposed the offer, but Mengli Gıray (1478-1514), who was the khân for the third time, accepted it, saying to the notables: "The Sultân, knowing that my son Sa'âdet Gıray is very important to me, asks to have him educated to be better able to govern Crimea after me .... If we do not accept, he will come against us with a huge army with his artillery and guns, etc. ...." Thus, Crimea, along with its other parts, became part of the Osmanlı Devlet.[419] At that time, Crimea was strong enough to resist Russian expansion towards the south. But afterwards Russia became very strong and was supported by the European Christian powers. Therefore, this annexation protected Crimea from being swallowed by Russia for two and a half centuries. Beginning in the second half of the sixteenth century, Russia occupied all the khânates that emerged as heirs of the Kök Orda (Golden Horde), first the khânate of Qazan in 1552 and then others.[i]

---

i   The *Kök Orda* (Golden Horde; *Zolotai Orda*) was founded by Batu Khân (d. 1255-56), grandson of Genghis Khân. The people living in that khânate were mostly the great-grandchildren of Köktürks, Huns,

## Chapter Six – The Struggle for Islamic Unity

### The Knights of St. John (Knights Hospitallers)

Adam is the first man and the First Prophet at the same time. Throughout history Prophets were sent to humanity to call them to live according to the Creator's laws. In the Qur'ân the Natural Laws are called *sunnatullâh* – the Way of Allah in His directing affairs. Islam means "submission" (to the commands of Allah, the Creator), and whoever accepts those principles is a "Muslim – one who submits to the will of Allah, the Creator". Therefore, according to Islam, all the Prophets, beginning with Adam, and including Noah, İbrâhîm (Abraham), Ayyûb, Ya'qûb (Jakob), Yûsuf (Joseph), Shu'ayb, Mûsâ (Moses), Dâvûd (David), Suleymân (Solomon), Yûnus (Jonah), Zakariyyâ, Yahyâ (John), and İsâ (Jesus), peace be upon them all, were sent at specific times to their peoples to direct them to the Right Way, and *thus, they are all Muslims*. The Final Messenger Muhammad ﷺ *was sent to all humanity* to show them the Right Way and call them to it. The Qur'ân addresses all humanity. And whoever confesses "There is no god but Allah, and Muhammad is His Messenger" becomes a Muslim by definition.

What is called "Christianity" was distorted by later generations. The language Jesus ﷺ spoke was Aramaic. There is no extant gospel

---

Bulgars, and Qıpchaq Turks. The Khân, commanders, and notables were of Tatar descent. Because of the fact that the Turkish population was a large majority, the Tatars also were Turkified, as the name of its last khân, Toktamısh, indicates. When Emîr Timur defeated Toktamısh, who was preparing for a campaign to Lithuania in 1396, the *Kök Orda* was dismantled, and four khânates emerged in its lands as its heirs: Qazan, Qırım (Crimea), Astrakhan, and Qâsım (Sibir). The dismantling of the Kök Orda gave the Slavs (Russians) who were under its dominion a golden opportunity to develop and, in the course of time, with the support of the European powers, they destroyed all these Turkish khânates.

in Aramaic; the earliest ones are in ancient Greek. Distortion and addition was so common that the number of the writings called gospels amounted to 72, and in 325 C.E. at Nicaea there were 319, but the "Church fathers" accepted four of them: Matthew, Mark, Luke, and John, and in addition the letters claimed to have been written by the disciples and by Paul, who was not a disciple.

These followers of the previous phase of religion distorted the Message and called themselves "Christians", ignoring and refusing to accept the Final Message, and over the centuries struggled against it. This is a tragic event in human history, especially in modern times. Western civilisation emerged "despite" Christianity after the Renaissance (which wasn't Christian as such) and the Reformation (a major movement against Church establishment and authority). Westerners deceive themselves and others, presenting themselves as a Christian civilisation. The dilemma of the Western world is that there is huge material prosperity and much less spirituality and they design events, politics, social affairs, etc. without solving human problems; the human being is lost in contemporary civilisation.

Having been thoroughly brainwashed by the priests of the distorted previous message, and prejudiced against the new and final phase of the Message, Europeans invaded Jerusalem and parts of Bilâdu'sh-Shâm (Syria) during the Crusades. When Salâhu'd-Dîn al-Ayyûbî subsequently reopened these areas to the Final Heavenly Message, Islam, some of the Crusaders settled on the island of Rhodes. Young men coming from every part of Europe entered the military-religious order of Saint John, and that fanatic and narrow-minded group was called the Knights of St. John. Being extremely well-trained plunderers, they used to attack Muslim ships and lands from their base on Rhodes. When Sultân Selîm revealed his intention to attack Iran once again and eradicate Shî'ism once and for all, the *ulemâ* reminded him that "it was far better to open a Christian village and gain its people over to Islam than to capture a vast country."

## Chapter Six – The Struggle for Islamic Unity

The administrative body also kept on urging Sultân Selîm to open the island of Rhodes to Islam, but he replied, "I want to open many countries to Islam, and you wish to keep me busy with capturing a thieves' den."[420] Those people who were called the Knights of St. John were viewed by the Muslim leader as nothing more than thieves.

### The Death of Sultân Selîm

Sultân Selîm set out for Edirne in July 1520, but fell ill *en route*. While on his deathbed, he asked Hasan Jan to recite Yâ Sîn, which he did. Both of them started to recite the same *sûrah* again, and when they reached the *âyah* "*salâmun qawlan min Rabbin Rahîm – Peace! a word of salutation from a Lord Most Merciful*" (Yâ Sîn (36): 58), Sultân Selîm passed away peacefully in 926/September 1520.[421]

The objective of the earlier European expansion in the East was to gain a stranglehold on Muslims through active collaboration with the Mongols. But this time the rulers of India had embraced Islam, and Europeans became mainly interested in the spice trade. Thus the commercial factor outweighed the religious motive in the European drive in the Indian Ocean and the Far East. "The Portuguese trading influence in the East continued after Albuquerque's death, but the Portuguese monopoly on the Eastern trade was broken by Dutch and English competitors whose commercial interests were not eluded by thecrusadingmotive."[422]

Sultân Selîm, on the other hand, had wanted to go to India, but not for commercial purposes as such. He was of the strong conviction that the humiliating capture by Emîr Timur of his great-grandfather represented a stain "on our dynasty" that could be removed only by the conquest of India, then ruled by Timur's grandchildren. His grand *vazîr* advised against the conquest of this distant country, arguing that more than a century had elapsed since this event, and that the Osmanlı Devlet had actively rubbed out this stain by its great success in opening vast areas to Islam. But Sultân Selîm replied that his wish was to go to India through a canal at al-Suwaysh (Suez), thus connecting the Mediterranean with the Red Sea and the Indian Ocean.[i]

---

[i] *Netâyij*, I, p. 81. It is interesting to note that the Turkish *Devlet* of Timur's descendants in India is always referred to by Western historians and writers as Mughal (Mogul).

# Chapter Seven

# The Superpower of the World

## 7.1 QÂNÛNÎ SULTÂN SÜLEYMÂN (THE MAGNIFICENT) (1520-1566)

Shâhzâda Süleymân was called from Manisa to İstanbul to become the Osmanlı sultân. But Janberdi Gazâlî,[i] the governor of Bilâdu'sh-Shâm (Syria), took advantage of this transfer of power to revive the Mamlûk Devlet. He proclaimed himself ruler with the title of Melik Eshref (Most Honourable King), made the *khutbah* in his name and issued coinage (*sikkah*). He sent envoys to Shâh İsmâîl and to the governor of Egypt, Khayri Beğ, asking for collaboration. Khayri Beğ perceived that the task was impossible, though at the same time he felt that it was in his interest not to provoke the hostility of Janberdi Gazâlî. He, therefore, informed him that he would join the rebellion if Janberdi Gazâlî besieged Aleppo. Janberdi Gazâlî besieged Haleb (Aleppo) with 20,000 men, but he met with very strong resistance. Meanwhile, Shehsuvâroğlu Ali Beğ arrived and defeated Janberdi Gazâlî, and the third *vazîr* Ferhâd Pasha came with the cavalry of some *sanjaqs* in Anatolia and janissaries; Janberdi Gazâlî was defeated and his head was sent to İstanbul. Janberdi's

---

i   Janberdi Gazâlî was a freedman of Melik Eshref Qayıtbay and was among the influential *beğs* of the Mamlûks during the Qansu Gawri and Tomânbây administrations. He was pardoned through Khayri Beğ's mediation and was appointed *beğlerbeği* of Bilâdu'sh-Shâm and *sanjaqbeği* of Jerusalem and Gazze: *OT*, II, pp. 307-308.

quick defeat upset Shâh İsmâîl's plans: when he heard that Janberdi Gazâli was defeated, he left his capital Tabrîz and went to the district of Qazvin under the pretext of spending the summer there.[423]

### The Opening of Belgrade to Islam (927/1521)

"The conquest of the Balkans opened the way for a two-centuries-long world war against the powers of Europe."[424] The Danube was the border between the Osmanlı Devlet, which represented Islam, and Christendom. The northern part of it belonged to Christian Europe, and the southern part to Muslims. The castle at Belgrade, which had very strategic importance, was situated on the southern bank of the Danube, thus making its annexation a dire necessity. The Osmanlıs had besieged it twice before but could not capture it. Qânûnî Sultân Süleymân marched upon Belgrade, then under Hungarian domination and of vital strategic importance to the Osmanlıs. About 50 ships transported supplies via the Danube. Belgrade was besieged for a month until it was finally opened to Islam in 927/1521.[425] Its inhabitants were given full freedom to leave or stay in Belgrade or in any of the Osmanlı lands by paying *jizyah*.[i]

### The Opening of Rhodes to Islam (928/1522)

The island of Rhodes on the İstanbul-Egypt route had been a continuous source of nuisance for the Muslims. Bilâdu'sh-Shâm (Syria) was also an Osmanlı country; therefore, this island was a focal area of unrest among the Osmanlı lands. Moreover, the Christians

---

i  Pechûyî İbrâhîm, *Târîkh-i Pechûyî* (İstanbul: Enderûn kitabevi, 1980), I, p. 70; *OT*, II, p. 312: "There were elephants in the Osmanlı army during the Belgrade campaign. The *softas* (students) of *madrasahs* in Edirne, Filibe, and Sofya participated in this first *jihâd* campaign of Qânûnî. Beginning with this date, Belgrade became one of the most important bases of the Osmanlı army in Europe and was called *dâru'l-jihâd*.

## Chapter Seven – The Superpower of the World

who called themselves the Knights of St. John helped the Mamlûks against the Osmanlıs from their base there during the battle of Raydâniyyah.[426] These knights were engaged in robbing and sacking Muslim merchants and pilgrims. In short, the island of Rhodes, with its lands, strong fortifications and castle, was a Christian outpost. It became a dire necessity for the Osmanlı Devlet to open it to Islam and to put an end to the aggressive acts of those pirates.

Qânûnî Sultân Süleymân had a strong navy that was built by his father Sultân Selîm. *Donanma-yı Hümâyûn* blockaded the island. Sultân Süleymân left the Anatolian shore to go to the island. Many fighters from Europe came to the island to participate in the defence.[427] The castle was so strong and well fortified that it took the Osmanlıs six months to open it to Islam. The knights surrendered the island on these conditions:

1. The Christians who stayed on the island would enjoy full freedom in their religious rituals;
2. None of the Christian inhabitants of the island would be taken as *devshirme* (to be brought up as Muslim and become janissaries);
3. The inhabitants of the island would not pay tax for five years.
4. Whoever wanted would be free to leave the island within three years; the knights would be transported on Osmanlı ships to the port of Kandiye on Crete.

That the Knights of St. John left Rhodes to the Osmanlı Devlet this way shows their trust in the Osmanlıs and that the Devlet was reliable, and kept its promises;

*The former president of the USA Ronald Reagan receives 'decoration of Malta' because of his opposition to curetting.*

the knights had no doubt or anxiety about their security after the surrender.

Those Christian fighters who were conveyed to Europe according to the stipulations of surrender later went to Malta, made it into a fortified base and continued their struggle against the Turks and Islam from there.

In this confrontation the Osmanlı artillery proved its superiority over Europe.[428] The Osmanlıs also controlled İstanköy (Kos) and Bodrum castles; thus no European pirates were left on Anatolian soil. Qurdoğlu Muslihiddîn Reîs was appointed *sanjaqbeği* of Rhodes in 928/1522.[429] Meanwhile the Osmanlı Sultân sent Selmân Reîs to establish law and order in Yemen and Aden.[430]

Thus, security was ensured in the eastern Mediterranean, but, before long, the rebellion in Egypt hindered the Osmanlı sultân from directing his attention to Europe for a while. Khayri Beğ of Egypt had remained loyal to the Osmanlı Devlet when Janberdi Gazâlî revolted. When Khayri Beğ died in 828/1522, Vazîr Ahmed Pasha was appointed in his place. But this *vazîr* was disappointed that he did not become *sadrâzam*. Thus, in him the Mamlûks found someone to lead the rebellion. Ahmed Pasha appointed his trusted men to the critical posts in Egypt and proclaimed himself Sultân of Egypt in Rebî'ulevvel 930/January 1524 and minted coinage (*sikkah*) and had the *khutbah* said in his name as tokens of his authority. But the janissaries in the castle of Cairo did not support him; on the contrary, they opposed him, and his arrogance turned many people against him. He was killed the next year, even before any official action was taken against him.

Süleymân the Magnificent sent İbrâhîm Pasha to Egypt to settle affairs. İbrâhîm Pasha suppressed the rebels, killed some of the Mamlûks, and appointed some others to posts in other parts of the country. He released people who had been unable to pay their debts and had been imprisoned, paying their debts from the treasury of the *devlet*, saw to it that justice was done, and thus tried to gain the people for the *devlet*. He repaired the canals, decreased the amount of taxes to be paid, established *waqfs*. He established the *sâliyâne* order all over Egypt to prevent any rebellion in the future. Every year, revenue would be divided, one part would be sent to al-Haramayn ash-Sharîfayn, a certain amount would be sent to İstanbul, and the remaining amount to Egypt. The *beğlerbeği* would be checked by the *defterdâr*, *muftî*, and the *subashı*. Every kind of tax in Egypt would be collected by official tax collectors. The *tımar* system was not practised in Egypt. Soldiers in Egypt would receive their salaries from the treasury; any Egyptian entering the service of the *devlet* would be employed in another part of the Osmanlı domain.[431]

## Battle of Mohacs (932/1526)

In Christendom, the crown of St. Stephen was the symbol of superiority. It was preserved by King Louis of Hungary who was consequently recognised in Europe as the Holy Roman Emperor. But the King of France wanted to have it for himself, and hence war erupted between the two Christian monarchs. With the support of the Spaniards, the Hungarians defeated the French, whose king was obliged to take refuge in a well-fortified castle. From there he sent an ambassador to the Osmanlı Sultân, urging him to divert the attention of the king of Hungary so that he could take his revenge on the king of Spain. On the other hand, the Hungarians proposed a treaty with the Poles and the *voyvodas* of Wallachia and Bogdan. It was the last straw to include Wallachia and Bogdan, which were in the Osmanlı domain, in the alliance. The development upset the balance of power and influence in the region.

Thus, the Osmanlı sultân, Süleymân the Magnificent, decided to march upon Hungary, and sent *Vazîr-i A'zam* (the Grand Vazîr) İbrâhîm Pasha (1523-1536) at the head of an advance force. After visiting the tombs of Eyüb Sultân, Shaykh Ebû Vefâ, Fâtih, Bâyezîd, and Sultân Selîm for blessing, Sultân Süleymân marched towards Hungary with the main body of the *Ordu-yu Hümâyûn* under *Sanjaq-ı Sharîf* (the Prophet's Standard).[432] The Hungarian army, which included knights from Germany, Poland, Bohemia, Italy, and Spain, was waiting at Mohacs. The *Ordu-yu Hümâyûn* and the Sultân of Islam crossed the Sava and Drava rivers and arrived at Mohacs.[433] The Hungarian cavalry of 60,000 men in armour assaulted the centre of the Osmanlı army *(Ordu-yu Hümâyûn)* at Mohacs on 20 Zilka'de 932/29 August 1526. Contrary to its previous practice, the Osmanlı army had placed its artillery in the centre, instead of on the flanks, on the advice of the *sanjaqbeği* of Semendire, Bâli Beğ of the *aqınjıs*. The Hungarian forces concentrated on the centre, and 300 guns were fired at them. Bâli Beğ quickly manoeuvred with the *aqınjıs* and encircled the Christian army, which was defeated and dispersed in a two-hour battle. King Louis of Hungary was among the dead, and Buda, the capital of the Hungarian kingdom, surrendered without any resistance.[434]

The Osmanlı Devlet did not annex all of Hungary but took over important strategic castles. They annexed the regions in Bosnia under Hungarian dominion. The Osmanlıs were apparently obliged to fight these wars because the Christians were determined to drive them back from the Dardanelles to Anatolia, if not to eradicate them altogether. There is still a popular saying in Serbia today that says that "no Muslim will survive from the Adriatic to Iran."[435] Apart from the *jihâd* motive, the Osmanlıs had therefore to fight their wars in Europe for survival against the aggressive, combined Christian force. So the historical background for the tragedy of Bosnia in the twentieth century becomes clear: the Serbians are frustrated at having been "out of history" for almost five centuries, and the Christian powers, through what is called the United Nations, tied the Muslims' hands through embargoes and other "diplomatic tricks" while the Christian Serbs were left free to massacre them.

## Chapter Seven – The Superpower of the World

Süleymân the Magnificent himself had expressed this conviction to the Hungarian (Transylvanian) ambassador in İstanbul, whom he received after this victory, by saying "Christendom used to accumulate threatening clouds over my ancestors, but those clouds did not result in rain. If they (the Europeans) had not caused these battles, that bloodshed would not have been necessary."[436] Had Christendom minded its own business, the Osmanlıs most likely would not have gone so far and would have instead concentrated their efforts in the East with their Sunnî brothers in Turkestan, even India. The *aqıncı* (raider) Ali Beğ of the famous house of Mihaloğlu expressed the same feeling in his *gazavât-nâme* where he says:

*Eğer def' olmaz ise bu beliyye*

أكر دفع اولمز ايسه بو بليه

*Ne İznik kala, ne Qostantiniyye.*[437]

نه ازنیق قالا نه قونسطنطینیه

If this challenge is not repulsed,
    Neither Nicaea remains nor Constantinople (in our possession).

### The First Siege of Vienna (935/1529)

Hungary lost its independence as a consequence of the Battle of Mohacs. The death of King Louis with no heir left the country in chaos: two claimants to the throne emerged. The Hungarian nationalists supported John Zapolya (d. 1540), the *voyvoda* of Transylvania, and some notables of Hungary supported Ferdinand, King of Bohemia and Duke of Austria, brother of the Holy Roman Emperor Charles V and brother-in-law of Louis.

In 932/1526 Sultân Süleymân the Magnificent appointed Zapolya King of the Osmanlı part of Hungary on condition he be a vassal of the Osmanlı Devlet.[438] But Ferdinand claimed that the throne of Hungary belonged to him.[439] Zapolya had been chosen king of Hungary by a majority of the nobles at the Tokay Diet (16 September 1527). Ferdinand defeated Zapolya at Tokay (27 September 1527). In response to the Habsburg invasion, Zapolya made an agreement with the Osmanlıs (February 28th, 1528) in which he re-acknowledged the Sultân's suzerainty so that he could drive Ferdinand out. Süleymân the Magnificent preferred to leave an autonomous Hungary under Zapolya's rule to act as a buffer against the Habsburgs rather than commit the troops and resources that would be needed for direct occupation and control of the country.[440]

Süleymân the Magnificent marched on Hungary again, retook Budapest, and appointed Zapolya king in 935/1529.[441] The *Ordu-yu Hümâyûn* took the castle of Esztergom, and besieged Vienna itself. Meanwhile, the French king, Francis I (r. 1515-1547), was harassed by Charles V and asked the Osmanlı sultân for help. The siege of Vienna put Charles V in a difficult position, and was thus a great help for Francis I. The Osmanlı sultân had, however, intended to teach Charles V and Europe a lesson with this siege and not to capture Vienna itself. Had he planned this, Süleymân the Magnificent would have brought heavy siege guns with his army, and proceeded directly to Vienna to reach it two months earlier and open it to Islam. Finally, however, he lifted the siege in October 1529 and returned to İstanbul.[442] "But the siege of Vienna did have a number of important results. First, it secured Ottoman possession of Hungary as well as the new vassal relationship with Zapolya. Second, it left Austria and northern Hungary so ravaged that Ferdinand was incapable of launching a successful counter-attack. Third, it did, therefore, enforce the status quo, with Habsburg rule continuing in the northern and western border areas of Hungary while the rest of the country remained under autonomous native rule, thus continuing to serve as a buffer between the superpowers to the north and the south."[443]

*Chapter Seven – The Superpower of the World*

**The Third Campaign against Hungary (938/1532)**

Ferdinand, the brother of Charles V, wanted Hungary to be left to him and besieged Budapest again. Süleymân the Magnificent was able to recognise Charles V as "King of Spain" but his brother Ferdinand only as "Governor of Vienna". Therefore, upon Ferdinand's attack on Budapest, he proclaimed war on Charles V directly since it was not convenient for him to address a governor. Thus, he challenged Germany, Austria, and one of the two naval superpowers of Christianity at the time, Spain. The Osmanlı sultân led the *Ordu-yu Hümâyûn* to Hungary in 938/April 1532 and headed for the north-western part of the country, taking a number of castles. He challenged Charles V to a confrontation, but the latter disappeared in terror. Charles V was at the head of an army composed of many nationalities, but he did not dare meet the challenge. He took into consideration that, if defeated, he would be in a very difficult position. Süleymân the Magnificent sent reproachful letters to both Charles V and his brother Ferdinand for their failure to appear.[444] The aim of the Magnificent in this campaign was to defeat Charles V and to destroy his empire.[445] Sultân Süleymân returned to İstanbul in 939/1532.

Ferdinand was able to resist the Osmanlı Devlet only with the help of his brother, Charles V. The emperor preferred to busy himself in western Europe and advised his brother to come to terms with the Osmanlı Devlet. Ferdinand therefore applied to the Osmanlıs for a peace treaty. The Osmanlı Devlet accepted the request because of the fact that campaigns to Hungary were a huge burden on the treasury and led to neglecting eastern Anatolia. Tahmasb Khân of Iran, who had succeeded his father Shâh İsmâ'il upon the latter's death in 930/1524, was stirring up some unrest in eastern Anatolia. Consequently, a peace treaty was concluded by which Zapolya was confirmed king of some parts of Hungary while Ferdinand was allowed to rule the rest. Ferdinand would not trespass on Janos Zapolya's domains, and would pay 30,000 gold pieces yearly to the Osmanlı treasury for the part of Hungary that he ruled.[446]

While Süleymân the Magnificent was in Edirne, a committee sent by Emîr Râshid of Basra, including his son Mâni and Vazîr Mîr Muhammad, arrived and presented the keys of Basra to him, declaring the Emîr's obedience to the Osmanlı Sultân on 26 Safer 944/24 July 1538.[447] Emîr Râshid was appointed *beğlerbeği* of Basra; a *berât* to this effect, *tuğ*, and *sanjaq* as tokens of his post, were sent to him. Thus, Basra and the surrounding area were protected against the Portuguese threat and danger.[448]

### The Fourth Campaign against Hungary (948/1541)

Zapolya died in 947/1540, leaving an infant son named Istvan, and Ferdinand once more besieged Budapest. Sultân Süleymân the Magnificent therefore set out again for Hungary in 948/1541. Ferdinand's forces tried to flee, but they were surrounded and annihilated. Istvan was sent with his mother to Transylvania (Hungarian: Erdely), his father's centre, and that part of Hungary that was under Zapolya was annexed to the Osmanlıs. It was called Budin Beğlerbeyliği, and Süleymân Pasha of Hungarian descent was appointed its first *beğlerbeği*.[449] After the victory at Mohacs, a part of Hungary had been annexed, but Budapest had been left to Zapolya, who paid *kharâj*, because it was a great distance from İstanbul, so it would have been difficult to maintain and defend it. But when Zapolya died, Budapest was attached to the centre because by that time it was easy to keep it.

### The Fifth Campaign against Hungary (950/1543)

Ferdinand tried his luck again and besieged Budapest with a force of 80,000 men. But Sultân Süleymân set out for Hungary at the head of the *Ordu-yu Hümâyûn* again in 950/1543, and

*Chapter Seven – The Superpower of the World*

when Ferdinand learned of his approach, he retreated. The Osmanlıs annexed some castles.⁴⁵⁰

Ferdinand requested peace in 954/1547. He was allowed to rule part of Hungary in return for an annual sum of 30,000 ducats paid to the Osmanlı treasury. Charles V, the Pope, the Republic of Venice, and France also signed this peace treaty, which was concluded for the duration of five years.⁴⁵¹

While the *Ordu-yu Hümâyûn* was subsequently engaged in a war with Iran, Ferdinand violated the peace terms and assaulted Erdel in 958/1551. Qara Ahmed Pasha, the second *vazîr* in the Osmanlı *Dîvân-ı Hümâyûn*, fought back, and the war continued until 970/1562 and in it he annexed Timişoara after a 35-day siege. Since the Osmanlı sultân was preoccupied with heretical Iran then, he left (Osmanlı Europe) only the local Osmanlı forces and a small number of troops from İstanbul in Rumelia to cope with the situation in Hungary. By that time and upon the abdication of Charles V, Ferdinand became the Holy Roman Emperor (1558-1564). A peace treaty for the duration of eight years was concluded, by which Ferdinand relinquished Erdel (Transylvania).⁴⁵²

**The Campaign against al-Irâqayn and the Fath of Baghdad**

Shâh İsmâîl of Iran died in 930/1524, and his son Tahmasb (r. 1524-1576) succeeded to the throne. He continued his father's aggressive policies and sent ambassadors to secure the collaboration of Charles V and Ferdinand against the Osmanlıs. By that time the Osmanlıs had already concluded their peace with Ferdinand and hence sent Sadrâzam İbrâhîm Pasha (1523-1536) with an army against Iran in September 1553. The Osmanlıs took over the castles of Adiljevâz, Erjish, Van, and Ahlat and took back Tabrîz in 941/1534. Sultân Süleymân the Magnificent led another Osmanlı army and took Baghdad in 941/1534. He identified the burial place of Abû Hanîfah Nu'mân b. Thâbit and built a tomb and a beautiful mosque in memory of this great imam. Sultân Süleymân also ordered the repair and maintenance of the tomb of 'Abdulqâdir Gaylânî, the great sûfî Shaykh, and visited the tomb of Mûsâ al-Kâzim, a descendant of Hazrat 'Ali and one of the Twelve Imams, and the tombs of other great Muslims.[453] All these acts and others indicate the benevolent and accommodating characteristic of Osmanlı-Turkish Islam. Meanwhile, Qatîf and Bahrayn were annexed to the Osmanlı Devlet.[454]

The most gifted Turkish poet Fuzûlî hailed this visit to Baghdad in a sentence:

كلدي برج أوليايه بادشاه نامدار
*Geldi Burj-ı Evliyâya Pâdishâh-ı Nâmdâr*
The Famous Sultân came to the citadel of Awliyâ.[455]

But while the Osmanlı Devlet was busy suppressing these internal troubles in the Islamic world, the greatest Christian naval power of the time, Portugal, was making an attempt to surround Muslim lands. Abbâs Hamdani describes this situation as follows: "Between 1517 and 1519 the Ottomans took Egypt, Syria, and Yemen and established their sovereignty over Makkah. In 1534 they took Baghdad and in 1546 Basra. As a result, they came to control the Red Sea and the Persian Gulf and were thus able to block a Portuguese advance from the Indian Ocean northward to Makkah or Cairo. Our attention is thus now drawn to Ottoman interest in North Africa and in the West, which in a way, constitutes Islâm's response to the discovery of America."[456]

On the other hand, France, having been engaged in a conflict with the Austrian Empire, sought an alliance with the Osmanlı Devlet; it thus wanted the Osmanlıs to keep the Austrian Empire preoccupied in the east and get some relief. "Now a French ambassador, Jean de la Forêt, reached the Sultân as he was returning from Iraq to Azerbaijan in May 1535, conveying offers of joint action against the Habsburgs. A

## Chapter Seven – The Superpower of the World

trade agreement, subsequently called the Capitulations, was reached (18 February 1536). Soon both the French and the Ottomans moved to carry out the obligations of their alliance in a joint attack on Italy: the former by land from the north, the latter by sea from the south. ... Süleymân set out of İstanbul toward Albania, leading an army of 300,000 men from where the fleet was to transport them to Italy. At this crucial point, however, with a mighty Ottoman armada off the Albanian coast poised to join France in an invasion of Italy, the Sultân learned what many of his successors were to find out in later years: that infidel friends would abandon all agreements when it suited their interests in Europe to do so. Under papal pressure Charles V and Francis ended their conflict, so that Europe could unite against Islam."[i]

### The Campaign against Iran

The Safavîs eventually recaptured Tabrîz, but Baghdad remained in Osmanlı domains, and no treaty was concluded with Iran. Shâh Tahmasb's brother, Elkas Mirza, the governor of Shîrvân, fought for the throne and when he was defeated in 954/1547, took refuge with the Osmanlıs[457] who treated him very well. Upon his advice, Sultân

---

[i] Shaw, *op. cit.*, I, pp. 97-99. When Süleymân the Magnificent gave some privileges to French merchants, in return for the same for Muslim merchants in France, it did not affect the sovereignty of the Osmanlı Devlet, as the Osmanlı Devlet was *the* superpower in 1536. These privileges were called *imtiyâzât* امتيازات at that time. But, over time, these privileges became an unbearable burden on the *devlet*, and were afterwards called "capitulations."

Another point to be corrected is that the Osmanlı army did not leave İstanbul as a whole; *qapıqulu* soldiers, the nucleus only, started from İstanbul; the huge body joined in the form of separate *tımarlı* units on the way, at several points, similar to streams joining a river.

Süleymân set out at the head of the *Ordu-yu Hümâyûn* in 955/1548 to retrieve the territories captured by Tahmasb, and in fact retook the castle of Van.[458] The Second Vazîr, Ahmed Pasha, was sent in 956/1549 to Gürjistân (Georgia), where he opened fifteen castles to Islam and annexed part of the province.[459]

Shâh Tahmasb entered Osmanlı territory and attacked some castles. Süleymân the Magnificent set out once again for Iran at the head of the *Ordu-yu Hümâyûn* in 960/1553 but could not find him. The Osmanlıs entered Nahchevan, Revân (Erivan), and Qarabağ. When he returned to Anatolia, however, the Sultân spent the winter at Amasya, where he negotiated a peace treaty with Tahmasb's envoys in 962/1555 that was observed by both sides until Tahmasb's death in 1576. This treaty stipulated that Azerbaijan, its capital Tabrîz, eastern Anatolia, and Irâq-ı 'Arab were all made part of the Osmanlı domain.[460]

### Naval Activities

The Osmanlı Devlet, the superpower of the sixteenth century, was superior on sea as well as on land. The most able naval commander in the world in the sixteenth century was perhaps Hızır Hayreddîn Pasha (his enemies called him: Barbarossa). On 3 Jumâda'l-Ûlâ 945/28 September 1538 he defeated the allied Christian navy under the famous Admiral Andrea Doria at Preveza. His father, Yâqûb Sipâhî, was from Vardar Yenijesi, but he settled on the island of Midilli when it was opened to Islam in 866/1462. Yâqûb had four sons: İshâq, Oruch, Hızır, and İlyâs. Though he was a *sipâhî* (cavalryman), his four sons were fond of the sea and navigation.[461] It is interesting to note that they were incited to *jihâd* by the Knights of St. John who martyred İlyâs Reîs.[462] One of them, Oruch Reîs, had his base in the island of Jerba near Tunis and concluded, with his brother Hızır Reîs, an alliance with Abû 'Abdillâh Muhammad, the Hafsî Sultân of Tunis, by which they were allowed to make

## Chapter Seven – The Superpower of the World

their operational base in Tunis in return for paying to the Sultân, in accordance with the Islamic practice, *khumsu'l-ghanâim*, one-fifth of what they took from the unbelievers.[463] Subsequently, they carried out successful naval operations in 919/1513 and became very famous, so other volunteer Turkish naval *gâzis*, including seven *reîs*, joined them. Among those seven were Qurdoğlu Muslihuddîn Reîs and Muhyiddîn Reîs, the nephew of Kemâl Reîs.[464] Baba Oruch, as he was called by his *mujâhids*, and his brother Hızır Hayreddîn Reîs sent gifts via Muhyiddîn Reîs in 921/1515 to Sultân Selîm, who sent them two ships as a present in turn. By that time the Muslim Devlet*s* in North Africa were moribund, and Spain was determined to make all North Africa another Andalusia: in line with the *Reconquista*, the Muslims were either to become Catholics or face massacre. There were Hafsîs in Tunisia, Banû Zeyân in al-Jezâyir (Algeria), and Merînîs in Merrâkesh, all of them weak.

The *'ulamâ* and a group of notables from al-Jezâyir approached Oruch Reîs and Hızır Reîs for help against the Spaniards who had already captured and garrisoned Bijâyah (Bougie) in al-Jezâyir. The brothers fought the Spaniards gallantly, but they could not

*Süleymâniye Mosque, İstanbul, by Mi'mâr Sinân, the greatest Osmanlı architect*

rescue this Muslim city from Christian domination, though they did take the cities of Jîjel and Jezâyir (Algiers) in 922/1516.⁴⁶⁵ The Spaniards fled to Penon Island, just before Jezâyir, and appealed to Charles V for help. He sent a fleet to Jezâyir, but the Spaniards were unable to recapture it. Establishing himself in Jezâyir, Oruch Reîs tried to expand towards the interior and proclaimed his dominion over the city.⁴⁶⁶ Then the Spaniards incited the Emîr of Tlemcen (Tilimsân) against Oruch Reîs. The latter, learning of this plot, took over Tlemcen, but the Spaniards besieged him there. They were supported in this by the local Muslim people of the area who were too ignorant to know that they were fighting with a powerful Christian enemy against their co-religionist *gâzis*, who were there to prevent the transformation of Muslim North Africa into a Catholic Latin Africa, a second Andalusia. Nevertheless, Oruch Reîs forced his way out, crossed a river with the bulk of his followers, and was about to destroy the bridge on the river and reach safety. It was at this critical last moment that Spaniards reached the wounded *gâzis* who shouted "Baba" (Father) for rescue from the enemy. Oruch Reîs stopped and turned back to rescue his fellow *gâzis*, but they were all martyred there in 924/1518.⁴⁶⁷ He was forty-four years old when he was martyred, and his brother Hızır Hayreddîn became the ruler of al-Jezâyir.ⁱ Had Oruch Reîs been a selfish and cowardly commander, he could have reached his ships safely. Rather than saving his life, he preferred to sacrifice it in honour and respect along with his fellow *gâzis* who had fought many battles with him against the infidels.

i   *OT*, II, p. 367, footnote 2: "Gazi Oruch Beğ of Anatolia took over the city Jezâyir (Jazâir-i Garb Diyârı: Bilâdu Jezâyiri'l Garb) and was called Sultân Oruch in 916/1510. After his death, his brother Hayreddîn Beğ replaced him and, coming (to İstanbul) with twenty ships, he became the servant of Hân, the Sultân and *mîrimîrân* (*beğlerbeği*) of that province" (Atayi, p. 94).

## Chapter Seven – The Superpower of the World

How striking it is to compare this magnanimous and courageous behaviour with that of Napoleon Bonaparte, who deserted his army suffering from the cold in Russia, and fled in disgrace in a carriage back to France in 1812.

After Oruch Reîs' martyrdom, his brother, Hızır Hayreddîn Reîs, defeated a Spanish army of 20,000 men who attacked the city of Jezâyir. But he could foresee the imminent danger from the Christians and therefore asked the Osmanlı Devlet for help in 925/1519.[468] Although he had been a volunteer naval *gâzi* until then, Hızır was in the process of becoming an Osmanlı official. He therefore sent four ships with a number of captives and presents to İstanbul. In fact he planned to go in person but the notables, *'ulemâ*, and merchants of Jezâyir begged him to stay and protect them from the aggressive Christian superpower of the time, Spain. They also sent a letter to the Osmanlı Sultân in which they praised Oruch Reîs for his martyrdom and the efforts of his brother Hızır Hayreddîn Reîs in protecting them. They also mentioned that the latter stayed behind at their request.[469] Sultân Selîm, the Osmanlı Sultân, who was overwhelmed with joy, sent a *berât* in which he made Hızır Hayreddîn Reîs an emîr and sent him good supplies of equipment and a standard. He also offered him a jewelled sword, and allowed him to recruit as many volunteer naval *gâzis* as he wanted from Anatolia.[i] Thus, Jezâyir became an Osmanlı province in 925/1519,

---

i  Kâtib Chelebi, *Tuhfetu'l Kibâr fî Esfâri'l Bihâr*, pp. 32-33; OT, II pp. 338. Stanford Shaw claims: "There are some indications that the French actually had encouraged Hayreddîn to enter Süleymân's service in the hope that he would indeed divert the Habsburgs from the west" (*op. cit.*, p. 97). He does not, however, specify those alleged "indications." Furthermore, Hızır Hayreddîn Pasha had already entered Osmanlı service in the khalifate of Süleymân's father, Yavuz Sultan Selîm. The reason why he attached his previously independent province to the Osmanlı sultan's

though the infidels were still in control of a rocky island, Penon, in front of Jezâyir that had a fortified castle on it. They would fire rifles and guns that made holes in the minarets whenever *muezzins* recited the *ezân* in Jezâyir. Hayreddîn fought them, took over the island, and destroyed the castle. Then he filled in the sea in between, leaving a bay and connecting the rock to the mainland. Thus the Bay of Jezâyir came into existence. Nine vessels had been sent from Spain to the aid of the Spanish troops on the island. Once they realised that the island was in Muslim hands, they hurriedly turned back, but Hayreddîn captured them.[i]

> country is explicitly expressed in *Tuhfetu'l Kibâr* of Kâtib Chelebi (p. 32), where it is reported that he said to the Algerians: "Up to now I protected you, repaired your castle, and installed these 400 guns. From now on install whomever you want as *vâli* (governor); I am departing by sea." Upon this, all of them requested him to stay on. Hayreddîn Beğ replied: "The emirs of Tunis and Tlemcen are against us. If the *khutbah* and *sikkah* (tokens of sovereignty in Islamic tradition) are changed into the name of the Osmanlı family, I will stay." They agreed, and he sent presents to the Osmanlı sultan, Selîm, and joined Algeria to the Osmanlı Devlet. Hızır Hayreddîn Pasha fought to rescue North Africa from the Spanish Christians. If France had invaded Algeria, he would have fought them too. It was sheer necessity to join Algeria with the powerful Osmanlı Devlet against the Christian superpower Spain.

i  Kâtib Chelebi, *Tuhtfetu'l Kibâr*, p. 37. It is a common fact that in all Osmanlı chronicles the European enemies are called "*kâfir*," "*kuffâr* – unbelievers" their ethnic peculiarity having no importance at all. So here also we find (when the ships were taken) the statement: "apart from those who fell in the fight, two thousand and seven hundred *kâfirs* came out." While describing the social structure of Venice, which had been a major naval power of Christendom in the sixteenth century, Kâtib Chelebi explains the Doge as the head of Patricia and goes on: "it means duke.

## Chapter Seven – The Superpower of the World

Muslims who remained in Andalusia under Spanish rule were at first allowed to practise their worship. But Charles V (1519-1558) banned this and tortured them. Hence they took refuge in the mountains and requested Hayreddîn Beğ of Jezâyir to rescue them. He sent 36 ships that repelled the Spaniards and took the Muslims on board. One thousand *gâzis* stood on guard, and the ships made seven journeys that brought about 70,000 *mudajjals* (Andalusian Muslims) to Jezâyir province. Hence, most Algerians appear to be of Andalusian descent.[470]

At the invitation of Sultân Süleymân the Magnificent, Hayreddîn Beğ went to İstanbul in 940/1533 and reiterated his standing in the Osmanlı service. He was appointed *beğlerbeği* of Jezâyir (Algeria) province and Qaptân of Gelibolu.[471] On his way back from İstanbul, he attacked the Italian coast.

Meanwhile, there was struggle for power between Hasan the Hafsî Sultân of Tunis and his brother Rashîd.[i] Charles V and Hayreddîn Pasha fought over this unstable region; the former wanted to annex

---

Among the Christians, it is equal to the rank of *beğlerbeği* among the Muslims." So, as far as the Osmanlıs, their ruling cadres, intellectuals, and the Muslim people were concerned, there were two different worlds, the *Nasârâ* (Christians) and the Muslims. It is significant that a great intellectual, Kâtib Chelebi, refers to the rank of *beğlerbeği* as a Muslim rank and not a Turkish rank because of the simple reason that nationalism as an idea or political drive did not exist in those centuries, and the Osmanlı Turks represented Islam.

i  The Hafsî sultân, Abû 'Abdillâh Muhammad, died in 1525, and his son Hasan succeeded him. He killed 42 of his 44 brothers. Rashîd and 'Abdulmu'min fled and hid among the Bedouin (nomads). Hasan was so dissolute that the people of Tunis called Rashîd. But Hasan was informed and tried to capture him. Rashîd took refuge with Hızır Hayreddîn in the city of Jezâyir: *OT,* II, p. 372, footnote 2.

it to his Holy Roman Empire, and the latter wanted to annex this Muslim region to the Muslim Osmanlı Devlet. Hayreddîn Pasha took over Tunis. Hasan asked for Charles V's help; the latter prepared a navy of 500 vessels under the famous admiral Andrea Doria in 942/1535, and he came in person with an army of 25,000 men to Tunis. Hayreddîn Pasha resisted for a long time, but was unable to hold out against that very numerous army and was forced to withdraw from Tunis to the city of Jezâyir.[472] Hayreddîn Pasha then set out from Jezâyir and near Majorca caught the Spanish ships carrying Muslim captives from Tunis. He freed the Muslim captives and made the Christians prisoners of war, burnt their ships, attacked the Balearic Islands, and returned to İstanbul.[473]

Sultân Hasan, who captured Tunis with the help of the Spaniards, was deposed in 947/1540 by his son Ahmad. The Spaniards, who came with Ahmad, committed every kind of atrocity in Tunis and built a bastion on the shore where the Catholics planned to settle forever. It was very well fortified; their intention was to make the Tunis region another Andalusia, a Spanish-speaking Catholic country, all within the framework of the *Reconquista*. But the Osmanlı *mujâhids* finally came with a *donanma-yı hümâyûn* under Sinân Pasha in 982/1574 and captured Tunis. They left 4,000 janissaries to protect Tunisia. By 999/1591 the period of *dayıs*[i] (or *deys*) began,[474] and they were succeeded by a *beğ*, who collected tax twice a year.[475]

Pope Paul III was making great efforts to reconcile the Christian powers and unite them against the major Muslim power, the

---

i  *Dayı* has two meanings in Turkish: maternal uncle, and brave, gallant, or courageous. In Tunis and Jezâyir, the *de facto* leaders, called *dayı*, emerged from among the soldiers and ruled those provinces in the name of the Osmanlı Devlet. Power shifted in Tunisia from the *dayı* to a *beğ* in the course of time, but in Jezâyir the *dayıs* retained authority until the French occupation in 1830.

## Chapter Seven – The Superpower of the World

Osmanlıs. He succeeded in making Francis and Charles V sign a treaty for ten years, incited them against the Osmanlı Devlet, and the Republic of Venice joined this alliance.[476]

While Hızır Hayreddîn Pasha was at Preveza as *qapudân-ı deryâ* (the commander-in-chief of the *Donanmayı Hümâyûn*),[477] the allied Christian navy, which was composed of the navies of the Pope, Portugal, Spain, Venice, Genoa, Malta, and other European powers, set up a blockade. There were 302 vessels, 60,000 men, and 2,500 guns in the Christian navy. There were 122 ships, 8,000 *mujâhids*, and 166 guns in the Muslim navy. The vessels of the Muslim navy sailed in the form of a crescent. In the centre was Hızır Hayreddîn Pasha, on the right flank Sâlih Reîs, on the left flank Seydî Ali Reîs. In the rear were the volunteer naval *gâzis* under the command of Turgut Reîs. The Christian navy was under the command of Andrea Doria; Admiral Vincent Capello of the Venetian navy and Admiral Marco Grimani of the Papal Navy fought under his command. The Christian navy was arranged in three lines, turning their sides to the *Donanmayı Hümâyûn* to be able to fire their guns. The first line was composed of huge warships as a defensive front. The fact that the Christian navy outnumbered the Muslim navy in terms of ships, manpower, and ammunition but preferred a defensive fight, shows Andrea Doria's fear of Hızır Hayreddîn.

Hızır Hayreddîn Pasha split the combined Christian navy and outmanoeuvred them, making the Christian ships unable to communicate with one another. The Christian navy suffered such a severe defeat that Andrea Doria gave orders to extinguish the lights and retreated in disgrace. Indeed it was a shameful and dishonourable act at that time for an admiral to behave like this for the sole purpose of saving his life. With this historic Battle of Preveza on 3 Jumâda'l-Ûlâ 945/28 September 1538, naval superiority in the

Mediterranean was finally secured for the Osmanlıs.[i] In this naval battle the commanders of the navy of volunteers Turgut Reîs, Murâd Reîs, Sâlih Reîs, and Güzelce Kaptan gained great fame.[478]

Charles V attacked Jezâyir with a very large army in 948/1541 even bringing many horses on the ships.[479] But Hasan Pasha, the adopted son of Hızır Hayreddîn Pasha, defeated him.[480] Papal soldiers and the Knights of Malta (previously Rhodes) fought together with Charles V. Hernando Cortez, who had occupied Mexico and subdued its people cruelly was also in this defeated navy and narrowly escaped death. The Spanish navy lost 160 ships in this adventure.[481]

Since the Osmanlıs were supporting France against Charles V, Hayreddîn Pasha set out on the Mediterranean with 115 vessels in the spring of 950/1543; the French Ambassador Polen de Lagard was on board Hayreddîn Pasha's ship. When the navy reached Rechio near Naples, Jezâyir's navy of 41 ships joined them. They captured Rechio and some other places, and the *Donanma-yı Hümâyûn* came to Ostia, a port of Rome; the people there were astonished but were soon put at ease. The Muslim soldiers paid the price of whatever they bought in coastal cities in full. The *Donanma-yı Hümâyûn* was joined by the French vessels at Marseilles. They went to Nice, which had been captured by the Duke of Savoy, an ally of Charles V. They captured the city of Nice in 950 (20 August 1543). While the siege of the inner castle of Nice was in progress, the French artillery stopped firing, ostensibly because they ran short of gunpowder. Hızır

---

i   Yılmaz Öztuna, *op. cit.*, I, pp. 295-296. It is interesting to note that in many books written by Europeans the very important and crucial Battle of Preveza is either not mentioned at all (as if it did not happen!) or is seriously underestimated. See for example: Kinross, *op. cit.*, p. 226, and Dorothy M. Vaughan, *Europe and the Turk: A Pattern of Alliances 1350-1700* (Liverpool: 1954), p. 124. They, on the other hand, elaborate on the Christians' defeat of the Osmanlıs at Lepanto in 1571.

## Chapter Seven – The Superpower of the World

Hayreddîn Pasha commented sarcastically, "What nice warriors! They fill their ships with wine and do not forget anything except gunpowder!" Turning to the French ambassador, he scolded him, "Were you joking when you told us in İstanbul that your country had made good preparations?"[482]

The Muslim navy came to Toulon to spend the winter, and Hayreddîn Pasha sent envoys to Genoa to secure the release of Turgut Reîs who had been a prisoner of war there for three years. When the latter was freed, Hayreddîn Pasha said, in appreciation of this great admiral, "Turgut is better than me." Hayreddîn Pasha, however, then passed away in 953/1546, and was buried on the seashore at Beshiktash in İstanbul.

Turgut Reîs, son of a peasant named Velî, was born in Menteshe, Anatolia. As a volunteer naval *gâzi*,[483] he made progress and became a *reîs*. He adopted Mahdiyye (Mahdia) on the African coast as his naval base for operations against non-Muslim powers and opened Tripoli (in today's Libya) to Islam in 958/1551, capturing it from the pirates called the Knights of St. John. He joined the Osmanlı Devlet and was appointed *sanjaqbeği* of Qarlieli[484] and went to Preveza, the centre of his *sanjaq*. He inflicted another defeat on the famous Admiral Andrea Doria at Ponza in 959/1552.[i] In support of the French against Charles V, Turgut Reîs landed at Corsica, which was under the Genoese, the allies of Charles V. He defeated the enemy forces who came to the help of the island and captured the well-fortified castle on 7 Ramadân 960/17 August 1553.[485]

Turgut Pasha afterwards became Beğlerbeği of Trablusgarb (Tripoli)[486] in 961/1554 and hence made a serious attempt to recapture the island of Jerba from the Spaniards. An allied Christian navy of 200 vessels under the command of Andrea Doria tried to challenge

---

i  *OT*, II, p. 386. There is no mention of this famous Christian admiral's defeat in Kinross' book.

the Osmanlı position on this island. But the Osmanlı Devlet sent Piyâle Pasha in command of 200 vessels, and the famous Battle of Jerba followed, in which the Muslims inflicted a heavy blow on the Christian navy. Andrea Doria fled in disgrace with only seven ships. The island of Jerba was thus reopened to Islam, and Turgut Pasha was appointed to govern it with full discretion to use it as a naval base.[487] The castle of Jerba was captured on 7 Zulka'de 967/30 July 1560.[488]

*Tomb of Hızır Hayreddîn Pasha, Beshiktash, İstanbul*

The *Donanma-yı Hümâyûn* blockaded the island of Malta in 972/1565, the central stronghold of the Knights of St. John, and besieged the secondary castle there. On his arrival, Turgut Pasha opted to besiege the main castle but was martyred during the battle[489] and buried in his tomb at Tripoli next to his mosque and *madrasah*.[490]

### Osmanlı Activities in the Indian Ocean

Since Vasco da Gama's discovery of the Cape of Good Hope in 1498, the Portuguese dominated the Indian Ocean and sailed to India and the Far East by this new route. By then, the Portuguese had captured some strategic sites on the Red Sea facing the Indian Ocean, and consequently confronted the Osmanlıs in Basra, the Hejâz, and Yemen. Bahâdur Shâh, the Sultân of Gujarat on the Indian sub-continent, approached the Osmanlı Sultân in 942/1535 for help against the Portuguese.[491] The Osmanlı Devlet prepared a navy at the port of Suwaysh (Suez) under the command of Süleymân Pasha who conquered Aden in Yemen[492] and arrived at the island

## Chapter Seven – The Superpower of the World

of Diu in 944/1537. But he could not capture it and returned to Yemen because the Portuguese murdered Bahâdur Shâh and his son, Mahmûd Shâh, who was allied with them. After Süleymân Pasha's return to Egypt, the Portuguese entered the Red Sea and even tried to capture Jeddah.[493] But they were repulsed, thanks to the gallant resistance of the commander of the castle and the timely arrival of the emîr of Makkah, Sharîf Numey. Had the Portuguese captured Jeddah, they could probably have marched on Makkah and threatened the Holy Places. The Osmanlıs' success in stopping this danger is alone enough to justify their presence in the Hejâz and Yemen as well. This great Muslim power was not there for the sake of oil, which was discovered later in the 20th century, or for any other form of exploitation, but to defend al-Haramayn ash-Sharîfayn against Portuguese aggression in the sixteenth century and subsequent European Christian imperialist activities in the area.

The Portuguese tried in vain to burn the Osmanlı fleet at Suez, though they did manage to burn the town of Tûr Sînâ in 950/1543.[i] In fact, Portugal and Spain were the two Christian superpowers

---

i   *OT*, II, p. 397. The Osmanlı presence in the Arabian peninsula was to defend the Holy Places of Islam. That is why it was important for the Osmanlıs to control Bâbul Mendeb, to prevent European Christian powers from entering the Red Sea. On the other hand, the Europeans' reason was exploitation. For example, the British East Indian Company was influential in British policy in the East and was the actual force that came to conquer India, which had been a rich country. It was much later in 1858 when the British displaced the East India Company and declared the Empire. What has happened after British rule there can now be seen; the poverty of that country is a good example of the British legacy. It should be noted that there was no such entity as 'Osmanlı-Yemen Coffee Company'. Therefore, Western historians should stop seeing Osmanlı expansion as similar to or the same as the West's imperialistic activities.

of the sixteenth century, which is why the Pope divided the world between them. South America is a very good example of this fact: Brazil speaks Portuguese, while the rest speak Spanish, all having been converted to Catholicism. And they have become *Latin America*. The Osmanlı Devlet fought these Christian powers on the one hand and had to cope with Iran who attacked from behind on the other.

The Portuguese, who had converted the Indian Ocean into the "Portuguese Ocean," occupied Aden, but the Osmanlı admiral of Suez, Pîrî Reîs (1465-1554), recaptured the town and proceeded with a naval force of 30 vessels to capture Masqat (Muscat) in 958/1551 after a fierce battle against the Portuguese in which 70 of their vessels were involved. The Portuguese fled to Hurmuz (Hormuz) castle, which Pîrî Reîs could not capture, and subsequently went to Basra. Once he knew of the Portuguese intention to blockade the bay of Basra, Pîrî Reîs left for Suez in 1553 with three vessels and then to Cairo. Nonetheless, he was punished because of his failure to continue the siege of Hurmuz and for leaving some ships and soldiers behind when he left Basra.[494] The Osmanlı Devlet was in the habit of generously rewarding success but at the same time punishing failure severely – in itself a sign of a healthy administration – even when committed, as in this case, by top officials.

Pîrî Reîs was one of the greatest admirals of his age, and his map of 1513 locates the American continent. Abbâs Hamdani writes, "All this goes to show that at a very early date the Ottomans were aware of and interested in the discovery of the New World, marked on Piri's map as '*Vilayet Antilia.*' The term *vilâyat* usually applied to an administrative unit of the Ottoman Empire.[i] As the Ottomans were engaged in a counter-Crusade in the Indian Ocean and the

---

i The writer carelessly uses this word (empire) and the distorted form (Ottoman) to describe the Osmanlı Devlet presumably out of sheer habit.

## Chapter Seven – The Superpower of the World

Mediterranean Sea against those very powers who had discovered these new lands, they appeared ready to pursue their enemies into and perhaps across the Atlantic. I would maintain that the Ottoman interest in North Africa and their drive toward the western shores of the Maghrib are themselves evidence of the Porte's[i] intentions. If the Ottomans did not reach America, it is because they failed to gain the Atlantic coast."[495]

After Pîrî Reîs, Murâd Reîs, the former governor of Qatîf, was appointed *qapudân* of Suez. He left Basra and fought a large Portuguese fleet off Hurmuz. But he was obliged to return to Basra[496] as the Portuguese ships were designed for crossing oceans and thus too large and high for the Osmanlı ships to confront. Nevertheless, the Osmanlıs continued to fight the Portuguese whenever they found a chance to do so.

> "From 1557 to 1562 the Turks made various raids into Abyssinia from Suakin. In 1557 all communication between Ethiopia and India was cut off."[497]

Seydî Ali Reîs (d. 1562), who was appointed *kapudân* (admiral) of Suwaysh (Suez), sailed from Basra in 1554 with 15 vessels, and met a Portuguese fleet of 25 vessels en route. He defeated it and took four of its ships. He also crushed another Portuguese fleet at a battle in Masqat, in which some of the Portuguese ships sank and the rest fled in the darkness of night. Sultân Jalâlu'd-Dîn Dînâr helped the Muslims against the Portuguese.[498]

Meanwhile, a storm swept Seydî Ali Reîs to India where he gave guns and equipment to Rajab Khân, the governor of Surat under the Sultân of Gujarât. Seydî Ali Reîs was the guest of Hümâyûn, the

---

i (The Sublime) Porte (Bâb-ı Ali) was used for the Osmanlı administration in later centuries. In the sixteenth century it was called the *Dîvân-ı Hümâyûn*.

pâdishâh of India, for three months.[499] He left behind the Osmanlı soldiers who preferred to stay in India and returned home with 50 friends after a journey that took three years for them to reach İstanbul in 963/1556.[500] He presented his book *Mir'ât-ı Memâlik* (Mirror of the Countries) in which he related this journey to Sultân Süleymân.

Meanwhile, in 972/1565 Sultân Alâu'd-Dîn of Acheh (Aceh), Sumatra, and Malacca asked the Osmanlı Sultân for help against the Portuguese. He readily sent equipment and staff to the Sultân to build ships and produce guns. Qurdoğlu Hızır Reîs, who was appointed *kapudân* of Suwaysh, would, moreover, have set out for the East had not İmâm Mutahhar of the Zaydî sect staged a revolt in Yemen and consequently directed his attention there. The staff and equipment arrived in two ships at Acheh, and many of the men even decided to settle there with their Muslim brothers. This demonstrates the strong brotherhood between Muslims at that time, which is expressed by the Islamic principle "A Muslim's homeland is where Islam exists," and in the Noble Qur'ân: *"Believers are only Brothers"* (*al-Hujurât* (49):10.) Those Osmanlı sailors, who relinquished their kin and land and opted to stay for good with people whom they met for the first time, must have certainly felt that they were among their brothers.

> "The counter-Crusade against Portuguese Malacca followed naturally from the origin of the Atjehnese state. Sustained for 120 years, it linked religion and patriotism more closely than elsewhere in Indonesia, and brought Atjeh into greater contact with Western Asia. Sultân Ala'ad-Dîn Riayat Shâh al-Kahar (1537-71) took the formal step of submitting to the suzerainty of the Turkish Sultân in return for military assistance against the Portuguese. The memory of this shortlived connexion was kept vividly alive in Acheh by the

## Chapter Seven – The Superpower of the World

*Hızır Khayraddin Pasha and his Sailors*

red Ottoman Flag, variants of which the Sultâns used, and by the great cannon *lada sejupak* guarding the *dalam* (royal enclosure) in Banda Acheh. These were revered as gifts from the Caliph in token of his protection over his most distant vassals."[501]

**The Jihâd on Sigetvar**

The Sigetvar castle bordered Muslim territory and was a source of constant trouble for them.[502] The Khalîfah-Sultân was advanced in age, an eventuality that encouraged Austria to delay paying tribute to the Osmanlı Devlet. Hence, in spite of his poor health, Süleymân the Magnificent decided to go on a *jihâd* against this great Christian empire. While leaving İstanbul, the people prayed, "O Allah! help the Sultân of Islam and support the Muslims." The Muslim Army besieged the well-fortified Sigetvar castle where the defenders had abundant ammunition and provisions. Nevertheless, the Muslim Army conquered the outer castle in a few days, and set the inner castle on fire. The Croatian general, Ruzunjuk, fled and was killed while fleeing. The Muslims opened Sigetvar to Islam shouting "*Nasrun min Allah wa Fathun Qarîb*[503] – *Help from Allah and an Immediate Victory*". But the Khalîfah-Sultân passed away during the siege in 974/1566,[504] and Shâhzâda Selîm, the *sanjaqbeği* of Kütahya, became the Osmanlı sultân.[505]

It was said:

شهید راه حق سلطان سلیمان *Sheiyd-i râh-ı Haq Sultân Süleymân*
Martyr in the cause of Haqq (Allah) Sultân Süleymân

The numerical values (974) of the letters in the line indicate the date (according to Islamic Hegira) of his death.

Incidentally, Sultân Süleymân the Magnificent was a poet whose *makhlas* or pen name was 'Muhibbî'. The following are some of his famous lines that have been memorised by many over the centuries:

خلق اجنده معتبر بر نسنه یوق دولت کبی
اولمیه دولت جهانده بر نفس صحة کبی

*Halq ichinde muteber bir nesne yok Devlet gibi*
*Olmaya devlet jihânda bir nefes sihhat gibi*
There is nothing as valuable among the people as the Devlet[i]
There could be no *devlet* in this world equal to only a breath of health.

Süleymân the Magnificent was famous for his splendour and pomp. It was reported that during his childhood he visited his father, Selîm, in pompous and fancy dress. Selîm reacted sarcastically "O Süleymân, you have put on all these beautiful things, so what can your mother put on (what did you leave for her to put on)?" This pomp continued during the era of Selîm II and reached its zenith at the time of Murâd III. The *vazîrs*' job was to help the Sultâns under the supervision and direction of *vazîr-i a'zam*. Süleymân the Magnificent gave the inexperienced İbrâhîm Ağa an exceptional promotion to the rank of *vazîr-i a'zam*, and empowered him with almost unlimited authority.

Towards the end of his sultanate, he vested all the important affairs of the Devlet in Sadrâzam (*Vazîr-i A'zam*) Rüstem Pasha (1555-1561). His successor, Selîm II, confirmed Sokollu Mehmed

---

i   In Osmanlı Turkish *devlet* means sovereignty, prosperity, power, good standing, and felicity.

# Chapter Seven – The Superpower of the World

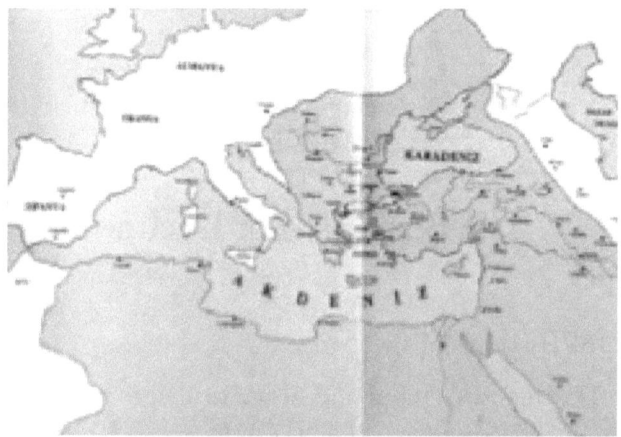

*Osmanlı borders at the death of Süleymân the Magnificent*

Pasha (1565-1579) as *sadrâzam* and gave him a free hand. But, with Sokollu's death, the manner and procedure of appointment to this post changed greatly. *Vazîrs* competed for the post through the presentation of precious gifts to the Sultân, his family, and his close friends. This led to intrigues, instability, and discontinuity that was detrimental to the Devlet.[506] Süleymân the Magnificent's deviation from the traditional method for appointing a *vazîr-i a'zam* was of particular harm to the structure of the Devlet.

# Chapter Eight

# The Beginning of Decline

## 8.1 SELÎM II (1566-1574)

Selîm II came to İstanbul and hence to Belgrade where he met the *Ordu-yu Hümâyûn* (The Heavenly Army) and received the *bay'at* (oath of allegiance) by which he was officially recognised as the Osmanlı Khalîfah-Sultân in 1566. In 1566 his father, Sultân Süleymân, on his way to Sigetvar, had sent Piyâle Pasha, Kapdân-ı Deryâ (1554-1568), at the head of the *Donanma-yı Hümâyûn* (The Heavenly Navy) to the Mediterranean. Piyâle Pasha opened the island of Sakız to Islam, taking it over from twelve Genoese notables who had failed to pay their due tribute to the Osmanlıs for the previous three consecutive years,[507] and had supported the Knights of St. John during the siege of Malta.[508] Selîm II consolidated his position, and envoys of some countries came to İstanbul to congratulate him, including the ambassador of the Austrian king. The peace treaty with Austria that had been infringed during the campaign of Sigetvar was renewed.[509]

### The Attempt to Build the Volga Canal (1569)

Ivan the Terrible of Moscow invaded Qazan in 1552. The Qazan Turks appealed to the Osmanlı government to dig a canal at the point where the Ten (Don) and İdil (Volga) rivers that flow into the Black Sea and the Hazar (Khazar or Caspian) Sea were nearest to each other (11.5 km).

## Chapter Eight – The Beginning of Decline

The Osmanlı *sadrâzam*, Sokollu, appointed Qâsım Pasha *beğlerbeği* of Kefe, and instructed him to initiate the project.[510]

D.E. Pitcher wrote the following about this project: "About 1560, the Turks began to realise the danger from Russia, and Süleymân conceived the bold plan of uniting the Don to the Volga by means of a canal. This was first mooted in 1563 and attempted by Sokollu Mehmed in 1569. It was a daring but not impossible scheme, which would have resulted in Turkish control of the lower Volga and the Caspian, and it would have provided a direct link with the Özbek enemies of Persia in Transoxania."[511]

This ambitious project showed that the Osmanlıs had great confidence in themselves and in their resources. Its implementation necessitated the capture of Astrakhan to keep the Russians out of the lower Volga basin and stationing a fleet in the Caspian through the new seaway to encircle the Caucasus and thus central Persia. Direct relations were also to be established with the khânates of Central Asia, and trade was to be revived along the route stretching from Khwarazm through Astrakhan to Crimea, which should be securely placed under Osmanlı control."[512] The Osmanlıs started work on this site, but they were unable to complete it.

Since the Osmanlıs had actually started digging this canal, this means that this area was under their dominion. But all Western maps place the Osmanlı border well south of this area, and exclude other Osmanlı territory in the Arabian Peninsula and Africa.

Sadrâzam Sokollu appointed unqualified staff for this job, and the Khân of Crimea, Devlet Gıray, was not enthusiastic about it because it would tighten Osmanlı control over his holdings. Being aware of the great potential Russian danger to their *devlet*, the Osmanlı administration used the Turks of Crimea very effectively against them. The semi-independent khans of Crimea were persuaded by the Osmanlıs to carry out frequent raids against Russia. Being excellent cavalrymen and masters of fighting, they raided Russia almost every week, even in winter, and had thus managed to keep it at bay for centuries.

## The Opening of Cyprus to Islam

The Eastern Mediterranean continued to be under Osmanlı sovereignty, but Cyprus represented a threat and nuisance to Osmanlı supremacy. Its pirates had even dared to seize a gift of horses sent by the *beğlerbeği* of Egypt to Selîm, then the *sanjaqbeği* of Qonya. In addition, Cyprus obstructed the pilgrimage route to Hejâz. Lala Mustafa Pasha and Piyâle Pasha were sent to deal with this threat. In 978/1570 they opened the capital, Lefqosha (Nicosia), to Islam while Girne (Kyrenia) and Baf (Paphos) surrendered. Having a very strong castle, Magosa (Famagusta) resisted for a while, but it was eventually opened to Islam in 979/1571.[513] This is expressed in a line:

الدي قبرس آطه سن شاه سليم

Aldı Kıbrıs adasın Shâh Selîm.
Shâh Selîm took the island of Cyprus.

The numerical values of the letters show the date: 978 (1571).

The Osmanlı administrative structure in Cyprus is described as follows: "The Ottomans reorganised Cyprus in accordance with their standard principles. The Latin Catholics who had formed the ruling class on the island were eliminated. The Greek Orthodox Church had its old privileges revived, and its property restored to it. Measures were taken to win over the local people and to develop economic and financial resources. The custom whereby serfs had to work two days a week for the landowners without pay was abolished. Large numbers of Turkish immigrants, 70,000 according to one calculation, were brought with their cattle and their implements from central Anatolia under the *sürgün* system of compulsory settlement, and settled on empty land in Cyprus."[514]

# Chapter Eight – The Beginning of Decline

## The Osmanlı Defeat at İnebahtı (Lepanto) (979/1571)

The Osmanlıs' annexation of Cyprus prompted the twelfth alliance of Christian powers against the Osmanlı Devlet. Papal, Spanish, and Venetian ships all assembled in 979/1571 against the Osmanlı Navy at İnebahtı (Lepanto) under the command of Don Juan, an illegitimate son of Charles V. The experienced sailor Uluch Alî Pasha suggested that the Osmanlı Navy should be on the defensive below the fortifications of İnebahtı, but Qaptân-i Deryâ Müezzinzâde Alî Pasha overruled him, and attacked the united Christian navy as instructed by İstanbul. Müezzinzâde, who was a very brave soldier but not a seaman, was martyred in the battle, and the Osmanlı navy was utterly defeated in 979/1571. Nevertheless, from his position as commander of the right flank of the Osmanlı navy, Uluch Alî Pasha attacked the left flank of the enemy navy and dispersed its vessels, capturing the flagship of the Knights of St. John. He was thus promoted to *qaptân-i deryâ* of the Osmanlı navy and named Qılıch (Sword) Alî Pasha. Europeans wishfully thought that the paralyzed Osmanlı navy would cease to operate effectively for at least a few years to come. But the Osmanlıs constructed more than two hundred vessels during the winter, and their navy was ready for combat next year. The Osmanlı Sadrâzam, Sokollu Mehmed Pasha, told the Venetian ambassador, Barbaro: "You see that the defeat at Lepanto did not discourage us, and there is a difference between your loss and ours; we captured a country (Cyprus) from you – thus, cut your arm, and you defeated our navy thus shaved our beard. – You cannot replace an arm, but a shaved beard grows even more thickly."[515]

Venice, a great naval power of that time, therefore deserted her allies and signed a peace treaty with the Osmanlı Devlet by which it recognised Osmanlı sovereignty over Cyprus and agreed to continue paying them an annual sum of 300,000 florins, which they had been paying since the time of Süleymân the Magnificent.

### The Attempt to Build the Suez Canal (980/1572)

The Osmanlıs sent equipment from Suwaysh (Suez) to the Sultân of Acheh. The Portuguese, who were in control of the Indian Ocean, seriously obstructed the pilgrimage from the East to Makkah. Being the spokesman of the Muslims and the protector of their Holy Land, the Osmanlı Devlet felt that the best means for securing the *hajj* route against Portuguese aggression would be by digging a canal at Suwaysh to connect the Mediterranean with the Red Sea, thus conveying the *Donanma-yı Hümâyûn* from the Mediterranean to the Red Sea and the Indian Ocean to fight the Portuguese there. The *beğlerbeği* of Egypt was instructed in 1568 to prepare a feasibility study that would show in particular the distance between the two spots, and the suitability of the soil for this venture. It is true that the Osmanlıs were unable to fulfil this plan, but their attempt to do this reveals their serious attitude and sense of responsibility towards all Muslims in the world, including those living in the Far East. While the Portuguese intervention in the affairs of the countries of the Far East was dictated by colonial ambitions, the Osmanlıs, on the contrary, wanted to carry out one of the essential duties of the khalifate, namely protecting the security of the Muslims in that part of the world and their *hajj* route against Portuguese aggression.

### The Annexation of Tunisia

Immediately after the conclusion of the peace treaty with Venice in 1573, the Osmanlıs sent Vazîr Sinân Pasha (1520? -1596) to Tunisia to break the Sicily-Malta-Tunisia triangle that separated Jezâyir from the rest of the Osmanlı territories in the East. Don Juan, the admiral of the Christian navy at Lepanto, exploited the contest between the members of the Hafsî ruling family by arriving with 90 ships on the shores of Africa, while Haydar Pasha, the *beğlerbeği* of Tunisia,[516] retreated to Qayravan (Kairouan). Rather than installing Ahmed as

## Chapter Eight – The Beginning of Decline

Hafsî sovereign of Tunisia, Don Juan exiled him together with his children to Naples and appointed his brother, Mevlây Muhammed, to this post in 980/1572. He left a group of Spanish soldiers in Tunisia.[517] A combined Muslim force of 300 vessels commanded by Vazîr Sinân Pasha, Qaptân-ı Derya Qılıch Alî Pasha, and the *beğlerbeği* of Jezâyir drove the Spaniards out in 982/1574, and thus saved Tunis from becoming a colony of Spain, i.e. the Holy Roman Empire of Charles V, which was then the most powerful Christian power in the world.[518] Had not the Osmanlı Devlet and the freelance volunteer naval *gâzis* done this, North Africa would have become a "Latin Africa" like "Latin America" as early as the sixteenth century. The Spaniards and the Portuguese imperialists had then seriously embarked on "Latinising" South America (i.e. Catholicising it, imposing their Catholic religion, language, and culture). While nobody came to the defence of the unlucky indigenous people of America, the North African people were fortunate to find this in the gallant Osmanlıs. Thus the Muslim Arab population of North Africa owe their distinctive presence there largely to the Osmanlıs. Otherwise, Jezâyir, Tunis, and Trablusgarb (Libya) would have shared the same fate as Andalusia (Spain and Portugal). The same applies to Fas (Fez – Maghrib), which was saved by the Battle of Vâdi's Seyl (986/1578) from being incorporated in the Catholic-Portuguese orbit like Brazil was.

Sultân Selîm II passed away in 972/1574.[519] His mother was Hurrem Sultân (Roxelana). Of Slav origin and a convert to Islam, she had conspired to get rid of the two better qualified *shâhzâdas*, Mustafa and Bâyezîd, so that her incapable and weak son would succeed Süleymân the Magnificent. Nevertheless, the Osmanlı momentum was so strong that the *devlet* continued during the time of Selîm II to fulfil its heavenly mission and opened new lands to Islam. Like his grandfather Sultân Selîm I, Selîm II loved Edirne and built his famous mosque, the Selîmiyye, there. This mosque and

*Selimiye Mosque, Edirne*

its complex (compound and *kulliyyah*) were built by the architect genius Sinan. Indeed, they are masterpieces of Osmanlı architecture.

## 8.2 SULTÂN MURÂD III (1574-1595)

Shâhzâda Murâd, the *sanjaqbeği* of Manisa, assumed the Osmanlı Sultanate and khalifate in İstanbul in 962/1574.[520]

### Relations with the Sultanate of Fes (Maghrib)

The Sa'dî Sharîfs continued to rule Fes in active collaboration with Spain, but when the latter became weaker they sought an alliance with Portugal. Rivalry and intrigue soon became evident among the ruling family, and the throne of Mevlây Muhammad was seriously contested by his uncle 'Abdulmelik. The latter appealed for Osmanlı support, and Muhammad was therefore driven into the hands of the Portuguese King, Sebastian. The Osmanlıs ordered Ramadân Pasha, the *beğlerbeği* of Jezâyir, to help 'Abdulmelik, while Sebastian himself came to the support of Muhammad at the head of a Christian army of 80,000 that was equipped with 300 guns. The Muslim forces of the Osmanlıs and 'Abdulmelik routed Sebastian at the Battle of Vâdi's Seyl in 986/1578.⁵²¹ 'Abdulmelik became the Sultân of Maghrib but died shortly after this victory. Sebastian was also drowned while fleeing. He left no sons, and his brother Henry assumed the throne of Portugal, though Philip II, the King of Spain, took it over in 988/1580.⁵²² If the Portuguese had defeated 'Abdulmelik and the Osmanlıs, Maghrib would have also become another Brazil, a Portuguese-speaking Catholic country.

Towards the end of the sixteenth century the Osmanlı Devlet was still vital enough to secure adequate naval strength for the defence of its long coastal territories, though not enough for any future confrontation with the Spanish and the Portuguese across the Strait of Gibraltar. "Spain and Portugal on their part got involved in the defence of their far-flung Empire and trade against new challengers such as England, Holland, and France. Prester John and the Great Khân had served their utopian purpose. Gold, slaves, and spices, as well as colonization in the newly-discovered lands, were now more important than Crusades against the Muslims. In the age of the East India companies, the recovery of Jerusalem faded as the prime motivating factor in their political activity. Yet the memory of those days still lingers in such American place-names as Matamoros (St. James, "the Moor-Killer")."⁵²³

**War with Iran (Persia)**

The death of Tahmasb, the Shâh of Iran, in 982/1574 was followed by a struggle for power that finally ended in the ascension of his son İsmâil II to the throne. Proclaiming that he was a Sunni, İsmâil killed a number of Shî'a shâhzâdas and notables. The life of Hudâbende, the almost blind *shâhzâda*, was saved, however, on compassionate grounds. İsmâil II breached the peace that was concluded between his father and the Osmanlıs and won over some *beğs* in eastern Anatolia. But he died or was killed in 985/1577⁵²⁴ and the time of his extravagant successor, Hudâbende, was characterised by tumult and disturbance in Iran. Husrev Pasha, the Osmanlı *beğlerbeği* of Erzurum, urged İstanbul that the time was very opportune for an attempt to annex some parts of Iran. Lala Mustafa Pasha marched on Iran in 985/1577, defeated the Iranian army at the Battle of Childir, and captured a number of Safavî notables and officers.[525] He advanced and took over Tiflis (Tbilisi) and Shirvân in 986/1578 while Özdemiroğlu Osman Pasha took over Dağıstan.[526] Ferhâd Pasha conquered Revân in 991/1583, and the Osmanlı army continued its campaign under Özdemiroğlu Osman Pasha until it took over the capital, Tabrîz, in 922/1584. Meanwhile, Abbâs Mirzâ (r. 1587-1629) became shâh, and the Sunnî Özbeks attacked Iran from the East. Faced with successive humiliating defeats, Iran was finally compelled to conclude a peace treaty with the Osmanlıs in 998/1590. The İstanbul treaty stipulated that Azerbayjân would remain under Osmanlı sovereignty, and the Shâh promised to stop the campaign of abuse and insult in Iran against Abû Bakr, Umar, and Aisha ﷺ.[527]

### War with Austria

An eight-year peace treaty was concluded in 972/1565 between the Osmanlı Devlet and Austria that stipulated the possibility of its renewal in future. Nevertheless, the commanders of the boundary on either side never failed to find excuses for skirmishes and other acts of hostility. The treaty was, however, renewed in 998/1590 for another eight years, though Austria did not pay the required tribute and incited the *voyvodas* of Eflak (Wallachia) and Bogdan to rebel against their suzerains, the Osmanlıs. In retaliation, Telli Hasan Pasha, the *vâli* of Bosnia, raided Austria three times, but he and many of his able commanders and soldiers were martyred in 1001/1593 during one of these *aqıns* (raids) in which a bridge collapsed.[528] After this tragedy, the Osmanlıs declared war on Austria, and Sadrâzam Sinân Pasha achieved some success in this campaign. After spending

## Chapter Eight – The Beginning of Decline

the winter in Belgrade, he set out again the next year, and the Khân of Crimea, Gâzi Gıray, came to his support with 40,000 cavalry. Muslim forces annexed the castle of Yanıkkale[529] (Raab) that was located between Budin (Budapest) and Vienna, and captured a lot of equipment. Faced with this serious Muslim threat, the Holy Roman Emperor and Archduke of Austria, Rudolf II, the King of Erdel and the *voyvodas* of Eflak and Bogdan concluded a treaty in 1003/1595 against the Osmanlıs. Since both these *voyvodas* were within the Osmanlı domain, their alliance with the Christian enemy was a real blow to the authority and prestige of the Osmanlıs that had to be dealt with immediately. While the Osmanlıs were engaged in subduing this rebellion, the Austrians were, however, successful in some areas of the conflict. But the *voyvoda* of Eflak was defeated and compelled to flee to Erdel. Hence, the Osmanlı army annexed both Bukresh (Bucharest) and Tirgovishte. On his way back, Sinân Pasha imposed taxes on the captive soldiers that were collected on a bridge on the Danube. Only those who paid were allowed to cross the river to the south. But the engagement of the Osmanlı army in this activity weakened it and enabled Mikhail to attack in 1595. The *aqınjıs*, who were still on the left shore of the river, had, however, fought courageously, and many of them were martyred in the battlefield while the Muslim army suffered other heavy casualties. This severe blow led to the virtual end of the *aqınjıs*[530] and the castle of Estergon (Esztergom) was captured by the Austrians as well.[531]

Just before his death in 1003/1595 Sultân Murâd III organised a fabulous festival on the occasion of the circumcision of his son Mehemmed[532] that lasted for 40 days. On his initiation, the entertainers at this festival requested that they be incorporated into the janissary corps as a reward. But the *yenicheri ağası* (commander-in-chief of this force), Ferhâd, refused to implement this ridiculous command and resigned in protest. His successor, Yûsuf, however, complied with this absurdity, which constituted a significant step towards the corruption of the janissary organisation. Until that time successive Osmanlı sultâns were very keen on keeping this force aloof and intact. Süleymân the Magnificent was, for example, furious to know that a member of this force repaired his silver bit that had broken during the *jihâd* of Sigetvar: he could not imagine that an artisan or tradesman could possibly be part of this *mujâhid* force and therefore immediately dismissed him and put him on a pension.[533]

## 8.3 SULTÂN MEHEMMED III (1595-1603)

On the insistence of the janissaries, Sultân Mehemmed III set out in 1004/1596 in command of the *Ordu-yu Hümâyûn*. He was accompanied by Sa'deddîn Efendi (1536-1599), the famous historian and author of *Tâju't Tevârîh* (The Crown of the Histories), teacher of the Sultân as well as of his father, Murâd III.

### The Opening of Eğri Castle to Islam 1004/1596

The *Ordu-yu Hümâyûn* arrived at Segedin where it became aware of the Austrian siege of the Osmanlı castle of Hatvan. A force was immediately dispatched, but the castle fell into the enemy's hand before its arrival. The Osmanlı army, however, besieged another castle, the castle of Eğri (Agriş), and the Sultân, like *Khalîfah* Umar b. Khattâb before him, sent an ultimatum to the enemy: that either they accept Islam or surrender and leave under safe conduct with their possessions. Otherwise they would face battle.[534] The Austrians decided to fight, and the Osmanlı Army recaptured the castle in 1005/1596.[535]

### The Battle of Hachova (Keresztes or Mezőkeresztes) 1005/1596

When the *Ordu-yu Hümâyûn* arrived at Hachova, it met a Christian force of 300,000 men commanded by Archduke Maximillian, brother of the Holy Roman Emperor. This army included Austrian, Hungarian, Spaniard, Czech, Polish, Florentine, Erdel, and papal

## Chapter Eight – The Beginning of Decline

troops, and had 100 guns. According to an eyewitness, the famous Osmanlı historian, Pechûyî İbrâhîm, the Osmanlı army consisted of 100,000 soldiers.[536] On the second day of the battle the Austrians attacked the centre of the Osmanlı army fiercely, confusing it, and its soldiers were dispersed, and many of the janissaries and *sipâhîs* fled. It was, to quote Na'îma, the same position in which the Muslims had found themselves at the time of the Battle of Trench in 5/627, which was described in the Qur'ân *"And the hearts gaped up to the throats"*[537] (*al Ahzâb* [33] *âyat*: 101). Sultân Mehemmed III was on horseback, wearing the *burde* of Hz. Muhammad ﷺ under Sanjaq-ı Sharîf (The Honourable Banner of the Prophet ﷺ). Sa'deddîn Efendi (1536-1599) held the reigns of the Sultân's horse tightly and told him: "O my Sultân! It is right that you hold your place firmly; it is war, and most of the battles in your ancestors' times took place that way, and *inshâ Allâh*, by the miracle of the Muhammad, peace be with him, the victory will be for the Muslims, be cheered." Sa'deddîn Efendi kept reminding the Sultân that "victory is achieved through endurance" and recited from the Qur'ân:

*Inna ma'al 'usri yusran*
*"Verily, with every difficulty there is relief."*[538]
(*al Inshirâh* [94] *âyat* 6)

The Austrian soldiers entered the Osmanlı headquarters and plundered it. But the cooks, woodchoppers, and other servants of the *Ordu-yu Hümâyûn* managed to attack with axes and to disperse the enemy in terror. They shouted often: *"Kâfir kachdı* – the *kâfir*, unbelievers, fled." This courageous act incited the Osmanlı soldiers to return and they defeated the Austrians in October 1596 and captured 95 of the enemy guns.[539] Sultân Mehemmed III then returned to İstanbul, and the Osmanlıs did not use this great victory to achieve any further advance. Pechûyî, an eyewitness of this battle, wrote: "It was almost certain that if the Sultân had spent that winter at Budin or Belgrade and had renewed the attack on the Austrians, it would have been possible to capture all the territory up to Vienna and conclude a peace treaty on very good conditions. But, the army returned to İstanbul. And there was leniency about war affairs, so the enemy utilised the opportunity to make up for the losses and madepreparations."[540]

Sadrazam İbrâhîm Pasha, together with Hasan Pasha, besieged the castle of Kanije (Nagykanizsa), which surrendered. But the Osmanlıs had magnanimously led its occupants to safety and allocated 200 camels to carry their property, including cradles and chicken crates.[541] Hasan Pasha was appointed *beğlerbeği* in 1600 and was left behind ascustodianofKanije.[542]

### The Siege of Kanije by the Christians

The next year, with a very large army, Archduke Ferdinand besieged the castle of Kanije that had, along with the surrounding lands, been made a *waqf* for al-Medînah al-Munawwarah.[543] Being the representative of the khalifate, the Osmanlıs frequently assigned large allocations to the *waqfs* of the sacred places of Islam.

Tiryâkî Hasan Pasha wisely played the Austrians off against the Hungarians. Consequently, their relations deteriorated and the Hungarians left the battlefield altogether and returned home. But Archduke Matyas, who had captured İstoni Belgrade from the Muslims, joined the besieging forces. Though the defenders of Kanije castle only numbered 4,000, Tiryâkî Hasan Pasha inflicted several blows on the besiegers, who lost 18,000 soldiers. The Pope's brother was wounded there and succumbed to his wounds. Hasan Pasha waged another daring raid on 18 October 1601 in which he captured 45 guns.[544] Archduke Ferdinand made another futile attack in which he lost another 30,000 soldiers, and finally fled in

## Chapter Eight – The Beginning of Decline

disgrace with 100 of his men, leaving his treasure and equipment on the battlefield. But the Osmanlıs had by then learnt from the bitter lesson the enemy taught them at Hachova, where its greed for the booty turned its initial victory into a crushing defeat. Hence Hasan Pasha firmly ordered the *gâzis* not to touch anything before the complete withdrawal of the enemy from the scene. Their respect for their leader was clearly demonstrated by their strict adherence to this directive. They even waited for the arrival of Hasan Pasha the next day to distribute the *ganîmet* to them. Finally, Hasan Pasha entered the great tent of Ferdinand, prayed two cycles of the *shukr* prayer, and shed tears of gratitude to Allah Almighty for this great victory. He struck the middle of Ferdinand's throne with his sword, and then sat upon it. He then summoned the first seven *mujâhids* who had entered the tent of Archduke, and said to them: "Everything, except for the throne and ammunition in this tent, belongs to you." The *ganîmet* they had was so large it took two months to convey it (guns, rifles, ammunition, and other wares) to Kanije Castle.[545] Tiryâkî Hasan Pasha was promoted to the rank of *vazîr*, and other instrumental persons in the achievement of this victory were also generously rewarded.[546]

The Osmanlı sultân, the *khalîfah* of the Muslims, sent the following *Khatt-ı Hümâyûn* (Heavenly Decree) to Hasan Pasha and the defenders of Kanije castle: "Praise be to Allah who preferred us to many of His believing slaves and gave us the keys to the affairs of the Muslims, and greetings to the Master of the Prophets. You are the *beğlerbeği* of Kanije and my experienced servant and thoughtful Vazîr Hasan Pasha. In this year of good omen, the Ummat of Muhammad has been supported by the Heavenly Help, and the service that you have rendered has been presented to the higher threshold, your relentless effort has been appreciated and your name has been inscribed among the notables. I wish you prosperity. I gave you rank of *vazîr* ..."[547]

Mikhail, the rebel *voyvoda* of Eflak had then realised that he could not resist the Osmanlı attacks and therefore fled to Erdel. But he was executed in 1010/1601 by Basta, the Austrian commander who saw his ambitions regarding Erdel.[548]

### External Relations

At that time the Osmanlıs received tribute from neighbouring countries. Venice paid tribute for the lands that it had near Osmanlı territory, while the Austrians paid 30,000 gold ducats yearly. They also gave presents to the commander of the Osmanlı Estergon castle, the governor of Budin, the *qâdi* of Budin, and the notables of the Osmanlı Devlet as well.

Poland had tried in vain more than once to incite the *voyvodas* of Bogdan against the Osmanlıs, but was itself finally plundered by the Osmanlıs and the cavalry of Crimea. Hence the Poles undertook to pay tribute to the Osmanlı Devlet as well as to the Khanate of Crimea. Conspicuously, this extraordinary event is not mentioned at all in Lord Kinross' book.

Russia did not have any significant relations with the Osmanlı Devlet in the sixteenth century, though the Russians sometimes fought the Khanate of Crimea and paid tribute to it. Eventually they invaded all the territories of the Qazan Khanate.

During the time of Süleymân the Magnificent, both the Austrians and the Spaniards were hostile to France, and the Osmanlı Devlet concluded a treaty with France against them.[549] While at the peak of its strength during the time of Süleymân the Magnificent, the Osmanlı Devlet used its influence and prestige to secure the release of Francis I, the French king, from imprisonment by Charles V. To prop up the French against their common enemies, Sultân Süleymân granted them some trade arrangements that exempted French merchants from paying anything in addition to customs tax, and gave them the right to settle their disputes by their own consuls.

They were also given the right to use interpreters, while all the cases that involved more than 44,000 *akcha* were to be dealt with before the *qâdıasker*.[550] These privileges did not have any serious impact on the strong Osmanlı Devlet of the sixteenth century but in the course of time caused great injustice and embarrassments, and even came to be known as *capitulations*.

### The Second Phase of the War with Iran (1603-1612)

The war between the Osmanlıs and the Austrians had been going on since 1001/1593, and the Osmanlı Devlet was also busy subduing some internal revolts. Shâh Abbâs (1586-1628) of Iran used these circumstances[551] to meet with Sir Antoine Shirley, one of the lieutenants of the Count of Essex who was then in Iran, and sent ambassadors to Europe in 1599 to conclude a treaty against the Osmanlı Devlet. He gave Shirley, who accompanied these envoys, letters addressed to the Pope, the Holy Roman Emperor, the queen of England, the kings of France and Poland, and the President of the Republic of Venice.[552] It was even reported that the Shâh wore a cross "under his shirt and round his neck, in token of the reverence and honour which he bears towards Jesus Christ."[553] Abbâs remained a Moslem, but certainly made serious effort to act in concert with western powers against the Turk.[554] Shâh Abbâs captured Tabrîz in 1603,[555] attained some towns in Âzerbeyjân, and captured Revân (Erivan) after a six-month siege. In the meanwhile, the Osmanlı sultân, Mehemmed III, died.[556]

## 8.4 SULTÂN AHMED I (1603-1617)

Ahmed, the son of Mehemmed III, succeeded his father to the throne. Sadrâzam Yavuz Alî Pasha marched against Austria, and Sinân Pasha, son of Jigala, was sent against Iran.[557] When the former died in 1604 Lala Mehemmed Pasha replaced him as *sadrâzam* (grand *vazîr*). He conquered some castles and besieged Estergon, which was re-opened to Islam in 1605.[558] Sinân Pasha was unable to retake the city of Revân[559] and spent the winter of 1605 at Van. He tried the following year without success to capture Tabrîz and later died at Diyarbakır. Shâh Abbâs captured Shirvân and Genje. Kuyuju Murâd Pasha killed the rioters in Anatolia and in 1019/1610 was appointed *serdâr* (commander-in-chief) of the campaign against Iran. He marched on Shâh Abbâs at Tabrîz, but neither side dared to engage in open battle. Murâd Pasha returned to Diyarbakır where he passed away.[560] Nasûh Pasha, the Osmanlı *sadrâzam*, accepted the Shâh's offer of peace. The subsequent peace treaty [561] stipulated that the Shâh would pay the Osmanlıs 200 loads of silk every year in return for their recognition of his sovereignty over the territories that he captured.

# Chapter Nine

# The Osmanlı Sultan's Descent to Equality With Emperors

## 9.1 THE TREATY OF ZITVATOROK (1606)

War with Austria had been going on for fourteen years. But the Osmanlıs soon opted for peace so that they could concentrate their energy on the pressing internal problems in their *Devlet*. Hence the peace treaty of Zitvatorok (Zsitvatorok) was concluded in 1015/1606 for a period of twenty years. It gave the title "Caesar" (emperor) to the Austrian sovereign instead of the previous title "king", and the Osmanlı ambassadors, who were Dîvân Chavushu, were promoted to *sanjaqbeği*. Austria's annual payment of 30,000 ducats to the Osmanlıs was, moreover, replaced by a one-off payment of only two-thirds of this amount. The Osmanlı Devlet gained the castles of Yanık (Raab), Estergon, Istoni Belgrade, and some other castles captured by the Austrians through this treaty. But in this treaty the Osmanlıs recognised for the first time the Austrian sovereign as an equal to the Sultân. Previously, all sovereigns were equated with the *sadrâzam* and not the Sultân as such. This treaty is therefore the first document that officially reduced the status of the Osmanlı sultân to the equal of a European sovereign.[562]

### The Third Phase of War with Iran (1615-1618)

Shâh Abbâs did not fulfil his promise to send 200 loads of silk to the Osmanlı Devlet and instead arrested the Osmanlı ambassadors who were sent to him to enquire about this delay.

Hence, Sadrâzam Mehemmed Pasha marched against Iran in 1024/1615. Though the Shâh hurriedly released the ambassadors, the *sadrâzam* continued his advance. He besieged Revân but could not conquer it, and he therefore concluded another peace treaty that obliged Iran to pay a hundred loads of silk to the Osmanlı Devlet every year. But Mehemmed Pasha was dismissed for his failure to conquer Revân, and his peace treaty was not ratified by the Osmanlı sultân. The new *sadrâzam*, Halîl Pasha, arrived at Tabrîz in 1617.

The cavalry of Crimea, which was reputed for its excellence over the centuries, raided Iran and forced the Shâh to withdraw to Erdebil (Ardabil) in 1618, and ask for a peace treaty. According to this treaty, Iran's tribute of two hundred loads of silk to the Osmanlı Devlet was reduced to only a hundred.[563]

Sultân Ahmed died in 1026/1617 at the age of twenty-eight, leaving no adult *shâhzâda*. He assigned a large number of villages in Egypt as a *waqf* for the poor of al-Haramayn ash-Sharîfayn.[564]

## 9.2 SULTÂN OSMAN II (1618-1622)

He was called Genç Osman (Young Osman), which was an appropriate title as he was active but inexperienced and under his mother's influence.

### The Campaign against Poland

The Turla (Dniester) River was the boundary between the Osmanlı Devlet and Lehistân (Poland). Though the khân of Crimea was instructed not to carry out any *aqın* (raids) into Poland, the Poles soon interfered in the political affairs of Bogdan, and occupied the castle of Hotin in 1617. Hence, İskender Pasha, the *beğlerbeği* of Özi, set out against them with Crimean cavalry and other forces, and in the battle near Yash that followed the Muslim forces defeated the *voyvoda* of Bogdan, who had been aided by 50,000 Polish

## Chapter Nine – The Osmanlı Sultan's Descent

soldiers.[i] The Cossacks of Poland had, however, travelled down the Özi (Dnieper) River to the Black Sea and plundered Yeniköy on the Bosphorus. This infuriated Sultân Genç Osman, who refused to receive the delegates of the Polish king and rejected the mediation of the British ambassador. Instead, he decided to fight Poland and led an army that left İstanbul in 1030/1621 and arrived at Edirne and Değirmenköyü where it was joined by some *beğs* and the *voyvoda* of Bogdan, Alexander. But the latter was dismissed because of his failure to repair the bridges and roads and to supply the army with grain. He was replaced in 1030/1621 by Istefan Tomsha, an arch enemy of the Poles.[565]

The *Ordu-yu Hümâyûn* arrived at Hotin in September 1621, but could not retake the castle. A force of 50,000 Crimean cavalry raided deep into Poland and frightened the population there. During the fourth attack on 14 September 1621, Karakash Mehmed Pasha, *vâli* of Budin, entered the enemy fortifications outside the castle, and was about to hoist the Osmanlı flag but was suddenly martyred.[566] Sadrâzam Hüseyin Pasha had not sent the expected reinforcements, apparently out of sheer jealousy. Hence, he was dismissed, and Vazîr Dilâver Pasha, *beğlerbeği* of Diyarbakır, was installed as *sadrâzam*. A peace treaty was finally concluded between the Osmanlı Devlet and Poland in 1030 (5 October 1621). It stipulated that Bogdan would regain the small castle of Hotin and that the border would remain as it was. Moreover, the Cossacks were not to intrude on Osmanlı territory, and the Poles were asked to continue paying 40,000 ducats to the Khân of Qırım (Crimea) as they had done since the time of Sultân Süleymân the Magnificent.[567]

---

i   Na'îmâ, *op. cit.*, II, pp. 175-176. Na'îmâ mentions that the *kâfir* had 53,000 soldiers while İskender Pasha had only 10,000. But the forces of Islam were victorious as promised in al-Baqarah [2] *âyat*: 249 "*How often by Allah's will a small force vanquished a big one.*"

### The Regicide of Genç Osman (1622)

The Muslim campaign in Poland was led by the Sultân himself and the Khân of Crimea, Janıbek Gıray (1610-1623), while the Polish army was commanded by the Polish king's son. The campaign was not a complete success, however, because of sharp differences between the Sultân and the janissaries. Sultân Osman II thought that the army needed to be reshuffled and renewed, or even replaced altogether by another body. But the janissaries maintained that the young sultân, who was under the influence of a black eunuch, was responsible for the deteriorating situation. Süleymân Ağa, the eunuch, and Ömer Efendi (1623-1625), the Sultân's teacher, had both urged him to set up an entirely new army composed of soldiers from Egypt, Syria, and Anatolia, and to leave İstanbul for the pilgrimage. Sheyhulislâm Es'ad Efendi, the Sultân's father-in-law, issued a *fetvâ* (legal opinion) that excused the Sultân from performing the pilgrimage that year so he could stay in the capital and implement justice. The very honourable spiritual master of the period, Shaykh Aziz Mahmûd Hudâî, also gave the same opinion.[568] But the Sultân defied these *fetvas* and decided to go ahead with his plans for the pilgrimage.

The janissaries and *sipâhîs* opposed the Sultân's decision to go on pilgrimage at that difficult time when the enemy was at the gates. They gathered in Sultân Ahmed Square, got a *fetvâ* from the Sheyhulislâm supporting their view, and asked for severe penalty for those who "misled" the Sultân. They wanted, in particular, Süleymân Ağa of the Harem to be dismissed and exiled. When the Sultân refused, they became more aggressive and asked for the execution of Sadrâzam Dilâver Pasha, the *defterdar*, Ömer Efendi, and Süleymân Ağa. They sent a group of scholars to negotiate their case with the Sultân, but he kept them in the palace. The soldiers then openly revolted, entered the palace, and reinstalled Mustafa as sultân by force. Osman II was then obliged to surrender Süleymân Ağa and

## Chapter Nine – The Osmanlı Sultan's Descent

Dilâver Pasha, but the soldiers forced the *ulemâ* to swear allegiance to Mustafa.[569] Osman II therefore took refuge with the janissaries who undertook to protect him, and save his life, though they made it clear that they would not accept him as *khalîfah* anymore.[570] But through the incitement of Dâvûd Pasha, the new *sadrâzam*, who saw in the person of the deposed sultân a potential danger for himself, some of the janissaries killed Genç Osman in 1031/1622.[571]

# Chapter Ten

# Rejuvenation

## 10.1 SULTÂN MURÂD IV (1623-1640)

Mustafa succeeded Genç Osman as sultân but was soon deposed because of ill health, and replaced by Murâd in 1032/1623. The following sentence in Osmanlı Turkish indicates the date of his ascension:

سلطان مراد رابع اولدي بادشاه

*Sultân Murâd(-ı) Râbi' oldı Pâdshâh*
Sultân Murâd the fourth became Pâdishâh.⁵⁷²

When the numerical values of the letters are added together, the sum is 1032 (1623 C.E.).

### The Capture of Baghdad by the Shâh of Iran

Bekir Subashı of Baghdad killed the *vâli* (governor) of Baghdad, Yûsuf Pasha, and assumed rule over the province in defiance of İstanbul. Hence, a force commanded by Hâfız Pasha, the *vâli* of Diyarbakır, was sent to Baghdad to deal with this deteriorating situation. Meanwhile, Bekir Subashı asked for the Shâh's help, but Hâfız Pasha shrewdly confirmed him in his position to avoid Iranian intervention in Osmanlı internal affairs.⁵⁷³ Though the Shâh of Iran had actually arrived with his army in Baghdad, Bekir Subashı saw no need for cooperation with him. He apologised to the Shâh, however, and gave him some gifts in an attempt to persuade him to withdraw from Baghdad. But the Shâh decided to make use of this opportunity, and besieged the city. Furthermore, he won to his side Mehmed, Bekir Subashı's son, by deceitfully promising that he would replace his father. Mehmed helped to open the gate of the castle, and the Persian forces entered the city. They committed all sorts of atrocities, including the oppression of the Sunnî population and killing both Mehmed and his father.[574]

### Sultân Murâd's Revân Expedition

Infuriated by the plunder of Baghdad, Sultân Murâd marched in 1045/1635 at the head of the *Ordu-yu Hümâyûn* towards Revân, and recaptured the castle there.[575] He then headed to Baghdad in 1048/1638 to find the Shâh hiding in terror at Qasr-ı Shîrîn.[576] The Osmanlı army besieged Baghdad and "Murâd led his men in person, worked in the trenches with his own hands, and, when the Persians sent a stalwart champion to defy the besiegers to single combat, it was Murâd himself who took up the challenge and after a hard fight clove the giant's skull from pate to chin. The chain armour in which he fought, a beautiful suit of interwoven steel and gold links, is still to be seen in the Treasury at Constantinople."[577] Baghdad surrendered after a month's siege, and the victorious Sultân visited the tomb of İmâm A'zam Abû Hanîfeh and repaired it, along with the tomb of Abdulqâdir Geylânî, the great *sûfî shaykh*, and the castle of Baghdad.[578] Finally, he returned to İstanbul in April 1048/1639[579] after concluding the peace treaty of Qasr-ı Shîrîn with Iran by which both sides agreed to demolish their castles along the border.[580] Being devout Sunnîs, the Osmanlıs insisted on adding the following warning to the terms of the treaty: "If the peace is to be honoured, the insulting of Abû Bakr, 'Umar, and the mother of the believers, 'Aisha, is to be stopped and prevented."[581]

Sultân Murâd died next year. He assumed the Sultanate at a very young age, and was therefore at first under the influence of his mother, Kösem Sultân. But he soon rid himself of her domination and asserted his authority over the Devlet. In a way, he resembled his predecessor Sultân Selîm, though he was not as knowledgeable and cultured as his ancestors.[582] Murâd officially prohibited the consumption of alcohol and tobacco, but this did not work.

# Chapter Eleven

# Decline and Restoration

## 11.1 SULTÂN İBRÂHÎM (1640-1648)

Sultân Murâd was succeeded by his brother İbrâhîm. The *sadrâzam* Kemankesh Qara Mustafa Pasha tried his best to keep up the administration.

### The Campaign in Girit (Crete)

While on his way to Egypt, Sünbül Ağa, an ex-officer of the Osmanlı palace, was intercepted by Christian pirates. He was martyred and all his property confiscated and sold in Girit (Crete), a Venetian island. In the spring of 1055/1645 the Osmanlıs sent more than 100 ships against Girit.[583] The *sanjaqbeğs* on the coast and in Garb Ojaqları (Trablus (Tripoli), Tunisia and Jezâyir) also joined the campaign with their naval forces. The castle of Hanya surrendered to the Muslims after a 54-day siege, and the Muslims recited *Ezân-ı Muhammedî* and flew Muslim flags. But the Osmanlıs allowed the Christians to go, assigned units to protect the market[584] and committed no plunder whatsoever. This recurrent behaviour towards the Christian ideological enemy shows the civility of the Osmanlıs and their society.

War between the Osmanlı Devlet and the strong naval Republic of Venice went on for years, during which the Venetian fleet blocked the Dardanelles Strait to prevent reinforcements for the *mujâhids* at Girit. Meanwhile, Sultân İbrâhîm was deposed in 1058/1648 because of insanity.

## 11.2 SULTÂN MEHMED IV (1648-1687)

Sultân Mehmed, following his family's custom, went to Eyüb Sultân's tomb for his inaugural ceremony called Qılıch Alayı (the girding on of the new sultân sword of Islam) and returned to the palace in procession.[585]

The currency of the Osmanlı Devlet gradually declined, though successive *sadrâzams* tried their best to arrest this deterioration. Tarhunju Ahmed Pasha, who was appointed from among them to this post in 1062/1652, deserves special credit for his efforts to stop wasteful expenditures and implement sound economic measures. With the help of the ships from Garb Ojaqları, the Osmanlı fleet defeated the Venetian fleet in 1064/1654, killed its admiral, Francesco Morosini, and captured his son. Thus the Venetian fleet was forced to temporarily leave the Dardanelles, which it had controlled for some time. But it came back in 1066/1656 when a storm inflicted losses on both the Osmanlı and Venetian fleets. Eventually, however, the Venetians gained control of the situation and captured the islands of Bozjaada, Limni, and Semendirek in the Aegean Sea, thus obstructing the İstanbul-Girit route.

### Köprülü Mehmed Pasha

On the advice of Mi'mâr Qâsım Ağa, the 70-year-old Köprülü Mehmed Pasha was appointed to the post of *sadrâzam* on September 14, 1656. But he insisted on certain conditions that gave him vast powers in running the machinery of the Devlet. The Sultân agreed to ratify all his recommendations and gave him absolute power to appoint able and honest people to public posts. *Vazîrs* and other palace notables were, furthermore, not allowed to have a dominant say in the affairs of the Devlet, and the Sultân undertook to ignore their advice and that of any other opponent.[586]

The notables were very determined to go to war with Venice because of its hostile attitude. But this task was quite difficult, particularly

## Chapter Eleven – Decline and Restoration

because of a serious shortage of funds to purchase equipment. This issue was discussed in an official assembly in which the Sultân himself was present. The *vâlide sultân*, Hadîje Turhân (mother of Mehmed IV), was reported to have said in this assembly: "Do your best to complete the opening of the Girit island to Islam, and I am going to give all my jewels, my gold and silver household utensils, and all my property for the sake of this campaign."[587]

Köprülü Mehmed Pasha led an Osmanlı fleet to the Dardanelles in 1067/1657, bearing the Sanjaq-ı Sharîf (The Prophet's Standard). A *waly*, called Muhammad Sâdiq, prayed, and, on his advice, 92 pious men, each of whose given name was Muhammad, were chosen from among the officials in the Osmanlı palace to recite Sûratal-Fath 92 times a week, a task that was to be completed on Friday at the time of *salât Jum'ah*. They should then all pray for help and victory.[588] (The numerical value of the name "Muhammad" is 92.)

The strong Venetian fleet anchored on the Anatolian shore face to face with the Osmanlı fleet. The Venetian admiral, Moceniko, tried in vain to capture the Osmanlı flagship, and a shell hit the gunpowder depot of his ship and destroyed it. Thus, the Venetian fleet was compelled to retreat. The Osmanlı *sadrâzam* performed *sajdat ash-shukr* and withdrew his fleet from the Dardanelles after retrieving the islands of Bozjaada and Limni.[589]

### Expedition to Erdel (1068/1658)

Meanwhile, Rakochi II, King of Erdel (Transylvania), concluded an alliance with Sweden, then the most powerful Christian country in Europe, and planned to capture Poland without the prior consent of his suzerain, the Osmanlı Sultân. The Poles appealed for help from the Osmanlı Devlet,[590] which opposed the incorporation of Poland into Erdel, and wanted a weak and troubled Poland on its northern borders that faced a constant threat from the horsemen of Qırım.

Rakochi, however, erroneously expected that the able Sadrâzam Köprülü would soon be replaced by another one with whom he would be able to settle his difficulties. Köprülü Mehmed Pasha set out for Erdel in 1068/1658 and annexed its strategic castle of Yanova. But he was obliged to return to İstanbul because of the danger of internal riots in Anatolia, and Seydî Ahmed Pasha, the *vâli* of Budin, was appointed commander-in-chief of the army. He defeated Rakochi,[591] and the *Dîvân-ı Hümâyûn* (literally: The Heavenly Dîvân, i.e. the Osmanlı government) endorsed the appointment of Apafi Mihal (r. 1661-1682) as king of Erdel.[592]

Köprülü Mehmed Pasha asserted the authority of the Devlet, and severely punished corrupt and tyrannical local administrators. He built the fortifications of Kumkale and Seddulbahr in the Dardanelles in 1071/1661, which were visited by the Sultân and his mother.

### War with Russia (1069/1659)

By the middle of the seventeenth century Russia was emerging as a powerful country in eastern Europe which harboured hostile intentions towards Ukraine. Though keen to keep Russia away from Ukraine, the Osmanlı Devlet was unable to respond to the appeals of Prince Vyogorsky of the Ukrainian Cossacks against the Russians. For it was then engaged in a bitter war with Venice on the question of Girit that continued for more than ten years, and, at the same time, was preoccupied with serious riots in Anatolia. Thus, the soldiers of Islam were distributed in many places, and could not therefore concentrate on the Russian threat. The Russian Czar decided to make use of this unique opportunity to crush the power of the Osmanlıs. He carefully prepared for this task for more than two years, and sent envoys to the Cossacks to incite them against the Muslims. He wanted in particular to destroy the powerful Crimean cavalry, which would make it easier for him to attack the Osmanlı Devlet effectively. But the Cossacks, who had attained their position and some of their lands with the active help of the Crimeans, informed Mehmed Gıray, the Khân of Crimea, of the Russian intentions. With his famous horsemen and the Osmanlı troops in Kefe, Mehmed thus marched on the Russian army in northern Ukraine, which was composed of some 350,000 untrained and vagabond soldiers. The Russians were defeated at the battle of Konotop in 1069 (12 July 1659), in which they lost 120,000 of their men, amongst whom was Prince Trubechkoy, the commander-in-chief. Fifty thousand others were captured. This decisive battle delayed the Russian invasion of Ukraine for half a century. The aged and tired Sadrâzam Köprülü Mehmed Pasha died in 1071/1661, and was replaced in fulfilment of his wishes by his son, Köprülü Fâzıl Ahmed Pasha.[593]

### Fâzıl Ahmed Pasha (1661-1676)

The Austrians never ceased interfering in the affairs of Erdel and had, in fact, built Zerinvar castle near the Kanije castle. When they refused the Osmanlı demand to demolish it, Fâzıl Ahmed Pasha led the Osmanlı army in 1073/April 1663 to the outskirts of the Uyvar castle in the middle of Hungary. Though it had been captured and fortified by the Austrians, Fâzıl Ahmed Pasha crossed the Danube and approached this castle to which the Austrian general Montecucculi came with further reinforcements. But he soon retreated in the face of a fierce Osmanlı attack, and the Austrians surrendered in 1073/1663. The Osmanlıs undertook to secure the life and property of the Austrians and had in fact provided them with four hundred carriages to transport their possessions. Furthermore, they addressed a letter to the Austrian sovereign that his soldiers had done their best to defend Uyvar castle. The Osmanlıs followed the maxim that "unless the *kuffâr* (infidel) soldiers came out of the castle the soldiers of Islam would not enter it." In addition to all these generous human gestures, the victorious Muslim army gave the departing Austrians food and treated the wounded soldiers in the castle.[594] The Osmanlı army conquered Zerinvar castle in 1077/1666 and demolished it. At the end of these battles, the Treaty of Vasvar was concluded.[595]

### The Expedition to Girit (Crete)

Sultân Mehmed IV summoned the *sadrâzam, sheyhülislâm, qazaskers* and other dignitaries of his *Devlet*, and told them: "Except for Kandiye castle, all Girit has been opened to Islam. Those in the Kandiye attack the merchant ships and those on their way to pilgrimage. Its *fath* (opening to Islam) is a dire necessity." In 1076/1666 the Sultân sent Fâzıl Ahmed Pasha to Girit and saw him off as far as Edirne.[596] Fâzıl Ahmed Pasha went to Girit through the Morea Peninsula. After a siege lasting two and a half years Kandiye castle was opened to Islam in 1080/September 1669,[597] and the Muslims converted its fourteen monasteries into mosques.[598]

Despite its declared peace with the Osmanlı Devlet, of all the European powers France helped the Venetians the most during the Girit war. A force of 15,000 French volunteers accompanied the Knights of St. John and the papal forces to Girit, and fought the Muslims. Finally, a peace treaty was concluded with Venice according to which Kandiye castle, along with all its guns and equipment, became an Osmanlı possession, and Venice undertook to abide by its obligations and to compensate for any Osmanlı ships lost in the Mediterranean.[599]

### The Sultân's Expedition to Poland

With the consent of the Osmanlıs, Ukraine was divided between Poland and the khân of Qırım, and the allegiance of its Cossacks' chiefs, who were titled *hatman*, alternated between the Osmanlı Devlet and occasionally Poland. In those years, France, Britain, Holland, and Sweden were all in the process of becoming great powers. As for Poland, it was still more powerful than Russia, but not as powerful as it used to be. Both Spain and Venice were also on the decline. While the Ukrainians were, like Russians, followers of Orthodox Christianity, the Poles were Catholics. But the Osmanlıs were keen on keeping both of them from interfering in the affairs of Ukraine. *Dîvân-ı Hümâyûn* had given the north-western part of Ukraine to Hatman Dorosenko, conferring upon him the rank of *sanjaqbeği*. He was a dependent of the Osmanlıs and participated in the expedition against Austria (Germany) with 15,000 horsemen under the command of the Khân of Qırım.

Upon Poland's attack on Dorosenko, the Sultân set out against it in year 1082 of Hegira/1672 C.E. The *Ordu-yu Hümâyûn* entered Poland and conquered Kamaniche. The Treaty of Bujash was finally concluded with Poland in 1083/October 1672 stipulating that the king of Poland would pay the Osmanlıs 22,000 ducats annually and that Podolya would surrender all its castles to the Osmanlıs. The Poles should, furthermore, leave Ukraine immediately, which would henceforth be under the administration of Hatman Dorosenko. Finally, Poland was asked to pay the annual tribute that was fixed at the time of İslâm Gıray to the khân of Qırım in return for his pledge to refrain from raiding Poland.[600]

Köprülü Fâzıl Ahmed Pasha died in 1087/1676, and Merzifonlu Qara Mustafa Pasha was appointed *sadrâzam* in his place.

## The Expedition to Chehrin

Hatman Dorosenko proclaimed himself a dependent of the Russians and planned to give them Chehrin, then capital of Ukraine. Hence, the Osmanlı army arrived there and faced a Russian army of 40,000 men, half of whom entered the castle. The castle was opened to Islam, and the Russian army fled. Finally, in 1681, a treaty was concluded with Russia by which the river Özi (Dnieper) became the dividing line between Osmanlı and Russian territory.[i]

## The Second Siege of Vienna 1683

The majority of the Hungarians were Catholic, but the rest lived in central Hungary and were Orthodox. The Austrians who dominated this area wanted to convert this minority to Catholicism, and when they rejected this, their king along with some princes were killed by the Austrian authorities in 1670. The king's son, Tököli İmre, revolted in 1673 in protest and took refuge with the Osmanlı Devlet. Sadrâzam Merzifonlu Qara Mustafa Pasha appointed Vazîr Uzun İbrâhîm Pasha, the *beğlerbeği* of Budin, commander-in-chief of an expeditionary force that reinstated Tököli İmre in return for an annual tribute of 40,000 ducats. The Osmanlı Devlet was then at the peak of its power, perhaps *the* superpower of the world. The status of *sadrâzam* and *sheyhülislâm* was equal in protocol to European heads of state with the exception of the Austro-Hungarian emperor. When officially writing to the Osmanlı sultân, European kings used to address the *sadrâzam* and *sheyhülislâm* as well. Being praised and flattered by Reîsul Küttâb Mustafa, Sadrâzam Qara Mustafa Pasha set out to Vienna at the head of a huge army.[601] This was against the advice of the veteran İbrâhîm Pasha, who was of the opinion that the advance on Vienna should be postponed until the capture of the castles en route. Tököli İmre was also of the same opinion.[602]

---

i  *Ibid.*, II, p. 80. Here Mustafa Nûrî Pasha relates a conversation between Sultân Murâd I and the first *vazîr*, Jendereli Halîl Pasha, in which it was decided that an expedition should only be carried out if it was a necessity and the probability of victory was high. But this was not the case with this expedition to Chehrin that Qara Mustafa Pasha carried out to prove himself and to secure his post.

## Chapter Eleven – Decline and Restoration

The siege finally began in 1094/July 14, 1683, and the Osmanlıs captured 40,000 Germans along the way, while the *aqınjıs* and the cavalry of Qırım dispersed in a vast area within this Christian domain. Leaving the city to an able general, the Emperor of Austria fled to Prague where he tried to muster soldiers.[603]

> "The Habsburgs had in fact held back in the hope of avoiding an open war with the Ottomans while they were fighting the French in the west, but Kara Mustafa was convinced by French agents that the time had come to take Vienna and thus achieve what the great sultâns of the past could not.
>
> While a vast army was being brought together at Edirne, the emperor formed a new European coalition to resist the threat. His most important ally was Jan Sobiyeski of Poland. Pope Innocent XI appealed widely for a new Christian Crusade against the infidel, going so far as to ask for help from the Shâh of Îrân, and while French opposition partly nullified the effects of the appeal, he still managed to secure men and money for the Habsburgs from Portugal and Spain as well as from Poland and various princes of Germany."[604]

Mustafa Pasha decided not to launch a massive attack on Vienna because he expected it to surrender after a siege of a few weeks, particularly as he had already subdued a great part of the Austrian Empire and was at the same time keen to avoid its inevitable plunder by the Osmanlı soldiers. But the city would have been successfully taken by the Osmanlı army if it attacked it rather than going on in this long siege.[605] For, as Defterdâr Sarı Mehmed Pasha says, "If a siege of a castle exceeds 40 days there is great probability of getting help from outside. The siege had been going on for more than 50 days and the Osmanlı soldiers had to go for a distance of 15-20 hours to find grass for their horses. The *sadrâzam* should have thought of providing water and grass."[606]

The Polish King Jan Sobiyevski led a large allied army in support of Vienna, and Mustafa Pasha was thus obliged to raise the two-month siege on September 12th. Subsequently, the Osmanlıs suffered a heavy defeat in which many soldiers died in battle, and the army left behind a large amount of ammunition and equipment,[607] while Estergon castle fell into Austrian hands in November 1683. For this humiliating defeat Mustafa Pasha blamed İbrâhîm Pasha, the commander of the right flank that collapsed first and punished him by execution. Before he was executed, however, İbrâhîm Pasha had magnanimously told his officers: "This man [Mustafa] is doing wrong to me. He is executing me unjustly. But, tell the Sultân not to execute him; as he is 'the' only man who can make up for the situation."[608] Afterwards, Mustafa Pasha was also executed in Belgrade as punishment.[609]

The policy of Qara Mustafa Pasha, who was admittedly a very able leader but stubborn and ambitious, may have been a major factor in this defeat. His opponents in the palace, however, hurried to take advantage of this critical situation to incite the Sultân to execute him. Once again the saying of the Prophet ﷺ, "Avoid jealousy, because jealousy eats up good traits as fire eats up wood" proved to be true. Perhaps more important than this was that the Islamic dynamic seems to have then begun to tarnish, and the army, whose *raison d'être* was "to fight for Islam," had progressively lost sight of its values. Scandalous and un-Islamic behaviour prevailed among the soldiers during the siege. They even consumed wine and committed adultery during the sacred months.[610] This disastrous behaviour, and the arrogance and conceit they exhibited during the siege, was similar to that of the Christian armies during the fourteenth century. An army that ignores its message and mission, and occupies itself with material and irrational pleasure is bound to be defeated.

The malicious and deceitful policy of the French government was another factor in this defeat and the inability of the Osmanlıs to recover from it. It was France who incited Qara Mustafa Pasha to attack Vienna, and then deserted her ally, the Osmanlı Devlet. Shaw has this to write in this respect: "Louis XIV used the Ottoman attack on Vienna to invade the Spanish Netherlands so that the Habsburgs were unable to follow up the Ottoman rout of 1683. If the French had continued their attack, the Ottomans might have been able to recover from the defeat. But as was to happen many times in their dealings with Europe, as soon as their ally achieved what it wanted in the West it made a separate peace, abandoning the Ottomans."[611]

## The Deposition of the Sultân

Sultân Mehmed IV was served during his youth by capable subordinates, particularly Sadrâzam Köprülü Mehmed Pasha and other reputable *vazîrs* from the same family. In the meantime, he was not taught the art of administration but grew up living an easy life and was particularly fond of hunting. The *ulemâ* reminded him several times of the need to be serious and behave, but he did not listen. Thus, the army in the European part of the Devlet rebelled against him, came to Silivri, near İstanbul, and asked for his *khal'* (removal). Sadâret Kaymakamı (Deputy Sadrâzam) Fâzıl Mustafa Pasha called an assembly of *Ahlul Hall wa'l 'Aqd* (religious authorities), *vazîrs,* and *pashas* at Ayasofya Mosque in 1098/1687 to discuss the issue. They decided to depose the Sultân, and went to the palace where they gave the *bay'at* (oath of allegiance on Islamic principles) to Süleymân. Mehmed was imprisoned and later died after five years in Edirne. He was carried to İstanbul to be buried there in the tomb at Bahchekapısı.[612]

## Financial Affairs

The Osmanlı Devlet was rich and prosperous during the reign of Murâd III. In spite of the wars of his successors with Austria and Iran, the Devlet remained solvent. In addition to the expenses of these wars, Ahmed I could afford to spend a huge amount of money in building his mosque and other auxiliary buildings. But on the accession of Mustafa to the Osmanlı throne in 1026/1617, the Devlet's finances deteriorated. This was partly due to the political instability that resulted from his replacement after only three months by Genç Osman, and then his re-ascension after another four years, after which Murâd IV became the Sultân, i.e. four ascensions to rulership in five years. During each ascension "gifts" were deferred to the soldiers while Mustafa's mother spent a huge sum of money on the military chiefs to secure her son's reign. The finances of the Devlet became so desperate that Sultân Murâd IV was obliged to melt the gold and silver utensils of the palace and to borrow money from some merchants to give the "ascension grant" to the janissaries and *sipâhîs*. Murâd IV, however, managed to make up for this deficit by slashing the number of janissaries and *sipâhîs*. But towards the end of the seventeenth century, top officials in the Devlet started to assign *tımar* and *ze'âmet* to those who paid them the highest fees. This led to a marked deterioration in military organisation. Moreover, through nepotism and corruption, many unqualified persons were incorporated into the janissary corps, and the Devlet had therefore to pay huge amounts of money to a large number of people, some of whom were not even professional soldiers. The deterioration of the *tımar* system in the seventeenth century was a further reason for military weakness, as those who illegitimately acquired it were unable or unwilling to recruit suitable soldiers. They even went to the extent of bribing some *beğlerbeğis* not to take part in the campaigns. This financial and military decline was, however, temporarily checked by Sadrâzam Kemankesh (archer) Mustafa Pasha, who was able to accumulate a good amount of money in the treasury. But after him fiscal disorder prevailed, and the number of soldiers in the centre increased. Köprülü Mehmed Pasha improved the financial situation once more, and during the next thirty years, i.e. until the defeat of Vienna in 1683, the finances of the Osmanlı Devlet remained on the whole fairly stable as the income acquired from exports (of grain and other commodities) was usually adequate to cover the expenditures of the Devlet's limited imports from Europe during the seventeenth century (i.e. clocks, sugar, etc.).[613] Nevertheless, extensive corruption among top officials had sometimes led to a budgetary deficit, as revealed in a report prepared by the famous administrator Tarhunju.[614]

## 11.3 SULTÂN SÜLEYMÂN II (1687-1691)

Sultân Süleymân was inaugurated in 1098/1687 at the tomb of Eyüb Sultân,[615] but after only one year the Austrians captured Erdel, Belgrade, and the castles of Uyvar and Eğri. Faced with this difficult situation, the new Sultân appointed Fâzıl Mustafa Pasha *sadrâzam* in 1100/1689. He reduced the taxes imposed on the people because of the ongoing wars, and amended some of the laws as a precautionary measure against a probable uprising of the Christian people in the Osmanlı domains who could be incited by the Austrians and the Venetians.[616] He also retrieved Nish, Semendire, and Belgrade in 1101/1690.[617] Sultân Süleymân II was very pleased with these victories achieved by the Serdâr-ı Ekrem (the title given to the *sadrâzam* when on a *jihâd* against the infidels, which means the most honourable commander-in-chief). In appreciation he took off his fur and dagger and put it on the *sadrâzam*, girded him with his own dagger, put his own crest on his head, and prayed for him weeping.[618] Though repulsing the Austrians beyond the Danube, Fâzıl Mustafa Pasha treated the Christian *ra'âyâ* there humanely and generously. He gave them grain, released their prisoners of war, and successfully persuaded the Muslim immigrants from those areas to return. Thus the Osmanlıs were successful in regaining the border lands.

## 11.4 SULTÂN AHMED II (1691-1695)

Sultân Süleymân II died at Edirne, and was succeeded by his brother Ahmed in 1102/1691.[619] Just about the time of his accession, Serdâr-i Ekrem Fâzıl Mustafa Pasha was engaged in a battle with the Austrian army at Salankamen. The Osmanlı army would have won had not its able leader been fatally wounded while encouraging his soldiers to fight. Upon his martyrdom the course of the battle was reversed, and the Osmanlı army retreated, taking with it the *sanjaq-ı Sharîf* (The Holy Prophet's standard), but leaving guns and ammunition behind in the battlefield. Nevertheless, the Austrians did not dare chase the Osmanlıs, though Mustafa Qaptân captured 800 of their boats full of grain and ammunition on the Danube.[620]

Fâzıl Mustafa Pasha had thus achieved substantial success and could probably have restored the previous strength and dynamism of the Osmanlı Devlet if he had lived a few years more. Meanwhile, Sultân Ahmed II set out with the *Ordu-yu Hümâyûn* but could not find the Austrians. He was, however, obliged to return in 1104/1692 to repair the castle of Belgrade. In 1693, Sadrâzam Bozoklu Mustafa Pasha led the Osmanlı army to Ruschuk and subsequently marched to Belgrade where he forced the Austrians to lift the siege of this city and retreat to the other bank of the Danube. He was succeeded by Sürmeli Ali Pasha in the post of *sadrâzam*, and he besieged the Austrian army in 1105/1694 that took refuge in the Varadin castle for 22 days. But he had to raise the siege and return because of constant rain. Meanwhile, the Venetian fleet attacked and captured the island of Sakız before İzmir in 1105/1694. The Osmanlıs were busy preparing themselves to retrieve this island when the Sultân died in 1106/1695.[621] He was succeeded by Mustafa II, son of Mehmed IV.

## 11.5 SULTÂN MUSTAPHA II (1695-1703)

During the time of Mustafa II the Osmanlıs recaptured Sakız island from the Venetians. In 1695 he led the *Ordu-yu Hümâyûn* to Belgrade while the Austrians assembled in Erdel (Transylvania). He crossed the Danube at Panchova to find the main body of the Austrian army under General Veterani at Sis. The Muslims defeated the enemy there and demolished the castles of Sis and Lugos.[622] But the Austrian army recouped its strength under the Prince of Saxony and besieged Tameshvar. Sultân Mustafa set out once more and crossed from Belgrade to Panchova, where he burned four Austrian galleys on the Danube. While retreating from Tameshvar, the Austrians tried to corner the *Ordu-yu Hümâyûn* at a narrow pass but failed, losing 15,000 of their men. The *Ordu-yu Hümâyûn* chased them for a while but finally returned. The Russians took advantage of the Osmanlıs' engagements in the Mediterranean, the Morea Peninsula, Hungary, and Poland to capture the castle of Azak (Azov) in 1108/1696, while the Poles besieged the castle of Kamaniche several times but could not capture it.[623]

Sultân Mustafa set out with the *Ordu-yu Hümâyûn* on his third expedition in 1108/1697. While the army was crossing the Tise river at Zanta, the bridge collapsed. Only one-eight of the Muslim Army managed to cross the river, and the rest – including the Sultân – were left behind. Nevertheless, Sadrâzam Elmas Mehmed Pasha, with some other pashas and about ten *beğlerbeğis* confronted the Austrians with the few soldiers at their disposal in a fierce battle in which they were all martyred after inflicting heavy casualties on the enemy. Sultân Mustafa, who was unable to participate in this battle, returned to Tameshvar. But the Austrians did not dare pursue him and instead retreated to Erdel (Transylvania). The Sultân appointed Amjazâde Hüseyin Pasha as the new *sadrâzam*. Amjazâde, the former custodian of the Belgrade stronghold, was an experienced general who knew the Austrians well. He had expressed his strong objection to the advance of the Osmanlı army in no uncertain terms by saying at the Dîvân assembly: "The Austrians' habit is to attack when we cross a river or while encamping, or departing. It is necessary to cross a few wide rivers to reach Tameshvar. It is not right to advance in that direction with such a large army as this: Let the Sultân stay at Belgrade and let us send small units to plunder the territory of Austria. Austria is thus compelled to divide its army into small units, and they will get tired and exhausted this way."[624] Had his advice been taken, the Osmanlı army would not have suffered those heavy casualties. The *vazîrs* seemed to have shared this view, but they appear to have ignored it deliberately out of sheer jealousy for their successful competitor, the *sadrâzam*. To ensure his embarrassment and failure, the *devshirme*[625] *vazîrs* urged him to take the fatal action of advancing and crossing several rivers. By the seventeenth century, the zeal and commitment for the cause and message of Islam had certainly and regrettably begun to fade among the ruling Osmanlı elite. Nevertheless, we can still reasonably argue that the Osmanlı Devlet remained fairly strong because it maintained *jihâd* on four fronts and against powerful enemies. The Austrians, who were obliged to fight the French in some battles, could not achieve a decisive victory in their wars with the Osmanlıs and therefore favoured peace with them. The Venetians achieved a measure of success at the Morea Peninsula, but their fleet was defeated by the Osmanlıs several times in the Mediterranean.

During their 15 years of war with the Osmanlıs, the Poles besieged the castle of Kamaniche several times, but they could not capture it, and the cavalry of Qırım had repeatedly plundered their country and inflicted heavy damages on its people. As for the Russians, they captured Azak (Azov) castle, though they pretended to be friendly towards the Osmanlı Devlet.

*Chapter Eleven – Decline and Restoration*

By the end of the seventeenth century the Osmanlı Devlet was thus able to fight four formidable socio-political bodies of Europe and Asia with a reasonable degree of success. But the heavy expenditures incurred in those wars compelled it to impose heavy taxes on its people. In due course, however, the Osmanlıs seemed to have lost hope of retrieving the lands they lost to these four strong Christian enemies.[626]

# Part Three

# Decline 1699-1922

## Chapter Twelve

## The Resumption of Decline

Sultân Mustafa was also too busy hunting at Edirne to perform his duties in a just and satisfactory manner. This drove the soldiers and some of the people to march to Edirne in protest and replace him with his brother Ahmed in 1115/1703. Sultân Mustafa spent the rest of his life in seclusion in the palace[627] until he died of a fatal disease, and was buried in his tomb in İstanbul.[628]

The first centuries in the history of the Osmanlı Sublime Devlet were characterised by administrative stability. Provincial governors remained in their posts for fairly long periods, ten to twenty years, and were thus able to perform their duties efficiently. But with the passage of time and weakness at the centre, their terms of service rarely reached three to five years. This insecurity led them to graft and corruption, and the Devlet thus contained the seeds of deterioration and decadence even at its zenith. Nevertheless, until the seventeenth century, it remained strong enough to open new areas to Islam, such as Girit, Ujvar, Kanije, Podolya, and Ukraine. This was largely due to the fact that its fiscal, military, and administrative affairs were still entrusted to able individuals, particularly in the centre. The *devshirme* children at first received a good education and were attached for a while to governors outside the capital to gain administrative and military experience that qualified them to be efficient *vazîrs*. But this order was progressively ignored during the course of the seventeenth century, and many of them found their way to top offices through nepotism and intrigues, and not because of their personal merits. Furthermore, they were self-indulgent and

## Chapter Twelve – The Resumption of Decline

lived lives of ease. The outcome was usually administrative and military failure, though some capable rulers occasionally found their way to power and tried their best to control this chaotic situation.[629] In this respect the situation in the Osmanlı Muslim Devlet during the seventeenth century was strikingly similar to that of Christian Spain: "In the 1600s, Spain, which had been one of the mightiest countries in Europe, began running huge deficits to pay for wars, a bloated civil service, and endemic corruption. By the end of the seventeenth century, revenues covered only half the state's spending.... Repeated currency devaluations, growing inflation, and a murderous tax burden killed off Spanish industry and agriculture. Impoverished Spain lost its global influence as its empire contracted to a fraction of its former size."[630]

## 12.1 SULTÂN AHMED III (1703-1730)

Sultân Ahmed came from Edirne to İstanbul where he restored law and order. But he was forced to distribute the largest accession grant ever paid to the soldiers who brought him to power. "Other soldiers who had not participated in the revolt then began to demand equal accession payments and influence. They gathered at Silivri near İstanbul with the intention of overthrowing the Osmanlı family and replacing it with a prince from the house of the *Han* of Qırım or, perhaps a descendant of the marriage between Sokollu Mehmet and the daughter of Selîm II, a line that continued well into the eighteenth century."[631] But the Sultân was able to suppress the mutiny and control the situation.[632]

### Battle of Prut (1711)

Since the Russians built some castles just outside Or, the gateway to Crimea, the Osmanlıs were encouraged to build Yeni Qale (the New Castle) on the shore on the Sea of Azov to deny them access to the Black Sea. By that time, the Russian Czar Peter, and the Swedish

King Charles XII (r. 1697-1718) were engaged in a bitter war in which the latter was defeated and wounded at Poltova in 1121/1709. He withdrew to Bender, an Osmanlı city at the border, but the Russians violated the border arrangements and pursued him into this city, inflicting heavy damage on its people. Hence the *Ordu-yu Hümâyûn* was sent against Czar Peter under Sadrâzam Baltajı Mehmed Pasha, while the *Donanma-yı Hümâyûn* (the Heavenly Navy) was sent to the Azak (Azov) Sea. The *Ordu-yu Hümâyûn* managed to cross the Prut River in 1123/1711 by building bridges over it, despite the fact that the Russian army tried to prevent them. And the Osmanlı army surrounded the Russian army; while the Khân of Qırım (Crimea) cut off the Russians' retreat.

Czar Peter retired to his corner in the tent because of the hopeless situation as he perceived it. Martha Rabe, who afterwards became Empress Catherine I of Russia, convened a meeting of the army generals, persuaded them to surrender by convincing them there was no other way out. Then she gathered all her money and jewels and, adding the amount she borrowed from others, prepared a ransom of 200,000 roubles and sent it to the Osmanlı *serdâr-ı ekrem* (commander-in-chief), asking for clemency. The claim that Catherine went in person to Baltajı Mehmed Pasha does not seem sound, but the claim that money along with jewels were a bribe is unfortunately true. The Osmanlı High level officials had become at that time fond of worldly gains. Omer Efendi, one of Baltaji's aids, was also guilty. General Ponyatofski advised that the Osmanlı Army should stay, doing nothing; because the Russian army was surrounded. It is true that the Osmanlı army did not fight well, there was corruption, but the Russians had no way to escape. The point is, if the Russian army had been captured, Russia would have become very weak, if not annihilated, but Baltaji would not have gained any wealth, only fame. It was the same disease among Osmanlı officials during that era: Qara Mustapha Pasha most probably would

## Chapter Twelve – The Resumption of Decline

have opened Vienna to Islam if he had acted immediately without wasting time, but in that case, spoils would have gone to the army; in case of the city surrendering, everything would have been *fay'*, and thus would have belonged to the treasury, which was in the hands of Mustapha Pasha. And he would have given precious gifts to high officials thus making his position well established.

When the Russian delegates came, Baltajı Mehmed Pasha convened a meeting of the Osmanlı commanders and the notables present in the army; they discussed the Russian proposal of peace that Russians would accept all the Osmanlı demands. The Osmanlı commanders and officials accepted the Russian offer; the reason was that they did not trust the efficiency of the Osmanlı army, so much so that the Osmanlı army retreated a little the day before because of the fierce shooting of the Russian artillery, but the Russians did not notice because it was dark.[633] "The builder of modern Russia and his army were completely surrounded and at the mercy of the Ottomans. While the Ottoman artillery peppered the Czar's camp, causing severe casualties, the Russians also were suffering from a lack of food and other supplies. With the Russians at his mercy it appeared that the grand vazîr could have demanded and obtained unconditional surrender and major territorial and other concessions. After lengthy negotiations, it was decided that the Russians were to demolish all the castles built after the Treaty of Karlowitz and return the castle of Azak to the Osmanlıs. It was also stipulated that they would not interfere in the affairs of the Cossacks, who were under the control of both Poland and the Khân of Crimea, and to secure the safe return of King Charles to his country, Sweden. The Russians were also asked to withdraw their ambassador from İstanbul, and to pay an annual tribute to the Khân of Crimea as they had done before.[634]

Sultân Ahmed sent Charles XII to his country with precious gifts,[635] and 10,000 ducats as travelling expenses. Both the Swedish King and the Khân of Crimea were dissatisfied with this peace treaty, and wanted to have the Russian army annihilated at Prut. But the Osmanlıs were content with the concessions they got from the Russians because they were aware of the fact that the Osmanlı army did not fight as well as it used to, and the decline had begun; the situation was not as good as it seemed in terms of the army's fighting ability. But, on the other hand, the Russian army was becoming hungry; the Russian soldiers were reduced to eating the leaves and bark of trees since they had run out of provisions. General Ponyatofski of Sweden recommended that they not attack the Russian army but wait for their surrender, but this view was rejected.[636] It seems that the Osmanlı palace people made this decision, but they could not evaluate the situation as it deserved; the Osmanlıs used to be good fighters in the battlefield but were, in general, great losers at the negotiation table.

**War with Austria**

Meanwhile, it became known that some lost Muslim ships in the Mediterranean were being assaulted by Venetian pirates. The people of Morea were Orthodox and were now under the rule of the Catholic Venetians and favoured the Osmanlıs. At that time Qaradağ (Montenegro) revolted against the Osmanlı Devlet, but Köprülüzâde Nu'mân Pasha, *vâli* of Bosnia, suppressed the revolt.

The Venetians gave refuge to the rebels from Osmanlı Qaradağ. Hence, Sadrâzam Ali Pasha marched on Morea, and the *Donana-yı Hümâyûn* was also sent to Morea. This peninsula was reopened to Islam together with all its castles in 1127/1715. Morea was divided into 1400 districts of *kılıch tımarı* and Aydınlı Mehmed Ağa was appointed the top official in Morea.[637]

Ali Pasha sent a letter to the Austrians to secure their neutrality while he was engaged in war with Venice, explaining that the Venetians had violated the Treaty of Karlowitz. But the Austrians

## Chapter Twelve – The Resumption of Decline

became apprehensive because of the Osmanlıs' recapturing Morea that had been given to the Venetians by the Treaty of Karlowitz, thinking that they too were about to lose what they gained by the same treaty. Austria had signed the Treaty of Rashtad with France in 1723 after the wars of inheritance and wanted to temporise to make preparations for war with the Osmanlıs. The Osmanlı envoy who was sent to them was detained for four months and then was sent back with a letter.

Austria signed a treaty with Venice on 15 April 1716 and sent a letter to the Osmanlı Devlet claiming that Morea should be given to Venice.[638] Hence, Sadrâzam Ali Pasha fought them at the Battle of Peterwaradin in 1128/1716 and was fatally wounded. The janissaries assaulted the Austrian troops and captured some of their guns, but they hurriedly retreated to Belgrade once they knew of the martyrdom of the *sadrâzam* and the collapse of the right flank of the Osmanlı army.[639] The Austrians did not pursue them but crossed the river Danube to the south, captured Timişoara after three months of siege, and continued their advance to besiege Belgrade in 1129/1717. Sadrâzam Halîl Pasha tried to rescue the city but was defeated, and Belgrade finally fell into Austrian hands in 1129/1717.[640]

The new *sadrâzam*, Nevshehirli İbrâhîm Pasha (1717-1730), witnessed the weak performance of the janissaries at Peterwaradin and was convinced that they were too corrupt to fight Austria. Hence he opted for the immediate conclusion of a treaty, the Treaty of Passarowitz (Poroffa) in 1130/1718, by which the Osmanlıs surrendered both Belgrade and Timişoara to Austria as well as some territory on the Adriatic coast to the Venetians.[641] Nevertheless Nevshehirli İbrâhîm Pasha improved the finances of the Devlet and was particularly successful in significantly slashing expenditure within a few years. But his initiation of the luxurious *Lâle Devri* (period of tulip festivals) incited the people against him, and ultimately led to his death in 1143/1730.[642]

### War with Persia

The Afghans revolted in 1135/1723 against the Safavîs, captured Isfahân, and put a final end to Safavî rule in Persia. This action encouraged the Sunnî emîrs of Dağıstân (Dagestan) to proclaim their allegiance to the Osmanlı Devlet, which appointed one of them, Dâvûd, Khân of Shirvân. The Osmanlı army captured Tbilisi and appointed Shehnevar khân over it as well as over Hemedân, Revân, Ganjah and Tabrîz.[643]

Sadrâzam İbrâhîm Pasha appointed many of his relatives to key positions in the Devlet. This nepotism incited the people to revolt and depose Sultân Ahmed III in 1143/1730. Mahmûd I succeeded him as the Osmanlı Sultân.[644]

# Chapter Thirteen

# The Attempt at Restoration

## 13. SULTÂN MAHMÛD I (1730-1754)

Meanwhile Ahmed Pasha, the *vâli* of Osmanlı Baghdad, defeated Tahmasb, the Shâh of Persia, and forced him to sue for peace. But Nâdir Ali, head of the Afshâr tribe, opposed any compromise with the Osmanlıs, deposed Tahmasb, and appointed his infant son in his place, with himself as regent. Nâdir Ali proceeded to besiege Baghdad, but Topal Osman Pasha, the Osmanlı *vâli* of Erzurum, defeated the Persian army in a battle in 1146/1733. The Persians were dispersed, and their leader was wounded and fled. Subsequently, however, Nâdir Ali took advantage of Osman Pasha's illness to come back and defeat the Osmanlı army near Kirkuk. Furthermore, he defeated Köprülüzâde Abdullah Pasha near Revân, and became the Shâh of Persia at the request of the notables of the country in 1148/1736.[645]

### War with Russia

The Russians gave back Derbend castle and other places to Persia and concluded a treaty with it against the Osmanlıs. This was a clever move by the Russians: by conceding small advantages it drew Persia to her side in the struggle with the Muslim Osmanlı Devlet. But it constituted a treacherous act on Persia's part, an act they could not be allowed to get away with. By that treaty Persia committed a blunder that put it on the side of a strong non-Muslim country against a Muslim Devlet.

In the meantime, the Russians violated their peace treaty with the Osmanlıs, attacked the castles of Azak (Azov) and Özi (Odessa) in 1143/1730 and assaulted Crimea. Hence, Sultân Mahmûd sent Sadrâzam Silâhdâr Mehmed Pasha to deal with the situation. The Osmanlı army arrived at Babadağı, but the Austrians delayed its advance on the pretence they were mediating for peace, while they themselves had, in fact, assaulted Osmanlı territory in flagrant violation of their recent peace treaty with the Osmanlıs.

Mehmed Pasha was not an experienced commander, and the affairs of the Devlet were therefore entrusted to Osman Hâlis Efendi. But the latter refused to send the necessary equipment and ammunition to the garrisons of Özi, Bender, and Vidin on the grounds that this would constitute unnecessary expenditures, while a treaty was, in his judgement, at hand. Eventually this shortage of armaments led to the surrender of the strategic castles of Azak (Azov), Özi, and Kılburun to the Russians. This defeat cost Osman Hâlis Efendi his life, while Silâhdâr Pasha was dismissed from his post as *sadrâzam* and the commander of Bender castle, Abdullah Pasha, appointed in his place. Here the Osmanlıs experienced the wisdom of the *hadith sharîf* that says:

> "If (important) affairs are entrusted to unqualified persons, then expect the calamity of it (failure)."

The Russian army assaulted the Crimean peninsula, but its people transferred their households to secure places in the mountains, burned the grain, and disturbed the Russian army whenever feasible. Nonetheless, the invading Russian army burned and destroyed the peninsula, but it was finally compelled to withdraw, leaving behind more than 20,000 dead or missing soldiers.[646]

### War with Austria

Meanwhile, the Austrians assaulted the Nish, Bosnia, and Vidin areas. They captured Nish but were defeated by Hekimoğlu Ali

## Chapter Thirteen – The Attempt at Restoration

Pasha in Bosnia, where they suffered heavy casualties – about 60,000 soldiers.[647] Ahmed Pasha, son of Köprülüzâde Shehîd Mustafa Pasha, retrieved Nish from the Austrians in 1150/1737, while İvaz Mehmed Pasha defeated the advancing Austrian army at Vidin. The latter crossed the Danube to the north, defeated the Austrian armies in the Muhadiye and Harshova areas and captured the island of Ada Kale in the Danube in 1151/1738.[648] He inflicted another crushing defeat on the Austrian army that forced it to conclude the Treaty of Belgrade on 14 Jumâdal Âhira 1152/18 September 1739,[649] by which Belgrade, Serbia, and Harshova were given back to the Osmanlı Devlet.[650] The Osmanlı Sublime Devlet, having recovered its lost territories through the Treaty of Belgrade, secured its Balkan borders, and the castle of Belgrade served to prevent the Austrians from coming south of the Danube.[651]

Meanwhile, the Russians assaulted the Crimean peninsula again and the Bender area, but they were repulsed. Nu'mân Pasha, the commander of the Bender area, inflicted another defeat on the Russians, who were then obliged to surrender the castles of Özi and Kılburun and to conclude a peace treaty with the Osmanlı Devlet in 1739. It stipulated the demolition of the Azak (Azov) castle, whose site would be a vacant neutral zone, while the Osmanlı Devlet was authorised to build a castle on the Don River and another near the Sea of Azak (Azov). The Russians were, on the other hand, prohibited from having warships or commercial vessels in the Sea of Azak or the Black Sea, and their commerce through the latter was to be transported by Osmanlı vessels.[652]

### The Attempt at Restoration

During the wars between 1683-1699 the Osmanlı central administration recruited soldiers from among shopkeepers, grocers, and the like into its janissary force. To get an *ulûfe* (the janissaries' salary), those recruits were obliged to participate in at least one *jihâd* to ensure their adequate military training. But when the buying and selling of *ulûfes* was permitted in 1740, the central military organisation of the Osmanlı Devlet suffered greatly. Most of the *ulûfes* were purchased by shopkeepers and relatives of notables who deemed them a source of revenue and a kind of investment.[653]

After the conclusion of the treaty of Belgrade and up to the campaign of 1768, a period of peace prevailed in the Osmanlı Devlet, and therefore there was no need to recruit new soldiers. The *ulûfes* of the dead soldiers were, in principle, to be cancelled and returned to the treasury, but this did not always take place, and they were often sold by the supreme commander of the janissaries himself to some notables.[654] Due to this inefficiency and corruption, some people illegitimately and undeservedly obtained money from the Devlet, and consequently accelerated its collapse. Until about 1000/1592 the Devlet-*i 'Aliyye* (Sublime Devlet) had about 80,000-100,000 skilled, able, and well-equipped cavalry *(tımarlı sipâhî)*. But this number had progressively diminished during the eighteenth century to a quarter, which was a tenth in terms of efficiency.[655]

The period between 1740-1768 was an exceptionally calm one in Osmanlı history, a matter that led to laxity and lack of discipline among the soldiers. Indeed, the Devlet sent 300,000 soldiers to war with Russia, but they were defeated and the castle of Khotin was lost. The Osmanlı army suffered another crushing defeat that convinced the administrators of the inability of the army to achieve any victory, particularly as its morale and equipment were at their lowest ebb.[656] It seems that complacency had set in.

### War with Persia

During a four-year truce, Nâdir Shâh achieved notable success in his Indian campaigns. In 1156/1743 he attacked Osmanlı territory, including Kirkuk and Baghdad. But his assault on the castle of Mawsil was repelled by Hüseyin Pasha, and the Iranians suffered

## Chapter Thirteen – The Attempt at Restoration

about 6,000 casualties. Nâdir Shâh was also cornered in 1158/1745 by Yeğen Mehmed Pasha between Qars and Revân, but he soon managed to overcome this difficulty after the sudden death of the commander of the Osmanlı army and the subsequent chaos and confusion in its ranks. Nevertheless, at the appointment of Hekimoğlu Ali Pasha as *serdâr* on the eastern front, Nâdir Shâh sued for peace, which was concluded in 1159/1746. In this treaty the border between the Osmanlı Sublime Devlet and Persia was maintained as it had been at the time of Sultân Murâd IV.

Sultân Mahmûd I, who died in Safer 1168/November 1754, was anxious to strengthen the army and enhance its prestige.[657] During his reign, the famous Claude Alexandre Comte de Bonneval (1675-1747), who became known after his conversion to Islam as Humbarajı Ahmed Pasha, entered Osmanlı service and rendered great service to Islam. The Osmanlı Sublime Devlet had a *humbarajı*[i] unit of 300 men who served in castles. Humbarajı Ahmed Pasha set up another *humbarajı* unit of 300 whom he brought from Bosnia under the *sadrâzam* and undertook their training and administration.[658]

---

i  A *humbarajı* was a group of soldiers belonging to the administration of the *jebeji* and *topchu*. They made explosives called *humbara*.

# Chapter Fourteen

# Crisis and Struggle

## 14.1 SULTÂN MUSTAFA III (1757-1774)

### War with Russia

When Sultân Mahmûd died, his brother Osmân III (1754-1757) succeeded him, but nothing important happened deserving mention. He died after three years and was succeeded by Mustafa, son of Ahmed III.

Sultân Mustafa III benefited from the services of Baron de Tott. He believed that Russian expansionism made war inevitable, but his knowledgeable and intelligent *sadrâzam*, Râgib Pasha, (1756-1763) argued that the Osmanlı army was too weak to go to war with Russia. "He was right in his evaluation about the military situation: the European armies had gained discipline and the Osmanlı army, on the contrary, was undisciplined. He should have taken necessary measures to make up for the situation, but did not. This may be due to either hopelessness, or it may have been seen as too dangerous to undertake to renew the army. His age also may have had its effect: he was between 60 and 70."[659] Therefore, it could be maintained that the Osmanlı Devlet had to a great extent lost its dynamism by the second half of the eighteenth century.

Meanwhile Czarina Catherine, of German origin, conspired in 1174/1761 to murder her husband, Czar Peter III, and succeeded him. To rally the Russian people behind her, she actively interfered in the affairs of Poland, and tried to expand towards Turkestan as well.

## Chapter Fourteen – Crisis and Struggle

The Polish notables (locally known as *bans*) appealed to the Osmanlı Sublime Devlet for help, arguing that once the Russians captured Poland they would attack the Osmanlıs. They also promised to give Podolya to the Osmanlıs.

This issue of war with Russia was hotly debated in the Osmanlı court, where some weak and hypocritical advisors supported the Sultân's view. But the experienced Sadrâzam Mehmed Pasha, son of Muhsin Pasha, who was in charge of Khotin and Özi (Odessa), argued strongly against this war without making the proper preparations and equipping the castles on the border and was dismissed and replaced by Hamza Pasha. The Russian ambassador was summoned in 1769 and warned that his country's troops should evacuate Poland immediately. He asked for some time to get instructions from his government, but the Osmanlıs felt that he was temporising and hence imprisoned him. The Osmanlıs had thus apparently wanted to hold him as a hostage to guarantee the safety of the Muslim merchants in Russia.[660] Subsequently, Hamza Pasha was dismissed because of psychiatric problems and Mehmed Emin Pasha was appointed in his place. The new *sadrâzam* marched towards the Danube, though the Osmanlıs were not very prepared for war. The Russian army besieged the castle of Khotin, but Moldovanjı Ali Pasha and the Khân of Crimea, Devlet Gıray (r. 1769-70, 1775-77), forced it to flee. Nevertheless the *sadrâzam*, who was also *serdâr-ı ekrem* (the most honourable commander-in-chief), realised the critical condition of his army and asked to be relieved of his post. He was succeeded by Moldovanjı Ali Pasha in 1183/1769,[661] who crossed the Turla (Dniester) river, and cornered the Muscovite units. This development put Catherine II in an awkward situation, and was about to cause an upheaval in St. Petersburg, then the capital of Russia, had not sudden heavy rains swelled the Turla river and destroyed the bridge over it. Some Osmanlı units came back on boats while the others were dispersed, and the castle of Khotin was therefore left to the

Russians without a fight. The Russian troops penetrated Wallachia and Moldova, and unsuccessfully attacked the castles of Bender and Özi (Odessa). Meanwhile, Ali Pasha was dismissed and replaced by Halîl Pasha, son of İvaz Pasha, who crossed the Danube and, with Qaplan Gıray, trapped the Russian army commanded by Romanov. Though the Russian army was placed in a desperate situation similar to that of Prut in 1711, the Osmanlı army wasted its time fortifying its positions instead of launching an immediate attack before the Russian troops organised themselves. Though inferior in numbers, the better trained and disciplined Russian forces eventually defeated the Osmanlı army in 1184/1770.[662]

### The Annihilation of the Osmanlı Fleet

France informed the Osmanlı Devlet at the beginning of the war that the Russians would send a fleet to the Mediterranean. While the Osmanlıs were engaged debating this possibility,[i] the Russians sent a few warships from the Baltic Sea, reinforced by others from Britain, Holland, and Venice. They also hired naval officers and seamen. They emerged near the Morea Peninsula and incited people to revolt against the Osmanlı Devlet. Mehmed Pasha, son of Muhsin Pasha, was sent to Morea, and he subdued the revolt. The Osmanlı *qaptân-ı derya*, Husâmeddîn Pasha, set out for the Mediterranean and confronted the Russian fleet in two battles. Jezâyirli Hasan Beğ would have captured the flagship of the Russian

---

i  "The claim that the Osmanlıs were ignorant of the possibility of access from the Baltic Sea to the Mediterranean is a fiction invented by Hammer. In fact, the Osmanlıs' opinion was that Russia was far from able to equip such a fleet and send it to the Mediterranean where they had no bases." Quoted in Kemâl Beydilli, *Türk Bilim ve Matbaacılık Tarihinde Mühendishâne, Mühendishâne Matbaası ve Kütüphânesi (1776-1826)* İstanbul, 1995, p. 365, footnote 1.

fleet, had not fire flared up and the two ships burned. The two fleets separated. The Osmanlı fleet arrived at the port of Cheshme near İzmir in 1184/1770. The Russians, with the help of British, Dutch, and Venetian naval officers, made a surprise attack and burned the Osmanlı ships.[663] Meanwhile, an able soldier, Jezâyirli Hasan was promoted to pasha, and was appointed *vazîr*; he proceeded to the Dardanelles. The Russian fleet besieged the castle of the island of Lemnos, but Hasan Pasha managed to convey his soldiers by casual ships to this island. He attacked the Russians and defeated them in battle, after which he was rewarded with the title of *gâzi*.[664]

## The Russian Attack on Crimea

Meanwhile, a huge Russian army attacked Crimea in 1185/1771, defeated its Khân, Selîm Gıray, and imprisoned the Osmanlı *vâli* of Kefe, İbrâhîm Pasha.[665] Field Marshall Romanov marched on Silistre in 1187/1773 but suffered heavy casualties and retreated north of the Danube. The people of Crimea asked for help, and the *muhassıl* (tax collector) of Janik (Samsun) al-Hâj Ali Beğ, mustered 20,000 soldiers supported by Crimean troops. The peninsula was about to be liberated by force when a peace treaty was concluded with Russia. Sultân Mustafa died in grief of apoplexy in 1188/1774, and his brother Abdülhamîd became the Osmanlı Sultân.[666]

# Chapter Fifteen

# Another Attempt at Restoration

## 15. 1. SULTÂN 'ABDÜLHAMÎD I (1774-1789)

Sultân 'Abdülhamîd I, son of Sultân Ahmed III, ascended the throne at a time when the battles with Russia were in progress. The Russians arrived at Shumna and surrounded the Osmanlı army, and, hence, the treaty of Küchük Kaynarja was concluded on 8 Jumâdal Ûlâ 1187/17 July 1774. It stipulated that Crimea would be independent and that the status of the Russian ambassador in İstanbul was equal to that of the German and Dutch ambassadors, while the Russians were given the right to visit Jerusalem and to build a church in Beyoğlu (Pera) in İstanbul. Furthermore, Russian vessels would have access to the Black Sea and the Mediterranean. The Osmanlıs, on the other hand, were given the whole Bujak country, and the castles of Aqkerman, Kili, and İsmâîl, as well as the islands that had been captured by the Russians. Having the castle of Azak, Russia also agreed to evacuate Wallachia and Moldova in return for the sum of 15,000 purses of *aqchas* to be paid by the Osmanlıs within three years.[667]

The Russians asserted that Crimea should be independent as its incorporation under Osmanlı rule would encourage its aggression against their country. But such independence would probably facilitate any prospective Russian attempt to occupy the peninsula, and would, in the Osmanlıs' view, lead to the existence of the un-Islamic practice of two *khalîfah*s at the same time: the Osmanlı *khalîfah* and a *khalîfah* for Crimea. But the Osmanlıs were obliged

## Chapter Fifteen – Another Attempt at Restoration

to relinquish the peninsula, though they continued to keep religious ties with Crimea so that the *khutbah* was delivered in the name of the Osmanlı Sultân, and the Osmanlı Qazasker was authorised to instruct the chief *qadı* of Qırım (Crimea) to implement the *Sharî'at*. And the person chosen by the people of Crimea would be appointed by the Osmanlı Sultân as the Khân of Qırım.[668]

### Sadrâzam Halîl Hâmid Pasha

The Osmanlı Devlet expected Russia to violate the peace treaty of Küchük Kaynarja. Therefore they fortified the castles on its border, and Sadrâzam Halîl Hâmid Pasha (1782-1785) tried to build a strong fleet as well. They direly needed – what was extremely difficult to achieve – a radical policy to strengthen the army by improving the *tımar* system. Some people had been utilising the *tımar* that they inherited from their forefathers, while some *tımar*s were purchased by others as a means of livelihood.[669]

Nevertheless, Halîl Hâmid Pasha, a brave and resolute leader, increased the number of the staff called "swift gunners" from 300 to 2,000, and accumulate food and equipment for the army at strategic points. He checked the registers of the soldiers stationed on the borders, and prohibited the very bad custom of selling soldiers' salaries. He also dared to decide that the soldiers whose salaries were purchased by shopkeepers should not be regarded as recruits in the army and therefore not paid. But these daring and heroic activities against corruption in the *tımar* system cost him his post and led to his martyrdom in Jumâdal Âhira 1199/April 1785.[670]

From the above account we may reasonably conclude that by the end of the eighteenth century the Osmanlı Devlet still had the potential to be a superpower, though this was a formidable task that needed a courageous, farsighted, and imaginative man like Halîl Hâmid Pasha. And notables whose interests were curtailed by such persons could not allow them to survive. But the Osmanlı Devlet was not unique in this respect in the world of the eighteenth century, as William Houston maintains in the following lengthy statement:

> "During the 1780s, France was run essentially by a council of aristocrats with the King at its head. It was in many ways a time of considerable prosperity: roads were the best in Europe, the administration was being reformed, industry was thriving, many peasants had been given their freedom, and torture was no longer being used to extract confessions.
>
> "Unfortunately, the country was also bankrupt. It had overspent on helping the American colonies win their War of Independence, and the administration was attempting to recoup its losses. The nobles and the church, however, refused to accept a rise in taxes. Instead, this was to fall primarily on the middle class and traders through the payment of *péages*, internal duties levied on the passage of goods along roads, rivers and canals.
>
> "It was also to fall on the peasantry with their seigneurial obligations to the manor or castles. What was worse, food prices were rising as a result of crop failures and, by 1789, those worst off were paying 80 per cent of their income for bread up from two-thirds at the start of the decade. Matters came to a head over the 14 July storming of the Bastille, which acted as a trigger for uprisings all over the country. A National Assembly was formed as the court council disintegrated."[671]

### Qırım (Crimea)

The Russians managed through intrigues and corruption to have their man Shâhin Gıray (1777-1782) installed as the Khân of an independent Crimea, though the weak Osmanlı Devlet was then in

## Chapter Fifteen – Another Attempt at Restoration

favour of his brother Selîm Gıray. But the Russians were engaged in propaganda against Shâhin Gıray whom they had caused to be installed. The Crimeans did not at all like the Eurocentric Shâhin Gıray who consumed wine in public and ate his meals seated at the table like Europeans. Thus, they revolted against him in 1782 and replaced him with Bahadır Gıray. By that time the political situation in Europe favoured Russia. While Britain was exclusively engaged in suppressing the American Revolution, France extended a friendly hand to Russia. Moreover, Franz Josef, the presumed stupid sovereign of Austria, naively believed the promise of the deceitful Russian sovereign Catherine II (1782-1796) to give him some Osmanlı territories, and consequently concluded a treaty with the Russians.[672] But Catherine II sent Marshal Potemkin to Crimea in 1197/1783 at the head of a large army that assembled the Crimean notables in the plain of Aqsu and forced them to swear allegiance to Shâhin Gıray. This amounted to *de facto* Russian sovereignty over Crimea and Taman. Infuriated by this trick, Shâhin Gıray took refuge within a few months with the Osmanlıs who sent him to the island of Rhodes to be executed for his treachery. The Osmanlı Devlet, however, recognised Russian rule over Crimea and Taman in the Treaty of Zishtovi of 1207/1792.[673]

**War with Austria and Russia (1201/1787)**

Sultân Abdülhamîd was not in favour of war as he was extremely touched by the hardship and tragedies that people suffered in the border areas. He used to pray, saying: "If the servants of Allah are trampled underfoot, may Allah take my soul." Nevertheless, the Osmanlı Devlet was obliged to declare war on Russia in view of the extensive and humiliating demands of the Russian ambassador in İstanbul, and the arrogant behaviour of Catherine who came to Crimea in 1786 with pompous ceremonies. Moreover, Britain and Prussia had urged the Osmanlıs to take this action that served their purposes, while the Austrians declared war on the Osmanlıs allegedly because of their treaty with Russia.

Sultân Abdülhamîd received Sadrâzam Qoja Yûsuf Pasha in the *Hırka-i Sa'âdet Dâiresi* (the quarter allocated to preserve holy relics in Topqapusu Sarayı – Topkapı Palace) and gave him Sanjaq-ı Sharîf, praying for him and telling him that he had absolute authority, even over his own son, Shâhzâda Mustapha.[674]

The Osmanlı army set out and reached Edirne, though it was not clear whom it was to fight, Russia or Austria. The Serbs had, in the meanwhile, been harassing the Osmanlıs and causing trouble for them, a policy that they pursued for a century whenever there was war between the Osmanlı Devlet and Austria. The advance of the Osmanlı army to Silistre on its way to Russia would expose Osmanlı Belgrade to virtual siege by Austrian forces. Thus the Osmanlıs assigned some of their forces under Shâhîn Ali Pasha to confront the Russians on land, and Qapudân-ı Deryâ Gâzi Hasan Pasha was assigned to defend the coastal areas against Russians, while the main body of *Ordu-yu Hümâyûn* headed towards Vidin.[675]

Sadrâzam Yûsuf Pasha (d. 1800) conquered the fortifications of Inlik, and defeated the Austrian imperial army while the commander of Osmanlı Belgrade crossed the Danube and captured the plain of Banat. The Austrians suffered heavy casualties (eighty guns), and the Osmanlıs captured 50,000 prisoners of war. Yûsuf Pasha wanted to preserve those areas, but the soldiers left them with huge booty, and the *sadrâzam* was thus obliged to retreat in October 1788 to winter encampment at Ruschuk, 1203/1788.[676]

### The Invasion of Özi Castle

Marshall Potemkin of Russia besieged the castle of Özi (Odessa) with 80,000 soldiers, but faced gallant resistance. Meanwhile, the Osmanlı fleet, led by the *qapudân-ı deryâ*, Jezâyirli Hasan Pasha (1774-1790), approached Özi. Though unable to advance because

## Chapter Fifteen – Another Attempt at Restoration

of shallow water there, he managed to defeat the Russian fleet that came from Aqyar (Sevastopol). Soon, however, he returned to İstanbul in 1203/1788 because of a violent storm that obstructed the path of auxiliary ships. Eventually, Potemkin captured the castle of Özi after a fierce three-day battle in which he lost 20,000 soldiers. He allowed Russian soldiers to plunder Özi for three days, during which they martyred 25,000 Muslims, including civilians. Sultân Abdülhamîd was so sorry for the loss of Özi (Odessa) and the massacre of its people that he died in grief in 1203/April 1789.[677] He, like his father before him, could not stand seeing the sufferings of his children, which was typical behaviour for an Osmanlı Sultân.

### 15.2 SULTÂN SELÎM III (1789-1807)

Selîm III, Abdülhamîd's nephew and son of Mustafa III, succeeded to the Osmanlı throne. He received *bay'at* in front of Aqağalar Qapısı, at Topqapusu Palace.[678] Due to a personal grudge, Shemseddîn, a certain top official, misguided the new young Sultân to replace the able Sadrâzam Yûsuf Pasha with Hasan Pasha in 1789. The latter was defeated at Boze in 1203/1789 by a combined Austrian and Russian army, and the Osmanlı Devlet lost the castles of Aqkerman and Bender to Russia[679] and Belgrade to Austria. A large Russian army attacked the city of İsmail, but was defeated by Jezâyirli Gâzi Hasan Pasha.[680] The latter executed Tayfûr Pasha for his cowardly withdrawal from the castles of Bender, Aqkerman, and Kili, which fell into the hands of the Russians. While actively preparing for war, the elderly (80 years old) Sadrâzam Hasan Pasha died of malaria at Shumna in 1204/1790. The new *sadrâzam*, Sharîf Hasan Pasha, repelled an Austrian siege of the castle of Yerköy led by Prince Koburg,[681] but he could not withstand another Russian assault by land and river on the castle of İsmail, which was captured by the enemy in 1205/December 1790 after heavy losses of 20,000 on each side.[682] Sadrâzam Sharîf Hasan Pasha himself was executed in February

1791 at Shumna for his failure. He had spent 50 days on the plain of Yerköy instead of immediately attacking the defeated Austrians; he had not been successful in his attack upon the Austrians because the war between them and Prussia had then ended and the former had gathered its forces together. This indicates that the Osmanlı Devlet dealt severely with catastrophic failure no matter who was at fault or what his position.

Qoja Yûsuf Pasha was appointed *sadrâzam* a second time. While aware of the weakness of the Osmanlı army, he tried to impress on the Russians his readiness for a bloody war if necessary, though at the same time he indicated his desire for peace as well. A treaty with the Russians was prepared in 1206/August 1791, but Sultân Selîm III strongly objected to its terms, particularly the Osmanlıs' surrender of Odessa, and instead opted for war. However, the pashas strongly advised the Sultân against this adventure because the army was not ready for it. Moreover, the impact of the French Revolution of 1789 was strongly felt throughout Europe, and Prussia did not honour her commitments to come to the support of her ally, the Osmanlıs, against Russia. Under these circumstances, the Osmanlı Devlet was obliged to endorse the Treaty of Iashi with Russia in February 1792, for which the Turla River marked the border. Russia got Odessa and the Osmanlı Devlet reluctantly accepted its annexation of Crimea and Taman, while they retrieved Bender, Kili, and Aqkerman.[683] The noticeable improvement in the strength of the Osmanlı army might have enabled it to deal with Russia in this war had it not been obliged to fight two enemies at the same time (Russia and Austria). The Osmanlı soldiers were brave and good fighters, and, when disciplined, proved to be a match for the very strong Russian army. The Osmanlı Devlet also concluded the Treaty of Zishtovi with Austria in 1206/August 1791, by which the Osmanlıs retrieved Belgrade in return for some boundary amendments in favour of Austria. Yûsuf Pasha was appointed *vâli* of Trebizond and *serasker*

## Chapter Fifteen – Another Attempt at Restoration

(Chief of Staff and Minister of War) of Anapa in May 1792, while Melek Mehmed Pasha became *sadrâzam*. When his friends criticised the laxity of the administration, the latter sarcastically replied, "During my first meeting with Sultân Selîm, I told him that my observation was that the high officials in the Devlet were very loyal to him and they were very dynamic. The next day many influential people sent me precious gifts and thanked me. So I understood that whatever I said to the Sultân, they would know about it and they would be consulted. Consequently, I have preferred to be on good terms with them."[684] This shows the unhealthy atmosphere within the Osmanlı administrative body in that period. The *sadrâzam* had, in fact, recklessly referred all of the affairs of the Devlet to those influential quarters, including official reports for improving the Osmanlı territorial and naval forces. Melek Mehmed Pasha remained in office for two and a half years. The Sultân, who at that time was keen to have a new army (*Nizâm-ı Jedîd* or the New Order) and an efficient arsenal, replaced him in October 1794 with a very able and honest man, İzzet Mehmed Pasha, the governor of Egypt.

### The French Invasion of Egypt in 1798

In 1209/1794 the Osmanlı Devlet recognised the republican regime that was set up in France after the success of the French Revolution of 1789. It appointed Ali Efendi as its ambassador to Paris, while France sent Ambassador Vertinac to İstanbul.

At the request of the French ambassador, in May 1796 the Osmanlıs concluded a fifteen-article treaty with France that provided for a general coordination between the Osmanlı Devlet and the French Republic in European wars and stated in particular the neutrality of the Osmanlıs in any future wars between France and Britain. The French ambassador had stated that such a treaty would have benefited both sides; he even mentioned the possibility of the Osmanlı Devlet retrieving Crimea. Some of the Osmanlı administrators were of the opinion that the French used to change their politics continually, and such a treaty between the Osmanlı Devlet and France would possibly incite the enmity of Russia and Austria towards the Osmanlıs; it would therefore be wiser to postpone concluding it. But the Sultân was in favour of the treaty, thus the *sheyhülislâm* and the *qâdıaskers* of Rumelia and Anatolia and other notables were summoned, the topic was discussed and the conclusion was presented to the Sultân. Nevertheless, the Sultân insisted on concluding the treaty immediately, and it was signed and exchanged on 17 Zil Qaʻdah 1210/24 May 1796.[685]

Shortly after that, France and Austria divided the Venetian territory between them, with France acquiring the Adriatic Sea, the Seven Islands, and Preveza, and thus had common borders with the Osmanlı Devlet, which had borders with Russia and Austria in Europe. Napoleon Bonaparte (1769-1821) was authorised by the republican government of France to set out into the Mediterranean at the head of 60,000 soldiers. He arrived first at Malta, which he blockaded with 25 warships and more than 300 auxiliary ships and gained control of it. He finished off the pirates who called themselves the "Knights of St. John";[686] they had gone there from Rhodes when it was opened to Islam in 1522 by Süleymân the Magnificent. This organisation was set up in 1070 in Jerusalem, moved to Cyprus in 1292, and then settled in Rhodes in 1306. "After the Muslim conquest of the Holy Land, the order had established itself as a fortified bastion against Islam, becoming the principal base for the pirates who raided Ottoman shipping in the Aegean and eastern Mediterranean and supported the various Crusader naval efforts in the environs."[687]

After that, Napoleon arrived in Alexandria, the port of Osmanlı Egypt, and, without any formal declaration of war, suddenly deployed his soldiers on Egyptian soil in July 1798. He tried to justify this unusual and out-of-place action, claiming that he came to Egypt

## Chapter Fifteen – Another Attempt at Restoration

to prevent the imperialistic activities of Britain by supporting the Osmanlı Devlet and to put an end to impertinent behaviour of the Mamlûks in Egypt; as if the Osmanlı Devlet had wanted him to do so. Vâli Bekir Pasha, Reîsul Umerâ İbrâhîm Beğ, and Murâd Beğ tried to defend Egypt with 30,000 soldiers, doing their best, but they were eventually defeated by the very well trained French army equipped with modern weapons.[688]

### Jezzâr Ahmed Pasha

After the invasion of Egypt, Napoleon Bonaparte wanted to have Syria also. He said, "I decided to march on Syria in the framework of colonialism. Syria and Egypt must be under the same government."[689] Napoleon tried to deceive Jezzâr Ahmed Pasha (d. 1804) of Osmanlı 'Akkâ, but the Pasha did not answer his letters.

Britain was not happy with the French invasion of Egypt. There was competition between these two imperial powers. After the Seven Years War (1756-1763) among the European powers, the Treaty of Paris (1763) stipulated that France give up its colonies in Canada and India to Britain. That France had Egypt, an important country in Africa situated along the passage to India, was not a situation that Britain could possibly accept. As a result, Admiral Nelson of Britain burnt the French ships.

General Napoleon Bonaparte advanced to Syria, taking Haifa castle by agreement and the castle of Jaffa by battle, but he massacred 5,000 Albanian and Arab soldiers. Arriving at 'Akkâ (Acre), Napoleon besieged the city for fifty days, during which he lost more than 15,000 soldiers, and was finally utterly defeated. This was Napoleon's first defeat. He buried the heavy guns of the French army there, and hurriedly retreated to Egypt after poisoning all the wounded and sick French soldiers. Had Napoleon not attacked 'Akkâ, the French occupation of Egypt would probably have lasted much longer. The siege of 'Akkâ and the humiliating defeat the French suffered there is indeed a turning point in the history of that region.[690]

The French occupation of Egypt had an important effect on world history; the centre of European politics shifted to the Mediterranean for three years. It was a failure for France: it could not have Egypt, it could not hinder Britain's route to India, it could not dominate the eastern part of the Mediterranean. But the scientists and learned men who came with Bonaparte to Egypt had an enormous impact on the people of Egypt and the future of the country.

The French adventure in Egypt was of great service to Britain; the danger of Napoleon, who threatened the British hold on the Orient, was gone; the British settled in Malta during this campaign, and thus had a second important stronghold in addition to Jabal Târiq (Gibraltar) to control the western part of the Mediterranean.[691]

### The Osmanlı Retrieval of Egypt

With the French occupation of Egypt, İzzet Mehmed Pasha was summarily dismissed, and the *vâli* of Erzurum, Yûsuf Ziyâ Pasha was appointed *sadrâzam* in his place. The Osmanlı Devlet concluded a treaty with Britain and Russia against the French in 1798, and in 1799 Russian ships joined Osmanlı ships in İstanbul under Shermet Kapudan. Together they recaptured the Jezâyir-i Seb'a (the Seven Islands) from France. Tepedelenli Ali Pasha (d. 1822) recaptured Preveza, Parga, and two other castles on the shore of the Adriatic. As was the case in Dubrovnik, a republic was set up on those Seven Islands under the sovereignty of the Osmanlı Devlet, to which it paid a tribute of 70,000 ducats every three years.[692]

Napoleon, stranded in Egypt due to the loss of his fleet, contacted Sidney Smith, the Admiral of the British Fleet, received permission from him to send some men to France, and, thus deceiving him, left Egypt himself on two small ships during Rabî'ul Âkhir 1214/ November 1799 and went to Marseilles. He left General Kleber

## Chapter Fifteen – Another Attempt at Restoration

behind in Egypt, who was authorised to conclude a treaty with Britain if no naval reinforcements reached him from France within six months, for Napoleon knew very well that France could probably not maintain its position in Egypt without a strong fleet.[i]

Yûsuf Ziyâ Pasha arrived in Damascus at the head of an Osmanlı army that was strengthened en route by new recruits. He reopened al-'Arish to Islam, and hence the French decided to withdraw from Egypt. Kleber, the British representatives, and a representative of Ziyâ Pasha concluded an agreement that specified the arrangements for this withdrawal in January 1801. By February 1801 the French had started to withdraw, but, on the very day they were to evacuate the castle, the British admiral received a sudden directive from London that they were to surrender it with all its weapons. This breach infuriated the French general and his soldiers, and they therefore carried out a surprise attack on British positions. But they were eventually defeated and forced to surrender Egypt in 1801, their weapons divided between the Osmanlıs and the British. Vazîr Hüsrev Pasha was appointed *vâli* of Egypt, and Sadrâzam Yûsuf Ziyâ Pasha returned to İstanbul, leaving behind 10,000 soldiers to deal with any trouble by the Mamlûk notables. The French occupation of Egypt lasted only about three years yet cost them dearly: 40-50,000 soldiers and a navy.[693] But it had, on the other hand, a tremendous impact on Egypt and the entire Muslim world. In due course, Egypt became stronger than the Osmanlı Devlet itself because the Egyptians adopted Western ideas and weaponry under the rule of Muhammad 'Ali and his dynasty.

---

i   The military genius Sultân Selîm knew this fact very well as early as 1517 when the Osmanlı Devlet took over Egypt; he waited for the arrival of the *Donanma-yı Hümâyûn* before sending a *fathnâmas* (declaration) to other countries, stating that he was taking over Egypt.

### The Beginning of Europeanisation: Nizâm-ı Jedîd

The Osmanlıs had begun to renew and improve their army during the time of Sultân Mahmûd I (1730-1754).

Comte de Bonneval, who converted to Islam and became known as Humbaracı Ahmed Pasha, was entrusted with the implementation of this policy. He trained *humbaracı* soldiers and was of the opinion that "an able general could conquer all the world with those soldiers."[694] During the time of Sultân Mustafa III, a Hungarian noble, Baron de Tott, was appointed to train the Osmanlı soldiers. Sultân Mustafa strongly believed that the janissary corps was no longer useful because of its lack of discipline. He set up the Mühendishâne-yi Bahrî-yi Hümâyûn (Naval Engineering College) in 1773 to train the officers, with Baron de Tott as a teacher.[695]

After the defeat of the Osmanlı navy at Cheshme in 1770, Gâzi Hasan Pasha emerged as an able figure. He was appointed *qapudân-ı deryâ*. "He understood that while modern ships were needed, they would not be enough unless they were manned by able officers and men trained in the new techniques of naval warfare. Hence his reforms proceeded on two fronts: firstly, new shipyards were built in the Golden Horn, the Black Sea, and the Aegean.... Secondly, Gazi Hasan also worked to build a career naval service. Sailors were enrolled from villages along the coasts of the Aegean and eastern Mediterranean, but the old system of allowing them to live unsupervised in bachelor quarters in Qasımpaşa and Galata was replaced with barracks at the naval arsenal itself, at Sinop on the Black Sea, and on Midilli island in the Aegean, where they were subject to constant discipline and training. To provide officers for the fleet he developed de Tott's school for mathematics into a full-fledged Naval Engineering School (*Mühendisâne-i Bahri-i Hümâyûn*), with instruction provided by de Tott, Campbell, and foreign and Ottoman specialists in geometry, navigation, and the like."[696]

## Chapter Fifteen – Another Attempt at Restoration

Once he came to power, Sultân Selîm began to actively implement his father's ideas, and in 1206/1792 ordered his top officials to present ideas to improve the situation. He also ordered extra training for the janissary corps, and at the same time began forming a new army. He improved the military institutions, set up *Mühendishâne-i Berrî-i Hümâyûn* (Land Engineering School) in Hasköy, İstanbul, in 1794. He built 45 new ships, and set up an organisation called *irâd-ı jedîd* (the new revenue) to deal with the financial affairs of the *Nizâm-ı Jedîd*.[697]

Meanwhile, a capable and ambitious soldier named Muhammad 'Alî emerged in Egypt. He was originally a soldier in the expedition that the Osmanlıs sent from Rumelia to Egypt during Napoleon's invasion of the country. Immediately after the French evacuation of Egypt, Muhammad 'Alî conspired against Hüsrev Pasha, the Osmanlı *vâli* of Egypt, and caused so much trouble for his successors they were unable to control the situation. He also managed to subdue the Mamlûk notables and in the end became an Osmanlı *vazîr* and *vâli* of Egypt in 1220/1805.

### The Deposition of Selîm III

During this time, unrest and instability spread throughout the Osmanlı Devlet. The Wahhâbîs became more of an influence in the Arabian Peninsula, while riots and uprisings spread in Greece, the Morea Peninsula, the Mediterranean, and Serbia. The Osmanlı Devlet was unable to cope with this dangerous situation, and the *ulemâ* blamed the *Nizâm-ı Jedîd* for this drastic failure. Nevertheless, having set up the *Nizâm-ı Jedîd* in İstanbul and Anatolia, Selîm III decided to introduce it in Rumelia as well. But Sadrâzam İsmâîl Pasha was adamantly against it, and had in fact secretly approached the notables to resist it. The failure of the *Nizâm-ı Jedîd* in Rumelia encouraged other provinces to actively oppose and conspire against it.

It seems that the *Nizâm-ı Jedîd* had been set up without lengthy thought and preparation. Many influential people were not convinced of its suitability, while others felt that the replacement of the janissaries with a new structure should be well-planned so that no room would be left to the janissaries to revolt and threaten the very existence of the Devlet.

Led by Kabakchı Mustafa, the soldiers on the Bosphorus revolted, and Sultân Selîm was forced to abdicate in 1807. Just before his abdication some of his advisers advised him to summon the Osmanlı army that had been sent via the Danube against the rebels. But he magnanimously refused, saying: "No, in that case the Russian armies could arrive at Chatalja (near İstanbul)."[698] This indicates that he placed the integrity of the Osmanlı Devlet well above his personal interest.

Sultân Selîm III had a fondness for the fine arts, poetry, and songs. He was a fairly good poet and a musical composer. He invented tunes of *sûz-i dilârâ* in classical Osmanlı music. But he and the notables of his *Devlet* loved extravagance and luxury. Perhaps this was a major reason for the people's dislike of the idea of *Nizâm-ı Jedîd*, which had been borrowed from Europe. Selîm's other blunder was his neglect of the views of the *'ulamâ* and learned men. For example, he, overruled their opinion of the necessity to discuss the question of concluding a treaty with France with the other Osmanlı leaders, and concluded a treaty forthwith. A short time later, the French ignored its provisions and invaded Egypt.

## 15.3 SULTÂN MUSTAFA IV (1807-1808)

Selîm III was succeeded in 1807 by Mustafa, who was not well educated and was obliged to be on good terms with those who deposed Selîm. The supporters of the *Nizâm-ı Jedîd*, on the other hand, had sided with 'Alemdâr Mustafa Pasha of Ruschuk,[699]

## Chapter Fifteen – Another Attempt at Restoration

who was originally a janissary promoted in 1221/1806 to the rank of *vazîr* because of his success in the battles against the Russians. While the *Ordu-yu Hümâyûn* was on its way from Edirne to İstanbul, 'Alemdâr joined the *sadrâzam* with 16,000 troops. Before entering İstanbul, the army sent Hajı Ali Ağa to execute Kabakchı Mustafa, then in charge of the Bosphorus. Subsequently, 'Alemdâr Mustafa Pasha controlled İstanbul in 1223/1808 with 15,000 soldiers. He planned to reinstate Selîm III, but, in an attempt to secure his position, Sultân Mustafa ordered the immediate execution of both Selîm and Shâhzâda Mahmûd. Selîm was killed, but Mahmûd managed to escape. In that same year the latter became the Osmanlı Sultân, and appointed 'Alemdâr his *sadrâzam*.[700]

### 15.4 SULTÂN MAHMÛD II (1808-1839)

Mahmûd II, the new young sultân, summoned the *a'yâns* (influential local authorities) from all the Osmanlı provinces and areas to a meeting in İstanbul. It was frankly and courageously addressed by 'Alemdâr Mustafa Pasha, who argued that the undisciplined janissary corps were the main cause of the disintegration of the Osmanlı Devlet and that this could only be arrested by the formation of a new army, called *Sekbân-ı Jedîd*.[701] He added that this rejuvenation was the wish of *Pâdishâh-ı güzîn ve Khalîfe-i Rûy-i Zemîn* (the Choice Sultân and the *Khalîfah* of the World).[702] This was an attempt to institutionalise the power and authority of the *a'yâns*, who produced a document called *sened-i ittifâq* (document of agreement), which enumerated some principles for strengthening the authority of the Devlet. The *Shaykhülislâm* issued a *fetvâ* declaring the authenticity and compatibility of the document with the *Sharî'at*, and the Sultân ratified it with his *Khatt-ı Hümâyûn* (Heavenly Decree).[703]

But one night in November 1808 the opponents of these novelties, together with some janissaries, attacked the home of 'Alemdâr

Mustafa Pasha. He was martyred, and the *Sekbân-ı Jedîd* organisation was thus abolished.[704] The rioters were planning to reinstate Mustafa, but he was executed[705] before they could do so.

The French emperor and the Russian czar took advantage of this disorder, and concluded an agreement against the Osmanlı Devlet. In 1810 the Russian army (for the first time) attacked Osmanlı territory from the Anatolian side. The Russians captured the castles of İsmâîl and İbrâil in the European part of the Osmanlı Devlet, though they were defeated at the battles that took place at Shumna[706] and Silistre.[707] The Russians also invaded Wallachia and Moldova on the Rumelian side, while the Serbs revolted under Qarayorgi against the Osmanlıs. But Napoleon suddenly attacked Russia and the Russians were thus compelled to conclude the treaty of Bucharest with the Osmanlıs in 1812. This treaty provided that the river Prut would demarcate the boundary between the two powers: the Osmanlıs gave up Bessarabia to Russia[708] but Hurshid Pasha subdued the Serbs and returned to İstanbul in 1229/1814.[709]

Once they settled their problems with Russia and the Serbs, the Osmanlıs directed their attention toward the rising danger of the Wahhâbîs in the Arabian Peninsula. Muhammad 'Ali Pasha of Osmanlı Egypt was asked to deal with this threat promptly and decisively. He sent his sons Tosun Pasha and İbrâhîm Pasha to Arabia at the head of a strong army. They defeated the Wahhâbîs in a number of battles and managed to assert the authority of the Devlet in that important peninsula.[710]

### Nationalism and Its Impact on the Osmanlı Devlet

Nationalism had begun to emerge in Europe by that time, and it was used to incite Osmanlı non-Muslim peoples against their government. Nationalism has been described as "a doctrine invented in Europe at the beginning of the nineteenth century" that "holds that humanity is naturally divided into nations, the nations are

## Chapter Fifteen – Another Attempt at Restoration

known by certain characteristics which can be ascertained, and that the only legitimate type of government is national self government."[711] This doctrine was used by Europeans to unite Germany as a nation and Italy, but to fragment the Osmanlı Devlet which consisted of so many national communities. It was, however, a political doctrine,[712] and it did not really matter whether it was an objective reality or not. Mussolini said about this doctrine: "We have created our myth. The myth is a faith, it is a passion. It is not necessary that it be a reality. It is reality by the fact that it is good, a hope, a faith, that it is courage. Our myth is the Nation, our myth is the greatness of the Nation! And to this myth, to this grandeur, that we wish to translate a complete reality, *we subordinate all the rest.*"[713]

Until the end of the eighteenth century the dominant motive in Europe as well as in the Osmanlı domain was faith: Christianity in the former and Islam in the latter. Nationalism emerged to provide a specific theory of political legitimacy. "Although it drew on earlier ideas, the theory was developed during the tumultuous period of the French revolutionary wars between 1789 and 1815 as a novel alternative to predominant modes of thought which grounded the authority of government in tradition, divine right, or natural law."[714] The western powers used this new doctrine to break up the Osmanlı Devlet by inciting first its non-Muslim *ra'âyâ* and then, in the First World War, its Muslim *ra'âyâ* too.

### The Greek Revolt

The Russians incited the Greeks and other Osmanlı non-Muslim peoples in Europe to revolt against Osmanlı rule. Riots started in Wallachia, and then spread in Morea in 1236/1821. They were easily suppressed in Wallachia, but acquired dangerous dimensions in Morea where the priests took an active role in encouraging this violence. The Greeks in Morea had been apprehensive of Tepedelenli Ali Pasha. But Hâlet Efendi, the *mühürdâr* of Sultân Mahmûd II, became angry with Tepedelenli because the latter stopped sending him the usual gifts. Moreover, Hâlet Efendi had served the Greek notables in İstanbul and he was a *mürebbî* of their children.

The person who encouraged and administrated the revolt was Alexander İpsilanti, aide-de camp of the Russian Czar. A secret society called Etniki Eterya was responsible for the revolt, and this society was directed by İpsilanti. The society was established in Odessa in 1814, with its alleged objective being to spread education among the Christians who lived in the Osmanlı domain. Its real objective was to revive the Byzantine empire under the leadership of the Orthodox Patriarch in İstanbul. Tepedelenli Ali Pasha received information about the Greek preparations to revolt in Morea and he obtained a letter written by the committee members to the despot of Yanya. He summoned the despot, giving him the letter and asking him to read it. The despot died on the spot out of shock and fear. Tepedelenli Ali Pasha reported the situation to İstanbul. Hâlet Efendi sent Nicola Moruzi, who was a translator at the *Dîvân* and a member of Etniki Eterya, to Morea to investigate. Naturally, Moruzi reported that the Rûm *ra'âyâ* were loyal to the Devlet. It was decided therefore, that Tepedelenli Ali Pasha should be punished. Thus, Tepedelenli was driven to the point of rebellion because of Hâlet Efendi's secret plans, and Hurshid Pasha was turned against him. The riots in Wallachia were subdued easily, and Alexander İpsilanti fled and took refuge in Austria. The Russian Czar criticised the revolt. But the situation in Morea reached dangerous dimensions because the priests took an active role in encouraging the violence. The Rûm Orthodox Patriarch in İstanbul was an influential member of the Etniki Eterya, but upon the Russian Czar's criticism of the rebellion, he became afraid and issued a proclamation, blaming those who had insisted on rebellion. This proclamation had some effect in İstanbul and Rumelia, but it did not have any effect in Morea. Hâlet Efendi, who continuously misled the Sultân and the *sadrâzam*, was

## Chapter Fifteen – Another Attempt at Restoration

sent to Qonya and then executed there.[715] "It became clear through papers that had been obtained that both the Patriarchate in İstanbul and the priests in the courtryside were involved in the rebellion, they were executed and *vazîrs*, officers were posted to the islands and the coasts."[716] The Rûm (Greek) Orthodox Archbishop Gregory in İstanbul, being a member of the Osmanlı *ra'âyâ*, was charged and executed in 1236/1821 for high treason;[717] a case that, even in our present day, would be repeated by any state without hesitation.[i]

To this day, the Rûm (Greeks) keep the doors of the gate in İstanbul from which he was hanged firmly closed, to remind their children of this incident whenever they go there and to instil in them a sense of hatred toward the country in which they live and enjoy full rights of citizenship.

Because Greek philosophy is one of the three elements of European culture, there was sympathy with the Rûms (Greeks who are "supposed" to be related to ancient Greeks, in fact, a myth) in Europe; thus, Colonel Fabvier served in the army of Napoleon, and Lord Byron aided the rebels in Morea.[718]

The Osmanlı Devlet was unable to subdue the rebellion in Morea; the janissary forces were of no use, and the attempt to set up a new army was unsuccessful. Therefore, the help of the *vâli* of Egypt Muhammad 'Ali Pasha was sought. His son, İbrâhîm Pasha, was appointed *vâli* of Morea with full authority, and the *vâli* of Vidin, Reshîd Pasha, was also appointed *beğlerbeği* of Rumelia and *serasker* (commander-in-chief), given responsibility and full authority to collaborate with İbrâhîm Pasha. İbrâhîm Pasha advanced from southern Morea with well-trained Egyptian forces and recaptured many places from the rebels. Reshîd Pasha advanced from the north and besieged the Missolonghi castle, which was very well fortified

---

i  Let us remember the attitude of the United States of America toward Texas when the latter wanted to secede!

and was protected by the sea. It was very difficult to take it. With the collaboration of Kapudân-ı Deryâ Hüsrev Pasha and İbrâhîm Pasha, this last stronghold of the rebels was subdued in 1241/1826.[719]

The Russian policy during Czar Nicholas I's reign was focused on destroying the Osmanlı Devlet. In fact, this policy was a continuation of Russian expansionism. Nationalism[i] began spreading among the Christian *ra'âyâ* of the Osmanlı Devlet.[720] Nicholas was closely involved in the following events directly or indirectly.

*The Weekend Gate. The locked gate at the Patriarchate.*

### Vaq'a-yı Khayriyye (1241/1826)

The discipline of the janissaries deteriorated grossly in the eighteenth century and especially in the first quarter of the nineteenth century. The deterioration reached such a level that many shopkeepers and

---

i  Nationalism emerged in Europe after the French Revolution as a political-ideological notion rather than depending on a real and rational base. Now, in Europe, the various nations are grouped under the name of "The European Union." But nationalism is still "employed" by Europeans and their followers among the other peoples of the world.

## Chapter Fifteen – Another Attempt at Restoration

artisans who held paid janissary posts were receiving *ulûfe* (the salary of the janissaries) but did nothing and were in fact troublemakers.

Sultân Mahmûd II had learned from the previous aborted attempts to abolish the janissary corps. Therefore he appointed the right people to the right places to accomplish his plan. Then he summoned Meclis-i Khâss on Shevvâl 17 1241/May 25 1826 to obtain a *fatwâ* on the "necessity of military training." They decided to organise "trained soldiers" under the name of *Eshkinji*, and also organise 150 persons from 51 janissary units to form this new military force. A document was prepared to this effect and the notables of the janissaries signed it together with those responsible for the administration.

The *eshkinjis* started their military training on 5 Zulka'de 1241/11 June 1826, putting on their new uniforms. It was most likely that the janissaries would resist this attempt too. Therefore, the Sultân won over the chiefs of the units of artillery, *humbarajı*, *lağımjı*, and the shipyard; in addition, Ağa Hüseyin Pasha and İzzet Mehmed Pasha, who were responsible for the shores of the Bosphorus, were prepared to interfere in case the janissaries attempted to riot.

The janissaries gathered at Etmeydanı, raising their cauldron as the sign of rebellion. The forces at the Bosphorus were summoned, the *Sanjaq-ı Sharîf* (The Standard of the Final Messenger) was flown, and the Muslims were invited to gather under it. The people, who were bored by the behaviour of the janissaries, came behind their *imâms* and *qâdis*. At the *Sheyhülislâm*'s invitation, about 3,500 *madrasah* students gathered under the *Sanjaq-ı Sharîf*. The barracks of the janissaries were smashed and burned down. The *fermân* concerning the abolition of the janissary corps was recited at the Sultânahmed Mosque on Zulka'de 11 1241/June 17 1826. This event was called *Vaq'a-yı Khayriyye* (The Good Event). Shortly afterwards, the *Bektâshi* order, to which the janissaries claimed to be related, was abolished and banned too.[721]

In a sense, the date 1826 refers to the time the Devlet-i 'Aliyye-i Osmâniyye ended, having lost the dynamism it had at the beginning, trying only to survive materially, and not depending any more on its original dynamics. It would not be wrong to view the events after this date as "attempts to hinder or postpone the decline." It should be noted that the decline occurred first in the minds of its administrators and intellectuals; they lost hope in Islam, the driving and reviving force and energy of the Devlet.

### The 'Asâkir-i Mansûre-yi Muhammediyye

A new army, named *'Asâkir-i Mansûre-yi Muhammediyye*, was established based on the European model. Sultân Mahmûd II, who was infuriated by recent French hostility toward the Osmanlı Devlet, employed Prussian and not French officers in this new army. Additionally, he sent students to Europe to be educated in the art of war.[722] In 1834 he opened the *Mekteb-i 'Ulûm-ı Harbiye* (School of Military Sciences) and opened a medical school in 1827 to train doctors for the new army. This school was relocated to its new building in 1838. The language of instruction in this school was French.[723]

### Greek Independence

The abolition of the janissary forces almost left the Osmanlı Devlet without an army. Czar Nicholas I wanted to make use of the Osmanlı Devlet's awkward situation to wipe it out and take the Balkans, the straits, and Anatolia, and began preparations for war. Meanwhile, the European powers decided to end Osmanlı suzerainty over Greece and declare it an independent entity. The French and British navies were sent to the Mediterranean to put pressure on the Osmanlı Devlet. The Russian Czar Nicholas I, sent his navy as well.[724] The governor of Osmanlı Egypt, Muhammad Ali Pasha, was anxious to attain independence; his navy was at the shores of Morea. The Greek

## Chapter Fifteen – Another Attempt at Restoration

revolt was subdued, and the castles were retrieved from the rebels. All that was left were some groups of vagabonds in some mountains. The Muslim forces took Athens in Zulka'de 1242 (5 June 1827), despite the fact that European forces helped the Greeks.[725]

The British did not like Muhammad Ali Pasha's presence in the eastern Mediterranean. There the presence of a weak Osmanlı Devlet and a small Greece was more convenient for Britain. The Russians and the British met in St. Petersburg on the pretext of discussing how to put an end to the alleged acts of injustice of İbrâhîm Pasha in Morea. They signed a protocol on 4 April 1827 that stated that Greece should be an autonomous country paying tribute to the Osmanlı Devlet and that all Turks should leave Greece. This was the first step towards the independence of Greece. The protocol was communicated to Austria, Prussia, and France. Austria rejected it, because it encouraged nationalism and Austria, being an empire containing several ethnic groups, could not possibly favour it. On the other hand, it would mark a Russian success. Prussia also rejected it.

But France informed them that it was in favour of that approach, aiming to break the Holy Alliance that was set up against it in 1815. And so Britain, Russia, and France signed the Treaty of London on July 6th, 1827. According to this treaty, if the Osmanlı Devlet accepted the Treaty of St. Petersburg, there would be a truce between it and the Greek rebels, and then a Greek state would be set up; if not, these three powers would help the Greek rebels and put pressure on the Osmanlıs.

The Osmanlı Devlet refused the Treaty of London, which it regarded as interference in its internal affairs. Then the navies of these three powers blockaded the Osmanlı and Egyptian navies at Navarin.[726] These three powers asked Muhammad Ali Pasha to withdraw, who informed them that his withdrawal depended on the annihilation of the Osmanlı navy; in that case, he would have an excuse to withdraw on the grounds that his forces had been stranded and their way back had been cut off.⁷²⁷ The admirals of the French, British, and Russian navies gave an ultimatum to İbrâhîm Pasha, asking for the withdrawal of Osmanlı and Egyptian fleets and the withdrawal of the Muslim soldiers from Morea. When the ultimatum was refused, the combined British, French, and Russian naval forces entered Navarin on the pretext of intimidating İbrâhîm Pasha, but in fact intending to annihilate the Muslim navy. They sank the Osmanlı and Egyptian fleets on November 20, 1827.

This event radically changed the situation: the Muslim forces in Morea found themselves in a defeated position. People in Europe celebrated the event of Navarin in great festivities; the alliance against national trends and the Russian project of the Holy Alliance were shattered. Metternich stated that "a new era in history began with Navarin." The Muslim people of the Osmanlı Devlet saw this event as a Crusade.⁷²⁸

The allies declared the independence of Greece in 1243/1828.⁷²⁹ As expected, the Osmanlı Devlet refused to recognise this move, but the Russians took this as an excuse to attack the Osmanlı Devlet in 1828. Since the latter was not prepared for war, the Russian army advanced quickly through Rumelia. On the other side it captured the castles of Ahıska and Kars in the eastern front, while Edirne in Europe fell into their hands in 1245/1829. The Osmanlı Devlet was hence obliged to conclude the Treaty of Edirne in 1245/1829, surrendering Ahıska and Circassia to Russia, and forced to recognise the independence of Greece,⁷³⁰ which at that time consisted of nothing more than the Morea Peninsula.

Meanwhile Muhammad 'Ali Pasha of Egypt attacked Bilâdush Shâm (what is called Syria today), and threatened the authority of the Osmanlıs there. Osmanlı troops were therefore sent against the Egyptian forces but were defeated at the battles of 'Akkâ and Qonya. Sultân Mahmûd II sent another army led by Hâfız Pasha that was also defeated by the well-trained Egyptian army at the battle of

*Chapter Fifteen – Another Attempt at Restoration*

Nisip in 1258/1839. Sultân Mahmûd II was perhaps fortunate to pass away before receiving that depressing news in İstanbul.[731]

### The Occupation of Jezâyir by France (1246/1830)

Jezâyir (Algeria) was governed on behalf of the Osmanlı Devlet by the gallant *mujâhid* soldiers called *dayı*. They were so powerful that when the representative of the Sultân arrived at Jezâyir, he was reminded that "he was at the Dîvân of Mujâhids." The Jezâyir Ojağı, as it was called, had a strong naval force; so much so that the American vessels entering the Mediterranean in the eighteenth century were obliged to pay tribute to Jezâyir Ojağı. Although the Europeans attacked Jezâyir seventeen times, they were not able to occupy it. Hence, they decided to call a truce during which they offered the *dayı* gifts to secure their commercial interests in the Mediterranean Sea.[732]

But industrialised France, which had become one of the major powers in the world, was determined to occupy the strategically important Jezâyir in order to challenge the authority of the British in the Mediterranean, who had already acquired Jabal Târiq (the pronunciation of which has been "distorted" into "Gibraltar") and Malta. They found an excuse to achieve this in the demands by some non-Muslim merchants in Jezâyir to receive their money from the French. While discussing the issue with the French consul general, Hüseyin Dayı (1765-1838, r. 1818-1830) furiously struck him in the face with a fan. France made use of this incident and its superior firearms to occupy Jezâyir in 1246/1830,[733] though the Muslims there offered organised resistance to the invaders.

Under Osmanlı rule education in Jezâyir developed fairly well, particularly at the primary and secondary levels.[734] When presenting the conclusions of the Commission d'Afrique in January 1834, General Valze emphasised that "all Arabs (Algerians) know how to read and write. There are two schools in each village."[735] Although

Algeria never had highly reputed religious schools such as the Zaytûna in Tunisia, the Qarawiyyîn in Fez, or al-Azhar in Cairo, the country had many educational centres of less significance. There were, for example, three thousand *kuttâb*s in different parts of Algeria.[736] These facts demonstrate the Osmanlıs' concern for the indigenous culture of Algiers and that the Osmanlıs did not invade in a way that made the local people feel they had "lost their identities," as happened with Western powers wherever they colonised a country. As is very well known, a native inhabitant of Jezâyir under French occupation was bound to starve if he did not know the French language and had no other source of income.

### The Treaty of Hünkâr İskelesi (1249/1833)

İbrâhîm Pasha, son of Muhammad 'Ali Pasha, advanced as far as Kütahya in Anatolia in 1832. Thus Sultân Mahmûd II applied to Nicholas I, the Russian czar, for help. The troops sent by the Czar landed on the Anatolian shore of the Bosphorus. Anxious that the Russian troops might occupy İstanbul, Britain, and France put pressure on Muhammad 'Ali Pasha, compelling him to come to terms with the Osmanlı Devlet. Thus the revolt of the Osmanlı *vâli* of Egypt was averted by the European powers who saw that the continuation of a weak Osmanlı Devlet was more favourable for them than a strong modernised Egyptian rule in Anatolia. Now that the question had been solved, the fleets of the foreign powers should have to leave İstanbul.

Before leaving İstanbul, the Russians concluded an eight-year treaty with the Osmanlı Devlet at Hünkâr İskelesi, Beykoz, where their headquarters were located. According to its secret clause, the Osmanlı Devlet undertook to block the straits to other fleets in case of a war. In this way, Russia made sure that no other fleet could enter the Black Sea. But Britain, Austria, France, and Prussia met with representatives of Russia in London, and concluded the Treaty of

*Chapter Fifteen – Another Attempt at Restoration*

London in 1840, putting the Osmanlı Devlet under the guarantee of these five powers. Thus Russia lost the advantages obtained with the Treaty of Hünkâr İskelesi.[737]

## 15.5 SULTÂN ABDÜLMEJÎD (1839-1861)

Upon the death of Sultân Mahmûd II in 1839, his son Abdülmejîd succeeded him at the age of eighteen. Mustafa Reshîd Pasha was the Sadrâzam and Nâzır of Foreign Affairs, and the Osmanlı Ambassador in London, also *vâli* of Egypt, Muhammad Ali Pasha, was in a strong position, and the Osmanlı Devlet was in danger of splitting into two. There was a dire need for external support to avert this problem.[738] But the re-organisation of the Osmanlı social structure contained many elements to please the European powers together with changes made to conform to the new conditions of the world. When the young sultân ascended the Osmanlı throne, Mustafa Reshîd Pasha came to İstanbul and "persuaded the Sultân, in secret meetings, of the dire need for the *Tanzîmât*."[739]

The structure of the Osmanlı Devlet had obviously deteriorated significantly in those years and was in dire need of well-considered adjustments and restructuring. But the recently introduced *Nizâm-ı Jedîd* or *Tanzîmât* proved to be ineffective and disastrous. The *Tanzimat* was worked out single-handedly by Reshîd Pasha and may even have been imposed on him by the foreign powers. The new Sultân was too young and inexperienced to know and appreciate their serious drawbacks. By then – the middle of the nineteenth century – the Osmanlı Devlet had virtually and practically come to an end, having been humiliated and defeated by a viceroy and an army that should have been under its firm control. Had he not been stopped by "European friends," İbrâhîm Pasha would certainly have entered İstanbul and taken over the Devlet. This would have led to the overthrow of the ruling family but not necessarily to any basic change in the main Muslim socio-political body. The Muslim

Devlet could even have emerged stronger and under a new energetic and committed leadership. The European powers do not seem to have stopped İbrâhîm Pasha out of sympathy for the Osmanlıs but only to prevent a dynamic and capable administration from taking over, and thus to retain their vital interests in the area.

The young and inexperienced Sultân hastily authorised Sadrâzam Mustafa Reshîd Pasha to read the *Hatt-ı Hümâyûn* during a ceremony that proclaimed the *Tanzîmât*. These rather superficial and naive administrative reforms guaranteed the life and property of everyone in the Devlet regardless of his religion and sect[740] and gave the treasury of the Devlet full responsibility for all expenditures and revenue. The *Hatt-ı Hümâyûn* was recited by Reshîd Pasha in Sha'bân 1255/November 1839 at Gülhâne. The Sultân, the *vazîrs*, and *'ulamâ* swore in the quarters of *Khirqa-i Se'âdet Dâiresi* (The chamber assigned to preserve the Cloak of the Final Messenger and Holy Relics) in the Topkapusu (Topkapı) Palace to conform to the rules of *Tanzîmât*. The Osmanlı Devlet was in fact in need of renewal. "It was stated in the *Hatt-ı Hümâyûn* that the Osmanlı Devlet acted in accordance with *ahkâm-ı Jelîle-i Qur'âniyye* and the *qawânîn-i Sher'îyye* from the beginning and rose to power, but those good rules were neglected because of unceasing difficulties and troubles and different motives in the last 150 years. It was added that the curse of bribery would be erased and the salaries of the officers would be raised."[741] Not as a concession to European powers, but by their imposition, equality between the Muslims and non-Muslims was accepted. As a result "all ranks and places in *devlet* structure became accessible to non-Muslims. They were not previously accepted as witnesses against Muslims, but now they became judges in courts that passed sentences on Muslims!"[742]

> "In fact, there is a 'dominant nation' in any great political entity: the German race in the Austrian Empire, the

## Chapter Fifteen – Another Attempt at Restoration

Russian race in the Russian Empire, the English race in Great Britain, and even in the United States of America the Anglo-Saxon element is the dominant, and existence of all these states depends on these dominances."743

"On the other hand, there was no such notion of a 'dominant nation' in the Osmanlı Devlet; there was no dominant nation but a dominant *ummat* during the period of 540 years between 1299/699, which is theoretically accepted as the beginning of independence for Osmân Gâzi, and 1839/1255."744

And incredible scenes were seen sometimes because of those awful changes: "There was a police station at Galata. Some Christians used to bring some Muslims there, complaining that the latter called themselves *gâvur* (the Turkish version of *kâfir*). And the commander of the station would reproach the accused: 'How many times have we told you that it is forbidden to call a *gâvur* a *gâvur* anymore?'"745

It was not only Muslims but some Christians as well who were not happy with some of the *Tanzîmât* regulations; the Rûm (Greek) Patriarch who attended the proclamation of the *Tanzîmât* at Gülhâne Garden stated when the *Hatt-ı Hümâyûn* was put into the satin purse: "I hope it will not come out of this purse again." Because they were privileged among the other Christian *ra'âyâ*, they had participated to some extent in the administration: they had been employed as translators of the *Dîvân-ı Hümâyûn*, translators of ambassadorial commissions, the *beğs* to Wallachia and Moldova were appointed from among the Greeks of Fener, İstanbul. The Rûm (Greek) Patriarch used to be responsible for all the Christians living within the borders of the Osmanlı Devlet.746

The Orthodox of the *ra'âyâ* applied to Russia, the Catholics to France, and the Protestants to Britain to make sure that their rights were guaranteed and upheld. And the European countries utilised these applications for their own political ends.

The previous efforts of renewal were in the field of military education and training and did not touch the essence, the structure, of the Devlet. But the *Tanzîmât* was a strong blow to the structure of the Devlet and it did break the historical line of conduct for it. It was certainly the first breaking point, deepening with *İslâhât Fermânı* in 1856, and continuing up until the end. In reality, the Osmanlı Devlet had lost its dynamism and life-giving drive at the administrative and bureaucratic level to some extent toward the end of the eighteenth century; therefore, it could be said that whatever had been done from the beginning of the nineteenth century, could be seen as "efforts to survive at any cost."

Mustafa Reshîd Pasha assigned two of the respected *'ulamâ* to explain the *Hatt-ı Hümâyûn* of Gülhâne in Rumelia and Anatolia. These two went from one city to another, carrying out their duty. The most difficult point in the *Tanzîmât* was the equality of the people regardless of their religion.[747] And this was only natural and reasonable; the Muslims had struggled generation after generation to maintain the Devlet, had been the "core" and the "main element" in the *Devlet-i 'Aliyye-i İslâmiyye*,[748] and now the *dhimmî* were promoted to the level of the Muslim. Muslim society had been living in accordance with the understanding that *"You are the best community that has been raised up for mankind. You enjoin what is good and forbid what is evil, and you believe in Allah. And if the People of Scripture had believed, it would have been better for them."* (Âlu 'Imrân [3], *âyat* 110)

There was a need to re-organise the structure, but this should have been achieved by the Osmanlıs themselves, without any external interference. This, however, would have necessitated a military and political strength the Osmanlı Devlet did not have at that time. Therefore, it begged interference by and even the imposition of

## Chapter Fifteen – Another Attempt at Restoration

"external" powers. In fact, its aim was "to solve the problem of Egypt connecting it with the accomplishment of the *Tanzîmât* – thus to correct European public opinion which had been tending to erase and wipe out the existence of the *Devlet-i 'Aliyye*."[749]

As a matter of fact, "the general feeling of Europe was that the ancient institutions and structure of the Empire[750] were barbarous and irretrievably bad, and that only the adoption, as rapidly as possible, of a European form of government and way of life would admit Turkey to the rank and privileges of a civilised state. This view was urged on Turkish statesmen with considerable vigour by the governments and embassies of the European powers and eventually came to be accepted, at least tacitly, by an increasingly larger proportion of a Turkish ruling class, which was deeply aware of the power, wealth, and progress of Europe as compared with their own backwardness, poverty, and weakness."[751]

But, on the other hand, to be a citizen in the Osmanlı Devlet was enviable. "Perhaps the most penetrating comments are those of Adolphus Slade, a British naval officer who visited Turkey many times from 1829 onwards, and acquired an intimate knowledge of the language, the country, and the people. His basic criticism is that the reformers destroyed an old order which was not in itself evil, but on the contrary contained much that was enviable: 'Hitherto the Osmanley (Osmanlı) has enjoyed by custom some of the dearest privileges of freemen, for which Christian nations have so long struggled. He paid nothing to the government beyond a moderate land-tax, although liable, it is true, to extortions, which might be classed with assessed taxes. He paid no tithes, the *vacouf* (*waqf*/ foundation) sufficing for the maintenance of the ministers of Islam. He travelled where he pleased without passports; no custom-house officer intruded his eyes and dirty fingers among his baggage; no police watched his motions, or listened for his words. His house was sacred. His sons were never taken from his side to be soldiers, unless war called them. His views of ambition were not restricted by the barriers of birth and wealth: from the lowest origin he might aspire without presumption to the rank of pasha; if he could read, to that of grand *vazîr*; and this consciousness, instilled and supported by numberless precedents, ennobled his mind, and enabled him to enter on the duties of high office without embarrassment. Is not this the advantages so prized by free nations? Did not the exclusion of the people from posts of honour tend to the French revolution?'"[752]

## The Treaty of London 1257/1841

The successful advance of İbrâhîm Pasha, son of Muhammad 'Ali, against the Osmanlı Devlet was stopped by its European allies, Britain, Austria, and Prussia. However, they conferred the governorship of Egypt on Muhammad 'Ali and his descendants, and gave him the castle of 'Akkâ during his lifetime. This ambitious viceroy refused these conditions and resumed his war with the Osmanlı Devlet. Britain, Austria, and Prussia met and decided on certain conditions concerning the straits, and Russia felt that it had to join it. Therefore, Britain, Austria, Prussia, and Russia concluded a treaty in London on 15 July 1840.

The Egyptian forces were defeated and Muhammad 'Ali Pasha was forced to sign the Treaty of London in 1841, by which he was given only the hereditary rule of Egypt, being part of the Osmanlı Devlet. The Bosphorus and Dardanelles Straits were closed to all warships, thus depriving the Russians of their previous privilege to navigate there.

## Enjümen-i Dânish

Thanks to the efforts of a *madrasah* graduate, Ahmed Jevdet Pasha, and those who knew the importance of science and education, the *Enjümen-i Dânish* (Academy) was set up in 1266/1850. Its purpose was to develop the Turkish language,

## Chapter Fifteen – Another Attempt at Restoration

to follow intellectual trends and currents, to translate scientific books, and to write new ones. It had 40 main members and 40 correspondent members. It met monthly.[753]

### The Straits

The Osmanlı Devlet had been in control of two very important straits for centuries: the Dardanelles and the Bosphorus. During the nineteenth century, the Christian powers, having undergone an industrial revolution and become very strong, showed interest in the Straits under the control of the Osmanlı Devlet, which seemed unable to defend them by itself. Russia had been following a policy of expansion in which the Osmanlı territory formed the greater portion. Its aim was to control the Black Sea and to reach the Mediterranean Sea through the Straits, thereby no longer being a land-locked empire. The Treaty of Qaynarja (1774) paved the way for Russia in that direction: it occupied Crimea in 1783 and became dominant in the Black Sea. Napoleon's attack on Egypt gave Russia another opportunity; the Osmanlı Devlet and Russia concluded a treaty against France in 1799 that gave Russia the right to go through the straits as a "friend" for eight years. Now the Russian administration began thinking that it was more convenient for them to take the Osmanlı Sultân under their protection instead of dividing the Devlet up and receiving only a share among the other European powers, or setting up a Greek government in its place. The treaty was renewed in 1805, according to which the Black Sea was shut to other powers; Russia and the Osmanlı Devlet exclusively had warships in the Black Sea. This treaty became nullified because of the war between Russia and the Osmanlı Devlet that began in 1807, but with the Treaty of Edirne in 1829 the Russians again gained the right of passage for their commercial vessels through the Straits. In 1833 with the Treaty of Hünkâr İskelesi Russia achieved the denial of passage to warships of other powers. But in 1841 the Russians lost this advantageous position with the Treaty of London.

France lost its colonies on the North American continent to Britain in the second half of the eighteenth century and followed a policy of making the Mediterranean Sea a French sea to make up for that loss. Austria and France divided the lands of the Venetian Republic after the Treaty of Campo Formio (1797), and Napoleon occupied Egypt in 1798. These were steps toward realising the French ambition towards the Mediterranean Sea. But this policy was against the ambition of the Russian czar, Alexander, of making the Black Sea a Russian sea, having control of the straits and dominating the eastern Mediterranean. Every attempt by Russia to control the straits was opposed by France, and every effort by France to expand toward the eastern Mediterranean was opposed by Russia.

Britain, as well, became very interested in the affairs of the eastern Mediterranean; its colony India needed protection against other powers. Thus Britain helped the Osmanlı Devlet drive French troops from Egypt. The shortest way between Europe and India was through the Mediterranean Sea; and Britain did its best to control the eastern Mediterranean by opposing Russia and France in their efforts to expand toward it and, during the nineteenth century, supporting the integrity of the Osmanlı territories that contained another route to India via the Tigris and the Euphrates valley to the Gulf of Basra.[754]

### The Crimean War (1853-1856)

The Russian czar, Nicholas I, thought that Britain and France would not enter a war against Russia in case it erupted because of his ambition to possess some parts of the Osmanlı territory. He thought that he could come to terms with Britain to divide the territories of the Osmanlı Devlet. He said to the British Ambassador Hamilton Seymour on 9 January 1853 in St. Petersburg, the then capital of Russia, that the "Osmanlı was a sick man, he was going to die shortly, and it was necessary for Russia and Britain to come to an

## Chapter Fifteen – Another Attempt at Restoration

agreement about dividing the territories." He added that he would never permit Britain to settle in İstanbul and that Russia was to occupy İstanbul temporarily. In disclosing his intention, the Czar erred in his calculations; Britain and France formed a block together with the Osmanlı Devlet.[755]

The external cause of the war was the problem of the holy places in Jerusalem, which were a source of conflict between the Catholics and the Orthodox. The keeping of the keys of these places and services concerning these places had been assigned to Catholics since the Süleymân the Magnificent era; but later conflicts between the Osmanlı Devlet and France were utilised by the Orthodox Patriarch, and the Orthodox Church obtained these privileges in 1634. From then on, the question of services in these places was a topic of conflict between the two churches.

Russia sent Prince Mechnikof to İstanbul in 1853. He behaved provocatively, visiting the Osmanlı *sadrâzam* not in his official uniform but in his causal clothes. He did not visit the Nâzir of Foreign Affairs Kecheji-zâde Fuâd who waited for him at his office. Kecheji-zâde resigned his post upon this disagreeable attitude. After much deliberation, a compromise acceptable to all parties concerned would have been forthcoming, had not the Prince insisted on the patronage of the Russian Czar over the 12 million Orthodox *ra'âyâ* of the Osmanlı Devlet.[756] Mustafa Reshîd Pasha set up a committee of 46 members to discuss the Russian claim, but it was rejected by an overwhelming majority of 43 to 3 and Prince Menchikof returned to Russia.[757]

Russian troops attacked Moldova and Wallachia in June 1853. An international congress was convened at Vienna, but it could not resolve the crisis, and the Russian fleet burned the Osmanlı fleet, off the coast of Sinop in Anatolia.[758] In the meantime, Ömer Pasha defeated the Russians at Oltaniche, and Britain and France entered the war in 1854 on the side of the Osmanlı Devlet. The

Allies defeated the Russians at Alma and entered Akyar (Sevastopol) in September 1855, while Ömer Pasha again defeated the Russians at Evapatoria.[759] The upshot of all these events was the conclusion of the Treaty of Paris in 1856, which left Russia with Crimea but obliged her to surrender Qars to the Osmanlı Devlet. The Black Sea was shut off to both the Russian and the Osmanlı fleets, while Wallachia and Moldova were given suzerainty over their internal affairs, and Serbia's independence was reiterated.

Crimea was very important for the Osmanlı Devlet; its loss was not like the loss of other provinces. The territories that the Osmanlıs lost earlier contained fewer Muslims than non-Muslims. But the two-million population of Crimea was Muslim; therefore, saving Crimea was a priority for the Osmanlı Devlet.[760] The point in deploying troops to Crimea was to prevent Russian intervention in İstanbul. In fact, the problem, as far as Britain was concerned, was to use the Osmanlı Devlet, which Nicholas I called the "Sick Man," as a buffer against Russian expansion. The main problem for Britain was not to save Crimea or the Caucasus from Russian occupation but to keep Russia at bay. As a matter of fact, Lord J. Russell said in a speech: "If we do not stop Russia at the Danube, we will have to stop her some day at the shores of Indus."[761]

With the Revolution of 1848, the labouring class emerged in France, trying to obtain some political rights. With Louis Philippe overthrown, the Republic was proclaimed.

The provisional republican government declared that it supported nationalist movements. And some organisations in various European countries rebelled against their sovereigns in order to obtain political and social rights. In a short period of time, there were rebellions in Spain, Italy, Ireland, Belgium, the Netherlands, Austria, and Hungary. The Hungarians rebelled in 1848 against Austria and were successful in the beginning. But they were defeated in the end because of Russian support in the form of 200,000 soldiers. Many of

## Chapter Fifteen – Another Attempt at Restoration

the Hungarians took refuge with the Osmanlı Devlet. The Austrian government asked the Osmanlı Devlet to give those Hungarians back, but the Osmanlıs refused. Thus the problem of Hungarian refugees emerged. The Poles, who cooperated with the Hungarians, also took refuge with the Osmanlı Devlet. Russia asked the Osmanlı Devlet to return those "vagabonds" who were her subjects, but the Osmanlıs refused; they did not see the refugees as "vagabonds," contrary to the claim of Austria and Russia. The Osmanlı Devlet published a report in Europe, stating that it defended the refugees out of mercy and humanitarian sentiments. The Osmanlıs resigned themselves to going to war if necessary for the sake of the refugees; it was dishonour for a *devlet* to surrender people who took refuge within it. Publishing this report by the Osmanlı Devlet had a great effect on public opinion in Europe. Demonstrations for the Osmanlı Devlet took place in Britain and France – to such an extent that British youth, when they met the Osmanlı Ambassador Mosurus Pasha in the street, untied the horses of his carriage and pulled the carriage up to the Osmanlı Embassy themselves.[762] Therefore, it can be thought that this public opinion in Britain and France also had its effect on these countries siding with the Osmanlıs during the Crimean War.

### The Fermân of İslâhât (1272/ 1856)

This *fermân* (decree) was prepared toward the end of the Crimean War, and proclaimed six months before the Treaty of Paris.[763] The most important point in the *fermân* of İslâhât is that it improved the status of the non-Muslim people of the Osmanlı Devlet by giving them equality in taxes and in every other aspect of life. Now the non-Muslim did not have to pay *jizyah* anymore. All the people living in the Osmanlı Devlet had the right to enter civil service regardless of their religion or sect. Non-Muslims could also be elected as members on the boards of *vilâyat*s and *sanjaq*s.[764]

Non-Muslims were given the right to enrol in military and civil schools.[765] This meant that a non-Muslim entering military school could become a general in the Osmanlı army and, if talented, could have command of the Osmanlı armies. A non-Muslim, could enter *mülkiye* (a class of senior civil servants) and become a *vâli* (governor), inspector, a minister of the interior, and even prime minister. All these would take place in a state whose official name was *Devlet-i 'Aliyye-i Osmâniyye*[766] or *Devlet-i 'Aliyye-i İslâmiyye*.[767]

On the other hand, there were some points in that *fermân* that non-Muslims did not like: military duty was not in the non-Muslims favour; they had been exempt from military service before İslâhât and had paid *jizyah* instead. The Muslims, particularly the Turks, had been fighting for the Devlet from the beginning, and non-Muslims were busy with their trades and work. The priests lost their advantageous position given to them by Fâtih Sultân Mehemmed; they had been receiving incomes as they liked from their communities, now they were to get salaries from the Devlet; they were to swear loyalty to the Devlet. Therefore, when the *fermân* was read and put into the purse, the bishop of İzmit said: "Let us pray God that this *fermân* should not come out of this purse again!"[768]

### The Financial Situation

Because of the huge expenditures of the Crimean War, for the first time the Osmanlıs had to borrow money from other states. With the agreement signed in London on 12 Shevvâl 1271/28 June 1855 the Osmanlıs borrowed five million pounds sterling from Britain and France, the annual interest being four per cent plus one per cent amortisation. The payments would take place every June and December.[769]

According to the Treaty of Paris of 1856, the integrity of the Osmanlı Devlet was placed under the guarantee of Britain, France, Prussia, Russia, Austria, and Sardinia.[770] But, Britain, France,

## Chapter Fifteen – Another Attempt at Restoration

and Austria, not trusting Russia's attitude toward the Osmanlı Devlet, signed another treaty in Paris on 9 Sha'bân 1272/15 April 1856, according to which the integrity of the Osmanlı Devlet was guaranteed by each of the three singularly and together; any assault on Osmanlı territories would be considered cause for war and these three states would use their armies and navies together with the Osmanlı Devlet against the transgressor.[771]

When the armies of the foreign powers left after the Treaty of Paris, the "disease of dissipation invaded the body of the Devlet, and its continuation caused greater calamities than war."[772] It seemed that the Osmanlı elite, having become acquainted with the Europeans over a period of three years, saw in them a people who had undergone an industrial revolution and exploited wealth all over the world, and had become very rich. The Osmanlı elite desired ardently to live like them; suffering from that "cultural shock"! … "The person who put into practice the manner of European civilisation in the Osmanlı Devlet and caused the public opinion to awaken is Mustafa Reshîd Pasha; being generous by nature he helped those who were in urgent need and opened the way of making the Treasury of the Devlet pay his debts, and others wanted to follow suit, hence the balance of income and expenditure was affected badly." "It was the custom to behave economically in the beginning of the Abdülmejid Era, but the expenditures of one wedding and one circumcision festivities, and the expenditures by the Harem-i Hümâyûn on the Treasury of the Devlet, and dissipation and gifts to the ministers caused the structure of the Devlet to be shaken at its foundations …. The loans were not spent for the Devlet, but for pleasure."[773]

On the other hand, Sultân Abdülmejîd was aware of the fact that Egypt had become stronger than the Osmanlı Devlet itself, thanks to the innovations Muhammad 'Ali Pasha achieved there. Therefore, he received Muhammad 'Ali Pasha several times when the latter came to İstanbul in 1848 and consulted him about administration. Muhammad 'Ali Pasha expressed his opinion: "First, even if the ministers demonstrated the need to borrow money from outside, the loan increases and does not decrease. The richness of the Treasury, the improvement of the country occurs by trade of the people and their wealth. Borrowing increasingly is harmful. Second, there are many places in the country that had been left wild and many rivers flowing without any use. If the lands belonging to the Devlet are given to people and the rivers are put to use scientifically, agriculture is improved. And if the nomads who go around aimlessly are settled at those places, fights among tribes because of income decrease and the income of the *devlet* increases. My third petition is that: the Europeans advanced considerably in science, education, and industry. It is not feasible to catch up with them immediately, but you should direct the people to set up schools starting with the villages up to the towns. Your ministers should be asked every year about what they have done in these three areas, and the work should be followed up this way so that desired development will be achieved."[774]

**Reactions to Change in the Structure**

The Osmanlı Devlet based its foundations on Islam from the beginning and represented Islam for centuries. But the reforms of 1839 and 1856 made non-Muslims equal to the Muslims, the founders and sustainers of this socio-political entity. In other words, the dates 1839 and 1856 indicate the great break in the historical line of conduct and existence of the Osmanlı Devlet. And this break caused great uneasiness and sorrow all over the Sunnî Muslim world. "The articles accepted in the Treaty of Paris for the benefit of the Christians in the Osmanlı Devlet caused general excitement and rage against non-Muslims. Some saw the main cause for the rebellion in India at that time was these articles in the Treaty of Paris; and the Christian elements who

## Chapter Fifteen – Another Attempt at Restoration

relied on the European powers and had been encouraged secretly were insolent.

"In that tense situation, during *hajj* season, people attacked Christians, and the consuls of Britain and France were killed during their intervention to protect their subjects. A British-French fleet came to Jeddah, and bombarded the city out of revenge. In addition, upon the British and French commanders' wish, ten of the notables of Jeddah were executed in August 1856 on the grounds of incitement. It should be remembered that, while all these murders were being committed, Britain and France were at peace with the Osmanlı Devlet, and they were even its allies."[775]

On the other hand, in Lebanon, where the foreign influence and intrigues were effective, the events of Jeddah caused trouble. The British were engaged in inciting the Durzîs (Druze), and the French the Mârûnîs (Maronites); the latter attacked the former and many Christians were killed.

There was trouble in Damascus too; among the dead were the American and Dutch consuls. The Foreign Minister Fuâd Pasha set up a military court and hanged more than a hundred people, among them officials, to prevent intervention by the European powers.[776]

### The Court of Quleli

The Muslims were not satisfied with the performance of Sultân Abdülmejîd and his government. All their efforts to improve the situation were fruitless. Top officials lived a luxurious and corrupt life, while the government borrowed substantial sums of money from European powers, and inflation reached unprecedented levels, particularly after the Crimean War. Under these circumstances, Shaykh Ahmed of the Bâyezîd *madrasah*, Ferîq Hüseyin Pasha, and some intellectuals formed a clandestine society that planned to overthrow the government and to reinstate the *Sharî'at*.[777] It should be noted that this attempt to form a secret society and acquire power to return the Devlet to its original, fundamental orbit was the first such attempt and was unique. Their initiative could be interpreted as a "non-governmental organisation" in the circumstances; they were aware of the fact that the Tanzîmât and İslâhât were events that contradicted the basic principles of the Devlet.

When Hasan Pasha was approached to join, he revealed the plot, and all 41 members of the society were arrested in 1859. They were tried at the Quleli barracks and the founders were given the death penalty, the others imprisonment. But the Sultân commuted the death penalties to imprisonment. The depressing conditions of the Osmanlı Devlet and the event of Quleli had a grave impact on the health of Sultân Abdülmejîd,[778] who died in 1861.[779] The notables swore *bay'at* (allegiance) to his brother 'Abdülazîz

Abdülmejîd had a very sensitive nature and it seems that he was not happy with what was going on in the Devlet. The *ser-qurenâ* (the chief chamberlain) Haji Ali Pasha saw Abdülmejîd in the Khirqa-i Sharîf Quarter praying one day: "Yâ Rabbî! save me from this man," referring to Reshîd Pasha.[780]

## 15.6 SULTÂN 'ABDÜLAZÎZ (1861-1876)

'Abdülazîz became sultân and *khalîfah* at the age of 30. He was healthy and well-built, being a good sportsman and a wrestler. He converted the palace theatre built by his brother into a stable,[781] presumably an indication of his sharp and unfavourable reaction to the Western cultural invasion. The Osmanlı Devlet had borrowed money from Europe during Fuâd Pasha's first term as *sadrâzam*, but now the paper money called *qaaime* (*kaime*) was abolished, and some irregular loans were paid back. Sultân 'Abdülazîz discouraged unnecessary expenditure, banned golden and silver utensils in the

## Chapter Fifteen – Another Attempt at Restoration

palace, and tried to prevent gifts and bribery. Some officials were sentenced on charges of bribery.[782]

It was only natural that Muslim public opinion was not in favour of the reform that had been put into practice without lengthy consideration but simply carried out off-handedly. And the Osmanlı Muslim people attached importance to Islamic values and ethics.

As an expression of frustration with the drift and unplanned drive toward Westernisation, Osmanlı society increasingly adhered to Islamic values and ethics. Osmanlı Turks and Muslims in general had sympathised strongly with the plight of their Muslim Turkish brothers in Turkestan. "In the 1860s the Ottoman Turks' awareness of other Muslim and Turkish peoples was increased by upheavals in inner Asia. The Panthais, Chinese Muslims in Yunnan province, revolted and set up a state of their own. Ya'qûb Bey successfully wrested Turkestan from Chinese control and governed it as a Muslim Devlet, centred on Kashgar."[783] Sultân 'Abdülazîz was recognised by the people of Turkestan as the *khalîfah*,[784] and Ya'qûb Bey sent Sayyid Mahmûd Ya'qûb to İstanbul as his envoy. Britain facilitated his journey via India because of the conflict with Russia over Turkestan. Sayyid Ya'qûb "returned to Kashgar with a group of Ottoman Turks, among them four army officers to act as military instructors, and a few light weapons. Sayyid Mahmûd Ya'qûb also brought back from İstanbul the title of *amîr* for Ya'qûb Bey and some kind of promise of protection, however unreal, from 'Abdülazîz as suzerain. Yaqûb proceeded to strike coins in the Sultân's name which bore the inscription 'Protected Kashgar,' and Abdülaziz's name was mentioned in the prayers. Again in 1875 the same envoy came to İstanbul, was well received by Abdülaziz, and returned with two thousand Suider breech-loading rifles and six fieldpieces."[785]

On the other hand, Russia was not content with the Treaty of Paris at all, but knowing that if it declared war directly on the Osmanlı Devlet the European powers would come to the latter's aid as during the Crimean War, it searched for an opportunity to intervene, inciting the Christian communities in the Osmanlı Devlet, encouraging national sentiments among them.[786] Russia secretly incited the Bulgarians and the people of Montenegro, and an uprising took place in Montenegro (Qaradağ) in 1280/1863 but was suppressed by Serdâr-ı Ekrem Ömer Pasha.[787]

### Events in Wallachia and Moldova 1861-1866

In accordance with the Treaty of Paris, a *fermân* was issued in 1278 (6 December 1861), entrusting the government of Wallachia and Moldova to Prince Cuza under the suzerainty of Osmanlı rule, thus marking the beginning of today's Romania. But its joint parliament rejected a bill presented by the Prince, who dismissed the parliament in retaliation. It was decided in 1281 (28 June 1864) that Osmanlı sovereignty would continue in Romania, though the latter was allowed to run its own internal affairs. The parliament elected Leopold, Count of Flanders and brother of the King of Belgium, to be the Prince of Romania,[788] but he refused. Hence France plotted to secure the election of Carol I to the post. He actually came to İstanbul in 1866 to offer his respects to the Sultân, who agreed to recognise his hereditary rule over Romania on the condition that this would be under Osmanlı sovereignty and that the Romanian army should not exceed 30,000 soldiers.[789]

### Events in Serbia

The Serbian government increased the size of its police force in 1278/January 1862, and killed some Turks during the months of February and March. This led to tumult and chaos during which the castle of Belgrade surrendered to the Serbs[790] in 1284/1867 without any resistance. The Osmanlı government was unable to do anything about this Serbian aggression because they knew that European powers would not allow them to crush the power of the Serbs.

# Chapter Fifteen – Another Attempt at Restoration

**The Uprising in Girit (Crete)**

Fifteen per cent of the population of Girit were Muslim while the rest were Christian. Some of those Muslims came from Anatolia, and the others were converts to Islam. The *Fermân* of *İslâhât* offered the Christians many privileges, and in 1866 they purchased extensive estates in Crete. Nevertheless, they revolted or were obliged to do so under the leadership of Michael, who threatened to burn down the houses of those who would not participate in this uprising, which was supported by Russia and Greece. In the meantime, European powers wanted an investigation and plebiscite to be held on Girit. But the Osmanlı Devlet refused this offer. The French ambassador Bourree was received by the Sultân, who replied to his insistence on investigation: "… There are three hundred thousand Rûm (Greek) people on Girit; while it is reasonable to take one piece of gold from each person a year as tax, the income would be three hundred thousand pieces of gold. But the tax is less than even half a lira, and since there is not a single country that receives such a little amount as tax, it has been continuously suggested that a commission be sent there for investigation."

The Osmanlı Devlet, however, contained this revolt on Girit in 1868 by blockading the coast of Greece to prevent any assistance from reaching the rebels and at the same time proclaimed a general amnesty. A conference was convened in Paris in 1869, endorsing the activities and policies of the Osmanlı Devlet in this respect.[791] In fact, during that time, Britain practised a tax policy in India that punished those who were unable to pay it by confiscating their property.

In 1867, the governments of Britain, Austria, France, and Russia examined the scope of realisation of the reforms promised by the Osmanlı Devlet, and found many shortcomings. They complained that the mixed courts were too few in number and that their methods of handling the cases were not satisfactory. Ahmed Jevdet Pasha was appointed head of the *Dîvân-ı Ahkâm-ı Adliyye* (the Supreme Court), whose members included both Muslims and non-Muslims.[792]

In 1867 Sadrâzam Âli Pasha suggested to Sultân 'Abdülazîz that the French civil law be translated and accepted as Osmanlı civil law. But Ahmed Jevdet Pasha (18221895), being a *madrasah* graduate, knew Islamic law very well, was well acquainted with Europe, and knew mathematics, history, and French civil law. Upon his offer, it was decided that a law-book would be compiled under the name of *Mejelle-i Ahkâm-ı Adliyye* for individual relations, with reference to *fiqh* books and taking the question of the age into consideration. A society was set up under the chairmanship of Ahmed Jevdet Pasha, which prepared Osmanlı Civil Law in about ten years as envisaged. The *Mejelle* consisted of one preface and sixteen books. The first fifteen books were completed in 1874, and the sixteenth in 1878.[793]

### The Young Osmanlıs (Yeni Osmânlılar)

Some Osmanlı intellectuals, having been influenced by the winds of freedom and liberalism blowing from Europe, set up a secret society named *Yeni Osmânlılar* (New or Young Osmanlıs). The Young Ottoman Society was organised in 1865; its members propounded their ideas in the *Tasvir-i Efkâr* and other newspapers in 1866. This secret society was organised on the basis of the Carbonari; among its members were Ziyâ, (Nâmık) Kemâl, Ali Suâvî, journalist Âgâh Efendi, and Shinâsi. Jean Pietri of Corsica played a crucial role in introducing members of this society to each other. Jean Pietri introduced a certain man called Sukkakini, who was, in fact, of Italian descent, to the Young Osmanlıs. Sukkakini, had been managing the commercial and secret political affairs of Mustafa Fâzıl Pasha of Egypt.[794] Mustafa Fâzıl Pasha, son of İbrâhîm Pasha, son of Muhammad Ali Pasha, opposed

## Chapter Fifteen – Another Attempt at Restoration

the Tanzîmât administrators because the *khedive* of Egypt İsmâîl Pasha changed the hereditary system, which was "the heir is the eldest male of the family," into "the heir is the son of the *khedive*," thus depriving Mustafa Fâzil Pasha of his inheritance. This change took place with the consent of the administrators of the Tanzîmât in İstanbul. He was very rich and gave financial support to the Young Ottomans Ziyâ Pasha, Nâmık Kemâl, Ali Suâvî, and Âgâh Efendi, who were in favour of the constitution.[795]

The Osmanlı government did not like the presence of these intellectuals in İstanbul, and appointed Nâmık Kemâl assistant of the *vâli* of Erzurum, and Ziyâ *mutasarrif* (governor of the administrative district) of Cyprus. But Sukkakini called them to Europe in the name of his superior to work there.[796]

Despite the fact that the young Osmanlıs were appointed to high posts outside İstanbul, they preferred Europe, guessing that the possibility of obtaining money and fame was more likely there. Kemâl and Ziyâ left the country from the Tophâne quay in disguise with the help of the French Embassy. Suâvî and Âgâh were also sent to Europe with Sukkakini's help, and Mustafa Fâzil Pasha accelerated his activities in Europe as protector of these "*jeunes*[i]."[797] They continued to write and send their works through foreign post offices that were beyond the control of the Osmanlı government. Some French newspapers described them as "the saviours of Turkey and the vanguard of the progressives."[798] "While 'these aged *jeunes*' wanted a freedom that would shake the Devlet in the fullest sense of the word for the benefit of the foreigners, 'the Osmanlı Devlet [was] the freest country of the world; everything [was] allowed in Turkey except to criticise Islam and the Sultân,' so reads the statement by Panait İstrati, a famous Romanian writer, which was a tributary realm to the Osmanlı Devlet."[799]

---

i  "Young people" in French.

The Young Osmanlıs began to propagate the constitution in Paris in Zilkade 1283/March 1867. There were sincere and dedicated persons among them, but some of them were in pursuit of their own personal interests. So much so that even Mustafa Fâzil Pasha, who was the general head of the society, was not a man of conviction;[800] he attempted to pressure the Sultân to appoint him crown prince and heir to the current *khedive* of Egypt.[801] And it should be remembered that some of them, including their forerunners Shinâsî, Nâmık Kemâl, and Ziyâ Pasha, were members of the Masons; this point is important and merits further study.

Mustafa Fâzil Pasha returned to İstanbul some years later and became a member of the *Hey'et-i Vükelâ* (Council of Ministers), subsequently restricting the financial sources of the Young Osmanlıs. They returned to Turkey after the death of Âlî Pasha, their arch enemy, and entered into the civil service of the administration they used to criticise.[802]

They made contact with Murâd Efendi, heir to the throne and a member of the Masons[803] like themselves. Sultân Abdülhamîd expresses in the *Muhtıra* of Dr. Âtıf Bey, published by İbnülemîn, "My brother (Murâd) was a friend of (Nâmık) Kemâl Bey; they used to drink alcohol at night until dawn, and to read and write. One day, I met Kemâl Bey, and said to him: 'Kemâl Bey, be aware that you will be the cause of my brother's death. Morally, do not encourage him to alcohol to that extent.' ... They used to meet in several places, but mostly at Kurbağalıdere Farm. Their business was to criticise Sultân 'Abdülazîz and to make plans to turn local and foreign public opinion against him, and to dethrone him as soon as possible and to put Murâd on the throne."[804]

### The Journey of Sultân 'Abdülazîz to Europe

The French emperor, Napoleon III, invited Sultân 'Abdülazîz to Paris on the occasion of the International Paris Fair; and conveyed

## Chapter Fifteen – Another Attempt at Restoration

to him through his ambassador in İstanbul the probability of using this opportunity to strengthen the general peace. At that time the problem of Girit (Crete) had been added to the troubles of the Balkans, and the Sultân therefore decided to go. He set out in Safer 1284/June 1867 by sea, arrived in Toulon and went to Paris. He was met by the Emperor at the station; but when Napoleon III told him that the best way to solve the Crete problem was to leave it to Greece, 'Abdülazîz replied that "the Devlet-i 'Aliyye, after fighting for 27 years and sacrificing so many souls, annexed the said island; I do not accept any offer to relinquish it and I am determined to fight for it to the end." Upon this statement, the emperor gave up his offer. Some ascribed this statement to Fuâd Pasha, who was famous for his quickness in reply; when he was asked during a friendly conversation for the price to sell Crete, he said: "the same price for which we have bought it!"[805]

Sultân 'Abdülazîz went to London and met Queen Victoria. The British Prime Minister Palmerston, who had made it a principle to support the Osmanlı Devlet against Russia, had died two years previously. The Sultân went to his house and visited his family; this attitude of faithfulness had a good effect on British public opinion. Sultân 'Abdülazîz returned via Brussels, Vienna, and Varna in Rabî'ul âkhir 1284/August 1867.[806]

### The Conference of London

With the defeat of France by Germany in 1870, it had lost its influence in the East. Britain kept its neutrality and there remained no power to oppose Russia in the East except Germany. Most likely, there was a secret agreement between the two about the Eastern Question. Russia was not content with the article in the Treaty of Paris which banned it from having warships in the Black Sea. Russia informed the states concerned that it regarded the said article null and void. After Sultân 'Abdülazîz became Sultân, the Devlet-i 'Aliyye had more than 20 armour-plated battleships and about 100 wooden battleships, which made Russia apprehensive. Russia therefore wanted the Treaty of Paris amended, and a conference was held in London in 1288/1871. At that conference, Russia's complaint was related to having warships in the Black Sea, but it was accepted that, in the case of the Osmanlı Devlet's wishes, the other states' warships would enter the Black Sea, and the right of the Osmanlı Devlet to keep the straits closed was confirmed.[807] After that conference Russian-backed Pan-Slavism gathered momentum.

### Toward the Independence of Egypt (1863-1882)

The Europe-oriented İsmâîl Pasha, a clever and adventurous young man, was installed as viceroy of Osmanlı Egypt in 1863. He came to İstanbul to present his regards and a steamboat to Sultân 'Abdülazîz who, for his part, visited Egypt in 1280/1863. In 1864-1865 İsmâîl reinforced the Osmanlı army with 4,500 troops to suppress a riot in the Hejâz, and in 1866 sent another 8,000 troops to support the Devlet in its struggle in Romania. He also sent 18,000 soldiers to Girit, and offered top Osmanlı officials very valuable gifts. Both the Sultân and Sadrâzam Fuâd Pasha were very grateful for his help, and remunerated İsmâîl by giving him a number of privileges, the most important of which was the title of *hidiv* (*khedive*) in 1293/1876, which empowered him to run the internal affairs of Egypt independently.[808]

With the permission of the Osmanlı government the digging of the Suez Canal started on 18 March 1866, and was completed in record time by August 1869.[809] But İsmâîl borrowed large sums of money from abroad, and hence in 1876 became obliged to establish an organisation for the administration of those loans. The British also bought some shares in the canal, thus becoming the second-largest shareholder after France. In the Egyptian government that was formed in 1878 under the premiership of Nobar Pasha, a Briton

*Chapter Fifteen – Another Attempt at Restoration*

and a Frenchman were appointed ministers of Finance and Public Works respectively.[810] But İsmâîl was dismissed in 1879 and, upon the initiative of Britain and France, his son Tawfîq was appointed *khedive*. By 1299/1882 Britain had firmly consolidated her position in Egypt.

Sadrâzam Fuâd Pasha passed away in 1286/1869, and his successor Ali Pasha died in 1288/1871. Mahmûd Nedîm Pasha was appointed to this post.[811]

**The Bulgarian Riots (1848-1876)**

The Bulgars, who were ethnically Turkish, advanced north of the Black Sea and established the Bulgar realm in 61/680-681. Afterwards, the Slav tribes came to the Balkans. By 251/865 all the people there had accepted Christianity, and the Turkic-Bulgars were gradually Christianised, their language switched to a Slavonic one, and their Turkish titles were dropped. The new Bulgarian realm became a vassal of the Roman Empire, but later the Osmanlı Turks came to control the entire area in the eighth/fourteenth century.[812] Although the Bulgarians remained under Greek patriarchs during Osmanlı rule, the Osmanlıs put an end to injustice and tumult there, and the villagers became far better off than their counterparts in Europe and Russia. During the war in 1245/1829 the Russians made contact with the Bulgarians, whom they perceived to be Orthodox as well, while the Greeks tried to win their allegiance through the GreekChurch.[813]

The riots and revolutions that shook Europe in 1848 affected the Bulgarians too. They rose in rebellion in Vidin in 1265/1849, but the Osmanlı Devlet subdued this revolt in 1267/1851.[814] In 1860 the Bulgarians approached the Osmanlı government to withdraw from the Greek Church, while the Austrian elements tried to win them over to Catholicism. But the Greek archbishop did not want the Bulgarians to become Catholics, and thus proclaimed that "the

379

Pope was a bishop of rejection and novelty." Nevertheless, many Bulgarians became Catholic, asserting that the Greek archbishop was himself an unbeliever, and those who remained Orthodox insisted on setting up their own independent church.[815] During this the Osmanlı Sultân issued the *fermân* of 1286 (11 March 1870) that reinstalled the exarch and proclaimed that all the religious affairs of the Bulgarian *millet* would be under his responsibility.[816] Thus, an independent Bulgarian church was established, and the Bulgarians were freed from Greek religious pressure. But the Bulgarians revolted against Osmanlı rule once again in 1293/1876. Though materially far better off than the Russians and other villagers, the Bulgarians seemed to have been aroused by an emotional national feeling and may also have been influenced by Bulgarian guerillas in Romania. The revolution began in Sofia and Filibe (Plovdiv), but an Osmanlı force of 18,000 soldiers, under the leadership of Midhat Pasha and with the help of Turks living in the area, managed to subdue the Bulgarians.[817]

### *Shûrâ-yı Devlet* (The Council of the Devlet)

A regulation called *teshkîl-i vilâyât* (forming *vilâyats*) was issued on 7 Jumâdal Âkhira 1281/7 November 1864 to reorganise the *eyâlets* into *sanjaq, qazâ,* and *nâhiye*. According to this regulation, each *vilâyat* was governed by a *vâli*, each *sanjaq* by a *mutasarrif,* and each *qazâ* by a *qaaimmakâm*; and each of them would preside over a *mejlis-i idâre* (council of administration) in their administrative area, and each *mejlis-i idâre* would contain Muslim and non-Muslim members who would be elected every two years, along with the governmental officials. Each *vilâyat* had a *mejlis-i 'umûmî* (general council) that met once a year; this *mejlis* (council) would contain members from all *qazâs* and would discuss and decide commercial, agricultural, industrial, educational, and civil affairs and works of the *vilâyat*.

*Chapter Fifteen – Another Attempt at Restoration*

Thus far the approach had always been *vahdet-i quvâ* (unity of power), but on 8 Zilhijje 1284/1 April 1868 the *Shûrâ-yı Devlet* was organised along the lines of *tefrîq-i quvâ* (distribution of power). Members from various *vilâyats* met on 17 Muharram 1285/10 May 1868. Sultân 'Abdülazîz gave a speech at the inaugural ceremony of the *Shûrâ-yı Devlet*.[818] We know that the Sultân's journey to Europe and his impressions there affected his quick acceptance of Âli Pasha's offer of this reorganisation.

### The Deposition of Sultân 'Abdülazîz 1876

The Russians invaded Tashkent in Turkestan in 1865, and Samarkand in 1868; the Emir of the Bukhâra region became a *vâli* of the Russian Czar. They occupied Hîve (Khiva) in 1873. Britain was not at all happy with Russian expansion towards India and kept the Russians busy in the Caucasus and the Balkans. The strife between Britain and Russia over Asia continued for some time in Persia and Afghanistan. This diminished somewhat after 1872 and Russia began to incite the people in the Balkans against the Osmanlı Devlet. Britain turned a blind eye to these activities because of balance of power problems in Europe, even encouraging them, and supported Midhat and his friends by means of their ambassador Elliot. This ambassador expressed the view that Midhat was elected in 1871 as head of the supporters of freedom and reform, in other words, "they" appointed him. He added that Midhat Pasha resided on his farm near the city walls and was busy making plans.[819] Elsewhere, Murâd Efendi was collaborating with the plotters through his special physician Kapolyon, his money changer Hristaki, and Ziyâ Bey.[820]

Unrest in Osmanlı Europe and the interference of the foreign powers in the affairs of the Devlet caused excitement and disillusionment within the Osmanlı domain. In general the people blamed Sadrâzam Mahmûd Nedîm Pasha for this deterioration, and the students were most likely incited to demonstrate on

May 11th, 1876 in front of Bâb-ı Âlî (Osmanlı government headquarters), demanding the immediate dismissal of the *sadrâzam* and the *Shaykhülislâm*. In a futile attempt to preserve his post, the *sadrâzam* replaced the *Shaykhülislâm* Hasan Fehmi Efendi, but the Sultân dismissed him summarily. To calm the situation, Sultân 'Abdülazîz reluctantly appointed Mütercim Mehmed Rüshdî Pasha as *sadrâzam*, while Hüseyin Khayrullâh Efendi became the *sheyhülislâm* and Hüseyin Avnî Pasha the *serasker* (Chief of Staff and Minister of War). Midhat Pasha also joined this government.[821] Presumably, the Sultân did not trust them at all, and it was only a matter of time before he would dismiss them and restore Mahmûd Nedîm Pasha to power. Hence, they conspired to depose the Sultân, and the idea was presumably the brainchild of Hüseyn Avni Pasha who persuaded Midhat Pasha to join the plot. Sadrâzam Mehmed Rüshdî Pasha was hesitant in the beginning, but was persuaded under threat.[i] The Shaykhülislâm was won over at Midhat Pasha's home,[822] and Serasker Hüseyin Avni Pasha persuaded Süleymân Pasha, the commander of the War College, and Qayserili Ahmed Pasha, the Naval Minister, to join too. The conspirators issued a *fetvâ* that declared 'Abdülazîz insane, with his khalifate considered harmful to the Devlet and the *millet* (the Muslims). They besieged the palace, swore allegiance to Murâd Efendi, and on 30 May 1876, the guns were fired announcing the deposition of 'Abdülazîz and the accession of the new Sultân, Murâd the Fifth.[823]

While the two most senior officials, Âlî Pasha and Fuâd Pasha borrowed huge loans from Europeans, Sultân 'Abdülazîz had tried his best to reduce expenditure. Nevertheless, he alone was held responsible[824] and deposed from his post, although he seems to

i   *Ibid.*, p. 105. It is clear that the "men of Westernisation had forgotten the meaning of *bay'at*"; Islamic values had faded immensely among "intellectuals."

## Chapter Fifteen – Another Attempt at Restoration

have still been popular among the masses. Jelâleddîn Pasha says in this respect: "If a brave official had taken Sultân 'Abdülazîz out of the palace door and the Sultân had spoken to the soldiers, explaining the real situation, the plot, the soldiers' bayonets would most probably have turned against the plotters, and those who organised the plot would have been defeated and dismissed. But those who surrounded him were not people who acted bravely; in general, they indulged in profit-making and graft."[825] Shortly after his deposition, the former Sultân allegedly committed suicide. Since both his wrists were cut,[826] however, 'Abdülazîz was most probably a victim of political murder.

### 15.7 SULTÂN MURÂD V (1876)

Allegiance (*bay'at*) was sworn to Murâd V, son of Abdülmejîd Khân.[827] He had received a classical Islamic as well as European education, and was well versed in both Arabic and French. During the 'Abdülazîz era, he lived a relatively free life and accompanied 'Abdülazîz on his journey to Europe. Because he was familiar with European manners and knew French, he became noteworthy in the French and British palaces. He befriended the British heir to the throne and was introduced to the Masons by him.[i] He became the Osmanlı Sultân and *khalîfah* on 30 March 1876. But the officials who installed him could not agree among themselves about the terms of the *Meshrûtiyyet* (Constitution), while Europe, on the other hand, urged its speedy proclamation.[828] This event and others explicitly show to what extent Europe had been interfering in the internal

---

i   Karal, VII, p. 352. Emphasis added. E.Z. Karal praises him for being a Mason and claims that he became famous among the rulers of Europe because of that. The Muslim *khalîfah* becomes a Mason, and Prof. Enver Ziyâ Karal praises him for this action – no wonder, because he himself was one!

affairs of the Osmanlı Devlet and the "design" of the structure of the Devlet!

The former sultân, 'Abdülazîz, died in 1293 (4 June 1876), but his fierce enemy Hüseyin Avni Pasha, because of his guilty conscience, would not allow a full post-mortem to determine the cause of death on the weak pretext that this should not be done to the "respected" Sultân 'Abdülazîz. The Sultân's death caused great excitement among the public who blamed Hüseyin Avni Pasha for this crime, and an angry officer killed him and wounded Qayserili Ahmad Pasha.[829]

Close to the end of his era, there were rumours that 'Abdülazîz was planning to amend the provisions of accession to the Osmanlı throne. This could have marginalised Murâd and endangered his status as the crown prince. Thus he cultivated a close relationship with the Young Osmanlıs, knowing at the same time that he would be executed if the attempt to depose Sultân 'Abdülazîz failed. When the deposition actually took place a day ahead of schedule, the sensitive Murâd was reported to have been terribly excited and confused, particularly as he realised his awkward status, whereby the responsibility was his, while power was actually in the hands of the triumvirate of pashas – Midhat, Rüshdi, and Hüseyin Avni. He could not stand this tremendous strain anymore,[830] and was therefore deposed by a *fetvâ* issued in 1293 (31 August 1876). The *bay'at* was sworn to Abdülhamîd on the same day.[831]

# Chapter Sixteen

# Preservation and Rejuvenation

## 16.1 SULTÂN ABDÜLHAMÎD II (1876-1909)

The new Sultân went to the Eyüb Sultân Mosque for the Kılıch Alayı ceremony; he was girded with the sword of Islam in the spiritual presence of this great *sahâbî*, and then he visited the tombs of his ancestors.[832] Midhat Pasha was appointed *sadrâzam*, but was too ambitious, and occasionally rather irresponsible. For example, he proposed that non-Muslim youth be admitted into the War College, but the Sultân adamantly refused.

### Proclamation of the Constitution (*Meshrûtiyyet*)

The "Problem of the Orient" entered a critical phase because of the Bulgarian riots and the sympathy of the European public opinion for them, as well as Russia's accumulation of armies at Bessarabia and on the border of Anatolia because it was not able to suppress the Serbian riots. Great Britain did not want Russia to become the main actor in that situation, and called for a conference with the signatories of the Treaty of Paris of 1856 in İstanbul.

"Meanwhile, the Osmanlı administrators decided to accept the principle of consultation and a committee was assigned under the chairmanship of Midhat Pasha to prepare a draft of the constitution.... But they were not aware of the fact that the aim of Europe was not to achieve reforms that would guarantee the safety and prosperity of the Osmanlı Devlet; on the contrary, in accordance with the triangle agreement, their aim was to divide the Osmanlı

Devlet into small entities and make them only outward vassals of the Osmanlı Devlet, and, in fact, to make them independent in their affairs ...."[833] The conference was convened at the Ministry of the Navy in Halich (the Golden Horn) and on 23 December 1876 Midhat Pasha quickly proclaimed the *Qânûnı-ı Esâsî* (Constitution) to impress the participants. Thus, Sultân Abdülhamîd complied with his promise of the Constitution made before his accession. This was a casual, and not a well-considered law; Sultân Abdülhamîd says in his notes about Midhat Pasha and this constitution:

> "In fact, he (Midhat Pasha) was in favour of the constitution heretofore. But this is partisanship on the basis of having heard its name and its praise only in books. When Midhat Pasha insisted on the proclamation of the Constitution regardless, he had not studied *any* constitution of *any* state and he did not have any sound idea about it. His guide was Odyan Efendi; and Odyan Efendi was not the most distinguished jurist. Moreover, he did not know the country's situation."[834]

> "The *Khatt-ı Hümâyûn* (Heavenly Decree) of the *Qaanun-ıEsâsî* (Constitution) was brought to Bâb-ı Âlî (the government headquarters) by Saîd Pasha, received by Midhat Pasha, and then recited and proclaimed by Mahmûd Jelâleddîn Pasha, with guns fired 101 times at the time of the proclamation. Foreign Minister Safvet Pasha said to the delegates of the conference who were in a meeting at that time that the guns were for the proclamation of the constitution and the rights of all elements in the Osmanlı Devlet were guaranteed. Therefore, there was no need for the conference to continue. But he was told that the conference was convened for the Balkan peace, and so they continued their works."[835]

> "It was a psychological mistake to proclaim the constitution in that manner. The Osmanlı government tried to surprise

*Chapter Sixteen – Preservation and Rejuvenation*

the European powers and abort the conference; but this important move should have been taken after preparing public opinion, possibly even inviting the ambassadors of European states and their delegates to the ceremony."[836]

The European states decided on some points concerning Serbia, Montenegro (Qaradağ), Bosnia-Herzegovina, and Bulgaria, but the Osmanlı government did not accept these decisions.[837]

"Sultân Abdülhamîd was of the opinion that the European states who withdrew their ambassadors from İstanbul upon the Osmanlı government's rejection of their decisions concerning the Balkan region should have been satisfied with some concessions to them. But he was aware of the fact that Sadrâzam Midhat Pasha was in no mood for reconciliation. On the other hand, the European states hinted that they regarded Midhat Pasha to be responsible for the failure of the conference."[838]

Midhat Pasha was too ambitious and was in the habit of behaving irresponsibly from time to time. He used to speak of the Republic indiscreetly during drinking parties. He dreamed of exchanging the Osmanlı line for his own, following the model of Napoleon III. It was well known that he used to say "until now it has been called 'Âl-i Osman' (the House of Osman), and what does it matter if from now on it is called 'Âl-i Midhat' (the House of Midhat)?"[839]

Midhat Pasha was in the habit of gathering Kemâl Bey, Ziyâ Bey, and other youths called "Young Osmanlıs" every night and disclosing secret affairs of the *devlet* to them. Ziyâ Bey and Kemâl Bey set up a committee at the military guesthouse on Bâyezîd Square, the head of which was Midhat Pasha. They began to enlist boys of the notables and others under the name of *millet askeri* (soldiers of the nation). Those who were enlisted there went to Midhat Pasha's home and demonstrated there. *Serasker* (Commander-in-Chief) Redîf Pasha was ordered to abolish that committee and to proclaim that those who wanted to volunteer were to enlist with the office of *serasker*. But those youths opposed that, saying "We do not accept being soldiers under the *serasker*, we want to be soldiers of the nation," and, going to Midhat Pasha's mansion, complained about the attitude of the *serasker*.

Midhat Pasha was ordered to send Ziyâ Bey and Kemâl Bey away, appointing them to some posts outside İstanbul. Midhat Pasha appointed Ziyâ Bey *vâli* of Syria with the rank of *vazîr*. Kemâl Bey did not want to go. Midhat Pasha was called to the palace, the *mühr-i hümâyûn* taken back, and he was dismissed. He was put on the steamer İzzeddin and exiled, put ashore at Brindisi upon his request.[840] It is ironic that article 113, which he had added and used to exile some people, was later applied to him himself to send him into exile.[841] Some poems were written about him when he was exiled, one of which was written by Kâzim Pasha, a conservative:

*Emîrul Mu'minîn sent Midhat away from his domain*
   *In the way that the Creator sent Satan away from Paradise*
*Because he did his best to seduce Adam*
   *And this one worked ceaselessly to make the world go astray.*

But Midhat Pasha was convinced that, if he was dismissed from the post of *sadrâzam*, the people would reinstate him, even asking – while the ship was passing through the Chanakkale Strait (Dardanelles) – if a revolution was taking place in İstanbul.[842] Nothing of the sort happened because people were happy he was leaving.[843] Kemâl Bey was sent to the island of Midilli.[844] Nâmık Kemâl Bey, died later on the island of Sakız, where he was *mutasarrif*, on 28 Rebî'ul Awwal 1306/2 December 1888, and was buried there. But when Sultân Abdülhamîd learned that he wished to be buried at Bolayır, he was conveyed there and buried near the tomb of Süleymân Pasha, with the expenses paid out of the Hazîne-i Hâssa.[845]

# Chapter Sixteen – Preservation and Rejuvenation

## The Osmanlı Parliament (Mejlis-i Meb'ûsân)

The Osmanlı Parliament was inaugurated with a ceremony on 4 Rabî'al Awwal 1294/19 March 1877. Ahmed Vefîk Pasha was elected as President of the Parliament.[846] The Young Osmanlıs committed a serious blunder with regard to representation in Parliament. According to the Constitution, the number of the members from each *vilâyat* should be in proportion to its population, but the Young Osmanlıs did not strictly abide by this with regard to the European part of the Osmanlı domain. This was explained by Stanford and Ezel Kural Shaw as follows: "While the Constitution required an equal ratio of representation for all the provinces of the empire, to impress the powers with the new privileges being given to Christians, the European provinces were considerably over-represented, receiving one deputy for every 82,882 males, while the Anatolian provinces had one for every 162,148 males, and those in Africa one for every 505,000."[847] Nevertheless, the first Osmanlı Parliament convened on 19 March 1877, and the Osmanlı elite were optimistic that this parliamentary system would solve all the problems of the Devlet.

## War with Russia

Despite the fact that the decisions of the conference had been rejected due to the influence of Midhat Pasha, hope for peace had not completely vanished. The Russian Czar, Alexander II, was apprehensive of Britain. Therefore, Ignatieff, the Russian Ambassador to İstanbul, visited the European capitals, discussed the situation, and the six big powers – Britain, France, Germany, Austria, Italy, and Russia – signed the Protocol of London on 16 Rabî'al Awwal 1294/31 March 1877. They telegraphed this short protocol to the Osmanlı government, demanding a piece of land for Montenegro (Qaradağ), reforms by the Osmanlı government in Bosnia-Herzegovina and Bulgaria, and a decrease in the Osmanlı army. Russia sent another note asking the Osmanlı government to send an ambassador to Saint Petersburg to discuss the reduction in the Russian army after the Osmanlı decreased the number of its soldiers. The Osmanlı government refused the land concession to Montenegro, wanted the decrease in the Osmanlı and Russian armies to occur simultaneously, and, while the Osmanlı ambassador was to be sent, a Russian ambassador should also be sent to İstanbul in reply on 26 Rabî'al Awwal 1294/10 April 1877.[848]

Russia, suspecting that the Osmanlı Devlet would reject the London Protocol, signed a secret treaty with Romania, according to which the latter would allow Russian armies to cross the Danube and help them attack the Osmanlı territory.[849]

Russia, having thus prepared the necessary political background and having completed military preparations, proclaimed war on the Osmanlı Devlet on 24 April 1877. Sultân Abdülhamîd II asked the signatories of the Treaty of Paris to hold to their commitment and come to his aid.[850] But the European states did not stir in response to the problem they themselves had caused by signing. After gaining control of the Black Sea, the Russian Czar planned to occupy part of Anatolia, reaching as far as İskenderun Bay on the Mediterranean. The Russian army captured Dobruja, Zishtovi, and Tırnova, and massacred most of the Muslim population there, while Nicopolis also fell after putting up a formidable fight. Outraged by these serious setbacks, Sultân Abdülhamîd II changed Osmanlı commanders, and Süleymân Pasha managed to keep the Russians at bay at Shipka Pass in Bulgaria for a long time.[851] A Russian army captured Vidin but was stopped at Pleven by Osman Pasha,[852] and the defences at Shipka and Pleven hindered the Russian onslaught on İstanbul. Ahmed Muhtar Pasha had, on the other hand, defended Qars on the eastern front against Russian aggression for a long time. To show his appreciation of their efforts, Sultân Abdülhamîd gave the title of *gâzi* to both Osman Pasha and Ahmed Muhtar Pasha.[853]

## Chapter Sixteen – Preservation and Rejuvenation

But the government was criticised in the Parliament that convened on 7 Zilhijjah 1294/13 December 1877 and was in fact put in an awkward and embarrassing situation by these Russian advances in Europe and the East. Sultân Abdülhamîd, however, argued that he had honoured his word to convene Parliament, but that the latter had behaved in an irresponsible manner and therefore deserved his decision to suspend it immediately.

### Treaty of San Stefano

With the Sultân's permission, the British fleet entered the Dardanelles and arrived at İstanbul. The Russian army reached Chatalja, near İstanbul, but was extremely exhausted, and the Treaty of San Stefano was therefore concluded on 3 Rabî'al Awwal 1295/3 March 1878, reiterating the Treaty of Edirne concluded a month previously. Montenegro and Serbia became independent, whereas the Osmanlı Devlet recognised the independence of Romania, and agreed to pay it an indemnity. Russia annexed southern Bessarabia, and Bulgaria was given the right to run its own internal affairs.[854]

### The First Chiragan Event

Immigrants from Bulgaria doubled the population of İstanbul. A former Young Osmanlı, the Pan-Turkist Ali Suavî, plotted with a group of immigrants to depose the Sultân as a protest against his acceptance of the peace treaty. He raided the Chiragan Palace on 20 May 1878, but was overpowered and killed. This encouraged the Sultân to pursue his policy of exercising power as he saw it convenient.[855] Ali Suavî seems to have had an interesting personality. Accepted as an idealist, it seems that he was ignorant of the principle that, if two *khalîfah*s were sworn allegiance to, the second was to be killed; in addition, Murâd, whom he wanted to make sultân, was not of sound mind and was dethroned for this very reason. One of his contemporaries, Mahmûd Jelâleddîn Pasha (1853-1903), said:

"When Sultân Abdülhamîd came to power, he appointed those who were partisans of the former Sultân Murâd, and important and impudent elements called New Osmanlıs to posts they did not deserve at all in the palace in order to keep them under control and prevent them from leaning to the other side. But it became clear that it was impossible to deal with them in that way; some of them, such as (Nâmık) Kemâl Bey, who had friends among the *vekîls* (members of the Osmanlı government), were appointed to governmental posts. A profligate man called Ali Suavî, who had stayed in Britain for a long time and married there and found a place among the notables thanks to his wife's beauty, remained unemployed."[856] A Mason historian, Enver Ziyâ Karal, says:

"Ali Suavî was born in İstanbul in 1839, was educated at Rüshdiyye School, worked as a teacher and then as an civil servant. After his dismissal, he went to Hejâz, and fled to Europe in 1867 with the help of Mısırlı Fâzil Qustafa Pasha, worked there in the Young Osmanlı Society together with Namık Kemâl and Ziyâ Pasha. When he fell out with them he went to Lyon in France, published newspapers and magazines there, and wrote books. When Abdülhamîd ascended the throne, he was allowed to return to his homeland, and was presented to the Sultân. He gained the trust of the Sultân and worked for a while as his private counsellor, and was appointed director of the distinguished Galatasaray Secondary School. But due to reasons unknown up until now, he lost his position and post and went back to journalism."

"Ali Suavî was a clever, dynamic and overly ambitious man, learning Arabic, Persian, French, and English. In Europe he propagated freedom and the constitution, and for a while criticised the Osmanlı government and the khalifate and was regarded as one of the leaders of Turkism because of his articles about the Turkish language and history. But after Abdülhamîd's accession, he began writing in favour of the Osmanlı line and against the constitution, and after he returned to İstanbul he continued to sing his praises, initiating a fierce battle with Midhat Pasha."[857]

## The Second Chiragan Event

The Masons wanted to inaugurate Murâd again, because he was a Mason too. Kelanti, the Master of the Masonic Prodos Lodge in İstanbul, set up a committee concerning Murâd V. This committee pasted manifestos on walls, praising Murâd throughout İstanbul. This committee planned to assassinate Sultân Abdülhamîd but could not implement the plan. According to a plan hatched in February 1878, they would secretly enter the Chiragan Palace through the plumbing and escape with Murâd. The committee was raided while in session, and, though Kelanti and Ali Shefqati were able to escape, others were caught and sentenced. "Ali Suavi and Kelanti are Masons. According to Sultân Abdülhamîd, Masons are people with a superficial European education."[858]

## The Congress of Berlin (13 July 1878)

Britain, Austria, and Prussia were all jealous of the huge territorial gains made by Russia and asked for an immediate congress to be held in Berlin. Russia reluctantly agreed, because it knew that its refusal to attend would lead to a major crisis, possibly war.

Britain asked the Osmanlı Sultân to allow it to govern Cyprus in his name on the assumption that this was necessary to defend eastern Anatolia against any Russian aggression, and warned that it would withdraw from the congress if the Sultân refused. The Sultân was thus obliged to concede this point in the Treaty of Cyprus that was signed on 4 June 1878. Britain, however, agreed to pay annually to the Osmanlı treasury whatever remained of the revenues it got from Cyprus, and the Osmanlı Devlet continued to administer the judicial, educational, and religious institutions of Cyprus. Britain in return promised to provide all necessary aid to defend eastern Anatolia if the Russians attacked.[859]

The Congress of Berlin convened on 12 Jumâdal Âkhira 1295/13 June 1878. The German Prime Minister Prince Bismarck was elected president. The chief of the Osmanlı delegation was Alexander Qara Todori; this Christian was given this position to impress the European powers. When they first met, Bismarck said to the Osmanlı delegates: "Do not deceive yourselves into thinking that the congress is convened for the Devlet-i Aliyye (Osmanlı Devlet). If the Treaty of San Stefano had not affected the benefit of the European states, it would have been left as it is."[860]

The Bulgarian – in fact, Russian – sphere of influence that had extended to the Aegean coast according to the Treaty of San Stefano was narrowed considerably at the Congress of Berlin. The Osmanlı Devlet took back Doğu Bayazit and Eleshkirt which it had handed to Russia according to the Treaty of San Stefano. But the Muslim population of Bosnia-Herzegovina did not accept the articles of this Congress, so Austria imposed a military regime there. Abdülhamîd, despite the fact that he was very sensitive to Islamic matters, was forced, on 21 April 1879, to recognise Austrian sovereignty over that area; the Muslims, however, would be completely free to carry out their religious duties, and the *khutbah* would be in the name of the *Khalîfah*. The natives would be employed in the administration, and those Muslims who wished to would be allowed to do so.[861] Sultân Abdülhamîd insisted on these matters, doing his best to protect the Muslims, his powers being limited to that extent.

# Chapter Sixteen – Preservation and Rejuvenation

## The French Occupation of Tunisia (1881)

Tunisia had technically been a part of the Osmanlı Devlet since 1574, but was ruled on its behalf first by *beğlerbeğis* and then by the *dayıs* and *beğs*. After 1591 the *dayıs* and then the *beğs* became the de facto rulers of the province, managed its internal affairs independently, though the tokens of sovereignty (*khutbah* and *sikkah*, coins) remained in the name of the Osmanlı *khalîfah*-sultân. Since the era of Ahmed Bey (r. 1837-1855), whose mother was originally a Genoese captive, Tunisia had started to drift away from Osmanlı authority. But Vazîr Hayreddîn Pasha, a prominent and capable statesman who was originally a Caucasian slave, struggled during the time of Sâdiq Bey to keep the province under Osmanlı rule. This loyalty to the Osmanlı Devlet exposed him to the bitter enmity of all the foreign consuls in Tunisia, and his political rivals finally forced him to leave the province. Sultân Abdülhamîd employed him in the Osmanlı central administration, but his departure weakened the Devlet's ties with Tunisia.

Meanwhile, Tunisia was heavily involved in foreign loans, and a committee for their administration was established in 1869. Britain gave France the green light to invade Tunisia in return for its recognition of the Treaty of Cyprus, and Bismarck expressed the view that "Germany would raise no objection to France if she occupied Tunisia." By this gesture Bismarck may have wanted to encourage France to swallow its pride with regard to the loss of Alsace-Lorraine to Germany, to keep it out of Europe, pushing it into conflict with Italy in Africa.[862]

With this international encouragement and persuasion, France attacked Tunisia on 4 April 1881 on the pretext of establishing law and order along the Algerian-Tunisian border that allegedly had been threatened by the attack of the Kurumir tribe on Algeria. They compelled Sâdiq Bey to sign the Treaty of Bardo on 12 May 1881 that stipulated French "protection" over Tunisia but remained silent about the presumed "aggressor".

The Osmanlı government protested this flagrant violation of the Treaty of Berlin, but it was powerless to confront the imperialist European powers.

**The Yıldız Court of Justice**

Mahmûd Jelâleddîn Pasha, who later became Nâzir of Finance and of Public Works, presented Sultân Abdülhamîd with a petition concerning the death of Sultân 'Abdülazîz. He claimed, based on the statement by Pervîn Felek Hanım, who came out of the palace after the death of 'Abdülazîz and was married to his son Münîr Bey (afterwards Pasha), that Sultân 'Abdülazîz did not commit suicide but had been murdered.

An extraordinary court of justice was formed under the leadership of Surûrî Efendi, chief justice of the court of appeal, the members consisting of Hristoforidi Efendi, the deputy head of the same court, Emin Bey, a German *mühtedi* (convert) who was famous for his straightforwardness, Tevfîk Bey, Hüseyin Bey, and Tekavur Efendi. Of the fifteen accused, the former Sultân Murâd and his mother were not called to court, and Niyâz Kalfa was pardoned on the grounds she was a woman. Müterjim Rüshdî Pasha, who was in Manisa serving his banishment, was interrogated in İzmir because of his illness. The most famous of the accused, Midhat Pasha, after being exiled, had held official meetings with the officials responsible in Britain and on the continent, despite having no official capacity. Having been pardoned through the intercession of Britain, he was appointed *vâli* of İzmir in 1880. Upon learning about the court case, he secretly left his home on the night of 16/17 May, taking refuge at the nearest foreign representative, the French Consulate. But upon the order of the French Foreign Minister, the French ambassador C. Tissot

## Chapter Sixteen – Preservation and Rejuvenation

in İstanbul telegraphed the French consul in İzmir, and Midhat Pasha was removed from the consulate.

After a three-day session, the court sentenced 10 of the 15 accused, including Midhat Pasha and Müterjim Rüshdî Pasha to capital punishment, and two others to confinement in a fortress. The sentence was ratified by the Supreme Court of Appeal and by the Office of the Chief Mufti.

But Sultân Abdülhamîd did not like execution and changed all the capital punishments to confinement in a fortress.[i] It was decided that they would serve their sentences at Tâif, and they were sent on board the steamer İzzeddîn.[863]

### The Düyûn-ı 'Umûmiyye (Public Loans)

On 20 November 1881 an institution called *düyûn-ı umûmiyye* was set up to arrange and administer the loans owed by the Osmanlı Devlet to European states. It operated much like an independent state within the Devlet. Its functionaries received higher salaries than their counterparts in the Devlet. This organisation was entitled to collect parts of the revenue of the Osmanlı Devlet to cover its debts to European states.[864]

### The British Occupation of Egypt (1882)

Khedive İsmâîl's reckless financial policy led to a difficult situation in Egypt. While all its revenue amounted in 1872 to 9.5 million liras, Egypt's external debt was 100 million liras, and its annual interest was 7.5 million liras. A commission representing the creditors was set up to check the country's finances, and two British and French ministers were appointed in 1878 to the Egyptian cabinet.[865] Faced

---

i   It is interesting to remember that his opponents and enemies labelled him the "Red Sultân"; this label was accepted by some without any further investigation.

with a public outcry, the *khedive* attempted to form an exclusively Egyptian government, but the British and the French intervened, and the *khedive* was compelled to abdicate on 26 July 1879, in favour of his son Tawfîq. Before his abdication, however, İsmâîl had cabled Sultân Abdülhamîd, requesting his protection, but the then Osmanlı *sadrâzam* Hayreddîn Pasha of Tunisia, insisted on his abdication as his stay in office would either incite a popular revolt or lead to external interference in the affairs of the Devlet.[866]

Infuriated by the foreign intervention in the affairs of their country, the Egyptian people revolted in 1881 under the leadership of Ahmad 'Urâbî Pasha. They took over the government, thus temporarily putting an end to European hegemony. Sultân Abdülhamîd convened a conference of ambassadors in İstanbul to discuss the Egyptian situation. Sadrâzam Sa'îd Pasha and other members of the Osmanlı government suggested that they attend, but the Sultân refused on the correct grounds that this would legalise foreign interference in Egyptian affairs. The ambassadors decided that the Osmanlı Devlet should try to resolve the Egyptian problem on its own, and determined that there would be no foreign interference "except in the case of unforeseen circumstances."[867] Sultân Abdülhamîd's political skill had thus saved Egypt from foreign interference for the time being. He summoned 'Urâbî Pasha and his companions to İstanbul for consultation, and sent Dervish Pasha to Egypt to strike a deal with the *khedive*. But while those talks were going on, European vessels appeared off the shores of Alexandria. This led to great excitement and riots among the people, and a few foreigners who happened to be in the streets were killed. Hence the British Admiral Seymour shelled Alexandria on 13 July 1882 even though the French warships had already left Alexandria bay in accordance with a directive from their Chamber of Deputies.[868] Faced with this disruption in the efforts of reconciliation, the Osmanlı government wanted to send troops to Egypt, but the Sultân refused. He felt that

## Chapter Sixteen – Preservation and Rejuvenation

the best course the Osmanlıs could follow in Egypt would be to settle the financial difficulties and appoint Egyptian nationalists to senior posts. They in their turn should take the necessary action.

While the Sultân's representatives were on their way to Cairo, the interventionists in Britain, led by the Minister of Trade, Joseph Chamberlain, wanted to crush the nationalists and occupy Egypt to secure the interests of the British creditors, and, at the same time, to obtain cheap Egyptian cotton for the textile industry in Chamberlain's hometown of Manchester. The French, on the other hand, opposed such military action, as it would bring the British to the eastern Mediterranean, and hence seriously jeopardise French economic and cultural dominance in the area. By then the liberal British Prime Minister Gladstone was about to quit his post, so the interventionists took the initiative in London. British troops landed at Alexandria, defeated the Egyptians at Tell el-Kebîr on 13 September 1882, and occupied Cairo four days later. The Osmanlı Devlet protested this occupation, but to no avail. Britain, however, claimed that its occupation was temporary and that it would withdraw once it solved the Egyptian problems, i.e. a policy of "rescue and retire." The Sultân had no option except to accept this "promise." An agreement was concluded on 24 October 1885, in which Osmanlı sovereignty over Egypt was theoretically maintained and Egypt agreed to pay an annual tax to the Osmanlı Devlet. Both the Osmanlıs and the British were to send high commissioners to Egypt to assist the *khedive* in internal affairs.[869] The Egyptian army was disbanded and its officers were either imprisoned or retired. British officials in Egypt wore the fez (*tarboush*) and adopted the Turkish title of *beğ*. "If they had been able to change their skin colour from white to olive, they would have done so."[870]

Sultân Abdülhamîd was in close contact with the Egyptian intelligentsia and political leaders through his high commissioner Ahmed Muhtar Pasha and the Khedive's family. The Egyptian notables were, for their part, very keen to be in touch with the centre, İstanbul. They sent their children there for education, bought summer mansions on the shores of the Bosphorus, and established matrimonial ties with Osmanlı notables to such an extent that the Osmanlıs "had far more influence in Egypt than was apparent to the British, who remained largely on the surface of Egyptian life through their long years of political and military control."[871]

There is no doubt that all this became possible because of the Islamic cultural unity between the two peoples; the substratum and background was convenient for this continuation. Foreign domination and occupation were unable to sever these strong relations, and it was only later that European imperialists succeeded in weakening these fraternal ties through one-sided education programmes and falsified history books written by their historians, depending not on local or Osmanlı sources but using their books following the model of "*nuqila 'an Nicola* – it was transmitted from Nicola."

### Bulgaria

In accordance with the decision taken at the Congress of Berlin, Bulgaria was divided into a principality under Osmanlı sovereignty and a *vilâyat* called "eastern Rumelia". The efforts of Bulgarian nationalists united the two parts on 18 September 1885. After discussion, the strategic Rouptcos and Kırjaali were returned to the Osmanlı Devlet. This can be regarded as a success for the Osmanlıs under circumstances at that time.[872]

### The Osmanlı-Greek War

The Treaty of 1830 defined the Osmanlı-Greek border. But a secret Greek society, *Ethniki Etaria*, organised an armed attack on the Osmanlı positions in Thessaly and Macedonia in 1897. Though stronger than its Osmanlı counterpart, the Greek navy was unable

## Chapter Sixteen – Preservation and Rejuvenation

to invade the islands in the Aegean Sea. Greek troops led by Constantine, the Greek king's brother, fought the Osmanlı forces under Müshîr (Marshall) Edhem Pasha but were defeated several times, and by the time of the victory of the Battle of Dömeke, on 17 May 1897, the road to Athens lay open for the Osmanlı army. In fact, it would have entered Athens had not the Russian Czar made a personal appeal to Sultân Abdülhamîd to stop military operations. Other European powers wanted the Osmanlı government to stop the war too. A truce was declared on 20 May 1897, and a peace treaty followed on 13 November 1897. The Osmanlı Devlet annexed some strategical points along the border of Thessaly, and the Greeks were forced to pay 100,000,000 franks as war compensation.[873]

*Ahmed Muhtar Pasha*

Though defeated in the battlefield, the Greeks continued to argue that Girit (Crete) belonged to them (the Osmanlı Devlet had, in fact, taken it from the Venetians and not the Greeks) and were supported in this claim by European powers. Due to troubles on Girit itself, its internal administration had been left to some local people in 1897. Prince George came to the island on 21 December 1898, and assumed power over it. Girit theoretically continued under Osmanlı sovereignty, but there was nothing to denote this sovereignty. A founding parliament was convened in 1899, and a committee of five persons was appointed to assist George. Most of the Muslims on Girit emigrated from the island to Anatolia. Thus, through a series of tricks and intrigues Girit was gradually Christianised.[874]

### Osmanlı-German Relations

Sultân Abdülhamîd was cautious towards Britain, belittled France, and never trusted the Russians, the latter having shown enmity towards the Turks and occupied large areas of Muslim-Turkish countries. "Sultân Hamîd's attitude in foreign policy was: handle Russia with tact, be careful not to have any problems with Britain, depend on Germany, do not forget that Austria had an eye on Macedonia, get along well with other states as far as possible, cause trouble in the Balkans, and enmity among the Bulgarians, Serbs, and Greeks."[875] He thus decided to work to win the support and goodwill of Germany. After a visit to Greece, the German Kaiser Wilhelm II came to İstanbul in 1899 and visited Damascus and Quds (Jerusalem) as well.

*German Fountain, Sultân Ahmed Square, İstanbul*

Though the British expressed their keen desire to construct the İstanbul-Baghdad-Basra railway, the Sultân gave this important assignment to Germany in 1903.[876] Apart from that, money was collected from people for the construction of the Hejâz railway, which connected the centre of the khalifate, İstanbul, to Medîna, the city of the Prophet Muhammad ﷺ, and it served the Muslim pilgrims. The intention was to continue with it to Makkah and later to Yemen.

The Osmanlıs were very careful to keep the silence in this holy city, so the route of the railway and the station were planned so as not to disturb the Prophet ﷺ.

## Chapter Sixteen – Preservation and Rejuvenation

Britain was not happy with the Sultân's friendly relations with Germany because that situation affected Britain's influence in the region negatively. The railway would have another branch – Baghdad-Basra-Kuwait; thus the Sultân increased the competition and rivalry between Germany and Britain.[877]

# Chapter Seventeen

# The İttihâd ve Teraqqî Society
# The Committee of Union and Progress

"While the educational explosion during Abdulhamit's reign produced hundreds of educated bureaucrats, doctors, officers, and writers willing to work within the system, it also introduced some Ottomans to the liberal political thought of western Europe. ...when the Sultân attempted to balance the budget by reducing the staffs of the ministries and the army, thus setting loose many graduates of his schools who, after having achieved their education, felt that they had a right to government employment at comfortable salaries."[878]

Students from the Military Medical School – İbrâhîm Temo, Abdullah Jevdet, Mehmet Reşîd, Hüseyin-zâde Ali, and İshâq Sukûtî – set up a secret society called *İttihâd ve Teraqqî Committee* (Union and Progress) on 21 May 1889 that enrolled members from among the students and army officers. Their programme was based on the principles of the constitution, Ottomanism, and freedom. "The Osmanlı İttihâd and Teraqqî Society was set up as a secret entity and developed in the course of time. Many methods and rules practised by Masons have been adopted."[i]

The number of members of this society rapidly increased. Ahmed Riza (1859-1930), one of its distinguished members, went to Paris

---

i   Karal, *op. cit.*, fourth printing, Ankara, 1995, VIII, p. 514. It is reasonable to trust Enver Ziyâ Karal's hint that the İttihâd and Teraqqî Society was founded by Masons or at least was initially under their influence if not control, keeping in mind that E.Z. Karal himself was a Mason.

## Chapter Seventeen – The İttihâd ve Teraqqî Society

and was deeply influenced by Pierre Lafitte, a disciple of Auguste Comte. He learned about positivism from Lafitte, which formed his attitude.[879] Ahmed Riza became the leader in course of time.

The Egyptian *khedive* supported this society by sending money to it, but stopped when he was told that its leader, Ahmed Riza, was allegedly an unbeliever.[880] The Osmanlı intelligentsia of that time naively assumed that immediate *meshrûtiyyet* (constitutional government) alone would solve all the problems of the Devlet.

**An Attempt at Assassination**

During the Russian-Osmanlı War of 1293/1877-78 there were Armenian generals and many Armenian officers and soldiers in the Russian army of the Caucasus. The Russian Armenians incited the Osmanlı Armenians, who had been living a very comfortable life and had been called *tebe'a-yı sâdıqa* (the loyal followers). The Russian Armenians tried to win the Osmanlı Armenians over for Russia. In fact, the Armenians had never lived under other sovereignties, including that of the Roman Empire, as comfortably as under the Osmanlıs; there were Armenian ministers and many high-level bureaucrats in the Osmanlı administration. Britain, in turn, seeing that the Russian ambition of reaching warm waters was possible because of the conditions accepted at Berlin Congress, decided to use the Armenians for its own interests and thus prevent a Russian advance that would endanger interests of Britain related to Egypt and India. Thus, the Armenians became a group used by the great powers for their own interests and were harmed.

The Osmanlı Armenians, incited and encouraged by foreign powers, acted. They spread propaganda in Europe claiming that they were oppressed in the Osmanlı Devlet, and also caused riots and acts of disobedience in the country. They were trying to pave the way for foreign interference. To set up an Armenia in Eastern Anatolia they decided to assassinate the Osmanlı Sultân, Abdülhamîd, by bombing his carriage and then blow up Bâb-ı Âli, the Osmanlı government headquarters, the Galata Bridge in İstanbul, the Osmanlı Bank, and the embassies in İstanbul. They hoped this turmoil would lead to European interference in the affairs of the Osmanlı Devlet. They constructed a carriage in Vienna, put 80 kilograms of melinite and 20 kilograms of mitraille (steel and iron pieces) in its chest. They set the time bomb for one minute and forty-two seconds, the time the Sultân took to reach his carriage after leaving the *Jumu'ah* prayer to his carriage during *Jumu'ah Selâmlığı*. While the Sultân was coming out of the Hamîdiyye Mosque on 18 Jumâde'l Ûlâ 1323/21 July 1905, after *salâtul Jumu'ah*, he spoke with the *sheyhülislâm*. He was thus delayed, while the bomb exploded with an awful noise heard throughout all of İstanbul.[881] "The Sultân understood from the noise and blast and the flying pieces that a terrible event took place. But he showed no sign of fear or alarm but only asked: 'What is the matter?' He rode in his carriage, taking the reins. Arriving at Chit kiosk, he entered it. He then received the ambassadors as was his custom, and spoke with them for about twenty minutes. The ambassadors told the interpreter pasha that they did not find anything extraordinary about the Sultân."[882] Twenty-six people died in this event. Many were injured, carriages were blown to pieces, and many horses were killed.

**Sultân Abdülhamîd and Freedom**

As far as Sultân Abdülhamîd was concerned, the "freedom" the Young Osmanlıs desired was "a destructive weapon for the Devlet." For, in his words, "Giving freedom was similar to giving a gun to a man who did not know how to use it. With that weapon that man could kill his father, his mother, his brothers, even himself. Thus, it is necessary to prepare the country for freedom before giving it, and I am trying to do this; the best way to achieve this objective is to improve education, and I am establishing schools."[883] "For Abdülhamîd, even

## Chapter Seventeen – The İttihâd ve Teraqqî Society

'Osmânlısm,' which he had adopted during his proclamation of the Constitution, did not count. The crux of the matter for him was Islam, the only strong tie that connected the Muslims to one another in the Osmanlı Devlet."[884] The above quotation is from the Turkish historian Enver Ziyâ Karal, who was not usually positively inclined toward Abdülhamîd. It is quite interesting to note that future events proved that Sultân Abdülhamîd was shrewd and right; the Osmanlı Devlet was viewed as a "Great Power" (it was considered one of the *düvel-i mu'azzama*/great states) in spite of all its weakness and problems. But after so-called "freedom," only ten years were enough to destroy it.

Sultân Abdülhamîd tried to bring the members of the İttihâd and Teraqqî, who were in some European cities and in Cairo, to reason through promises. Some came back and entered civil service. But the idea of "freedom" had become an "ideal" for the Osmanlı intelligentsia. European states supported those naive people who believed that the proclamation of the constitution alone would immediately abort European projects of dividing the Osmanlı Domain![885]

*Osmanlı Railway Station at al Madina al Munawwarah*

The Ittihâd and Teraqqî Society, using Masonic methods and the tactics of plotters, won over the young army officers in Rumelia, which was where the Sultân sent the best ones because of the importance of the region. Marshall Shemsî Pasha was sent to put down the rebel bands led by army officers to Manastır, where he was assassinated on 7 Jumâdal Âkhira 1326/7 July 1908. Marshall Osman Fevzi Pasha replaced him, but he was kidnapped. He was treated with great respect by the kidnapping soldiers, but it was firmly stated that they wanted the Constitution to be proclaimed.[886] And telegrams poured from Rumelia to the Sultân with extremely respectful but firm demands that they wanted the constitution to be proclaimed. They stated that not only soldiers but shopkeepers and all the people were determined to see to it that the constitution be proclaimed.[887] Sultân Abdülhamîd was about to turn 66 by then, had been in power for 32 years and was tired.[888] Therefore, because of the threats and blackmail of the İttihâd ve Teraqqî Committee Society, he was forced to proclaim the second Constitutional Administration for the second time on 23 July 1908. "When it finally did take place, the young Turk Revolution was one of the strangest events of its kind ever seen in history. It was not planned, at least not in that manner, and by the time it finally occurred, it really did not even happen, and it certainly did not depose Abdülhamîd. Yet it forced him to recall the Parliament and, for all practical purposes, to give up most of his powers."[889]

On 3 April 1909 there was a violent response in İstanbul against the İttihâd ve Teraqqî Committee that sought to dismiss Ahmed Riza from the chairmanship of the Assembly and to install a real and true Muslim in this position. The crowd attacked the Assembly, and, while the members were fleeing, two innocent people were killed, mistakenly thought to be Ahmed Riza and Hüseyin Jâhid, the latter a famous writer and journalist. The İttihâd ve Teraqqî Committee was not well established in İstanbul, and so its members fled the

## Chapter Seventeen – The İttihâd ve Teraqqî Society

city. The government resigned and the power that remained was the Sultân's. He appointed İsmâil Kemâl President of the Assembly. The senior officers of the Osmanlı Macedonian Army gathered under the leadership of Mahmûd Shevket Pasha and vowed to establish law and order anew. They called themselves *Hareket Ordusu* (the Operational Army) and departed for İstanbul by train. But when the parliamentarians met them at Yeshilköy station, a new development took place since they decided to depose the Sultân himself. On the other hand, it seems that all these events were planned by some groups and staged.

### 17.1 THE DEPOSITION OF THE SULTÂN

The Assembly met on 27 April 1909 and decided to depose the Sultân. Abdülhamîd was sent immediately to Selânik (Thessaloniki) by train.[890] Among the four representatives who broke the sad news to the Khalîfah-Sultân, two were non-Muslims: Emmanuel Carasso (a Jew) and Aram (an Armenian). "The worst act by the İttihâd ve Terakki Committee was deposing Abdülhamîd, who was a master of European diplomacy with 32 years of experience. The British ambassador Nicholas O'Connor said that all the peoples of Europe ought to pray for him [Sultân Abdülhamîd II] in order to escape the trial of a world war. And

*Sultân Abdülhamîd II*

409

the French ambassador, Maurice Bompard, expressed the view that there was no diplomat of his calibre in any state in Europe."[891]

Abdülhamîd was put under house arrest in Alatini's mansion in Selânik, but was brought to İstanbul in 1912 during the Balkan War, where he stayed at Beğlerbeği Palace until his death on 10 February 1918. While there, Enver Pasha, one of the three leaders of the İttihâd and Teraqqî, visited him; the experienced former sultân observed that he "would make a good colonel."

While the İttihâd ve Teraqqî Committee leaders were engaged in the election campaign, the Europeans inflicted serious blows on the weak and impotent Osmanlı Devlet. Austria annexed Bosnia and Hercegovina on 5 October 1908. Bulgaria proclaimed independence, and Greece occupied Crete, which the European powers evacuated on 27 July. The Osmanlı Devlet appealed for help to the guarantors and signatories of the Berlin Treaty, but to no avail. It then tried to resolve the problem itself by concluding a treaty with Austria, whereby it accepted Austria's annexation of Bosnia and Hercegovina in return for getting back the town of Novi Pasar from Austria, who would also pay them war compensation. A treaty was also concluded with Bulgaria on 19 April 1909 by which the Sultân acquired control over the Muslim institutions in Bulgaria, Bosnia, and Hercegovina and religious leaders (*qadıs* and *muftis*) for them. Both Austria and Bulgaria guaranteed that they would support the Muslim schools and mosques in their countries financially.

## 17.2 SULTÂN MEHMED V RESHÂD (1909-1918)

Mehmed Reshâd, Abdülmejîd's son, became sultân-*khalîfah* on 27 April 1909. A revolution broke out in Albania in 1910. It was masterminded by the Catholics, but Muslim Albanians subsequently joined. Sultân Reshâd went to Kosova in June 1911 to calm the situation, declaring a general amnesty. The revolt came to an end on 4 September 1912.[892]

# Chapter Seventeen – The İttihâd ve Teraqqî Society

## The Tripoli War (1911)

Britain and France occupied most of the Muslim countries in North Africa, and the political atmosphere was conducive for an Italian adventure in Tripolitania (Libya), where many Italian merchants resided. France was ready as early as 1900 to recognise Italian supremacy over Tripolitania in return for Italy's acceptance of the French occupation of Morocco. In 1909 Italy supported the persistent Russian demand for freedom to navigate the Straits of İstanbul and Chanakkale (Dardanelles) in the hope that this would persuade the latter to support the Italian invasion of Tripolitania.[893]

The Italian government proclaimed war on Tripolitania on 29 September 1911 on the pretext that its subjects were badly treated there. Italian troops invaded the coast but were not able to advance any further. Sultân Abdülhamîd, knowing about the Italian intentions with regard to Tripolitania, had formed a unit of 5,000 soldiers composed of *kulogliyye*[i] and volunteers from among the local people. Rejeb Pasha had formed a cavalry unit of 1,200 men composed of *kulogliyye*, thus securing the defence of the country

*Meshed-i Hüdâvendigâr, Kosova*

i   *kuloğlu*: born of marriages between Turkish soldiers and local women.

until the arrival of the Osmanlı army in case of a sudden Italian attack.[894] Some Osmanlı army's officers went there and joined the resistance movement. Kushchbashı Eshref, one of the founders of *Teshkilât-i Makhsûsa*, settled in Cairo in disguise; he mastered the Arabic language, and organised the transfer of Osmanlı officers from there to Libya, and went there himself as well. Enver, Mustafa Kemâl, Fethi (Okyar), Nûri (Jonker), Ali (Chetinkaya), and Ömer Nâji (*khatîb*) were among those volunteer officers. Those officers were regarded as on leave, because the Osmanlı Devlet was not "officially" at war with Italy. They went to Libya voluntarily and took part in the resistance.[895]

Unable to occupy Libya, Italy tried its might at the Dardanelles and shelled Beirut. It also occupied Rhodes and twelve islands in the Aegean Sea, the Dodecanese. These serious military setbacks forced the Osmanlı Devlet to the negotiation table, and on 15 October 1912 a treaty was concluded with Italy. The Osmanlı Devlet accepted Italian sovereignty over Libya, but the *khutbah* in the mosques of Libya remained in the name of the *khalîfah*, thus maintaining some sort of Islamic connection. A *nâib* (deputy) was also to represent the Sultân in Libya, and Italy surrendered Rhodes and the twelve islands to the Osmanlı Devlet. Shortly afterwards, however, the Balkan War broke out, and Italy failed to honour her pledge.[896] "Fâzıl Beğ, a member of the Osmanlı delegation that would conclude the Treaty of Ushi with Italy, visited Minister of War Nâzım Pasha. While discussing that treaty, Fâzıl Beğ told Nâzım Pasha: 'There are traitors among us. During the debate, I tried to get some concessions from the Italian delegates and they consented. But during the second session I found them changed. When I asked the reason, they told me that their ambassador in İstanbul had had a talk with our Minister of Foreign Affairs G. Norodongıyan, who told the ambassador that "we are in a bad situation, and are obliged to give whatever you want; insist on your demands and do not miss this opportunity," and that the Italian ambassador in İstanbul reported the information to the Italian delegation.'"[897]

## The Balkan Wars (1912-1913)

Sultân Abdülhamîd II, a very clever and skilful statesman, intelligently exploited the religious differences between the Greeks and Bulgarians. But the inexperienced government of the İttihâd ve Teraqqî Committee issued a decree on 10 July 1910 that settled these differences, although there were great and chronic differences between Greeks and Bulgarians about many churches and schools in Macedonia since the separation of the Bulgarian Church from the Greek Orthodox Church, to such an extent that the Greek Patriarchate excommunicated the Bulgarian Church.

Oppressed by the İttihâd ve Teraqqî Committee and incited by the European states, riots in Albania flared up again. The İttihad ve Teraqqî organisation sent an army to Albania. Some army officers, however, established a group called *khalâskârân* (saviours) and took to the hills as Enver and Niyâzi of the İttihâd ve Teraqqî Committee had done in 1326/1908. The members of this group in İstanbul put pressure on the government, causing Sa'îd Pasha to resign on 1 Sha'bân 1330/16 July 1912 and leaving the İttihâd ve Teraqqî organisation in power.[898]

The Osmanlı government discharged well-trained soldiers from 120 battalions in Rumelia because of the false guarantee given by Russia to the Osmanlı Foreign Minister Noradungiyan Efendi. On the other hand, the İttihâd ve Teraqqî organisation wanted the Osmanlı army to be defeated in Rumelia, thereby coming into power once again.

Greece, Bulgaria, Serbia, and Montenegro united together after having solved the problems thanks to the decree of July 3rd, 1910, and attacked Osmanlı territory in October 1912. They occupied large territories in Osmanlı Europe; the ex-Interior Minister of the İttihâd ve Teraqqî organisation, Talât Bey, became a volunteer soldier, came to Edirne, but tried to dissuade the soldiers from fighting. In other words, the İttihâd ve Teraqqî organisation was engaged in defeatism.

Shükrî Pasha defended Edirne for 155 days, after which the city fell. King Ferdinand gave this hero his sword back.[899] The Second Balkan War ended 52 days later because of differences among the allies; Romania, Greece, Serbia, and Montenegro fought against Bulgaria. The Osmanlı Devlet entered the war and recovered Edirne.[900] The Osmanlı army retrieved only some parts of the territories that had been occupied by the Balkan allies, and the future status of those parts was not clear.

On the other hand, the members of the İttihâd ve Teraqqî Committee met with War Minister Nâzım Pasha, who was chief of the *khalâskârân* at the same time, and promised him that they would not interfere with politics any more. Enver and Jemâl were appointed to key positions in İstanbul, thereby controlling an important part of the soldiery in İstanbul.[901] Enver Bey raided Bâb-ı Âli (the government building) on 14 Safer 1331/23 January 1913 and forced Sadrâzam Kâmil Pasha to resign.[902] Mahmûd Shevket Pasha replaced him and was assassinated. Jemâl Pasha, one of the three leaders of the İttihâd ve Teraqqî Committee (İttihâd ve Teraqqî Komitesi), imposed martial law in İstanbul. "The Committee of Union and Progress appointed one of its members, Mehmet Sait Halim Paşa, an Egyptian prince and a grandson of Muhammad Ali, as grand *vazîr*, and four other committee members were assigned key cabinet positions. Thus began the CUP dictatorship ... (12 June 1913),"[903] ultimately leading to a catastrophe in the Osmanlı Devlet.

A group of officers attempted to acquire the post of War Minister for Enver Bey; he was given three years' seniority for his participation in the wars of Libya and the Balkans so he immediately became *pasha* while he was only a lieutenant-colonel and was appointed War

## Chapter Seventeen – The İttihâd ve Teraqqî Society

Minister on the same day, 3 January 1914. İzzet Pasha had already resigned from the posts of War Minister and Deputy Commander-in-Chief. Jemâl Bey was also given the same favours and became a *pasha*. These two pensioned off all the senior officers, who were more senior than themselves, claiming that they were rejuvenating the army and the navy. From then on, the administration was held in the hands of Enver Pasha, who was married to Nâjiye Sultân, daughter of Süleymân Efendi, one of Abdülmejîd's sons and thus married into the Osmanlı line.[904]

### The First World War (1914-1918)

The end of the Industrial Revolution and the subsequent failure of European powers to share the resources and raw materials of the world intensified their differences, disputes, and conflicts. As a result, a large-scale war was imminent and perhaps inevitable. Since European powers were competing mainly over Osmanlı territory, the most advisable course for the Osmanlı government was to try its best to be neutral and stay out of the conflict. The conflict was among the industrialised powers with regard to sharing and plundering the world's resources; the Osmanlı Devlet was in no position to make a claim, nor did it have the financial, military, or political resources for it.

Britain, France, and Russia concluded the Triple Entente, while Germany, Austria, and Italy forged a counter-alliance and were called the Central Powers. Italy, however, proclaimed its neutrality, leaving its allies on 1 August 1914.[905] The direct cause for the outbreak of the First World War was the assassination of the crown prince of Austria-Hungary on June 28, 1914 at Saray-Bosna (Sarajevo). The İttihâd and Teraqqî had three leaders: Enver, Talat, and Jemâl. While Enver and Talat favoured Germany, the third leader, Jemâl Pasha, preferred neutrality, if not outright support of the Entente powers, though this was not in their interests at that time. Nevertheless, Saîd Halîm Pasha and Enver Pasha concluded a secret treaty with Germany on 2 August 1914.[906] Britain refused to honour a previous agreement to deliver two battleships, the Sultân Osmân and the Reshâdiye, to the Osmanlı Devlet even though it had paid for them in full. Two other German battleships, Göben and Breslau, were chased from the Mediterranean by British warships into the Dardanelles, and Enver Pasha admitted them into Osmanlı territorial waters on 11 August 1914. As a cover-up, it was declared that the warships had been bought by the Osmanlıs, and their names were changed to Yavuz and Midilli, while the German Admiral Souchon and his crew were dressed in Osmanlı uniforms. Germany wanted the Osmanlı Devlet to enter the war formally on its side, thus engaging her enemies, the Russians at Odessa and the British at the Suez Canal. Britain and Russia were, on the other hand, naturally anxious to secure the neutrality of the Osmanlıs, and thus offered them guarantees to secure the integrity and independence of all their territories. On 14 September 1914 the Bahriye Nâzırı (Minister of the Navy) Jemâl Pasha, gave the order to Admiral Souchon to set out for the Black Sea and to shell any Russian ships that he might encounter, but this was stopped by the Osmanlı Government. On 11 October, the German ambassador offered the Osmanlı government 2 billion *qurush* to fight on the side of the Central Powers, and the money was actually received on 21 October. Enver Pasha and his friends cancelled the capitulations[i] on 7 September, thus inflicting a serious blow to the economic interests of the Entente Powers.

---

i  Some privileges given by Süleymân the Magnificent to French merchants called *imtiyâzât*, to support France against Charles V, the Holy Roman Emperor, and thus prevent European unity against the Osmanlı Devlet became known as "capitulations" because of weaknesses in the Osmanlı administration.

## Chapter Seventeen – The İttihâd ve Teraqqî Society

Without consulting other Osmanlı ministers, Enver and Jemâl Pasha once more ordered Admiral Souchon to attack the Russians in the Black Sea, which he did on 29 October 1914, and sank several Russian ships. Russia therefore declared war on the Osmanlı Devlet on 2 November 1914, and Britain and France followed suit. Moreover, Britain had annexed Cyprus and unilaterally ended Osmanlı suzerainty over Egypt, which was declared a British protectorate on 18 December 1914. On 11 November 1914 the Osmanlı Khalîfah-Sultân, Reshâd, declared a *jihâd* (Holy War) against the Entente Powers, asking all Muslims, particularly those in the British and Russian possessions, to join in the campaign against the infidel.[907] But the British in India and Egypt and the Russians in Central Asia were successful in suppressing the Sultân's call for a Pan-Islamic movement. Nevertheless, the Sultân's call for the *jihâd* achieved more success than is generally admitted, as it compelled the powers to maintain large garrisons in those countries to prevent the Muslim *ra'âyâ* from revolting against the Entente powers.[908]

The entry of the Osmanlı Devlet into the First World War marked the Devlet's virtual end. Having lost its dynamism, it had been trying to survive since 1826 by making some not very well-considered reforms in the country and playing the big powers against each other internationally. Sultân Abdülhamîd was very successful in external policy. But the İttihâd ve Teraqqî leaders, who, despite their good intentions, could not balance their abilities with their ambitions, dragged the Devlet towards catastrophe. Russia attacked in November 1914. Though the Osmanlıs repelled this attack and launched a counter-attack on 21 December, Russia made another large-scale offensive in January 1915 that routed the Osmanlı army and opened the way for the Russian army to advance into eastern Anatolia. The most powerful navies of that time, the British and the French, together with a Russian warship, tried to enter the Strait of Chanakkale (Dardanelles) but suffered heavy casualties on 18 March 1915, and the battle continued at Gallipoli where they landed but were finally forced to retreat. Had they captured the Dardanelles, they would have occupied İstanbul, the Osmanlı capital, and German attempts to expand eastward would have been paralysed. Furthermore, this would have enabled Britain to dominate Mesopotamia and consolidate its hold over Egypt, while the Allies could have sent ammunitions and help to Russia through the Black Sea. But these battles at the Dardanelles cost the Osmanlıs dearly: 250,000 lives, of whom 50,000 were officers. The British also advanced on the Iraqi front in the hopes of uniting their forces with those of the Russians in the Caucasus. But the Osmanlı army defeated them at Qûtu'l Amârah (Kut al-Amara) in April 1916, which was a great blow to the greatest Christian empire, causing the loss of thousands of soldiers, surrendering into captivity 5 generals, 481 officers and 13,300 soldiers. The British Empire received reinforcements and captured Baghdad on 11 March 1917.[909] The Osmanlı army also advanced towards the Suez Canal in 1915. The British were defeated twice at Gazze (Gaza) but were eventually victorious in

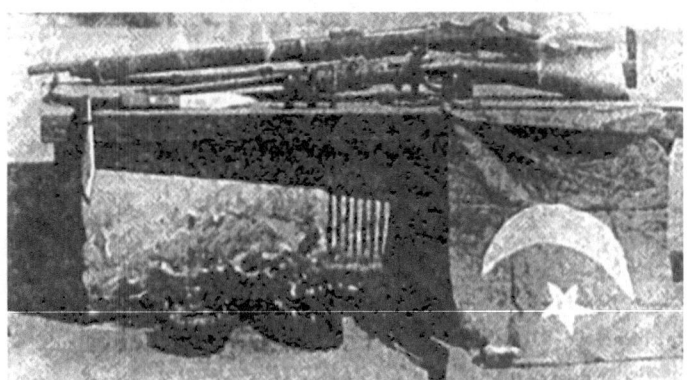

*Souvenir of the two Muslims who fought Anzacs in Australia carrying out the Khalîfah's call for jihâd*
*Now on display at a museum in Australia*

## Chapter Seventeen – The İttihâd ve Teraqqî Society

the third battle in 1917. Meanwhile, in 1916 the British bribed Sharîf Hüseyin of Makkah to betray and rise in revolt against the Osmanlı *Khalîfah*. T.E. Lawrence, a graduate of Oxford University who was extremely fluent in Arabic, was instrumental in this revolt, and perhaps even the brain behind it.[i]

The Russians occupied eastern Anatolia, but the Osmanlı Devlet was relieved of their occupation by the outbreak of the Communist Revolution of 1917 in Russia. An interesting topic is that there are rumours that Lenin's coming to Russia for revolution was assisted – even arranged – by the Osmanlı Teshkilât-ı Makhsûsa (Special Organisation); this merits more thorough study.

### 17.3 MEHMED VI VAHÎDEDDÎN

*Fountain of Abdülhamîd II*

Sultân Mehmed Reshâd died on 28 June 1918 and was succeeded by Mehmed Vahîdeddîn, in whose era the British and the French made other attacks on the Osmanlıs on several fronts. The Osmanlı troops fought bravely, but they were outnumbered and enemy weaponry was much more advanced and superior. The Osmanlı Devlet fought on many fronts in the First World War: the Caucasus, the

---

i    It is interesting to note that the European powers used Arab nationalism against the Osmanlı Devlet. But when they entered Damascus, the Christian commander went to the tomb of Salâhuddîn Ayyûbî, who crushed the Crusaders in the twelfth century, kicked it and said: "Stand up, O Saladin, we have arrived!" The establishment of Israel as a *religious* entity is another reward(!) given by the British to Arab nationalism.

Dardanelles, Palestine, and Sinai peninsula, Iraq, İzmir, and Antalya, Galicia, Romania and Dobruja, and the Hejâz. Three million lives were lost, but the Devlet finally collapsed, and the humiliating Truce of Mondros was imposed on 30 October 1918. Osmanlı troops began to surrender their weapons, Greece joined the allies at the last moment, and İstanbul was occupied by the Entente powers.[910] The Osmanlı Devlet officially ceased to exist[911] on 4 November 1922 when the Tevfîk Pasha cabinet resigned.

# Conclusion

It should now be obvious that Western literature on the Osmanlı Devlet, however scholarly it may appear, comprises a huge monument of distortion. Since "... For too long the Ottomans have been studied without the use of any of their sources, resulting in serious distortion and error. No history of France would be considered methodologically sound and balanced if it were written on the basis of English and Italian observations."[912] This methodologically wrong attitude has been maintained about Osmanlı history.

The Osmanlıs emerged as a major Islamic power in the fourteenth century, and by the sixteenth century had become *the* superpower in the world, which had successfully confronted both Europe and Iran. They had aspired from the very beginning to unite all the Muslims under their Khalifate. Sultân Murâd I (1362-1389) was the *de facto Khalîfah*, and was recognised as such by some Muslim powers, while his son Yıldırım Bâyezîd defeated the combined European armies and represented the supreme power of Islam. Fâtih Mehemmed (1451-1481) was the *Khalîfah*,[913] and his grandson Sultân Selîm combined both the "actual" and the "official" Khalifate. Until the end of its days, the Osmanlı Devlet represented the Sunnî Khalifate, and the Republic of Turkey retained the Khalifate for a while even after the collapse of the Devlet and the abolition of the Sultanate. Eventually, however, the Grand National Assembly of Turkey abolished the Khalifate on 3 March 1924. According to Hayrullah Efendi, "a major achievement of the Osmanlıs was their success in uniting the Sultanate and the Khalifate, which had long existed as separate institutions."[914]

The Osmanlıs were engaged in *jihâd* in Europe until the end of their Devlet, but they were confronted by almost all the European powers who wanted to drive them back to, if not altogether out of, Anatolia.

*Jihâd* represented the cornerstone of the policy of the Osmanlı Devlet that it carried out with enthusiasm throughout the centuries. Thus, the Osmanlı Devlet should not be viewed as isolated from its predecessor, the Selçuklu Devlet. On the contrary, the Selçuklu sultân had given Osman Gâzi the *berât*, and appointed him *beğ*. He urged him to implement Islam in every walk of life and to take care of the *ra'iyyet*. The Osmanlı Devlet was thus a continuation of the Selçuklu Devlet, which in its turn was a continuation of the 'Abbâsî khalifate. All its social, economic, educational, and judicial institutions were adopted from the Selçuklu model that was itself based on Islam. Like the Selçûkis of Anatolia under Alâeddîn Keykubâd I, the Osmanlıs achieved the highest level of civilisation. The success or failure of a civilisation should be judged by the well-being of its people. When young, a human being can face hardships, but when he ages, he cannot, and should therefore be given comfort. Indeed the welfare of human beings was the primary concern of the Osmanlı Devlet even during and after its disintegration. People under Osmanlı administration lived most comfortably throughout their lives. The grandfather remained throughout his life *the* authority in the household, and no one dared oppose him, including his married sons. This situation prevailed in Osmanlı territories even half a century after the official collapse of the Osmanlı Devlet. Such human behaviour towards old people is unthinkable in "modern" times where they usually live boring and lonely lives in isolated institutions far away from their own families.

The Osmanlı Devlet was essentially and exclusively Islamic. Its army was called "the Army of Islam," and all other institutions, especially its *madrasahs*, were Islamic too. For more than five centuries Arabic continued to be taught as the language of learning and of Islam. The Osmanlıs used the Muslim (*hijrî*) calender and Quranic Arabic letters for the Osmanlı-Turkish language. In fact, their identity was submerged in Islam to a great extent, as David Kushner noted, "The Osmanlıs associated themselves over centuries with Islam, and did not even show interest in their ancestral race until the second half of the 19th century. For example, a textbook published in 1877 for secondary schools still did not even mention the Turkish ancestry of the Osmanlıs."[915]

Nationalism was regarded as a matter of great concern contradictory to the basic Islamic concept of the *Ummat*. Sultân Abdülhamîd II had warned as late as 1907 that it seriously undermined the Muslim-Osmanlı entity. The Sunnî feature of the Devlet was too important to be neglected. Even in the proclamation of the Tanzîmât in 1839, which officially initiated the process of Europeanisation, it was mentioned that "The Osmanlı Devlet implemented the Qur'ân and *Sharî'at* from the very beginning and achieved a very high standard of living and the people were prosperous, but for the last 150 years there had been leniency and relaxation, even disregard, concerning *Sharî'at* and laws, resulting in the weakening of the Devlet."[916] We should emphasise here that nationalism was a very late phenomenon in the Osmanlı Devlet, and appeared with the İttihâd and Teraqqî Party that ruled the Devlet for only a decade (1909-1918). Walter L. Wright, Jr. has this to say about the Osmanlı Devlet in its last days: "Facing the attack of forces new both to it and to the world, such forces as nationalism and democracy, steam and electricity, it wasted away little by little. The Ottoman was the last of the great empires of the Nearer Orient[i] and perhaps the strongest. Never did it lack sufficient strength,

---

i   "Nearer Orient" or Near East, from the Western point of view, another aspect of West-centralisation of the globe and events.

even in the worst periods of degeneracy, to guarantee its existence so far as oriental competitors were concerned."[917]

As *the* Muslim Power, the Osmanlıs saved North Africa from Catholicism, defended al-Haramayn ash-Sharîfayn against Portuguese and subsequent British aggression, and controlled Babel Mendeb in Yemen. The Osmanlı presence in Yemen was not for the sake of oil, which was explored and utilised later in the 20th century, but for the defence of the sacred lands of Islam, i.e. al-Haramayn ash-Sharîfayn. It is interesting to note here that the great Muslim Uways al-Qarnî (in Turkish: Veysel Qarânî), who lived in Yemen during the time of the Final Messenger Muhammad ﷺ, is quite famous in Turkey today, although he is not known to many in Yemen. There is a well-known hymn about him, and a *maqâm* (a place containing a symbolic tomb) in his name in Anatolia. Significantly, when the railway reached the Osmanlı Devlet, it did not take the Devlet long to connect the sacred city of the Final Messenger ﷺ to the centre of the Khalifate. This Hejâz railway was built not by public funds but by private contributions from the Muslim people.

The emergence of Shî'ite Iran in the sixteenth century had seriously obstructed the Osmanlı advance into Europe, and the Osmanlıs lost more than thirty *vazîrs* in their wars with Christian Europe and Shî'ite Iran.

Sultân Abdülhamîd II inherited a weak and disintegrating *Devlet*, but he managed to hold it together. He exercised absolute power, but he used this authority to pay off a large part of the external loans, while his predecessors were unable to pay even the interest. Furthermore, he strongly emphasised education and established many schools. The Osmanlı intelligentsia of the time were obsessed with constitutional reform, but this was, as their bitter experience proved, inappropriate and unsuitable to the Osmanlı situation of that time. The İttihâd and Teraqqî Society (later Party) was founded by persons from various races, but none of them were Turkish. It advocated and adopted Turkish nationalism as a means of holding the disintegrating Osmanlı Devlet together, yet without any success. Some of its leaders were brave and patriotic, but they should all be held responsible for the collapse of the Osmanlı Devlet after a period of only ten years. Bravery and patriotism were not enough to "save" the Devlet but needed to be accompanied by administrative and leadership skills. Tal'at Pasha, for example, was a very honest man in his private life, and his food was even reported to be similar to that of ordinary Osmanlı citizens. But he was a clerk after all, and hence did not have the necessary skills and talent to be a *sadrâzam* (prime minister) of one of the great (weak but still great) world powers of the time. Enver Pasha was an honest and brave officer who was martyred in 1922 while fighting the Russian army in Turkestan. But excellence in military service is not alone enough to govern a big *devlet* with many complex problems like that of the Osmanlıs. When meeting him for the first time, the experienced and shrewd ex-sovereign, the former Sultân, Abdülhamîd II, prophetically said, "He would have made a good colonel!"[918] Indeed Enver became Minister of War, and an acting Commander-in-Chief of all Osmanlı (9 in total) armies. In short, if a sergeant is put in charge of a brigade, the consequences are to be expected. A similar situation took place during the last decade of the Osmanlı Devlet.

Perhaps the best way of understanding and evaluating social and historical events is through comparison. Therefore it may be appropriate to make a comparison between the Osmanlı Devlet and some other socio-political entities:

The Greek and Roman Empires had in many respects brought catastrophe to humanity; Europeans converted the whole of America into English-Spanish-Portuguese speaking Christian countries, and annihilated the indigenous people; in the whole continent of Australia the British left only a small number of its original inhabitants, and it is now practically an extension of the

British sphere of influence, speaking English, adopting British culture and Christianity, although Christianity itself is losing ground in Europe, and churches are being put up for sale in Britain. This sweeping cultural invasion is also evident in other parts of the world, particularly throughout the continent of Africa. In striking contrast, the Osmanlı Devlet through its creative *millet* system respected and preserved the cultural identities of all its non-Muslim and non-Turkish peoples and refrained from oppression and cultural exploitation. Hence it is misleading and a great blunder to call it an "empire" in the Western sense of the word.

The Osmanlı Devlet remained in what today is called Greece for four centuries. The Osmanlı presence in the former Yugoslavia continued for five hundred years. Today, there are people in those countries and they have their identity, language, everything, while all the indigenous peoples of America and Australia are a very tiny minority with no place in society in their homeland. And now, great-grandsons of those suppressors, exploiters, and imperialists in Europe and America write "scholarly" works about the Osmanlı Devlet, presenting it as an "exploiter," and calling it an "empire."

⁂

The reasons for the collapse of the Osmanlı Devlet may be summarised as follows:

The first ten Osmanlı sultâns, i.e. up to and including Süleymân the Magnificent, were energetic and capable leaders. Their personalities and leadership were decisive in the consolidation and expansion of the Devlet. But with the exception of a few, such as Murâd IV, Mustafa III, and Abdülhamîd II, subsequent sultâns generally were not of great calibre. Moreover, during the period between 1595 and 1687 senior administrative posts including *beğlerbeği* were given to *kethüdâs* (employees and representatives) of *vazîrs* and *mültezims* who accumulated huge sums because of these positions.[919] "When a *tımar* or *ze'âmet* became available, *Mirlivâs* conferred it upon those who offered the largest bribe."[920] The wars with Austria and Persia that took place after 1592 necessitated the recruitment of new soldiers every year. On top of that, the regicide of Osman II in 1622 entailed ten years of chaos during which the *sipâhîs* recruited their own children and relatives under the title of *veledesh* (his son). The grand vazîr and the commander-in-chief also recruited their entourage into the army. Thus the numbers of the paid soldiers reached more than 100,000. Murâd IV reduced them sharply to 50,000-55,000, but this still represented a huge burden that was a major factor in the financial collapse of the Devlet.[921]

Second, the *jihâd* was the mission of and basic driving force for the Osmanlı Devlet. But, from the seventeenth century on, devotion to it, and for Islam itself, gradually faded among the administrators and *vazîrs*. The Osmanlı Devlet was, moreover, mainly staffed by people of *devshirme* descent who were engaged in jealousy and the distribution of the posts to their supporters rather than in *jihâd*. An industrialist is like a man riding a bicycle: if he does not go forward, he falls. It is the same for a political entity with a mission that loses its drive.

Third, with the exception of the period 1740-1768 (only 28 years), all generations of the Osmanlıs were engaged in battles against all of Europe, including the new emerging Russia. This, no doubt, cost the Devlet a great deal in terms of lives and property and was therefore a further factor in its disintegration.

Fourth, the exploration of new sea routes and the discovery of America in the fifteenth century enriched the opponents and enemies of the Osmanlıs, and made it difficult for the Devlet to challenge the imperialist Christian powers. The flow of cheap American silver through Europe into the Osmanlı Devlet contributed to the financial turmoil, particularly as the Osmanlıs used silver for their coinage.

Fifth, the industrial revolution made Europe financially and technologically very strong in contrast to the Osmanlı Devlet, which could no longer match the Europeans. This was particularly so in the field of armaments and weaponry.

The intervention of palace women in the affairs of the Devlet was another important cause of its deterioration and eventual collapse. Beginning with the Magnificent's spouse Hurrem Sultân, they endeavoured to secure the throne for their own sons, regardless of their qualifications and leadership ability.

Luxury and extravagance had also its role in undermining the Osmanlı Devlet. During the reign of Abbâs Pasha of Egypt (1848-1854), many rich *pashas* and *beğs* came from Egypt to İstanbul with huge amounts of money. The palace women and wives of the *vazîrs*, *pashas*, and other offensively wealthy people adopted the luxurious and corrupt European style of life. In a short time, the palace was unable to pay its debts to the bankers, and the Devlet went bankrupt during Abdulmejîd's reign.[922]

Abdülhamîd II miraculously succeeded in arresting this economic deterioration and achieved a noticeable degree of solvency. During his time, the Osmanlı Devlet was still among the *Düvel-i Muazzama* (superpowers). But, unfortunately, the elite drastically failed to understand his role and appreciate his achievements and conspired to depose him. It took the leaders of the İttihâd and Teraqqî only ten years to wipe the Osmanlı Devlet off the world map altogether.

# Osmanlı Sovereigns

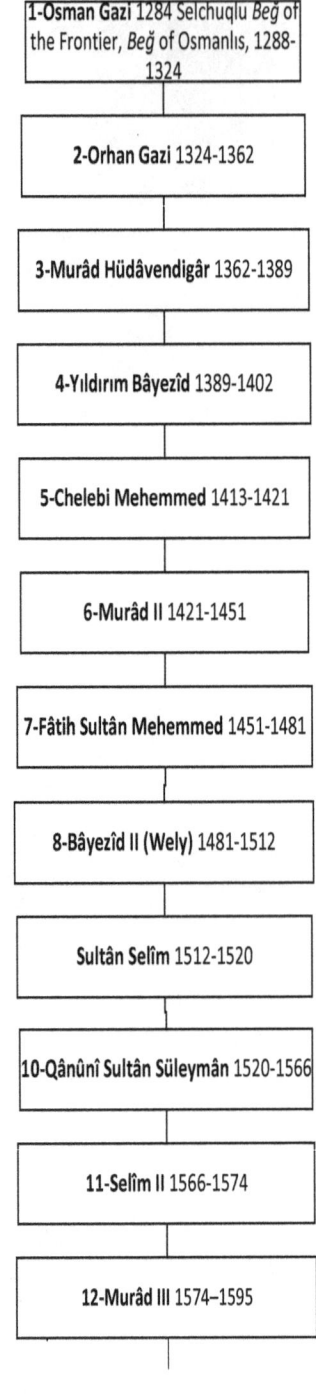

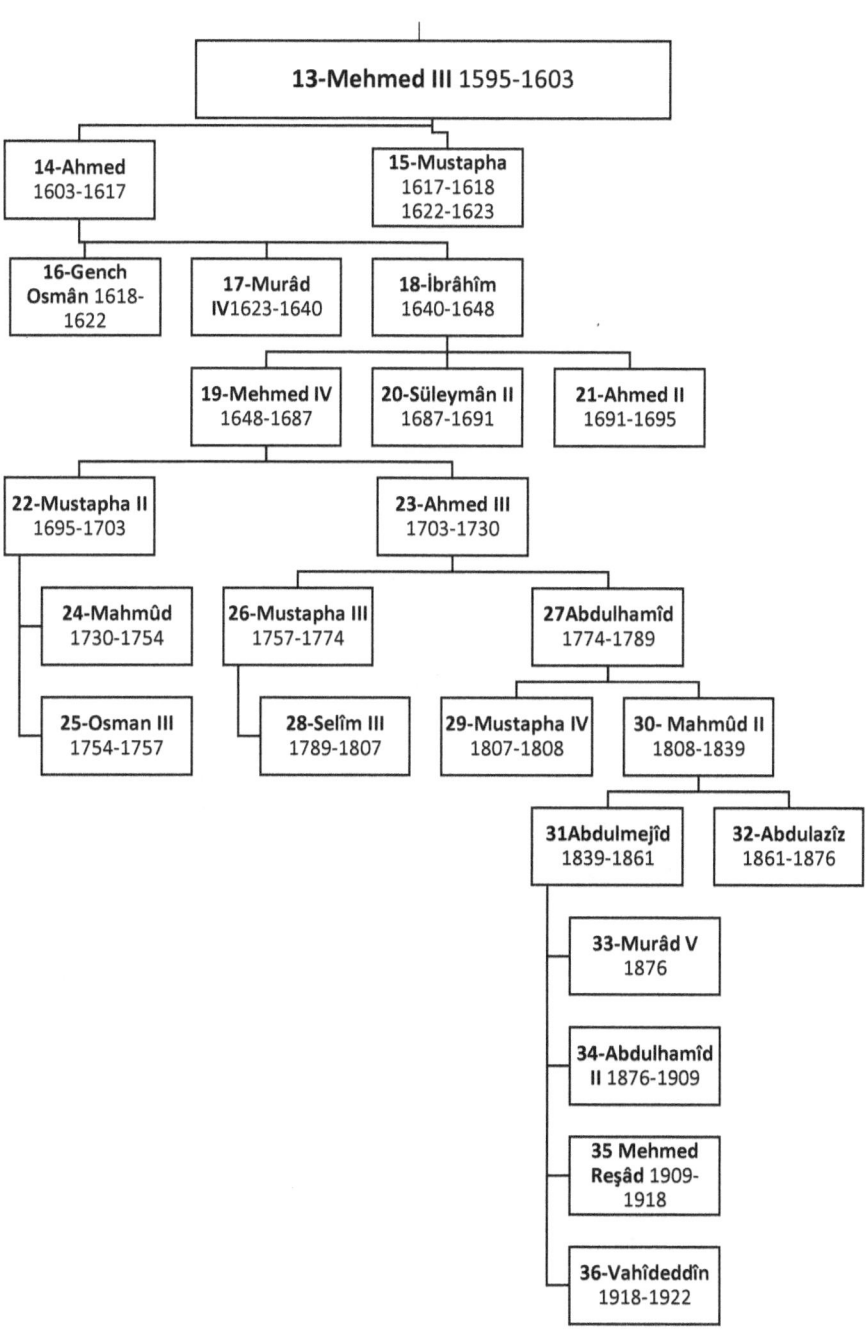

# Addendum

# The Osmanlı Socio-Political Entity: Empire or Devlet?

In this paper[i] we will attempt to discover what specific term the Osmanlıs preferred in referring to their socio-political entity. This is attempted chiefly on the basis of documents now preserved in the Osmanlı Archives in İstanbul.

Generally speaking, the Osmanlı socio-political entity is referred to by modern historians and other writers as "The Osmanlı Empire"; hence, the term "empire" will be defined in the light of the relevant literature on the topic to see what it really signifies and whether this term is applicable to the Osmanlıs or not. On the basis of both its connotative and denotative meaning, however, it becomes evident that this particular term is not applicable to the Osmanlıs. On no occasion did they use the term "empire". Instead, the term they used to describe themselves in all their documents, records, *fermâns, demarches*, and official correspondence was *devlet*. The use of the word "empire" here means the foisting of a term generally used pejoratively in the modern political context – a term, moreover, that is alien to the nature, quality, and structure of their (Osmanlı) rule and administration. This has obviously been done by Western scholars and writers, who, when it comes to

---

i  First published in *Hamdard Islamıcus*, (Hamdard Foundation Pakistan, Summer 1995), v.XVIII No.2 pp.41-53.

others, pay little heed to the fact that "countries and peoples are unique and are not so easily lured into identity with each other save on limited, and specific, points."[923]

To name any institution or social entity differently from its original, proper name involves subjective evaluation and even implies hostility towards it. For example, Sunnî Muslims called a certain sect *Mu'tazilah* while this sect used the name *Ahlul 'Adl, Ahlut Tawhîd* or *Ahlul Haqq*. If the Sunnîs had accepted that sect's own preferred nomenclature, they would also have called it *Ahlul 'Adl, Ahlut Tawhîd*, or *Ahlul Haqq*. But throughout the centuries, right up to the present, they have called this sect *Mu'tazilah*, following the great scholar, Hasan al-Basrî, who said about the first *mu'tazili*, Wâsil b. 'Atâ: "*I'tazala 'anna Wâsil* – Wâsil has withdrawn from us." On the other hand, the name 'Amr b. Hishâm means nothing to anybody. But if one mentions Abû Jahl (Symbol of Ignorance), almost every Muslim will have heard of him and his keen hostility toward Islam and the Prophet ﷺ.

So if we look at the Osmanlı documents and books written and printed in the Osmanlı era, we do not see the phrase "Osmanlı Empire" or its Turkish equivalent *Osmanlı İmparatorluğu* or *İmparatoriyye-yi Osmâniyye*. Instead, they call their social entity *Devlet-i 'Alîyye-i 'Osmâniyye* – The Sublime Osmanlı Devlet or *Devlet-i Senîyye* – The Brilliant Devlet. They never called their rule or territory *İmparatoriyye-yi Osmâniyye* or *Osmanlı İmparatorluğu* – the Osmanlı Empire. The head of an empire would be an "emperor." But the Osmanlıs never called their sovereign *imperator* (emperor).

In fact, the Osmanlıs never called their social and political entity "an empire." In the huge corpus of original documents housed in the Osmanlı Archives (T.C. Başbakanlık Osmanlı Arşivi, İstanbul), which, among other things, includes the official correspondence of the Osmanlıs, and in the treaties, this entity is always referred to as دولت عليه عثمانيه – *Devlet-i Alîyye-i Osmâniyye*/The Sublime Osmanlı

## The Osmanlı Socio-Political Entity: Empire Or Devlet?

Devlet, or سلطنت سنیه – *Saltanat-ı Senîyye*/The Brilliant Sultanate, etc. This name was used not only in the Osmanlı documents but also in the works of official Osmanlı historiographers. So common was its usage that, when the Osmanlı Bank was founded in Turkey, the qualificative title شاهانه (*Shâhânah*) and not *"Imperial"* was affixed, the actual name being بنك عثماني شاهانه – *Bank-i Osmânî-i Shâhânah*.

When reading almost any scholarly work about the Osmanlıs, however, one very frequently comes across the phrase "The Osmanlı Empire." Now, the question is: Why has the Osmanlı Devlet come to be referred to as "Osmanlı Empire"? It would be interesting to find out how this misnomer acquired currency in Western literature on the Osmanlıs. And what, if any, is the motive for foisting the term "Empire" on them?

But let us first look at a few documents, chosen at random, to sustain our contention that the Osmanlıs throughout their history used for themselves the Turkish term Devlet:

> "Concerning the telegram line that we have decided to have installed and extended between my domain of *Devlet-i Alîyye* (Sublime Devlet) and the domain of Naples through (underneath) the sea..." (1858).[924]

> *Biz ki bilütfil Mevlâ Turkistan ve shâmil olduğu memâlik ve buldânın Padishâhi es Sultân ibnus Sultân es Sultân el Gâzi Abdülmejîd Hân ibnus Sultân el Gâzi Mahmûd Hân ibnus Sultân el Gâzi Abdülhamîd Hanız. İshbu Tasdîqnâme-i Hümâyûnumuzla beyân ve ilân ederiz ki Devlet-i Alîyyemizle hashmetlû Nederlanda ve Bibao Kralı Hazretleri beyninde mevjûd olan revâbit-i dûstîyi te'yîd ile....*[925] which translates as:

> "We, by the Grace of the Lord, Pâdishâh of Turkestan and the territories it contains, sultân, son of Sultân Gazi (Warrior

in Holy War) Abdul Majid Khân, son of Sultân Gazi Mahmûd Khân, son of Sultân Gazi Abdülhamîd Khân, express and proclaim by this Heavenly Ratification of ours that, galvanising the existing friendly relations between our Sublime Devlet and his Majesty King of the Netherlands and Bibao..."

Here the Osmanlı sultân, 'Abdul Majîd Khân, ratifies a consular agreement between the Osmanlı Sublime Devlet and His Majesty the King of the Netherlands in 1857.

"The Budapest General Consul of the Brilliant Sultanate...."[926]

The Osmanlıs used the word *Senîyye* (brilliant, fine and glorious) as an adjective of their *devlet* and not the word Imperial. The Osmanlıs were not unaware of the common usage of the word "emperor", but they used it for those who called themselves emperors, for instance:

"*Hashmetlu Alamanya Imparatoru* ..."[927] (a reference to the *Emperor* of Germany conferring a medal from the Osmanlıs on the emperor's chief aide-de-camp);

"*Fransa Imparatoru Hazretleri* ..."[928]

This is with reference to the French emperor's journey to Algeria and the Osmanlı Minister's opinion that the Pasha-Governor of Osmanlı Tunisia should not be ordered to welcome the Emperor;

"The Palace Minister of His Majesty, the *Emperor* of Japan";[929]

"...*Hashmetlu Avusturya imparatoru*... – His Majesty, the *Emperor* of Austria ..."[930];

"*Hashmetlu Japonya Imparatorichesi* – Her Majesty, the *Empress* of Japan ...";[931]

## The Osmanlı Socio-Political Entity: Empire Or Devlet?

"The Holy Roman *Emperor*, the late Charles VI ...."[932]

And when the Osmanlıs made an agreement with a socio-political entity whose form of government was republican, they called it a "republic":

> "...the Pact concerning the change in citizenship, which was concluded between the Sublime Devlet and the Republic of America..."[933]

The official historians who wrote the history of the Osmanlıs spoke of them as *devlet*. For instance, consider the following:

الكلام في ظهور الدولة العلية العثماني

*el Kelam fi zuhurid Devletil Aliyyetil Osmaniyye.*

> "Information about the Emergence of the Sublime Osmanlı Devlet."[934]

Na'ima (1655-1716), the first official historian of the Osmanlıs, uses the normal and proper name "the Devlet" for the Osmanlı administration and domain. Had the Osmanlı Sultân or other high officials deemed it "an empire", he would certainly have used the term "empire" (امباراطورية).

The relevant passage from Ahmed Wasif, reads as follows:

> "Printing of the new history and useful work entitled *Mahâsinul Âsar wa Hakâyiqul Akhbâr*, compiled by the official *historian* of the *Osmanlı* Sublime Devlet دولت عليه عثمانية مؤرخ has been finished..."[935]

For the Osmanlıs, their *devlet* was "sublime" and "brilliant," and they added عثمانية *osmaniyye* (pertaining to Osman) as an adjective. It means that the Osmanlı socio-political entity is *devlet*, and this *devlet* is sublime, and, as a matter of secondary importance, it belongs to the Osmanlıs: the followers of Osman Gâzi. In fact, it is really impossible to find another nation or people who had so submerged their identity in Islam as the Osmanlıs did. For the Osmanlıs the concept of *Devlet* entailed that people can live as human beings only within its framework, a concept that made sure that law and order prevailed in all walks of life, a concept that has come to mean happiness, felicity itself. It encompasses much more than the concept of "state". This fact can be clearly seen in Süleymân the Magnificent's poem:

خلق ايچنده معتبر بر نسنه يوق دولت كبي
اوليه دولت جهانده بر نفس صحة كبي

*Halk içinde mu'teber bir nesne yok devlet gibi*
   *Olmaya devlet cihanda bir nefes sihhat gibi*
There is nothing equal in worth to *devlet* in this world.
   In fact, there can be no *devlet* (felicity) in this world worth of only a breath of health.

And the Osmanlıs would not give up this meaningful word, *devlet*.

It would be instructive to refer to the document concerning the ratification by Sultân 'Abdülazîz in 1870 of the amendments made by the representatives of the Osmanlıs, Germany, Austria, France, Great Britain, Italy, and Russia, in London, to modify the Treaty of Paris (1856). This document, which mentions the official titles of the heads of governments that were involved in the treaty of 1870, helps to corroborate our thesis. The document says:

"We hereby express and declare by our Heavenly Ratification that those who met in London to make amendments to the Treaty of Paris, representing:
Our Sublime Devlet (دولت عليه مز) and:
1. His Majesty, the Emperor of Germany and King of Prussia;
2. His Majesty, the Emperor of Austria and King of Bohemia and Hungary;

3. The Honourable President of the Executive Government of the Republic of France;
4. Her Majesty the Queen of the United Kingdom of Great Britain and Ireland;
5. His Majesty, King of Italy, and;
6. His Majesty, the Emperor of all the Russias.[936]

As is evident from the document itself, the Osmanlı ruler is referred to as *padishâh,* sultân, khân, and not "emperor," while here in this passage cited emperors are referred to as "emperor", kings as "king", and the head of a republic as "President".

Another document from the Osmanlı Archives, ratifying the agreement between the Osmanlı Sublime Devlet and the King of Bavaria about establishing consulates, says:

"This is a ratification of the consular agreement between the *Devlet-i 'Aliyye* and His Majesty, King of Bavaria:

We, by the Grace of the Lord, Padishâh of Turkestan and the countries it includes, Sultân, son of sultân, Sultân 'Abdülazîz Khân, son of Sultân Gazi Mahmûd Khân, son of Sultân Gazi 'Abdul Hamîd Khân, Hereby express and proclaim that between our Sublime Devlet and his Majesty, the King of Bavaria ...."[937]

Having established the official titles relating to the external correspondence and agreements, let us look at some of the documents concerning internal affairs and correspondence:

"The petition that has been sent over to the Divan-ı Hümâyûn has been perused. Concerning the vessels carrying the Flag of the Sublime Osmanlı Devlet...";[938]

"Concerning the promotion of Colonel Feyzi Bey, instructor in internal diseases at the Shâhâne Medicine School, to the rank of Brigadier ...";[939]

"...employed in the Second *Heavenly* Brigade"[940] (heavenly, and not imperial);

"Teacher of drawing at the *Shâhane* High School ...";[941]

"... Because of the fact that the cloth merchant Mr. Ohannes, a *ra'iyyet* (who is cared for) of the Sublime Devlet, has had conferred upon him the *Majeedy* Medal of the fifth rank ...";[942]

"The Seventh Heavenly Army...."[943]

The Osmanlıs believed they bore a Heavenly Message – Islam – and thus called their army *Ordu-yu Humayun* (The Heavenly Army).

The *huma*, the bird believed to live in the sky without ever coming down and touching the earth, was what the Osmanlıs felt described their army, which they called *humayun,* i.e. pertaining to that bird, which thus entailed "heavenly" and not "imperial".

These documents establish beyond any doubt that the Osmanlıs did not use the words "empire" or "imperial" about themselves. Now let us examine some aspects of empire to discover if the Osmanlı entity was characterised by those features.

### a) The Political Aspect

An empire comprises the main body of the ruling nation or race and the other defeated and governed nations. Likewise, it comprises the heartland of the empire and other territories and dominions. The heartland is inhabited almost exclusively by the ruling nation, which produces governors, administrators, and representatives and imposes on the governed people whatever it sees convenient.

In the Osmanlı domain, the Grand *Vazîrs* came from people of countries opened to Islam since the fifteenth century, the graduates of *Enderun* (The Palace University), which recruited students from among the *devshirme*. The commander-in-chief of the janissaries, even the janissaries themselves (the core of the Osmanlı Army), also

## The Osmanlı Socio-Political Entity: Empire Or Devlet?

came for the most part from the *devshirme*. The very word janissary (in Turkish: *yeni ceri*, the new soldier) reveals their origin. At first, the janissaries were exclusively from the *devshirme* (boys taken from the Christians of Bosnia Herzegovina, Albania, etc). Later, however, Turks were also admitted. Some *vazîrs*, members of the *Divan-i Humayun* (the supreme governing body of the Osmanlı administration) kept their native tongues despite the fact that they had converted to Islam.

Let us look at what non-Muslim Westerners say about imperialism:

"Imperialism (deriv. Lat. imperium, power): acquisition and administration of an empire, often as a part of general commercial and industrial expansion. From the 15th century onwards, Spain, Portugal, Holland, France and Britain began building overseas empires."[944]

"The ruling of alien peoples and other lands by Europeans was the most striking demonstration of the European hegemony. In spite of enormous argument about what imperialism was and is, it seems helpful to confine the notion of it to such direct and formal overlordship, blurred though the boundaries with other types of power over the non-European world may be .... In the nineteenth century European imperialism was carried further and became more effective than ever before. This happened in two distinguishable phases, and one running down to about 1870 can conveniently be considered first. During this, some of the old imperial powers continued to enlarge their empires impressively, such were Russia, France and Great Britain. Others stood still and found theirs reduced; this group included the Dutch, Spanish and Portuguese."[945]

Now let us look at what a famous Western non-Muslim scholar writes about the Osmanlı case:

"Until the nineteenth century the Turks thought of themselves primarily as Muslims; their loyalty belonged, on different levels, to Islam and to the Ottoman house and state. The language a man spoke, the territory he inhabited, the race from which he claimed descent, might be of personal, sentimental, or social significance. They had no political relevance. So completely had the Turks identified themselves with Islam that the very concept of a Turkish nationality was submerged – and this despite the survival of the Turkish language and the existence of what was in fact, though not in theory, a Turkish state. Among the common people, the rustics and the nomads, a sense of Turkishness survived, and found expression in a rich but neglected folk literature. The governing and educated groups, however, had not retained to the same degree as the Arabs and Persians an awareness of their identity as a separate ethnic and cultural group within Islam."[i]

---

i  Bernard Lewis, *The Emergence of Modern Turkey*, second edition (London: Oxford University Press, 1968), p. 2 (emphasis added).
*Devlet* is different even from the 'state' which has 3 powers : legislative, executive and judiciary. But '*Devlet*' has only 2 powers: executive and judiciary. Islamic *Devlet* does not legislate: legislation has already been made by Allah: the *Sharî'at*. The *Qânûnnâmas* are only instructions about application of the *Sharî'at* to different circumstances. They are certainly not legislation. When *qânûnâmas* were issued, there was no parliament in the Osmanlı Devlet! It is one of the incurable diseases of many orientalists that they insist on trying to put Osmanlı Devlet, which has a completely different structure from their socio-political bodies, (together with the concept of *devlet* itself) in the same form as their political/administrative entities! As if there had been an obligation for all

## The Osmanlı Socio-Political Entity: Empire Or Devlet?

It is noteworthy that this submergence of their identity in Islam occurred in harmony with the Islamic ideology of which they were supporters, and the *raison d'être* of their existence as an organised socio-political body was Islam:

To quote Bernard Lewis again:

> "[I]ts people thought of themselves first and foremost as *Muslims*. Both Ottoman and Turk are, as we have seen, terms of comparatively recent usage, and the Ottoman Turks had identified themselves with Islam – submerged their identity in Islam – to a greater extent than perhaps any other Islamic people. It is curious that while in Turkey the word Turk almost went out of use, in the West it came to be a synonym for Muslim, and a Western convert to Islam was said to have *turned Turk*, even when the conversion took place in Fez or Isfahan."[946]

Hence, it is indeed baseless to claim that Osmanlı Turks used Islam only or mainly to show the Arab and other populations that they were Muslims and to govern them.

The Osmanlıs organised the other peoples according to their beliefs, in the *millet* system. Each *millet*, i.e. community of believers or followers of a religion, had its place in the Osmanlı Devlet and entertained complete freedom of belief and the freedom to carry out their rituals throughout the centuries.

Let us look at another Western non-Muslim scholar's opinion of the Osmanlıs:

> "Taking a long view, the Ottomans must be praised for maintaining such politically crippling but morally praiseworthy Islamic practices as the *millet* system, low

---

peoples of the world to follow their social structure and administrative forms!

tariffs and the concept of *imtiyaz* or capitulations, which ultimately prevented the Ottomans from modernising rapidly or absorbing religious minorities into the Ottomani polity."[947]

Under imperial rule, the defeated people are not happy at all. They try very naturally to get rid of the central administration whenever possible. If the Osmanlı Devlet had been imperialistic, all the European territories, which were under Osmanlı rule until 1402, would have revolted against it. As is well known, when the Osmanlıs were defeated by Tamerlane at Ankara in 1402, the Osmanlı Devlet seemed to have come to an end. The sons of the captured Yıldırım Bâyezîd were engaged in continuous civil war among themselves, which went on for eleven years. There was no Osmanlı navy worth mentioning. So, the European part of the Osmanlı Devlet was cut off from its Asian part, and the Christian Roman Empire was at its centre.

It is noteworthy that during this period no revolt against the Osmanlıs took place in the European part of the Osmanlı Devlet, which was inhabited mostly by non-Muslim subjects. So, how can it be justly claimed that Osmanlı sovereignty was imperialistic? In contrast, Christians – Serbs, and Croats – fought each other mercilessly in the last quarter of the 20th century. Under the Osmanlıs, even when the central authority collapsed in 1402, the Christians in the Balkans and the countries in Europe newly opened to Islam did not fight one another, nor did they revolt against the Osmanlıs. This fact shows how justice prevailed in those areas under the Islamic rule of the Osmanlıs which allowed the People of the Book to live according to their own beliefs and to exercise religious freedom in full. On the other hand, we can observe the attitude of the subjected races in an imperial structure in what went on in the former USSR when its grip on the people relaxed a little.

## The Osmanlı Socio-Political Entity: Empire Or Devlet?

Curiously enough, among the representatives of the Osmanlıs in other countries, there were many Christian, non-Turkish officials. For instance, the person who represented Osmanlı interests as the official consul of the Osmanlı Devlet in Bavaria was Aristarki Bey, who was of Greek origin and a Christian. The Osmanlıs were represented by their Christian subject, Konstantin Pasha, in the peace conference of 1876 that was held in London to make amendments to some articles of the (1856) Treaty of Paris.

It is possible to find more of such instances. It is a fact that the Osmanlı Devlet that stood for Islam was tolerant towards its non-Muslim subjects. We see Christian Armenian ministers and *pashas* in the Osmanlı Cabinet. Now, is this a feature of an Imperial power? Does this produce a picture of Turkish Imperialism?

### b) The Cultural Aspect

It is a characteristic feature that an imperial power always imposes its own language on the nations it governs because language is the most important basis of culture. And there is no doubt that culture is the most influential among the elements in a person's life. Consequently, a human being belongs to a people in whose culture he is brought up. In this way, the colonised native peoples of Africa very nearly lost their identity under European colonial powers. Those who were educated and the people at large spoke English or French. The British prepared such an attitude of mind among the colonised peoples in Africa that a native African under British rule, when asked if he had been to Britain, would reply: "No, I have never been home." Under French rule a native of Algeria or Tunisia was nearly doomed to starvation if he did not know French. In the Soviet Union of Russia, almost all of the non-Russian peoples could speak Russian.

In contrast, a non-Muslim from the Balkans area came to Divân-ı Hümâyûn and made his complaint in his tongue, translators of the said Dîvân helping him in his case. The Osmanlı Devlet did not assimilate other people, did not cause them to lose their identity, which is the most important human value. Serbs who had lived for 500 years and Greeks more than 400 years under the Osmanlı administration, living and practising their faith, speaking their own languages, became independent in the 19th century. In the Millet system of Osmanlı Devlet all non-Muslims preserved their identities, languages, cultures, traditions, and religions. In the 21st century, the so-called civilised, materially developed countries cannot even imagine this tolerant attitude toward other religions and cultures, especially Islam.

The Osmanlıs, in contrast, used Arabic widely in their schools and universities for at least five centuries. Only in the nineteenth century did they begin to use French as the language of instruction in some of the faculties, but Arabic continued to be taught in *madrasahs* until the end of the Osmanlı Devlet, and they used the Arabic script for Osmanlı Turkish. Education and cultural life in the Osmanlı Devlet adopted the Arabic script for the sole reason that the Osmanlıs stood for Islam, that Islam was the *raison d'être* for them, and that the Arabic language is the language of the Qur'ân.

At least 60 per cent of the words in Osmanlı Turkish are of Arabic origin. Even today, about 30 per cent of the Turkish language contains words that are of Arabic origin.

There is no need to mention how important names are for people. A proper name is called *'alam* in Arabic, which also means a flag. Therefore, the flag represents a socio-political entity, state, and a proper name represents a person.

When we look at the names of the Osmanlı sovereigns we find the following: Othman, 1288; Ikhtiyarud Din Orkhan, 1326; Murâd, 1360; Bâyezîd, 1389; Mehemmed, 1402-1421; Süleymân, 1403; Musa, 1410; Murâd, 1421; Mehemmed the Opener of Constantinople to Islam, 1451; Bâyezîd, 1481; Selîm, 1512; Süleymân

## The Osmanlı Socio-Political Entity: Empire Or Devlet?

the Magnificent, 1520; Selîm, 1566; Murâd, 1574 Mehemmed, 1595; Ahmed, 1603; Mustafa, 1617 & 1622; Othman, 1618; Murâd, 1623; Ibrahim, 1640; Mehemmed, 1648; Süleymân, 1687; Ahmed, 1692; Mustafa, 1695; Ahmed, 1703; Mahmûd, 1730; Othman, 1754; Mustafa, 1757; Abdul Hamid, 1773; Selîm, 1789; Mustafa, 1807; Mahmûd, 1808; Abdul Majîd, 1839; Abdul Aziz, 1861; Murâd, 1876; Abdul Hamid, 1876; Mehmed Reshad, 1909; and Mehmed Vahided Din, 1918-1922. All Muslim names and Arabic.

The greater part of North Africa was ruled by the Osmanlıs. If they had not gone there, Algeria, Tunisia, and Libya would have become Spanish-, French- or even Italian-speaking Catholic countries just like Spain (Andalusia) and most of South America. Egypt was first occupied by France, then by Britain. Is there a single sovereign among British or French kings or emperors with an Arab name? There is not one. It would be unimaginable. This indicates how alien these imperialistic powers were to native Arabs. On the other hand, even today, the proper names of people in Turkey are mostly Arabic-Islamic names. That is purely from their attachment to Islam, as the Arabs never conquered them. In countries that had been colonised by Western powers, there are many native peoples with proper names of European origin today, a fact that indicates how deeply rooted cultural imperialism is there.

In summary: Is it possible to find an imperial power, an empire, that teaches its own nation the language of the nation ruled, using the language of those ruled as the language partly in education over the centuries, naming its own sovereigns and citizens with the names of those ruled? Is it possible to find an empire using the script of those ruled as its own language?

Even today, the most beautiful calligraphy in Arabic letters is carried out by Turkish calligraphers, because the art of *khatt* has been a tradition in Turkey for many centuries. Is it possible to imagine Arabic being used as the language of instruction in Britain and in France, the English and French languages written in Arabic script officially over the centuries? It did happen as far as Turkish goes. The Osmanlı Turks submerged their identity in Islam, and neglected the Turkish language; the first compiler of Turkish grammar was a French scholar, Jean Deny. For the Turks who were educated in *madrasahs*, grammar (morphology and syntax) was a science pertaining only to Arabic. The Arabic and Islamic cultures were the basis for Osmanlı intellectual life. One of the most talented poets, Fuzuli, wrote his famous *Su Kasidesi* (poem of the water) in praise of the Prophet Muhammad ﷺ.

Almost every Osmanlı Turkish family's home had a *Shamâil-i Sharîfa*, which are descriptions in Arabic and in very elegant forms and compositions of the person of the Prophet ﷺ, rather than the names or *Tughras* of the Osmanlı Sultâns.

Let us quote a non-Muslim Arab about the Turkish language in the Osmanlı administration.

> "A servant of the Ottoman Sultân who used Turkish would not necessarily have thought of himself as a Turk; a subject of the Sultân who did not speak Turkish would not until the very last years of the empire have thought of himself as being shut out of the political community."[948]

Finally, in terms of the importance of teaching language in a country, we should remember what happened when De Gaulle of France and Gamal Abdunnasir of Egypt were alive. For some reason, Gamal Abdunnasir decided to replace English in Egyptian schools with another Western language. Charles de Gaulle immediately decided to send four hundred teachers of the French language to Egypt, all expenses and salaries paid by France.

### c) The Economic Aspect

An imperial power uses its merchants and tradesmen to exploit the

## The Osmanlı Socio-Political Entity: Empire Or Devlet?

resources and materials of the dominions as much as possible, but all through the centuries there were no Turkish Muslim merchants who exploited the wealth of the conquered countries. Until the fall of the Osmanlı Devlet, trade was in the hands of its non-Muslim peoples because, to quote Bernard Lewis, "The Muslims knew only four professions – government, war, religion, and agriculture. Industry and trade were left to non-Muslim conquered subjects, who continued to practise their inherited crafts."[949]

Is this a characteristic of an Empire? If the Osmanlı Devlet were an imperialistic power, the main body, i.e. the Turks, would have been the richest. Imperial powers have started wars for the sake of trade and market. The history of nineteenth-century Europe is full of the European drive towards free markets. On the contrary, the Osmanlı Devlet stood for another principle: namely, Islam. It is interesting to remember that Huseyin Dayi of Osmanlı Algeria insulted the French representative for the sake of a *dhimmî*, an Osmanlı subject, a Jewish merchant. And his action brought about the loss of Algeria to France in 1830.

# Osmanlı Institutions

# Introduction

Osmanlı institutions are the embodiment of Osmanlı civilisation, which is rooted exclusively in Islam. Islam is the unique source and lifeblood of the Osmanlı socio-political entity, which is the continuation of and a component part of Islamic civilisation.

It should be remembered that Western civilisation has emerged in lands where Christianity prevailed. Although it contains some Christian elements, in the main and in essence, it emerged and developed despite Christianity after bitter struggles with the latter in the form of Catholicism. Western civilisation has reached a stage where the very "human being" is lost, with the "material" or "thing" occupying the centre and the human being pushed to the periphery. One aspect of this is the weakening interest that human beings have in Christianity; churches are for sale in Britain. Other aspects are shattered human relations, violence, a growing number of children born out of wedlock (they may outnumber legitimate ones in a few decades, and legitimacy may become "out of date" or "old fashioned" in some Western countries in the not so very distant future), homeless people spending nights on shopping streets in makeshift cardboard shelters.

Each and every civilisation produces its own type of human being. Beginning with Mevlâna Jelâleddîn Rûmî, al-Hâj Bektâsh Wely, and Yûnus Emre, Anatolia had been under the spiritual control of great *shaykhs* throughout the Osmanlı era. Mevlâna Jelâleddîn and Horâsân Erenleri (The Awliyâ of Horâsân) came to Anatolia during the last decades of the Seljûqlu *Devlet*. The founder of the Osmanlı Devlet, Osmân Gâzi's father-in-law

Edebalı, was one of the *Akhiyyatul Fityân shaykhs*.[950] The great *sûfî shaykh* Geyikli Baba lived during the era of Osmân Gâzi's son, Orhân Gâzi. Al-Hâj Bektâsh Wely adorned the time of the third ruler, Murâd Hüdâvendigâr. His son Yıldırım Bâyezîd's daughter was married to another great *shaykh*, Emîr Sultân Muhammed Bukhârî. Al-Hâj Bayrâm Wely adorned the epoch of Murâd the Second, and his *Khalîfah* Aq Shemseddîn was the spiritual master of Mehemmed Fâtih, the opener of Constantinople to Islam in 1453. Later, there were Shemseddîn Sivâsî, Üftâde, Azîz Mahmûd Hüdâî, and many other great *sûfî shaykhs* right up to the end of the Osmanlı Devlet. Since "sûfîsm is the latest, earliest, simplest, quickest, and the most successful of all mystical systems in the world. It advocates full participation in worldly affairs, unlike other mystical disciplines that are characterised by world renunciation and asceticism,"[951] the Osmanlı society was a very healthy one under the guidance of great spiritual masters who earned profound respect from the Sultâns, *vazîrs*, and *pashas* as well as from the public. Many sultâns were girded with the sword of Islam by *sûfî shaykhs* after visiting the tomb of *mujâhid sahâbî* Abû Ayyûb al-Ansârî in their accession ceremony.[952]

A Western scholar has this to say about the Osmanlı political entity:

> "From its foundation until its fall the Ottoman Empire was a state dedicated to the advancement or defence of the power and faith of Islam. For six centuries the Ottomans were almost constantly at war with the Christian West, first in the attempt – mainly successful – to impose Islamic rule on a large part of Europe, then in the long-drawn-out rearguard action to halt or delay the relentless counter-attack of the West. This centuries-long struggle, with its origins in the very roots of Turkish Islam, could not fail to affect the

whole structure of Turkish society and institutions. For the Ottoman Turk, his Empire, containing all the heartlands of Islam, was Islam itself. In the Ottoman chronicles the territories of the Empire are referred to as the 'lands of Islam,' its sovereign as 'the Padishâh of Islam,' its armies as 'the soldiers of Islam,' its religious head as 'the *Sheyh* of Islam'; its people thought of themselves first and foremost as Muslims. Both Ottoman and Turk are, as we have seen, terms of comparatively recent usage, and the Ottoman Turks had identified themselves with Islam – submerged their identity in Islam – to a greater extent than perhaps any other Islamic people. It is curious that while in Turkey the word Turk almost went out of use, in the West it came to be a synonym for Muslim, and a western convert to Islam was said to have 'turned Turk,' even when the conversion took place in Fez or Isfahan."[953]

# I. Administrative Organisation

## 1 THE KHALIFATE

Khalifate is the central institution in the Islamic political entity. Because Islam is the final message,[i] not only to humanity on this earth, but to the whole universe,[ii] and the first human being Adam ﷺ was also the *khalîfah* (vicegerent)[954] of Allah on earth and the First Prophet, the notion of the Khalifate (vicegerency) has the central position in Islam. Since Adam ﷺ, humanity has never been deprived of heavenly guidance: throughout its existence on earth, humanity has been spiritually replenished by thousands of Prophets of whom twenty-five are named in the Qur'ân (on certain occasions; the Qur'ân is not a history book). *Ulu'l 'Azm* (the greatest, most important) Prophets are: Adam, Noah, Moses, Jesus ﷺ, culminating with the Final Messenger Muhammad ﷺ. Allah supported His Messengers with miracles. When Moses ﷺ was sent, magic was at its zenith; it was the most important aspect of knowledge or skill, and Moses ﷺ defeated Pharaoh's magicians. When the Prophet Jesus ﷺ was sent, the prevailing skill was in the field of medicine, and he, by the permission and support of Allah, opened the eyes of the blind and revived the dead. When the Final Messenger Muhammad ﷺ was sent, the prevailing skill was in literature. Beside other miracles,

---

i  Muhammad ﷺ is the Final Messenger and *"'Seal of the Prophets'"*; al-Qur'ân, al-Ahzâb [33] *âyat* 40.

ii  A practising Muslim reads in *salât* (prayer) five times a day, and each time during *qiyâm sûrat al-Fâtiha* (the first *sûrah* of the Glorious Qur'ân). This *sûrah* begins with the sentence: *"Praise be to Allah, the Lord of the Worlds."*

his outstanding miracle is the Qur'ân, the word of Allah the Sublime. "The Qur'ân is singularly distinctive in its style compared to any human composition. Human eloquence, with its remarkable history in the composition of poetry, has failed to compose even a single verse like that of the Qur'ân. The Qur'anic composition is a living challenge for human beings to imitate its miraculous style."[955] A human being has no chance, no opportunity to observe, to experience the miracles of Moses and Jesus 🙏, but he has the chance and opportunity to experience the Last Miracle: the Qur'ân.

This situation of the human being as vicegerent of the Creator on earth puts humanity in a very realistic and harmonious position: everything has been put at his service; he is entitled to use and utilise everything on earth[956] and in the heavens.[957] Therefore, when given the *wahy* (revelation, inspiration) made manifest in the Qur'ân, the human being need no longer be in a dilemma regarding, for example, the consumption of animal products. In a way, it is very "human" to be a vegetarian, thinking that one should not take away a living creature's life for one's food. But in reality it is in contradiction with "actual" life and events observed in the vegetarian Hindus' attitudes towards other "human beings" in Kashmir and in India itself. The human being is entitled to use everything good[958] on earth, and his life becomes and remains meaningful in his obedience to Allah's Laws, i.e. the natural laws.

With the establishment of Muslim society and polity in enlightened, radiant Medîna, the greatest revolution in world history took place: an entirely new, relevant, "human" and contemporary concept, the *Ummat*, was formed; a concept that modern Europe has only partially realised in the last decade of the twentieth century by forming the European Union. *Ummat* is a far more comprehensive concept: it embraces all who believe in the same principles and share the same worldview and values regardless of their place and position in world geography. An individual becomes a full member of the

*Ummat* the moment he or she becomes a Muslim, regardless of race, colour, language, and part of the world he or she inhabits. Being a member of the *Ummat*, the believer is entitled to all the rights other co-believers have, and shares in the duties and obligations with all other members of the *Ummat*. It is not socialism, but it provides immense solidarity among the believers.

It is incumbent upon the *Ummat* to have a leader. The first leader of the Ummat was the Final Messenger Muhammad ﷺ. He was succeeded by Abû Bakr ﷺ (622-634) and he was called Khalîfahtu Rasûlillâh (Vicegerent of the Messenger of Allah). When he was succeeded by 'Umar b. al-Khattâb ﷺ (634-644), it would have been too cumbersome to call him Khalîfatu Khalîfati Rasûlillâh (vicegerent of the vicegerent of the Messenger of Allah), and so he was called Amîrul Mu'minîn (Prince of the Believers). Then succession, vicegerency, continued as khalifate in the Muslim political entity. The leadership of the *Ummat*, the Khalifate, was converted by the Umawîs (661-750) into a dynastic succession and continued with the 'Abbâsîs (750-1258) in the same way until the invasion of Baghdad by the Mongols in 1258. Aside from the Bulgar Turks who embraced Islam en masse in 910 under Yaltavar oğlu Almush Khân, in the wide lands north of the Caspian Sea, other Turk masses had also embraced Islam in Turkestan and Afghanistan by that time. The Muslim Turkish Qarahanlı *Devlet* (840-1212) converted to Islam en masse in 944. Muslim Turks set up the Gazne *Devlet* (the Ghaznavids) in Afghanistan in 963, and it lasted until 1186. The Gazne *Devlet* carried out seventeen *jihâd* campaigns into India, as a result of which the *Ordu* (in Turkish: army) language came into existence. Since the Muslim *ordu* (*urdu* is a distorted form, much like Uzbek for Özbek) consisted mainly of Turks, including other local people as well, their languages became mixed and resulted in the *ordu* language.

Then the Turks under Selçuk (Seljuk) emerged in Jand, and as a Muslim, Selçuk refused to obey the non-Muslim Turkish Oğuz

# I – Administrative Organisation

Yabgu (the sovereign) and set up his own *devlet* in 1038, which lasted until 1157. Selçuk's grandson Muhammed Tuğrul Beğ, as a champion of Sunnî Islam, entered Baghdad in 1055, and aided the Sunnî 'Abbâsî *khalîfah* against the Shi'î Bûyîs. When Baghdad was invaded by Mongols in 1258, the Selçuklu (Seljuk) sultâns acted as *khalîfah*s. On the other hand, there was a Mamlûk sultân of Egypt and Bilâdush Shâm.[i] Baybars installed a member of the 'Abbâsî family as *khalîfah* in al-Qâhira in 1261. But this *khalîfah* was a "symbolic" one, having only the "title" without any military, political, financial, or actual power whatsoever.[ii]

After the Great Selçuklus (1038-1157), the Anatolian Selçuklu Devlet (1075-1308) represented Islam and its sultâns acted as *khalîfah*s. The khalifate, as the actual unity of the Muslims world over and representative of united Muslim power, is the nightmare of

---

i At that time the proper name for the region was, and among the people of the region still is, "Bilâdush Shâm," with Damascus as its capital. At the time we are talking about, the region was called Bilâdush Shâm, until almost the middle of the twentieth century.

ii Bernard Lewis, *The Arabs in History* (New York: Harper Torchbook, 1967), p. 155. This is true; but, on the other hand, we should keep in mind that, in *hadith* criticism – called *al-Jarh Wa't Ta'dîyl* – even a Muslim, a believer in Islam and Muhammad's status as Messenger 🌸 is sometimes rejected, and a *hadîth sherîf* related by him is not accepted if he had some minor shortcomings. For example, *fartu'l gaflet* is enough reason to reject a *râwi* (a Muslim narrator). In case of his shortcoming or neglect of prayer, his relating is not taken seriously, is not accepted. So, what about someone who does not believe in Muhammad's status as a Messenger 🌸? It is only fair to disregard and discard claims, views, and assertions of orientalists with regard to *ahâdîth sharîfa*. No discerning Muslim can take their views seriously. Dealing with al-Qur'ân and Sunnat is the task of believers, not of unbelievers.

those who oppose Islam. Consequently, to undermine and even to eradicate the very "concept" of khalifate, they always repeat the wrong claim that the khalifate came to an end in 1258, and they even try to cast doubt about the very "institution" of the khalifate. In actual fact, the Muslim community, *Ummat*, did have leadership throughout its existence. That leadership was generally called the khalifate. Besides, it is simply and certainly impossible for the Muslims not to have a *Khalîfah*. There are several *ahâdîth sharîfa*[959] about the obligation of Muslims to swear allegiance (*bay'at*) to a *Khalîfah*.

Actually, the Great Selçuklu sovereigns, representing military and political Islamic power, were justified in acting as Khalîfah-Sultâns. After them, Anatolian Selçuklu Sultâns assumed this duty. After the death of the last Anatolian Selçuklu Sultân Mes'ûd II in 1308, this *devlet* ceased to exist, giving way to several principalities in Anatolia. The largest and strongest of those *beğliks* (principalities, emirates) were Qaramân and Germiyân. Since it is impossible for Muslims not to have a leader, a *khalîfah*, the sovereign of the largest and strongest *beğlik*, Qaramân, was accepted as the *Khalîfah*.

Orhan Gazi's son Murâd, the third leader of the Osmanlı Devlet, refers to his capital Bursa as "Dâru'l Khilâfah" (Seat of the Khalifate) in his letter to the sovereign of the Qaramân Beğlik, dated 1 Rabî' Thânî 767/16 December 1365, informing him that the Osmanlı *mujâhids* had opened new areas in Europe to Islam.[960]

The fourth Osmanlı leader, Yıldırım Bâyezîd, continued to maintain the position of *Khalîfah* and was addressed as *Zillullâhi fi'l Khâfiqayn* (Shadow of Allah over the Two Seas), *Râfi'u A'lâmi'sh Sharî'ati'sh Sharîfati's Sunniyyati* (Raiser of the Flags of the Honourable Sunnî *Sharî'at* [Islamic Law]) and, *Sultânu Arzillâh* (Sultân of Allah's territory) by the sovereign of Egypt, Hâjj b. Sha'bân, in a letter written on 6 Shawwâl 793/6 September 1391.[i]

---

i  *Munsheât*, I, p. 116. The "institution" of the khalifate is a nightmare

*I – Administrative Organisation*

It is very significant that the symbolic 'Abbâsî *Khalîfah* was in Egypt, and that the leader of this entity addressed the fourth Osmanlı Sultân Yıldırım Bâyezîd as *khalîfah*; a fact that clearly shows Osmanlı leaders' being accepted by the sovereign of the Mamlûk Devlet, a major Islamic power at that time, as *Khalîfah*. Fâtih Mehemmed (1451-1481) was called the "Sultân of the Two Continents, Khâqân of the Two Seas, Amîru'l Mu'minîn"[961] (Prince of Believers). İstanbul, the Osmanlı capital, was the seat of Khalifate:

> for non-Muslim Western "scholars," some of whom keep close ties with their respective foreign ministries. They always repeat and insist on the false topic of the khalifate's coming to an end. They are very keen on luring Muslims to believe that, when the last 'Abbâsî *khalîfah* was killed in 1258 in Baghdad by Mongols, the "Institution" of the Khalifate came to an end. The Abbâsî *Khalîfah*, who was installed in Egypt by Mamlûk Sultân Baybars in 1261, was a symbolic one with no actual power. When Sultân Selîm took over Egypt in 1517, he did not perform any ceremony of taking over the khalifate; consequently, the Osmanlıs did not represent the khalifate as they claimed later on.
> 
> The simple, plain and certain facts:
> 1. Even in post-Christian Europe, they regard Christianity as a "culture" and "part of their cultural-historical identity." Catholic and Orthodox Christians have their heads of faith.
> 2. Muslims do not have a "head," but they are dispersed in their secular national states. The khalifate means unity of Muslims, which is in stark contrast to Western interests in Muslim country. Therefore, in their view, everything must be done to nip the "concept" of Khalifate in the bud.
> 3. Those "scholars" do not look at original sources but continue to quote from one another's published works, repeating incorrect evaluations.
> 4. When Selçuklu Sultân Muhammed Tuğrul Beğ entered Baghdad in 1057, he attained authority from the 'Abbâsî *khalîfah* to govern the Muslims in his domain according to *Sharî'at*.

"in the spring of 886/1481 they left İstanbul, which is his Dâru'l Khilâfah, and crossed to Üsküdar."⁹⁶²

His son Bâyezîd II (1481-1512) was acknowledged, for example, by Husein Bayqara, Pâdishâh of Khurâsân, to be *Khalîfahtullâhi fi'l enâm*⁹⁶³ (Vicegerent of Allah among people). What Sultân Selîm (1512-1520) did after annexing Bilâdush Shâm and Egypt in 1516 and 1517, sending the last "symbolic" 'Abbâsî *khalîfah* to İstanbul, was, in fact, combine the actual, real khalifate with the symbolic one, taking over the latter.⁹⁶⁴ The leadership of the Sunnî Muslim world was represented by the Osmanlıs throughout the following centuries. The Osmanlı sultâns were "the" leaders of the sunnîs, the great majority of the Muslims. And they were very well aware of their position as such. When Tiryâkî Hasan Pasha defeated the besieging Christian armies, which far outnumbered him, at Kanije castle in 1601 and utterly routed them, he received a decree from the Osmanlı sultân in which the Sultân promoted him to the rank of *vazîr*, and wrote: "Praise be to Allah who preferred us to many of His believing servants and gave us the keys to the affairs of the Muslims."⁹⁶⁵ Certainly, he who has been given "the keys to the affairs of the *Muslims*" is undoubtedly none other than the *Khalîfah*.

When Osman II was deposed and took refuge with the janissaries in 1622, the soldiers shouted in unison that they would not accept him anymore as *Khalîfah*, but neither would they agree to his being killed.⁹⁶⁶ The Osmanlı Khalîfah-Sultâns were recognised by other Sunnî rulers as such, and there was no Muslim sovereign of a major power in the heartlands of Islam other than the Osmanlı sultân. While Osmanlı leaders put more emphasis on the titles of "sultân," "pâdishâh," etc., which indicate "real", "actual," "political," and "military" power, they used the title of "*Khalîfah*" as well and they were addressed by other Muslim rulers as such.

To give only a few examples, we quote here some relevant passages from the Osmanlı Archives:⁹⁶⁷

*I – Administrative Organisation*

Osmanlı Khalîfah-Sultân Süleymân II informs the French King Louis of his accession to the throne of the Osmanlıs, which is the Seat of the Khalifate;[968]

And when the Osmanlı Sultân writes to the Khân of Qırım (Crimea), inviting him to participate in *jihâd*, he mentions the fact that the Khân had been very loyal to the *Khalîfah* in 1107/1696.[969]

The Khalifate was maintained and represented by the Osmanlı Devlet until the end; when Khalîfah-Sultân Mehmed Reshâd proclaimed *jihâd* against the allies during the First World War, responses came from Muslims as far away as Australia. Two Muslims who had been living there started fighting the British and Australians against whom the *Khalîfah* had proclaimed a *jihâd*. Those brave Muslims caused a great deal of trouble, and it took some time for the Christian authorities to deal with them. At last they were martyred and the carriage from which one of them used to sell ice-cream is on display today in a museum in Australia.

The institution of the Khalifate is the pivotal one in Islamic civilisation; all other social, religious, educational, sanitary, judicial, military, economic institutions are related and connected to this central institution.

## 2 THE VIZÂRATE

There are two kinds of vizârate[970] in Islamic practice: *tafwîz* (delegation) and *tanfîz* (executive). A *vazîr* of *tafwîz* (وزير مفوض) has full authority and responsibility. The office of *vazîr* was established very early in the Osmanlı administration. Being the continuation of the Anatolian Selçuklu Devlet, the Osmanlıs established their main administrative and social institutions on the Selçuklu model.

The very word *vazîr* is mentioned in the Qur'ân: "*And appoint a wazîr for me from my family, my brother Hârûn,*"[971] Mûsâ ﷺ implores Allah the Almighty. In the Islamic understanding, Mûsâ ﷺ is a Muslim Prophet since Islam is the one and only religion, its first

Prophet being Adam ﷺ and its final Messenger Muhammad ﷺ. Therefore, the *vazîr* of Mûsâ ﷺ is a Muslim one and the institution of vizârate is Islamic as well. The concept of *vazîr* had always been present in the Islamic mind, so much so that we find the same word in the sayings of the Final Messenger Muhammad ﷺ: "If Allah wants good for an *amir* (administrator), he gives him an upright, trustworthy *vazîr*. When he forgets, he reminds him, when he remembers, he helps him."[972]

The *Vazîr* is a quite different concept from that of the Western "minister." The latter is invested with authority while the former implies accountability and responsibility.[973] The very word *vazîr* stems from *wzr* in Arabic, which is related to "burden," "load" as stated in the Qur'ân: " وَلَا تَزِرُ وَازِرَةٌ وِزْرَ أُخْرَىٰ - *wa lâ taziru wâziratun wizra ukhra*[974] – No one bears the burden, the responsibility for others". *Vazîr* literally means "one who has been loaded with a burden, responsibility" because the Muslim Devlet is responsible for the well-being of the governed people, regardless of their race, colour, religion, language, traditions, etc. The governed people are significantly called *ra'iyya* (cared for), in sharp contrast with the Western concept of *subject*, who was sold together with the land as if he or she was a farm animal.

Like all other Muslim Devlet*s*, the Osmanlıs also had *vazîrs*, having adopted the model of administration from their predecessors, the Anatolian Selçuklus. The first Osmanlı *vazîr* was Alâeddin Pasha,[975] who lived during Orhân Gâzi's era (1326-1362). Then Orhân Gâzi's son, Süleymân Pasha, was appointed *vazîr* in 733/1332. Towards the middle of Sultân Murâd's era (1362-1389), Jendereli Halîl was appointed *vazîr*, with the title of Hayreddîn Pasha.

When he died in 787/1385, his son Ali Pasha replaced him. Afterwards, when Timurtash Pasha and some other high-ranking *mujâhid* commanders were promoted to the rank of *vazîr*, Ali Pasha was called *vazîr-i a'zam* (the greatest vazîr).[976] When Ali Pasha died,

*I – Administrative Organisation*

his son İbrâhîm Pasha became *vazîr-i a'zam*. Upon his death, his son Halîl Pasha was appointed *vazir-i a'zam* and he remained in this post for more than 25 years.⁹⁷⁷

Then Mahmûd Pasha Wely became *vazîr-i a'zam*, and he was followed by Gedik Ahmed Pasha.⁹⁷⁸

During the Khalifate of Süleymân the Magnificent (1520-1566), the title of *vazîr-i a'zam* was changed into *sadr-ı a'zam (sadrâzam)*.⁹⁷⁹ This title continued to be used until the end.

Osmanlı *vazîrs* were empowered with full authority. The *sadrâzam* carried *mühr-i hümâyûn* (the Heavenly Seal: Seal of the Khalîfah-Sultân) and acted in the name of the Sultân, sealing official documents with that seal. Even the *vazîrs* were entitled for some time to write *fermân*s (decrees by Sultâns) and to put *tuğra* (the elegantly written name of the Sultân) on it.⁹⁸⁰ In other words, *vizâret* (the post of *vazîr*) in Osmanlı administration was *vizâret* of *tafwîd*, the *vazîr* was *vazîr mufawwad* (authorised *vazîr*)[i] with full responsibility.

Since Islam[ii] is "the" religion of mankind, starting with the

---

i Stanford Shaw (*History of the Ottoman Empire and Modern Turkey*, CUP 1991, I, p. 24) refers to the first Osmanlı *vazîr* as "chief minister." As there was no other *vazîr* at that time, the "chief" part is irrelevant. But *vazîr* should not be translated as "minister"; the terms are not the same. A *vazîr* was also an army general, a *beğlerbeği* (general governor of Anatolia or Osmanlı Europe). Mahmûd Pasha was the *beğlerbeği* of Rumeli (Osmanlı Europe) and *vazîr-i a'zâm*: *Netâyij*, I, p. 58; Lala Shâhin Pasha, and then Timurtash Pasha were *beğlerbeği*s of Rumeli, and both were given the rank of *vazîr*: *op. cit.*, I, pp. 15-16. Another important mistake Shaw makes is thinking of them within the framework of *vazir-i tenfîdh* (executive *vazîr*). "Minister" may be used as a translation for *nâzır*.

ii Islam means "submission" to the will of the Creator. In Islam, physical (natural) laws are called *Sunnatullah*, i.e. the way Allah governs the universe.

first human being and the First Prophet Adam ﷺ, continuing throughout the ages with other Prophets such as Nûh (Noah), İbrâhîm (Abraham), Mûsâ (Moses), and Îsa (Jesus) ﷺ, and Sulaymân (Solomon) ﷺ was one of the Muslim Prophets, his wise *vazîr*, Âsaf b. Berkhiyâ had been accepted by the Osmanlıs as the master and model of their *vazîrs* – so much so that the seat of *sadrâzam* was referred to in Osmanlı usage as "Bâb-ı Âsafî" (the Gate of Âsaf). The title of a famous book written by Lutfi Pasha, *sadrâzam* of Süleymân the Magnificent, is *Âsafnâme* (*Book of Âsaf*), in which he relates his experience in office and gives advice to his successors. In short, the Osmanlı *sadrâzam* is conceived of as related to Âsaf, son of Berkhiyâ. And Âsaf, as a proper name, is still used in Turkey as part of the Osmanlı heritage.

It should be remembered that the late S. Shaw was one of the most sympathetic of the orientalists.

## 3 THE DÎVÂN

As the legal and natural continuation of the Anatolian Selçuklu Devlet, the Osmanlıs adopted all their Islamic institutions. As early as the second sovereign Orhân Gâzi's era, the *dîvân* became the central administrative-judicial body the Osmanlıs.

### 3.1 The Dîvân-ı Hümâyûn

Over time, the Osmanlı central *dîvân* became the *Dîvân-ı Hümâyûn*. The *hümâ* is a bird believed to always live in the sky and not touch earth at all. *Hümâyûn* means pertaining to the *hümâ*, hence "Heavenly." As representatives of the Final Heavenly Message, Islam, the Osmanlıs called important institutions and objects *Hümâyûn* (Heavenly). Thus, the decree of the Osmanlı Khalîfah-Sultân is *Khatt-ı Hümâyûn* (the Heavenly Decree), his seal is *Mühr-i Hümâyûn* (the Heavenly Seal), the Osmanlı army is *Ordu-yu Hümâyûn* (the Heavenly Army), the navy is *Donanma-yı Hümâyûn* (the Heavenly

*I – Administrative Organisation*

navy), and even the first gate of the Topkapusu (Topkapı) Palace is *Bâb-ı Hümâyûn* (the Heavenly Gate of the Seat of the Khalifate). Therefore, *Dîvân-ı Hümâyûn* should not be distorted into "Imperial Council."[i]

In the *Dîvân-ı Hümâyûn*, there were a few other *vazîrs* called the second *vazîr*, the third *vazîr*, etc. There were two *qâdiaskers*, a *qâdıasker* of Rumelia (the European part of the Osmanlı Devlet) and a *qâdıasker* of Anatolia and Qâdi (Judge) of İstanbul. *Qâdiaskers* were responsible for appointing *qâdis* and they represented a higher authority in their respective areas. The highest judicial authority was the *sheyhülislâm*, who was equal in protocol to the *sadrâzam*. The *sheyhülislâm* was the head of the whole judicial system and was the supreme head of education as well. The *Dîvân-ı Hümâyûn* had to acquire his *fetvâ* (legal opinion and permission given in accordance with *Sharî'at*) on every important issue. The *nishânjı*, who put the *tuğra* (an artfully written signature of the Khalîfah-Sultân) on documents, was in charge of official correspondence. Another member of the *Dîvân-ı Hümâyûn* was the *defterdâr*, who was responsible for financial affairs. The supreme commander of the janissaries (*yenicheri ağası*) was also a member. And then there were also the commanders of units of the central army the (*bölük ağaları*) and the scribes (*khâjegân*) of the *Dîvân-ı Hümâyûn*.[981]

---

i    Stanford J. Shaw, *op. cit.*, pp. 25, 26, 101, 102, 108, 115, 117, 118, 120, 121, 122, 123, 131, 137, 163, 164, 258, 280, 281, 282, 288, 289. A very good example of showing how an alien and incorrect term is foisted upon Osmanlıs. Proper names and nomenclatures are *not* translated. Moreover, "Countries and peoples are unique and are not so easily lured into identity with each other save on limited, and specific points" (Rupert Emerson, *From Empire to Nation*, Cambridge, Massauachussets: Harvard University Press, 1967, vii).

Until the time of Fâtih Mehemmed, the Osmanlı Khalîfah-Sultân presided over the meetings of the *Dîvân-ı Hümâyûn*. One day when the *Dîvân-ı Hümâyûn* was meeting, a Turkish peasant came and asked: "Which of you is the Sultân? I have a matter to complain about." The Sultân was displeased with that intrusion and afterwards it became the custom for the Sultân to listen to the deliberations of the *Dîvân-ı Hümâyûn* behind a window covered with a curtain, adjacent to the room.[982] From then on, the seal of the Sultân was given to the *vazîrs* who held the post of *sadrâzam* and were given the responsibility of administrating the affairs of the Devlet.[983]

The *Dîvân-ı Hümâyûn* met after the *fajr* prayer every day except on holidays. After listening to the *mehter*, they would discuss affairs of *Devlet*. At the *Divan-ı Hümâyûn*, important matters were decided on and this institution acted as the Sublime Court as well. Since people could take their complaints to the *Dîvân-ı Hümâyûn*; there was no need in the Osmanlı administration for the *Dîvân-ı Mezâlim* (administration for restitution for injustices).

### 3.2 The Vazîr-i A'zam's Dîvân

Apart from the *Dîvân-ı Hümâyûn*, there was another *dîvân* called the *Dîvân-ı Âsafî*. It was the *sadrâzam*'s *dîvân*. They discussed and decided matters and cases that were not concluded in the *Dîvân-ı Hümâyûn* and were of secondary importance and which thus did not need to be presented to the Khalîfah-Sultân.

This *dîvân* was called the *Dîvân-ı Âsafî* (*Âsaf's Dîvân*); the Osmanlıs, being bearers of the Heavenly Message, Islam, perceived Âsaf b. Berkhiyâ, the wise *vazîr* of the Prophet Süleymân ﷺ, as a Muslim *vazîr*. Thus, the Osmanlı *sadrâzam*'s model was based on that wise *vazîr*.

The *Dîvân-i Âsafî* met at the residence of the *sadrâzam* a few days a week, after the mid-afternoon prayer (*'asr salât*). For this

*I – Administrative Organisation*

reason it was also called the *dîvân* of the mid-afternoon (*ikindi dîvânı*).⁹⁸⁴

## 4 THE QALEMIYYE

One of the members of the *Dîvân-ı Hümâyûn* was the *nishânjı*. His office was responsible for conveying decisions taken and orders issued by the *Dîvân-ı Hümâyûn*. He would put the *tuğra* (a very elegant piece of work, almost a masterpiece: the calligraphic signature of the Khalîfah-Sultân) on documents. He would write decrees of appointments for military posts, decrees allocating *tımâr* to deserving people. He would supervise cadastral surveys of lands newly opened to Islam. He was in charge of external correspondence as well. The the chief scribe (Reîsu'l Küttâb), who became influential afterwards, was previously under his jurisdiction. The scribes of the *Dîvân-ı Hümâyûn* (*khâjegân-ı Dîvân-ı Hümâyûn*) were responsible for the accounts of the army and internal correspondence.⁹⁸⁵

## 5. COMMUNICATIONS

There is no need to emphasise the importance of communications as being vital for any socio-political body in maintaining its existence and active development. The communications organisation in Muslim Devlet*s* was called *berîd* (postal service). *Berîd* originally referred to a distance of 12 miles. One *fersakh* is three miles, thus one *berîd* equals four *fersakhs*.

The *berîd* organisation in Muslim administration was first founded by Mu'âwiya b. Abî Sufyân, and later improved upon by Abdulmalik b. Marwân. Extremely important for any socio-political entity, the *berîd* was maintained by other Muslim Devlet*s*. The Osmanlı Devlet adopted this organisation, among others, from the Anatolian Selçuklu Devlet.

469

The Osmanlı Devlet set up a wonderful network of communications reaching every part of its extensive territory. The seat of the Khalifate, İstanbul, was the centre of the road network.

From İstanbul three main roads went to Europe and another three to Asia. The directions in Europe were:

1. a) *sağ qol* (right hand): İstanbul – Qırqlareli – Aydos – Prevadi – Babadağ-İsaqchi – Aqkerman – Özü;
2. b) *orta kol* (middle course): İstanbul – Silivri – Chorlu – Edirne – Filibe – Sofya – Belgrade;
3. c) *sol qol* (left hand): İstanbul – Silivri – Tekirdağ – Gelibolu (Gallipoli) – Keshân – Gümüljine – Selânik (Selonica) – Yenişehir.

In the Asian part of the Osmanlı domain, the three main roads were:

1. a) *sağ qol* (right hand): Üsküdar – Eskişehir – Aqshehir – Qonya – Adana – Antaqya (Antioch) – Halab (Aleppo);
2. b) *orta qol* (middle course): Üsküdar – Gebze – İznik – Sapanca – Geyve – Hendek – Düzje – Bolu – Hajıhamza – Merzifon – Amasya – Turhal – Toqat – Sivas – Malatya – Diyarbakır;
3. c) *sol qol* (left hand): Üsküdar – Gebze – İznik – Sapanca – Geyve – Hendek – Düzje – Bolu – Hajıhamza – Merzifon – Qarahisâr-ı Sharqî – Bayburd – Terjan – Erzurum – Qars.

In addition to the main roads, there was a network of secondary roads that connected the centre to other parts of the Osmanlı Devlet. The central government built the main roads while the secondary roads were built by the holders of *tımâr* and *ze'âmet* (those able people who had been given the right to collect taxes (*'ushr*) in the name of the Devlet and who were obliged to maintain a certain number of soldiers with full equipment ready for *jihâd*).

The Osmanlı Devlet set up institutions called *menzilhâne* along the roads. *Menzil* means a station or a stop. Orders from the centre and other correspondence went to distant places through those

# I – Administrative Organisation

roads and officers changed their horses at *menzilhâne*. Villages near a *menzilhâne* were given the responsibility of maintaining a certain number of horses for the officials to go from one *menzilhâne* to another, provide food for them, and take other measures for their comfort.

The organisation of the *menzilhâne* was used for military purposes as well: before a *jihâd* campaign, the Khalîfah-Sultân sent his orders as to the directions, and in the *menzilhâne* enough food, etc. was stocked for the mobile army's need. People also came to these centres to sell their merchandise, causing these places to become lively trade centres.

The *menzilhâne* were administered by a *menzilhâne emîni* who was appointed for one year. Under him were other officials and a group of people who inhabited a village or a town near that *menzilhâne*, called a *menzilkesh*. The *menzilhâne emîni* was in charge of the administration of the *menzil*, responsible for providing lodging and food to troops that stopped at the *menzil* along their way. In return, those who served the *menzil* were exempt from paying taxes. The *menzil* organisation was checked by *qâdis*, their *nâibs* or by a *muhtesib*. The *menzil* institutions were promulgated after a postal organisation was set up in 1834.[986]

The *menzil* was a two-way communications organisation: orders, letters from the centre to the periphery and letters, information about enemies, and local affairs were carried from the periphery to the centre through these points. Confidential correspondence was carried by one *ulâq*, who changed his horse at the *menzil* and continued on his journey post-haste. The horse belonging to a *menzil* was taken back from there by a functionary called a *sürüjü* (driver) to his *menzil*.

On the other hand, it was also a one-way communication: some *aqınjı beğs* knew more than half a dozen local languages in their area of operation. They would enter the enemy territory and would send pigeons with information tied to their leg to İstanbul. As a result, the Osmanlı *Dîvân-ı Hümâyûn* was aware of almost every political meeting that took place in Christendom in the sixteenth century.

# II – Economic Institutions

## 6. ADMINISTRATION OF THE LAND

In the Osmanlı administration, there were two ways of profiting from the land:

a) a right to cultivate (*haqq-ı zirâ'at*): Those who had the right to use the land were given a deed of *tapu*, and they possessed the right to cultivate the land. They lived on what they produced through agriculture.

b) a judicial right to one-tenth in accordance with *Shari'at* (*'ushr-ı sher'î*): this is the right of the Devlet. The *Devlet* gave this right (called *tımar*) to soldiers who proved their bravery in *jihâd*, or to notables or high officials (called *ze'âmet*), or kept for the Khalîfah-Sultân or *vazîrs* (called *khâss*). *Tımar*, *ze'âmet* and *khâss* are all *iqtâ'* in different sizes. Those who were entitled to hold those *iqtâ'ât* had the right to collect the one-tenth (*'ushr*) share of the Devlet on the crops produced; it was their revenue instead of a salary. On many occasions, the *'ushr* from land was allocated to pious foundations (*awqâf*: plural of *waqf*). For example, the land of a village had been given by deeds of *tapu* to 80-100 people to cultivate, and the right of the Devlet (*'ushr*: one-tenth of the crops produced) had been given to a *sipâhî* as *tımâr* or to a *za'iym* as *ze'âmet*, or to a notable or high commander as *khâss*, or this revenue was allocated as *waqf*.[987] Muslims under the Osmanlı administration founded *awqâf* for very different humane purposes: to feed the poor, to look after orphans, to provide marriage expenses and furniture for orphan girls, to maintain mosques, *zâwiyas* (hospices for *sûfis*), to maintain caravanserai (*kervânsarâys* – fortified buildings on caravan routes with provisions of food, etc., and fodder for their animals), to care for migrating birds that were unable to continue their migrations and had to alight, and even to care for hungry wolves that approached villages during the winter; they provided food for them from the *waqf* that was set up for this purpose.

People in the second group, i.e. those who had the right to collect the *'ushr* on behalf of the Devlet, are called *sâhib-i arz*. Any peasant who wanted to sell his land would give a *taqrîr* in the presence of the *sâhib-i arz*, whose permission was needed for the transaction.[988]

## 7. TRADE

The Osmanlı Devlet facilitated commercial activities in its domains. Security on the roads was extremely important. Therefore, following the Anatolian Selçuklu model, the Osmanlıs built *kervânsarâys* on main roads. A *kervânsarây* is a stone building, a fortified place with all the facilities needed for travellers and their animals, including their merchandise. They were built at certain distances from one another. A caravan (*kervân*) would set out from one of them immediately after the morning prayer (*salât fajr*) and would reach the next about mid-afternoon, or in any case certainly before sunset. The people and animals would spend the night there, would rest, and continue the journey during the day.

Notables and rich Muslims built *kervânsarâys* as institutions of *waqf*. They allocated shops, land, orchards, etc., whose revenues were used to maintain a *kervânsarây*. Travellers, merchants, and their animals were entitled to stay in a *kervânsarây*, lodged and fed at no charge for up to three days. A *kervânsarây* usually had a *mesjid*, an imam, a *muezzin*, cooks, servants, and a small band of cavalry to protect the area.[i]

---

i   *Netâyij*, II, pp. 105-106. All these activities were inspired by *ahâdîth-i*

## 7.1 Akhiyya-Fityân

Artisans and craftsmen were organised into professional institutions called *akhiyya-fityân*. *Fityân* means youth. There were *akhîs* in every city and town. The organisations cared for training apprentices, making sure they were good Muslims and the quality of production – thus protecting not only the people involved in the profession but the rights of consumers as well.[i] The *shaykh* of a *lonja* (guild) was the spiritual head of his profession at the same time.

The *akhîs* had a *sandıq* (box) for giving financial support to the artisans and craftsmen who had completed their training and who were entitled to set up their own businesses. The support was granted in the form of gift from one's colleagues; neither loan nor interest was involved.

## 8 – FINANCE

As a matter of fact, the Osmanlı financial system depended on the Islamic concept of administration and was in accordance with the Islamic tradition that they had inherited from the Anatolian Selçuklus.

---

*sharîfa* of the Final Messenger. These activities fall under the concept of *sadaqa jâriya*. The three-day time limit for guests was also stated by the Final Messenger Muhammed ﷺ.

i  A Muslim must not deceive; there is a *hadîth sherîf* that means: "he who deceives, is not one of us." So the *lonja* organisation was very keen on the quality of production and securing the rights of consumers. That the master of the *lonja* was a *sûfî shaykh* was itself a guarantee of straightforwardness and trustworthiness.

## Osmanlı History and Institutions

### 8.1 Beytu'l Mâl

In Osmanlı practice the Beytu'l Mâl (Public Treasury) was called *Khaziyne-i Âmire*. The high official who was responsible for finance of the Devlet was the *defterdâr*. He was a member of the *Dîvân-ı Hümâyûn*. The Osmanlı central administration kept registers carefully and so detailed that they knew how many people lived in which village and what they owned in terms of animals and other possessions.

Over time, as the domain of the Osmanlı Devlet expanded and fiscal affairs overburdened one department, they appointed two other *defterdârs*: one for Rumeli (the European part of the Osmanlı domain) and one for Anatolia (the Asian part of the Osmanlı domain) with the titles Rumeli Defterdârı and Anadolu Defterdârı, respectively, and they were called the Second and Third Defterdârs, the chief *defterdâr* being called *Bash Defterdâr*.[989] This institution was abolished after 1826.

### 8.2 Zakât

In implementing *Sharî'at*, the Sacred Islamic Law, the Osmanlı Devlet pursued economic affairs according to the Qur'ân and *Sunnah* (practice of the Final Messenger ﷺ). The economic policy of Islam is explained in the Qur'ân: "... *so that this (wealth) may not circulate solely among the rich from among you.*"[990] Islam tolerates the rich but imposes heavier obligations on them: they have to pay taxes to help the poor and are prevented from practising immoral means of exploitation, hoarding, and the accumulation of wealth.[991]

Being the Islamic political entity, the Osmanlı Devlet collected *zakât* from the Muslims and *jizyah* from the non-Muslims in its domains. Since Islam encompasses all aspects and activities of human life, provides for the well-being of humans in this world and

*II – Economic Institutions*

in the hereafter as well, *zakât*, the main means of financial solidarity and social harmony and security, is significantly mentioned in the Qur'ân in many places together with *salât* (prayer): *"Establish (the performance of) the salât (prayer) and give zakât …"*[992] *Zakât* was collected by the Devlet and was spent on specific people as mentioned in the Qur'ân.

*Zakât* has two main meanings:

a) cleanliness, purity;

b) increase.[993]

When a Muslim pays *zakât* on his wealth, he purifies it from the right of the Creator and other Muslims and his wealth increases just as a pruned plant does. Undoubtedly, the best way to understand and evaluate any social institution is juxtaposition; in this special case, observing other societies that do not have an institution such as *zakât*. The last three centuries or more in world history have been dominated by Western powers. Since their background is a distorted belief (Christianity being a distorted form of what the Prophet Jesus had taught), those societies lack socio-economic institutions. Because they do not have *Sharî'at*, they produced and succumbed to either a liberal-capitalist economic system or a totalitarian-socialist one. The latter has proved, after a bitter experiment on a large section of humankind, insufficient, and major socialist countries are now in the process of getting rid of it.[i] The former is still prevalent, but it is very difficult to claim that the liberal-capitalist system has brought satisfaction and happiness to the "majority" of the people: it is bound to collapse in the long run because it depends on exploitation, a fact that has given rise to socialism as a reaction.

---

i   Since the author wrote this book, communism has made a major comeback with the appearance of China as a world power. Ed.

## 8.3 'Ushr

*'Ushr* means one-tenth (its plural: *a'shâr*). The Osmanlı Devlet collected this tax from Muslims in its domain. The amount that was collected was one-tenth of the crops produced. This amount was, in the case of grain, produced only by rain or spring water. If human effort and watering was involved, then the ratio was one-twentieth.

## 8.4 *Jizyah*

Non-Muslims were exempt from military service and paid *jizyah* instead. It was paid by able-bodied non-Muslims; the poor, women, children, priests, monks, hermits, and elderly were exempt. *Jizyah* was practised by other Muslim political entities before the Osmanlı Devlet, which had modelled its structure on the Anatolian Selçuklu Devlet, which in turn, had followed the example of previous Islamic communities.

*Jizyah* is mentioned in the Holy Qur'ân:[994] "*Fight those who do not believe in Allah nor the Last Day, nor hold that forbidden which has been forbidden by Allah and His Messenger, nor acknowledge the Religion of Truth, from among the People of the Book, until they pay jizyah with willing submission, and feel themselves subdued.*" And the Final Messenger Muhammed ﷺ took *jizyah* from the bishop of 'Aqabe (Eyle) during the *jihâd* campaign to Tabûk in 9/630.[995]

In Osmanlı practice, in addition to the poor, females, children, elderly, religious officials, clergy, those families who were employed as functionaries by the Devlet and people of some islands and important places were exempted from *jizyah*.

*Jizyah* had three levels: *a'la* (for the rich), *awsat* (for the middle class), and *adnâ* (for the poor). The *jizyah* papers were sent to towns. Those papers were distributed to the relevant people in Muharram (the first Islamic Lunar Month of the year). Apart from this time, *jizyah* was not collected.[996]

Non-Muslims in the Osmanlı Devlet enjoyed full rights as *ra'iyyet* by paying *jizyah*. When a non-Muslim man converted to Islam, *jizyah* was automatically cancelled, and women were already exempt. It has nothing to do with poll-tax.

*Jizyah* was a sort of tax that was paid by non-Muslim, able-bodied males; it was, undoubtedly, an indirect encouragement to embrace Islam. A *dhimmî*'s life, honour, and property were protected by the Islamic *devlet*, and the *dhimmî* enjoyed full freedom of religion. He was not oppressed, but he must certainly have felt a sense of inferiority. There were no regulations hindering anyone who wanted to become a Muslim, submitting themselves to the will of the Creator, thus being in harmony with the universe as well as with themselves and being able to attain one of the most important posts in the Osmanlı Devlet.

## 8.5 *Kharâj*

Non-Muslims paid *kharâj* to the Osmanlı Devlet whereas Muslims paid *'ushr*. The land classified as land of *kharâj* had to pay more than the land that was accepted as land of *'ushr*. *Kharâj* was one of the main revenues of the Osmanlı Devlet.

Non-Muslims were happy under Islamic Osmanlı administration because the Osmanlıs treated them well, did not interfere with their beliefs and religious practices – in dramatic contrast with the European-Christian practice toward non-Christians. Osmanlıs eased non-Muslims' living conditions as well. For example, the regulations of Stephan Dushan, the Serbian King, required a Christian villager to work for his lord two days a week, i.e. 104 days a year, without payment. The same villager worked only three days a year for the Osmanlı *sipâhî*, the local authority. It was an Osmanlı essential principle to prevent usurpation of the villagers by local chieftains.[997]

### 8.6 Ganâ'im, Fay

Ganâ'im formed a substantial part of revenue for the Osmanlı *Beytu'l Mâl* (public treasury), together with tributes received from European countries such as the Roman Empire, Nemsa (Austria), Venice, Raguza (Dubrovnik), Eflak, Poland, and Russia. The last two countries, however, paid to the khânate of Qırım (Crimea) mainly, which was part of the Osmanlı Khalifate.

Representing the final phase of the Heavenly Message, Islam, Osmanlı society was in a position to implement the Heavenly Commands, *Sharî'at*, and in line with the Heavenly Statement أَنَّ ٱلْأَرْضَ يَرِثُهَا عِبَادِيَ ٱلصَّٰلِحُونَ – "*My righteous servants will inherit the earth.*"[998] Indeed, the Osmanlı Devlet perceived itself as responsible for the order of the world (*Nizâm-ı Âlem*) and did not hesitate to protect the Republic of Raguza (Dubrovnik) in the fifteenth century when it sought Osmanlı protection against their Christian neighbour, the Republic of Venice, which was one of the strongest empires of the world at that time. The Republic of Raguza voluntarily gave the Osmanlı Devlet a piece of land, a walking distance of one and a half hour in width on its border with the Republic of Venice, thus inserting Osmanlı territory between itself and Venice and securing its territory and even its existence. One of the lines started from the port of Klek, the other from the port of Storina, and both joined at Croatia, thus creating an Osmanlı territory between the Republics of Raguza and Venice. So they lived safe and secure under Osmanlı protection for more than 400 years. The Republic of Raguza paid the Osmanlı Devlet 75,000 *gurush* every three years as tribute. It was not the Osmanlıs but Napoleon Bonaparte who invaded that republic in 1215/1800.[999]

It was not only military power that the Osmanlıs relied on. In the fourteenth, fifteenth, and sixteenth centuries, they were the protectors of justice and order. Juxtaposition is the best way to

## II – Economic Institutions

understand, appreciate, and evaluate events. In the fifteenth century the Christian people of the Republic of Raguza themselves offered to shelter under Muslim Osmanlı protection, voluntarily giving them territory and paying them tribute. In the twentieth century, in the same region, the Muslim population of Bosnia suffered for years because of the games of Western powers.

As for spending the revenue obtained from *ganâ'im* (booty), the Osmanlı Devlet followed the Noble Qur'ân, which states: *"And know that out of all the booty that you may acquire (in war), a fifth is assigned to Allah, and to the Messenger, and to near relatives, orphans, the needy, and the wayfarer."*[1000] Therefore, the rule is that a share of one fifth is set aside for the leader of the Muslim Devlet. This one fifth was for the expenditure of the Devlet, which was a tool to implement the Heavenly Commands. The *mujâhids* who actually participated in *jihad* could share four-fifths.

# III – The Legal System

In dealing with the legal system, it is necessary to understand the worldview of Islam. The very word "Islam" means "submission," and "obedience." Therefore, a Muslim is one who submits himself to and obeys the commands of the Creator of the Universe. In this sense, the sun, the moon, all heavenly bodies, water, the soil are all Muslims, i.e. they obey natural laws that have been ordained by the Creator for them to obey. What science calls "physical laws" Islam calls *Sunnatullâh* (Allah's way of governing the universe). It is very significant that in the Qur'ân the human being is ordered to be "just" in "measuring," immediately after mention is made of the sun and the moon being followers of precisely calculated courses, the sky being raised high, and the Creator as the one who has set the balance: "*The sun and the moon follow computed courses. And the herbs and the trees bow in adoration. And the firmament has He raised high, and He has set up the balance (of justice), in order that you may not transgress (due) balance. So, establish weight with justice and do not fall short in the balance.*"[1001]

The most beautiful names belong to Allah, the Creator. One of His names is Haqq.[1002] There is no single word in Western languages that corresponds to this word and concept. The concept of *haqq* is a central topic in Islamic thought and practice, and has several meanings such as "right," "due," "share," "just," "true," and "real," ….. Therefore, all of the legal system in Islamic civilisation is devised to be in line, to comply with, and implement this issue of *haqq*. In Islam human life is conceived as a whole: this worldly life is called *al-hayâtu'd dunyâ* (the nearer life), and the hereafter is called *al-hayâtu'l âkhirah* (the latter, everlasting life). In other words, human life does not terminate with death; the worldly life is a stage of testing and preparation for the hereafter. Consequently, if someone wrongs another and justice is not implemented properly, the wronged one will receive justice from the wrongdoer in the hereafter if the former does not forgive the latter. And, to carry out justice properly in this life, there are conditions for being qualified as a witness, such as not having consumed alcohol, carrying out daily prayers, complying with moral values, etc. It was not exceptional that the *qâdi* of Bursa, Molla Fenârî, refused the fourth Osmanlı sovereign, Yıldırım Bâyezîd, as a witness in the court, on the grounds that the victor of Nicopolis (1396) sometimes neglected not prayers (for a Muslim may pray privately, whereas participation in the service is highly encouraged) but the *jamâ'at* (the meeting of believers in the mosque). The Sultân then built a mosque near his palace in order to be able to attend *jamâ'at*.[1003]

In the Osmanlı administration all of the legal system was set up to secure the well-being of the people. The governed people, regardless of race, religion, colour, and language, were called *ra'âyâ* (singular: *ra'iyyat*). *Ra'iyyat* literally means those who are looked after, cared for. From the very beginning the Osmanlı administration had been very careful about *haqq* and the *ra'iyyat* and its right as *amânah ilâhiyyah* (heavenly, religious responsibility)[1004] (*ri'âyat-i huqûq-ı ra'âyâ*).

## 9. *QAZÂ'* (JUSTICE)

The Osmanlı administration was sensitive about maintaining justice in Osmanlı domains. From the beginning they appointed knowledgeable, trustworthy and well-educated scholars as *qâdis*.

The first Osmanlı *qâdi* was Tursun Faqîh, another son-in-law of Shaykh Edebalı. The *qâdi* was responsible not only for maintaining justice, acting as public prosecutor as well, but for security and educational institutions of his area as well as the administration of *waqfs*. He had been given such an immense authority that:

"The medieval Muslim Qâzi cuts a miserable figure beside his Ottoman colleague. Appointed by and answerable to the central authorities, he was compelled to abandon to them important fields of jurisdiction, and he was wholly dependent on their rather dubious co-operation for the execution and enforcement of his judgements. The Ottoman Qâzi, on the other hand, *was* the central authority in the area of his jurisdiction, which in the Ottoman system of provincial administration was known, significantly, as a *qazâ* – the area administrated by a Qâzi, as a *vilâyat* was governed by a Vâli. Moreover, he was one of a proud and powerful hierarchy of judicial and theological authorities, who were ready to support him in any clash with the military and political institutions, and presided over by the *Shaykhülislâm* (or Chief Mufti) and the two Qâdıaskers in the capital, so great and revered, that the Sultân himself rose to his feet to receive them when they came to offer him their greetings at the Bayram festival."[1005] To keep the *qâdi* above society and to protect his standing from being impugned, there were strict rules: a *qâdi* was prohibited from engaging in commercial activities, from lending money or borrowing, from receiving presents or gifts, from accepting dinner invitations, etc. In addition, a *qâdi* could not hold his office for more than twenty months. In the case of higher offices, the duration was limited to one year. This measure was implemented to prevent them from becoming too intimate with people, which could affect their judgement during a case if those people were involved. On the other hand, following Islamic practice, a *qâdi* would be regarded as removed from his post after that period, and would wait for another post, going to İstanbul; during that waiting time he would refresh his knowledge and improve his learning.

The *Khalîfah* was in a position to accept the verdict of a *qâdi*. Having a very well-established and stable society, the Osmanlı administration appointed *qâdis* who had graduated from top-level *madrasah*s (universities). Since the common *madhhab* was *hanefî*, *qâdis* judged according to their *madhhab*. The *shâfi'î*-populated areas had *shâfi'î qâdis* and they judged according to that *madhhab*. In North Africa there were *hanefî* and *mâlikî qâdis*.

In the Osmanlı Devlet it was possible for an individual with certain abilities to become *sadrâzam*, even if he did not have a proper education. But it was absolutely impossible for anyone to become a *qâdi* even for a small town if he had not been qualified through a *madrasah* education.

## THE NAQIYBU'L ASHRÂF

Descendants of the Final Messenger Muhammed ﷺ came down through his daughter Fâtima ؉ and her two sons: Hasan and Huseyn ؉. Those who are descendants of Hasan ؉ are called *shurafâ'* or *ashrâf* (plural of *Sharîf*) and those who are descendants of Huseyn ؉ are called *sâdât* (plural of *Sayyid*). These titles were used under the Abbâsîs beginning in the fourth/tenth century and continued in other Muslim polities. They wore green turbans and green *jubbah* during Hârûn Rashîd's era. The Turkish Mamlûk Sultân of Egypt Ashraf Sha'bân revived this custom in 773/1371 by ordering *Sayyids* and *Sharîfs* to wear green turbans. The women in this group also wore something green on their heads.

When the Osmanlı Devlet assumed leadership of the Muslims, *Sayyids* and *Sharîfs* also came to their domain. Osmanlı sultâns respected them very much. Yıldırım Bâyezîd (1389-1402) appointed Sayyid Ali Natta' b. Muhammed as their chief in Ramadân 802/ May 1400. During Sultân Bâyezîd II's time (1481-1512), Sayyid Mahmûd was appointed chief of this honourable group in 900/1494 with the title *naqiybu'l ashrâf*. The post of *naqiybu'l ashrâf* continued until the end of the Osmanlı Devlet.

*Sayyids* and *Sharîfs* were exempt from taxes in the Osmanlı Devlet. *Naqiybu'l ashrâf* was paid a salary from Beytu'l Mâl. When the new Sultân-Khalîfah was installed, the *naqiybu'l ashrâf* was to carry out *bayʻat* (swearing allegiance) first, and then the other notables followed suit. He was the first to congratulate the Sultân on the occasions of Bayram (*ʻiyd*). When *naqiybu'l ashrâf* went on *jihâd* together with the Sultân, he would be under *Sanjaq-ı Sharîf* (The Honourable banner of the Final Messenger Muhammed, ﷺ). *Sayyids* and *Sharîfs* would recite *tekbîr* and *salavât* when the *Sanjaq-ı Sharîf* was taken out of its quarter in the Topkapusu Palace, and they would recite *tekbîr* and *salavât* under the *Sanjaq-ı Sharîf* during the *jihâd*.

If any of them committed any wrong, they would be taken not to the *qâdi* but to the *naqiybu'l ashrâf* in İstanbul or to his *qaymaqam* (representative, who was also a *sayyid*) in the provinces and would be judged and imprisoned by him.[1006]

### 9.1 The Sheyhülislâm

The title *sheyhülislâm* came into use in the second half of the fourth century A.H./tenth century C.E. and was given to those erudite scholars who were able to deliberate about the judicial problems discussed among the *fuqahâ*. Being "the" Muslim political superpower, the Osmanlı Devlet institutionalised the post of *sheyhülislâm*. This post gained tremendous importance such as no other Muslim political entity had ever seen.[1007]

Since the Khalîfah-Sultân (the *mashrû'*/legal imam) was the vicegerent of Allah on earth and responsible only to Him, and obliged to act in accordance with the Qur'ân and Sunnah, if he neglected this course of action he would lose his right to be obeyed. His authority is limited to the framework of *Sharîʻat*,[1008] and therefore it was imperative for him to appoint an erudite scholar to consult in *Devlet* affairs that had to conform to the *Sharîʻat*.

In the Osmanlı administration, the *sheyhülislâm* was equal to the *sadrâzam*. In every important matter the Devlet needed to obtain a *fetvâ* from the *sheyhülislâm*. In other words, the *sheyhülislâm* was the top official for issuing legal opinions about important affairs of the Osmanlı Devlet. Even the deposition of the Osmanlı sultân was possible only through his *fetvâ*.

The *sheyhülislâm* was the head of the judicial system as well as education and *awqâf* (pious foundations) in the whole Osmanlı Domain. In 962/1574 Sheyhulislâm Ebussu'ûd Efendi began to appoint *muderrises* (professors in *madrasahs*), *qâdis* and *muftis* of towns and cities, imams and *muezzins* of mosques.[1009] In the course of time the *sheyhülislâm* also appointed a *qâdıasker* after consulting the *sadrâzam* on the matter.[1010]

The *sadrâzam* visited the *sheyhülislâm* in 992/1584 and this action became a regulation afterwards. The *sheyhülislâm* visited the *sadrâzam* only on the occasion of latter's appointment. The *sadrâzam* would go to the *iftâr* (having dinner at the end of fasting day) given by the *sheyhülislâm* on the invitation of the latter.[1011]

At times the *sheyhülislâm* would go on *jihâd* together with the Sultân-Khalîfah, beginning at the end of the sixteenth century and during the seventeenth century. During a *jihâd* campaign, it was customary to place three *tuğs* (banners mounted with horsetails) in front of the *sheyhülislâm*'s tent – the same number of *tuğs* as in front of the *vazîrs*' tents.[1012]

The *sheyhülislâm* and the *sadrâzam* would carry out *zuhr* prayer on the 15 Ramadân at Ayasofya Mosque, then they would visit the Sultân-Khalîfah, who would, with great ceremony attended by the top officials of the Osmanlı Khalifate, open the cloth case (*bohcha*) of the *Hırqa-i Sharîf* (the Honourable Mantle of the Final Messenger, ﷺ) in the Topkapusu Palace.[1013]

Muhammed Shemsuddîn Fenârî (751-834/1350-1431) was appointed as the first *mufti* (*sheyhülislâm*) in 1424.[1014] He was succeeded in this post by Molla Yegân and Fahreddîn Ajemî.[1015] The most famous Osmanlı *sheyhulislâms* are: Molla Husrev, Molla Gürânî, Ali Jemâlî Efendi (1503-1525), Kemâl Pashazâde (1525-1533), and Ebussuûd Efendi (1545-1574).

After attempts at Westernisation, the post of the *sheyhülislâm* began to lose its importance. In 1839 an organisation called the Consultative Council (*Shurâ-yı Devlet*) was established, thus diminishing the importance of this post. When the Ministry of Justice (*Adliye Nezâreti*) was established in 1879, it entailed another move to curb the jurisdiction of the *sheyhülislâm*.[i] The *sheyhülislâm*, however, continued to be a member of the Osmanlı government until the end of this socio-political entity in 1922.

The *sheyhülislâm*'s position is better understood if shown in a table:

## SULTÂN-KHALÎFAH[II]

| *Sadrâzam* | *Sheyhülislâm* (Mufti of İstanbul) |
|---|---|
| Temporal Administration | Religion / Law |
| Scribal, military | education, *awqâf* |
| *Kâhyâ Beğ* | Naqiybu'l ashrâf |
| Minister of War and the Interior | Inspectors |
| *Reîsul Kuttâb* (Minister of Foreign Affairs) | *Qudât* (Judges) |
| *Chavush Bashı* (Minister of Police)[iii] | *Nuvvâb* |

i J.H. Kramers, *op. cit.*, p. 488. The Osmanlı sovereigns had been *real khalîfah*s since Murâd I (1362-1389). His son Bâyezîd (1389-1402) was "the" leader of the Muslim domains, who defeated combined Crusader armies at Nicopolis in 1396. Fâtih Mehemmed (1451-1481) was *khalîfah* as mentioned by Kemâl Pashazâde (*Tevarih-i Âl-i Osman* VII, p. 194, 296), i.e. even before Sultân Selîm (1512-1520)'s taking over the "symbolic" 'Abbâsî khalifate when he defeated the Mamlûks. But the Osmanlıs put emphasis on the titles of *sultân*, *pâdishâh*, and *khâqân*, which indicated "actual" and "real" power.

ii The Osmanlı sultâns were actual and legal *khalîfah*s.

iii Summarised with modification from Stanley Poole, *Turkey* (London , 1966), p. 324.

## 9.2 The Qâdıasker (Qazasker)

In Osmanlı practice the chief *qâdi* (*qâdilqudât*) was called *qâdıasker* (military judge). But he was not only a military judge; he also appointed *qâdis* and was responsible for all judicial and educational institutions under his jurisdiction.

When the Osmanlıs needed a post for administering the judicial affairs of the numerous soldiers and the Muslim population who inhabited large areas, they created the post of *qâdıasker* around the year 1360 when Jendereli Kara Halîl, the *qâdi* of Bursa, was appointed *qâdıasker*.[1016]

Over time the Osmanlı Devlet had two *qâdiaskers*: one for Rumelia (the European part of the Osmanlı Devlet), and one for Anatolia (the Asian part of the Osmanlı Devlet). The *qâdiaskers* were members of the *Dîvân-ı Hümâyûn*. Their duty encompassed appointing *qâdis* and *muderrises* in their region.

At the same time they acted as judges of the high court. Unless otherwise authorised or ordered, the *qâdi(qâzi)asker* of Rumelia acted as a judge. Because the Osmanlı Devlet expanded in the direction of *dârulharb*, Europe, the *qâdiaskers* and *beğlerbeğis* of Rumelia had priority in the administration and ceremonies over their counterparts, who were responsible for Asian part.

When eastern and south-eastern Anatolia were annexed by Sultân Selîm (1512-1520) in 922/1516, a third *qâdıasker* was installed in Diyarbakır for the Arab and *Ajem* (Persian) areas. When Bilâdush Shâm (what is now called Syria) and Egypt were annexed, the jurisdiction area of this third *qâdıasker* was widened and his seat was shifted to the capital. Later, this post was abolished and its area of jurisdiction merged with that of the *qâdıasker* of Anatolia. The post of the *qâdıasker* continued to exist until the end of the Osmanlı Devlet.[1017]

The *qâdıasker* was appointed from among the experienced *qâdis* holding high posts. His tenure was for one year.[1018] *Qâdiaskers* were

## Osmanli History and Institutions

members of the *sadrâzam*'s *dîvân* as well. *Vazîrs* in this *dîvân* would sit on the right side of the *sadrâzam*, while the *qâdiaskers* would sit on his left.[1019]

The *qâdiaskers* themselves would hold a *dîvân* everyday except Tuesday and Wednesday and would pass judgement in their jurisdiction.[1020]

The *qâdıasker* was the head of a vast organisation, and he had many helpers and functionaries. The most important of them was the military *qassâm*, who represented him in the provinces with full authority. Others were *tezkireji, berât kâtibi, ahkâm kâtibi, muhzir, muhâsebeji*.[1021]

### 9.3 The İhtisab Ağası

*İhtisab* means "devotion," "action to please the Creator, not expecting any rewards from creatures." This institution is exclusively an Islamic one, taking its roots from the Islamic principle of *al-Amr bi'l Ma'rûf wa'n Nahy 'ani'l Munkar* (enjoining that which is good and forbidding, preventing what is evil). Unlike individuality or socialism, which put the emphasis on the individual and society respectively, Islam strikes a nice balance between emphasis on the individual and society. On the one hand, each person is accountable for himself; on the other hand, there is a pronounced social responsibility in Islam: وَٱتَّقُوا۟ فِتْنَةً لَّا تُصِيبَنَّ ٱلَّذِينَ ظَلَمُوا۟ مِنكُمْ خَاصَّةً "*Fear the trial that affects not only those of you who do wrong* ...."[1022] Therefore, maintaining justice in every walk of life was the central point in the Osmanlı administration.

Every civilisation produces its own type of human being, and that type of human being, in turn, contributes to his society and civilisation. Islam envisages believers as responsible, caring, aware of their accountability as the Last Messenger ﷺ states: "Anyone of you who sees an evil, let him change (prevent) that evil with his hand; if not able, then with his tongue (advising the wrongdoer); if he is not able to do so, then let him be angry in his heart; and this is the weakest category of faith."[1023] Islam does not produce people with the mindset: "It's none of my business." Each and every Muslim is supposed to follow this very natural course of consciousness.

As an organised society, this aspect of responsibility was embodied in the institution of *ihtisâb*. The well-educated person who fulfilled this position was called *ihtisâb ağası* (master of the *ihtisâb*) in Osmanlı practice. Because he was an important official, an *ihtisâb ağasi* had to possess certain qualifications. First of all, he had to be a Muslim. Since he carried out duties derived from the Qur'ân, it would have been a flagrant contradiction to assign those duties to someone who does not accept the Eternal Message, Islam. He had to be a male adult, with his main concern to seek the pleasure of Allah ﷻ. Piety, good behaviour, being upright, having a strong character, a sound knowledge of *Sharî'at* as well as of general culture, and the power to implement and enforce his verdict were the other conditions for being appointed *muhtesib* (*ihtisâb ağasi*).[1024] In principle, he was appointed for one year, but sometimes his tenure reached three or four years.[1025]

The *ihtisâb ağasi* had assistants who helped him in implementing his verdicts. They also had good qualities. If any of them committed any fault, he would immediately be dismissed. The *ihtisâb ağasi* (*muhtesib*) would travel around the town, stopping whatever evil he encountered. His authority and responsibility included seeing to it that imams recited the Qur'ân correctly, without distorting the pronunciation of the *âyat*s for the sake of musical harmony, checking the measures and balances in the market, checking the quality of goods and prices, preventing people from obstructing pedestrians by putting loads on the pavements, preventing builders from narrowing the roads by transgressing the limits, preventing people from overburdening animals, checking public baths, providing for enough stock of foodstuff for the town, issuing permission to open shops, etc. The *ihtisâb ağasi* arranged for *jum'ah* prayers to be held wherever there were forty male Muslims since this is the number needed for the *jum'ah* prayer, according to the Hanefî view. He had the authority to interfere with any action that was not in line with Islamic values. He received his authority from the *qâdis*.

One of the duties of the *muhtesib* was to collect tax from the market. It began as early as Osmân Gâzi's time.[1026] We know that Fâtih Mehemmed (1451-1481) arranged the duties and responsibilities of the *muhtesib*. During Sultân Mahmûd II (1808-1839)'s time, in 1242/1826, this institution became a ministry (*ihtisâb nezâreti*) and the *muhtesib* was called the Minister of İhtisâb (*İhtisâb Nâzırı*). When the police organisation was founded in 1261/1845 and the *zaptiye müshiriyyeti* in 1262/1846, some of the duties of the *ihtisâb nâziri* were transferred to them, and the *ihtisâb nâziri* remained responsible for commercial activities and setting prices (*narh*). It was abolished in 1271/1854 when the *shehremâneti* (municipality) of İstanbul was founded.[1027]

# IV – Military Organisation

## 10. THE ARMY

Being founded on the concept of and devotion to the principle of *"İ'lâ-yi Kelimeti'llâh"* (to uphold the commands of Allah), the Osmanlı Devlet was in need of a strong army. Since the beginning of the Osmanlı Devlet great emphasis was placed on having a standing army, and they initiated and developed a fantastic system for having a strong and very well-organised army without putting a great financial burden on the *Beytü'l mâl*, the Central Treasury. They had a central army and a much larger provincial army; together these armies comprised the *Ordu-yu Hümâyûn* (Heavenly Army).

*Hümâ* is a mythical bird that was said to live always in the sky, and *hümâyûn* means pertaining to *hümâ*, heavenly. As bearers of the Final Heavenly Message, Islam, the Osmanlıs named every important institution and object of theirs *hümâyûn*:

*Dîvân-ı Hümâyûn* (the Heavenly Divan);
*Donanmayı Hümâyûn* (the Heavenly Navy);
*Khatt-ı Hümâyûn* (the Handwriting of the Khalîfah-Sultân);
*Mühr-i Hümâyûn* (the Seal of the Sultân);
*Otâğ-ı Hümâyûn* (the Khalîfah-Sultân's tent pitched during *jihâd*);
*Bâb-ı Hümâyûn* (the First Gate of the Khalîfah-Sultân's residence: Topqapı Palace.

Needless to say, the nomenclatures are *not* and ought *not* to be translated as "imperial," and to speak of, for example, the *Dîvân-I Hümâyûn* as the "Imperial Council" is no doubt a great distortion. The Osmanlı Devlet was *not* an imperialistic power; it was founded on the basis and principle of *jihâd*: spreading Islam, upholding the Creator's Heavenly Commandments.

During the course of time, the *Ordu-yu Hümâyûn* (the Heavenly Army) consisted of several elements:

| CENTRAL ARMY (Qapuqulu Askerleri) | | PROVINCIAL ARMY (Eyâlet Askerleri) | |
|---|---|---|---|
| Infantry | Cavalry | Yerli Qulu | Serhad Qulu |
| (Qapuqulu Piyâdesi) | | Yaya | Tımarlı Suvâriler |
| 1. *Yenicheri* | 1. *Sipâhi* | 1. *Azeb* | 1. *Aqınjı* |
| 2. Jebeji | 2. Silâhdar | 2. Sekbân | 2. Deli |
| 3. Topchu | 3. Sağ Ulûfeji | 3. İjâreli | 3. Gönüllü |
| 4. Humbarajı | 4. Sol Ulûfeji | 4. Lağımjı | 4. Beşli |
| 5. Lağımjı | 5. Sağ Garibler | 5. Müsellem | |
| 6. Sol Garibler | | | |

The terms in the table are explained in the paragraphs below.

### 10.1 The Central Army (Qapuqulu Askerleri)

The Osmanlı troops were initially cavalrymen. Every able-bodied man was supposed to be a *gâzi* (warrior in *jihâd*). After skirmishes the *gâzis* would return to their villages, to raising herds and cultivating their lands. They were administered according to the *iqtâ'* system.[1028]

Orhân Gâzi (1326-1362) initially founded the regular Osmanlı army, composed of Turkish youth: infantry troops were called *yaya*,[1029] consisting of 1000 *mujâhids*, and cavalry units were called *müsellem* (which means exempt from taxes). *Yayas* had one leader for every ten soldiers, and a *yüzbashı* for one hundred. Thirty *müsellems* were seen

## IV – Military Organisation

as one *ojak* (unit). *Yaya* and *müsellem* troops rendered great services until the middle of the fifteenth century C.E. The *yaya* of the Osmanlı Devlet wore a white *börk* (headgear made of felt) to distinguish them from soldiers from other Turkish emirates in Anatolia.

On the other hand, the boundaries of the Osmanlı Devlet expanded greatly during the time of Orhân Gâzi and his son Murâd Khân. The spacious lands that were opened to Islam were inhabited mostly by Christians. Thus there was a need to increase the Muslim population in these newly acquired lands. On the advice of a scholar, Qara Rüstem, they initiated taking one captive out of five as share of the Devlet in accordance with *Sharî'at* Law: وَٱعۡلَمُوٓا۟ أَنَّمَا غَنِمۡتُم مِّن شَىۡءٍ فَأَنَّ لِلَّهِ خُمُسَهُۥ وَلِلرَّسُولِ (*al-Qur'ân*, *al-Anfâl* [8], *âyat* 41) in 763/1361.[1030] Captive youths were given to peasants to help them with their work, thus becoming accustomed to hardship, and they adopted the Islamic way of life, learning Turkish. This practice was called *Türke vermek* (giving to Turks). A few years later they were recruited into the army, and called *yenicheri*s (new soldiers). Initially, the captives of the Devlet's share were put to work on the ships that conveyed the cavalry together with their horses from Anatolia to Europe. But some of them escaped. Consequently, the Osmanlı Devlet developed a system called *devshirme* (collection): they collected children and, after their conversion to Islam and learning the Turkish language, they were put into the *ajemi ojaği* and, after having been trained there, they became *yenicheri*s. Youths between ten and twenty years were trained in the *ajemi ojaği*.[1031] Then they were recruited as *yenicheri*s and *sipâhî*s. They were the Sultân's personal slaves, as the word *kapıkulu* indicates: slave of the Porte. They were paid *ulûfe* every three months.

### 10.1.1 The Yenicheri

The *yenicheri* organisation was founded as such in 1362 and took its new form under Murâd I (1362-1389). Their units were called *orta*, its commander was *chorbajı*. The general commander was *Yenicheri Ağası*.[1032] The Osmanlı Sultân was the first *yenicheri*. *Börk* (the headgear made of felt of the *yenicheri*) was originally the headgear of the *akhîs*.

During *jihâd* the *yenicheris* stood in the centre, together with the Sultân. They were very well-trained, excellent soldiers, and rendered great service during the sixteenth and seventeenth centuries. Some *yenicheri* units were stationed in the castles as well.

### 10.1.2 The Jebeji

The duty of the *jebeji* was to provide and maintain the battle equipment of the *yenicheris* – their arrows, bows, rifles, swords, powder, bullets, armour, lances, etc. During a *jihâd* they carried that equipment to the front and distributed it to the *yenicheris* there. After the battle was over, they collected all the equipment and repaired whatever needed repair. They had a depot in İstanbul called *cebehâne* and storehouses in castles and places near the front.[1033]

### 10.1.3 The Topchu

The task of the *topchu* was to manufacture guns and to use artillery on the battlefield. The Osmanlıs used artillery for the first time during the Battle of Kosova in 1389. They used this new weapon at the Battle of Nicopolis (1396) as well.

The Osmanlıs also placed artillery in the castles. It is noteworthy that they used mortars during Fâtih's time (1451-1481).[1034]

Small guns were transported on camels, horses, etc. But when large guns were manufactured, they transported them on carriages.

### 10.1.4 The Humbarajı

This group of soldiers belonged to the administration of the *jebeji* and *topchu*. They made explosives called *humbara*.

Some of their units were not paid salaries but were given *tımar* and

*IV – Military Organisation*

served in castles. Their *tımars* were in the vicinity of the castles they served in.

A French nobleman, Count Bonneval, took refuge in the Osmanlı Devlet in 1142/1729, embraced Islam, and was named Ahmed. He is the famous Humbarajı Ahmed Pasha, who reformed and developed the *humbarajı* units in 1144/1731.[1035]

A *humbara* was a small bomb filled with explosives and launched by mortar. There was another version that was thrown by hand. A *humbara* was thrown by a mortar at targets that were not necessarily seen. These soldiers provided great service when besieging castles and opening them to Islam.

### 10.1.5 The Lağımjı

This group was a highly skilled technical unit. Part of it was placed under the jurisdiction of the head of the *jebejis* and another part owned *tımars*.

The duty of the *lağımjıs* was to dig tunnels underground towards the castles that were being besieged by the *Ordu-yu Hümâyûn*. They dug tunnels underneath the walls of the besieged castles, placing explosives and demolishing the walls and towers. This task necessitated great skill in geometry and engineering.

If the *lağımjı* personnel present in the capital were insufficient, the administration would order *lağımjı* personnel from the provinces to come. For example, Süleymân the Magnificent (1520-1566) ordered *lağımjıs* from some towns to join the *Ordu-yu Hümâyûn* when he went on a *jihâd* campaign to Sigetvar in 1566.

The *lağımjı* units played a major role in 1078/1667 in the opening of Kandiye castle on Girit (Crete), which was very well fortified.[1036]

The *Lağımjıs* repaired bridges along the way for the *Ordu-yu Hümâyûn* and built new bridges when necessary.

### 10.1.6 The Qapuqulu Süvârisi

The *qapuqulu süvârisi* (cavalry) consisted of six *bölüks* (units). The first two *bölüks* were called *sipâh* and *silahdâr* and had been founded during Sultân Murâd's (1362-1389) time. The other four units were added later.

The *qapuqulu süvârisi* were also personal slaves and attendants of the Sultân. They were cavalry and were better paid than *yenicheries*. *Süvâris* were chosen by the *Yenicheri Ağası* from the senior *yenicheries* who provided good service. Some *devshirme* youths were educated in the Palace University called *Enderûn*, becoming high officials, commanders, *vazîrs*, and *sadrâzam*. Also some were recruited as *qapuqulu süvârisi* from the staff of *Enderûn*. They were well educated and were extremely skilful in riding and fighting on horseback.[1037]

All the *qapuqulu* soldiers, infantry, and cavalry units were disbanded in 1826.

### 10.2 Provincial Army (The Eyâlet Askerleri)

These were soldiers in the *eyâlets* and *sanjaqs*. They comprised the majority of the *Ordu-yu Hümâyûn* and were maintained by *tımar* and *ze'âmet* holders.

### 10.2.1 The Yerli Qulu

They were regular military personnel who were paid salaries, and were soldiers of the *pashas* of *eyâlets* and *sanjaqbeğis*.

10.2.1.1 The Azeb

The origin of this word is the Arabic *a'zeb* (bachelor, unmarried). These soldiers were of Turkish descent in Anatolia. They functioned as an advance guard in front of the *Ordu-yu Hümâyûn*. They were unmarried young men, selected on the basis of one from twenty to thirty five houses in the towns, according to need. The *azebs* were disbanded during Süleymân the Magnificent's time.

*IV – Military Organisation*

On the other hand, there were *azebs* in the castles; this group was initiated by Fâtih and abolished in 1826.

### 10.2.1.2 The Sekbân and Tüfenkji

The *sekbâns* were volunteers collected from villages when need arose. They used swords and rifles. Over time, a group called *tüfenkji* replaced them. The latter were also volunteers.

### 10.2.1.3 The İjâreli

These were artillery personnel. They lived in the castles and towns on the border. Because they were paid *ujret* (Arabic: *ujrat* – a fee), they were called *ijâreli*. Their commander was called *topchu ağası*.

### 10.2.1.4 The Lağımjı

They lived in the castles on the boundaries. Their duty was to counteract the enemy's attempts to dig tunnels and trenches. Their commander was appointed from İstanbul and was called *lağımjıbashı*. When the *lağımjıs* met the enemy in tunnels underground, fierce clashes took place.

### 10.2.1.5 The Müsellem

They were not combat troops. Their duty was to even out the roads that the *Ordu-yu Hümâyûn* would travel on, and to repair bridges along the road of the army, etc. They were exempted from taxes, and hence were called *müsellem*. In the European part of Osmanlı Devlet, Christian people were employed as *müsellem*.

## 10.2.2 The Serhad Qulu

The most important part of these *mujâhids* were the *aqınjı ojağı*.

### 10.2.2.1 The Aqınjıs (Raiders)

These *mujâhids* were light cavalry-commando units composed of

Turks. Their leader was called the *Aqınjı Beği*, and he was directly responsible to İstanbul; the *pasha* of an Eyâlet had no jurisdiction over him. He had complete freedom to choose his volunteer soldiers; nobody could interfere with his recruitment. The *aqınjıs* were named after their *beğs*, of whom the most famous were the *Evrenos Beğ oğulları* (sons of Evrenos Beğ), the *Mihaloğulları* (sons of Mihâl Gâzi) and the *Malqochoğulları* (sons of Malqoch Beğ). An *aqınjı beğ* was fluent in up to ten local languages in his area of operation. They were robust, extremely brave, very well-trained *mujâhid* commandos. Some of them were *tımarlı* (given the right to collect *'ushr* from a certain area), and some were exempt from taxes. An *aqınjı beğ* commanded 30,000 to 50,000 *aqınjıs*. Mihaloğlu Mehmed Beğ had more than 50,000 *aqınjıs* during the *jihâd* campaigns in Germany in 1530 and 1532.

*Aqınjıs* preceded the *Ordu-yu Hümâyûn* by several days. When they entered the enemy's territory in Europe, they divided into small groups, and subdivided into smaller groups, like the branches of a tree. Consequently, 20 to 30 *aqınjı* entered each enemy village, and greater numbers entered the towns of the enemy in border areas, and even beyond. The result was an almost complete demoralisation of the enemy. For example, the *Aqınjıs* raided "as far afield as Motting (1408) in the extreme north-west."[1038] In the sixteenth century C.E. no village in central Europe could be sure that it would not be raided by *aqınjıs* at night. In Poland, they still preserve a tower on which a guard was killed by an *aqınjı's* arrow. The *aqınjıs* suffered a great loss in 1595 when Sinân Pasha ordered the collection of a tax on *ganîmet* on a bridge along the way, thus dividing the whole army into two. When Voyvoda Mihail of Eflak (today's southern Romania) was raided, most of the *aqınjıs* were guarding the rear of the army and were martyred. They were still important to some extent in the first half of the seventeenth century C.E. Later, the excellent horsemen of Qırım (Crimea) were employed instead of them.

## 10.2.2.2 The Deli

The origin of this word is the Arabic *delîl* (guide). They were extremely brave, so they were called *deli* (crazy). They were light cavalry and traditionally it is believed that they were followers of Hazrat Umar b. al-Khattâb's line.

They operated in the European part of the Osmanlı Devlet, their units composed of Turks and Muslim Serbs, Croats, and Bosnians. They wore headgear made of hyena skin and mounted with eagle wings; their trousers (*shalvar*) were made of bearskin or wolfskin – an appearance that filled the enemy with fear right from the start.

They were very effective in the sixteenth century. They were disbanded in 1826.

## 10.2.2.3 The Gönüllü (Volunteer)

These were light cavalry units. They were comprised of the people living on the border in the European part of the Osmanlı Devlet. Their duty was to protect the towns and cities in border areas. They were paid a salary as well. They used rifles and were very useful until the first quarter of the nineteenth century.

## 10.2.2.4 The Beshli

*Besh* means five in Turkish, and *beshli* means pertaining to five. They were recruited on the basis of one soldier from every five houses, hence the name.

They were light cavalry and they participated in raids (*aqıns*) whenever necessary. They were paid salaries.

## **10.2.3 The Tımarlı Süvâri**

From the beginning the Osmanlı administration adopted the Islamic *iqtâ'* system, inheriting it from the Anatolian Selçuks. A commander, a soldier who rendered good service during *jihâd*, was assigned a certain piece of land with a number of villages, even towns on it. He did not possess this piece of land but was given the right to collect the Islamic *'ushr* tax in the name of the Devlet. In return for this revenue, he was to prepare, train, and maintain a certain number of *mujâhids* with full equipment, and be ever ready to participate in *jihâd* whenever called (in practice, every summer). The force that he prepared was called *jebelu*.

Because the majority of the Osmanlı Devlet was subject to that practice, these *mujâhid* soldiers comprised the bulk of the Osmanlı army. They were skilled cavalry and the most important part of *Ordu-yu Hümâyûn* until the end of the sixteenth century C.E.

This *tımar* system was a fantastic institute; when the owner of a *tımar* died or was martyred, his son would inherit the *tımar*. When some of the *mujâhid* soldiers were martyred, there were many waiting for recruitment. As a result, the Osmanlı Devlet had a huge army of *mujâhids* at its disposal, without spending *any* amount from the *Hazîne-i Âmire* (the Public Treasury: *Beytü'l mâl*). And, however long the wars continued, it did not affect the Osmanlı Devlet in terms of manpower; new recruits were available in abundance, to be trained and maintained by the owners of *tımars*.

## 11. THE NAVY

### 11.1 The Central Navy

The Osmanlı Navy was called *Donanma-yı Hümâyûn* (Heavenly Navy). The chief admiral was *qapudân-ı deryâ*. They used ships propelled by oars and by sails. Ships were built in several *tersâne*s. The word *tersâne* (arsenal) was adopted by the Osmanlıs from Western nations such as the Spaniards, the Portuguese, and the Venetians, who used a form of *darsena*, which the Osmanlıs transformed into *tersâne*. *Darsena* comes from the Arabic *Dâru's Sinâ'ah*.[1039] It seems that Europeans adopted *dârus sinâ'a* and pronounced it *darsena*; in

*IV – Military Organisation*

the same way, Jabal Târiq became Gibraltar, al-Vadil Kebîr became Guadalquivir, and al-Kuhûl became alcohol, etc.

The central Osmanlı *tersâne* was in İstanbul and was called *Tersâne-i Âmire*. In addition to İstanbul, they had ship building *tersânes* in Gelibolu, Sinop, Iznikmid (Izmit), Suwaysh, Birecik, Basra, Rusçuk, Samsun, and Kefken.[1040]

The Osmanlı navy became a sizable force during the time of Sultân Murâd II (1421-1451). At that time, the Osmanlı navy put pressure on the Pontus Empire of Trebizond and levied taxes from them.[1041] Before the opening of İstanbul to Islam in 1453, the Osmanlı navy had about 350 ships.[1042] But the golden age of *Donanma-yı Hümâyûn* is the sixteenth century, when three quarters of the Mediterranean was a Muslim Sea under the Osmanlıs. Superiority in the Mediterranean shifted from Christendom to Islam on 28 September 1538, when the crucial battle of Preveza took place. The *Donanma-yı Hümâyûn* under Qapudân-ı Deryâ Hızır Hayreddîn Pasha defeated the combined Christian navy under the famous Admiral Andrea Doria, who was able to save himself only by extinguishing the lights of his flagship and taking refuge in the darkness of the Mediterranean; this action was seen as degrading and dishonourable, even for a captain, let alone a grand admiral.[i]

Osmanlı superiority on the Mediterranean continued until the death of Kılıch Ali Pasha in 995/1587, who was trained by Hızır Hayreddîn Pasha.[1043] Muslim superiority on the Mediterranean was revived by Mezomorta[ii] Huseyin Pasha at the beginning of the eighteenth century.

---

i   It is very interesting to note that this crucial naval battle is either downplayed or never mentioned in the serious "scholarly" books written by Westerners, whereas they elaborate on Lepanto (Inebahtı, 1571), when Europe destroyed the Osmanlı Navy.

ii  This naval *mujâhid* was seriously wounded during a naval *jihâd*; he hovered between life and death for a considerable time, hence this nickname:

Apart from the main navy, the Osmanlıs had river ships on the Tuna (Danube) and the Fırat (Euphrates), called *inje donanma*.[1044]

The *mujâhid* soldiers on central ships were called *azap* (from Arabic *a'zeb*: bachelor). They had their *reîs* (head, chief). The supreme commander of the navy was *qapudân-ı deryâ* (*qaptan pasha*). The rank of *qaptan pasha* was equal to that of *beğlerbeği*, beginning with Hızır Hayreddîn Pasha. Later, the rank of *qaptan pasha* became equal to that of *vazîr*.[1045] Under the *qaptan pasha* there were *sanjaqbeğis* who were called *derya beği*. Each *derya beği* participated in naval *jihâd* with one, two, or three ships, together with the owners of *tımars* in their regions.[1046]

In 1502 Bâyezîd II (1481-1512) initiated the practice of the *Donanma-yı Hümâyûn* setting out on the Mediterranean in the spring of every year, and it became a tradition that continued until the middle of the nineteenth century. Its purpose was to protect the shores of the Muslim Devlet against enemy and pirate assaults. Later, they sent the navy to patrol the Black Sea as well when Russia emerged as a threat.[1047]

The Osmanlı Devlet had a navy in the Indian Ocean as well. Pîrî Reîs (1465-1554) was one of the Osmanlı captains who operated in the Indian Ocean, fighting the Portuguese, then the major Christian naval power. The first known map of America came from Pîrî Reîs, dated 1513, drawn by him at Gelibolu.[1048]

He refers in his map to America as *Vilâyat-i Antilia*. Pîrî Reîs compiled a book about navigation in the Aegean and Mediterranean Seas, called *Kitâbı-ı Bahriyye*.

---

*mezomorta*. The Osmanlı Muslims were not keen on using Turkish words, but they did not mind borrowing words related to the sea, naval activities, etc. from the Europeans they fought, such as the word *mezomorta*. Naval *mujâhids* mastered the main European languages such as Spanish, Portuguese, etc.

*IV – Military Organisation*

## 11.2 Volunteer Naval Mujâhids

Volunteer naval *mujâhids* comprised a very important part of Osmanlı sea power. The first known volunteer naval *mujâhid* who commanded some ships in *jihâd* against European infidels was Kemâl Reîs. Later, he was appointed by Bâyezîd II (1481-1512) as *qapudân-ı deryâ* and rendered great services to the Osmanlı Devlet. Commissioned by Bâyezîd II, he attacked the shores of Spain, and conveyed thousands of Muslims from Andalusia to Dârulislâm.[i] His nephew Pîrî Reîs participated in *jihâd* activities under his command and also entered the Osmanlı Devlet's service afterwards.

The most famous volunteer naval *gâzis* of the sixteenth century are Oruch Reîs and Hızır Reîs. They were sons of Yâkûp Sipâhi. They had two other brothers: İshâq and İlyâs. Born on the island of Midilli, they grew up fond of the sea and engaged in commercial activities. When their ship was intercepted by the pirates of Malta called the Knights of St. John, one of the brothers, İlyâs was martyred.[1049] This

---

i One of the "traps" that orientalists set regarding the Osmanlı-Muslim Devlet is: "Why did the Osmanlıs not save Andalusia?" The answer is very clear and simple: it was impossible for *any* side (Muslim or infidel European) to dominate the *whole* of the Mediterranean exclusively. The Mediterranean was too large to be dominated by only *one* of the fighting sides. In addition, the Osmanlıs did help the Andalusian Muslims by carrying thousands of them to Darulislâm. Plus, naval superiority was not on the Osmanlı side in 1492, when the last Muslim part of Andalusia fell into the infidels' hands: Superiority shifted to Osmanlı Muslims only on September 28, 1538 when they defeated the combined Christian Navy at Preveza. On the other hand, it was absolutely impossible to go through all of Europe on land and annex Spain and Portugal, who were not small powers at all in the last decade of the fifteenth century.

hostile action prompted them to become naval *gâzis*, and they began fighting the European infidels at sea. Oruch Reîs and Hızır Reîs went to North Africa, repulsed the Spaniards from Jezâyir (Algeria) and Tunisia, and Oruch Reîs was martyred in 1518 near Tlemcen in Jezâyir. Hızır Reîs and other naval *gâzis* saved Jezâyir and Tunisia from becoming Spanish-speaking Catholic countries, as occurred in South America. Hızır Reîs was awarded by the Osmanlı Khalîfah-Sultân Selîm (1512-1520) the right to recruit as many volunteers as he wanted from Anatolia. Hızır Reîs became Sultân of Jezâyir but, realising that it was impossible for him to defend this part of the Muslim world against the then very powerful Holy Roman Empire, he voluntarily presented it to the Osmanlı Devlet during the time of Süleymân the Magnificent (1520-1566), who appointed him *qapudân-ı deryâ* of the Osmanlı Devlet: Hızır Hayreddîn Pasha. He is the Muslim admiral who defeated Andrea Doria at Preveza on 28 September 1538 – a date that European powers prefer to forget and do their best to make others forget too.

Turgut Pasha, whom Europeans, out of fear, call Dragut (a distortion of the word dragon), was another very able naval *mujâhid* of the sixteenth century. The son of a peasant by the name of Wely, from the Menteshe province in Anatolia, he joined the naval *mujâhids* when he was very young. He became a *reîs* and a nightmare for European sailors and the population living on the Mediterranean coast. He saved Trablusgarb (Tripoli, Libya) from the pirates of Malta.[i] Joining the service of the Osmanlı Devlet, he became the

---

i   Those pirates, as Sultân Selîm named them, were trained very well. They came from every part of Europe to fight "infidel Turks" as they called them because the Osmanlı Muslims did not accept the Prophet Îsa 🕊 as God, like the Europeans did. For more information, the reader is kindly referred to what has been written by Stanley Lane-Poole, *Turkey* (London, 1886), pp. 142-151.

*IV – Military Organisation*

*beğlerbeği* of Trablusgarb with the rank of Pasha. He was martyred during the siege of Malta in 1565 and was conveyed to Trablusgarb and buried near his mosque there. He is considered a *waly* (singular of *awliyâ*) and it was the custom of people in Trablusgarb to mention him not by his temporal title Pasha, but his pious title: *Sîdî Turgut* (*Sayyidî*: title of a *sûfî shaykh* in North Africa).

Qurdoğlu Muslihiddin Reîs, Sâlih Reîs, and Mezomorta Hüseyin Reîs are some of the other famous volunteer naval *gâzi* leaders.

They would recruit volunteers from Anatolia from time to time, and would train them completely. They were engaged in continuous *jihâd* activities against the Europeans.

Each *reîs* had his own flag. Hızır Reîs had a green flag with a drawing of *Zulfiqâr* (the sword of 'Ali, *karramallahu wajhahu* – may Allah honour his face) and the seal of Suleymân ﷺ (*Mühr-i Süleymân*, a double triangle) on it. The *hilâl* (crescent) was common as a symbol of Islam.

Over time and due to distance, Trablusgarb, Tunisia, and Jezâyir, called *Garb Ojakları*, became *de facto* semi-independent provinces. Volunteer *gâzis* were administrators and the central authority endorsed their governors. These provinces actively participated in the *jihâd* activities of the Osmanlı Devlet by sending several warships to its service during naval battles. Tunisia sent several warships to the Osmanlı Devlet as late as the Crimean War (1853-1856) to fight the Russians.

It is interesting to mention as an example of their power that when American sailors entered into the Mediterranean in the eighteenth century, they had to pay tribute to the *gâzis* in Jezâyir.

# V – Social Institutions

Osmanlı society was very well-organised. There was immense solidarity among the people; they took care of everyone through well-established social institutions.

## 12. WAQF

The *waqf* institution is the embodiment of Islamic social charitable solidarity. It is the greatest financial act one can achieve in one's life. This institution is, so to speak, the crystallisation of the spirit of *Ummat*: a believer allocates the revenue of a property such as a building, shops, orchards, etc. for the profit of others. He or she makes his or her property into a *waqf*, of which the revenue is spent according to conditions set by him or her for specific purposes. The one who allocates his property is called a *wâqif*, the allocated property *waqf*, the document in which the conditions are written *waqfiyye*, and the appointed administrator of the *waqf* a *mutawally*.

*Waqf* is rooted in the Noble Qur'ân:

> "By no means will you attain birr (righteousness) unless you give (freely) of that which you love; and whatever you give, Allah does know it well."[1050]

The word *birr* (righteousness) that occurs in the *âyat* is explained in detail in *Sûrat al-Baqarah*:

> "It is not righteousness that you turn your faces towards East or West; but it is righteousness to believe in Allah and The Last Day, and the Angels, and the Book, and the Messengers; to spend of your substance out of love for Him, for your kin, for orphans, for the needy, for the wayfarer, for those who ask, and

*for the ransom of slaves; to be steadfast in prayer, and give zakât, to fulfil the contracts which you have made; and to be firm and patient (in pains for suffering) and adversity, and throughout all periods of panic. Such are the people of truth, the God-fearing."* (*Sûrat al-Baqarah* [2] (*âyat*: 177))

And there are sayings of the Final Messenger encouraging Muslims to establish *waqfs*. For example: "When a son of Adam dies his charitable and good deeds cease except three: knowledge that people benefit from, good descendants, and *sadaqah jâriyah* (continuing charity)."

Muslims established *waqfs* already in the time of the Final Messenger ﷺ and continued to do so throughout the centuries. This practice became a firmly established tradition and continued down to the Osmanlıs. The first Osmanlı to make a *waqf* was the second ruler Orhân Beğ (r. 1326-1362). He built a *madrasah* in İznik and allocated real estate to maintain the building as well as to take care of the *müderris*' (professor) and students' needs. The first *müderris* of that *madrasah* was Dâvûd-ı Qayserî, who was educated in his home town Qayserî, and then later in Egypt. Tâjuddîn Geredî and then Alâuddîn Esved later became *müderris* at that *madrasah* from which able scholars and administrators graduated.[1051]

Orhân Gâzi built a mosque and *madrasah* in Adapazarı, a mosque, a *zâwiya* (hospice), an *imâret* and guest house, and another mosque in Qandıra. He allocated real estate for all of these institutions to maintain them and for people such as the *müderris*, *imâm*, *khatîb*, cook, servant, porter, etc.[1052]

The *waqfiyye* of the *zâwiya* in Bursa bears the date of 761/1359. It is mentioned in this *waqfiyye* that the *'ushr* of some villages, the revenue of inns, *hammâms* (public baths), shops, mills, orchards was allocated to maintain the building, to pay the staff there, to accommodate people by providing free food and lodging for three days with the *mutawally*'s permission. If any amount remained after spending on the above mentioned purposes, it would be spent on the needs of the personnel of the mosque and *zâwiya*. If the *zâwiya* became disused and ruined, then the revenue would be spent on poor Muslims. The first *mutawally* of this *waqf* was Sinân Pasha with the proviso that, after his death, the *qâdi* of Bursa would be the *mutawally*.

Juxtaposition is the best way to differentiate between "history" and "story." Therefore, we should look at Europe at that time when the Muslims had institutions such as *hammâms*. We see Europe in this position as described by Europeans themselves: "Self-torturing monks gloried in their own filth. In his *History of the Inquisition*, Llorente mentions many instances of converts from Mohammedanism being scourged almost to death, then thrown into filthy prisons because they continued the daily ablutions of their faith." The same westerner goes on to say: "The streets and dwellings were foul with human and animal excretions. Filthy, louse-ridden Christians, from kings to commoners, were infested with sores and riddled with disease."[1053]

The Osmanlıs established *waqfs* for easing problems faced by people, covering almost everything imaginable: they allocated *waqfs* for household utensils and other needs of orphan girls (this should not be confused with the dowry of non-Muslims), to look after migrating birds that were unable to continue on their journey and rested, even to feed hungry wolves that approached villages in winter.

Apart from the *waqf* institution, the Osmanlıs used stone pillars called *sadaqa tashı* (stone of charity) on which to put money in several places in towns; the needy would go to one of these pillars, which was about a metre and half high, after *'ishâ* (at night) when people had gone to bed, and would take some money from the top of the stone, not knowing who had put it there, without any embarrassment.[i] One

---

i   It is a great pleasure for me to repeat my warm thanks and gratitude to the International Islamic University, Malaysia, for commissioning me to colof those stones that has survived up to the present is in Doğancilar, Üsküdar. Several others are in İznik (now in the museum), which was opened to Islam by the Osmanlıs in 1331. It proves that the Muslims had helped the needy in the first half of the fourteenth century without causing any embarrassment on the part of the latter.

Allowing the building and maintenance of educational and sanitary institutions, bridges, etc. by members of the public greatly relieved the Treasury of the Osmanlı Devlet.

## 13. ZÂWIYA-TARÎQATS

Osmân Gâzi's father-in-law Edebalı was a knowledgeable well-educated *sûfî shaykh*, and had a *zâwiya*. Osmân Gâzi once had a dream in which he saw a moon emerging from Edebalı's navel and entering his own bosom, and immediately a tree grew out of Osmân's navel spreading over a vast area, with mountains and flowing rivers under its shadow. When he related his dream the next day to Shaykh Edebalı, the latter explained that Allah Almighty had vested sovereignty over the whole world in Osmân and his descendants, and that his own daughter had become *halâl* to Osman, and he gave her in marriage to Osmân Gâzi.

There were other *sûfî shaykhs* like Turgud Shaykh, one of whose *murîds* (disciples) was present when Shaykh Edebalı explained Osmân Gâzi's dream, and when he asked for something as a gift for this wonderful herald, Osmân Gâzi gave him a village.[1054]

During Osmân Gâzi's son Orhân Gâzi's era, there was another famous *sûfî shaykh*, among others, by the name of Geyikli Baba. Orhân Gâzi's son Sultân Murâd was himself an *akhî shaykh*. His

---

lect material in Turkey from the respective capitals of the Osmanlı Devlet, during which I had the chance to take photographs of several *sadaqa taşhı* in İznik (Nicaea), dating back to first half of the fourteenth century, and a *sadaqa taşhı* in İstanbul (Üsküdar, Doğancilar, in front of a barber's shop).

*The thrree marble pillars that were erected by Sultân Murâd II on the spots where three angels alighted to prevent people from stepping on them.*

grandson Murâd II (1421 – 1451) was at such a high spiritual level that he saw in his dream three angels alighting in the courtyard of the mosque known as *üsch sherefeli jâmi* in Edirne, and he erected a marble pillar at each spot to protect it from being stepped on by human beings. The three green marble pillars are still there in the courtyard of the mosque, which at the time was called *üch sherefli jâmi* (mosque, owner of three honourable ones; referring to the three angels). Over time it came to be called *üch sherefeli* (owner of *uch sherefe*: places for reciting *ezân*); in fact, its *sherefes* are not three in number.

Sûfî *shaykhs* rendered great services throughout Osmanlı history: they educated people in their *zâwiyas* and trained them to live in accordance with the Creator's laws. It is interesting to note that *sûfî shaykhs* went to the Balkans, settled there, and spread Islam even before those areas were opened to Islam by the Osmanlı army.

A *zâwiya* was a building in which a *sûfî shaykh* lived with his family. He educated people along Islamic lines, affecting others with his pious, concentrated personality through *hâl* (attitude) more than *qawl* (utterance). In other words, he was such a wise, pious, refined, knowledgeable person that his influence on his visitors and disciples emanated from his clean, pure, illuminated personality.

Some *zâwiyas* (*tekkes*) contained rooms for *murîds* (disciples) to live in and to practise *khalwat* training: fasting certain days and practising *dhikr*. In the Osmanlı practice of Islam, belonging to a *sûfî tarîqat* (order) was regarded as an increase in commitment and dedication. As a result, *sûfî tarîqats* were common all over the Osmanlı domain, and they had their *tekkes* or *zâwiyas* with fairly rich *waqfs* devoted to them by the administration as well as by the public. The Osmanlı Devlet, being a Sunnî champion of Islam, tolerated and encouraged Sunnî *tarîqats*.

## 14. İMÂRET

The *imâret* tradition goes back in the Osmanlı Devlet to the time of its founder, Osmân Gâzi. Osmân Gâzi was a very good, committed Muslim. "It was his custom to gather the poor and pious people every three days and treat them with dinner and to clothe the needy and support the widows."[1055]

An *imâret* is a building where the poor would be fed every day. It was built by individuals and not by public funds, and had enough revenue from the shops, fields, orchards, etc. that had been made into a *waqf* for this institution. The person who founded the *imâret* would put in its *waqfiyye* what sorts of food and the amount of food to be served daily. In the *waqfiyye*, the administrative set-up of the *imâret* was also listed. It would be in the charge of a well-bred man, and the servants were to be of a certain quality. For example, when Orhân Gâzi (1326-1362) built an *imâret* in İznik upon opening that historical town to İslâm in 1331, he appointed *al-Hâj Hasan*, who was a *murîd* of Shaykh Edebalı, as the *shaykh* of this imâret.[1056] Therefore, the *imâret* was intended not only to feed people physically free of charge but to refine their souls as well at the hands of well qualified *sûfî* masters. It means that as early as the first half of the fourteenth century C.E., the Islamic *Devlet* of the Osmanlıs did not neglect the individual: he was looked after well, his spiritual needs were also met, and he was spiritually elevated.

There were *imârets* all over the Osmanlı Devlet. Even after more than a half century after the Osmanlı Devlet, there was still a continuation of this very beautiful and humane tradition: in almost every village in Anatolia, there was someone who built a building from the same material as his house and allocated this building to guests, people coming from outside his village. For three days, food was also sent there from the home of that person, free of charge. Sometimes, a room in his own house was allocated for guests. In some cases, the villagers built a guest room and sent food there from different homes. As is well known, the three-night period for guestship was set by the Final Messenger ﷺ.

## 15. KERVÂNSARÂY

The Osmanlı Devlet was very concerned with the well-being of the *ra'iyyet*. Internal security had an outstanding priority with the Osmanlı administration. In addition to security measures in cities, towns, and villages, they put special emphasis on road safety in the countryside. People of that time travelled in *kervân*s (caravans), in groups, on horseback or on camels. Merchandise was conveyed on camels. There were strongly-built buildings called *kervânsarây* (palaces as resting places for *kervân*s) along main roads.

A *kervânsarây* contained rooms for travellers, place for their animals and merchandise, a *masjid*, a *hammâm* (bath building), and whatever else the travellers needed. The *kervânsarây*s were built at such a distance from one another along the main roads that if a *kervân* left a *kervânsarây* shortly after the morning (*subh* or *fajr*) prayer, at dawn, it would reach another one by mid-afternoon (*'asr*) and spend the night there. A *kervânsarây* was much more than an inn; it was fortified, and travellers did not pay anything for food or lodging there for up to three nights.

There is a *hadith sharîf* of the Final Messenger Muhammad ﷺ about the duration of being a guest:

> "A believer should not stay as a guest with his brother more than three days; he should not cause him to feel embarrassment."

So, Muslim people living under the administration of the Osmanlı Devlet were very careful to follow the Final Messenger's orders; they observed the period of guest-ship as three days in the *kervânsarây* that they built.

A *kervânsarây* was not built with public funds; wealthy Muslims built it at their own expense and allocated a source of revenue for its maintenance, administration, and other expenses, following the Islamic concept of pleasing the Creator, the utmost ideal of every Muslim.

Sayyid Mustafa Nûrî Pasha, who was *defter-i hâqânî nâzırı* during Sultân Abdülhamîd II's time, quotes a good example of how a *kervânsarây* came into being and how it was maintained: "According to the *waqfiyye* of Enishte Hasan Pasha, who was *sadrâzam* during the time of Sultân Ahmed III, there was a place called Qaramurt in the region of Shaykhu'l Hadîd that belonged to the Uzeyr administrative unit. This Qaramurt was on the way to the Arabian Peninsula and al-Harameyn ash-Sharifayn. Over time, its villages were abandoned by their inhabitants, left to ruin, and the place became a home for thieves. The *defterdâr* (Finance Minister) of that time assessed this place at 5,000 *gurush*, but the *sadrâzam* purchased it for 7,500 *gurush* and turned it into a *waqf*. He built a castle there with a mosque inside it, two *hammâms* (one for men, and the other for women), a *khân* (inn) with 90 fireplaces (one in each room), a *madrasah*, an *imâret*, 30 shops, and houses for guards of the castle, the *mutawally* of the *waqf* (administrator), the *kâtib* (scribe), the *vâ'iz* (preacher), the *muezzins*, and the *qayyim* (those who clean the mosque and maintain it).

He made allocations for:

26 cavalrymen each of whom received 15 *akcha* daily;
1 commander (*süvâri ağası*) who received 30 *akcha* daily;
1 *kethüdâ* (commander's assistant and deputy) who received 20 *akcha* daily);
1 *alemdâr* (flag bearer) who received 17 *akcha* daily;
1 *chavush* who received 16 *akcha* daily to protect passers-by.

In addition, he allocated the following for manning the castle:

15 soldiers each of whom received 10 *akcha* daily;
1 *dizdâr* (their commander) who received 15 *akcha* daily;
4 *bewwâbs* (doorkeepers) each of whom received 12 *akcha* daily.

Moreover, he allocated certain salaries for the servants of the *imâret*, and certain amount of money for the food cooked and served free of charge in the *imâret*. All the soldiers, their commanders, and the employees of the *waqf* were to eat at the *imâret* free of charge. He allocated 50 *akcha* daily to each of his sisters from the *waqf*. So he also ensured good living conditions for his sisters.

> "Thus, the establishment of this *waqf* served three purposes: developing the countryside, the safety the roads, and the spread of knowledge."[1057]

## 16. HAMMÂM

Since Islam puts great emphasis on cleanliness, throughout the centuries Muslims had *hammâms*. When they opened a town to Islam or when they built a new city, they put the mosque where the *jum'ah* prayer was held in the centre. Near to it there was a *hammâm* and governmental buildings.

## V – Social Institutions

This tradition was passed on to the Anatolian Selçuklus and the Osmanlıs. Being representatives of Islam, they were very keen on cleanliness – so much so that even during *jihâd* campaigns they did not neglect to bathe. There was a special kind of organisation called the *hamâmjı esnâfı* that provided for a huge army on the move, with warm water and movable bathing places.

A *hammâm* was among the very first buildings to be built in a town newly opened to Islam in the Osmanlı era. For example, there is still a *hammâm* in use in İznik (Nicaea) that dates back to the early fourteenth century. Apart from public *hammâms*, houses had their private bathing rooms called *gusl-hâne* (room to perform major ablution).

Perhaps the Külliye of Selîmiyye in Edirne is a good example of Osmanlı practice. Even before starting to build the mosque, which is a masterpiece by Sinân the greatest Osmanlı architect, they first built the *hammâm* to enable the workers on the mosque to keep clean throughout their work. Then the mosque and other buildings were built.

They were keen on keeping the streets clean as well. Some people allocated *waqfs* for this purpose. The employee of that *waqf*, carrying a sack of ash on his shoulder or back, would go round the town. If he saw someone spitting, he would take a large tablespoonful of ash from the sack (which is called a *heybe*) and cover the dirt with ash.

It goes without saying that comparison is the best way to understand and evaluate the level of civilisation in societies. So, when we look at Europe during that period, which is really the Dark Ages for the West, although a brilliant age for the Muslim world, we have this picture: "All over the Mediterranean coastlands the free public baths fell into ruins. The belief that dirt was next to godliness spread throughout Europe.... This form of Christian insanity prevailed until the middle of the eighteenth century."[1058]

On the other hand, as mentioned elsewhere in this book, building *hammâms* even in *kervânsarâys* along roads was common practice in the Osmanlı Devlet. Apart from common public baths, people went to *kapılıjas* and *ichmejes* to maintain good health – a practice that continues in Turkey nine decâdes after the Osmanlıs. A *kaplija*, where people take regular baths, has special mineral water that cures rheumatism and some other diseases. An *ichmeje* is a place with facilities where people drink the water that contains a variety of elements that cleanse the body; a practice that modern medicine advises and people in the Osmanlı Devlet exercised throughout the centuries. With this practice of cleanliness, people were by and large healthy. Wrestling was a very common sport. On every occasion there were wrestling competitions: at festivities, *bayrams* ('*iyds*), marriages and circumcision ceremonies, etc. – villages even had wrestling competitions.

It is interesting to note that venereal disease came to the Osmanlı Devlet from Europe. The Osmanlıs called it *frengistân*. Venereal disease in Osmanlı Turkish is from *frengî* (belonging, related to the Franks).

## 17. HOSPITALS

The Osmanlıs inherited the hospital tradition from the Anatolian Selçuklus who had hospitals, called *dâru'sh shifâ* (house of healing), in many major cities in Anatolia. A *dâru'sh shifâ* was built, and a *waqf* assigned to it from which the administrator, doctors, and servants received their salaries. Patients were treated free of charge – regardless of their race and faith. Apart from the *dâru'sh shifâ*, the Selçuklus had a *bîmâristân* for the cure of mental diseases and the care of the mentally handicapped. A *dâru'sh shifâ* building from the Selçuklu period is still standing in Amasya city, Anatolia.

The Osmanlıs continued with the hospital tradition of the Selçuklus.[1059] Sultân Yıldırım Bâyezîd built a *dâru't tibb (*house of medicine*)* in Bursa and appointed Hoja Husnî (1389-1412) as *tabîb*

*V – Social Institutions*

(doctor) there.¹⁰⁶⁰ They had a *dâru'sh shifâ* in main cities as a part of *külliyes*. A *külliye* contained a mosque, a *hammâm*, several *madrasahs*, a library, and an *imâret*, etc.

The Osmanlıs had a *bîmâristân* institution as well. There was a *bîmârhâne* (hospital) in Manisa, built in the early sixteenth century. There was a *bîmârhâne* in the *külliye* of Haseki Hürrem Sultân, built in 946/1540 together with mosque, an *imâret*, a *sibyân mektebi* (school for children), and a *madrasah*.¹⁰⁶¹ The *Bîmârhâne* of the Süleymâniyye was built in 957/1550 by Süleymân the Magnificent in his *külliye* of Süleymâniyye. The *bîmârhâne* of Vâlide-i 'Atiyq, the mother of Sultân Murâd III, was built in 991/1583 in her *külliye* at Toptashı, Üsküdar. In the *külliye* of Sultân Ahmed (built in 1086/1617) there was a *bîmâristân* as well.

A *bîmâristân* housed the mentally handicapped as well. The doctors used water and music to treat the mentally handicapped. There was a table-like area, from the top of which water flowed slowly to its lower slopes and the patients listened to it. Music was also used to treat them.

Doctors observed that it was necessary to use different types of music for different types of people. So, they assigned certain *maqâms*ⁱ of music for certain diseases. For example:

*Rast*: was considered beneficial for paralysis;
*Irâq*: for people with a hot nature;
*Isfahân*: to improve intelligence;
*Rehâvî*: for headaches.¹⁰⁶²

In the seventeenth century a vaccination for chicken pox

---

i   A *maqâm* is equivalent to a 'key' in European music except that the latter has twelve tones and semitones, whereas the former can have twenty-four notes with the addition of quarter tones, and indeed can even have microtones. There is evidence to suggest that the *maqâm* tradition is the source of the European tradition of keys.

was conveyed from the Osmanlı Devlet to Europe. At first the Europeans were apprehensive, but Voltaire (1696-1778) was immensely helpful in dispersing that apprehension.[1063]

Osmanlı doctors were also *'ulamâ* (scholars) of *sharî'at*. They were interested in the *Tibb-ı Nebevî* (Prophetic Medicine) by Abû Naîm. The first medical book written in the Osmanlı Devlet was *Khawâssu'l Edwiye (*Special Properties of Medicines*)* by İshâq b. Murâd in 792/1390.[1064] Then Ahmed Dâ'î wrote *Kitâb-ı Tibb* and Ahmedî compiled *Muntekhâb-ı Shifâ* in 800/1397.

According to Ahmedî, cities should be surrounded by open space, their *qibleh* should not be obstructed, closed in by mountains like Bursa.[1065] Mumin b. Mukbil wrote *Zahîre-i Murâdiyye* in 841/1437 in the name of Sultân Murâd (1421-1451). He also wrote *Miftâhu'n Nûr ve Hazâinu's Surûr* and *Kitab-ı Tibb* in the field of medicine.[1066] Fâtih Mehemmed's (1451-1481) spiritual master Shaykh Akshemseddîn was a great doctor as well. As early as the fifteenth century he pointed out the hereditary factors in certain diseases[1067] and objected as early as that time to the acceptance of the effect of the stars on malaria,[1068] which was a novelty at that time. His contemporary, Altunjuzâde, made great contributions in the field of urology.[1069] Hâjı Pasha (fifteenth century) was a medical genius; he studied medicine in Egypt where that science was at a very high level, worked there in a *mâristân* (hospital) and, when he came back to Turkey, he wrote *Teshîl-i Shifâ* and *Shifâu'l Esqâm wa Dawâu'l Âlâm*.[1070] It should be remembered that İbn Sina's *al-Qânûn fit Tibb* was studied in European universities up until the seventeenth century. Then superiority in medicine shifted to Europe; they did not mind dissecting the human body for research and made progress that way.

The *waqfiyye* of each hospital was designed with utmost care: how much doctors, clerks, and functionaries would be paid, what sort of food would be served according to seasons, etc.; all of this was very explicit and stated in detail.

On the other hand, it is really hair-raising to remember what European practices were during that same period regarding the mentally ill: some of the poor folk were burnt alive "to rid them of the evil souls inside their bodies."

In 1312/1896 the Osmanlı Khalîfah-Sultân, Abdülhamîd II, founded a *dâru'l 'ajeze* (home for the disabled). This (still in use with some modifications) is an institution where the elderly and poor, even children, are looked after, regardless of race and religion. This excerpt from *Taqvîm-i Vaqayi'*, the official gazette of the Osmanlıs, dated January 1906, gives a good example of the residents in that institution:

|          | Muslim | Greek | Armenian | Catholic | Jews | Bulgarian |
|----------|--------|-------|----------|----------|------|-----------|
| male     | 270    | 92    | 51       | 4        | 35   | 1         |
| female   | 197    | 27    | 11       | 14       |      |           |
| children | 296    | 2     | 1        |          |      |           |

## 18. EDUCATION

Osmanlıs rated learning and learned men very highly. Two examples are worth quoting about how the Osmanlıs respected learned men.

The famous Osmanlı writer and encyclopaedist Kâtib Chelebi's (d. 1067/1657) intention was to become a *sipâhî* (cavalryman) in the Osmanlı army. But when he observed the respect paid to an *'âlim* (scholar) who visited his home town, he changed his mind and became a great scholar.

The second example is the famous historian Kemâl Pashazâde Ahmed Shemsuddin (1468-1534). He also wanted to become an officer in the best army of the world at that time. But when he saw that a young *'âlim*, Mollâ Lutfî-i Tokâdî, was treated with more respect than even very high commanders, he changed his mind, and became an *'âlim, qâdıasker,* and *sheyhülislâm*.

The Osmanlı educational system had these institutions: mosque, *tekke*, *sibyân mektebi* (*küttâb*) for children, *madrasah*, and *enderûn* for the education of the brightest.

## 18.1 The Mosque

Muslims received their religious instructions in *mesjids* from preachers. A *mesjid* occupied a central position in each quarter. There were regular *vâ'z* (admonition and exhortation) activities in the mosques carried out by well-qualified preachers.

Apart from the preachers, imams of the mosques also had educational functions. An imam was a sort of head man in his district. He was in charge of the marriage of couples according to Islamic custom. He watched over the poor and widowed in the district and found those who could help them.

In addition to the mosque, there was the *tekke* (*zâwiya*), where people from every walk of life went, listened to the *sûfî shaykh*, participated in *dhikr*, learned about their responsibilities, and refined their souls.

## 18.2 The Sibyân Mektebi (Children's School)

A Turkish Muslim child received its first lesson when it was born: *ezân* was recited in its ears while being held towards Ka'ba in the naming ceremony. If the child was male, the mother would say to him while suckling him for the first time: "*Yâ shehid ol yâ gâzi*" (Be either a martyr or survive *jihâd*). When the child was 4 years, 4 months, and 10 days old it would be sent with great ceremony to the *sibyân mektebi* to learn how to read the Noble Qur'ân, and how to write. When the child completed reading the Qur'ân from beginning to end, there was a great ceremony called the *hatim jemiyeti* (gathering to celebrate the *khatm* conclusion of the reading of the Qur'ân).

The *sibyân mektebi* was similar to the *kuttâb* in early Islam. There was a *sibyân mektebi* in every place where people lived and in every district of big cities. Children of 5 to 6 years went to these primary schools, called *dâru't ta'lîm*, *mu'allimhâne*, or *mekteb*, *mektebhâne* in the *waqfiyyes*. There they learned the *elifbâ* (alphabet), writing, reading, reciting the Noble Qur'ân, and arithmetic. The teacher was called the *mu'allim*, his assistant was the *qalfa*. The amount of schooling they would receive daily was expressed in the *waqfiyye* of that school.

The *sibyân mektebi* was very common, and there was one in every unit of habitation, even in villages. Evliyâ Chelebi informs us that there were 1993 *sibyân mektebi* in İstanbul in the seventeenth century.[1071] There were many educational institutions not only in the capital or major towns in the Osmanlı Devlet but at its periphery as well. For example, in Jezâyir (Algeria) there were two schools in each village when France occupied the region in 1830.[1072] Before 1830, primary and secondary education flourished in Jezâyir (Algeria).[1073] Needless to say, the educational situation was similar in other provinces.

## 18.3 The Madrasah

The *madrasah* was a relatively late development in Islamic education. The earliest stage was that of the mosque schools that had originated during the time of the Final Messenger Muhammad ﷺ and his pious *khalîfah*s. The Holy Qur'ân, the *hadîth*, the Arabic language, and sciences related to Islam were taught in the mosque.

The next stage was private schools located mostly in the houses of intellectuals and scholars. Those schools were an embryonic form of academy for advanced studies.

The third stage was the establishment of *dâru'l hikmat*. But during the Fâtimî period, this development was used for Shi'ite propaganda in particular, ignoring its main purpose of acquiring knowledge, self-realisation, and then service to mankind.

Thus, it was mainly in order to combat wrong ideas and distortions in religion that Sunnî Muslims established the *madrasah*. One of the most remarkable educational institutions of its time was the celebrated Nizâmiyye Madrasah in Baghdad. This *madrasah* was founded by Nizâmul Mulk, who was the grand *vazîr* of the Selçuklu Sultân Alp Arslan, and his son Melik Shâh. This *madrasah* served a double purpose: spreading knowledge and purifying Islamic thought.[1074]

The Osmanlı Devlet adopted the *madrasah* system, inheriting it from the Anatolian Selçuklus. It was necessary to have a diploma called an *ijâzet* to be entitled to teach in a *madrasah*. A *müderris* (professor) was a very well qualified scholar with a working knowledge of Arabic, being fairly well versed in *tefsîr, hadîth, siyret, fiqh,* in addition to his field of specialisation.[1075]

The first Osmanlı *madrasah* was built in İznik by Orhân Gâzi. Its first *müderris* (professor) was Dâvûd Qayserî (d.751/1351), who was educated, after leaving his home town Qayseri, in Qâhira (Cairo) where he studied *tefsîr, hadîth, usûl* (methodology), *bedi'*, and other sciences. Orhân Gâzi built another *madrasah* in Bursa in 736/1335. His son Sultân Murâd built a *madrasah* in Chekirge in Bursa in 767/1365-1366. Yıldırım Bâyezîd established another *madrasah* in Bursa.[1076] Chelebi Sultân Mehemmed (1413-1421) established a new *madrasah* in Bursa, which was later named the Sultâniyye Madrasah, and whose first *müderris* was the brilliant scholar Muhammed Shâh, then only 18 years old, a son of the famous scholar Shemsuddîn Fenârî.[1077]

Sultân Murâd II (1421-1451) founded the *Dâru'l Hadîth* in 838/1435 and *Üch Sherefli Madrasah* in 851/1447-48, both in Edirne, the then capital of the Osmanlı Khalifate. He built another *madrasah* called *Murâdiyye* in Bursa as well.[1078] Sultân Fâtih Mehemmed (1451-1481) established his eight *madrasahs* called *el-Medârisu's Semâniyye* around his mosque in İstanbul. Süleymân the Magnificent (1520-1566) built his *madrasah* in the compound of *Külliye-i Süleymâniyye* in İstanbul. His son Selîm II (1566-1574) established his *madrasah* at *Selîmiyye Külliyye* in Edirne.

"The students were first given lessons in the Arabic language. When a sufficient knowledge of Arabic language had been acquired, the students took up the study of commentaries on the Holy Qur'ân, the Traditions, and related literature and Muslim jurisprudence, and sociology and law. The chief commentary on the Holy Qur'ân was that of al-Baidâwî (*Anwâr al-Tanzeel*), a commentary called *Tafseer-i Qâdi*.[1079] The sovereigns and notables were very respectful towards scholars. Most of the *Shâhzâdas* (sons of the Sultâns) and members of the nobility worked very hard in the pursuit of knowledge under the direction of their private tutors, who were selected from among the distinguished scholars of their time."[1080]

The students, as well as their *müderris*, received an allowance from the *waqf* of the *madrasah*. The *mutawally* of the *waqf* appointed the *müderris*.

There were two kinds of *madrasah*: common *madrasahs* and specialised *madrasahs*. Common *madrasahs* were built in every place where people lived, even in villages in the Osmanlı Devlet. Islamic sciences and other disciplines were studied in those *madrasahs* at different levels. Those who studied certain Islamic and other sciences at a high level in those *madrasahs*, were appointed as *qâdis*, *muftis*, or *müderris*. The specialised *madrasahs* were: *dârul hadîth*, *dârut tibb*, and *dârulqurrâ*.

The *dârul hadîth* was a *madrasah* specialising in the Final Messenger's words, actions, and endorsements (*taqrîrs*). In those *madrasahs* they studied narration (*rivâyat*), comprehension (*dirâyat*), chains of transmission (*isnâd*), biographies of *râwîs*-narrators (*terâjimu'l ahvâl*). They read masterpieces in the science of *hadîth*, such as the *Sahîh* of Bukhârî and the *Sahîh* of Muslim, and their commentaries (*sherhs*). The requirement for acceptance in this *madrasah* was graduation from a common *madrasah* or having a sound knowledge at an acceptable level.

### Daru't Tibb

*Tibb* (medicine) was studied in *dâru'sh shifâs* (hospitals) during the Selçuklu period and during Osmanlı rule until Süleymân the Magnificent. When he established an independent *madrasah* for medicine in the *külliye* of Süleymâniyye, the study of medicine shifted to the *madrasah*, with *dâru'sh shifâ* becoming a place for training and practice. In *tibb madrasahs* they studied books by previous doctors, as well as books written by Osmanlı doctors.[1081]

### The Dâru'l Qurrâ' (school for reciters/readers)

When a student completed his education in a *sibyân mektebi* (children's school) or had received private education, he first entered a low-level *dâru'l qurrâ'* where he memorised the whole of the Holy Qur'ân. Then he entered a higher level *dâru'l qurrâ'* where he studied *'ilm-i qirâat* (the science of recitation) and *makhâriju'l hurûf* (articulation of the letters). Those who graduated from these *madrasahs* were employed in mosques.[1082] The month of Ramadân was a vacation period for *madrasahs*. It was customary for the students to spend their vacations going to villages, carrying out *va'z* (admonition and exhortation) and *imâmet* of *terâvîh* prayer there, thus putting in practice what they had learnt at the *madrasahs*.

## 18.4 The Enderûn

The *enderûn mektebi* was a unique, original educational institution set up by the Osmanlı Devlet; there is no similar institution to it, not in the Selçuklu administration nor in the west. It is true that ruling family members received a special kind of education in both the Selçuklu Devlet and in European practice, but the *enderûn* is completely different: it is a large school with hundreds of select students set up in the *Topqapusu Sarayı* (Topqapı Palace) to educate the elite and train a very large number of bright students to assume responsibilities as a *sadrâzam, vazîr, pasha, beğlerbeği,* or *kaptanpasha,* etc. It was an academy specialising in military, administrative, and political sciences.

The *enderûn* recruited its students from the *ajemi oğlanlar* (young converts). They were first trained in one of these palaces: the Edirne Sarayı, Galata Sarayı, İbrâhîm Pasha Sarayı, or the İskender Chelebi Sarayı.

Sultân Murâd (1362-1389) built a number of rooms for those youths in the Edirne Sarayı. Clever and able-bodied young converts were selected for this school. They were taught reading and writing and were given a military training as well.

The Galata Sarayı was founded by Sultân Bâyezîd II (1481-1512) in 1481 on the advice of a *sûfî shaykh* by the name of Gül Baba. A mosque and three hostels with the capacity of two hundred students each, three *hammâms*, an administrative building, and kitchens were built. The students were educated by Gül Baba and other scholars. Students were engaged in sports activities as well, such as archery, *jirit*,[i] etc.

İbrâhîm Pasha Sarayı and İskender Chelebi Sarayı were built in the sixteenth century. The İskender Chelebi maintained six thousand slaves. Six of those slaves became *vazîrs*. Among them was the famous *sadrâzam* Sokollu Mehmed Pasha.[1083]

Students who were trained in those schools were sent to *kapukulu süvârî*[ii] units, and the best ones were sent to the *Enderûn* for further training. *Enderûn* had six units; the supreme one was *hâs*

---

i   a traditional Turkish equestrian team sport played outdoors on horseback in which the objective is to score points by throwing a blunt wooden javelin at opposing team's horsemen.

ii   a corps of elite cavalry soldiers in the army of the Osmanlı devlet.

*oda*, numbering about 40 students from which the top officials emerged.[1084]

# Conclusion

The Osmanlı institutions were rooted in Islam. As champions of Sunnî Islam, the Osmanlıs were very keen on implementing the "commands of the Creator" in every aspect of life. Therefore, their institutions were founded on and geared to the Islamic way of life. In other words, all Osmanlı institutions were set up, arranged, and maintained to facilitate a way for the created to live in accordance with the Creator's commands.

The Osmanlı institutions were the lifeblood of Osmanlı civilisation. Every civilisation may be assessed by the type of human being it produces and how happy human beings are in that environment. The Osmanlı civilisation was a perfect one: it produced brave, gallant soldiers for the battlefield, and, on the other hand, the *osmanlı efendisi*, very refined gentlemen. The *ra'iyyet* (the governed people) lived happily – regardless of race and religion. The elderly were greatly respected. An elderly Osmanlı was the authority and pillar of his household until his death. He had full authority, even over his married sons with children and grandchildren. Even half a century after the Osmanlı Devlet's destruction, murder was a rare occurrence in İstanbul, their capital, and people would talk about it for weeks, astonished and disapproving.

> "The life and death of a civilization depend in an equal measure on the quality of its basic teaching. If it invites its adherents to renounce the world spiritually man will certainly make great progress, yet the other constituent parts of man, his body, his intellectual faculties, etc., will not be allowed to perform their natural duties and will die even before their season of bloom. If, on the other hand, a

civilization lays emphasis only on the material aspects of life man will make great progress in those aspects at the expense of others; and such a civilization may even become a sort of boomerang, causing its own death. For materialism often engenders egoism and lack of respect for the rights of others, creating enemies, who await their chance for reprisals. The result is mutual killing."[1085]

Since the Osmanlı civilisation depended on Islam, it envisioned securing happiness in this world and in the hereafter as well: "Well-being in this world and well-being in the hereafter;"[1086] "Islam will certainly not satisfy the extremists of either school, the ultra-spiritualists (who want to renounce all worldly things and mortify themselves as a duty) and the ultra-materialists (who do not believe in the rights of others), yet it can be practised by an overwhelming majority of mankind, which follows an intermediate path, and seeks to develop simultaneously the body and the soul, creating a harmonious equilibrium in man as a whole. Islam has insisted on the importance of both these constituents of man, and on their inseparability, so that one should not be sacrificed for the benefit of the other."[1087] Therefore, when the Osmanlıs built an *imaret,* for example, there was a responsible spiritual master, a *sûfî shaykh,* to refine the souls of the people in addition to feeding their material bodies.

Perhaps, the lop-sided, imbalanced, over-materialistic, modern civilisation has a great deal to learn from and can emulate the Osmanlıs who represented the last and the longest link of the "balanced" Islamic civilisation.

# Bibliography

## A. DOCUMENTS

Başbakanlık Osmanlı Arşivi (Prime Ministry's Osmanlı Archives), *Mühimme Defteri* 5

Başbakanlık Osmanlı Arsivi, *Mühimme Defteri* 7

Başbakanlık Osmanlı Arşivi, *Nâme-i Hümâyûn Defteri* 5

Başbakanlık Osmanlı Arşivi, *Nâme-i Hümâyûn Defteri* 7

Başbakanlık Osmanlı Arşivi, *Nâme-i Hümâyûn Defteri* 9

Başbakanlık Osmanlı Arşivi, *Nâme-i Hümâyûn Defteri* 12

Topkapı Sarayı Müzesi Kitaplığı *E/6456* (Translation of the letter sent by *hatîb, fuqaha, imâms,* merchants, and notables of Jezâyir (Algeria) on the *jihâd* activities of Oruch Reis to the Osmanlı Sultân in 925/1519)

## B. BOOKS AND ARTICLES

### 1. Turkish

Abdullah Battal Taymas, *Qazan Türkleri*, İstanbul, 1341/1925.

Ahmed 'Âsım, *Târîh*, İstanbul, Jerîde-i Havâdis n.d.

Ahmed Cevdet Paşa, *Mâruzat*, ed. Yusuf Halaçoğlu, İstanbul, Çağrı Yayınları 1980.

Afetinan, *Piri Reisin Hayatı ve Eserleri* (Ankara: Türk Tarih Kurumu Basımevi, 1992).

Akgündüz Ahmed, *Osmanlı Kanunnamelerinin Hukukî Tahlilleri*, İstanbul: 1990, I.

Aknerli Grigor, *Mogol Tarihi*, transl. by Hrand D. Andreasyan, İstanbul Üniversitesi Edebiyat Fakültesi, İstanbul, 1954.

Akkutay Ülker, *Enderun Mektebi*, Ankara: 1984.

Aşıkpaşaoğlu Tarihi, ed. Nihal Atsız, Ankara, 1985.

Baltacı Cahit, *XV-XVI. Asırlarda Osmanlı Madrasahleri*, İstanbul: 1976.

Baykal, Bekir Sıtkı, "Mustafa III", *M.E.B. İslâm Ansiklopedisi*, İstanbul, 1993, v. VIII, p. 701.

Berki, Ali Himmet "Vakıf Kuran İlk Osmanlı Padişahı" *Vakıflar Dergisi*, Ankara: 1962, V.

Beydilli, Kemâl, *Türk Bilim ve Matbaacılık Tarihinde Mühendishâne, Mühendishâne Matbaası ve Kütüphânesi (1776-1826)*, İstanbul, 1995.

Bilge Mustafa, *İlk Osmanlı Madrasahleri*, İ.Ü.Edebiyat Fakültesi Basimevi, İstanbul, 1984.

Bostan İdris, *Osmanlı Bahriye Teşkilâtı XVII. Yüzyılda Tersâne-i Amire*, Ankara: Türk Tarih Kurumu Basımevi, 1992.

Dânişmend, İsmâil Hâmi, *İzahlı Osmanlı Tarihi Kronolojisi*, I-IV, İstanbul, I, 1971.

Defterdar Sarı Mehmed Pasha, *Zübde-i Vakayi'ât*, İstanbul, Tercüman Yayınları, 1977.

Jelâlzâde Koja Nishânjı Mustafa (d. 975/1567), *Kitâb-ı Meâsir-i Selîm Khânî*, TSMK, H 1415.

Khoja Sa'deddîn, *Tâju't Tevârîh*, İstanbul, 1279.

Kramers, J.H. "Seyhulislam," *İslam Ansikpedisi* XXI, İstanbul: 1979.

Kuran Aptullah, *Mimar Sinan*, İstanbul: 1985.

Köprülü, F. Orhan-Mustafa Uzun, "Akşemseddin," *Türkiye Diyânet Vakfı Ansiklopedisi*, v. II, pp. 299-301.

Levend, Agâh Sırrı, *Gazavatnâmeler ve Mihaloğlu Ali Beyin Gazavatnâmesi*, İstanbul, 1956.

Lutfi Pasha, *Tevârîh-i Âl-i Osmân*, İstanbul, 1341.

Mahmûd Jelâleddîn Pasha, *Mir'ât-ı Haqîqat* İstanbul, 1326.

Maksudoğlu, Mehmet, "Tunusta Dayıların Ortaya Çıkışı," in

*Ankara Üniversitesi İlâhiyat Fakütesi Dergisi,* Ankara, 1967, vol. XIV, pp. 189-202.

_____, "Tunusta Hâkimiyetin Dayılardan Beylere Geçişi," in *Ankara Üniversitesi İlâhiyat Fakültesi Dergisi,* Ankara, 1968, vol. XV, pp. 173-186.

_____, "Osmanlı Socio-Political Entity: Empire or *Devlet?*" *Hamdard Islamicus,* vol. XVIII, 1995.

_____, "Empire or *Devlet?* The Ottoman Polity Revisited," *International Islamic University Malaysia*, Research and Information Bulletin, January 1994 and February 1994.

Çifci, Fâzıl, *Candaroğlu İsmâil Bey, Şahsiyeti ve Eserleri,* Kastamonu, 1996.

Enverî, *Düstûrnâme,* ed. M. Halîl Yinanç, İstanbul, 1928.

Fâiq Reshâd, *Târîh-i Edebiyyât-ı Osmâniyye,* İstanbul, n.d.

Ferîdûn Beğ, *Münshe'ât-i Selâtîn,* İstanbul, 1274.

Fındıklılı Mehmed Ağa, *Silâhdâr Tarihi,* İstanbul, 1928.

Halacoğlu Yusuf, "Osmanlı İmparatorluğunda Menzil Teşkilâtı Hakkında Bazı Mülahazalar," *Osmanlı Araştirmaları,* İstanbul: 1981, II.

Hamidullah Muhammad, *Introduction to Islam,* 5th ed., Lahore: 1979.

İbn-i Kemâl (Kemâl Pasha-Zâde), Shemsu'd Dîn Ahmed b. Süleymân, *Tevârîh-i Âl-i Osmân, I. Defter,* ed.Şerâfettin Turan, Atatürk Kültür, Dil ve Tarih Yüksek Kurumu, Ankara, 1991. İbn Kemâl (1468-1534) wrote his *Tevârîh-i Âl-i Osmân* by order of Bâyezîd II (r.1481-1512).

_____, *Tevârîh-i Âl-i Osmân, VII. Defter,* ed. Şerafettin Turan, Atatürk Kültür, Dil ve Tarih Yüksek Kurumu, Ankara, 1991.

İnalcık, Halîl – Mevlüt Oğuz, *Gazavât-ı Sultân Murâd b. Mehemmed Hân,* Ankara, 1978.

Jelâlzâde Koja Nishanjı Mustafa, *Kitâb-ı Ma'âsir-i Selîm Khâni* (manuscript) TSMK H.1415.

Karal, Enver Ziyâ, *Osmanlı Tarihi*, vols. V-IX, Ankara: Türk Tarih Kurumu, 1983-1996.

Kâtib Chelebi, *Tuhfetu'l Kibâr fî Esfâri'l Bihâr*, İstanbul, 1329.

Kazıcı Ziyâ, *Osmanlılarda İhtisab Müessesesi*, İstanbul: 1987.

Keşfî Mehmed Çelebi, *Keşfî'nin Selîm-Nâmesi*, ed. by Şefâettin Severcan, Kayseri: 1995.

Mehmed Râshid Efendi, *Târîh*, İstanbul, 1867, II.

Mehmed Süreyya, *Sijill-i Osmânî*, İstanbul, 1308.

Mehmed Tevfîq, *Târîh-i Osmânî*, İstanbul, 1305.

Mustafa Nûrî Pasha, *Netâyiju'l Vuqû'ât*, I-IV, İstanbul, 1327.

Mustakimzade Süleymân Sadeddîn, *Devhatu'l Meşâyih*, İstanbul: 1978.

Müneccimbaşı Ahmed b. Lütfullah, *Câmiüd Düvel, Osmanlı Tarihi (1299-1481)*, ed. Ahmet Ağırakça, İstanbul, 1995.

Na'îmâ, *Ravzatu'l Huseyn if Khulaâati Akhbâri'l Khâfıqayn* (*Târîh-i Naîmâ*), 2nd ed., İstanbul, 1280.

Neşrî (Mehmed), *Kitâb-i Cihân-Nümâ*, I-II, ed. F.R. Unat and M.A. Köymen, Ankara: Türk Tarih Kurumu, 1949.

*Oruç Beğ Tarihi*, İstanbul: Tercüman Yayınları, 1972.

Otmanbölük, Günvar, "Fâtihin Annesi Özbeöz Türktür" (Fâtih's mother is purely of Turkish Stock), in *Türkiye* (newspaper), January 13, 1992, p. 8. (Bursa Sher'iyye Sijilleri, Nos. 31 (p. 35), 201 (p. 64), and 375 (p. 40).

Öztuna, Yılmaz, *Osmanlı Devleti Tarihi*, I-IV, Faisal Finans Kurumu, İstanbul, 1986.

Parmaksızoğlu, İsmet, "Kemâl Reis" *İslâm Ansiklopedisi* (Encyclopaedia of Islam in Turkish, published by Ministry of Education) VI, pp. 566-569.

Pechûyî İbrâhîm, *Târîh-i Pechûyi* İstanbul: Enderun Kitabevi, 1980.

Pîrî Reîs, *Kitâb-ı Bahriye*, İstanbul, 1935.

Qarachelebizâde (Sheyhulislâm) Abdulazîz, *Ravzatu'l Abrâr*, Bulaq, 1248.

*Bibliography*

Şâhin, Kâmil, "Edebalı," *Türkiye Diyânet Vakfı İslâm Ansiklopedisi*, X, 393-4.

Shânizâde Mehmed 'Atâullâh, *Târîh*, İstanbul, 1284.

Selânikî Mustafa Efendi, *Târîh-i Selânikî*, 2 vols, ed. Mehmet İpşirli, İstanbul, 1989.

Silahdâr Solaqzâde Mehmed Hemdemî, *Solakzâde Târihi*, İstanbul, 1298.

Togan, Zeki Velîdî, "İbn Fadlan," *M.E.B. İslâm Ansiklopedisi*, İstanbul, 1993, v. V, part II, pp. 730-731.

Turan, Osman, *Türk Cihan Hâkimiyeti Mefküresi Târihi*, I-II, İstanbul: Nakışlar Yayınevi, 1979.

Tursun Beğ, *Târîh-i Ebu'l Feth*, İstanbul: Fetih Cemiyeti, 1977.

Uludağ Osman Şevki (ed. ilter Uzel), *Beş Buçuk Asırlık Türk Tababeti Tarihi*, Ankara: 1991.

Uzunçarşılı, İsmail Hakkı, *Osmanlı Tarihi*, I-IV, Ankara: Türk Tarih Kurumu, 1947-1959.

_____, *Osmanlı Devleti Teşkilâtından Kapukulu Ocakları*, I, Ankara: TTK, 1984.

_____, *Osmanlı Devletinin İlmiye Teşkilatı*, Ankara: 1984.

_____, "Gâzi Orhan Bey Vakfiyesi," in *Belleten*, Ankara: Türk Tarih Kurumu, 1941, v. 19, pp. 280-283.

_____, *Osmanlı Devletinin Merkez ve Bahriye Teşkilâtı*, Ankara: Türk Tarih Kurumu Basımevi, 1984.

_____, *Osmanlı Tarihi*, I.

Yazıjızâde, *Selchûqnâme*, TSMK, Revân, 1391.

Yüce, Nuri, "Bulgar" (Batı Hun Devleti içindeki Türk kavimlerinden biri), *Türkiye Diyânet Vakfı İslâm Ansiklopedisi*, İstanbul, 1992, v. VI, p. 390.

M. Zeki Pakalın, *Osmanlı Tarih Terimleri ve Deyimleri Sözlüğü*, İstanbul, 1983, I-II.

Ziyâ Kazıcı, *Osmanlılarda İhtisab Müessesesi*, İstanbul: 1987.

## 2. Arabic

*al-Qur'ân al-Karîm.*

Abû Bakr Muhammad b. Aziz as Sijistani, *Garîbu'l Qur'ân (al Musamma bi Nuzhati'l Qulûb)*, Beirut: Daru'l Fikri'l Arabi, 3rd printing, 1402/1982.

Abû Dâwûd, *as Sunan.*

Abû Ya'lâ Muhammad b. al-Husayn al-Farrâ, *al-Ahkâmu's Sultâniyyatu,* Surubaya, Indonesia, 1394/1974.

Ahmad b. Hanbal, *al-Musnad.*

Akkutay Ülker, *Enderun Mektebi,* Ankara: 1984.

al Bukhârî, *al-Jâmi'u's Sahîh.*

İpşirli Mehmet, *XVII. Yüzyıl Başlarına Kadar Osmanlı İmparatorluğunda Kadıaskerlik Müessesesi* (Unpublished post-doctorate dissertation: İstanbul Üniversitesi, Edebiyat Fakültesi).

Hallâq, Hassan 'Alî, *Târikhu'n Nuqûd wa'd Dawâwîn,* Beirut, 1986.

Hraydi, Muhammad 'Abdullatîf, *al-Hurûbu'l 'Uthmâniyyatu'l Fârisiyyatu wa Âthâruhâ fi İnhisâri'l Maddi'l İslâmiyyi 'an Urubbâ* (The Ottoman Persian Wars and Their Share in Retreating the Islamic Tide from Europe), al-Qâhira, 1408/1987.

Harb, Muhammad, *Mudhakkirâtu's Sultân 'Abdi'lHamiyd* (translation & commentary), Egypt, 1978.

İbn Battuta, *Rihlatu'bni Battuta (Tuhfatu'n Nuzzâr),* Beirut, 1384/1964.

İbn Hishâm, *as Siyratu'n Nabawiyyatu,* al-Qâhira, 1375/1955.

İbn Iyâs, *Badâiu'z Zuhûr fi Waqâi'id Duhûr,* ed. Mohammad Mustafa, Cairo, 1960.

Maksudoğlu, Mehmet, "Zuhûru'd Dâyâti bi'l Qutri't Tûnisiyyi," in *Ankara Üniversitesi Ilâhiyat Fakültesi Dergisi,* Ankara, 1967, vol. XIV, pp. 202-210.

Mâlik b. Anas, *al-Muwatta.*

al-Mâwardî, *al-Ahkâmu's Sultâniyyatu,* al-Qâhira 1983 XIV, pp. 203-213.

*al Mâwardî, *al-Ahkâmu's Sultâniyyatu,* Egypt: 1973.
Muhammad Farîd Bey, *Târikhu'd Dawlati'l 'Aliyyati'l Uthmaniyyati,* Beirut, 1986.
*Muslim, *as Sahîh.*
Nasaî, *as Sunan, al-Bay'at.*
Öztuna, Yılmaz, *Târikhu'd Dawlati'l Othmâniyyati* I, (transl. 'Adnân Mahmûd Salmân, checked by Dr. Mahmûd al-Ansârî), İstanbul: Faisal Finance Institution Inc., 1408/1988.
ash Shâzulî, Mahmûd Thâbit, *al-Mas'alatush Sharqiyyatu, Dirâsatun Wathâiqiyyatun 'ani'l Khilâfati'l Othmâniyyati,* Maktabatu Wahba: al-Qahira, n.d.
ash Shinnâwî, 'Abdulazîz Muhammed, *ad Dawlatu'l 'Uthmâniyyatu Dawlatun İslâmiyyatun Muftaran 'Alayha,* I-III, al-Qâhira, 1980.
Tashkoprizâde Ahmed İsâmeddîn, *ash Shaqâ'iqu'n Nu'mâniyyatu fi 'Ulemâi'd Dawlati'l 'Aliyyati'l Othmâniyyati,* Beirut: 1975.

## 3. English

Aly Bayoumy Aly Oteify, "Interrogative Utterances in Surah Al-Baqarah," *Intellectual Discourse,* The Journal of the Faculty (*Kulliyah*) of Islamic Revealed Knowledge and Human Sciences, International Islamic University Press, Malaysia, October 1993, I, number 1, p. 70.
Bariun Fawzia, *Malik Bennabi, His Life and Theory of Civilization,* Kuala Lumpur: 1993. İbn Battûta, *Travels in Asia and Africa 1325-1354,* translated by H.A.R. Gibb, London, 1983. Bariun, Fawzia, *Mâlik Bennabi, His Life and Theory of Civilization,* ABIM, Kuala Lumpur, 1993.
Bryer, Anthony, *Peoples and Settlement in Anatolia and Caucasus 800-1900,* Variorum Reprints, London, 1988.
Davison, Roderic H., *Reform in the Ottoman Empire 1856-1876,* New York: 1973.

Dunn, Ross E., *The Adventures of İbn Battuta: A Muslim Traveler of the 14th Century,* London: 1986.

Emerson, Rupert, *From Empire to Nation,* Cambridge, Massachaussets: Harvard University Press, 1967.

Ferriman, Z. Duckett, *Turkey and the Turks,* London: Mills and Boon Ltd., 1911.

Figgie, Jr. Harry E., and Gerald J. Swanson, *Bankruptcy 1995: The Coming Collapse of America And How to Stop It,* Boston/New York: Back Bay Books, 1992.

Gibb, H.A.R., *A History of Ottoman Poetry,* London, 1900, reprinted 1958.

Gibbons, H.A., *The Foundation of the Ottoman Empire, A History of the Osmanlıs up to the Death of Bâyezîd I 1300-1403,* Frank Cass & Co. Ltd., 1968.

Goldsmith Jr., Arthur, *A Concise History of the Middle East,* Boulder, Colorado, 1988.

Hamdani, Abbas, "Ottoman Response to the Discovery of America and the New Route to India" in *Journal of American Oriental Society,* vol. 101 (1981), pp. 323-330.

Houston, William, *Meltdown, The Great '90s Depression and How to Come Through it a Winner,* London: 1994.

İnalcık, Halîl, *The Ottoman Empire* (translated by Norman Itzkowitz & Colin Imber), London: 1973.

_____, "The Heyday and Decline of the Ottoman Empire," in *The Cambridge History of Islam,* IA, Cambridge University Press, 1988, pp. 324-353.

Jay, Richard, "Nationalism," in *Political Ideologies,* London: Unwin Hyman, 1990.

Jenkins, R.J.H., "Social Life in the Byzantine Empire", *The Cambridge Medieval History,* vol. IV, part II, ed. by J.M. Hussey, Cambridge University Press, 1967, repr. 1978, pp. 78-103.

Köprülü, M. Fuad, *The Origins of the Ottoman Empire*, translated and edited by Gary Leiser, New York, 1992.

Kushner, David, *The Rise of Turkish Nationalism 1876-1908*, London: 1977.

Lane-Poole, Stanley, *Turkey*, repr., London: 1986.

Lapidus, Ira M., *A History of Islamic Societies*, Cambridge University Press, 1988.

Lewis, Bernard, *The Emergence of Modern Turkey*, second edition, London: Oxford University Press, 1968.

Lewis Bernard, *The Arabs in History*, New York: Harper Torchbook, 1967.

_____, *The Emergence of Modern Turkey*, 2nd ed., Oxford University Press: 1968.

Lings, Martin, *Muhammad ﷺ: His Life Based on the Earliest Sources*, London: George Allen & Unwin, 1983.

Lord Kinross, *The Ottoman Centuries, the Rise and Fall of the Turkish Empire*, New York: Morrow Quill Paperbacks, 1977.

Muller, Herbert J., *The Uses of the Past; Profiles of Former Societies*, New York: New American Library, 1954.

Pitcher, Donald Edgar, *An Historical Geography of the Ottoman Empire*, Leiden: E.J. Brill, 1972.

Pixley Michael M., "The Development and the Role of Seyhulislam in Early Otoman History," *Journal of the American Oriental Society*, vol. 96,

Nr. 1, January-March 1976.

Reid, Anthony, *The Contest for North Sumatra, Atjeh: The Netherlands and Britain 1858-1898*, Oxford University Press/University of Malaya Press, 1969.

Repp R.C., *The Mufti of İstanbul: A Study in the Development of the Ottoman Learned Hierarchy*, Oxford University Computing Service, 1986.

Savory, R.M., "Safavid Persia," in *The Cambridge History of Islam*, Cambridge, CUP:1980, IA, pp. 394-429.

Scrutton, Robert, *Nature's Way to Nutrition & Vibrant Health*, California, Willshire Book Company, 1977.

Shaw, Stanford, *History of the Ottoman Empire and Modern Turkey*, CUP, 1991, I.

Shaw, Stanford J., and Ezel Kural Shaw, *History of the Ottoman Empire and Modern Turkey*, vol. II, Cambridge: 1977.

Scrutton, Robert J., *Nature's Way to Nutrition and Vibrant Health*, Hollywood, California: Melvin Powers, 1977.

Spuler, Bertold, *The Muslim World, Part I: The Age of the Caliphs*, Leiden: E.J. Brill, 1960, translation by F.R.C. Bagley.

Stripling, George William Frederic, *The Ottoman Turks And the Arabs 1511-1574*, Philadelphia: Porcupine Press, 1977.

*Sûfî Path* (articles related to sûfîsm), published in Malaysia by A.S. Noordeen, 1991, back cover.

Taylor, A.J.P., *The Course of German History*, London: Routledge paperback, 1988.

Uğur, Ahmet, *The Reign of Sultân Selîm I in the Light of the Selim-Nâme*

*Literature*, Berlin: Klaus Schwarz Verlag, 1985.

Vaughan, Dorothy, *Europe and the Turk, A Pattern of Alliances 1350-1700,*

Liverpool: 1954.

Wright, Jr., Walter Livingstone, *Ottoman Statecraft: The Book of Counsel for Vazirs and Governors of Sarı Mehmed Pasha, the Defterdar*, Princeton: Princeton University Press, 1935.

## 4. FRENCH

Cahen, Claude, *La Turquie Pre-Ottomane*, İstanbul/Paris, 1988.

# Endnotes

## Introduction

1. Stanford J. Shaw, *History of the Ottoman Empire and Modern Turkey* (Cambridge University Press, 1991) Vol.I, p.vii.
2. Stanford J. Shaw and Ezel Kural Shaw, *History of the Ottoman Empire and Modern Turkey* (Cambridge University Press, 1977) Vol. II, p. x. .
3. Rupert Emerson, *From Empire to Nation* (Cambridge, Massachusetts: Harvard University Press, 1967), p. vii.
4. Bernard Lewis, *The Emergence of Modern Turkey*. 2 nd edition. (London: Oxford University Press, 1968), p.2.
5. This mistake is very common among all the orientalists, for example, one of them who is very famous: Bernard Lewis, *The Emergence of Modern Turkey*, (Second Edition, Oxford University Press:1968) pp. 5, 13, 36, 46, 106.
6. Chris Cook, *Dictionary of Historical Terms* (London: Macmillan, 1983), p. 152
7. J.M. Roberts, *The Hutchinson History of the World* (London: Hutchinson, 1987), p. 835.
8. Ahmad ibn Hanbal, *al-Musnad*, VI, p. 240.
9. Hassan 'Ali Hallâq, *Târikhun Nuqûd wa'd Dawâwîn* (Beirut: 1986) p.86.
10. Bukhârî, *as Sahîh, Kitâbul Jihâd wa's Siyar*, 181.
11. Abû Dâwûd, *as Sunan, Imârah*, 14.
12. Mâlik b.Anas, *al-Muwatta', Zakât*, 4.
13. al Mâwardî, *al-Ahkâmu's Sultâniyyah* (Cairo: 1983) p. 172.
14. In his translation of the elaborate work of Sarı Mehmed Pasha, *Nasâihul Vüzerâ ve'l Ulemâ* under the title *Ottoman Statecraft: the Book of Counsel for Vazirs and Governors of Sarı Mehmed Pasha, the Defterdar* (Princeton: Princeton University Press, 1935), Walter Livingson Wright Jr. erroneously translates "Rikâb-ı Hümâyûn" as "the Imperial Gate" (p. 71, footnote 48) and understands "Divân-ı Hümâyûn" as "the Imperial Divan" (p. 17).
15. S. Shaw, *History of the Ottoman Empire and Modern Turkey* (C.U.P. 1976), pp. 25, 26, 101, 102, 108, 115, 117. And Shaw is one of the very rare "objective" orientalists.
16. *al-Qur'ân al-Karîm, Tâ Hâ* (20) âyats 29, 30.

17    Abû Dâwûd, *as Sunan, al-İmârah,* 4.
18    Nasaî, *as Sunan, al-Bay'ah,* 33.
19    *al-Qur'ān al-Karim, al-An'âm* (6) *âyat* 164.
20    Shaw, *op. cit.*, I, p. 25.
21    *al-Qur'ân al-Karîm, Tawbah* (9), 60.
22    Tashköprüzâde Ahmed 'Isâmeddin, *ash Shaqâ'iqun Nu'mâniyyah fi 'Ulemâi'd Dawlati'l 'Uthmâniyyah.* Incidentally his name is not Husameddin, as Shaw reads it: *op. cit.*, p. 145.
23    Neşrî (Mehmed), *Kitâb-ı Cihân-Nümâ* (ed. by F.R. Unat and M.A. Köymen) Ankara; Turk Tarih Kurumu, 1949, I, p. 186.
24    D.E. Pitcher, *An Historical Geography of the Ottoman Empire* (Leiden: E.J. Brill, 1972) p. 5.
25    Şerâfettin Turan, İbn Kemâl, *Tevârîh-i Âl-i Osman VII. Defter,* Atatürk Kültür Dil ve Tarih Yüksek Kurumu, Ankara 1991, IX-XXII.
26    Neşrî, *op. cit.*, p. 108, line 13.
27    Neşrî, I, 108-110; İbn Kemâl, *Tevârîh-i Âl-i Osmân,* ed. by Şerafettin Turan, TTK, (Ankara : 1991) I, 107.
28    İbn Hishâm, *as Siyratun Nabawiyyah,* al-Qâhirah : 1375/1955, second printing, v.I, p.494.
29    *Munsheât,* I, 48.
30    Abû Ya'lâ al-Farrâ Muhammad, *al-Ahkâmus Sultâniyyah* (Surabaya: 1394 /1974 ), p. 20.
31    *Munsheât,* I, 69.
32    35 *Ibid,* I, p. 116.
33    Tursun Bey, *Tarih-i Ebul Feth* (İstanbul: İstanbul Fetih Cemiyeti, 1977) p. 33.
34    *Ibid,* I, pp. 307, 326.
35    *Ibid,* I, pp. 375-377.
36    *Munsheât,* I, p. 87.
37    Neşrî, *Cihânnümâ,* I, p. 294.
38    Kâtib Chelebi, *Tuhfetu'l Kibâr fi Esfâri'l Bihâr* (İstanbul: 1329), p. 37.
39    Neşrî, *op. cit.*, I, p. 196.
40    *al-Qur'ân al-Karîm, al-Anfâl* (8) *âyat* 41.
41    Naîmâ, *Ravzatul Huseyn fi Khulâsati Akhbâril Khâfiqayn* (İstanbul: 1280) I, p. 257.
42    Kâtib Chelebi, *Tuhfetul Kibâr Fî Esfâril Bihâr* (İstanbul: 1329) p. 40.
43    Mustafa Jenâbî, *Târîh,* Ragib Pasha Ktb. nr. 986, 339b, cited in İsmet Parmaksizoğlu, "Kemâl Reis" *IA,* VI, pp. 566-569; Pîrî Reîs, *Kitâb-ı Bahriye* (İstanbul: 1935) p. 17; D.E. Pitcher is also aware of this fact, see: *An Historical Geography of the Ottoman Empire* (Leiden: 1972) p. 98.
44    Translation of the invitation letter: TSMK E 6456.

*Endnotes*

45 Cited in Osman Turan, *Türk Cihan Hakimiyeti Mefküresi Tarihi* (İstanbul: Nakışlar Yayınevi, 1979), II, p. 422.
46 Agâh Sırrı Levend, *Gazavatnâmeler ve Mihaloğlu Ali Beyin Gazavatnâmesi* (İstanbul: 1956), pp. 246, 254 and 295, cited in *ibid.*, p. 422.

## Part One – The Foundation of the Osmanlı Devlet 1288-1453

### Chapter One – Islam in Anatolia

47 Yazıjızâde, *Selchûqnâme*, TSMK, Revân 1391, 3a.
48 Nuri Yüce, "Bulgar (Batı Hun Devleti içindeki Türk kavimlerinden biri)"*T.D.V. İslâm Ansiklopedisi*, İstanbul 1992, v. VI, p.390.
49 *Loc. cit.*
50 *Loc. cit.*
51 Yazıcızâde Ali, *Tevârîh-i Âl-i Selçuk*, ed. Abdullah Bakır (İstanbul: 2009), p. 51.
52 Ahmad Mukhtâr al-'Abbâdî and as Sayyid 'Abdulazîz Sâlim, *Târîkhu'l Bahriyyati'l Islamiyyah*, Beirut, 1972, pp. 32-33.
53 Yılmaz Öztuna, translated by Adnan Mahmûd Selmân and edited by Dr.Mahmûd Ansârî: *Târikhu'd Dawlati'l 'Othmâniyya* (İstanbul 1408/1988) p. 68.

### Chapter Two – The Foundation of the Osmanlı Devlet

54 İsmail Hakkı Uzunçarşılı, *Osmanlı Târihi*, Ankara, Türk Tarih Kurumu, 1982, v. I, p. 103.
55 Neşrî (Mehmed), *Kitâb-ı Cihân-Nümâ*, edited by F.R.Unat and M.A.Köymen, Ankara, TTK 1949, v. I, pp. 78. Neshrî informs that Osmân's uncle Tundâr also performed *bay'at* (swore allegiance in the Islamic fashion).
56 İbn-i Kemâl, *Tevârîh-i Âl-i Osmân*, ed. by Şerafettin Turan, Atatürk Kültür, Dil ve Tarih Yüksek Kurumu (Ankara: 1991), vol. I, p. 60.
57 *Âlu Imrân* (3), 26.
58 Neşrî, I, 82.
59 İbn Battûtah, *Travels in Asia and Afrca, 1325-1354* (London: 1983), translated by H.A.R. Gibb, p. 125. İbn Battûtah (703-770/1304-1369) travelled extensively all over the Muslim world.
60 İ.H.Uzunçarşılı, *Osmanlı Tarihi*, I, 106.
61 M. Fuad Köprülü, *The Origins of the Ottoman Empire*, tr. and ed. by Gary Leiser (New York: 1992), pp. 68-69.
62 İ.H. Uzunçarşılı, *Osmanlı Devleti Teşkilâtından Kapıkulu Ocakları* (Ankara: T.T.K., 1984), vol. I, p. 1.
63 M. Fuad Köprülü, *The Origins of the Ottoman Empire*, pp. 69-70.

64  Neşrî, *op. cit.*, pp. 72-74.
65  Müneccimbaşı Ahmed Lütfullah, *Câmi'ud Düvel*, ed. by Ahmet Ağırakça, İstanbul, 1955, p. 56.
66  İbn Kemâl, I, p. 106.
67  Neşrî, I, p. 108.
68  Neşrî, I, 108; İbn Kemâl, I, 107.
69  İbn Kemâl, *Tevârîh-i Âl-i Osmân*, ed. by Şerâfettin Turan, TTK, Ankara: 1991, I, 112-113; Neşrî, *op. cit.*, I, 110.
70  İbn Hishâm, *as Siyratu'n Nabawiyyah*, al-Qâhirah: 1375/1955, second printing, v.I, p. 494.
71  İbn Kemâl, I, 112.
72  İbn Kemâl, I, 113.
73  Neşrî, *op. cit.*, I, 108.
74  R. Emerson, *From Empire to Nation* (Cambridge, Massachusetts: Harvard University Press, 1967), p. vii.
75  Uzunçarşılı, *op. cit.*, I, 107.
76  Neşrî, I, 114-116.
77  Uzunçarşılı (*OT*), I, 110.
78  *OT*, I, 111.
79  *OT*, I, 117.
80  Neşrî, *op. cit.*, I, 145.
81  *Aşıkpaşaoğlu Tarihi*, ed. by Nihal Atsız, Ankara, Ministry of Culture and Tourism, 1985, pp. 28-29.
82  *OT*, I, 118.
83  Neşrî, I, 154; *Mufassal Osmanlı Tarihi*, vol. I, p. 69.
84  Hoca Sa'deddîn Efendi, *Tâcu't Tevârîh*, İstanbul 1279, I, 43; *OT*, I, 120.
85  *Loc. cit.*
86  Neşrî, I, 163-165.
87  Neşrî, I, 162.
88  *Loc. cit.*
89  Robert J. Scrutton, *Nature's Way to Nutrition and Vibrant Health* (California, 1977), p. 16. Emphasis added.
90  *Loc. cit.* quoted from Henry Buckle, *History of Civilization*, vol. II, p. 44.
91  Robert J. Scrutton, *op. cit.*, p. 17.
92  Neşrî, I, 186.
93  Ferîdûn Beğ, *Mecmû'a-i Münsheât-ı Selâtîn*, İstanbul, 1274, v.I, p. 69.
94  Michael H. Hart, *The 100: A Ranking of the Most Influental Persons in History* (Malaysia:Golden Books Centre Sdn. Bhd. 1989), p. 164.
95  *OT*, I, 119.
96  Neşrî, I, 162.

*Endnotes*

97 Neşrî, I, 165.
98 Neşrî, I, 166.
99 *OT*, I, 123.
100 Neşrî, I, 172.
101 *Aşıkpaşaoğlu Tarihi*, p. 55; Neşrî, I, 184.
102 *OT*, I, 157-158.
103 İsmâil Hâmi Dânişmend, *İzahlı Osmanlı Tarihi Kronolojisi*, İstanbul 1971, v. I, p. 32.
104 *Münsheât*, I, 69-70.
105 *Loc. Cit.*
106 Neşrî, I, 186.
107 According to Neşrî, Murâd Khân became ruler in 760/1359: I, 190.
108 *OT, I*, 531.
109 *OT, I*, 159.
110 İbn Battûtah, *Travels in Asia and Africa, 1325-1354*, translated by H.A.R. Gibb (London: 1983) pp. 125-126.
111 Neşrî, I, 190-192.
112 *Tarih vesikaları dergisi 4*, December 1941, cited in *OT*, I, 531: Murâd Gâzi, appointed a certain Mûsâ as *Akhî* at Malkara in Rajab 767/ March 1366.
113 *OT*, I, pp. 161-162.
114 *Aşıkpaşaoğlu Tarihi*, p. 56.
115 İsmâil Hâmi Dânişmend, *İzahlı Osmanlı Tarihi Kronolojisi*, İstanbul 1971, I, 39.
116 Halîl İnalcık, *The Ottoman Empire*, translated by Norman Itzkowitz and Colin Imber (London, 1973), p. 13.
117 For this sort of attitude of mind see Ferîdûn Beğ, *Münsheât-i Selâtîn*, I, p. 72.
118 Ferîdûn Beğ, *Münsheât-i Selâtîn*, I, p. 90, line 25.
119 *Münsheât*, I, 87.
120 al-Farrâ', Abû Ya'lâ Muhammad ibn al-Husayn, *al-Ahkâmus Sultâniyyah* (Surabaya, Indonesia, 1394/1974), p. 20.
121 *OT*, I, 165; Stanford J. Shaw, *History of the Ottoman Empire and Modern Turkey* (reprinted), Cambridge 1976, v. I, p. 18.
122 İsmail Hâmi Dânişmend, *İzahlı Osmanlı Tarihi Kronolojisi*, I, 42
123 *OT*, I, 167.
124 *OT*, I, 168.
125 Stanford J. Shaw, *History of the Ottomam Empire and Modern Turkey*, CUP, Cambridge 1988, I, 18.
126 Dânişmend, I, 42; *OT*, I, 168.
127 *OT*, I, 169.
128 *OT*, I, p. 166.

129 Neşrî, *op. cit.*, I, p. 196.
130 Qurân, al-Anfâl [8] *âyat* 4. The *âyat* goes on to explain where this should be spent by the Islamic *devlet*.
131 Neşrî, *op. cit.*, I, p. 198.
132 Dânişmend, I, 43-45.
133 Dânişmend, I, 45-46.
134 Dânişmend, I, 46.
135 Stanford J. Shaw, *History of the Ottoman Empire and Modern Turkey*, Cambridge: 1991 (reprint), vol. I, p. 19.
136 Shaw, *op. cit.*, I, 19.
137 *OT*, I, p. 170.
138 *OT*, I, 173.
139 Dânişmend, *op. cit.*, I, 51-56.
140 *OT*, I, 174.
141 *OT*, I, 175.
142 *OT*, I, 176.
143 H.A. Gibbons, *The Foundation of the Ottoman Empire, A History of the Osmanlıs up to the Death of Bâyezîd I, 1300-1403* (Place: Frank Cass and Co. Ltd., 1968), pp. 162-163.
144 Shaw, *op. cit.*, I, 17.
145 *OT*, I, 184.
146 Dânişmend, I, 7
147 *OT*, I, 46. The correct name is Melek Hâtûn, not Nefîse Sultân.
148 Neşrî, *op. cit.*, I, pp. 216-230.
149 *OT*, I, 249.
150 Shaw, I, 21.
151 Mustafa Nuri Pasha, *Netâyijul Vuqû'ât*, İstanbul, 1327, I, 13.
152 *OT*, I, 253.
153 Shaw, *op. cit.*, I, 21.
154 Neşrî, *op. cit.*, I, pp. 278-282.
155 al-Qur'ân, Âl-i 'Imrân [3]: 26.
156 Neşrî, *op. cit.*, I, 284-286.
157 Neşrî, *op. cit.*, I, 304; *OT*, I, 256.
158 Neşrî, *op. cit.*, I, 306; *OT*, I, 257.
159 Shaw, *op. cit.*, I, 22.
160 *Netâyij*, I, pp. 15-16.
161 Dânişmend, *op. cit.*, I, 87.
162 Dânişmend, *op. cit.*, I, 85.
163 Dânişmend, I, 86.
164 Dânişmend, I, 86, 88.
165 *Aşıkpaşaoğlu Tarihi*, ed. by Nihal Atsız (Ankara, 1985), p. 67.
166 Neşrî, *op. cit.*, I, 312.

167 Dânişmend, *op. cit.*, I, 89-91.
168 *Aşıkpaşaoğlu Tarihi*, p. 69; Dânişmend, *op. cit.*, I, 95.
169 *Aşıkpaşaoğlu Tarihi*, p. 72; Dânişmend, I, 123.
170 Shaw, I, 31.
171 Dânişmend, I, 98.
172 Dânişmend, I, 98; Shaw, I, 31.
173 Dânişmend, I, 102.
174 *OT*, I, 276.
175 *OT*, I, 298-299.
176 *Aşıkpaşaoğlu Tarihi*, p. 74.
177 *Aşıkpaşaoğlu Tarihi*, p. 72; *Oruç Beğ Tarihi*, p. 55.
178 *OT*, I, 286.
179 Shaw, *op. cit.*, I, p. 33.
180 Dânişmend, I, 104-106.
181 *OT*, I, 289.
182 *Aşıkpaşaoğlu Tarihi*, p. 73; *Oruç Beğ Tarihi*, pp. 55-56.
183 *OT*, I, 295-296.
184 *OT*, I, 277-278.
185 Mustapha Nûrî Pasha, *Netâyijul Vuqû'ât*, I, pp. 11-12.
186 *Netâyij*, I, p. 11.
187 Stanley Lane-Poole, *Turkey* (London: 1986), p. 65.
188 Feridun Emecen, "Kuruluştan Küçük Kaynarcaya," *Osmanlı Devleti Tarihi*, vol. I, p. 19, publication of *Zaman*, İstanbul, 1999.
189 *OT*, I, 306-307.
190 Dânişmend, I, 127.
191 Neşrî, I, 350.
192 Mustapha Nûrî Pasha, *Netâyijul Vuqû'ât*, I, 24.
193 *OT*, I, 313.
194 *Aşıkpaşaoğlu Tarihi*, p. 80; Neşrî, I, 358.
195 Stanley Lane-Poole, *Turkey*, pp. 72-73.
196 *OT*, I, 314.
197 Mustapha Nûrî Pasha, *Netâyijul Vuqû'ât*, I, p. 21.
198 Stanley Lane-Poole, *op. cit.*, p. 74.
199 Mustapha Nûrî Pasha, *Netâyijul Vuqû'ât*, I, pp. 13-15.
200 Dânişmend, I, 142-143.
201 *Aşıkpaşaoğlu Tarihi*, p. 84.
202 *OT*, I, 325-326.
203 Donald Edgar Pitcher, *An Historical Geography of the Ottoman Empire* (Leiden: E.J. Brill, 1972), p. 58.

# Chapter Three – Restoration

204 *OT*, I, p. 351.

205  *OT,* I, 350-351; Dânişmend, I, 176.
206  Dânişmend, I, 173.
207  *OT,* I, 352-353.
208  *OT,* I, 354-355; Dânişmend, I, 174-175.
209  *OT,* I, 355.
210  Dânişmend, I, 175-176.
211  *OT,* I, 357.
212  *Netâyij,* I, p. 30.
213  *OT,* I, 370-371.
214  *Netâyij,* I, 54-55.
215  *Netâyij,* I, 55.
216  *OT,* I, 372.
217  Oruç Beğ, p. 78; *Aşıkpaşaoğlu Tarihi,* p. 93.
218  Oruç Beğ, p. 78.
219  *OT,* I, p. 376-377.
220  *Aşıkpaşaoğlu Tarihi,* p. 93.
221  *Aşıkpaşaoğlu Tarihi,* p. 95.
222  *Aşıkpaşaoğlu Tarihi,* p. 98; *Netâyij,* I, 32.
223  *OT,* I, 388-389.
224  *Aşıkpaşaoğlu Tarihi,* p. 99; *Netâyij,* I, p. 33.
225  Stanley Lane-Poole, *Turkey,* p. 83. He uses "empire" instead of sultanate.
226  Neşrî, *Cihân-Nümâ,* Ankara, Turkish Historical society, 1957, Vol. II, p. 578; *Netâyij,* I, p. 36.
227  Dânişmend, I, p. 19.
228  *OT,* I, 393-394.
229  Neşrî, II, 586; *OT,* I, p. 400.
230  *OT,* I, p. 401.
231  Neşrî, II, p. 592; *Netâyij,* I, p. 34.
232  Neşrî, II, pp. 604-606.
233  Dânişmend, I, p. 194.
234  *Netâyij* I, p. 35.
235  *OT,* I, pp. 408-411.
236  *Aşıkpaşaoğlu Tarihi,* p. 114; Neşrî, II, p. 616.
237  Neşrî, II, p. 618; *Netâyij,* I, p. 36.
238  She was Maria Branković, her father was George Branković, and her mother the sister of the emperor of Trabzon; *OT,* I, 413.
239  Neşrî, II, p. 620.
240  *Oruç Beğ Tarihi,* p. 85.
241  *OT,* I, p. 416.
242  Neşrî, II, p. 622.
243  Dânişmend, I, p. 204.

244 Aşıkpaşaoğlu, *op. cit.*, p. 118; Oruç Bey, *op. cit.*, p. 87.
245 *OT,* I, p. 416 and the footnote 2.
246 *OT,* I, p. 418.
247 S. Shaw, *op. cit.*, I, pp. 50-51.
248 OT, I, p. 419.
249 *OT,* I, pp. 419-427; Dânişmend, *op. cit.*, I, pp. 209-210.
250 *OT,* I, p. 428, footnote 1.
251 Dânişmend, I, p. 213.
252 *Netâyij,* I, p. 38.
253 Shaw, *op. cit.*, I, p. 52.
254 *OT,* I, p. 434.
255 Shaw, *op. cit.*, I, p. 53.
256 Ferîdûn Beğ, *Münsheât*, vol. I, pp. 233-235.
257 Oruç Bey, *op. cit.*, p. 93; *Netâyij,* I, p. 39.
258 Neşrî, *op. cit.*, II, p. 665.
259 Hammer, translated by Atâ, v. II, p. 237 cited in *OT,* I, p. 447.
260 Lütfi Paşa Tarihi, p. 163 cited in *OT,* I, p. 447.
261 *Ban* means "prince" or "minor sovereign" in Slavic: Mehmet Zeki Pakalın, *Osmanlı Tarih Deyimleri ve Terimleri Sözlüğü*, İstanbul 1993, v. I, p. 158.
262 *Netâyij,* I, p. 40.
263 Neşrî, v. II, p. 672.
264 Neşrî, *op. cit.*, II, p. 662.
265 Neşrî, II, p. 674.
266 Neşrî, II, p. 676.
267 *Netâyij,* I, p. 40.

## Part Two – Expansion 1453-1699

### Chapter Four – Expansion

268 Neşrî, *op. cit.*, II, p. 682; Tursun Beğ, *Târîh-i Ebül Feth* (İstanbul, 1977), pp. 36-37.
269 Fâzıl Çifci, *Candaroğlu İsmail Bey, Şahsiyeti ve Eserleri*, Kastamonu 1966, s. 61-62, 64.
270 *OT,* I, p. 415, footnote 4.
271 Dânişmend, *op. cit.*, I, pp. 200-202.
272 *Netâyij,* I, p. 40.
273 Tursun Bey, *op. cit.*, p. 38.
274 *OT,* I, p. 453.
275 Aşıkpaşaoğlu, *Târîh*, p. 137; Neşrî, *op. cit.* II, p. 688.
276 Ahmad b. Hanbal, *al-Musnad* 4/335.
277 *OT,* I, p. 464.

278  *OT*, I, pp. 465-467.
279  Dânişmend, I, p. 235.
280  İbn-i Kemâl, *Tevârîh-i Âl-i Osmân, VII. Defter*, ed. by Şerâfettin Turan (Ankara: Türk Tarih Kurumu, 1991), p. 57. 311
281  *OT*, I, pp. 477-478.
282  Dânişmend, *op. cit.*, I, p. 246.
283  *OT*, I, p. 482.
284  315 *OT*, I, p. 483.
285  *OT*, I, p. 485.
286  İbn Kemâl, *op. cit.*, VII, p. 62.
287  İbn Kemâl, *op. cit.*, VII, p. 73.
288  Müneccimbaşı, *Camiü'd Düvel*, p. 247.
289  Tursun Beğ, *op. cit., p. 33*.
290  *Netâyij*, I, p. 55.
291  A.J.P. Taylor, *The Course of German History* (London: Routledge paperback, 1988), p. 2.
292  Ferîdûn Beğ, *Münsheât-i Selâtîn*, I, pp. 235-239.
293  *Münsheât*, I, pp. 239-243.
294  *Münsheât*, I, pp. 245-249.
295  Abbas Hamdani, "Ottoman Response to the Discovery of America and the New Route to India," *Journal of the American Oriental Society*, vol. 101 (1961), p. 325.
296  Dânişmend, I, pp. 263-268.
297  S. Shaw, *op. cit.*, I, pp. 60-61.
298  Dânişmend, I, pp. 272-278.
299  Neşrî, *op. cit.*, II, pp. 723-725 ; Tursun Beğ, *op. cit.*, pp. 80-83.
300  Dânişmend, I, pp. 279-280.
301  Tursun Beğ, *op. cit.*, pp. 91-105.
302  Dânişmend, I, p. 283.
303  Uzunçarşılı, *Osmanlı Tarihi*, Ankara 1983, v. II, p. 52, footnote 1.
304  İbn Kemâl, *Tevârîh-i Âl-i Osmân*, v. VII, p. 179.
305  Tursun Beğ, *op. cit.*, pp. 107-108; *Netâyij*, I, p. 42.
306  *Netâyij*, I, p. 42.
307  Neşrî, II, p. 752.
308  *OT*, II, pp. 55-57.
309  *OT*, II, pp. 64-67.
310  Dânişmend, I, pp. 305, 311, 339.
311  Tursun Beğ, *op. cit.*, p. 111.
312  İbn Kemâl, *op. cit.*, VII, p. 217.
313  *Ibid.*, p. 118.
314  Tursun Beğ, *op. cit.*, pp. 121-128; Dânişmend, I, pp. 300-301; *OT*, II, p. 82.

*Endnotes*

315 *OT,* II, pp. 84-85
316 *Netâyij,* I, pp. 69-70.
317 Neşrî, II, p. 780.
318 Dânişmend,I, p. 306.
319 *Netâyij,* I, p. 43.
320 Oruç Beğ, *op. cit.,* p. 123; Neşrî, II, p. 802.
321 *OT,* II, p. 96, footnote 1.
322 *OT,* II, p. 97.
323 Tursun Beğ, *op. cit.,* p. 166; Neşrî, II, 816; İbn Kemâl, VII, p. 354.
324 *OT,* II, p. 103.
325 *Netâyij,* I, 45.
326 Dânişmend,I,pp.333-334
327 *Aşıkpaşaoğlu Tarihi,* pp. 184.
328 Dânişmend, I, pp. 332, 336, 342-343.
329 S. Shaw, *op. cit.,* I, pp. 69-70.
330 *Netâyij,* I, p. 47.
331 Neşrî, II, p. 842.
332 *Netâyij,* I, p. 62.
333 *Netâyij,* I, p. 69.
334 Lord Kinross, *The Ottoman Centuries, the Rise and Fall of the Turkish Empire* (New York: 1977), p. 120.
335 Neşrî, II, pp. 838-840.
336 R.J.H. Jenkins, "Social Life in the Byzantine Empire," in *The Cambridge Medieval History,* vol. IV, part II, ed. by J.M. Hussey (Cambridge University Press, 1967; reprint 1978), pp. 88–89.
337 *Loc. cit.*
338 Arthur Goldschmidt, Jr., *A Concise History of the Middle East* (Boulder, Colorado, 1988), p. 123.
339 Abbas Hamdani, "Ottoman Response to the Discovery of America and the New Route to India," *Journal of the American Oriental Society,* vol. 101 (1981), pp. 323-330.

## Chapter Five – Sultân Bâyezîd Velî (1481-1512)

340 Mustafa Nuri Pasha, *Netâyijul Vukû'ât,* I, p. 47.
341 İsmail Hakkı Uzunçarşılı, *Osmanlı Tarihi,* II, p. 166.
342 Stanley Lane-Poole, *Turkey* (reprint), London, 1986, p. 142.
343 *Ibid.,* p. 145.
344 *Ibid.,* p. 146.
345 *Turkey,* p. 151.
346 Donald Edgar Pitcher, *An Historical Geography of the Ottoman Empire* (Leiden: E.J. Brill, 1972), p. 98.
347 Dânişmend, *op. cit.,* I, pp. 390-397.

348  Dânişmend, I, p. 406.
349  *Netâyij*, I, p. 48.
350  Bîmârhâne is a specialised hospital for the mentally ill. The patients were cured through music; they were made to listen to a special *maqaam* for various illnessess. At that time in Europe the mentally ill were burnt on the grounds that "they were possessed" by *jinn*! It should be indicated here that this practice has been revived by Assist. Prof. Dr. Rahmi Oruç Güvenç, Marmara University, İstanbul (Alemdar Cad. No: 18/3 Sultânahmet-İstanbul, Tel: 00 90 212 526 90 31).
351  Lütfi Pasha, *Tevârîh-i Âl-i Osmân*, İstanbul, 1341 AH, p. 192.
352  *OT*, II, pp. 182-184.
353  Solaqzâde, *op. cit.*, pp. 310-311.
354  Kâtip Çelebi,*Tuhfetu'l Kibâr fî Esfâri'l Bihâr* (İstanbul:1329), p. 40.
355  Dânişmend, *İzahlı Osmanlı Tarihi Kronolojisi* (İstanbul: 1971), v. I, p. 391.
356  *OT*, II, pp. 184-185.
357  Tursun Bey, *Târîh-i Ebu'l Feth*, p. 201; Kâtip Çelebi, *op. cit.*, p. 22.
358  *OT*, Ankara 1983, v.II, p. 224.
359  R.M.Savory, "Safavid Persia," *The Cambridge History of Islam*, (Cambridge: C.U.P., reprint 1980), vol. I A, p. 398.
360  *Ibid.*, p. 394.
361  Ahmet Uğur, *The Reign of Sultân Selîm I in the Light of Selim-Nâme Literature*, Berlin: Klaus Schwarz Verlag, 1985, p. 192.

## *Chapter Six – The Struggle For Islamic Unity*

362  Jelalzâde Qoja Nishanjı Mustafa, *Kitâb-ı Meâsir-i Selîm Khânî TSMK*, H. 1415, 63 a.
363  30 *Ibid.*, 64 a.
364  Abbâs Hamdani, "Ottoman Response to the Discovery of America and The New Route to India," *Journal of the American Oriental Society*, vol. 101 (1981), p. 325. Emphasis added.
365  *Ibid.*, p. 327.
366  *Netâyij*, I, p. 72.
367  Fâik Reşâd, *Târîh-i Edebiyyât-ı Osmâniyye* (İstanbul, n.d.), p. 230.
368  İbn İyâs, *Badâi'u'z Zuhûr fî Waqâi'id Duhûr*, ed. by Muhammad Mustapha (Cairo: 1960), vol. IV, p. 191.
369  *Ibid.*, IV, pp. 372-376.
370  Qoja Nishanjı, *op. cit.*, 93 b.
371  Lütfi Pasha, *Tevârîh-i Âl-i Osmân*, p. 208.
372  *OT*, II, p. 263; Solaqzâde, *Târîh*, p. 369; *Netâyij*, I, p. 73.
373  *OT*, II, p. 264, footnote 2.
374  *OT*, II, pp. 266-268.

375 İ.H. Dânişmend, *İzahlı Osmanlı Tarihi Kronolojisi,* İstanbul 1971, vol. II, pp. 15-16.
376 Lütfi Pasha, *Tevârîh-i Âl-i Osmân,* İstanbul 1341 AH, p. 230.
377 Qoja Nishanjı, *op. cit.,* 102a-105 a.
378 *OT,* II, pp. 264-268.
379 D.E. Pitcher, *An Historical Geography of the Ottoman Empire* (Leiden: E.J. Brill, 1972), p. 124.
380 Solaqzâde, *op. cit.,* p. 376; *Netâyij,* I, p. 75.
381 Solaqzâde, *op. cit.,* pp. 383-388; Lutfi Pasha, *op. cit.,* pp. 249-250.
382 George William Frederic Stripling, *The Ottoman Turks and the Arabs, 1511-1574* (Philadelphia: Porcupine Press, 1977), p. 15.
383 *OT,* II, p. 287, footnote 1.
384 Mahmûd Thâbit ash Shâzulî, *al Mas'alatush Sharqiyyah: dirâsah wathâiqiyyah 'anil Khilâfati'l 'Osmâniyyah* (Cairo: Maktabat Wahbah, n.d.), pp. 73-74.
385 *OT,* II, p. 288.
386 Ferîdûn Beğ, *Mejmû'a-i Münsheât-i Selâtîn,* İstanbul: 1274 AH, vol. I, pp. 484-485.
387 Lütfi Pasha, *op. cit.,* pp. 256-257; Khoja Sa'deddîn Efendi, *Tâju't Tevârîkh,* İstanbul 1862, vol. II, p. 354.
388 Lütfi Pasha, *op. cit.,* p. 264.
389 Solaqzâde, *Tarih* (İstanbul: 1297), p. 400; Dânişmend, *op. cit.,* vol. II, pp. 32-36. The Osmanlı historian and *qâdi* (qâzi)asker (afterwards ShaykhulIslam) Shamsuddîn Ahmed ibn Kemâl dated: *Fâtihu Mamâlikil'Arab* (923); *OT,* II, p. 290, footnote 1. Actually: *fâ* 80, *alif* 1, *tê* 400, *hâ* 8, *mîm* 40, *mîm* 40, *alif* 1, *lâm* 30, *kâf* 20, *alif* 1, *lâm* 30, *'ayn* 70, *râ* 200, *bâ* 2: 923.
390 Münejjimbâshı, *Sahâifu'l Akhbâr,* III, p. 567; *OT,* II, p. 290, footnote 1.
391 *Netâyij,* I, p. 78.
392 *OT,* II, p. 292.
393 Jelâlzâda Qoja Nishanjı Mustapha, *Kitâb-Maâsir-i Selîm Khânî (manuscript)* (TSMKH, 1415), 43 a.
394 Hoja Sa'deddîn, *Tâju't Tevârîh,* İstanbul, 1279, II, 371-379 ; *Netâyij,* I, p. 82.
395 'Abdu'l 'Azîz Muhammad ash Shinnâwî, *ad Dawlatu'l 'Uthmâniyyatu dawlah muftaran 'alayhâ* (Cairo: 1980), vol. I, pp. 20-21.
396 *OT,* II, pp. 426-427.
397 al Muslim, *al-Jâmi'u's Sahîh, Kitâbu'l İmârah,* 58.
398 *Münsheât,* I, p. 90, line 31.
399 *Münsheât,* I, p. 96, line 27 and p. 97, line 8.
400 *Münsheât,* I, p. 97, the last line.
401 *Münsheât,* I, p. 116.

402 İbn Kemâl, *Tevârîh-i Âl-i Osmân*, vol.VII, p. 194, 296.
403 *Münsheât*, I, p. 306, lines 25, 28.
404 *Münsheât*, I, p. 307.
405 *Münsheât*, I, p. 326.
406 *Münsheât*, I, p. 327.
407 *Ibid.*, I, p. 330.
408 *Ibid.*, I, pp. 345-346.
409 *Ibid.*, I, p. 365.
410 *Ibid.*, I, pp. 375-377.
411 *Ibid.*, I, p. 379.
412 Keşfî Mehmed Çelebi, *Keşfî'nin Selîm-nâmesi* (ed. by Şefâettin Severcan), Kayseri, 1995, p. 189.
413 *Münsheât*, I, pp. 500, 515, 519.
414 Solaqzâde, *op. cit.*, p. 412; *OT*, II, p. 295.
415 *Hürriyet* (Newspaper), 30 March 2001; *Akit* (Newspaper), 31 March 2001.
416 Dânişmend, II, p. 45.
417 *OT*, II, 298-300.
418 Solaqzâde, *op. cit.*, p. 428.
419 *Op. cit.*, p. 429.
420 *Netâyij*, I, p. 80.
421 Solaqzâde, *Târîh*, p. 421.
422 Abbas Hamdani, *op. cit.*, p. 327.

## Chapter Seven – The Superpower of the World

423 *OT*, II, p. 308-309.
424 I.M. Lapidus, *A History of Islamic Societies* (Cambridge: C.U.P., 1988), p. 311.
425 Lütfi Pasha, *Tevârîh-i Âl-i Osmân* (İstanbul: 1341), p. 303.
426 *OT*, II, p. 313.
427 Qarachelebizâde (Shaykhu'l Islâm) 'Abdülazîz, *Ravzatu'l Abrâr* (Cairo: 1248 A.H.), p. 66.
428 *OT*, II, p. 315.
429 Kâtib Chelebi, *Tuhfetu'l Kibâr fî Esfâri'l Bihâr*, p. 24.
430 Kâtib Chelebi, *op. cit,*. p. 25.
431 Stanford J. Shaw, *History of the Ottoman Empire and Modern Turkey* (Cambridge: 1976), vol. I, pp. 89-90.
432 Solaqzâde, *Târîkh*, pp. 451-452.
433 *Ibid.*, pp. 453-454; and Lütfi Pasha expresses that the Christian army included Russians as well: *Tevârîkh-i Âl-i Osmân*, p. 324.
434 Solakzâde, *Târîkh*, 459; *OT*, II, pp. 324-326.
435 *od Jadrana do Irana nece biti Müslimana*.

436 Osman Turan, *Türk Cihan Hâkimiyeti Mefkûresi Târihi* (İstanbul: Nakışlar Yayınevi, 1979), vol. II, p. 422.
437 Agâh sırrı Levend, *Gazavatnâmeler ve mihaloğlu Ali beyin Gazavatnâmesi* (İstanbul: 1956), p. 246, 254, 295; cited in O. Turan, *Loc. cit.*
438 Dânişmend, II, p. 127.
439 Qarachelebizâde (Shaykhulislâm) 'Abdülazîz, *Ravzatu'l Ebrâr* (Bulaq, Cairo: 1248 H.), p. 99.
440 Shaw, I, pp. 92-93.
441 Solaqzâde, I, p. 471; *OT*, II, p. 329.
442 Lutfi Pasha, *op. cit.*, p. 338; Karachelebizâde, *op. cit.*, p. 104; Solaqzâde, *op. cit.*, p. 473; *OT,* II, p. 330.
443 Shaw, I, p. 93.
444 *OT,* II, p. 334.
445 Dânişmend, II, p. 144.
446 *OT,* II, p. 336.
447 Dânişmend, II, pp. 205-206.
448 *OT,* II, pp. 352-353, footnote 2.
449 *OT,* II, p. 339.
450 *OT,* II, p. 339.
451 *OT,* II, p. 340.
452 *OT,* II, p. 342.
453 *OT,* II, p. 352
454 Qarachelebizâde, *op. cit.*, p. 120.
455 Solaqzâde, *op. cit.*, p. 487. The numerical value of the sentence in Turkish is **941** (1534 C.E.): *Kâf* (*gâf-i fârisî*): 20, *lâm*: 30, *dâl*: 4, *yâ*: 10, *bâ*: 2, *râ*: 200, *jîm*: 3, *alif*: 1, *wâw*: 6, *lâm*: 30, *yâ*: 10, *alif*: 1, *yâ*: 10, *hê*: 5, *pâ*: 2, *alif*:1, *dâl*: 4, *shîn*: 300, *alif*: 1, *hê*: 5, *nûn*: 50, *alif*: 1, *mîm*: 40, *dâl*: 4, *alif*: 1, *râ*: 200 (941).
456 Abbas Hamdani, "Ottoman Response to the Discovery of America and the New Route to India," *Journal of the American Oriental Society* 101, p. 327.
457 Solaqzâde, *op. cit.*, pp. 507-508.
458 *Ibid.*, p. 510.
459 *Ibid.*, p. 513.
460 *OT,* II, pp. 360-361.
461 *OT,* II, p. 363.
462 Kâtib Chelebi, *Tuhfetu4l Kibâr fî Esfâri'l Bihâr* (İstanbul: 1329 H), p. 25.
463 *Ibid.*, p. 26.
464 *OT,* II, p. 366.
465 *OT,* II, 366. Oruch Reîs was nicknamed "Barbarossa" (Redbeard) by the Europeans because of his reddish hair and beard.

466 Gabriyel Kolen, *Korpüs* (Paris: 1910), p. 12; cited in *OT*, II, p. 368, footnote 1: The inscription on the tower of Jîjel, dated 924/1518 reads: *al-Qâ'im bi-Amrillâh al-Mujâhid fî Sabîlillâh* Oruch b. Ya'qûb.
467 . *OT*, II, p. 367.
468 *OT*,II,p. 368.
469 The Library of Topkapı Sarayı Museum, E/6456.
470 Kâtib Chelebi, *Tuhfetu'l Kibâr*, p. 40.
471 *OT*, II, p. 372.
472 *OT*, II, p. 373.
473 *OT*, II, p. 374.
474 For detailed information about the emergence of the *Dayıs* in Tunisia. see: Mehmet Maksudoğlu, "Tunus'ta Dayıların Ortaya Çıkışı", *Ankara Üniversitesi İlâhiyat Fakültesi Dergisi*, 1967, XIV, pp. 189-202. (Its Arabic in the same issue: *Zuhûru'd Dâyât bi'l Qutri't Tûnisî*.)
475 For the transfer of power from the *Dayıs* to the *Beys*, see: Mehmet Maksudoğlu, "Tunus'ta Hâkimiyetin Dayılardan Beylere Geçişi," *Ankara Universitesi İlahiyat Fakültesi Dergisi*, 1968, XV.
476 *OT*, II, p. 374.
477 Heavenly Donanma: Osmanlı Navy.
478 *OT*, II, pp. 377-379.
479 Lütfi Pasha, *op. cit.*, pp. 392-395.
480 *OT*, II, p. 398.
481 *OT*, II, p. 380.
482 II, p. 382.
483 Solaqzâde, *Târîh*, p. 540.
484 *Ibid.*, p. 540; *OT*, II, p. 386.
485 Dânişmend, II, p. 277.
486 Solaqzâde, *op. cit.*, p. 541.
487 *OT*, II, p. 388.
488 Dânişmend, II, p. 320.
489 Solaqzâde, p. 570.
490 *OT*, II, pp. 389-390.
491 *OT*, II, p. 392.
492 Solaqzâde, *Târîh*, p. 500.
493 Lütfi Pasha, *Tevârih-i Âl-i Osmân*, pp. 420-422.
494 Solaqzâde, *op. cit.*, p. 534.
495 Abbas Hamdani, *op. cit.*, p. 329.
496 Solaqzâde, *op. cit.*, pp. 534-535.
497 Stripling, *op. cit.*, p. 97.
498 Solaqzâde, *op. cit.*, p. 536.
499 Solaqzâde, p. 537.
500 *OT*, II, p. 399.

501 Anthony Reid, *The Contest for North Sumatra, Atjeh, the Netherlands and Britain 1858-1898,* Oxford University Press-University of Malaya Press: 1969, pp. 2-3.
502 Solaqzâde, *op. cit.*, p. 571.
503 *al-Qur'ân, as Saff* [61] *âyat*: 10.
504 Selânikî Mustafa Efendi, *Târîh-i Selânikî* (ed. by Mehmet İpşirli, İstanbul: 1989), p. 39.
505 Uzunçarşılı, *op. cit.*, II, p. 575.
506 *Netâyij*, I, p. 116.
507 BOA, *Mühimme Defteri* 5, p. 543; Kâtib Chelebi, *op. cit.*, p. 81.
508 İ.H. Uzunçarşılı, *op. cit.*, III, I, p. 6.
509 *Netâyij*, I, p. 98.

## Chapter Eight – The Beginning of Decline

510 Uzunçarşılı, *OT*, III, part I, p. 35.
511 Donald Edgar Pitcher, *op. cit.*, p. 122.
512 Halîl Inalcık, *op. cit.*, I A, p. 335.
513 *Netâyij*, I, p. 100.
514 Halîl Inalcik, "The Heyday and Decline of the Ottoman Empire," *The Cambridge History of Islam*, Cambridge University Press, 1988, I A, p. 337.
515 Uzunçarşılı, *op. cit.*, III, I, p. 23.
516 BOA, Muhimme Defteri, 7, p. 258 (R 975) (1568); Uzunçarşılı, *op. cit.*, III, part I, p. 33.
517 *Ibid*, III, I, p. 29.
518 Selâniki, *op. cit.*, p. 97; Solaqzâde, *Tarih* (İstanbul: 1297), p. 594.
519 Selânikî, *op. cit.*, p. 98.
520 *Ibid.*, p. 99; Solaqzâde, *op. cit.*, p. 597.
521 *Netâyij*, II, pp. 102, 103.
522 Uzunçarşılı, *op. cit.*, III, I, pp. 46-48.
523 Abbâs Hamdânî, *op. cit.*, pp. 329-330. Emphasis added.
524 Uzunçarşılı, *op. cit.*, III, I, pp. 55-56.
525 Solaqzâde, *op. cit.*, p. 599.
526 *Netâyij*, I, pp. 103-104.
527 Uzunçarşılı, *op. cit.*, III, I, p. 63.
528 Uzunçarşılı, *op. cit.*, III, I, p. 63.
529 Solaqzâde, *op. cit.*, p. 620.
530 Naîmâ, *Ravzatu'l Husayn fi Khulâsati Akhbâri'l Khâfiqayn*, I, p. 133.
531 *Ibid.*, I, p. 134.
532 Solaqzâde, *op. cit.*, p. 620.
533 *Netâyij*, I, pp. 140-141.
534 Naîmâ, *op. cit.*, I, p. 145.

535  Uzunçarşılı, *op. cit.*, III, I, p. 75.
536  *Ibid.*, III, I, p. 76.
537  Na'îmâ, *op. cit.*, I, p. 157.
538  *Ibid*, pp. 157-158.
539  Uzunçarşılı, *op. cit.*, pp. 76-79.
540  Cited in *Netâyij*, II, p. 6.
541  Na'îmâ, *op. cit.*, I, p. 234.
542  Uzunçarşılı, *op. cit.*, III, I, p. 83.
543  Na'îma, *op. cit.* (İstanbul), I, p. 257.
544  Uzunçarşılı, *op. cit.*, III, I, p. 88.
545  *Ibid.*, III, I, p. 89.
546  Na'îmâ, *op. cit.*, I, p. 274; *Netâyij*, II, p. 14.
547  Na'îma, *op. cit.*, I, p. 279.
548  *Ibid.*, III, I, p. 94.
549  *Netâyij*, I, p. 151.
550  *Ibid.*, I, p. 152.
551  Na'îmâ, *op. cit.*, I, p. 327.
552  Uzunçarşılı, *op. cit.*, III, I, p. 64.
553  Pincon, *Relation*, 162, cited in Dorothy M. Vaughan, *Europe and The Turk* (Liverpool, The University Press: 1954, reprint: 1976), p. 210.
554  *Loc. cit.*
555  Na'îmâ, *op. cit.*, I, p. 334; Dorothy Vaughan, *Loc. cit.*
556  Na'îmâ, *op. cit.*, I, p. 350; Uzunçarşılı, *op. cit.*, III, I, p. 65.
557  *Netâyij*, II, p. 21.
558  *Ibid.*, II, p. 22.
559  Uzunçarşılı, *op. cit.*, III, I, pp. 65-66.
560  *Ibid.*, III, I, p. 66.
561  *Ibid.*, III, I, p. 67.

*Chapter Nine – The Osmanlı Sultan's Descent to Equality With Emperors*

562  Uzunçarşılı, *op. cit.*, III, I, p. 98.
563  *Ibid.*, III, I, p. 68.
564  Solaqzâde, *Târîh*, pp. 696-697.
565  Uzunçarşılı, *op. cit.*, III, I, p. 131.
566  Solaqzâde, *op. cit.*, p. 702.
567  Na'îma, *op. cit.*, II, p. 201.
568  *Ibid.*, II, p. 211.
569  *Ibid.*, II, p. 218.
570  *Ibid.*, II, p. 227.
571  *Ibid.*, II, p. 229.

## Chapter Ten – Rejuvenation

572  Solaqzâde, *op. cit.,* p. 737.
573  Na'îmâ, *op. cit.,* II, p. 278.
574  *Ibid.,* II, pp. 284-288.
575  *Ibid.,* II, p. 247.
576  *Netâyij,* II, p. 53.
577  Stanley Lane-Poole, *Turkey,* p. 220.
578  İ.H. Uzunçarşılı, *op. cit.,* III, I, p. 204.
579  *Netâyij,* II, p. 53.
580  Uzunçarşılı, *op. cit.,* III, I, p. 206.
581  BOA, *Nâme-i Hümâyûn Defteri,* No. 7, pp. 4-6.
582  *Netâyij,* II, pp. 53-54.

## Chapter Eleven – Decline And Restoration

583  Na'îmâ, *op. cit.,* IV, p. 112.
584  *Ibid.,* IV, pp. 142-149.
585  *Netâyij,* II, p. 58.
586  Na'imâ, *op. cit.,* VI, p. 223.
587  *Netâyij,* II, p. 68.
588  Na'îmâ, *op. cit.,* VI, p. 278.
589  *Netâyij,* II, p. 69.
590  *Na'îmâ, op. cit.,* VI, p. 331.
591  Uzunçarşılı, *op. cit.,* III, I, pp. 382-385.
592  *Ibid.,* p. 386.
593  Mehmed Râshid Efendi, *Târîh* (İstanbul: 1281), I, pp. 16-20.
594  *Ibid.,* I, p. 47.
595  *Netâyij,* II, p. 76.
596  Uzunçarşılı, *op. cit.,* III, I, p. 414.
597  Ibid., III.I, p. 419.
598  Silâhdâr Fındıklılı Mehmed Ağa, *Târîh,* I, p. 525, İstanbul 1928.
599  *Netâyij,* II, p. 78.
600  *Netâyij* II, p. 79. Uzunçarşılı, *op. cit.,* III, I, pp. 424-425.
601  Silâhdâr, *op. cit.,* II, pp. 18-19.
602  Râshid, *op. cit.,* I, p. 402.
603  *Netâyij,* II, pp. 82-83.
604  S. Shaw, *op. cit.,* I, 214.
605  Silahdâr, *op. cit.,* II, p. 93.
606  Defterdâr Sarı Mehmed Paşa, *Zübde-i Vakâyi'ât* (Tercüman 1001 Temel Eser, İstanbul: 1977), p. 223.
607  Uzunçarşılı, *op. cit.,* III, I, p. 453.
608  Uzunçarşılı, *op. cit.,* III, I, p. 459.
609  Silahdâr, II, 121; *Netâyic,* II, 84.

610 Silahdâr, II, 91.
611 S.Shaw, *op. cit.*, p. 217.
612 *Netâyij*, II, p. 87.
613 *Ibid.*, II, p. 99.
614 *Ibid.*, II, p. 100.
615 Râshid, *op. cit.*, II, p. 21.
616 Uzunçarşılı, *op. cit.*, III, I, p. 523.
617 *Ibid.*, III, I, p. 527.
618 *Ibid.*, p. 530.
619 *Netâyij*, III, p. 7.
620 Uzuncarşılı, *op. cit.*, III, I, p. 535.
621 *Netâyij*, III, p. 10.
622 *Ibid.*, III, p. 11.
623 *Ibid.*, III, p. 12.
624 Râshid, *op. cit.*, II, pp. 407-412.
625 These were taken as Christian children and raised in the Islamic way of life.
626 *Netâyij*, III, p. 15

## Part Three – Decline 1699-1922

### Chapter Twelve – The Resumption of Decline

627 Shaw, *History of the Ottoman Empire and Modern Turkey*, I, p. 228.
628 Mustafa Nûri Pasha, *Netâyicu'l Vukûât*, İstanbul 1327 H., III, p. 19.
629 *Netâyij*, II, p. 89-90.
630 Harry E. Figgie, Jr. with Gerald J. Swanson, *Bankruptcy 1995: The Coming Collapse of America and How to Stop It* (New York and Toronto: Back Bay Books: 1993), p. 146.
631 S. Shaw, *Loc. cit.*
632 *Netâyij*, III, p. 19.
633 İsmâil Hâmi Dânişmend, *İzahlı Osmanlı Târihi Kronolojisi*, İstanbul 1972, v. IV, pp. 3-4.
634 *OT*, IV, I, p. 85.
635 *Netâyij*, III, pp. 23-24.
636 *OT*, IV,I, p. 89. Ankara 1995.
637 *OT*, IV, I, pp. 99-107.
638 *OT*, IV, I, pp. 110-111.
639 Rashid, *Târîh* (İstanbul: 1281), IV, p. 263.
640 *Netâyij*, III, p. 26.
641 Râshid, *Târîh*, V, p. 20.
642 *Netâyij*, III, p. 31
643 *Netâyij*, III, p. 29.
644 *Netâyij*, III, p. 32.

*Chapter Thirteen – The Attempt at Restoration*

645  *Netâyij*, III, pp. 33-34.
646  *Netâyij*, III, 35.
647  *OT*, IV, I, p. 276.
648  *Netâyij*, III, p. 36.
649  Dânişmend, *op. cit.*, IV, p. 28.
650  *Netâyij*, III, p. 39.
651  *OT*, IV, I, p. 326.
652  *OT*, IV, I, p. 293.
653  *Netâyij*, III, pp. 85-86.
654  *Netâyij*, III, p. 86.
655  *Ibid.*, III, 94.
656  *Ibid.*, III, pp. 95-96.
657  *Ibid.*, III, p. 41.
658  *OT*, IV, I, pp. 322-323.

*Chapter Fourteen – Crisis and Struggle*

659  *Netâyij*, III, p. 43.
660  *Netâyij*, III, pp. 43-49.
661  Netâyij, III, p. 46.
662  *Netâyij*, III, p. 47.
663  *Netâyij*, III, p. 48.
664  *Netâyij*, III, p. 49.
665  *Netâyij*, III, p. 51.
666  *Netâyij*, III, p. 54.

*Chapter Fifteen – Another Attempt at Restoration*

667  *Netâyij*, III, pp. 56-70.
668  *Netâyij*, III, pp. 52-53.
669  Ahmed Âsım, *Târîh* (İstanbul; printed at Jerîde-yi Havâdis), I, p. 34.
670  *Netâyij*, IV, pp. 5-6.
671  William Houston, *Meltdown: The Great '90s Depression and How to Come Through It a Winner* (Warner Futura: London 1994), p. 69.
672  *Netâyij*, IV, pp. 9-11.
673  *Netâyij*, IV, pp. 12-13.
674  İsmail Hakkı Uzunçarşılı, *Osmanlı Tarihi*, vol. V, sec. I, p. 525.
675  *Netâyij*, IV, p. 18.
676  *Netâyij*, IV, p. 19.
677  *Netâyij*, IV, p. 21.
678  Dânişmend, IV, p. 68.
679  *Netâyij*, IV, pp. 23-25.

680  *Ibid.*, IV, p. 25.
681  *Ibid.*, IV, p. 26.
682  *Ibid.*, IV, p. 2.
683  *Netâyij*, IV, p. 33.
684  *Netâyij*, IV, p. 34.
685  *Netâyij*, IV, p. 36.
686  *Ibid.*, IV, p. 37.
687  Shaw, *op. cit.*, I, p. 69.
688  *Netâyij*, IV, p. 37.
689  Enver Ziyâ Karal, *Osmanlı Tarihi*, Ankara 1994, sixth edition, v, p. 39.
690  *Netâyij*, IV, p. 38.
691  Karal, *op. cit.*, V, p. 42.
692  *Netâyij*, IV, p. 39.
693  *Netâyij*, IV, pp. 40-41.
694  Enver Ziyâ Karal, *Osmanlı Tarihi* (Ankara: Türk Tarih Kurumu Basımevi, 1994), v. V, p. 57.
695  Bekir Sıtkı Baykal, "Mustafa III," *Millî Eğitim Bakanlığı İslâm Ansiklopedisi*, İstanbul 1993, v. V, III, p. 701.
696  Shaw, *op. cit.*, I, p. 252.
697  Karal, V, p. 67.
698  Karal, *op. cit.*, V, p. 83.
699  Karal, *op. cit.*, V, p. 85.
700  Karal, *op. cit.*, V, pp. 88-89.
701  Mehmed Tefvîq, *Târîh-i Osmânî* (İstanbul: 1305), p. 293.
702  Karal, *op. cit.*, V, 91.
703  Karal, *op. cit.*, V, 93.
704  Karal, *op. cit.*, 96.
705  *Netâyij*, IV, 60.
706  Shânizâde Mehmed Atâullah, *Târîh* (İstanbul: 1284), p. 371.
707  *Netâyij*, IV, 64.
708  M. Tevfîq, *op. cit.*, p. 295.
709  *Netâyij*, IV, 70.
710  M. Tevfîq, *op. cit.*, p. 296.
711  E. Kedorurie, *Nationalism* (London: 1960), p. 9. Cited in Richard Jay, "Nationalism," in *Political Ideologies* (co-authors Robert Ecclashall, Vincent Geoghegen, Richard Jay, and Rick Wilford, London: Unwin Hyman, 1990), p. 185. Emphasis added.
712  *Loc. cit.*
713  Benito Mussolini (1922), quoted in R. Finer, *Mussolini's Italy* (New York: 1935), p. 218, cited in *ibid.*, p. 185. Emphasis added.
714  *Ibid.*, pp. 185-86.
715  Karal, *op. cit.*, V, pp. 111-13.

716   *Netâyij,* IV, 74.
717   M. Tevfîq, *op. cit.,* p. 297; Karal, *op. cit.,* V, 113.
718   Karal, *op. cit.,* V, p. 114.
719   *Netâyij,* IV, p. 75; Dânişmend, *op. cit.,* IV, pp. 108-09.
720   Akdes Nimet Kurat, *Rusya Tarihi,* Atatürk Kültür, Dil ve Tarih Yüksek Kurumu, Ankara, 1987, second printing, p. 323.
721   Dânişmend, *op. cit.,* IV, pp. 110-11; Karal, *op. cit.,* V, p. 150.
722   Enver Ziyâ Karal, *Osmanlı Tarihi,* V, p. 151, Ankara 1994, 6th printing.
723   Bernard Lewis, *The Emergence of Modern Turkey,* Oxford University Press, 1968, pp. 84-85.
724   Akdes Nimet Kurat, *Rusya Tarihi,* p. 324.
725   Dânişmend, *op. cit.,* IV, p. 112.
726   Karal, *op. cit.,* V, pp. 116-18.
727   *Netâyij,* IV, p. 91.
728   Karal, *op. cit.,* V, p. 118.
729   *Netâyij,* IV, p. 91; M. Tevfik, p. 299.
730   *Netâyij,* IV, p. 80.
731   *Netâyij,* IV, p. 93.
732   *Netâyij,* IV, p. 82.
733   Muhammad Farîd Bey, *Târîkh'd Dawlati'l 'Aliyyati'l 'Uthmâniyya (Beirut: 1086),* p. 447.
734   Alf Andrew Heggoy, "Arab Education in Colonial Algeria," *Journal of African Studies,* VII, 42, summer 1975, p. 149, cited in Dr. Fawzia Bariun, *Malik Bennabi, His Life and Theory of Civilization* (Kuala Lumpur: 1993), p. 12.
735   Nevill Barbour (ed.), *A Survey of North West Africa (The Maghrib),* Oxford University Press, 1962, p. 239, cited in Dr. Fawzia Bariun, *op. cit.,* p. 12.
736   Ahmad Tawfîq al-Madanî, *Hâdhihi Hiya al-Jezâyir* , Maktabat al-Nahdah, Cairo (n.d.), p. 139, cited in Dr. Fawzia Bariun, *op. cit.,* p. 12. For the French record regarding education in Algeria, see Dr. Fawzia Bariun, *op. cit.,* pp. 13-22.
737   Akdes Nimet Kurat, *op. cit.,* pp. 325-26.
738   Mahmûd Jelâleddîn Pasha, *Mir'ât-ı Hakîkat,* İstanbul 1326, v. I, p. 15.
739   Dânişmend, *op. cit.,* IV, p. 123.
740   M. Tevfik, *op. cit.,* p. 304.
741   Dânişmend, *op. cit.,* IV, pp. 124-126.
742   Abdurrahman Şeref, *Tarih Söyleşileri (Musâhabe-i Târihiye),* ed. by Mübeccel Nâmi Duru, İstanbul 1980, p. 56.
743   Dânişmend, IV, pp. 126-127.
744   Dânişmend, IV, p. 127. In fact ,foundation of Osmanlı Devlet

happened in 1288 at the minute when *khutbah* of *jum'ah* was recited in the name of Osman Gâzi at Qaraja Hisâr. The writer repeats the commonly accepted but wrong date.

745  Karal, *Osmanlı Tarihi*, V, p. 186.
746  Karal, V, p. 187.
747  Karal, V, p. 171.
748  Mahmûd Jelâleddîn Paşha, *Mir'ât-ı Haqîqât*, İstanbul 1326, v. I, p. 7.
749  Mahmûd Jelâleddîn Pasha, *Mir'ât*, I, p. 7.
750  Bernard Lewis still thoughtlessly calls the Devlet an Empire.
751  Bernard Lewis, *The Emergence of Modern Turkey*, second edition, 1968, p. 124. Emphasis added.
752  A. Slade, *Record of Travels in Turkey, Greece etc.*, second edition, 1854, p. 145, cited in Lewis, *Emergence,* p. 125.
753  Karal, VI, pp. 176-177.
754  Karal, *Osmanlı Tarihi*, V, pp. 205-208.
755  Akdes Nimet Kurat, *Rusya Tarihi, Başlangıçtan 1917'ye Kadar,* Atatürk kültür, Dil ve Tarih Yüksek Kurumu, Türk Tarih Kurumu, second printing, Ankara, 1987, p. 327.
756  Dânişmend, IV, p. 142.
757  Karal, *op. cit.,* V, p. 230.
758  Karal, V, p. 235.
759  Karal, V, p. 240.
760  *Netâyij,* IV, p. 97. Emphasis added.
761  Karal, V. p. 221.
762  Karal, V, pp. 213-217. Emphasis added.
763  Karal, V, p. 248.
764  Dânişmend, IV, p. 175. Emphasis added.
765  Dânişmend, IV, p. 176.
766  Mustafa Na'îmâ, *Ravzatul Huseyn fî Khulâsati Akhbâril Khâfikayn,* İstanbul 1280, c. I, s. 6.
767  Mahmûd Jelâleddîn Pasha, *Mir'ât-ı Hakîkat*, İstanbul, 1326, c. I, s. 7.
768  Dânişmend, IV, p. 167.
769  Dânişmend, IV, p. 167.
770  Karal, V, p. 243.
771  Dânişmend, IV, p. 182.
772  Mahmûd Jelâleddîn Pasha, *Mir'ât-ı Hakîkat*, I, p. 20.
773  *Loc. cit.*
774  Karal, VI, pp. 100-101.
775  Dânişmend, IV, p. 186. Emphasis added.
776  Dânişmend, IV, pp. 191-192.
777  Dânişmend, IV, p. 189. Emphasis added.
778  Enver Ziyâ Karal, *Osmanlı Tarihi,* Ankara, Türk Tarih Kurumu, 1983, v. VI, p. 96.

*Endnotes*

779 M. Tevfik, *op. cit.*, p. 308.
780 Karal, *op. cit.*, VI, p. 107. Emphasis added.
781 Enver Ziyâ Karal, *Osmanlı Tarihi* (third printing, Ankara, Türk Tarih Kurumu, 1983), v. VII, p. 2.
782 *Ibid.*, p. 3.
783 Roderic H. Davison, *Reform in the Ottoman Empire 1856-1876* (New York: 1973), p. 272.
784 *Loc. cit.*
785 R.H. Davison, *op. cit.*, pp. 273-274.
786 Mahmûd Jelâleddîn Pasha, *Mir'ât-ı Hakîkat*, v. I, p. 21.
787 E.Z. Karal, *op. cit.*, VII, pp. 3-7.
788 Karal, VII, p. 10.
789 Karal, VII, pp. 11-13.
790 Karal, VII, pp. 14-17.
791 Karal, VII, pp. 18-36.
792 Karal, VII, p. 166.
793 Karal, VII, pp. 172-173.
794 Ziyâ Nur Aksun, *Osmanlı Tarihi*, İstanbul, 1994, v. IV, p. 6.
795 Dânişmend, IV, pp. 212-213.
796 Ziyâ Nur Aksun, p. 6.
797 Ziyâ Nur Aksun, p. 6.
798 Aksun, p. 8.
799 Aksun, IV, p. 10.
800 Dânişmend, IV, pp. 212-213.
801 Stanford J. Shaw and Ezel Kural Shaw, *op. cit.*, II, p. 131.
802 Aksun, IV, p. 12.
803 Karal, *OT,* VII, p. 352.
804 Aksun, IV, pp. 12-13.
805 Dânişmend, *op. cit.*, IV, p. 219.
806 Dânişmend, IV, p. 222.
807 Mahmûd Jelâleddîn Pasha, *Mir'ât-ı Hakîkat*, I, pp. 31-32.
808 Karal, VII, p. 43.
809 *Ibid.*, pp. 44-46.
810 *Ibid.*, p. 52.
811 *Ibid.*, p. 69.
812 E.Z. Karal, *Osmanlı Tarihi,* Ankara, 1983, VII, p. 83.
813 *Ibid.*, p. 84.
814 *Ibid.*, p. 89.
815 *Ibid.*, p. 92.
816 *Ibid.*, p. 93.
817 *Ibid.*, p. 98.
818 Dânişmend, IV, pp. 226-227.
819 Z.N. Aksun, IV, p. 130.

820   Z.N. Aksun, IV, p. 133.
821   Mahmûd Jelâleddîn Pasha, *Mir'ât-ı Hakîkat*, İstanbul, H. 1326, v. I, p. 94.
822   *Ibid.*, p. 106.
823   Karal, VII, p. 109.
824   Karal, VII, pp. 110-112.
825   Mahmûd Jelâleddîn Pasha, *op. cit.*, I, p. 112.
826   *Ibid.*, I, p. 120.
827   *Mir'ât*, I, p. 116.
828   Karal, *op. cit.*, VII, pp. 352-353. Emphasis added.
829   *Ibid.*, VII, pp. 357-360.
830   Karal, VII, p. 364.
831   Karal, VII, p. 366.

## *Chapter Sixteen – Preservation and Rejuvenation*

832   Dânişmend, IV, p. 285.
833   *Mir'ât-ı Hakîkat*, I, p. 220.
834   Dânişmend, IV, p. 293. Emphasis added.
835   Dânişmend, IV, p. 294.
836   Karal, *Osmanlı Tarihi*, Atatürk Kültür, Dil ve Tarih Yüksek Kurumu, Türk Tarih Kurumu, Ankara, 1995, 4th printing, VIII, p. 29.
837   Dânişmend, IV, p. 296; Karal, VIII, p. 34.
838   Karal, VIII, pp. 36-37.
839   Dânişmend, IV, p. 297.
840   Z.N. Aksun, IV, p. 264.
841   Z.N. Aksun, IV, p. 251.
842   Z.N. Aksun, IV,p. 264.
843   There was also a folk-song about him: ***Midhat Pasha sells soldiers Wake Sultân Azîz wake!***
844   Mahmûd Jelâleddîn Pasha, *Mir'ât-ı Hakîkat*, I, pp. 266-269.
845   Dânişmend, IV, p. 329. Emphasis added.
846   Dânişmend, IV, p. 298.
847   Stanford J. Shaw and Ezel Kural Shaw, *History of the Ottoman Empire and Modern Turkey* (Cambridge, 1992), v. II, p. 181.
848   Dânişmend, IV, p. 299.
849   Mahmûd Jelâleddîn Pasha, *Mir'ât-ı Hakîkat*, Dersaâdet 1326, v. II, p. 10.
850   Shaw and Shaw, II, p. 183.
851   M. Jelâleddhin Pasha, *op. cit.*, II, pp. 170-174.
852   *Ibid.*, II, pp. 205-210.
853   Shaw and Shaw, II, p. 184.
854   M. Jelâleddîn Pasha, *Mir'ât-ı Hakîkat*, v. III, p. 89.

*Endnotes*

855 S. Shaw and Ezel Kural Shaw, *op. cit.*, II, p. 189.
856 Mahmûd Jelâleddîn Pasha, *Mir'ât,ı Hakîkat*, III, p. 138.
857 Enver Ziyâ Karal, *Osmanlı Tarihi*, Ankara, 1983, second printing, v. VIII, p. 499.
858 Karal, *OT,* VIII, pp. 501-504.
859 Shaws, *op. cit.*, II, p. 190. Emphasis added.
860 *Mir'ât-ı Hakîkat*, III, pp. 175-176.
861 Shaws, *op. cit.*, II, p. 192.
862 Karal, *op. cit.*, VIII, p. 85.
863 Dânişmend, IV, pp. 319-321.
864 Dânişmend, IV, pp. 321-322.
865 Karal, *op. cit.*, VIII, p. 88.
866 *Ibid.*, VIII, p. 89.
867 S. Shaw and Ezel Kural Shaw, *op. cit.*, II, p. 194.
868 *Loc. cit.*
869 *Loc. cit.*
870 Karal, *op. cit.*, VIII, p. 98.
871 S. Shaw and Ezel Kural Shaw, *op. cit.*, II, p. 195.
872 Dânişmend, IV, p. 328.
873 Karal, *op. cit.*, VIII, p. 118.
874 Karal, *op. cit.*, VIII, p. 125.
875 Tahsin Paşa, *Abdülhamit ve Yıldız Hatıraları*, İstanbul, 1931, p. 62.
876 Karal, *op. cit.*, VIII, pp. 173-177.
877 Tahsin Paşa, *op. cit.*, p. 286.

## *Chapter Seventeen – The İttihâd ve Teraqqî Society – The Committee of Union and Progress*

878 S. Shaw and E.K. Shaw, *op. cit.*, II, pp. 255-256.
879 Bernard Lewis, *The Emergence of Modern Turkey*, Oxford University Press, 1968, pp. 197-198.
880 Karal, *op. cit.*, VIII, p. 517.
881 Dânişmend, IV, pp. 349-350.
882 Tahsin Paşa (Mâbeyn Başkâtibi), *Abdülhamit ve Yıldız Hatıraları*, İstanbul, 1931, p. 203.
883 Karal, *op. cit.*, VIII, p. 537.
884 Karal, *op. cit.*, VIII, p. 538.
885 Dânişmend, IV, p. 360.
886 Dânişmend, IV, p. 361.
887 Tahsin Paşa, p. 263.
888 Dânişmend, IV, p. 362.
889 S. Shaw and E.K. Shaw, *op. cit.*, II, p. 266.

890  Ibid., p. 282.
891  Dânişmend, IV, p. 379.
892  Ibid., pp. 288-293.
893  Ibid., p. 289.
894  Tahsin Paşa, op. cit., p. 278.
895  Karal, OT, Ankara, 1966, IX, pp. 276-277.
896  S. Shaw and E. K. Shaw, op. cit., II, p. 293.
897  Tahsin Ünal, Türk Siyâsî Tarihi, Ankara 1978, pp. 403-404, cited in Nuri Ünlü, İslâm Tarihi, İstanbul, 1994, vol. III, p. 197.
898  Dânişmend, IV, p. 388.
899  Dânişmend, IV, pp. 391-392.
900  Dânişmend, IV, p. 406.
901  Ünlü, op. cit., III, p. 214.
902  S. Shaw and E.K. Shaw, op. cit., II, p. 295.
903  Ibid., p. 296.
904  Ünlü, III, p. 221.
905  Dânişmend, op. cit., IV, p. 418.
906  Stanford Shaw and Ezel Kural Shaw, op. cit., II, p. 310.
907  S. Shaw and E.K. Shaw, op. cit., II, p. 312.
908  Ibid., II, p. 319.
909  Stanford Shaw and Ezel Kural Shaw, II, 319.
910  Stanford J. Shaw and Ezel Kural Shaw, op. cit., II, p. 328.
911  Ibid., p. 365.

*Conclusion*

912  S. Shaw, and Ezel Kural Shaw, *History of the Ottoman Empire and Modern Turkey* (Cambridge University Press, 1992), II, X. Emphasis added.
913  Solakzâde Mehmed Hemdemî, *Solaqzêde Târihi* (İstanbul, 1298), p. 266, line 10, and p. 270, line 15; İstanbul is referred to as "**Dârul Khalifate.**"
914  *Târîh-i Devlet-i 'Aliyye-i Osmâniyye*, pp. 13-14, cited in David Kushner, *The Rise of Turkish Nationalism 1876-1908* (London, 1977), p. 37.
915  David Kushner, *The Rise of Turkish Nationalism 1876-1908* (London: 1977), p. 29. Emphasis added.
916  E.Z. Karal, *Osmanlı Tarihi* (Ankara: Türk Tarih Kurumu, 1983), VIII , p. 255.
917  Walter Livingstone Wright, Jr., *Ottoman Statecraft: The Book of Counsel for Vazirs and Governors of Sarı Mehmed Pasha, the Defterdar* (Princeton: Princeton University Press, 1935), VIII.
918  Muhammad Harb 'Abdul Hamid (translation & comments by), *Mudhakkirâtu's Sultân 'Abdil Hamiyd*, Egypt, 1978, p. 128.

919   *Netâyij*, II, 90.
920   *Ibid.*, II, 91.
921   *Ibid.*, II, 93.
922   Ahmed Cevdet Paşa, *Ma'rûzât* (ed. Yusuf Halaçoğlu, İstanbul: Cağrı Yayınları, 1980), pp. 7-17.

## Addendum – The Osmanlı Socio-Political Entity: Empire or Devlet?

923   Rupert Emerson, *From Empire to Nation* (Cambridge, Massachusetts; Harvard University Press, 1967), p. vii.
924   Başbakanlık Osmanlı Arşivi (The Osmahlı Archives), *Nâme-i Hümâyûn Defteri*, 12, 196 (hereafter BOA).
925   BOA, *Nâme-i Hümâyûn Defteri* 12, 159.
926   BOA, *AMD* 257, p. 163.
927   BOA, *AMD* 256, p. 14.
928   BOA, *AMD* 216, p. 37.
929   BOA, *AMD* 257, p. 154.
930   BOA, *İrâde-Hariciye* 6, 1693, 26; Sevval, 1332.
931   BOA, *AMD*, 257, p. 169.
932   BOA, *Nâme-i Hümâyûn Defteri*, 8, p. 71.
933   BOA, *AMD*, 218, p. 139.
934   Na'ima, *Ravzatul Huseyn fi Hulâsati Ahbâril Hâfiqayn*, I, p. 6.
935   Ahmed Wâsif, *Mahâsinul Âsâr ve Haqâyiqul Akhbâr*, II, p. 257. Bulaq (Egypt) 1243/1827.
936   BOA, *Nâme-i Hümâyûn Defteri*, 13, p. 73.
937   BOA, *Nâme-i Hümâyûn Defteri*, 13, p. 71.
938   BOA, *Mukteza Defteri* 21, p. 114.
939   BOA, *AMD*, 257, p. 72.
940   BOA, *AMD*, 257, p. 71.
941   BOA, *AMD*, 256, p. 29.
942   BOA, *AMD*, 257, p. 149.
943   BOA, *AMD*, 256, p. 149.
944   Chris Cook, *Dictionary of Historical Terms* (London: Macmillan, 1983), p. 152.
945   J.M. Roberts, *The Hutchinson History of the World* (London: Hutchinson, 1987), p. 835 (emphasis added).
946   *Ibid.*, p. 13.
947   C.M. Kortepeter, Comment on Halîl Inalcik's "The Turkish Impact on the Development of Modern Europe," in Kemâl Karpat (ed.), *The Ottoman State and its Place in World History* (Leiden: Brill, 1974), p. 59.

948 Albert Hourani, "The Ottoman Background of the Modern Middle East," in Karpat, *op. cit.*, p. 67.
949 Lewis, *op. cit.*, p. 35.

## Osmanlı Institutions

### Introduction

950 Mehmed Neşrî, *Kitâb-ı Cihân-nümâ* (Ankara: Türk Tarih Kurumu, 1949), I, pp. 80-84.
951 *Sûfî Path* (articles related to Sûfîsm), published in Malaysia by A.S. Noordeen, 1991, back cover.
952 Mustafa Nûrî Paşa, *Netâyiju'l Vuqû'ât*, I (İstanbul, 1327), II, p. 58.
953 Bernard Lewis, *The Emergence of Modern Turkey*, 2nd ed., Oxford University Press, 1968, p. 13.

### *I. Administrative Organisation*

954 *al-Qur'ân, al-Baqarah* [2] *âyat* 30.
955 Aly Bayoumy Aly Oteify, "Interrogative Utterances in Surah Al-Baqarah," *Intellectual Discourse* (The Journal of the Faculty (*Kulliyah*) of Islamic Revealed Knowledge and Human Sciences) (Malaysia: International Islamic University Press, October 1993), I, number 1, p. 70.
956 *al-Qur'ân, al-Hajj* [22 ] *âyat*: 65.
957 *al-Qur'ân, Luqmân* [31] *âyat*: 20; *al-Jâthiyah* [45] *âyat*: 13.
958 *al-Qur'ân, al-Baqarah* [2] *âyat*: 172.
959 Ahmad b. Hanbal, *Al Musnad*, 3: 111; al-Bukhârî, *as Sahîh*, al-Anbiyâ: 50; Muslim, *as Sahîh*, Imârah: 44; al-Bukhâr, *as Sahîh*, Shehâdat: 33; see also: Abû Ya'lâ Muhammad b. Husayn al-Farrâ, *al-Ahkâmu's Sultâniyyah* (Surubaya, Indonesia: 1394/1974), p. 20.
960 Ferîdûn Ahmed Beğ, *Mejmû'a--yı Munsheât-I Selâtîn* (İstanbul: 1274), I, p. 90.
961 Tursun Beğ, *Târîh-i Ebu'l Feth*, ed. by Mertol Tulum (İstanbul: 1977), p. 33; İbn Kemâl, *Tevârîh-i Âl-i Osman*, VII, pp. 194, 196.
962 Solaqzâde, *Târîh* (İstanbul: 1298), p. 266.
963 Munsheât, I, p. 306.
964 Keşfî Mehmed Çelebi, *Keşfî'nin Selîm-Nâmesi*, ed. by Şefâettin Severcan (Kayseri: 1995), p. 198. Recitation of the *khutbah* of the khalifate in the name of Sultân Selîm at al-Qâhira in 923/1517.
965 Na'îmâ, *Ravzatu'l Huseyn fî Khulâsati Akhbâri'l Khâfiqayn*, 2nd ed. (İstanbul: 1288), v. I, p. 290.
966 Naîmâ, II, 229.
967 BOA, *Nâme-I Hümâyûn Defteri* (henceforth: *NMH*) 9, p. 101. İstanbul

is called *Dâru'l Khilâfeti'l 'Aliyye* (Seat of the Sublime Khalifate). Hüseyin Bayqara, the pâdishâh of the fourth Osmanlı sovereign with the Khorasân, addressed Yıldırım Bâyezîd as *zillullâh* (shadow of Allah): Muusheit, I, p. 306.
968 BOA, *NMH*, 5, p. 18.
969 BOA, *NMH*, 5, p. 205.
970 al Mâwardî, *al-Ahkâmu's Sultâniyyah* (al Qâhira: 1380/1960), p. 6.
971 al-*Qur'ân, Tâ Hâ* [20]: 29-30.
972 Nasaî, *as Sunan, al-Bey'at,* 23; Abû Dâvûd, *as Sunan, al-İmârat,* 4.
973 al Mâwardî, *al-Ahkâmu's Sultâniyyatu* (al Qâhira: 1327/1909), p. 6.
974 *al An'âm* 6, 164.
975 *Netâyij,* I, p. 15.
976 *Netâyij,* I, p. 16.
977 *Netâyij,* I, p. 56.
978 *Ibid.,* I, 57.
979 *Ibid.,* I, 115.
980 *Ibid.,* II, 91.
981 *Netâyij,* I, 58.
982 Solaqzâde, *Târîh* (İstanbul: 1298), p. 268.
983 *Ibid.,* pp. 268-269.
984 M. Zeki Pakalın, *Osmanlı Tarih Terimleri ve Deyimleri Sözlüğü* (İstanbul, 1983), II, pp. 47-48.
985 *Netâyij,* I, p. 58.
986 Yusuf Halacoğlu, "Osmanlı İmparatorluğunda Menzil Teşkilâtı Hakkında Bazı Mülahazalar," *Osmanlı Araştırmaları* (İstanbul: 1981) II, pp. 123-132.

## II – Economic Institutions

987 *Netâyij,* I, p. 119.
988 *Netâyij,* I, p. 120.
989 *Netâyij,* I, p. 115.
990 *al Hashr* [59] *âyat*: 7.
991 M. Hamîdullah, p. 122.
992 *al Baqara* (2), 43; *al-Baqara* (2), 83; *al-Baqara* (2), 110; *an-Nisâ* (4), 77 and 162; *al-Mâide* (5), 12 and 55; *al-A'râf* (7), 156; *at Tawba* (9), 5, 11, 18, 71; *al-Kahf* (18), 81; *Maryam* (19), 13, 31, 55; *al-Anbiyâ'* (21), 73; *al-Hajj* (22), 41, 78; *al-Mu'minûn* (23), 4; *an Nûr* (24), 37, 56; *an Naml* (27), 3; *ar Rûm* (30), 39; *Loqmân* (31), 4; *al-Ahzâb* (33), 33; *Fussilat* (41), 7; *al-Mujâdila* (58), 13; *al-Muzzammil* (73), 20; *al-Bayyina* (9).
993 Abû Bakr Muhammad b. Aziz as Sijistânî, *Garîbu'l Qur'ân (al Musammâ bi Nuzhati'l Qulûb)* (Beirut: Dâru'l Fikri'l Arabî), 3rd printing, 1402/1982, p. 102.

994 *at Tawba* [9] *âyat* 29.
995 İbn Hishâm, *as Siyratu'n Nabawiyyatu* (al-Qâhira: 1375/1955), II, p. 525.
996 *Netâyij* III, p. 100.
997 Halîl İnalcık, *The Ottoman Empire*, translated by Norman Itzkowitz and Colin Imber (London: 1973), p. 13.
998 *al Qur'ânu'l Karîm, al-Anbiyâ* [21] *âyat*: 105.
999 *Netâyij*, I, pp. 69-70.
1000 *al Qur'ânu'l Karîm, al-Anfâl* [8], *âyat* 41.

## III – The Legal System

1001 *ar Rahmân* [55], âyats: 5-9.
1002 For different meanings of *haqq*, see: Dr. Wahbah al-Zuhayly, *al-Fiqhu'l Islamî wa adillatuhu*, Dimashq, Dâru'l Fikr, second printing, 1409/1989, p. 8.
1003 Tashkoprîzâde Ahmed 'Isâmeddin, *ash Shaqâ'iqu'n Nu'mâniyyatu fî 'Ulemâi'd Dawlati'l 'Aliyyati'l Othmâniyyati* (Beyrût: 1975), p. 19.
1004 Ferîdûn Beğ, *Munsheât-ı Selâtîn*, I, p. 69.
1005 Bernard Lewis, *The Emergence of Modern Turkey*, second edition, Oxford University Press, 1968, p. 14.
1006 İ.H. Uzunçarşılı, *Osmanlı Devletinin İlmiye Teşkilatı* (Ankara, 1984), pp. 161-170.
1007 J.H. Kramers, "Seyhulislam," *İslam Ansiklopedisi* XXI (İstanbul, 1979), p. 486.
1008 Ahmed Akgündüz, *Osmanlı Kanunnamelerinin Hukukî Tahlilleri* (İstanbul: 1990) I, p. 47; Uzunçarşılı, *op. cit.*, p. 179. *Ibid.*, p. 181.
1009 Uzunçarşılı, *op. cit.*, p. 179.
1010 *Ibid.*, p. 181.
1011 *Ibid.*, pp. 187-188.
1012 *Ibid.*, p. 206.
1013 *Ibid.*, p. 207.
1014 Mustakimzade Süleymân Sadeddin, *Devhatu'l Meşâyih* (İstanbul, 1978), pp. 3-4; Michael M. Pixley, "The Development and the Role of Seyhulislam in the Early Ottoman History," *Journal of the American Oriental Society*, vol. 96, Nr. 1, January-March 1976, p. 92.
1015 R.C. Repp, *The Mufti of İstanbul: A Study in the Development of the Ottoman Learned Hierarchy* (Oxford University Computing Service, 1986), pp. 98-105.
1016 Uzunçarşılı, *Osmanlı Tarihi*, I, p. 166.
1017 Uzunçarşılı, *Osmanlı Devletinin İlmiye Teşkilâtı* (Ankara, 1984), p. 152.

1018  Loc. Cit.
1019  Ibid., p. 153.
1020  Ibid., p. 154.
1021  Mehmet İpşirli, *XVII. Yüzyıl Başlarına Kadar Osmanlı İmparatorluğunda Kadıaskerlik Müessesesi* (unpublished post-doctorate dissertation: İstanbul Üniversitesi, Edebiyat Fakültesi), pp. 186-187.
1022  al Qur'ânu'l Kerîm, al-Anfâl [8] âyat 25.
1023  Muslim, *as Sahîh, Kitâbul İmârah, 20.*
1024  al Mawardî, *al-Ahkâmu's Sultâniyyatu* (Egypt, 1973), p. 241.
1025  Ziyâ Kazıcı, *Osmanlılarda İhtisab Müessesesi* (İstanbul, 1987), pp. 54-61.
1026  Mehmed Neşrî, *Kitâb-ı Cihân-Nümâ*, ed. by F.R. Unat and M.A. Köymen (Ankara: Türk Tarih Kurumu, 1949) I, p. 110.
1027  Z. Kazıcı, *op. cit.*, p. 33.

## IV – Military Organisation

1028  Uzunçarşılı, *Osmanlı Devleti Teşkilâtından Kapıkulu Ocakları* (Atatürk Kültür, Dil ve Tarih Yüksek Kurumu,; Ankara, 1984) I, p. 1.
1029  Neşrî, *op. cit.*, I, pp. 154.
1030  Uzunçarşılı, *op. cit.*, I pp. 6-7.
1031  Uzunçarşılı, *op. cit.*, pp. 11-13.
1032  *Netâyij*, I, p. 142; *Kapıkulu Ocakları*, I, pp. 145-146.
1033  *Kapıkulu Ocakları*, II, pp. 3-5.
1034  *Ibid*, II, pp. 35-36.
1035  *Ibid*, II, pp. 117-119.
1036  *Ibid*, II, pp. 131-132.
1037  *Ibid*, II, pp. 137-139.
1038  Donald Edgar Pitcher, *An Historical Geography of the Ottoman Empire* (Leiden: E.J. Brill, 1972), p. 5.
1039  İdris Bostan, *Osmanlı Bahriye Teşkilatı XVII. Yüzyılda Tersâne-i Âmire* (Ankara:Türk Tarih Kurumu Basımevi, 1992), p. 1.
1040  *Ibid.*, pp. 14-24.
1041  İ.H. Uzunçarşılı, *Osmanlı Devletinin Merkez ve Bahriye Teşkilatı* (Ankara: Turk Tarih Kurumu Basımevi, 1984), p. 391.
1042  *Ibid.*, pp. 391-392.
1043  Uzunçarşılı, *Osmanlı Devletinin Merkez ve Bahriye Teşkilatı*, p. 392.
1044  Uzunçarşılı, *op. cit.*, pp. 403-404.
1045  *Ibid.*, p. 414.
1046  *Ibid.*, p. 421.
1047  *Ibid.*, p. 437.
1048  Afetinan, *Piri Reisin Hayatı ve Eserleri* (Ankara: Türk Tarih Kurumu Basımevi, 1992), p. 27.

1049 Kâtib Chelebi, *Tuhfetu'l Kibâr fî Esfâri'l Bihâr* (İstanbul, 1329), p. 25.

## V – Social Institutions

1050 *Âlu 'İmrân* [3] *âyat:* 92.
1051 Ali Himmet Berki, "Vakıf Kuran ilk Osmanlı Padişahı," *Vakıflar Dergisi* (Ankara: 1962), V, p. 127.
1052 *Ibid*, V, pp. 128-129.
1053 Robert J. Scrutton, *Nature's Way to Nutrition and Vibrant Health* (Hollywood, CA: Melvin Powers, 1977), pp. 16-17.
1054 Neşri, I, p. 82.
1055 *Ibid*, I, p. 72.
1056 *Ibid*, I, p. 162.
1057 Sayyid Mustafa Nûrî Pasha, *Netâyiju'l Vuqû'ât* (İstanbul: 1324), II, pp. 105-106.
1058 Robert J. Scrutton, *op. cit.*, p. 16.
1059 Osman Şevki Uludağ (ed. İlter Uzel), *Beş Buçuk Asırlık Türk Tababeti Tarihi* (Ankara: 1991), p. 25.
1060 *Ibid.*, p. 161.
1061 Aptullah Kuran, *Mimar Sinan* (İstanbul: 1985), pp. 38-39.
1062 Osman Şevki Uludağ, *op. cit.*, pp. 140-141.
1063 *Ibid.*, pp. 143-151. Voltaire's *Philosophical Writings* (the eleventh letter refers to this vaccination: *Loc. cit.*, footnote 19 by.O.Ş.U.), 13.
1064 *Ibid.*, p. 24.
1065 *Ibid.*, pp. 32-33.
1066 *Ibid.*, pp. 33-34.
1067 *Ibid.*, p. 48.
1068 *Ibid.*, p. 47
1069 Fuat Kamil Beksan, "Beş Asır Evvel Türkiyede Üroloji," *Üroloji Kliniği Dergisi* 1935 (2) 2, pp. 73-89; cited in *Ibid.*, p. 49.
1070 Osman Şevki Uludağ, *op. cit.*, pp. 50-51.
1071 C. Baltacı, *XV-XVI. Asırlarda Osmanlı Madrasahleri* (İstanbul: 1976), p. 19.
1072 Nevill (ed.), *A Survey of North West Africa (The Maghrib)* (Oxford University Press, 1962), p. 239; cited in Dr. Fawzia Bariun, *Malik Bennabi, His Life and Theory of Civilization* (Kuala Lumpur, 1993), p. 12.
1073 Fawzia Bariun, *Loc. cit.*
1074 Mustafa Bilge, *İlk Osmanlı Medreseleri* (İstanbul: İ.Ü.Edebiyat Fakültesi Basımevi, 1984), pp. XI-XII.
1075 *Ibid.*, p. XII.
1076 C. Baltacı, *op. cit.*, p. 15.
1077 M. Bilge, *op. cit.*, p. XIII.
1078 C. Baltaci, *Loc. cit.*

1079  M. Bilge, p. XIV.
1080  *Ibid.*, p, XIII.
1081  C. Baltacı, pp. 21-22.
1082  *Ibid*, p. 23.
1083  B. Miller, *The Palace School of Muhammad the Conqueror* (Cambridge: 1941), p. 78; cited in Ülker Akkutay, *Enderun Mektebi* (Ankara: 1984), p. 86.
1084  This chapter is a short summary of *Enderun Mektebi* (pp. 1-105) by Ülker Akkutay (Ankara, 1984).

## Conclusion

1085  M. Hamidullah, *Introduction to Islam,* 5th ed.(Lahore: 1979), pp. 38-39.
1086  *al Qur'ânu'l Karîm, al-Baqarah* [2], *âyat*: 201.
1087  M. Hamidullah, *op. cit.*, p. 39.

# Glossary

**ahî:** The Akhiyya-Fityân was a voluntary religio-military police force in Anatolia in the thirteenth and fourteenth centuries that was composed of traders and artisans. They were not paid by the Osmanlı Devlet, though they were exempt from paying taxes.

**aqınjı:** Volunteer boundary forces under the Aqınjı Beği. These commandos were fit, very well trained, and extremely brave *mujâhids*. They were used to demoralise the enemy.

**alp, alperen:** spiritually and physically trained *mujâhid*.

**beğlerbeği:** *Beğ* (Bey) of *beğs*. The Osmanlı Devlet had two main beğlerbeğis during the classical period: one for Rumeli (Osmanlı Europe) and the other for Anatolia. Each of them was to take a position on the right flank of the army when a *jihâd* was fought in his region.

**berât:** Decree of authorisation.

**beytülmal:** (Ar. *baytu'l mâl*) Public treasury of the Muslim Devlet.

**börk:** Headgear of Turks. Its shape varied according to climate and time. The Göktürks had *börks* (or *börüks*) made of lambskin with wool on them. Turks who lived north of the Caspian Sea and the Black Sea had *börks* made of tailored lambskin, which were also called *qalpaq*. Turks in Anatolia

|  |  |
|---|---|
| | had *börks* made of felt. The janissary corps set up by Orhan Gâzi had white *börks*. |
| dervish: | (Per. *Darvish*) A follower of a *sûfî* order. |
| devshirme: | Non-Muslim children who were converted to Islam and recruited into the military service known as *yenicheris* (janissaries). Those who were educated in the *Enderûn* (Palace School) became *pashas, vazîrs,* and *sadrâzams*. |
| dhimmî: | Non-Muslims living under the protection of the Muslim Devlet. |
| dizdâr: | Commander of a castle. |
| enderûn: | (Per. *andarûn*) Palace School. |
| eren: | A pious man who attains an outstanding spiritual level, and is regarded as a *velî* (Muslim saint). |
| eyalet: | sometimes translated as province or governorate. |
| ezân: | (Ar. *adhân*) The Islamic call to prayer. |
| fermân: | Sultânic decree. |
| fetâ: | (Ar. *fatâ*) Young, strong, able and virtuous. |
| fetvâ: | (Ar. *fatwâ*) Legal opinion given by the SheyhülIslam or mufti. |
| gazâ: | (Ar. *ghazâh*) In Osmanlı usage it means *jihâd*. *Jihâd* and *mujâhadah* are infinitives of the verb *jâhada* in Arabic, which means to struggle. *Jihâd* means to struggle with infidels, and *mujâhadah* means to struggle with one's ego, own self to attain a higher degree of spirituality. |
| gâzi: | (Ar. *Ghazi*): *Mujâhid,* fighter for the cause of Islam. |
| gusl: | (Ar. *ghusl*) Great ablution. |
| hâjet namâzı: | Two cycles of prayer to implore the Creator regarding some need (*salât al-hâjah*). |
| hâfız: | (Ar. *hâfız* pl. *huffâz*): One who memorises the whole Glorious Qur'ân. |

**hajj:** Pilgrimage to the Ka'bah in Makkah al-Mukarramah.

**hamam** (Ar. *hammâm*): Public bath.

**hamamjı esnâfı:** People who provided hot water and convenient places for the Osmanlı army to take a bath during a *jihâd*.

**harâch** (Ar. *kharâj*): Tax on land paid by non-Muslims living in the domain of the Muslim Devlet.

**ijâzet** (Ar. *ijâzah*): Permission to carry out an action.

**iqtâ** (Ar. *iqtâ'*): Allocating a piece of land to individuals. This practice was initiated by the Final Messenger and later adopted by the Osmanlıs under the name of *tımâr*. Larger *tımâr*s were called *ze'âmet* and the largest were called *khâss*.

**imâret** (Ar. *'imârah*): A building constructed to feed the poor and sometimes give them shelter. Its revenue came from the *waqf* allocated to it. This *imâret* tradition continued in Turkey after the collapse of the Osmanlı Devlet. In almost every village there was a special room called *köy odası* assigned to visitors who could have food and lodging for three nights without charge. The period of time is specified in a *hadith sharîf* (saying of the Final Messenger).

**jihâd:** Holy Islamic war.

**jizye** (Ar. *jizyah*): Derived from Arabic root *jazâ*, which means to compensate. *Jizyah* was thus a tax levied on non-Muslims who lived under the protection of a Muslim Devlet. It has no relation with poll-tax; westerners commit this mistake by asserting a resemblance to their society's practice. It varied in amount, and there were exemptions for the poor, women, children, slaves, monks, and hermits. It was ordained by the Creator in the Qur'ân Karîm (Sûrat al-Tawbah [9] *âyat*: 29), and was first adopted by the Final Messenger when he went on a *jihâd* to Tabûk in 9/630; the Bishop of 'Aqabah (Aylah) Yuhanna came to him with a golden cross on his chest and paid *jizyah*, thus obtaining the protection of the Muslim Devlet.

**qadı (Ar. *qâdî*):** A Muslim judge who had to act in accordance with the *Sharî'at* (the Holy Islamic law).

**qazasker (Ar. *qâdî 'askar*):** A military judge. The Osmanlı Devlet, which was based on the ideal of *jihâd*, set up the post of *qazasker* at an early stage in its history. Over time there were two main *qazaskers*; one for Rumeli and the other for Anatolia.

**qaptân-ı deryâ:** Supreme commander of the Osmanlı naval forces.

**mehter:** Osmanlı military band that was derived from the Selçuklu tradition and played music every afternoon. It was used effectively during *jihâd*. It became a model for future European bands.

**menshur (Ar. *manshûr*):** Decree issued by the Sultân giving the rank of *vazîr*, *beğlerbeği*, etc., or appointing someone commander-in-chief of the army. It is a synonym of *fermân*.

**müjâhid:** Fighter in a *jihâd*.

**müderris (Ar. *mudarris*):** A professor or teacher in a *madrasah*.

**mükâshefe (Ar. *mukâshafah*):** A *velî*'s spiritual approach to attain knowledge of the unknown.

**müsellem (Ar. *musallam*):** A soldier who was exempted from paying taxes. Originally a member of the infantry corps set up by Orhan Gâzi.

*Glossary*

mütevellî (Ar. *mutawallî*): Administrator of a *waqf*.

nâhiye: a district, a subunit of a *qazâ*

nedîm (Ar. *nadîm*): A knowledgeable and pleasant man with whom Sultâns loved to converse.

öshür (Ar. *'ushr*): One-tenth. A Muslim pays *öshür* on his crops, an amount that may be reduced to one-twentieth if human and other expenses were involved.

qazâ: a subdivision of a *sanjaq* corresponding roughly to a city with its surrounding villages, and subject to the legal and administrative jurisdiction of a *qaaimmakâm*

raîyyet (Ar. *ra'iyyah* pl. *ra'âyâ*): Those who are cared for and looked after. The ruled people in Islamic administration are not *subjects* but were called *ra'âyâ*. The word implied the *devlet*'s responsibility towards the governed people.

sadrâzam (Ar. *sadr a'zam*): Chief *vazîr*.

salât (Per. *namâz*): Muslim worship (five times a day). The Final Messenger was taught by Jibrîl (Gabriel) how to worship.

sanjaq: an administrative division of an *eyalet* province

sipâhî: A cavalryman. *Sipâhi* units were founded during Sultân Murâd's era (1362-1389). Apart from the *sipâhî* units in the capital, there were other provincial cavalry units called *sipâhî* as well.

sûfî: A devoted, pious man, belonging to one of the spiritual orders called *tarîqat*.

sürre (*mahmal*) (Ar. *surrah*): Gifts and money presented to the people of the two Holy Cities of Islam, Makkah al-Mukarramah and Madînah al-Munawwarah (Medîna). The first Osmanlı sultân to send a *sürre* was Chelebi Mehemmed (1413-1421). Since

> 1517 and until and during the First World War the Osmanlıs regularly sent an annual *sürre* to the Hejâz. And the *sürre emîni* (head of the *sürre* group) performed *hajj* (pilgrimage) on behalf of the Sultân.

**sünnah** (Ar. *sunnat*): The tradition of the Final Messenger.

**shâhzâda** (Per. *shâhzâdah*): Son of the Sultân.

**sheyh** (Ar. *shaykh*): A spiritual master in a *sûfî* order. Most of the Osmanlı sultâns and *vazîrs* greatly respected the *sheyhs*.

**sheyhülislam** (Ar. *shaykhu'l islâm*): The highest judicial and educational authority in the Osmanlı Devlet. He was on equal footing with the *sadrâzam* in the hierarchy, and the Osmanlı Devlet had to obtain his approval on important issues.

**tablhâne** (Per. *tablkhânah*): *Mehter*, the Osmanlı military band.

**tarîqat** (Ar. tarîqat): A *sûfî* order.

**tekke:** Home of the *sheyh* and the gathering place of a *sûfî* order where spiritual training is practised and passed on to followers.

**tekfur:** Roman governor of a city or town.

**tımar:** Osmanlı *iqtâ* system.

**tuğ:** Post decorated with three horsetails signifying its owner's high standing.

**ulûfe** (Ar. *'ulûfah*): The stipend given to the *yenicheris* (janissaries) every three months.

**vakıf** (Ar. *waqf*): Endowment allocated by wealthy people for pious and social purposes.

**velî pl. evliyâ** (Ar. *walî* pl. *awliyâ'*): A very beloved, pious, refined and pure man who attains a very high spiritual level.

**vazîr** (Ar. *wazîr*): In Islamic understanding, one who assumes

|  |  |
|---|---|
| | responsibility and accountability for the affairs of the *devlet*, having much more power than a government minister today. |
| **yenicheri:** | A "new soldier". The Osmanlı Devlet trained its converted captives to be soldiers. They were called *yenicheris*, which was Anglicised as "janissaries." |
| **voyvoda** | a title denoting a "military-leader" or "warlord" in Central, Southeastern and Eastern Europe since the Early Middle Ages. |
| **zakât** (Ar. *zakât*): | Religious offering that had to be paid by wealthy Muslims. *Zakât* has been ordained by the Creator in various places in the Noble Qur'ân. When a Muslim pays his *zakât*, his property is purified and increased. |

# Places Mentioned in the Text

The Osmanlıca language is written in Arabic script. Since the "reforms" undertaken by Atatürk rewriting it in Latin script there are sometimes considerable variations in the spellings which we have tried to accomodate in the following.

| | |
|---|---|
| **Ada Kale** | Ada Kaleh was a small island on the Danube in what is modern Romania |
| **Adana** | a major city in southern Turkey. The city is situated on the Seyhan River, 35 km (22 mi) inland from the north-eastern coast of the Mediterranean Sea. |
| **Adapazarı** | a city in north-western Turkey and the central district of Sakarya Province. |
| **Adiljevâz** | Adilcevaz is a town and district capital of the district of the same name within Bitlis Province, Turkey. The city is on the shore of Lake Van. |
| **Ahıska** | Akhaltsikhe is a small city in Georgia's south-western region (mkhare) of Samtskhe–Javakheti. |
| **Ahlat** | a town and district in Turkey's Bitlis Province in the Eastern Anatolia Region. |
| **Akhisâr** | a town and district in Manisa Province in the Aegean Region of western Turkey; also the ancient city of Thyatira |
| **Alajahisâr** | Kruševac, a city and today the administrative centre of the Rasina District in central Serbia. |

| | |
|---|---|
| Alâiye | Alany, formerly Alaiye, is a city and a district of Antalya Province on the southern coast of Turkey, in the country's Mediterranean Region |
| Alaşehir | in Antiquity and the Middle Ages known as Philadelphia "the city of him who loves his brother", is a town and district of Manisa Province in the Aegean region of Turkey. |
| Amasra | a district in the province of Bartın in the Western Black Sea Region |
| Antaqiyya | Antioch |
| Antalya | the capital of Antalya Province. Located on Anatolia's southwest coast bordered by the Taurus Mountains, on the Mediterranean coast outside the Aegean region |
| Aqkerman | Akkerman or Aqqerman. Bilhorod-Dnistrovskyi, a city, municipality and port in Odessa Oblast of south-western Ukraine |
| Aq Qoyunlu | a Persianate Sunni Turkoman tribal confederation that ruled parts of present-day eastern Turkey from 1378 to 1503. |
| Aqsaray | Aksaray, a city in the Central Anatolia region of Turkey, the seat of Aksaray Province and District. |
| Aqchây | Akçay |
| Aqshehir | Akşehir, a town and district of Konya Province in the Central Anatolia region of Turkey. |
| Aras | A river that rises in eastern Anatolia and flows into the Caspian Sea. |
| Armutlu | a district of Yalova province, located in the north of Gemlik Bay in the east of the Sea of Marmara. |
| Atjeh | Acheh or Aceh |

## Places Mentioned in the Text

| | |
|---|---|
| **Avlonya** | Vlorë is located in south-western Albania, and sprawls along the Bay of Vlorë. |
| **Aydın** | a *beğlik* in South-Western Anatolia between Saruhan and Menteshe |
| **Aydos** | Aydos Hill (Turkish: Aydos Tepesi) is a hill in the north of the Kartal district of Istanbul. |
| **Azaq/Azak** | Azov, previously known as Azak, is a town in Rostov Oblast, Russia, situated on the Don River. |
| **Âzerbeyjân** | Azerbaijan |
| **Babadağı** | Babadağ (ancient Mount Anticragus) is a mountain near Fethiye, in Muğla Province, southwest Turkey |
| **Bahrayn** | Eastern Arabia was historically known as *al-Bahrayn* until the 18th century. This region stretched from Southern Iraq along the Persian Gulf coast and included regions in Iraq, modern-day Bahrain, Kuwait, Eastern Saudi Arabia, United Arab Emirates, Qatar, and Northern Oman. The entire coastal strip of Eastern Arabia was known as "Bahrain" for ten centuries. |
| **Balıkesir** | a province in north-western Turkey with coastlines on both the Sea of Marmara and the Aegean. |
| **Banat** | a geographical and historical region straddling between Central and Eastern Europe that is currently divided among three countries: western Romania, north-eastern Serbia and south-eastern Hungary. |
| **Balqans** | Balkans. |

| | |
|---|---|
| Basarabia/Bessarabia | a historical region in Eastern Europe, bounded by the Dniester river on the east and the Prut river on the west. about two thirds of Bessarabia lies within modern-day Moldova |
| Bayburd | a town in eastern Anatolia |
| Beğshehri | A city in south-western Anatolia |
| Bergama | a district in İzmir Province in western Turkey |
| Beykoz | also known as Beicos and Beikos, a district in Istanbul, at the northern end of the Bosphorus on the Anatolian side. |
| Beğpazarı | a town and district of Ankara Province in the Central Anatolia region of Turkey, approximately 100 km west of the city of Ankara |
| Berat | a city, the centre of the province of the same name in central southern Albania. |
| Biga | a town and district of Çanakkale Province in the Marmara region of Turkey. |
| Bilejik | Bilecik, the provincial capital of Turkey's Bilecik Province in north-western Anatolia. |
| Birecik | a town and district of Şanlıurfa Province of Turkey, on the River Euphrates. |
| Bitola | a city in the south-western part of North Macedonia, known to the Osmanlı as Manastır or Monastir. One of the oldest cities in North Macedonia. |
| Bodrum | a port city in Muğla Province, south-western Turkey, at the entrance to the Gulf of Gökova. |
| Boğazkesen | (meaning "Strait-Blocker Castle" or literally "Throat-Cutter Castle") or Rumeli Hisârı is a fortress located in Istanbul, on a series of hills on the European banks of the Bosphorus. |

*Places Mentioned in the Text*

| | |
|---|---|
| Bolayır | a town in the Gallipoli district |
| Bolu | a city, and administrative centre of Bolu Province, on the old highway from Istanbul to Ankara. |
| Boze | Boże is a village in the administrative district of Gmina Stromiec, within Białobrzegi County, Masovian Voivodeship, in east-central Poland. |
| Bozjaada | Bozcaada is an Aegean island, municipality, and district governorate in Çanakkale Province, Turkey |
| Budin | Buda was the historic capital of the Kingdom of Hungary and since 1873 has been the western part of the Hungarian capital Budapest, on the west bank of the Danube. |
| Bujak | Budjak or Budzhak, historically part of Bessarabia until 1812, is a historical region in Ukraine and Moldova, lying along the Black Sea between the Danube and Dniester rivers. |
| Campo Formio | Campoformido, a town and commune in Friuli-Venezia Giulia, north-eastern Italy. |
| Çankırı | historically known as Gangra, the capital city of Çankırı Province, north-east of Ankara |
| Chaldiran | a plain in Iranian Azerbaijan |
| Chanaqqale | Çanakkale, ancient Dardanellia, a city and seaport in Turkey in Çanakkale province on the southern shore of the Dardanelles at their narrowest point |
| Chanqırı | the capital city of Çankırı Province, northeast of Ankara. |
| Chatalja | Çatalca, a city that is today a rural district in Istanbul. |
| Chehrin | Chyhyryn is a city and historic site located in Cherkasy Raion of Cherkasy Oblast of central Ukraine. |

| | |
|---|---|
| Cheshme | Çeşme is a coastal town and the administrative centre of the district of the same name in Turkey's westernmost end. |
| Chıldır | Çıldır is a district of the Ardahan Province of Turkey. |
| Chiragan | Çırağan Palace is located on the European shore of the Bosphorus, between Beşiktaş and Ortaköy in Istanbul. |
| Chirmen | The Sanjak of Çirmen or Chirmen was a second-level Ottoman sanjak (or liva) encompassing the region of Ormenio in Thrace. |
| Chorlu | Çorlu is a north-western Turkish city in inland Eastern Thrace. |
| Chuqurova | Çukurova or the Cilician Plain is a large fertile plain in the Cilicia region of southern Turkey. |
| Dârende | a district of Malatya province whose centre is north-west of Malatya |
| Darıja (Darıca) | a town and district of Kocaeli Province. |
| Değirmenköy | a village in the Güroymak district of Bitlis province in Turkey |
| Derbend | Derbent is a city in Dagestan, Russia, located on the Caspian Sea. |
| Dimetoka | or Didymoteiho, a district in Western Thrace. |
| Dinyester River | the Dniester, a river in Eastern Europe. |
| Diu | the Battle of Diu was a naval battle fought on 3 February 1509 in the Arabian Sea, in the port of Diu, India |
| Divriği | a district of Sivas |
| Diyârbakır | a city in south-eastern Anatolia, situated around a high plateau by the banks of the Tigris river. |
| Dobruja | or Dobrudja is situated between the lower Danube River and the Black Sea, and includes |

## Places Mentioned in the Text

| | |
|---|---|
| | the Danube Delta, Romanian coast, and the northernmost part of the Bulgarian coast. |
| Doğu Bayazit | Doğubayazıt is a district of Ağrı Province, the easternmost district of Turkey, lying near the border with Iran. |
| Domanich | Domaniç, a town and district of Kütahya Province in the Aegean region of Turkey. |
| Drech | (Dıraç or Duraç) Durrës is the second most populous city of the Republic of Albania. |
| Dreczny | A town in Poland |
| Dulkadir | Dulqadir and Dulqadiroğlu, Kadirli is a town and district of Osmaniye Province in the Mediterranean region of Turkey. |
| Düzje | Düzce, the capital city of Düzce Province which is situated on the Black Sea between Ankara and Istanbul. |
| Edremit | a city and district of Balıkesir Province in the Aegean region of Turkey |
| Egine | Aegina, one of the Saronic Islands of Greece in the Saronic Gulf. |
| Eğriboz | the island of Euboea or Evia |
| Elbasan | or Ilbasan, the centre of Elbasan province in Central Albania located next to the Iskomi River. |
| Eleshgird | a city in Anatolia to the east of Erzurum |
| Eleshkirt | Eleşkirt is a town and district of Ağrı Province in Turkey. |
| Emet | a town and a district of Kütahya Province in the Aegean region of Turkey |
| Epir | Epirus, a historical region located in the Balkans between Albania and Greece |

| | |
|---|---|
| Erdek | a town and district of Balıkesir Province in the Marmara region of Turkey. |
| Erdel | the historical name of Transylvania in Turkish. |
| Erjish | Erciş, a town and district located in Van Province, Turkey on Lake Van. |
| Erzinjan | Erzincan is located on the historical Silk Road in the Upper Euphrates section of the Eastern Anatolia region. |
| Eskihisâr | a village in Gebze district of Kocaeli province. |
| Eskişehir | a city in north-western Turkey and the capital of the Eskişehir Province. |
| Filibe | Plovdiv is the second-largest city in Bulgaria, standing on the banks of the Maritsa river in the historical region of Thrace. |
| Focha | Foça, a district of İzmir, north-west of İzmir city centre. |
| Gebze | a district in Kocaeli Province, southeast of Istanbul. |
| Gelenbanya | A castle and town in Poland |
| Gelibolu | Gallipoli |
| Gemlik | a district of Bursa |
| Germiyân | a prominent Anatolian *beğlik* established by the Oghuz Turkish tribes |
| Geyve | a town in Sakarya Province in the Marmara region of Turkey. |
| Glagori | a castle in Poland |
| Gümüljine | Komotini is a city in the region of East Macedonia and Thrace, north-eastern Greece. It is the capital of the Rhodope. |
| Hajıhamza | A small town between Bolu and Merzifon in Anatolia |
| Hamîd | the *beğlik* of Hamîd was one of the 14th century |

*Places Mentioned in the Text*

|   |   |
|---|---|
|  | Anatolian *beğliks* in the regions around Eğirdir and Isparta in south-western Anatolia. see Hamîdeli |
| Hamîdeli | the country administered by Hamîdoğulu Beğlik containing İsparta, Burdur and Antalya, cities in South and south-western Anatolia |
| Harmankaya | Harmanköy, today a village in the District of İnhisar, in Bilecik Province, Turkey. |
| Harshova | Hârşova is a town located on the right bank of the Danube, in Constanța County, Northern Dobruja, Romania. |
| Hatvan | a town in Heves county, Hungary |
| Hayrabolu | a district of Tekirdağ province and one of the oldest settlements in Thrace |
| Hemedân | Hamadan, the capital city of the province of the same name in Iran. |
| Hendek | a town and district of Sakarya Province in the Marmara region of Turkey. |
| Hereke | a town in Kocaeli province. |
| Hermanstad | Sibiu or Sibin is a city in the Erdel region of Romania. |
| Hive | Khiva, a city in the province of Khwarezm, Uzbekistan. |
| Horasân | Khorasan |
| Hotin | Khotyn is a city in Dnistrovskyi Raion, Chernivtsi Oblast of western Ukraine. |
| Iashi | Iași the second largest city in Romania and the seat of Iași County, in the historical region of Moldavia |
| İbrâil | Brăila, a city in Moldova, eastern Romania, is a port on the Danube. |
| İhtiman | a town in western Bulgaria, in Sofia Province. |

| | |
|---|---|
| Ilgın | a town and district of Konya Province in the Central Anatolian region of Turkey. |
| İnlik | a castle on the shores of the Danube |
| İnegöl | a district of Bursa province in the Marmara Region. |
| İpsala | a district in the Edirne province of the Thrace part of the Marmara Region. |
| İshkodra | Shkodër, one of the continuously inhabited cities in the Balkans, it was founded under the name Scodra. |
| İsfendiyâr | principally in the regions corresponding to present-day Kastamonu and Sinop provinces of Turkey, also covering parts of Zonguldak, Bartın, Karabük, Samsun, Bolu, Ankara and Çankırı provinces in the Black Sea region of modern-day Turkey. |
| İskenderun | a city in Hatay Province on the Mediterranean coast of Turkey. |
| İsmail | Izmail, a city and municipality on the Danube river in Odessa Oblast in south-western Ukraine. |
| Isparta | a city in western Turkey and the capital of the province of the same name. |
| Istanköy | Kos or Cos, a Greek island, part of the Dodecanese island chain in the southeastern Aegean Sea. |
| Istirya | Istria is the largest peninsula within the Adriatic Sea at the head of the Adriatic between the Gulf of Trieste and the Kvarner Gulf. |
| İzladi | or İzladin, a city and municipality located in the İzladi-Pirdop valley in the Sofia province of Bulgaria. |

*Places Mentioned in the Text*

| | |
|---|---|
| **İzmit** | the central district of Kocaeli province, Turkey. |
| **Jandaroğlu Beğlik** | a *beğlik* lying along the southern coast of the Black Sea and including Sinop |
| **Janik** | the *beğlik*s of Canik, a name given to a group of small Turkoman principalities in northern Anatolia during the fourteenth and fifteenth centuries. |
| **Jezâyir-i Seb'a (Seven Islands)** | the Ionian Islands are a group of islands in the Ionian Sea, west of mainland Greece traditionally called the Heptanese Islands. |
| **Kamaniche** | Kamianets-Podilskyi is a city on the Smotrych River in western Ukraine, to the north-east of Chernivtsi. |
| **Kandiye** | Heraklion or Iraklion, the largest city and the administrative capital of the island of Crete and capital of the Heraklion regional unit. |
| **Kanije** | Nagykanizsa is a medium-sized city in Zala County in south-western Hungary. |
| **Karacabey** | formerly Mihaliç, a district of Bursa located to its west. |
| **Karajahisâr** | Karacahisar Castle, a Byzantine castle on a plateau near the Porsuk River, southwest of Eskişehir, Turkey |
| **Karlowitz** | Sremski Karlovci, a town and municipality on the banks of the Danube in the South Bačka District of the autonomous province of Vojvodina, Serbia. |
| **Kars** | a city in northeast Turkey and the capital of Kars Province |
| **Kartal** | a city on the shore of the Marmara Sea, now a part of Istanbul. |

| | |
|---|---|
| Kefe | Feodosia, also called Theodosia, is a port, a town in Crimea on the Black Sea coast. |
| Kefalonya | Kefalonia or Cephalonia, formerly also known as Kefallinia or Kephallenia, is the largest of the Ionian Islands in western Greece. |
| Kefken | Kefken Island, lies off the Black Sea coast of Turkey. |
| Kemah | known historically as Ani-Kamakh, a town and district of Erzincan Province in the Eastern Anatolia Region of Turkey. |
| Keşan | both the name of a district of Edirne Province, Turkey, and of the largest town in the district. |
| Khokand | Kokand, a city in Fergana Region in eastern Uzbekistan, at the south-western edge of the Fergana Valley |
| Khotin | Khotyn, a city in Dnistrovskyi Raion, Chernivtsi Oblast of western Ukraine, south-west of Kamianets-Podilskyi. |
| Khwarazm | a large oasis region on the Amu Darya river delta in western Central Asia, bordered on the north by the (former) Aral Sea, on the east by the Kyzylkum Desert, on the south by the Karakum Desert, and on the west by the Ustyurt Plateau. |
| Kiklad islands | Cyclades Islands |
| Kılburun | a medieval castle built on the eastern edge of the mouth of the Dnieper river to the northwest of the Black Sea. |
| Kili | Kili, Kiliia or Kilia, the central city of Kiliya Rayon in Odessa Oblast, in southwest Ukraine, in the delta of the Danube, on the territory of historical Bessarabia. |

*Places Mentioned in the Text*

| | |
|---|---|
| **Kilikya** | Cilicia is a geo-cultural region in southern Anatolia (Turkey), extending inland from the north-eastern coasts of the Mediterranean Sea. |
| **Kırjaali** | Kırcaali is Kardzhali, sometimes spelt Kardžali or Kurdzhali, a town in the Eastern Rhodopes in Bulgaria |
| **Kırklareli** | Qırqlareli, a province on the Thrace side of Turkey's Marmara Region |
| **Klek** | a peninsula in the Adriatic Sea southwest of Neum, Bosnia and Herzegovina. |
| **Kocaeli** | a province to the north of the Gulf of İzmit, near Istanbul. |
| **Koron** | a town of ancient Cappadocia, inhabited in Byzantine times, near Çömlekçi, Altunhisar district, Asiatic Turkey. |
| **Köstendil** | Kyustendil, a town in the far west of Bulgaria, the capital of Kyustendil Province |
| **Kroya** | Krujë, also Kruja in English, Akçahisâr is a small city to the north of the capital city of Tirana |
| **Küchük Kaynarja** | a town in Southern Dobruja, a historical region in the Balkans between the lower Danube River and the Black Sea. |
| **Kumkale** | is located in the central district of Çanakkale, within what is today the National Park of Troy. |
| **Kütahya** | the capital of Kütahya Province, a city in western Turkey, lying on the Porsuk river. |
| **Lârende** | Karaman (Qaramân), historically known as Laranda, is a city in south central Turkey, in Central Anatolia, the capital district of the Karaman Province. |

| | |
|---|---|
| **Lesh Alessio** | Lezhë, a city in the Republic of Albania historically known as Lissos, Lissus or Lissum and seat of Lezhë County and Lezhë Municipality. |
| **Limni** | Lemnos or Limnos, a Greek island in the northern part of the Aegean Sea. |
| **Lugos** | Lugoj, a city in Timiş County, Romania. |
| **Lüleburgaz** | a district in Kırklareli province of Turkey. |
| **Malatya** | a large city in the Eastern Anatolia region of Turkey |
| **Mangup** | also known as Mangup Kale (kale means "fortress" in Turkish), a historic fortress in Crimea, on a plateau about 13 kilometres due east of Sevastopol (ancient Chersones). |
| **Maltepe** | a district in Istanbul, on the northern shore of the Sea of Marmara |
| **Malqara** | Malkara, a town and district of Tekirdağ Province in the Marmara region of Turkey. |
| **Manisa** | historically known as Magnesia, a large city in Turkey's Aegean Region and today the administrative seat of Manisa Province. |
| **Mawsil** | Mosul |
| **Mekeje** | Mekece, a town in Pamukova, a district of Sakarya Province in the Marmara region of Turkey. |
| **Menteshe** | a *beğlik* in South-Western Anatolia |
| **Meriç** | Maritsa or Maritza also known as Evros, a river that runs through the Balkans in Southeast Europe. |
| **Merzifon** | a town and district in Amasya Province in the central Black Sea region of Turkey. |

*Places Mentioned in the Text*

| | |
|---|---|
| Midilli | Lesbos or Lesvos, a Greek island located in the north-eastern Aegean Sea. |
| Mihalıç | the old name of the Karacabey district of Bursa. |
| Missolonghi | or Messolonghi is a municipality in western Greece, the site of a dramatic siege during the Greek War of Independence, and of the death of poet Lord Byron. |
| Morea | a first-level province of the Osmanlı devlet centred on the Peloponnesian peninsula in southern Greece |
| Mudanya | the site of ancient Apamea Myrlea, a town and district of Bursa Province in the Marmara region of Turkey, on the Gulf of Gemlik |
| Muğla | formerly Mobolla, a city in south-western Turkey. |
| Muqattam | the name of a range of hills and a suburb in south-eastern Cairo, Egypt. |
| Nahchevan | Nakhchivan: a region and its capital city in Azerbaijan. |
| Navarin | Navarino, Pylos, is a town and a former municipality in Messenia, Peloponnese, Greece. |
| Niğbolu | Nicopolis |
| Niğde | the capital city of Niğde Province in the Central Anatolia region of Turkey |
| Nish | Niš in the southern part of Serbia is the third largest city in Serbia and the administrative centre of the Nišava District. |
| Nisip | Nizip is a district and city of Gaziantep Province of south-eastern Turkey. |
| Novi Pasar | Novi Pazar ("New Bazaar") is a city in the Raška District of southwestern Serbia. |

| | |
|---|---|
| Novobërda | Novo Brdo or Artana, a municipality in the Pristina district of Kosovo |
| Ohrid | a city in North Macedonia, the seat of the Ohrid Municipality. |
| Or | the Isthmus of Perekop, literally Isthmus of the Trench is the strip of land that connects the Crimean Peninsula to the mainland of Ukraine. |
| Ostrovicha | Sivrice Hisâr, a small fortified town built on one of the peaks of Rudnik mountain, to the north-west of the town of Rudnik |
| Özi | Ochakiv, Ochakov, a small city in Mykolaiv Oblast (region) of southern Ukraine. |
| Özü | the Eyalet of Silistra or Silistria, later known as Özü Eyalet meaning Province of Ochakiv, was an eyalet of the Osmânlı devlet along the Black Sea littoral and south bank of the Danube River in south-eastern Europe. |
| Panchova | Pančevo is a city and the administrative centre of the South Banat District in the autonomous province of Vojvodina, Serbia, on the shores of the Tamiš and Danube rivers. |
| Parga | a town and municipality in the north-western part of the regional unit of Preveza in Epirus, north-western Greece. |
| Pendik | a five-walled city outside Istanbul. |
| Pera | Beyoğlu, a district on the European side of İstanbul, separated from the old city by the Golden Horn. It was known as the region of Pera (meaning "Beyond" in Greek) surrounding the ancient coastal town Galata |

*Places Mentioned in the Text*

| | |
|---|---|
| **Petervaradin** | Petrovaradin, a historic town in the Serbian province of Vojvodina, now a part of the city of Novi Sad. |
| **Pleven** | a city in northern Bulgaria. |
| **Podolya** | Podolia Eyalet was an *eyalet* of the Osmanlı devlet whose capital was Kamianets-Podilskyi |
| **Ponza** | the largest island of the Italian Pontine Islands archipelago, south of Cape Circeo in the Tyrrhenian Sea. |
| **Poltava** | a city on the Vorskla River in central Ukraine. |
| **Pravadi** | Provadia, a town in north-eastern Bulgaria, part of Varna Province |
| **Preveza** | a city in the region of Epirus, north-western Greece, on the northern peninsula at the mouth of the Ambracian Gulf |
| **Prut River** | Pruth, a long river in Eastern Europe. It is a left tributary of the Danube, which for part of its course forms Romania's border with Moldova and Ukraine. |
| **Qalecik** | Kalecik, a town and district of Ankara Province in the Central Anatolia region of Turkey |
| **Qandıra** | a small town near İzmit (ıznikmid) |
| **Qanczuga** | Kańczuga, a town in Przeworsk County, Subcarpathian Voivodeship, Poland |
| **Qarabağ** | Karabakh, a geographic region in present-day south-western Azerbaijan and eastern Armenia, extending from the highlands of the Lesser Caucasus down to the lowlands between the rivers Kura and Aras. |
| **Qarahisâr-ı Sharqî** | Karajahisâr or Karacahisâr |

| | |
|---|---|
| Qaramân | one of the Anatolian *beğlik*s, centred in South-Central Anatolia around the present-day Karaman Province. |
| Qaresi | Karesi, an Anatolian *beğlik* in the area of classical Mysia centred in Balıkesir and Bergama |
| Qars | Kars, a former village in the Khizi Rayon of Azerbaijan. |
| Qasımpaşa | Kasımpaşa, a quarter within the Beyoğlu district of Istanbul. |
| Qastamonu | Kastamonu capital district of the Kastamonu Province, Turkey, just south of the Black Sea |
| Qatîf | Qatif or al-Qatif is a governorate and urban area located in the Eastern Province, Saudi Arabia. |
| Qaynarja | Kaynardzha, a village in northeastern Bulgaria, part of Silistra Province, and location of the signing of the Treaty of Küçük Kaynarca on 21 July 1774 |
| Qayseri | Kayseri, a city in Central Anatolia, Turkey, and the capital of Kayseri province. |
| Qipchaq | the Kipchaks, also known as Kipchak Turks, Qipchaq or Polovtsians, were a Turkic nomadic people and confederation that existed in the Middle Ages, inhabiting parts of the Eurasian Steppe. |
| Qazan | the Khanate of Kazan was a medieval Tatar Turkic state that occupied the territory of former Volga Bulgaria between 1438 and 1552, covering contemporary Tatarstan, Mari El, Chuvashia, Mordovia, and parts of Udmurtia and Bashkortostan, and whose capital was the city of Kazan. |

*Places Mentioned in the Text*

| | |
|---|---|
| **Qırqlareli** | Kırklareli, a city within Kırklareli Province in the European part of Turkey. |
| **Qızılja Tuzla** | Tuzla or Kızılca Tuzla, a city in present-day Bosnia and Herzegovina |
| **Qonya** | Konya |
| **Qoyunhisâr** | Koyunhisâr castle in Kocaeli Province, Turkey |
| **Quleli** | Kuleli, a district of Istanbul |
| **Rakovitza** | a town near Nikopol, in Bulgaria |
| **Ramazanoğlu** | the Ramadanid Emirate (Modern Turkish: Ramazanoğulları Beyliği) was an autonomous administration and a de facto independent emirate that existed from 1352 to 1608 in Cilicia, taking over the rule of the region from the Armenian Kingdom of Cilicia. |
| **Rashtad** | Rastatt, a town in the district of the same name, in Baden-Württemberg, Germany. |
| **Raydâniyyah** | one of the villages belonging to the Mansoura Centre in the Dakahlia Governorate in the Arab Republic of Egypt. |
| **Revân** | Yerevan, the capital and largest city of Armenia |
| **Rumelia** | etymologically "Land of the Romans", was the name of a historical region in Southeastern Europe that was administered by the Osmânlı devlet, corresponding to the Balkans. |
| **Rusçuk** | Ruse, the fifth largest city in Bulgaria, in the north-eastern part of the country, on the right bank of the Danube, opposite the Romanian city of Giurgiu. |
| **Safranbolu** | (Greek: Saframpolis), a town and district of Karabük Province in the Black Sea region of Turkey, north of the city of Karabük |

| | |
|---|---|
| Sakız | Chios, the fifth largest of the Greek islands, in the northern Aegean Sea. |
| Salankamen | Stari Slankamen, a village in the Inđija municipality, in the Syrmia District of Serbia. |
| Samandıra | a district in the Sancaktepe municipality on the Anatolian side of Istanbul. |
| Samokov | a town in Sofia Province in the southwest of Bulgaria. |
| Samsun | a city on the north coast of Turkey and a major Black Sea port. |
| Santamavra | Santa Maura but today known as Lefkada, also Lefkas or Leukas and Leucadia, is a Greek island in the Ionian Sea on the west coast of Greece. |
| Sapanca | a town and district in the Sakarya Province in the Marmara region of Turkey near Lake Sapanca. |
| Saruhan | a *beğlik* in Western Anatolia |
| Sawâkin | see Suakin |
| Seddulbahr | Sedd el Bahr, a village in the district of Eceabat, Çanakkale Province, at Cape Helles on the Gallipoli peninsula in Turkey. |
| Segedin | the Sanjaq of Segedin or Szeged, an administrative territorial entity of the Osmânlı devlet located in the Bačka (Bácska) region |
| Selânik | Thessaloniki, also known as Thessalonica, Saloniki or Salonica |
| Semendire | Smederevo, a city and today the administrative centre of the Podunavlje District in eastern Serbia. |
| Semendirek | Samothrace, a Greek island in the northern Aegean Sea. |

*Places Mentioned in the Text*

| | |
|---|---|
| Serez | Serres (Siroz), a city in the Central Macedonian region of Greece and the centre of the province of the same name. |
| Seydishehri | A town in Qonya district |
| Shabinqarahisâr | Şebinkarahisâr, the administrative seat of the Şebinkarahisâr District, Giresun Province in the Black Sea region of north-eastern Turkey. |
| Shipka | a town in central Bulgaria |
| Shumna/Shumnu | Shumen, the tenth largest city in Bulgaria and the administrative and economic capital of Shumen Province. |
| Sigetvar | Szigetvár, a town in Baranya County in southern Hungary. |
| Silifke | a town and district in south-central Mersin Province, Turkey, west of the city of Mersin, on the west end of Çukurova. |
| Silistre | Silistra is a town in north-eastern Bulgaria on the southern bank of the lower Danube river. |
| Silivri | a city and district in Istanbul Province along the Sea of Marmara outside the urban core of Istanbul |
| Simav | a town and a district of Kütahya Province in the Aegean region of Turkey on the Simav River |
| Sinop | a city on the Black Sea coast |
| Sivas | a city in central Turkey and the seat of Sivas Province |
| Sivrihisâr | ("a pointed castle"), a town and district of Eskişehir Province in the Central Anatolian Region of Turkey. |
| Sofya | Sofia, the capital and largest city of Bulgaria. |

| | |
|---|---|
| Söğüt | a town and district in Bilecik Province, Turkey in the Marmara region in the north-west of the country. |
| Söğütlüdere | a village in the Havsa District of Edirne Province in Turkey |
| Sozopol | a town and municipal centre close to the city of Burgas in western Bulgaria. |
| Storina | a small town in Montenegro |
| Suakin | Sawâkin, a port city in north-eastern Sudan, on the west coast of the Red Sea. |
| Taraklı | formerly known as Dablar, a historic district in north-western Turkey, approximately midway between Istanbul and Ankara in the Sakarya Province of the Marmara region. |
| Taman | a rural locality (a *stanitsa*) in Temryuksky District of Krasnodar Krai, Russia, on the coast of Taman Bay. |
| Tasheli | a province in southern Anatolia |
| Tameshvar | see Timişoara |
| Tavşanlı | a town and district of Kütahya Province in the Aegean region of Turkey. |
| Teke | an Anatolian *beyliğ* with its capital at Antalya |
| Tekirdağ | a city in Turkey that is a part of the region historically known as East Thrace, located on the Balkan peninsula in south-eastern Europe. |
| Terjan | a town in the municipal area of Plandište. |
| Tesalya | Thessaly, one of the 13 regions that make up Greece whose centre is the city of Larisa. |
| Timişoara | the capital city of Timiş County. It lies on the Bega River. |
| Tırnova | a city in Bulgaria, the capital of the Second Bulgarian Empire |

*Places Mentioned in the Text*

| | |
|---|---|
| Topqapusu/Topqapı | Topkapı |
| Toqat/Tokat | the capital city of the Tokat Province of Turkey in the mid-Black Sea region of Anatolia. |
| Tosya | previously called Theodosia under the Byzantine Empire, a town and district of Kastamonu Province in the Black Sea region of Turkey. |
| Transoxania | or Transoxiana, an ancient name referring to a region and civilisation in lower Central Asia roughly corresponding to modern-day eastern Uzbekistan, Tajikistan, southern Kazakhstan and southern Kyrgyzstan. |
| Turhal | a town and district of Tokat Province in the Black Sea region of Turkey. |
| Turla | the river Dniester |
| Ujvar | Uivar, a commune in Timiş County, Romania. |
| Ulubâd | a settlement near the town of Karacabey in the Bursa Province of north-western Turkey. |
| Üsküdar | a large and densely populated district of Istanbul, on the Anatolian shore of the Bosphorus. |
| Üsküp | Skopje, the capital and largest city of North Macedonia. |
| Urfa | officially known as Şanlıurfa (known in ancient times as Edessa), a city in south-eastern Turkey and the capital of Şanlıurfa Province. |
| Urla | a town and the centre of the district of the same name in İzmir Province, in Turkey. |
| Vardar Yenijesi | Giannitsa, the largest city in the regional unit of Pella and the capital of the Pella municipality, in the region of Central Macedonia in northern Greece. |

| | |
|---|---|
| Varna | today the third-largest city in Bulgaria on the Bulgarian Black Sea Coast and in the Northern Bulgaria region in the Gulf of Varna. Historically known as Odessos. |
| Vidin | a port town on the southern bank of the Danube in north-western Bulgaria close to the borders with Romania and Serbia. |
| Yanbolu | Yambolu, the city of Yambol province, Bulgaria along the Tunca valley neighbouring Edirne province on the border with Turkey |
| Yalvach | Yalvaç, a town and district of Isparta Province in the Mediterranean region of Turkey. |
| Yanova | Janjevo or Janjevë, a village or small town in the Lipljan municipality of eastern Kosovo. |
| Yanya | Ioannina, often called Yannena within Greece, is the capital and largest city of the Ioannina regional unit and of Epirus, an administrative region in north-western Greece. |
| Yarhisâr | a village in the District of Yenişehir, Bursa Province. |
| Yash | a city in north-eastern Romania |
| Yenişehir | Larissa, the capital and largest city of the Thessaly region in Greece. |
| Yergöğü (Giurgiu) | a city in southern Romania |
| Yerköy | a town and district of Yozgat Province in the Central Anatolian region of Turkey. |
| Zağra | Zagora, a city that is the administrative centre of the Old Zagora Province in Bulgaria |
| Zanta | Zakynthos is a Greek island in the Ionian Sea, the third largest of the Ionian Islands. |
| Zishtovi | a city in northern Bulgaria. It is located south of the Danube in the province of Veliko Tarnovo. |

# Full Table of Contents

Terms and Names ... ix

Pronunciation of Turkish Sounds ... ix

Abbreviations ... ix

Footnotes and Endnotes ... x

## Introduction ... 1
    Sources ... 11
    Important Observations ... 14
    Outline of the Book ... 22

## Part One: The Foundation of the Osmânlı Devlet 1288-1453 ... 25

Chapter One: Islam in Anatolia ... 27
    1.1 Islam and the Turks ... 29
    1.2 The Opening of Anatolia to Islam ... 33
    1.3 The Mongolian Occupation of Anatolia ... 38

Chapter Two: The Foundation of the Osmânlı Devlet ... 41
    2.1 Ertuğrul Gâzi ... 42
    2.2 Osmân Gâzi (1288-1324) ... 43
    2.3 Orhan Beğ (1324-1362) ... 58
    2.4 The Khalifate: The Osmânlı Goal and Ideal ... 63
    2.5 Gâzi Sultân Murâd (1362-1389) ... 70
        The Situation in the Balkans ... 72
        The Eastern Roman Empire Becomes Subordinate to the

## Osmanli History and Institutions

| | |
|---|---|
| Osmânlı Devlet | 75 |
| The Battle of Sırpsındığı (Rout of the Serbs) 1364 | 76 |
| The Opening of Biga to Islam | 78 |
| Dubrovnik Enters Osmânlı Protection (1365) | 79 |
| The Loss of Gallipoli (Gelibolu) | 80 |
| The Return to Opening New Lands in Europe | 82 |
| The First Battle of Kosova (791/1389) | 89 |
| The Osmânlı Administrative Structure | 92 |
| 2.6 Sultân Yıldırım Bâyezîd Khân (1389-1402) | 93 |
| The Battle of Niğbolu (Nicopolis) (798/1396) | 99 |
| Emîr Timur and Yıldırım Bâyezîd | 106 |
| Evaluation | 111 |
| The Period of Tumult (1402-1413) | 112 |
| Chapter Three: Restoration | 115 |
| 3.1 Mehemmed Chelebi (1413-1421) | 115 |
| The First Osmânlı-Venetian Naval Conflict | 118 |
| Tribute of Mircea, the Voyvoda of Wallachia | 118 |
| Jandaroğlu Beğlik | 119 |
| Mustafa Chelebi as a Hostage | 119 |
| The End of the Interregnum | 120 |
| 3.2 Sultân Murâd II (1421-1451) | 122 |
| The Situation in Rumelia | 126 |
| The Situation in Anatolia | 126 |
| The Annexation of the Menteshe Beğlik 829/1425 | 126 |
| The Annexation of Aydınoğlu Beğlik 829/1426 | 127 |
| Qaramânoğlu Beğlik | 127 |
| The Annexation of Germiyân Beğlik 832/1429 | 128 |
| The Opening of Selânik and Yanya to Islam | 128 |
| The Serbian-Hungarian and Qaramân Alliance | 130 |
| Campaign in Rumelia | 131 |
| 3.3 The Abdication of Sultân Murâd | 135 |

The Second Battle of Kosova (852/1448)     140

# Part Two: Expansion 1453-1699     147

## Chapter Four: Expansion     149
### 4.1 Fâtih Sultân Mehemmed Khân (1451-1481)     149
The Opening of Constantinople to Islam (857/29 May 1453)     153
The Jihâd against Serbia     168
Victory at Berat in Albania     169
The Siege of Belgrade     169
The Opening of Serbia to Islam (863/1459)     171
The Opening of Pontus to Islam (865/1461)     172
The Opening of New Lands to Islam in Albania     175
Prince Vlad of Wallachia, the Impaler     177
The Opening of Bosnia to Islam     178
The Republic of Raguza     179
The Opening of Morea to Islam     180
The Annexation of the Beğlik of Qaramân     181
The Battle of Otluqbeli (878/1473)     182
The Opening of Kefe and Azak (Azov) to Islam (880/1475)     184
The Opening of New Regions in Europe to Islam     185
The Death of Sultân Fâtih     188

## Chapter Five: Sultân Bâyezîd Velî (1481-1512)     195
The Expedition to Bogdan     201
Aid for the Muslims of Andalusia     203
The Jihâd in Lehistân (Poland)     204
Osmânlı-Mamlûk Relations     205
The Completion of the Opening of Morea to Islam     205
The Spread of Shî'ism in Anatolia     206

Osmanli History and Institutions

Chapter Six: The Struggle For Islamic Unity 209
  6.1 Sultân Selîm Khân (1512-1520) 209
    The Struggle Between Selîm and İsmâîl 211
    The Campaign against the Mamlûks 218
    The Osmânlı Khalifate 226
    Naval Affairs 231
    The Annexation of Crimea 231
    The Knights of St. John (Knights Hospitallers) 233
    The Death of Sultân Selîm 235

Chapter Seven: The Superpower of the World 237
  7.1 Qânûnî Sultân Süleymân (The Magnificent) (1520-1566) 237
    The Opening of Belgrade to Islam (927/1521) 238
    The Opening of Rhodes to Islam (928/1522) 238
    Battle of Mohacs (932/1526) 241
    The First Siege of Vienna (935/1529) 243
    The Third Campaign against Hungary (938/1532) 245
    The Fourth Campaign against Hungary (948/1541) 246
    The Fifth Campaign against Hungary (950/1543) 246
    The Campaign against al-Irâqayn and the Fath of Baghdad 247
    The Campaign against Iran 249
    Naval Activities 250
    Osmânlı Activities in the Indian Ocean 260
    The Jihâd on Sigetvar 265

Chapter Eight: The Beginning of Decline 268
  8.1 Selîm II (1566-1574) 268
    The Attempt to Build the Volga Canal (1569) 268
    The Opening of Cyprus to Islam 270
    The Osmânlı Defeat at İnebahtı (Lepanto) (979/1571) 271
    The Attempt to Build the Suez Canal (980/1572) 272

| | |
|---|---:|
| The Annexation of Tunisia | 272 |
| 8.2 Sultân Murâd III (1574-1595) | 274 |
|    Relations with the Sultânate of Fes (Maghrib) | 274 |
|    War with Iran (Persia) | 275 |
|    War with Austria | 276 |
| 8.3 Sultân Mehemmed III (1595-1603) | 278 |
|    The Opening of Eğri Castle to Islam 1004/1596 | 278 |
|    The Battle of Hachova (Keresztes or Mezőkeresztes) 1005/1596 278 | |
|    The Siege of Kanije by the Christians | 280 |
|    External Relations | 282 |
|    The Second Phase of the War with Iran (1603-1612) | 283 |
| 8.4 Sultân Ahmed I (1603-1617) | 283 |
| Chapter Nine: The Osmânlı Sultan's Descent to Equality With Emperors | 285 |
| 9.1 The Treaty of Zitvatorok (1606) | 285 |
|    The Third Phase of War with Iran (1615-1618) | 285 |
| 9.2 Sultân Osman II (1618-1622) | 286 |
|    The Campaign against Poland | 286 |
|    The Regicide of Genç Osman (1622) | 288 |
| Chapter Ten: Rejuvenation | 290 |
| 10.1 Sultân Murâd IV (1623-1640) | 290 |
|    The Capture of Baghdad by the Shâh of Iran | 290 |
|    Sultân Murâd's Revân Expedition | 291 |
| Chapter Eleven: Decline and Restoration | 293 |
| 11.1 Sultân İbrâhîm (1640-1648) | 293 |
|    The Campaign in Girit (Crete) | 293 |
| 11.2 Sultân Mehmed IV (1648-1687) | 294 |
|    Köprülü Mehmed Pasha | 294 |
|    Expedition to Erdel (1068/1658) | 295 |

| | |
|---|---|
| War with Russia (1069/1659) | 296 |
| Fâzıl Ahmed Pasha (1661-1676) | 297 |
| The Expedition to Girit (Crete) | 298 |
| The Sultân's Expedition to Poland | 298 |
| The Expedition to Chehrin | 299 |
| The Second Siege of Vienna 1683 | 300 |
| The Deposition of the Sultân | 303 |
| Financial Affairs | 303 |
| 11.3 Sultân Süleymân II (1687-1691) | 305 |
| 11.4 Sultân Ahmed II (1691-1695) | 306 |
| 11.5 Sultân Mustapha II (1695-1703) | 307 |

## Part Three: Decline 1699-1922     311

| | |
|---|---|
| Chapter Twelve: The Resumption of Decline | 312 |
| 12.1 Sultân Ahmed III (1703-1730) | 313 |
| Battle of Prut (1711) | 313 |
| War with Austria | 316 |
| War with Persia | 318 |
| Chapter Thirteen : The Attempt at Restoration | 319 |
| 13. Sultân Mahmûd I (1730-1754) | 319 |
| War with Russia | 319 |
| War with Austria | 320 |
| The Attempt at Restoration | 321 |
| War with Persia | 322 |
| Chapter Fourteen: Crisis and Struggle | 324 |
| 14.1 Sultân Mustafa III (1757-1774) | 324 |
| War with Russia | 324 |
| The Annihilation of the Osmânlı Fleet | 326 |
| The Russian Attack on Crimea | 327 |

Chapter Fifteen: Another Attempt at Restoration 328
   15. 1. Sultân 'Abdülhamîd I (1774-1789) 328
      Sadrâzam Halîl Hâmid Pasha 329
      Qırım (Crimea) 330
      War with Austria and Russia (1201/1787) 331
      The Invasion of Özi Castle 332
   15.2 Sultân Selîm III (1789-1807) 333
      The French Invasion of Egypt in 1798 335
      Jezzâr Ahmed Pasha 337
      The Osmânlı Retrieval of Egypt 338
      The Beginning of Europeanisation: Nizâm-ı Jedîd 340
      The Deposition of Selîm III 341
   15.3 Sultân Mustafa IV (1807-1808) 342
   15.4 Sultân Mahmûd II (1808-1839) 343
      Nationalism and Its Impact on the Osmânlı Devlet 344
      The Greek Revolt 345
      Vaq'a-yı Khayriyye (1241/1826) 348
      The 'Asâkir-i Mansûre-yi Muhammediyye 350
      Greek Independence 350
      The Occupation of Jezâyir by France (1246/1830) 353
      The Treaty of Hünkâr İskelesi (1249/1833) 354
   15.5 Sultân Abdülmejîd (1839-1861) 355
      The Treaty of London 1257/1841 360
      Enjümen-i Dânish 360
      The Straits 361
      The Crimean War (1853-1856) 362
      The Fermân of İslâhât (1272/ 1856) 365
      The Financial Situation 366
      Reactions to Change in the Structure 368
      The Court of Quleli 369
   15.6 Sultân 'Abdülazîz (1861-1876) 370
      Events in Wallachia and Moldova 1861-1866 372

| | |
|---|---|
| Events in Serbia | 372 |
| The Uprising in Girit (Crete) | 373 |
| The Young Osmânlıs (Yeni Osmânlılar) | 374 |
| The Journey of Sultân 'Abdülazîz to Europe | 376 |
| The Conference of London | 377 |
| Toward the Independence of Egypt (1863-1882) | 378 |
| The Bulgarian Riots (1848-1876) | 379 |
| *Shûrâ-yı Devlet* (The Council of the Devlet) | 380 |
| The Deposition of Sultân 'Abdülazîz 1876 | 381 |
| 15.7 Sultân Murâd V (1876) | 383 |
| | |
| Chapter Sixteen: Preservation and Rejuvenation | 385 |
| 16.1 Sultân Abdülhamîd II (1876-1909) | 385 |
| Proclamation of the Constitution (*Meshrûtiyyet*) | 385 |
| The Osmânlı Parliament (Mejlis-i Meb'ûsân) | 389 |
| War with Russia | 389 |
| Treaty of San Stefano | 391 |
| The First Chiragan Event | 391 |
| The Second Chiragan Event | 393 |
| The Congress of Berlin (13 July 1878) | 393 |
| The French Occupation of Tunisia (1881) | 395 |
| The Yıldız Court of Justice | 396 |
| The Düyûn-ı 'Umûmiyye (Public Loans) | 397 |
| The British Occupation of Egypt (1882) | 397 |
| Bulgaria | 400 |
| The Osmânlı-Greek War | 400 |
| Osmânlı-German Relations | 402 |
| | |
| Chapter Seventeen: The İttihâd ve Teraqqî Society – The Committee of Union and Progress | 404 |
| An Attempt at Assassination | 405 |
| Sultân Abdülhamîd and Freedom | 406 |
| 17.1 The Deposition of the Sultân | 409 |

*Full Table of Contents*

| | |
|---|---|
| 17.2 Sultân Mehmed V Reshâd (1909-1918) | 410 |
| The Tripoli War (1911) | 411 |
| The Balkan Wars (1912-1913) | 413 |
| The First World War (1914-1918) | 415 |
| 17.3 Mehmed VI Vahîdeddîn | 419 |
| Conclusion | 421 |
| Osmânlı Sovereigns | 430 |
| Addendum: The Osmânlı Socio-Political Entity: Empire or Devlet? | 433 |
| a) The Political Aspect | 440 |
| b) The Cultural Aspect | 444 |
| c) The Economic Aspect | 448 |

## Osmânlı Institutions  451

| | |
|---|---|
| Introduction | 453 |
| I. Administrative Organisation | 456 |
| 1 The Khalifate | 456 |
| 2 The Vizârate | 463 |
| 3 The Dîvân | 466 |
| 3.1 The Dîvân-ı Hümâyûn | 466 |
| 3.2 The Vazîr-i A'zam's Dîvân | 468 |
| 4 The Qalemiyye | 469 |
| 5. Communications | 469 |
| II – Economic Institutions | 473 |
| 6. Administration of the Land | 473 |
| 7. Trade | 474 |
| 7.1 Akhiyya-Fityân | 475 |
| 8 – Finance | 475 |

| | |
|---|---|
| 8.1 Beytu'l Mâl | 476 |
| 8.2 Zakât | 476 |
| 8.3 *'Ushr* | **478** |
| 8.4 *Jizyah* | 478 |
| 8.5 *Kharâj* | 479 |
| 8.6 *Ganâ'im, Fay* | 480 |
| III – The Legal System | 482 |
| 9. *Qazâ'* (Justice) | 483 |
| The Naqiybu'l Ashrâf | 485 |
| 9.1 The Sheyhülislâm | 486 |
| Sultân-Khalîfah | 488 |
| 9.2 The Qâdıasker (Qazasker) | 489 |
| 9.3 The İhtisab Ağası | 490 |
| IV – Military Organisation | 493 |
| 10. The Army | 493 |
| 10.1 The Central Army (Qapuqulu Askerleri) | 494 |
| 10.2 Provincial Army (The Eyâlet Askerleri) | 498 |
| 11. The Navy | 502 |
| 11.1 The Central Navy | 502 |
| 11.2 Volunteer Naval Mujâhids | 505 |
| V – Social Institutions | 508 |
| 12. Waqf | 508 |
| 13. Zâwiya-Tarîqats | 511 |
| 14. İmâret | 513 |
| 15. Kervânsarây | 514 |
| 16. Hammâm | 516 |
| 17. Hospitals | 518 |
| 18. Education | 521 |
| 18.1 The Mosque | 522 |
| 18.2 The Sibyân Mektebi (Children's School) | 522 |

| | |
|---|---|
| 18.3 The Madrasah | 523 |
| Daru't Tibb | 526 |
| The Dâru'l Qurrâ' (school for reciters/readers) | 526 |
| 18.4 The Enderûn | 526 |
| Conclusion | 529 |
| Bibliography | 531 |
|   A. Documents | 531 |
|   B. Books and Articles | 531 |
|     1. Turkish | 531 |
|     2. Arabic | 536 |
|     3. English | 537 |
|     4. French | 540 |
| Endnotes | 541 |
|   Introduction | 541 |
|   Part One – The Foundation of the Osmânlı Devlet 1288-1453 | 543 |
|   Part Two – Expansion 1453-1699 | 549 |
|   Part Three – Decline 1699-1922 | 560 |
|   Addendum – The Osmânlı Socio-Political Entity: Empire or Devlet? | 569 |
|   Osmânlı Institutions | 570 |
|   Introduction | 570 |
| Glossary | 577 |
| Places Mentioned in the Text | 584 |
| Full Table of Contents | 608 |

www.ingramcontent.com/pod-product-compliance
Lightning Source LLC
Chambersburg PA
CBHW022005300426
44117CB00005B/37